HUDSON'S
HISTORIC HOUSES & GARDENS
MUSEUMS & HERITAGE SITES

HUDSON'S

D0532735

Bringing Britain's Heritage to You

Published by Hudson's Media Ltd
35 Thorpe Road, Peterborough PE3 6AG
Telephone: 01733 296910
Email: info@hudsons-media.co.uk
www.hudsonsheritage.com

Front Cover: The Ornamental Garden at The Alnwick Garden, Northumberland, looking from above the Grand Cascade to the roof of the Visitor Centre.

Back Cover: (left) Alnwick Castle in springtime, *photo: Sean Elliott*; (right) Following a Nature Trail in the park at Holkham Hall, Norfolk.

2015

28

467 811 180

Discover untold stories and hidden treasures

Explore 1,000 years of history in over 340 beautiful churches

- Stunning art, architecture and artefacts
- Romantic ruins and deserted villages
- Dazzling stained glass
- Astonishing monuments
- Tall tales and local legends
- *Free entry*

THE CHURCHES
CONSERVATION TRUST

visitchurches.org.uk

Welcome to HUDSON^s

In Britain since the 1940s those in charge of our heritage places have been working out how to share them with us, the visitors. A day out today is different from one our parents might have taken. There is more access to parks and gardens, more freedom to find the answers for ourselves and more chance to see what our ancestors would have been up to below stairs as well as above. *Hudson's Heritage Awards* is shining a light on some of the best experiences you can have as a visitor and showing that it is not just the biggest attractions that can be innovative and interesting to visit.

It seems that a love of the past starts for many by watching the Antiques Roadshow with their mums or granddads. On set with Fiona Bruce at Chenies Manor House, we found an audience of all ages. Anniversaries from Magna Carta to the 1715 Jacobite Rising will be fun to explore around the country

this year. The truly inspiring poppy installation at the Tower of London has set off remembrance of the First World War and we learn here of the crucial role country houses played in two world wars. It's 40 years since the V&A exhibition *The Destruction of the Country House*, so we asked why two brave owners took up the challenge and I talked to Jenny Abramsky about the future of heritage funding. You can't fail to enjoy Simon Jenkins' stunning choice of English views.

So use this book to find out where to go and what to see, how to get there and how to get from place to place and get some inspiration to make discoveries of your own. Tell us what you think in our survey (p.413) and don't miss our new *Hudson's Short Breaks* programme for a weekend away with some of the best historic houses and gardens.

Sarah Greenwood,
Publisher

Pictures: Top, from left to right: Bodnant Gardens, Wales; Alnwick Castle, Northumberland. Above, from left to right: Apsley House, the London residence of the Duke of Wellington; Craigevar Castle, Aberdeenshire; The Old Laundry, Traquair House, Borders.

Heating your home the oil fashioned way

...is putting its future at risk

As fuel prices have increased, the ability to heat historic houses to comfortable levels, to protect the fabric of the building, art and furniture collections has been reduced.

Modern renewable heating can run at a cost and efficiency that allows low levels of always on heating to create the desired comfort and protection.

At Kelmarsh Hall, Ecovision have installed a Water Source Heat Pump to lower running costs and provide a stable environment to combat the damp that permeates the fabric of the walls, furniture and works of art.

Kelmarsh will not only benefit from a reduced carbon footprint but also a 60% decrease in its consumption of oil. Qualifying for the Renewable Heat Incentive Scheme, the system will pay for itself in five years.

Renewable services for country houses

Contact us to discuss how renewable energy can protect your home.

Call: **0845 003 8004**
Visit: **www.ecovisionsystems.co.uk**

Inside

Pictures: Top, from left: Helmingham Hall, Suffolk; Plas Newydd, Denbighshire; Stratfield Saye Gardens, Hampshire; Tudor chimneys at Chenies, Bucks; Dalemain House, Cumbria.

Thanks to everyone at Cadw, Churches Conservation Trust, English Heritage, the Historic Houses Association, Historic Royal Palaces, Historic Scotland, the National Trust, the National Trust for Scotland, the Royal Collection, private owners and local authorities who help us compile Hudson's and keep it accurate and up to date. All images are copyright to Hudson's Media Ltd, the owner or property depicted.

Hudson's Historic Houses & Gardens team:
Editorial: Sarah Greenwood; Neil Pope
Production Manager: Deborah Coulter
Product Manager: Rebecca Owen-Fisher
Creative team: Neil Pope; Jamieson Eley
Publishing Manager: Sarah Phillips
Advertising: Rebecca Owen-Fisher; James O'Rawe 01733 296913;
Hall-McCartney Ltd, Baldock, SG7 5SH
Printer: Stephens & George, Merthyr Tydfil CF48 3TD
Distribution: Compass DSA, London W4 1RX
Hudson's Media Ltd, 35 Thorpe Road, Peterborough PE3 6AG 01733 296910

What's new?

Watch out for some highlights of the heritage year in 2015.

Champing

Camping chic has gripped the nation, after glamping, famously available at Leeds Castle, Warwick Castle or Layer Marney Tower, comes champing, camping in an historic church! Thanks to the Churches Conservation Trust, you can now book in for a weekend at the picturesque medieval All Saints' Church in Aldwincle, Northamptonshire. Comfortable bedding laid out in the North and South aisles welcomes you after a hearty supper and a candlelit walk through the village. An evening with a professional story teller will set you up for a good night's sleep before an optional day's canoeing on the nearby River Nene. Breakfasting in the coloured lights cast by the stained glass windows promises to be a highlight.

Go to www.visitchurches.org.uk/champing or call 0845 303 2760.

Agincourt!

Today we remember the Battle of Agincourt most easily from Shakespeare's play, Henry V, *"We few, we happy few, we band of brothers"* etc. In 1415 this was an astonishing victory for the English over the French. The battle established the legendary English longbowmen as the most effective force of the period, striking down ten times as many French knights in a hail of arrows as were killed on the English side. At Leeds Castle in Kent, the 600th anniversary of the battle offers a chance to revisit the castle's lively medieval past. A new 4-D medieval experience will open at the castle this year, where you will be surrounded by the sights and sounds of battle. Hands on displays and exhibitions around the Castle and grounds will help visitors relive the world of 1415. Expect longbows aplenty!
Leeds Castle, Kent (p.152)

Left: The Battle of Agincourt from Enguerrand de Monstrelet's *Chronique de France*, around 1500.

Centenary of the WI

2015 is the centenary year of the Women's Institute. The WI was formed in 1915 as a direct response to the First World War which emptied rural communities and needed women to focus on producing food. Since then the organisation's aims have broadened and the WI is now the largest voluntary women's organisation in the UK with 212,000 members in 60 societies. Traditionally great supporters of historic houses and heritage places, this is the year to look out for exhibitions and events that celebrate the centenary. Kiplin Hall in Yorkshire for one, is hosting 100 Shades of Green which will show off the skills of the

theWI
INSPIRING WOMEN
FOR 100 YEARS
1915   2015

various WI Federations of North Yorkshire West and Northumberland in May.
Kiplin Hall, North Yorkshire (p.287)

INVITATION TO VIEW

Invitation to View is a co-operative of private historic houses which invites visitors to buy tickets to visit by appointment on pre-advertised dates just as you might buy a theatre ticket. You do not need to be part of a group but can visit as individuals. Many properties do not open for anyone else and, frequently, the owner takes charge of the tour.

Places which do open to the general public make sure that Invitation to View visitors get something extra, often getting behind closed doors. Check the calendar at www.hudsonsheritage.com or book at 01206 573948 or www.mercurytheatre.co.uk.

Spreading Enlightenment

A visit to one of England's grandest and most beautiful neo-classical palaces will take on a new 'wow factor' once an innovative learning and discovery centre has been completed. Due to open in April 2015, the new centre will contain cutting-edge multimedia experiences that will transport visitors into the worlds of the historic occupants of the House and new gallery spaces for temporary exhibitions. The project, 'Enlightenment for All' at Stowe House in north Buckinghamshire, is being made possible by a grant of more than £800,000 by the Heritage Lottery Fund (HLF) and by grants from the World Monuments Fund and Esmée Fairbairn Foundation.

Sir John Vanbrugh, William Kent, Capability Brown, Robert Adam and Sir John Soane all left their mark on Stowe House and its surrounding landscape.

The Stowe House Preservation Trust will also transform visitor access and enjoyment of the 18th century palace by creating new ways by which people can understand and experience the historic building and its stories. Key improvements will include imaginative new resources for all ages, full access for disabled people and working with the surrounding community on creative projects to produce exciting new displays and installations for visitors.

→

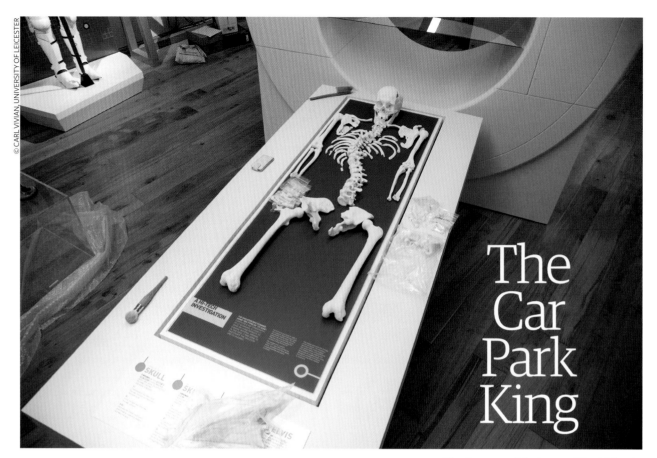

© CARL VIVIAN, UNIVERSITY OF LEICESTER

The Car Park King

© CARL VIVIAN, UNIVERSITY OF LEICESTER

The discovery of the bones of King Richard III in Leicester in 2013 filled headlines worldwide as few stories of medieval England have done before. The new Richard III Visitor Centre is now open in Leicester and while there is not much here that is authentic, you can see the excavated car park grave which held his remains for nearly 600 years. The new exhibition has also helped to save the old Leicester Grammar School building and regenerate this quarter of town. There is a 3-D printed replica of Richard III's skeleton, twisted by scoliosis, and a controversial white suit of armour that was merrily compared to a Star Wars storm trooper by detractors. If you were in doubt that this was big heritage news, 10,000 people visited the centre in the first month. The King's bones will be finally laid to rest in Leicester Cathedral just opposite in March 2015.

heritage open days

Heritage Open Days Weekend
10-13 September 2015
Look out for lots of heritage
places to visit!
www.heritageopendays.org.uk

Magna Carta 800

800 years ago this year, a reluctant King John met his angry Barons at Runnymede and signed a document we know as Magna Carta – the Great Charter. It contained key clauses outlining the idea that the law took precedence over the king, and so gave birth to some of the freedoms that underlie modern concepts of democracy and human rights which have been exported all over the world. Of the Charter drawn up in 1215 only 4 copies remain, at the British Library, at Salisbury and at Lincoln. On 1 April this year, Lincoln will become a major destination with the opening of Lincoln Castle Revealed, linking a new dedicated Magna Carta Vault built between the Norman Castle and the restored Victorian prison building. You will be able to hear the story of the original Magna Carta alongside the important original 1217 Charter of the Forest which repeats the key clauses. On the restored castle ramparts, among the best preserved in Britain, you can complete the Wall Walk with far reaching views particularly to Lincoln Cathedral where the Magna Carta was protected for 800 years. It is a great medieval complex which vividly recalls the dispute between King John and his Cardinal Archbishop, Stephen Langton, educated at Lincoln Cathedral and a signatory of Magna Carta.

Lincoln Castle, Linconshire (p.252)
Other copies of Magna Carta: Bodleian Library, Oxford (p.165)
Durham Cathedral, Co Durham (p.320)

Mrs Hudson's Grand Day Out...

ILLUSTRATION: CLARE MACKIE

Mrs Hudson and dog, Walpole, spent the summer holidays staying with family and friends. Poor Walpole took second place in favour of family fun.

June

Off to the Midlands for a weekend with old friends. Aiming for Warwick Castle but not sure about the theme park razzmatazz but my companions, two children, 4 & 6, their parents, two travelling Australian students, and grandma are up for anything.

At the gates, there's already a choice, Dad wants to quiz the costumed archery demonstrator and the kids spot their favourite Horrible Histories. All satisfied, we finally make it through the gatehouse, struck by what a fantastic medieval castle Warwick is, the walls and towers full of history; Piers Gaveston, Warwick Kingmaker, Edward IV, Richard III were all here and the architecture of the dungeons, towers, and ramparts is impressive.

Here we split up, Dad and 6 year old to the Merlin's Tower, Mum and 4 year old to the Princess Tower, Aussies to the Warwick Dungeon and Grandma joins a traditional guided tour with an enthusiastic member of the History Team.

Joining up again for lots of laughs and history shared as we picnic by the lake on a mix of home food and supplies from the plentiful food stalls (more Horrible Histories en route).

The students are full of horrors from the medieval town's past, loved all the pantomime and special effects. They plan a Dungeon tour of Britain. The 4 year old now sports a tiara and the 6 year old a sword and are full of stories.

After lunch we pick up coffee and ice cream and watch the eagles flying from the Towers in the sunshine, before more exploring, some hands on archery and for Mum and Grandma a visit to Daisy Greville's House party, a waxwork display in the Victorian state apartments which is surprisingly entertaining, partly because the maid who greets us is real, and we feel transported to Edwardian elegance (and scandal!).

We just make it to the firing of the Trebuchet – well, it awed me and the kids – before a restorative cup of tea and home via the cobbled streets of Warwick town.

A full day with lots left to do and what a lot of real history we all learned, from face-to-face chat, AVs, cheery costumed interpreters, experiences of all sorts and awe-inspiring surroundings. Next year, let's try glamping in the King's tent!

July

In London with relatives seeking a country escape on a hot weekend and entertainment for an adored toddler and 9 year old godchild. History buff Mum steers us to English Heritage's Audley End, just over an hour from town up the M11.

Every bit the stately mansion, Audley End offers a welcome escape from the traffic and a stroll across the bridge over the Cam bring us to a haven of lawns and mature trees.

Drinks and cake in the old Servants'

Hall fuels us to explore the many service rooms – the Servants' Bells and the Lamp Room most intrigue the godchild. In the house, magnificent suites of Jacobean revival and Adam rooms with tinkling piano in the Library culminate in a gallery of Victorian stuffed animals and birds which proves a big hit with the godchild.

Most fun for the children is the 1830s nursery with Victorian toys and dressing up. On the lawns both

children get caught up in traditional games – you need skill to bowl a hoop Victorian style.

Lunch in the café and plenty of time to be enchanted by the sight of a handsome grey horse lunging in the stable yard, before testing out sidesaddle on a dummy, hide and seek in the walled kitchen garden and a spell in the playground. We rejoin the traffic feeling a real sense of having been part of this great house, not just as onlookers.

TM PICTURE LIGHT

TRINITY HALL BRING THEIR ART TO LIGHT WITH ENERGY EFFICIENT, HIGH COLOUR DEFINITION, **LED PICTURE LIGHT**

Trevalsa Court Country House Hotel & Restaurant, Cornwall

76th EDITION

SIGNPOST
SELECTED PREMIER HOTEL

SIGNPOST

RECOMMENDING THE UK'S FINEST HOTELS SINCE 1935

Every hotel featured in this guide has that something special, no run-of-the-mill hotels included

•

Available from Signpost hotels and all good book shops

•

Visit our website for up-to-date special offers and a chance to win a weekend stay at a Signpost hotel

'Gem of a guide... covers hotels of character'
EXECUTARY NEWS

'For anyone doing any extensive motoring in Britain, this guide would seem invaluable'
NEW YORKER MAGAZINE

'The British Hotel guide for the discerning traveller'
PERIOD LIVING

www.signpost.co.uk

August

Up in the North of England beyond Hadrian's Wall, so to Northumberland for Alnwick Castle and The Alnwick Garden. This time I'm with five Harry Potter fanatics from 5 to 15 and their parents.

Through the town gate to the Castle, the children are immediately distracted by Harry Hotspur and the Knight's Quest and are soon resplendent in tabards and cloaks for much rushing around, bashing the quintain, pelting each other in the stocks and squabbling over who sits on which throne.

We, adults, sit and chat in the sun while they wear themselves out. Dragon Quest proves almost too scary for the 5 year old (who refuses to leave) though the 15 year old is cynical so we rush to the main courtyard for broomstick training.

A robed wizard with a sergeant-major voice makes this totally absorbing and everyone manages to get off the ground with photos to prove it! We swear to return when all the Harry Potter characters are here at the Bank Holiday.

All go to the State Apartments; while the adults would rather have lingered over the Titians and Van Dycks, the kids speed through with just time to count the stuffed dogs. The children show off their discoveries of Queen Elizabeth's gloves in little drawers in the 1st Duchess exhibition. Lunch (and local ice cream) in the café and then a stroll through a flock of guinea fowl to The Alnwick Garden.

Our local child shows her friend the garden she works with her Durham school in Roots and Shoots in the Walled Garden. They harvested and ate their potatoes in June.

In the Garden, the 5 year old commandeers a big truck and plays in the water at the Cascade (I supervise) while the rest tour the Poison Garden with a humorous guide. Parents wander in the Ornamental Garden, thick with roses and salvias, some of the more unusual labelled and available in the plant shop later.

The 15 year old takes the kids off into the Bamboo Labyrinth where they encounter Splash Alnwick! and find themselves in a wild water fight. The Serpent Garden is only mildly calmer with much splashing (and a bit of science) around the smooth metal sculptures. A change of clothes and a refuelling stop at the rather magical café in the Treehouse Restaurant and 50% are asleep in the car on the way home, imaginations all tired out. We agree that Castle OR Garden is quite enough for one day!

Mrs Hudson is a pseudonym, she is no relation of Norman Hudson, Chairman of Hudson's Heritage Award panel, nor of other Hudsons we know. The dog is real and wants to be included next time.

© SEAN ELLIOTT/ BY KIND PERMISSION OF THE NORTHUMBERLAND ESTATES

In Scotland in September at Craigevar Castle with in-laws in their 80s and cousins from 13 to 19. The castle featured in NTS's TV ad with costumed attackers but all is quiet today. Turrets and walls harled in pink make this a perfect fairy tale castle perched on a hill and it even has the required secret staircase.

Narrow stone spiral staircases prove a bit of a challenge for our 80 year olds and the marvellous renaissance plasterwork ceilings don't wow the teenagers but this is the real thing – an ancient Scottish castle with the requisite dungeons and Mary Queen of Scots' bedspread, minstrel's gallery and atmospheric 17th century interiors. Highlights for the cousins are Queen Victoria's mahogany lavatory and some very convincing ghost stories. Portraits of be-ruffed Danzig Willy – William Forbes of Corse – and his descendants, tell an interesting story of riches from trade in the Baltic and the changing Autumn tints in the Glen Garden draw everyone to explore outside.

What a summer! A chance to see that places planned for entertainment and quieter places can be great for all generations with a taste of our past and plenty of fun.

Warwick Castle, Warwick (p.277)
Audley End, Essex (p.224)
Alnwick Castle (p.321)
The Alnwick Garden (p.323)

Blenheim Palace, Oxfordshire

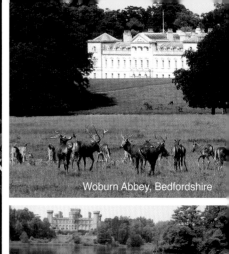

Woburn Abbey, Bedfordshire

Eastnor Castle, Herefordshire

Blair Castle, Pitlochry, Scotland

Highclere Castle, Berkshire

Arley Hall Gardens Cheshire

Sausmarez Manor, Guernsey

Benvarden, Northern Ireland

Bolton Castle, Yorkshire

Your Paintings

The development of an online catalogue called ***Your Paintings***, a collaboration between the Public Catalogue Foundation and the BBC has shown us paintings we never knew existed. Here ***Hudson's*** shares the story of the project.

The UK holds one of the largest and finest collections of publicly owned oil paintings in the world, but only 20% are on display. The Public Catalogue Foundation (PCF), a small arts charity, believes that the public should be able to access the art it owns for enjoyment, learning and research.

Through a ten-year cataloguing and photography project, the PCF has created a comprehensive record of this rich, diverse national collection. In partnership with the BBC, the PCF developed *Your Paintings*, a free website where people can discover 212,000 paintings from 3,200 locations across the UK. There is also an accompanying series of 85 beautifully illustrated books.

Started in 2003, taking Kent and Leeds as pilot areas, the project was completed in 2012. The PCF field teams tirelessly explored storerooms, offices and forgotten corridors in public buildings across England, Northern Ireland, Scotland, Wales, the Isle of Man and the Channel Islands. Whilst local authority and national museum collections make up the majority of the institutions represented, paintings held by universities, hospitals, town halls, libraries and even a lighthouse, a swimming baths and an aquarium are included in the project. Also included are the stately homes and castles of the National Trust, National Trust for Scotland, CADW and English Heritage, and the colleges of Oxford and Cambridge.

Many intriguing discoveries were made during the cataloguing process. At Lacock Abbey, Wiltshire, PCF photographer Dan Brown discovered a painting in the attic with a large, octagonal hole in its centre.

© THE BOWES MUSEUM

The *Portrait of Olivia Boteler Porter,* lady-in-waiting to Queen Henrietta Maria, was in storage at the Bowes Museum and covered in layers of varnish and dirt. Now identified through the PCF by expert, Dr. Bendor Grosvenor, as by Sir Anthony Van Dyck, the restored painting (right) is insured for up to £1 million.

A View of the South East Elevation of Haddon Hall in Derbyshire from the River Wye by David Payne, identity confirmed online by Vikki Stronge of Haddon Hall and held by Atkinson Art Gallery.

Downstairs, in the dining room, Dan found the missing section of the painting set into the wall. The portrait from the centre of the painting had been used to fill an empty frame after the original, more valuable painting had been removed and sold, possibly to settle a debt.

Perhaps the biggest surprise of the project was a 28ft-high altarpiece by William Hogarth found hanging in the offices of Bristol and Region Archaeological Services. Originally intended for St Mary Redcliffe church in Bristol, the painting now belongs to Bristol Museum and Art Gallery, but remains on the wall in the archaeology offices.

Your Paintings is a treasure trove of mysteries waiting to be solved. There are nearly 30,000 paintings on the website where the artist is not known and over 15,000 works where the attributions are uncertain. Some 8,000 portraits remain anonymous and thousands of other paintings are missing information about the places or events they depict.

After spotting a portrait of Olivia Boteler Porter on *Your Paintings*, Dr Bendor Grosvenor re-attributed the work as an original Van Dyck. Held by the Bowes Museum, County Durham, it was originally thought to have been an undistinguished 19th century copy.

To help solve more mysteries, the PCF has launched *Art Detective*, an online digital network connecting public art collections with providers of specialist knowledge. Since its launch, many fascinating discoveries have emerged. Landscapes from Glencoe to Deal have been located, and works have been reunited with their creators, most notably a work by French Belle Époque artist Jacques Emile Blanche. The identities of several sitters have been confirmed, including an unknown soldier depicted in a portrait held by Carmarthenshire Museums Service. The solider has been identified as Second Lieutenant Paul Chancourt Giradot who perished in the First World War. *Art Detective* research has also identified a portrait of an unknown rheumatologist at the Royal Free Hospital, London, as Dr Charles Brehmer Heald (1882–1974).

Second Lieutenant Paul Chancourt Giradot by unknown artist identified by *Art Detective* public user Martin Gillott with a full history of the death of this officer in the First World War.

A Terrible Shipwreck: 12 February 1870 at Kingsdown near Deal by Thomas Longley Mourilyan records a Channel storm and was identified for Compton Verney from a detailed online discussion on *Art Detective*.

The question from the Shakespeare Birthplace Trust about their *Portrait of an Unknown Man and Woman* is still open on *Art Detective*. Is this Thomas and Elizabeth Nash (Shakespeare's granddaughter) or John and Susanna Hall (Shakespeare's daughter) or someone else entirely?

Bristol City Council archaeology office (above) is home to a vast altarpiece painted by William Hogarth in 1756 for St Mary's, Redcliffe. Put in storage in 1910 the painting had been all but forgotten but can now be viewed from Monday to Friday, during office hours, by appointment only on 0117 903 9010.

Sketch for *'Valve Testing: The Signal School, Royal Navy Barracks, Portsmouth'* by Arthur David McCormick (1860–1943). The link with the original in the Imperial War Museum was spotted by *Art Detective* public user Toby Bettridge.

Other PCF initiatives include *Masterpieces in Schools*, which enables school children to experience great art close up. In 2013, 26 oil paintings by artists such as Gainsborough, Lowry, Monet and Turner were lent to primary and secondary schools for a day. As many UK schools are not able to arrange museum visits, this was for many children their first encounter with a painting.

The PCF also runs a successful commercial digitisation section offering cataloguing and photography services to private and public collections. Clients include St Paul's Cathedral and Bristol Museum and Art Gallery.

Looking forward, the PCF is planning their next major project – cataloguing and photographing the nation's collection of sculpture; arguably the finest in the world and would be interested in helping any other heritage collection, large or small, with cataloguing.

USEFUL WEBSITES

The national collection of oil paintings offers a remarkable insight into the history, landscape and culture of the United Kingdom. Visit the *Your Paintings* website to discover the art you own.
www.thepcf.org.uk
www.bbc.co.uk/yourpaintings
www.thepcf.org.uk/artdetective

THE TETLEY WORKSHOP

Specialising in the Conservation of Carpets.

We are Accredited Conservators and listed on the Conservation Register,
www.tetleyworkshop.co.uk.   01364649029.   Info@tetleyworkshop.co.uk

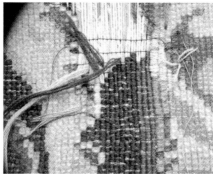

Our client list is diverse, crossing the public & private sector. We have worked closely for 30 years
with members of Historic Houses Association, The Treasure Houses, English Heritage
The National Trust, The Royal collection & private owners.

We have long experience in the care of historic carpets and collections, offering a service
of high quality cleaning, repair and preventive treatments for carpets.

Dame Jenny Abramsky holds a crumpled gold cross, part of the Staffordshire Hoard which is now on public display in a dedicated gallery in Birmingham after an HLF contribution of £704,500 in 2013. The Hoard is the largest collection of Anglo-Saxon treasure ever discovered.

Funding the future

Dame Jenny Abramsky was appointed Chair of the Heritage Lottery Fund in 2008, after a career at the BBC. Retiring in 2014, she talked to Sarah Greenwood about the Fund, the National Heritage Memorial Fund and the impact heritage funding has had on Britain.

Dumfries House, Ayrshire rescued for the nation in 2007 in a campaign led by HRH the Prince of Wales, with a £45 million fund to which the National Heritage Memorial Fund was a major contributor. The HLF monitored project has proved successful for this great Scottish Enlightenment house and its unique collection of Chippendale furniture.

How do you define the purpose of the Heritage Lottery Fund?

I think it is helping people make sure that the places, spaces and things that they value are there for the future. Heritage is a critical part of the future. It helps define who we are; it helps create communities; it is the places we live in; it is our collective memory. It's as much about red kites in Yorkshire and butterflies in Hampshire as lochs in Scotland and our industrial heritage.

Where do historic houses and heritage gardens fit into this?

They are absolutely a part of our heritage but I have always felt that heritage is not just about our historic houses and gardens. They are a very important part of what this country is and the more accessible and the more welcoming they are to us all, the more they will play a part in that future.

What do you think the HLF has contributed to the current state of the UK environment?

In my view the state of the UK's heritage before the HLF was created was a national disgrace. Since 1994, the Heritage Lottery Fund has distributed £6 billion of lottery income to nearly 37,000 heritage projects all over the UK.

How is the Heritage Lottery Fund organised?

We are managed by a board of trustees and rely on expert advice. The board bring their own skills, in the natural environment, in museums, in philanthropy, in archaeology, in history. We always have a regional view of a project before we take decisions. We won't fund anything unless there is clear consultation, the community is involved and there is a sustainable future for it.

"My hope is that heritage remains one of the good causes for the lottery distributor because its work is never done"

What is the relationship between the National Heritage Memorial Fund and the Heritage Lottery Fund?

The NHMF is the mother organisation that effectively distributes the HLF. The NHMF is the fund of last resort and has far less money, only £5 million a year. There is £20 million in the NHMF endowment which we tapped into, for example, when we had only three weeks to save Dumfries House but we had to pay it back within five years. The HLF has £375 million to distribute this year but remember that between £500 and £600 million has been taken out of the heritage sector every year since 2010, through cuts to the RDAs, to local authority funding, to English Heritage, to the NHMF (it was cut by 52%). There has been a significant decline in public funding of heritage but there has been an increase in funding from philanthropic donors, trusts and foundations and fortunately from lottery funding. The Coalition restored our share of the Lottery to 20%, it had been cut to 16.6%, so that gave us another £50-60 million per year – not to be sneezed at!

How do you monitor and maintain your investment?

We assign project monitors, including one of the trustees and the head of nation/region. Occasionally there have been projects where we have held back money until a particular problem is sorted out. We have clawed back money from projects but one of the astonishing things about HLF is that in 20 years no project has totally failed, I think because all are monitored and questioned and challenged. There are times when we have turned down projects for things that people have truly loved but we just don't believe that it will be sustainable.

The Romantic vista to Thomas Archer's baroque pavilion at the viewpoint of the Long Water at English Heritage's Wrest Park, Bedfordshire which received £1.14 million from the HLF in 2011.
© ENGLISH HERITAGE

Of the £3.6 million required for the restoration of The Swiss Garden, £2.8 million was contributed by the Heritage Lottery Fund. The Regency garden and its 13 buildings, a unique example of the fashion for Swiss Picturesque, opened to the public in 2014.

The Hon Charles Hamilton's landscape garden at Painshill Park in Surrey was boosted by £47,400 from the HLF which helped to restore its buildings including the Gothic Temple.

The new Mary Rose Museum at Portsmouth Historic Dockyard, opened in 2013, vies with the Cutty Sark as the recipient of the largest HLF grant. Built to display Henry VIII's flagship, The Mary Rose, raised from the seabed in 1982, is the only 16th century ship on display in the world.

What has been the change in patterns of applications over the past six years?

Over the last two years applications have gone up by 40% and there has been a switch away from local authority applications, as their budgets shrink so they can't produce matched funding. Local authorities do recognise that heritage can be a force for growth. People who think that heritage is just a drain are completely misunderstanding the positive impact it can have on a community and how important it is for economic health.

Do you ring fence funds for a particular sector?

We have a series of programmes where we ring fence a certain amount of money. For landscapes we put £20million aside; for places of worship we put £30million aside; for townscapes, we put £20 million aside. People can apply for up to £3million for a townscape up to £5 million for a landscape. Open programmes are for any kind of project. Theoretically we could be deciding between the Peak District National Park, Stonehenge and Stubbs' portrait of *Whistlejacket* at one meeting with only money for one. How do we decide? We have a series of measures: Is it at risk? Is it at immediate danger of loss? Is it of high heritage value? Will the outcome be sustainable?

And do you hold things over?

No, or you end up with a backlog. But a huge number of projects get rejected but come back a second time. We reject between 65% and 70% of applications at board level but we give feedback. In our last major grants programme we funded Canterbury Cathedral even though we had turned them down a year before.

How do you balance funding across private and public projects?

We can only fund up to £100,000 for buildings in private ownership and it has to deliver something for the public good. Emergency repairs are the responsibility of English Heritage not us. People have to deliver on a whole series of outcomes: that they have volunteers; that they are widening access; that there are learning opportunities.

You place a lot of emphasis on volunteers; do you worry that the volunteer population will decline as people retire later?

The voluntary sector is the backbone of our heritage. It is very difficult to predict what life is going to be like over the next 15 to 20 years, and, yes, that is clearly one of the great dangers, so the more young people we can get involved in volunteering the better.

Looking back over your six years as Chairman, what are you proudest of?

I think HLF has become far more responsive since the financial crash. For example, we started a programme called *Skills for the Future*. So far we have spent £47 million to give roughly 2,200 people proper craft and conservation qualifications. Of graduates of the programme, over 80% have got jobs using skills like dry stone walling, hedgerow laying, textile conservation and stone masonry. I'm very proud of the heritage enterprise programme that we launched last year. It encourages partnerships between not-for-profit organisations and private enterprise where we pay the conservation deficit. So where a building has remained empty for 20 years because no developer could find a financially sensible proposition, it is now viable. I'm very proud that we recognised that organisations would find fund raising more difficult as other sources of funding dried up, so we reduced the amount of matched funding we expected. The average award is still only about 64% but potentially for some projects we can now go up to about 90%. There are still very few projects in this category but it was a psychologically important thing to do.

What have you personally brought to the Fund?

I brought a desire for the organisation to become more nimble and more responsive and I brought a passion for training. I also think that to be a good communicator is an essential part of the job.

What do you think the future holds?

My hope is that heritage remains one of the good causes for the lottery distributor because its work is never done. I hope that the heritage sector will constantly reinvent itself, because there is no doubt that the challenges over the next few years are going to get tougher and people are going to have to think of new visitor models. We are not going to go back to the world before 2008 so we need to think forward and think differently.

The restoration of Britain's only surviving tea clipper, The Cutty Sark, required nearly £25 million funding from the HLF and opened in 2012 in Greenwich.

© NATIONAL TRUST IMAGES

Tyntesfield, the home of the late Lord Wraxall, was bought by the National Trust with help of a £17.5 million grant from the National Heritage Memorial Fund. A further grant of £20 million from the Heritage Lottery Fund has contributed to its restoration and reinterpretation for visitors.

Ys Ysgwrn, home of the Welsh bard, Hedd Wyn was granted £2.8 million in May 2014 for the Snowdonia National Park to restore and open the house. Hedd Wyn's death in World War I and his posthumous award of the Chair of the 1917 Eisteddfod came to symbolise the loss of his generation in Flanders.

Traquair House from the Bear Gates.

"Dool an' sorrow hae fa'en Traquair
An' the Yetts that were shut at Chairlie's comin'
He vowed wad be opened nevermuir
Till a Stuart King was crooned in Lunnon"

The Old Pretender

The mark left on history by the Jacobite movement of the early 18th century is a curious mixture of romance and tragedy, memorably combined at Traquair House in the Borders. Catherine Maxwell Stuart, 21st Lady of Traquair, recounts her family's involvement in 1715 and the impact of later events.

© THE NATIONAL PORTRAIT GALLERY

Remembered simply as 'the Fifteen', the First Jacobite Rising, occurred 300 years ago this year in 1715. It was not the start nor the end of my family's involvement with the cause of the Stuart kings in exile, but the relics that it left loom large in the history of the house and my family. The Jacobite movement was born two decades earlier with the flight of the last Stuart King, James II & VII and the accession of William of Orange in 1689. A group of Scots, mostly catholic and Episcopalian, declared themselves for James and became known as Jacobites. My ancestor the catholic 4th Earl of Traquair had allied himself to the Jacobite cause from the beginning and was imprisoned twice in 1692 and 1708.

Things heated up again after the death of the last Stuart monarch, Queen Anne, and the accession of the Hanoverian dynasty in the person of George I in 1714. At this stage, the focus of attention was the son of King James, James Edward Stuart later known as The Old Pretender. His support was strongest in Scotland where he could claim loyalty not only from Catholics but from Scots whose ancient loyalty to the Stuart line of kings remained strong but there were also risings in this year in Northumberland, Wales and the West Country. In Scotland support for James Edward included many of the Highland clans and Lowland lairds and the 4th Earl of Traquair certainly provided funding.

Pictured above: Prince James Francis Edward Stuart by Anton Raphael Mengs. Portraits and engravings of the Stuart kings in exile were handed out to their supporters and several hang at Traquair.

→

The 4th Earl of Traquair and his countess Mary Maxwell in oval frames in the Dining Room at Traquair. Below: Winifred, Lady Nithsdale, whose daring rescue of her Jacobite husband from the Tower in 1716 became the talk of the town.

The 1715 rising was led by the Earl of Mar whose forces were defeated at the Battle of Sheriffmuir by government troops led by the Duke of Argyll. By February 1716, it was all over and Mar and James Edward had fled to France.

For us, the main players in the Fifteen were the 4th Earl of Traquair, his wife, Mary Maxwell, her brother, William, the Earl of Nithsdale and her sister in law Winifred. This time the 4th Earl managed to stay at home and look after his estates but he sponsored his brother-in-law to go and fight. Lord Nithsdale was immediately captured and imprisoned in the Tower of London under sentence of death.

We have their own account of what happened in the correspondence preserved in the family archive. Lady Nithsdale determined to rescue her husband and travelled through the winter snows to London. Once there, she petitioned the King for her husband's release and visited him repeatedly with a maidservant or with friends. They made a point of crying and covering their faces whenever they left until on one occasion, one of them swapped clothes with Lord Nithsdale and he was smuggled out disguised in a large cloak. Winifred even had the nerve to go back and extract the companion and the three of them escaped to France.

They joined the Stuart court in exile in France and Italy and were never able to return. Their estates and titles were forfeit and without the continued support of the Traquair family, who bought back their lands, they would have had no income. Winifred wrote an extraordinary account of this great escape which had such currency at the time that the style of cloak worn became a fashion item known as a Nithsdale. The actual cloak passed down through several families and ended up with a sister of the Duke of Norfolk who turned up here 20 years ago and handed me the cloak in a plastic carrier bag. It has since been conserved and will be a centre piece of an exhibition on the 1715 rising at Traquair this year. I can't think of an object which so vividly brings back the desperate atmosphere of the time.

The Library founded by the 4th Earl of Traquair and expanded by the 5th Earl which contains many Jacobite documents.

The Traquair Amen glass used for the traditional Jacobite toast *"To the King over the Water"* and inscribed:

*"God Bless the Prince of Wales
The True born Prince of Wales
Sent us by Thee
Send him soon over
And kick out Hanover,
And then we'll recover
Our Old Libertie"*

Catherine Maxwell Stuart and her family at Traquair.

Prince Charles Edward Stuart leaving Traquair by Tom Scott.

The Jacobites had many of the characteristics of a secret society. The correspondence uses code names – the 4th Earl and Countess were Mr & Mrs Young, the Nithsdales, Mr & Mrs Joanes and the Old Pretender, Mrs Arther's son. The house is full of Jacobite symbolism. We have a collection of Jacobite glass, including a rare Amen glass, engraved with roses, sunflowers, butterflies, oak leaves and acorns, all symbols of Jacobite resistance dating from after the 1745 Rising. The family's alliances with Jacobite families continued. The 5th Earl's sister, Catherine, married her cousin, William, son of Lord Nithsdale of the great escape, while another sister, Mary, married John Drummond, Duke of Perth, whose portrait with a Jacobite white cockade at his throat, hangs in our Lower Drawing Room.

The family continued to support the Jacobite cause and we know that the Young Pretender, Charles Edward Stuart, grandson of James II & VII was entertained here by Charles, 5th Earl of Traquair in 1745. As his guest left, no doubt admiring the recently erected gates, the 5th Earl famously declared that the gates would be closed until another Stuart monarch was on the throne. The Rising went badly, the Jacobite troops were defeated at Culloden and Charles Edward fled abroad. The 5th Earl was arrested at his new wife's home in Yorkshire and imprisoned in the Tower but was released after eighteen months without charge. The gates remain shut to this day, waiting for the next Stuart King, and ever since we have had to approach the house at the side. There is no more potent or romantic symbol of the Jacobite cause.

"The gates remain shut to this day, waiting for the next Stuart King..."

The portrait of the Duke of Perth to the right of the fireplace in the Lower Drawing Room shows him with a white Jacobite cockade at the neck.

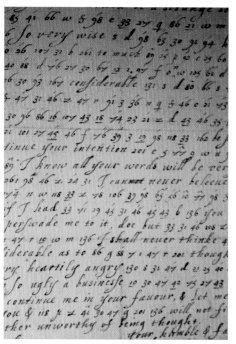

Above left: Detail of a coded letter received at Traquair during the Forty Five and never deciphered.

Jacobite Ale brewed to an 18th century recipe at Traquair commemorates the Traquair family's Jacobite history.

Traquair House, Borders (p.330)

Other houses with Jacobite associations:
Abbotsford House, Borders (p.329)
Glamis Castle, Tayside (p.338)
Huntingtower Castle, Tayside (p.339)
Kildrummy Castle, Grampian (p.344)
Fairfax House, York (p.290)
Bamburgh Castle, Northumberland (p.323)
Nunnington Hall, Yorkshire (p.289)
Chiswick House, London (p.126)

The Bear Gates – Charles Edward Stuart, 'Bonnie Prince Charlie' was the last person to pass through them in 1745.

A Glowing Report

Derek Tarr rambles through the quintessentially English countryside of the North Cotswolds.

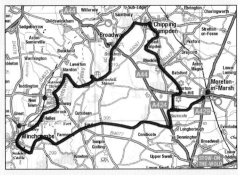

DEREK'S WALKS
DAY BY DAY

Walk 1: Winchcombe to Stanton
Walk 2: Stanton to Chipping Campden
Walk 3: Chipping Campden to Moreton in Marsh
Walk 4: Moreton in Marsh to Winchcombe

Photos: Nicola Burford

Fine views over the Vale of Evesham. Bottom left: Among the cloister arches at Hailes Abbey.

Stanway House from the restored 18th century water gardens.

Nestling in a corner of South West England, The Cotswolds stretch from Warwickshire in the north to Somerset in the south. The underlying Oolitic Jurassic Limestone has a beautiful golden hue giving the stone buildings their distinctive colour. Cotswolds means 'sheep enclosure in rolling hills' and the region's prosperity derived from the wool trade from the Middle Ages.

WALK 1
Winchcombe to Stanton
6 miles approx

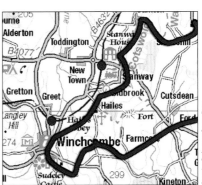

On leaving, the sun shone through threatening clouds and I anticipated an afternoon of mixed weather. I joined the Cotswolds Way and after a mile or so reached the remains of the Cistercian Hailes Abbey. Founded by the Earl of Cornwall in 1246, in thanks for surviving a shipwreck, it was a medieval pilgrimage destination to see a 'phial of holy blood'. The abbey was destroyed in 1539 during the Reformation. A few yards away stands the 12th century Hailes Church, older than its neighbour and possessing beautiful faded wall paintings.

Heading north through recently ploughed fields, the shrill whistle of a steam train on the nearby Gloucestershire/ Warwickshire Railway signalled the start of heavy rain. My next destination was Stanway House and as if my arrival was expected the clouds cleared and the afternoon sunshine streamed through. The gabled house, home of the Earl of Wemyss, is a beautiful Jacobean residence with a warm homely feel. The estate boasts a brewery and a fully working watermill. However, for me, the most spectacular feature is the fountain in the grounds, which at 300ft is the highest in Great Britain and the tallest gravity fountain in the world.

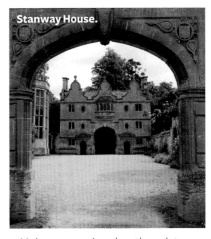

Stanway House.

My journey continued northwards to Stanton and my stop for the night. This pretty village has many B&Bs and The Mount Inn, with fine views over the Vale of Evesham, is a good place to eat and refresh yourself.

The Great Fountain at Stanway House.

WALK 2
Stanton to Chipping Campden
8 miles approx

Contains Ordanance Survey Data
© Crown copyright and database right 2012

The following morning started with a steep climb through woodland to Shenberrow Hill and a pleasant walk to the village of Snowshill. Here is, to my mind, one of the National Trust's gems, the quirky Snowshill Manor. Purchased by architect Charles Paget Wade in 1919, it became the home for his eclectic collection. Samurai armour, old bicycles, industrial machinery and toys clutter the rooms. He was inspired to begin collecting after seeing his grandmother's Chinese cabinet of curiosities which can be seen today in the Zenith Room. Graham Greene, Virginia Wolf and Queen Mary were among his visitors and he was partial to dressing up and performing dramatic productions with his friends.

The arrangement of the gardens was influenced by the Arts and Crafts Movement. Originally Wade constructed a model village around the pond called Wolf's Cove and some of these fragile buildings survive within the property. The National Trust is raising funds to construct a replica of the village.

After lunch in the café I continued on my way to Broadway Tower. The route follows the road for about two miles as there is no direct footpath through Broadway Country Park but the views are worth the effort. Set on the second highest hill in the Cotswolds, 16 counties can be seen from this point.

The folly, built by the Earl of Coventry for his wife, is today a small museum. The artists William Morris and Edward Burne-Jones rented the tower as a country retreat and one floor is dedicated to Morris' work. The Tower also has military connections. It is the location of a Cold War nuclear bunker and was used by the Observer Corps to track enemy planes. Close by is a memorial on the site where an AW 38 Whitley bomber crashed in 1943.

I rejoined the Cotswolds Way and after some gentle walking reached the elegant town of Chipping Campden. With its stone buildings mellowed by the evening sunlight, I stood in the High Street and admired the towering St James', a superb example of an early perpendicular wool church. Located by the church and just beyond the gateway to old Campden House, destroyed by fire during the Civil War, is Court Barn. This small but enjoyable museum is dedicated to the Arts and Crafts Movement. Influential designer, Charles Robert Ashbee moved The Guild and School of Handicraft here from London in 1902 to create jobs for local artisans. In the centre of the town is the Market Hall of 1627, with splendid arches and a remarkable cobbled floor.

The Noel Arms, an old coaching inn and my resting place, is famous for its award winning curries, which I can vouch are delicious!

"Rooms which inspire a thousand fancies" at Snowshill Manor.

Broadway Tower, folly, antiquarian library, inspiration for William Morris and wartime viewpoint.

"Quirky Snowshill Manor is one of the National Trust's gems"

The elegant town of Chipping Campden.

Mature trees at Batsford Arboretum and (below) the Japanese Bridge.

WALK 3
Chipping Campden to Moreton in Marsh
10 miles approx

Contains Ordanance Survey Data
© Crown copyright and database right 2012

The next day I headed south on the Monarch's Way through delightful Broad Campden and on to Blockley, a village which has a mixed industrial past. Following the decline of the wool trade it turned to silk production. Today it is the home of Watsonian Squire, the largest manufacturer of sidecars for motorcycles in the UK and Mill Dene Garden. It is also the main location for the filming of the 'Father Brown' BBC television series.

With the mid-morning sun beginning to warm me I climbed out of Blockley and reached the boundary wall of Batsford Arboretum. I stood awhile taking in the view through the trees to the Vale of the Evenlode before continuing to the estate. This wonderful arboretum was the result of the work of the 1st Lord Redesdale, grandfather of the Mitford sisters, at the turn of the 19th century and later by the 2nd Lord Dulverton. The 56 acres contain one of the country's largest private collections of trees and shrubs including giant redwoods and Japanese cherries with a constantly changing array of colours throughout the year.

The Falconry at Batsford is also well worth a visit where exotic birds, including golden eagles, hawks and falcons, star in a impressive demonstration.

I lunched at the Visitor Centre before heading down the drive towards Bourton-on-the-Hill where I had a brief stop to enjoy the topiary in the pretty gardens of Bourton House. From here I followed the Heart of England Way and after a short walk the onion dome of Sezincote beckoned from between the trees. This extraordinary building was constructed by the Cockerell brothers in the Mogul style of Rajasthan in the early 1800s. It was the inspiration, following a visit by the Prince Regent, for the transformation of the Brighton Pavilion. I started my visit with a cup of tea and a piece of cake in the sweeping Orangery before a guided tour of the house. The interior is more classical in style. The Oriental theme continues in the grounds with the Indian Bridge, the Persian Garden and the Snake Pool.

Bustling Moreton-in-Marsh, two miles east, has an impressive Georgian High Street with many independent shops. Locally produced St Eadburgha cheese was recommended by the friendly staff of the Cotswold Cheese Company. I stayed at the White Hart Royal Hotel which sits at the junction of the Fosse Way and the A44. Good food – I had exceptional duck with tempura pak choi – and fine beer make this a most pleasant of stops. The hotel runs 'Treesleep', a worthwhile scheme which raises money for the local Woodland Trust.

Raj-inspired Sezincote in its turn inspired The Brighton Pavilion.

Above clockwise: The Orangery Tearoom at Sezincote affords views across the gardens; shopping in the Cotswold Cheese Company; the White Hart Royal Hotel. Below: Topiary at Bourton House Gardens.

OFFICIAL TOURIST BOARD GUIDE

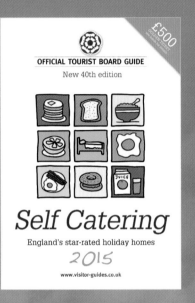
FIND A GOLDEN TICKET TO WIN A UK SHORT BREAK WORTH £500

Special 40th Anniversary Edition
featuring 'golden ticket' promotion

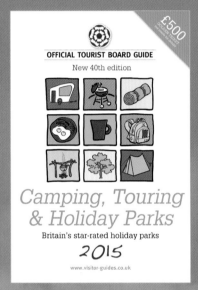

THE official national guide to quality-assessed B&Bs, Hotels and other guest accommodation in England

Packed with information and easy to use, it's all you need for the perfect English break

- Web-friendly features for easy booking
- Events, attractions and other tourist information
- National Accessible Scheme accommodation at a glance

To celebrate the 40th anniversary edition, 6 lucky readers will be in with a chance of finding a Golden Ticket for a UK short break worth £500.

AVAILABLE FROM ALL GOOD BOOKSHOPS AND ONLINE RETAILERS

Now book your star-rated accommodation online at

www.visitor-guides.co.uk

Sudeley Castle, the East Garden.

WALK 4
Moreton in Marsh to Winchcombe
15 miles approx

Contains Ordanance Survey Data © Crown copyright and database right 2012

An early start was needed for the 14 miles to Sudeley Castle. I retraced my steps back to Sezincote and headed towards Hinchwick, passing an unusual slate memorial to Hase and Michael Asquith; he was the grandson of World War 1 Prime Minister, Herbert Asquith. The Gloucestershire Way led me through the middle of Jackdaw's Castle, J. J. McManus' horse-racing yard where Jonjo O'Neill is the trainer. Just beyond the stables lies the village of Ford and the Plough Inn, 'Racing Pub of the Year' in 2008, displaying pictures dedicated to the sport, including A. P. McCoy's welcome following his Grand National success in 2010.

Continuing westward to a superb view at the edge of the Cotswolds Hills, I glimpsed Sudeley Castle nestled in the valley below. Sudeley can trace its history to before the Norman Conquest but for me the most fascinating period was the 16th century when it became the home of Sir Thomas Seymour and his bride Katherine Parr, the last wife of King Henry VIII. For a time the couple lived here

Tomb of Queen Katherine Parr in St Mary's Church.

The Knot Garden at Sudeley Castle.

with a large retinue including the future Queen Elizabeth and Lady Jane Grey. In 1548 Katherine gave birth to a daughter, Mary, but sadly died from puerperal fever. Her beautiful marble tomb is in St. Mary's Church in the grounds.

Following heavy damage during the English Civil War the castle was 'slighted' and remained a ruin until the 19th century when it was bought by brothers John and William Dent, prosperous Worcester glovemakers. The restored house is today the home of Lord and Lady Ashcombe and their family. The interior includes the Emma Dent textile display, although it was the romantic rose strewn garden outside which captured my imagination.

A short stroll from the castle brought me back to Winchcombe and a well-earned pint of Stanway bitter at The Lion, my final night's accommodation. Following a much needed dinner I wearily retired to my comfortable bed.

The North Cotswolds is beautiful and unspoiled with well signposted footpaths and bridleways. Whilst rarely demanding, it offers good walking with spectacular views and a host of places to visit. I passed through 'chocolate box' villages, sweetly scented gardens and historic houses brimming with fascinating collections. Bathed in the glow of golden limestone and the warmth of the summer I left reluctantly but will return soon to savour this most enticing of regions.

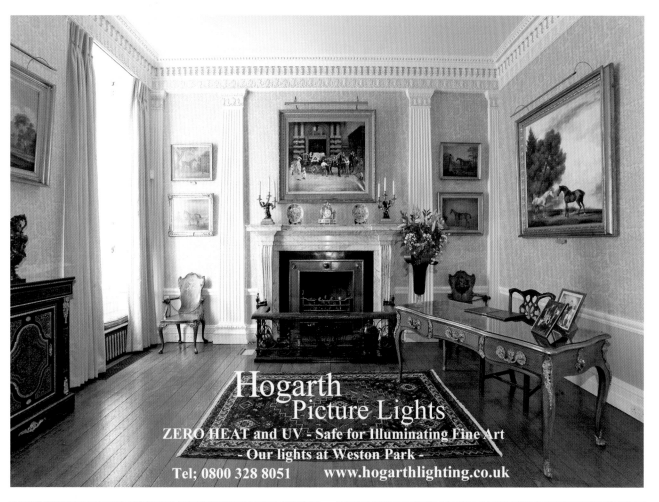

Hogarth
Picture Lights

ZERO HEAT and UV - Safe for Illuminating Fine Art

- Our lights at Weston Park -

Tel; 0800 328 8051   www.hogarthlighting.co.uk

The Landmark Trust

"A marvellous coffee table dream book. It can never be replaced by anything digital. If I had a fire, it's one of the few books I'd save."

The 50th anniversary edition of the Landmark Trust Handbook is a book to treasure. 276 pages with beautiful colour photographs of all our Landmarks.

1965 - 2015
50 YEARS
RESCUING BUILDINGS

http://www.landmarktrust.org.uk/giftshop/

Transform your landscape
with semi-mature trees, specimen shrubs & instant hedging

Wykeham Mature Plants

...from bare ground to this in a single day!

Larger plants for instant results

Experienced horticulturalists to help and advise so that your planting scheme will thrive on your site

Nationwide delivery

All stock fully hardy & guaranteed (terms & conditions apply)

150 acre nursery supplying trade & public for over 30 years
The Walled Garden, Wykeham Abbey, Scarborough, N. Yorks.

01723 862406   enquiries@wykeham.co.uk

www.wykehammatureplants.co.uk

THE PERSIAN CARPET STUDIO

Specialists in the sale of antique and new handmade rugs and carpets

- Extensive showroom with stunning traditional and contemporary rugs, runners and room size carpets
- Expert advice on colour, style, wearing quality and care
- Home and on-site consultations
- Carpet copying service of old, antique and historic carpets

Conservation and restoration of rugs and carpets

- Experienced and accredited conservators offering a complete conservation service for owners of historic houses, museums and private collections
- On-site evaluations. Full written and photographic reports, condition and treatment surveys, collection cataloguing and historical research
- Purpose built workshops equipped with specialist facilities for treatment of both small and oversized carpets
- Advice on display, handling, packing and storage
- Preventative conservation, emergency treatments and aftercare services
- Flexibility to treat carpets during closed season

The Persian Carpet Studio, The Old White Hart, Long Melford, Sudbury, Suffolk CO10 9HX

01787 882214 | info@persiancarpetstudio.co.uk

www.persiancarpetstudio.co.uk

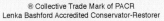
® Collective Trade Mark of PACR
Lenka Bashford Accredited Conservator-Restorer

Waterloo!

This year is the 200th anniversary of the Duke of Wellington's
victory over Napoleon at the Battle of Waterloo.
Lucy Denton has been searching for evidence.

O n 18th June 1815, the Battle of Waterloo – the *'closest
run thing you ever saw in your life'* according to the
victorious 1st Duke of Wellington – would end more
than twenty years of terrible conflict and change
forever the dynamics of European politics.

Arthur Wellesley, introverted, sensitive, musical, and perhaps
somewhat neglected, grew up in Ireland in a house now in
ruins. He would become one of history's greats despite his
initial reluctance to pursue a military career. Much of his
story and the consequences of his triumph over the Emperor
Napoleon, amidst the battered farmsteads of Hougoumont
and La Haye Sainte, can be traced in surviving historic houses,
through associations, artefacts, collections and memorials.

**Pictured above
left: The Duke
of Wellington
by Sir Thomas
Lawrence hangs
at Apsley House,
London, near his
great adversary,
Napoleon by
Robert Lefévre
(right).**

Evidence of the Duke of Wellington's formative years survives in and around Wales. Brynkinalt Hall near Chirk on the Welsh border, is a Jacobean house remodelled in 1808 in the Gothick style. The young Arthur Wellesley made frequent visits to his grandparents at Brynkinalt, the seat of the Trevor family, and reminders include a family portrait depicting his mother Anne, Countess of Mornington as a girl and various objects that belonged to them.

Wellesley returned from military service on the Indian subcontinent with two stone lions, now installed at nearby Plas Newydd in Denbighshire as a gift for the celebrated 'Ladies of Llangollen', Sarah Ponsonby and Eleanor Butler, in whose diaries he was described as *'handsome, fashioned, tall and elegant'*. Their modest cottage, transformed into an extraordinary Gothic fantasy of carved black oak timbers, was the setting for Regency intrigue, literary gatherings and tea with luminaries including Wellesley and Wordsworth.

Of the same name, but located on Anglesey, is another Plas Newydd, the home of Henry Paget, 2nd Earl of Uxbridge, later 1st Marquess of Anglesey, who commanded the cavalry at Waterloo. In its military museum is Uxbridge's innovative articulated wooden leg, one of the first prosthetics ever made and one of many discovered in the cellars, each designed for different purposes; he was cruelly injured by one of the last cannon shots of the battle. This, along with his unwashed uniform, his sword and a piece of paper 'liberated' from Napoleon's carriage are among the highlights.

At Windsor Castle we can explore the sequence of events that led up to the battle, its key figures, and the outcome in a series of military objects exhibited in a trail throughout the State Apartments. The Waterloo Chamber was built in 1830 in tribute to the victory of Wellington and his Allied forces, featuring specially commissioned portraits by Sir Thomas Lawrence depicting the main characters, including Tsar Alexander I of Russia and Emperor Francis I of Austria.

Left: Brynkinalt, home of the Duke of Wellington's maternal grandparents.

Above: An enamel bracelet given by the young Arthur Wellesley, later Duke of Wellington to his mother, in the collection at Brynkinalt.

"At Windsor Castle we can explore the sequence of events that led up to the battle, its key figures, and the outcome in a series of military objects exhibited in a trail throughout the State Apartments"

Plas Newydd, Llangollen, home of the accomplished Ladies of Llangollen who frequently entertained Arthur Wellesley as a young man.

The Anglesey Leg displayed at Plas Newydd, Anglesey, with the uniform the Earl of Uxbridge wore at Waterloo.
Uxbridge: *"By God, Sir. I've lost my leg."*
Duke of Wellington: *"By God, Sir. So you have."*

The Duke of Wellington in uniform by Sir Thomas Lawrence hangs in the Music Room at Plas Newydd, Anglesey.

© NATIONAL TRUST IMAGES/EDDY REYNOLDS

© HUDSON'S MEDIA IMAGES

French cavalry stream past the farm of La Haye Sainte in the Battle of Waterloo laid out in The Model Soldier Collection at Houghton Hall.

The Cholmondeley Collection of Model Soldiers at Houghton Hall, Norfolk is a unique display of figures amassed by the 6th Marquess from 1928. One of the largest and most comprehensive collections in the world, the miniature soldiers are laid out in formation as though they were engaged in the Sudan Wars, the Battle of Culloden and, of course, Waterloo. Here, the adversaries oppose each other from either side of the farm of La Haye Sainte, captured in the terrifying moments prior to the arrival of the Prussians.

The National Trust's Mount Stewart in Ireland has on show arms and armour from Waterloo – and this year hosts an exhibition displaying several of the twenty two giltwood chairs used at the Congress of Vienna. This meeting between national representatives which took place between 1814 and 1815 was instigated to redress an imbalance of power between European countries arising from the French Revolutionary and Napoleonic Wars. Viscount Castlereagh, adept and distinguished Foreign Secretary, his half-brother, Charles Stewart, and the Duke of Wellington were among the attendees whose final Act was signed just nine days prior to Napoleon's ultimate defeat.

The Percy Tenantry Museum housed in the Constable's Tower at Alnwick Castle, Northumberland, is an exceptional exposé of the historic collaboration between landed estate and the local population described in personal records of volunteers raised to defend the Castle from the French. In the Lower Guard Chamber is a display of their uncomplicated paraphenalia: pistols, powder flasks and horns. Major the Honourable Henry Percy, an aide to Wellington, who carried the official Dispatch to London declaring defeat of the French, is here commemorated by the purple velvet wallet used for the purpose, his ink bottle and case, and his coatee, worn during Waterloo.

Stratfield Saye in Hampshire was built in the 17th century for the Pitt family, then sold to the nation and gifted to the Duke of Wellington in 1817 in tribute to his military accomplishment. Extending the house, rather than expensively demolishing and rebuilding, the Iron Duke made Stratfield his home and it is where today's Duke of Wellington lives. Here the tour is devoted to his life – and death – including maps, weapons and his colossal cast bronze funeral carriage made out of French cannon.

Top: The grave of Wellington's charger, Copenhagen, at Stratfield Saye, Hampshire.

Above left: Stratfield Saye, Wellington's unassuming home.

Above: Hugh, Earl Percy in the uniform of the Percy Tenantry Volunteers.

©ENGLISH HERITAGE

Walmer Castle, where the Duke of Wellington died in 1852.

"For many of the British, Napoleon's downfall was as engrossing as Wellington's victory"

The grave of Copenhagen, Wellington's chestnut war horse of just fifteen hands, who is said to have bitten the Duke when he dismounted after the battle, is in the gardens. Of him the Duke remarked, *'there may have been many faster horses, no doubt many handsomer, but for bottom and endurance I never saw his fellow'*.

For many of the British, Napoleon's downfall was as engrossing as Wellington's victory. Among the spoils of war, some macabre, many intriguing, was the Emperor's personal carriage. Seized by the Prussians at the end of the battle, and looted of its most valuable contents, it was handed over to the British Government in October 1815 before being sold, along with four of Napoleon's horses, to museum entrepreneur William Bullock who exhibited it and its remaining contents at the Egyptian Hall on Piccadilly. Waning interest led Bullock to auction the contents in 1816. One of the buyers was John Powell Powell of Quex Park in Kent, a keen purchaser of Napoleonic memorabilia. Still at Quex House are the carriage watch Napoleon reputedly used to time the start of battles, his compass, a cannon, and a lock of his hair. It is likely he named the Waterloo Tower of 1819 in the Park in honour of the battle, one of the most unusual commemorative secular monuments complete with twelve bells, and viewed by tour only.

Apsley House, nicknamed No 1 London because of its location at the Knightsbridge turnpike, was sold to the Duke of Wellington in 1817. Wellington, who was Prime Minister twice, used the townhouse as a political base, the opulently dazzling Regency interiors reflecting his status. The Waterloo Gallery, a room commissioned shortly after Wellington became Prime Minister in 1828, was the scene of the annual banquet held to celebrate the Iron Duke's achievement, due to be recreated by English Heritage this year. Wellington Arch, designed by Decimus Burton in 1826, will feature a new exhibition displaying a pair of the famous leather Wellington Boots. Once surmounted by a statue of the Duke, this was replaced in 1912 by the largest bronze in Europe depicting Peace descending on the four-horse chariot of war.

Quex Park, Kent, where Napoleon's carriage can still be seen.

From left to right: Napoleon's carriage watch, captured at Waterloo; one of several objects at Quex Park; The Waterloo Tower at Quex Park from a watercolour of 1820; A lock of Napoleon's hair, still treasured as a souvenir of Waterloo.

The Waterloo Barracks at the Tower of London, built by the Duke of Wellington in 1841.

As Constable of the Tower of London for twenty six years, the Duke of Wellington was the last man actively to fortify its defences. A space within the newly opened Bowyer Tower, never before seen by the public, is being used to show three films about the Duke's extraordinary tenure here, revealing details about his influence, a devastating fire in 1841 and the threat of revolution which prompted his building of the Waterloo Barracks for 1,000 soldiers. So robust was his construction, is it where the Crown Jewels are now on display.

It was at Walmer Castle in Kent that Pitt the Younger met with his ministers to orchestrate defences against Napoleon; later it would become the summer residence of the Duke as Lord Warden of the Cinque Ports. It was here in 1852 that he died, in a chair still on display. An exhibition featuring his state funeral which saw more than a million people line the route to St Paul's Cathedral opens in 2015.

It is easy to see the historical impact of Waterloo, something of the brutality of early 19th century warfare and the Duke of Wellington's political accomplishments revealed at a selection of historic houses and castles commemorating his victory, as many did two hundred years ago.

The Battle of Waterloo by Denis Dighton in the Cavalry Room at Plas Newydd, Anglesey.

The Lady of Seville

Jane Hasell-McCosh has spent the last 10 years on a mission to revive the fortunes of marmalade. Each year, the World's Original Marmalade Festival attracts crowds to her home, Dalemain in Cumbria, for two days of tasting, music, lectures and enjoyment of all things marmalade. At the Festival, the winners of the annual World's Original Marmalade Awards are announced. This international competition now attracts over 2,000 entries from 30 countries, as well as sponsors from Fortnum & Mason and Mackays of Scotland to Paddington Bear. She shared some favourite recipes with *Hudson's*.

WHAT IS MARMALADE?

Every spoonful of marmalade serves up a bite of British history. Marmalade started out as a quince paste imported from Portugal (the Portuguese word for quince is marmelo). The oldest mutual alliance still in force is the Anglo-Portuguese Alliance of 1373 and the first imports arrived in Britain at least as early as the 1490s from the Iberian peninsula. From the start it was purported to have health and aphrodisiac properties. The same long established trade also brought 'suckets', pieces of candied oranges and lemons, to Britain and by the 17th century recipes appear which describe a citrus preserve closer to today's marmalades. Scottish companies like James Keillor & Son of Dundee developed marmalades in jars ready for distribution to the growing urban populations of industrial towns in the late 18th century so that, 100 years later, it was appearing on every breakfast table in the nation.

JANE'S 5 TOP TIPS

1 Use the best ingredients
The best Seville oranges begin to arrive into the shops after Christmas. The season is short so make time in January. Other citrus fruits are available all year but make sure to choose fruit that is a good colour, heavy with juice and with a smooth skin.

2 Clean equipment
If you haven't used your equipment since last year, wash it thoroughly before use. You don't want your hard work to be undermined by musky undertones. To create award winning marmalade, small details matter.

3 Plan your recipe
Decide what sort of marmalade you are going to make and how you would like it to taste. I invented my own recipe which I absolutely adore and produce every year.

4 Setting point
At Dalemain, our judges taste marmalade blind; out of its jar or on a plain white saucer. It's therefore important that it has set correctly. Don't be tempted to overcook your marmalade into a solid, unpleasant lump. Have confidence in your recipe and remove it from the heat when it states that you should.

5 Settling time
Make sure that the peel doesn't all rise to the top. After your marmalade has reached its setting point leave it to settle in your preserving pan for 15 minutes before it is poured into a jar.

ROUGH CUT MARMALADE

INGREDIENTS

2.5 kg Seville Oranges
Juice of 2 lemons
2.5 litres cold water
2.5 kg sugar

METHOD

Wash the oranges. Peel off the shred taking care not to peel the pith and then cut finely. Peel off the pith and put into a muslin bag with the pips. Chop the flesh roughly. Put the shred, muslin bag and flesh into a preserving pan with the water.

Boil gently until the peel is tender (about 2 hours; it will reduce by half). Meanwhile warm the sugar. Add the sugar and stir until dissolved and boil rapidly. Test for setting point by dropping a spoonful onto a saucer from the fridge, push gently to see if a skin has formed. It will reach setting point after about 15-20 minutes.

Allow to stand for about 15 minutes and pot in clean warm jars.

THREE CITRUS FRUIT MARMALADE

INGREDIENTS

1.5 kg mixed sweet oranges, grapefruit and lemons (I like a dominant orange flavour)
3 times the quantity of water to fruit
1.5 kg granulated sugar

METHOD

Chop up fruit roughly and remove pips. Put pips in muslin bag and leave in with the fruit to sit for 24 hours. Add three times the amount of water to fruit. Simmer for 2 hours until the shred is tender. Warm the sugar. Add 1kg of sugar to every 1 litre of liquid and fruit.

Boil rapidly until setting point is reached (see left). Allow to stand for about 15 minutes and pot in clean warm jars.

The World's Original Marmalade Festival 2015 at Dalemain Cumbria on Saturday 28 February and Sunday 1 March 2015.

WORLD'S ORIGINAL
DALEMAIN
MARMALADE AWARDS

Smell the roses

Gardening with roses has a long pedigree as **Hudson's** discovered when we asked some of our best heritage gardeners to describe their rose gardens and to propose their favourite rose.

Lady Xa Tollemache, owner, Helmingham Hall Gardens

The new rose garden at Helmingham was created in 1982. With the advice of Peter Beale, I planted the four outer beds with collections of roses within their particular group. I underplanted these with masses of geraniums, adding other perennials for late summer interest when these old fashioned roses are over. These beds are edged with Hidcote lavender. The four inner curved beds encircling a statue of Flora are planted densely with repeat flowering roses, mainly David Austin New English roses.

After five years the roses were established and I was very pleased with the planting schemes, but one night, in a terrific rainstorm, all the roses were split and all the blooms left lying on the ground. In desperation, I designed a rose support, retaining the natural shape of the shrub but holding it in place by tying down the new growths. These have now been in place for nearly 20 years and have proved exceptional, allowing the rose to flower all the length of the stem so they resemble huge ballgowns. My favourite rose trained in this way is *R. Madame Plantier*, a white rose with small green eye.

R. Munstead Wood, a delicious deep red rose that repeats continuously is my favourite David Austin rose. We also have huge borders devoted to hybrid musks planted in 1963 and underplanted with *Campanula Lactiflora* and *London Pride* (*Saxifrage Urbium*) and climbing roses on training wires in the walled garden and on all the walls.

Modern repeat flowering roses surround the statue of Flora. Right: *R. Madame Plantier* blooms on a hidden rose support.

Multiple blooms cover old fashioned roses in beds edged with lavender.

Elizabeth, Lady Ashcombe, owner, Sudeley Castle & Gardens

From May onwards every year, the gardens at Sudeley Castle & Gardens explode in an exuberant display of roses with their subtle variety of colours, textures and fragrances, weaving enchantment for all to enjoy. I love roses and I particularly love this time of year at Sudeley.

Twenty years ago I embarked, with renowned rosarian Jane Fearnley-Whittingstall, on an ambitious project to re-create a rose garden on the original Tudor parterre. The hundreds of roses which we selected for the Queen's Garden reflect every period of Sudeley Castle's history – from a time when Katherine Parr and Lady Jane Grey would have strolled along rose petal-strewn paths, right the way through until the present day.

The castle has won honours for this garden and last year Jane returned to replant many of the species which had seen the height of their splendour, introducing new varieties into the collection.

My favourite of all the glorious roses found in the Queen's Garden is the *Rosa Mundi*. With its ancient lineage, subtle scent and magically stripped pink and white petals, it evokes for me a romantic time when Henry VIII visited Sudeley Castle & Gardens with his then Queen, Anne Boleyn. The *Rosa Mundi* is also said to have been her favourite rose.

Lady Ashcombe with a bed of *R. Mundi*, a favourite of hers and of Anne Boleyn. Below: The Queen's Garden at Sudeley Castle.

Pergolas in the Ornamental Garden support a profusion of climbing roses.

Trevor Jones, head gardener, The Alnwick Garden

Well known for the UK's only Poison Garden, magnificent wooden treehouse and as an innovative contemporary garden, The Alnwick Garden also provides visitors with a spectacular surprise of flora and fauna, including two rose gardens.

The largest of these rose gardens is created from an informal planting of three thousand David Austin English shrub roses. Austin has bred the qualities of the old rose, with its multi petal head and rich fragrances, with roses that have all those qualities but also repeat-flower throughout the season to create a blanket of scent and colour across the north west corner of the garden.

Together with climbers that scramble overhead on pergolas, the roses are grown in good loamy soil and foliar fed with a sea weed based fertilizer, which keeps the plants healthy with little attack from pests or diseases.

The most fragrant of these roses, *"Jude the Obscure"*, is a medium yellow incurved cup shaped rose, but this (in my opinion) fades into insignificance when compared with *"Chandos Beauty"*,

The Duchess of Northumberland, the innovator behind The Alnwick Garden.

which is grown in The Ornamental Garden above The Grand Cascade. Here in a formal rose garden of squares, each containing one variety of rose, this shell-pink hybrid tea possesses forty petals to each flower, opening in a spiral whorl to give rise to a true rose fragrance that drifts in the atmosphere.

Colour themed roses in the Ornamental Garden include Trevor Jones' favourite, *R Chandos Beauty* (inset).

R. Adelaide d'Orleans on the pergola in the Walled Garden but *R.Mrs Oakley Fisher* (below right) is a favourite.

Johnny Bass, head gardener, Mottisfont Gardens

"Heaven!" As far as I'm concerned this is the only word that gives an accurate description of the Rose Garden here at Mottisfont. Designed by Graham Stuart Thomas in the early 1970's and then planted with his own collection of rare, forgotten and thought-to-be extinct roses, this really is a special place to be. A revolutionary design that combined what were considered to be old fashioned roses with a whole host of companion planting, this now seems common place but at the time was not the done thing. Home to the National Collection of pre 1900 shrub roses and with a collection of roses that has grown from some 250 to over 650 different varieties it really is a sight to behold. One of my favourites is *Mrs Oakley Fisher*, a rose that is the epitome of beautiful simplicity.

On opening the door into the Rose Garden, particularly at dawn or soon after, I am filled with a feeling of tranquillity and peacefulness. Much like a weary traveller after a long journey I feel that I have arrived home. All the problems in the world seem to evaporate and disappear, and I am left standing in perfect silence to soak up the horticultural masterclass that is before my eyes.

Chris Wardle, garden advisor,
Crathes Castle

The gardens of Crathes are an exceptional example of the arts and crafts style of gardening dating from the early 20th century, particularly special so far north. The gardens were put together in their current form by Sir James and Lady Sybil Burnett, who were influenced by the designs and planting schemes of Gertrude Jekyll and the high Victorian style, meshing together the two to create a formal structure with effervescent and billowing plantings full of rare and unusual plants. Within the many garden rooms, the rose garden is an oasis of colour and scent.

Stunning views up to the castle provide a backdrop to the bright displays of hybrid Tea roses such as *Rosa Friend for Life, R. Rob Roy* and *R. Iceberg* as well as the heady aromas of the old fashioned bourbon and moss roses as well as traditional scotch briar roses. The impressive yew hedges give the garden a sense of enclosure as well providing the climbing support for masses of flame creeper *Tropeolum speciosum* which flowers in abundance with quantities of red flowers in mid-July.

Ancient yew hedges set off the delicacy of the hybrid and species roses in the Arts and Crafts gardens at Crathes Castle.

Adam Salvin on the Upper Rose Terrace.

Adam Salvin, acting head gardener, Bodnant Gardens

I have long had a passion for roses. During a walk around Bodnant Garden for my job interview some years ago the garden foreman pointed out the magnificent Rosa Gardenia which is trained down the wall of the White Garden and it reminded me of the waterfall for which Bodnant is so well known. From this very first, impressive statement of the impact which roses can make, I've found myself at the centre of a large project renovating our rose terraces, which are now flourishing into what I believe is the best display of roses in Wales.

We are fortunate at Bodnant in having not one rose garden but two – part of the five famous Italianate terraces which sweep west down our hillside garden, overlooking the Snowdonian mountains. The Upper Rose Terrace is where the renovation work began in 2006. I was asked by garden manager Michael McLaren which project was the most important that coming winter and without hesitation I replied the Upper Rose Terrace. So the garden team and I set about replacing 150 tonnes of soil and replanting the beds with mainly David Austin English Roses.

In 2012 we renovated the Lower Rose Terrace; this is the larger of the two rose terraces and with this space we've been able to create a more relaxed, informal area and the *Rosa Gardenia*, planted en masse on the central pergola will, I hope, become as powerful and memorable a feature for visitors as that first encounter I had all those years ago.

Newly replanted *R. Gardenia* on the pergola surrounding the Pin Mill on the Lower Terrace.

Kirklinton Hall

The entrance front of Kirklinton Hall with Jacobean gables and the 19th century wing to the right.

Take 2

What motivates someone to rescue a doomed country house and open it to the public? Luckily for all of us, such individuals do exist. **Hudson's** considers two such cases.

The warm sandstone of the West front picked out by early winter sun.

Wentworth Woodhouse

Wentworth Woodhouse once rivalled the finest stately homes in the country. Planned as the largest house in Britain, its gilded rooms held a priceless collection of art by Van Dyck, Lely and Stubbs, set in a park designed by Humphry Repton for the Fitzwilliam family. Targeted by the post-war Labour government, the formal gardens and part of the Repton park were largely destroyed by the largest open cast mining operation in the country from 1946.

The façade is breathtaking; 615ft of Palladian magnificence whose flanking pavilions each form a substantial country house in their own right. Conceived by local architect Ralph Tunnicliffe in the 1730s and embellished by Henry Flitcroft and John Carr, this house, like Stowe, is a tribute to the taste and ambition of the Whig party in parliament. In the 1750s, it was home to the Whig prime minister, the 2nd Marquess of Rockingham. With stables by John Carr of York and numerous garden buildings and follies in the extended park, it is still possible to glimpse the glories of Wentworth Woodhouse in its heyday.

It was this glimpse that excited Clifford Newbold one weekend in London as his family gathered for Sunday lunch. He was retiring from a successful London architectural practice and looking for a 'project'. The sale details of the house caught his eye and his three sons agreed that here indeed was a project. The house was purchased in 1999, the family moved to Yorkshire and found themselves owners of the largest private house in Britain. There are said to be 365 rooms – one for every day of the year - and 250,000 ft² of floor space behind the longest façade in Europe. But the Newbolds discovered that Wentworth Woodhouse is really two houses, behind the Palladian front lies another house, a Baroque confection of brick and pilasters which only predates the Palladian part by a few years but is in a more conservative style.

→

"There is a terrible irony that the coal that helped fund the building of this great palace should still be destroying it"

By living in the Baroque section and restoring the Palladian enfilade of state rooms, the Newbold family felt that there was potential to develop a business use for the house, which would generate funds to maintain the structure and secure it for the future, while enjoying the building and establishing a family base. This mix of business sense and passion for the house has brought Clifford Newbold's younger son Giles to champion Wentworth Woodhouse with as much fervour as his father. Their joint vision is to create a new tourist destination in South Yorkshire, to restore the stable block as business units and to welcome people into the 82 acres of parkland. The ornate interiors designed by Henry Flitcroft largely survive, so even if there are no Van Dycks in the Van Dyck Room, the beauty of the decoration and proportion shines through. The Marble Hall is unchanged now that the Newbolds have restored the inlaid floor hidden beneath later floorboards. In 1768, it was described by writer, Arthur Young as *"Beyond all comparison, the finest room in England"*. Many of the garden buildings have been swallowed up by surrounding villages but Humphry Repton's landscape design still provides a fine setting for the house.

With over 5 million people living within a 40-mile radius of the house, the plan looks viable except for one problem: the house is subsiding into unseen mine workings by approximately 1cm every year. The family has challenged the Coal Authority in court since the extent of the mine workings was not previously disclosed. The case continues. There is a terrible irony that the coal that helped fund the building of this great palace should still be destroying it. Can the passion of one family reverse the decline?

The Long Gallery which joins the Palladian and Baroque wings of the house.

The neoclassical Marble Hall at Wentworth Woodhouse, with bas-reliefs added by James 'Athenian' Stuart in 1755.

The East front of Wentworth Woodhouse only fits on this page thanks to a fish eye lens.

Giles Newbold at the foot of the steps to the baroque East front of the house. Coalmining operations came to within 15 feet of these steps in the early 1950s.

Roses blooming once more by the ornate front door.

An enigmatic face carved into the bedrock at The Captain's Seat recalls a local legend of Maelgwyn the Fair, a faerie princess who pined away for love of the first de Boyville to make Kirklinton his home.

Kirklinton Hall was never grand or stately, rather it is a fine example of 17th century baroque architecture, built for the aspiring Cumberland gentry as the turbulent border region finally enjoyed the first peace for 200 years. The house is a ruin, roofless for 30 years and with a chequered history as an officers' mess, flats, a hotel and a nightclub frequented by the notorious Kray twins. Not exactly a promising prospect for a family home.

London barrister, Christopher Boyle QC inherited a farm in the next valley where he has restored the farmhouse, whose core is a fortified bastle house, embellishing the interiors with fine craftsmanship in the aesthetic of country house architects like Lutyens and Lorimer. When the property crash of 2008 put paid to a controversial planning scheme for 22 dwellings at Kirklinton, he realised that he could both save the ruined house from inappropriate development and create a new canvas for his flair with interiors. Kirklinton has, he says *"All the amenities of civilised living"*.

Designed by Edward Addison, who had worked with the great Baroque architect Talman at Lowther Castle, Kirklinton Hall was built as a showpiece house in the 1680s when the local Appleby family married a Dacre heiress from nearby Lanercost. A Victorian wing later doubled the house in size but Kirklinton, tucked into the lee of a wooded hillside, still feels intimate.

Together with his wife, Ilona, Christopher Boyle has already embued Kirklinton with a sense of fun. Resplendent in a new 'Chinese Chippendale' style pigsty, are Monica Simmons and the Empress of Kirklinton, Middle White pigs with a heritage as old as the house. The gardens are already being reclaimed with an organic vegetable garden, formal herb garden, orchard, nuttery, quince grove, rose terraces and a long border backed by a surviving 19th century garden wall. A Pell-Mell allée encourages visitors to play a game beloved by Charles II, a pre-cursor of croquet. Restoring a Victorian wilderness walk to a viewpoint above the river, they discovered that Kirklinton has a distinct mystical quality, one they have exploited to captivate children in their 'Fairie Glen'. A temporary roof has opened up the Victorian wing for weddings.

The house has been cleared of rubble and trees and work on the interior can begin. Originally, it had a central hall with a great chamber above and a book room in the third storey in the Scottish tradition. Christopher Boyle hopes that the creation of new interiors will allow a flowering of local craftsmanship married with new technologies to heat and light the

Temporary roofing on the Old Ballroom looking through to the Bride's Border on the top terrace.

Gardens planted on the 17th century principle of 'dulce et utile' so that beauty is balanced with productivity.

house on environmentally sound principles. He admits *"I resent the break with tradition that modernism represents"*, so plans to sponsor traditional craft skills in his recreation of the interior rooms. It will take time; the Boyles' children are not yet teenagers and this purchase was certainly for the long term. The first family to live here were the de Boyvilles 900 years ago; it looks as if the Boyle family have now re-established an ancient connection at Kirklinton Hall.

Wentworth Woodhouse, S Yorkshire (p.299)
Kirklinton Hall, Cumbria (p.308)

A Good View

Simon Jenkins has been described as 'the supreme champion of England's heritage'. His published compilations of England's 1000 Best Churches and England's 1000 Best Houses are popular best sellers. He has now taken a step back to consider views and he shared with **Hudson's** a selection of his favourite views of historic buildings in England.

The Queen's House, Greenwich, with the domes of the Royal Naval College framing the view of Canary Wharf beyond.
Photo © Visit England Images

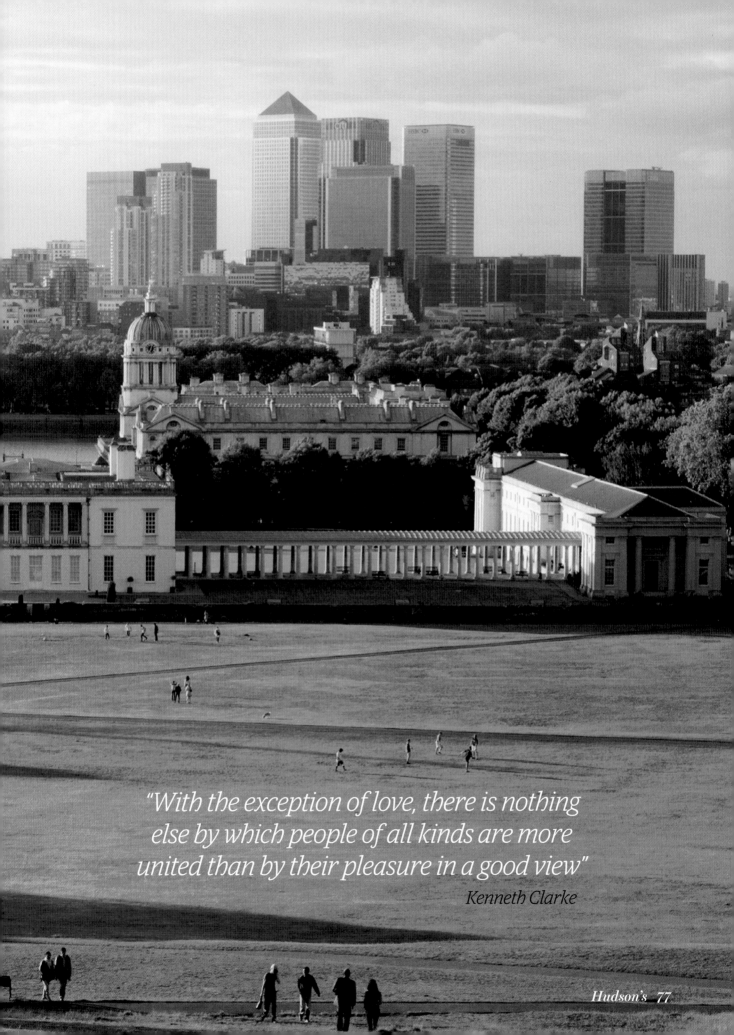

"With the exception of love, there is nothing
else by which people of all kinds are more
united than by their pleasure in a good view"

Kenneth Clarke

In England's 100 Best Views, I celebrate the hills, valleys, rivers, woods and settlements that are the landscape of England. I came to marvel at them while seeking out the best of England's churches and houses. I realised that a building's appeal is not intrinsic, but is a collage of the contexts from which it draws historical and topographical reference.

A view is not a picture. It is a contract between people and nature, nature harnessed to the needs of humans. I have seen and described hundreds of such contracts. Some are scenes of intense loveliness; most I have just marvelled at, marvelled that somewhere in England I could gaze over so much we have inherited from the past that remains so beautiful.

← GREENWICH

London does not lend itself to views. Not so Greenwich. The most celebrated view is by Canaletto from across the Thames. It shows Wren's great palace with barges gliding before it over a sunlit river, a picture of regal serenity recognisable today. This view is now rivalled by that in the opposite direction, downhill from Greenwich Park. The palace remains in the foreground but as a gilded gateway to the new commercial London of Docklands rising in the distance. It is the one London view that can accurately be described as sensational and I give it precedence. The vantage point is from the top of Greenwich Park, reached from Blackheath by the Royal Observatory. The park falls suddenly away at our feet, a greensward flanked by trees and rolling steeply downhill with all the eastern half of London beyond. In the foreground is the Queen's House, commissioned in 1616 for Anne of Denmark, wife to James I. It is simple and lovely, flanked by 19th century colonnades drawing the eye to the later buildings of Greenwich Palace below.

ARUNDEL

Grey sombre Arundel lies on the flank of the Downs like a cat waiting to prey on the valley below. Arundel is a marriage of Middle Ages and 19th century, a monumental expression of the aristocratic pomp and Catholic faith of the Howards, Dukes of Norfolk. Arundel Castle became the Windsor of the south coast, a sequence of halls, state rooms and private apartments surmounted by battlements and fortifications. The adjacent cathedral is almost more prominent than the castle, built at Norfolk expense in 1868 to celebrate the Catholic emancipation of forty years earlier. These two great buildings are attended by an immaculate small Sussex town, a packed cluster of tile roofs and red-brick walls surrounding a high street that winds around the castle mound. It appears at first more French than English, a lofty citadel on a defensible cliff on a bend in a river. But from across the fertile flood plain of the Arun from Crossbush, the scene acquires the softer outlines of Sussex and the South Downs. From here, Arundel could only be in England.
Arundel Castle, Sussex (p.171)

"From across the fertile flood plain of the Arun, the scene acquires the softer outlines of Sussex and the South Downs"

Arundel: Victorian variations on a medieval theme.

CHATSWORTH

"The eye was instantly caught by Pemberley House...a large handsome stone building standing well on rising ground, and backed by a ridge of high woody hills"

So wrote Jane Austen. This can only be a view of Chatsworth. Chatsworth does not float in the sky like Castle Howard, or roar defiance at the world, like Blenheim. For all its wealth and beauty, it seems at peace with nature and Derbyshire in one. The house seems at first conspicuously retiring, set off-centre at the side of its valley, glowing beneath a wooded hanger on the hill above. There is no grand avenue, obelisk or belvedere to lead the eye to the house. Chatsworth borrows privacy from its surroundings. Only at night does the view from across the Derwent burst into magnificence, indeed literally electrified by the Chatsworth floodlights. Then the house becomes a golden palace in a darkened gallery.
Chatsworth, Derbyshire **(p.244)**

Chatsworth, the respectful marriage of architecture, landscape and nature.

Holkham sits grand on its pedestal and is left as if set in the park at random.

HOLKHAM

I stood at Holkham's obelisk and looked out over the park towards the sea, across one of the most crafted 'natural' countrysides in England. The far horizon was hazily lined with coastal pines, punctuated by a distant monument. Views east and west were closed by thickly planted woods. The land in the middle distance fell away at my feet, a grassy savannah dotted with trees and groves, deer drifted across it like clouds forming and dissolving in a breeze, interrupted by a gentle game of cricket. In the centre of it all lay Holkham, the quintessential English palace in a landscape. It was a scene of the most exquisite beauty. Corpulent, cultured and liberal-minded, its creator Thomas Coke was also rich. He spent six years from the age of fifteen on a Grand Tour of France, Germany and Italy. The exterior of Holkham was Coke's own work, aided by Kent and his assistant Matthew Brettingham. Holkham was supremely fortunate in passing to his nephew, 'Coke of Norfolk', a true radical. Under his aegis, Holkham came to exemplify the transformation of the English landscape over the 18th and 19th centuries. The house was left as if it had been set in the park at random, with grass up to its walls. Holkham is Italy for sure, but Italy at ease with English countryside.
Holkham Hall, Norfolk (p.230)

Up-along, Down-along's industry may now be tourism rather than fish and smuggling but Clovelly continues to please the eye.

© VISIT ENGLAND IMAGES

Ruins "of infinite use to the landscape of England" to quote Jane Austen's comment on the legacy of the Dissolution of the Monasteries.

RIEVAULX

Rievaulx was founded in 1132 in a burst of monastic patronage under Henry I. The abbey was a success, growing to 350 monks in its first decade and 640 at its peak. For all its proclaimed asceticism, the residential quarters were among the most sumptuous in northern Europe. While the best view of the ruins is from the valley floor, it was the prospect over them down the valley that appealed to the Georgians. They should be set *'picturesque'*, overwhelmed by nature swelling up behind them as a backdrop. The owner of the embracing Helmsley estate, Thomas Duncombe of Duncombe Park, decided in 1758 to lay out a serpentine terrace to capture this scene. His guests would drive out after dinner to admire vistas carefully crafted to be seen through the trees. At one end of the main promenade is a Doric temple, at the other a banqueting house in the form of an Ionic one. While the monastic buildings have been merely stabilised in their ruined state, 'as found', the classical temples have been grant-aided for their splendid restoration. Conservation is a strangely biased ideology.

Rievaulx Abbey, Yorkshire (p.299); Terrace and Temples (p.293)

CLOVELLY

Clovelly is famously attractive. A single cobbled street, known as Up-along, Down-along, shambles down an isolated coastal ravine to a bay and small harbour. Halfway downhill, the street reaches a small plateau from where there is a view both up and down. Upwards, the curve of the street is defined by cottage walls, lime-washed white, cream, lemon and pink. Devon slates cover the roofs and windows are wooden casements. From every crevice erupt petunia, geranium, hydrangea and fuchsia. As the eye travels upwards, the street line is broken by an intimation of courtyards and alleys, everywhere backed by the trees of the surrounding cliff. The view downhill to the harbour is quite different. It is a Mediterranean prospect, contrasting starkly with Hartland Point to the South-West with its crashing Atlantic rollers. Village business takes place where it always did, round the harbour below. Nothing can detract from the intrinsic charm of the place. It has the quality of a Greek island settlement while remaining unmistakably English.

Clovelly Village, Devon (p.195)

PRIOR PARK

Ralph Allen was Bath's principal developer, one of the triumvirate, with Beau Nash and John Wood, on which the town's wealth was built. Prior Park was located near his quarry and gave a view down a steep and narrow valley to the town below. A contemporary called in 'a noble seat, which sees all Bath, and which was built for all Bath to see'. The prospect over central Bath is as Allen would have known it. We see his terraces swirling along the contours opposite, rising to Royal Crescent in the distance, like regiments manoeuvring for battle. An added delight of the view from Prior Park is the immediate foreground, where parkland sweeps down the valley to the river. The wider park was later redesigned by Capability Brown as a tumbling slope of grass between flanking woodlands. It culminates in two lakes framed by a colonnaded bridge. Another characteristic of the view is from below, looking up through the silhouetted bridge to Prior Park above. In mist or snow, when the surroundings slip into the background, it seems to float on the hillside.

Prior Park Landscape Garden, Somerset (p.211)

From the lake, looking through the Palladian bridge at Prior Park across Capability Brown's landscape.

BEESTON & PECKFORTON

The twin castles of Peckforton and Beeston rise above the Cheshire plain like mounted knights rearing and wheeling for battle. They occupy an outcrop of the long Marches ridge, now so coated with trees that I searched for an hour for a clear view of the castles in line. The castles are chiefly the creation of a man described by the historian Mark Girouard as 'one of those tremendous, rock-hewn Victorians who seem built on a larger scale than ordinary men'; Lord Tollemache was eccentric and progressive, believing everyone should own 'three acres and a cow'. He built himself, on a bluff at Peckforton, the last deliberately fortified mansion in England, designed in 1844 by the medievalist, Anthony Salvin. Not content with his own castle, Tollemache restored another, the ruins of Beeston a mile away on the neighbouring crag, ideally sited to enhance his view from Peckforton. It was Ludwig of Bavaria meets Crac de Chevalier.

Beeston Castle, Cheshire (p.307)

"The Michelin Green Guides give as many stars to views as to buildings..."

© VISIT ENGLAND IMAGES

**Bamburgh and Lindisfarne (opposite page)
Castles guard the Northumbrian shore,
redolent of the Middle Ages.**

www.hudsonsheritage.com

© PETER STYLES

Beyond Peckforton (foreground) and Beeston Castles lie the Dee Valley and distant Snowdonia in the West and the tower of Liverpool Cathedral to the East.

LINDISFARNE & BAMBURGH

Holy Island lies offshore at the end of a long shingle causeway, one of a line of Northumbrian citadels from Berwick southwards to Bamburgh, Dunstanburgh and Warkworth to Newcastle. The island was home to one of the earliest and, for a time, most civilised centres of Christianity in northern Europe, the monastery at Lindisfarne. The castle on the far tip of the island is everything a castle should be, lonely on a rock, vertical and imposing in outline, with a wild sea beyond. While the most popular view is from the coast, with the castle isolated across the sands, the best prospect is from the castle itself, south to Bamburgh on its own lonely outcrop. Both castles are creations largely of the 20th century when owners and

© VISIT ENGLAND IMAGES

architects could let their imaginations run free and before the law froze every ruin in time. The view south, as along most of England's eastern shore, depends heavily on the weather. It is of an expanse of seas and sky, misty and moody on all but the brightest day. Bamburgh looks impregnable above the surrounding dunes, gazing out to the Farne Islands.

Lindisfarne Castle, Northumberland (p.324)
Bamburgh Castle, Northumberland (p.323)

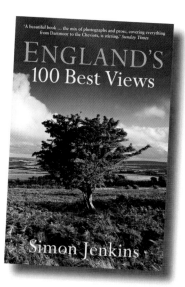

'A beautiful book ... the mix of photographs and prose, covering everything from Dartmoor to the Cheviots, is stirring.' *Sunday Times*

ENGLAND'S 100 Best Views

Simon Jenkins

This article is an extract from England's 100 Best Views by Simon Jenkins, published by Profile Books at £25 (hardback) and £15 (paperback).

Lilford Hall today.

© KAREY DRAPER

Country Houses in Wartime

In 2015, Britain continues to mark not only the centenary of the First World War but the end of the Second World War in 1945. Historian, Karey Draper, has spent the last few years considering the impact of war on Britain's country houses and shares some of her research with **Hudson's**.

U.S. Army 303rd Station Hospital around Lilford Hall in place for D-Day, May 1944.

© 303rd BOMB GROUP AND THE BRIAN MCGUIRE FAMILY

Soldiers and nurses on the Chinese Dairy veranda at Woburn Abbey during the First World War.

There is no shortage of documentation of the individual heroism displayed in the two world wars, but it may be surprising to learn of the critical and often unheralded role played by Britain's historic houses in the defence of this nation.

Spacious mansions could accommodate large numbers of residents with ample space outdoors for other occupations. This made them uniquely suitable as military hospitals and convalescent homes during WWI and several estate owners patriotically volunteered their homes for such uses.

The Duke of Bedford offered his indoor Riding School at Woburn Abbey as a hospital for wounded soldiers in 1914. Remarkably, Duchess Mary financed the installation of the 80-bed hospital where she also worked as a nurse. Waldorf Astor volunteered part of the estate lands at Cliveden, in Buckinghamshire, to the Canadian Red Cross for building a hospital at the outbreak of WWI. The Marquess of Bath offered Longleat in Wiltshire as a hospital while a portion of the surrounding land was used to train war horses. Blenheim Palace, Harewood House and Lotherton Hall also served as hospitals. In many cases the estates and hospitals operated with a predominantly female staff as the male population was vastly depleted during the war.

In World War II, Britain's country estates proved to be a distinct asset, particularly in the build up of forces leading to D-Day in June 1944 when nearly two million foreign military troops were stationed here, all requiring accommodation and space to train. Indeed, Britain's country estates were essential to the Allied defeat of Nazi Germany in 1945. Whilst several were again volunteered for wartime use, such as Longleat, Cliveden and Woburn, the government requisitioned the majority of country houses, confirming their crucial importance to the war effort.

Country estates served a wide variety of purposes including billeting for troops, training, secret operational and intelligence centres, treasure repositories, airfields, hospitals and housing for schools, evacuees and prisoners of war. Often estates fulfilled several wartime needs at once. Boughton House, Northamptonshire home of the Duke of Buccleuch, acted as a repository for the British Museum whilst the estate housed troops, German prisoners of war and an American airfield.

It was the billeting of troops, which led to much of the post-war decline of country houses in the latter half of the 20th century. As historian John Martin Robinson noted in his book, *The Country House at War*, 'it was generally agreed that soldiers were the worst possible occupants of fragile historic buildings.' The sentiment of the day was summed up succinctly by Sir Archibald Sinclair, Air Minister, who remarked

The Chinese Dairy at Woburn Abbey today.

in 1940: *"We are out to win this war and should not be put off by a desire to maintain intact the stately homes of England."*

One aspect of country houses that made them less than ideal, they often lacked central heating and modern plumbing. An army of engineers was employed by the Ministry of Works to prepare sites for occupation. This alone involved a measure of intrusion and damage to house and landscape, such as the installation of sewage works and water pipelines to accommodate the new inhabitants.

Winter months in a country house could be particularly cold, and wood was in high demand. Finely carved staircases, paneling and furniture were occasionally appreciated less for their beauty and more for the warmth they could provide when fed to a fire. At Rolls Park in Essex nine battalions of soldiers stayed in the house, causing extensive damage, the worst of which was chopping up the Tudor staircase. The house was finally demolished in 1953.

Parkland was often roughly used under requisition. Concrete bases were constructed for temporary shelters such as Nissen huts, necessary for accommodating so many armed forces. Lilford Park in Northamptonshire, still carries the concrete vestiges of its wartime occupation. Once world famous for its gardens and Victorian aviaries established by the ornithologist Baron Lilford, Lilford Hall served as an

Lt Virginia Hanning sunbathing on the roof of Lilford Hall in 1944. Around 75 American nurses were stationed at the Hall caring for up to 1500 casualties.

Lydiard Park, Wiltshire, was requisitioned early in World War II and sold to Swindon Borough Council in 1943. Nissen huts housed a hospital first for the American 101st Airborne Division, then up to 200 German prisoners of war. Below: The prison guards pose in the park.

American field hospital during WWII. The original design was for 750-beds but this number doubled to 1500 after D-Day, when so many wounded were sent here for treatment.

If historic buildings were too fragile for wartime uses, their historic setting often had a positive impact on wartime occupants. Country estates were essentially the culmination of the pursuit of aesthetic perfection. For the soldier billeted or convalescing on a country estate, away from the chaos of war, it must have seemed a kind of oasis. One American upon arriving at Lilford in January 1944 wrote in a letter home, *"My dearest, I really feel that all this is rather a dream… The grounds are beautiful with enormous trees, beautiful pheasants wandering about and attractively arranged buildings. It is more than picturesque. I could not feel any happier over here."*

The billeting, training and logistical support that

The Great Hall at Boughton House today, in 1941 a narrow central aisle allowed passage through British Museum packaging cases stored three deep on either side.

Above: *Boughton House, The Great Hall,* as a repository for *the Antiquities of The British Museum* by C.O. Waterhouse, December 1941.

Right: Mary, Duchess of Bedford in her nurse's uniform. She financed and founded four hospitals at Woburn and remained a nurse until the 1930s.

country estates provided in support of two world wars was not without a price. It is estimated that between 1945 and 1955 demolition companies wiped away nearly a thousand country houses that had been damaged during wartime requisition, culminating in 1955 with one country house demolished every two and a half days. The declining state of a majority of country houses in the post-war years led to debates at a national level about whether the country house should be saved as a matter of national interest. As we remember the sacrifices made by Allied forces during WWI and WWII, we would do well to also remember the largely forgotten contributions made by country estates throughout Britain. Many paid a heavy price, sustaining damage rendering them beyond repair and resulting in their ultimate destruction. But without these silent contributions, the outcomes of both world wars may well have been very different.

HUDSON'S
HISTORIC HOUSE&GARDEN
SHORT BREAKS

Hudson's and renowned travel experts, Martin Randall Travel, have teamed up to offer a new range of short break holidays.

The 3 day tours take you to celebrated stately homes and little known country houses where you will be able to explore the history of Britain through great architecture, family stories, interior decoration and stunning works of art.

Add glimpses below stairs, spectacular gardens and landscaped parks, our first three tours can fill your weekends or join two to make a week's adventure.

Tours will be led by expert lecturers, Dr Andrew Moore and Dr Adam White.

Let Hudson's Short Breaks help you discover Britain's unique country house heritage.

Grimsthorpe, steel engraving c. 1830.

The Lecturers

Dr Andrew Moore

Andrew is Keeper of Art at Norwich Castle Museum & Art Gallery. In 2013 he co-authored the award winning exhibition "Houghton Revisited" with Houghton Hall and the State Hermitage Museum, St Petersburg. He is a Visiting Fellow in the School of World Art Studies & Museology at the University of East Anglia.

Dr Adam White

An art historian and museum curator who has worked at the Leeds Museums and Galleries since 1983. He is Fellow of the Society of Antiquaries of London and has published widely on British art, particularly sculpture.

Rutland

8–10 May 2015 (EB 322)
3 days • £530
Lecturer: Dr Andrew Moore

The rich agricultural land of the East Midlands, with its broad undulations and endless skies, is home to many of the finest country houses in England. Burghley, designed and built by Elizabeth I's Lord High Treasurer, William Cecil, is one of the great palaces of the age. Described by Daniel Defoe as *'more like a town than a house'*, its 35 principal rooms contain an astonishing array of treasures, from fine Italian Old Masters to exquisite Oriental ceramics, while its vast Tudor kitchen captures the scale of country-house entertaining.

Burghley set a high benchmark, matched by succeeding generations. Grimsthorpe Castle, a country house rather than a fortification, was Vanbrugh's last masterpiece; its monumental, arcaded Great Hall, described by Pevsner as: *'unquestionably Vanbrugh's finest room'*.

Not all the houses on the tour are on this imposing scale. At Rushton, Sir Thomas Tresham, High Sheriff of Northamptonshire, used a tiny triangular folly to express his Catholic devotion in elaborate symbolism. While Deene Park is as renowned for its inhabitants as its architecture. Here, the home of the Brudenell family for the past 500 years, contains myriad memories, particularly of its most famous son, Lord Cardigan, hero of the Charge of the Light Brigade.

Itinerary

Day 1: Deene Park. Leave Peterborough Railway Station at 1.50pm. Largely 16th century, Deene Park is still very much the home of the Brudenells. A house as flamboyant as the family that has occupied it for almost 500 years, it is filled with fascinating mementoes of the family and of the hero of the Charge of the Light Brigade, Lord Cardigan. Overnight Barnsdale Lodge.

Day 2: Rockingham, Elton, Rushton Triangular Lodge. A former royal castle and hunting lodge in Rockingham Forest, with views of the Welland Valley, Rockingham Castle has the familiar medieval hall with outbuildings inside the bailey of a Norman keep. The Tudors divided the hall and added wings at either end. The medieval bake house, brewery, larder and dairy are still intact. Dickens was a regular guest here and the house is arguably the inspiration for Chesney Wold in *Bleak House*. Elton Hall is a fascinating mixture of styles with excellent furniture and painting collection from the 15th to the 19th century. The 15th century tower and chapel built by Henry VIII was enlarged in the 17th century. 16th century Rushton Triangular Lodge is a testament to Roman Catholicism. The number three, symbol of the Holy Trinity, is echoed in all the detailing. Overnight Barnsdale Lodge.

Day 3. Grimsthorpe, Burghley. *Grimsthorpe Castle's Baroque front of 1715, a northern Blenheim, is Vanbrugh's last masterpiece. A country house rather than a castle, in 3000 acres the park was landscaped by 'Capability' Brown. Grimsthorpe has been the home of the de Eresby family since 1516. One of the few baronies able to descend through the female line; the present owner is the granddaughter of Nancy Astor, who died here. The grandest of Elizabethan prodigy houses, Burghley was built by the queen's chief minister and magnificently remodelled internally a hundred years later. The paintings and furniture are superb, the Hell Staircase a highlight. Return to Peterborough Railway Station by 4.45pm.*

Practicalities

Price: £530 (deposit £100). Single supplement £60 (double room for single occupancy).
Included meals: One dinner with wine.
Accommodation: Barnsdale Lodge Hotel (www.barnsdalelodge.co.uk) is housed in an extended old farmhouse close to Rutland Water. Public rooms and bedrooms are arranged around a courtyard and have a traditional, country décor. Bedrooms vary in size and outlook. There is a restaurant and lounge; service is friendly. There is no lift.
How strenuous? Unavoidably there is quite a lot of walking on this tour and it would not be suitable for anyone with difficulties with everyday walking and stair-climbing. Coaches can rarely park near the houses, many of the parks and gardens are extensive, the houses visited don't have lifts.
Average distance by coach per day: c. 50 miles.
Group size: Between 14 and 30 participants.

Derbyshire

16–18 June 2015 (EB 364)
3 days ● £530
Lecturer: Dr Adam White

In *Pride & Prejudice*, Jane Austen's Elizabeth Bennet travelled into Derbyshire, not in search of Mr Darcy, but on the already celebrated trail of the Peak District, with its romantic vistas and wealth of stately homes. This tour offers a carefully chosen sample of first-rate houses of almost every era, from the Elizabethan masterpiece Hardwick Hall, created by the formidable Bess of Hardwick, then the richest woman in England after the queen, to the grand Roman Baroque of

Hardwick, wood engraving c. 1880.

Kedleston, which Robert Adam designed in the 18th century to showcase the might of the Curzons.

The romance of medieval and Tudor Haddon Hall rests not just with its mellow ancient walls and rich interiors but with the stories of the inhabitants; while Renishaw, transformed from its Jacobean roots into 19th century neo-Gothic with cold cash from nails and coal, became a hub of style and creativity in the early 20th century under the influence of the extraordinary Sitwell siblings, Osbert, Edith and Sacheverell.

Itinerary

Day 1: Kedleston. One of the supreme monuments of Classical architecture and decoration in England, recreating the glories of Ancient Rome in the foothills of the Peak District, Kedleston Hall (1759–65) was the creation of Sir Nathaniel Curzon and, initially, three architects, of whom Robert Adam emerged the victor. The sequence of grand rooms for entertainment and show are homogeneous and complete (with furnishings designed by Adam), an impeccable manifestation of aristocratic wealth, education and taste. Overnight Derby.

Day 2: Renishaw, Hardwick. Grade 1-listed Renishaw Hall has been in the Sitwell family for over 400 years. The famous literary trio, Edith, Osbert, and Sacheverell Sitwell were all patrons of the arts and played a significant part in the artistic and literary world at the beginning of the 20th century. Set in eight acres of Italianate gardens, the house was built in 1625 and altered several times, more recently by Lutyens in 1908. Hardwick Hall (1590) is the finest of all Elizabethan great houses, a highpoint of the

English Renaissance, the façade famously more glass than stone. The unaltered interiors are decorated with stucco reliefs and filled with contemporary textiles and furniture. Overnight Derby.

Day 3: Tissington, Haddon. A rare survival of a village scattered around the country house of its squire, Tissington has a population of 100 and is the home of the FitzHerbert family who have owned the house and estate since the 15th century. Built in the early 17th century the hall has been added to many times, most notably in the early 18th century and in c. 1900. *'The most perfect English house to survive from the Middle Ages'*, Haddon Hall evolved from c. 1370 to the 17th century after which nearly 300 years of disuse preserved it from alteration. The gardens are exceptional. Return to Derby Railway Station by c. 5.45pm.

Practicalities

Price: £530 (deposit £100). Single supplement £70 (double room for single occupancy.
Included meals: One dinner with wine.
Accommodation: Jurys Inn hotel in Derby is within walking distance of the Cathedral Quarter of the city. Bedrooms are comfortable with all mod cons.
How strenuous? Unavoidably there is quite a lot of walking on this tour and it would not be suitable for anyone with difficulties with walking and stair-climbing. Coaches can rarely park near the houses, many of the parks and gardens are extensive, the houses visited don't have lifts.
Average distance by coach per day: c. 42 miles.
National Trust: Members refunded c. £20.
Group size: Between 14 and 32 participants.

HUDSON'S
HISTORIC HOUSE & GARDEN
SHORT BREAKS

Yorkshire

19–21 June 2015 (EB 366)
3 days ● £560
Lecturer: Dr Adam White

Yorkshire is England's largest and one of its most beautiful counties, renowned for the spectacular countryside of the North York Moors and Yorkshire Dales. But it is also a county blessed by an outstanding range of country houses. This tour provides the opportunity to explore some of the best.

Visitors will focus on houses that were really homes, the creation and vision of powerful dynasties over centuries. Some (Sledmere, Newby Hall) are still in the hands of the families who created them; the majority contain museum-quality treasures. Amongst the artistic highlights are the Gobelins tapestries at Newby Hall and the Joseph Rose plasterwork at Sledmere, but these are also houses that reflect the serendipity of everyday life, from the rooms crowded with British Empire memorabilia at Lotherton Hall to the working chapel at Markenfield.

Guests will also be able to explore York, a city with one of the finest concentrations of historic buildings in England.

Itinerary

Day 1: Lotherton. The coach leaves York Railway Station at 1.30pm. Lotherton Hall is a charming Edwardian country home rich in collections of paintings, furniture, silver, china, costume and oriental art, set in beautiful grounds. Overnight York.

Day 2: Markenfield, Newby. Markenfield Hall is the best surviving medieval moated manor house in England. Parts date to c. 1290, while the crenellations were licensed in 1310. A William-and-Mary house (1693), Newby Hall was subject for the next two centuries to refurbishment and extension of the highest quality, one set of rooms (by Adam) was designed to house a collection of Roman sculpture. Overnight York.

Day 3: Sledmere, Scampston. Designed and built in the mid- to late-18th century by Sir Christopher Sykes, Sledmere remains in the Sykes family today. It was destroyed by fire in 1911, but the Joseph Rose plasterwork has been restored. Scampston Hall is a wonderful example of an English country house set in 'Capability' Brown parkland. The walled garden is a magnificent example of contemporary design. Return to York by c. 5.00pm.

York, wood engraving c. 1880.

Practicalities
Price: £560 (deposit £100). Single supplement £110 (double room for single occupancy).
Included meals: One dinner with wine.
Accommodation: Guests will stay at the award-winning boutique hotel The Grange in York, a beautifully restored grade II-listed Georgian townhouse, and the decoration and furnishings combine period and modern; very good restaurant; there is no lift.
How strenuous? Unavoidably there is quite a lot of walking on this tour and it would not be suitable for anyone with difficulties with everyday walking and stair-climbing. Coaches can rarely park near the houses, many of the parks and gardens are extensive, the houses visited don't have lifts.
Average distance by coach per day: c. 54 miles.
Group size: Between 14 and 32 participants.

Booking
Book online at www.martinrandall.com or contact Martin Randall Travel to make a provisional booking, or use the booking form at the back of this book, complete and return with your deposit to the address, fax number or email address at the bottom of this page (for security, we ask that you do not send credit or debit card details by email).

Cancellation: If you have to cancel your participation on a tour, there would be a charge which varies according to the period of notice you give. Up to 57 days before the tour the deposit only is forfeited. Thereafter a percentage of the total cost of the tour will be due:
between 56 and 29 days: 40%
between 28 and 15 days: 60%
between 14 days and 3 days: 80%
within 48 hours: 100%

Please make sure that you also read our full booking conditions at www.hudsonsheritage.com/shortbreaks

Turn to page 414 for the Booking Form

Martin Randall Travel Ltd, Voysey House, Barley Mow Passage, London W4 4GF
Telephone: 020 8742 3355   Fax: 020 8742 7766   Email: info@martinrandall.co.uk

AITO: 5085   ATOL: 3622   ABTA: Y6050

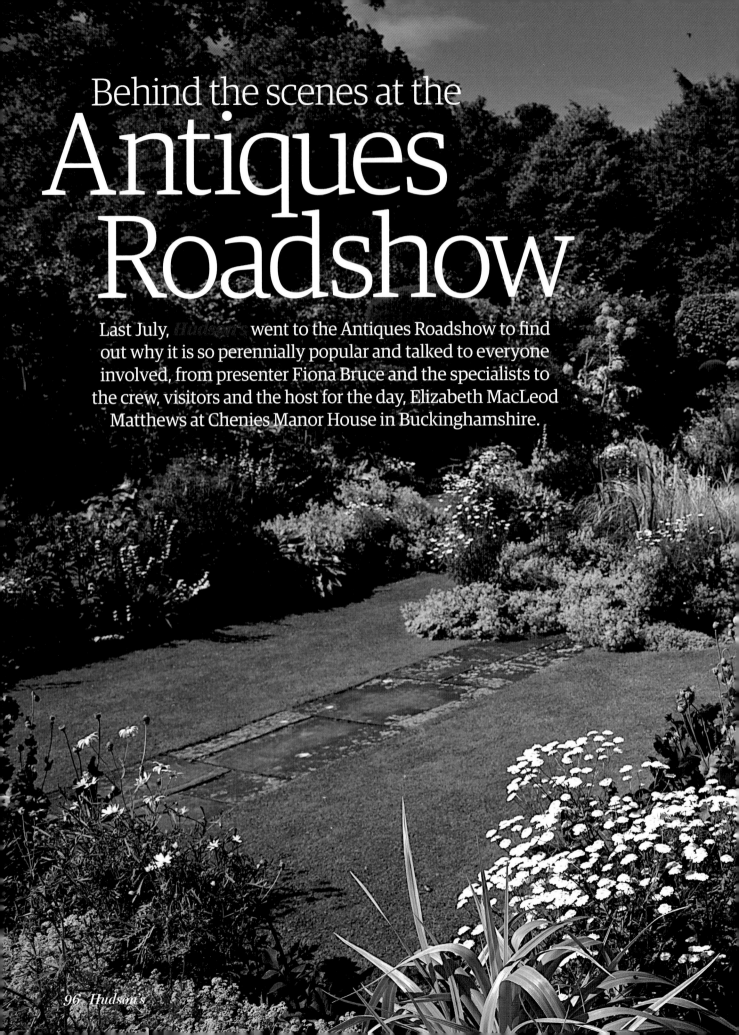

Behind the scenes at the
Antiques Roadshow

Last July, *Hudson's* went to the Antiques Roadshow to find out why it is so perennially popular and talked to everyone involved, from presenter Fiona Bruce and the specialists to the crew, visitors and the host for the day, Elizabeth MacLeod Matthews at Chenies Manor House in Buckinghamshire.

Paul Atterbury (Miscellaneous) uncovers some memories of the Somme.

Photos: Gary Hope

In its 37th season, the format for the Antiques Roadshow remains virtually unchanged. Programmes broadcast over the winter of 2014/5 were filmed in 13 venues all over the UK from ruined castles (Lowther Castle) and cathedrals (Durham and Liverpool Metropolitan) to art galleries (Kelvingrove), industrial spaces (Derby Roundhouse) and Walthamstow Town Hall. Fronted by Fiona Bruce for the last 6 years, the show attracts Sunday night audiences of nearly 6 million viewers. We all know how it works. You turn up, carrying Great Aunt Edna's bit of china and hope it will be worth not £4 but £4,000. Last year Fiona Bruce spotted a study for The Magistrates of Brussels by Sir Anthony Van Dyck, bought in a Cheshire antiques shop for £400 and, now restored, worth £400,000. Everyone dreams of that moment, surely, but what is it really like?

Fiona Bruce is tall. Add 1 inch platform sandals to 5 foot 10 and she seems slightly intimidating even in an English country garden. But her ease and dimply smile soon take over and she moves easily through the crowd dispensing charm; *"Well, here's a perfect Roadshow moment!"* she greets a woman heaving a man-sized teddy bear. She loves the Antiques Roadshow and the chance it gives her to visit so many historic places *"This show absolutely fits with my natural instincts. I'll keep doing it for as long as they keep asking me!"* Asked for a favourite venue, she remembers *"One that really sticks in my mind is Leeds Castle in Kent, because we stayed in it. We all had supper, they said, 'We're off now, the castle is yours'. It was a beautiful evening and we had a drink on the ramparts. I'm not sure I can top that really."*

THE SPECIALISTS

Mark Poltimore (Prints & Pictures).

Clive Stewart-Lockhart (Miscellaneous).

Lisa Lloyd in red (Miscellaneous).

Rupert Maas (Pictures & Prints).

Philip Taubenheim (Collectables).

Christopher Payne (Furniture).

→

From left: David Battie (Ceramics) on screen; Simon Shaw, series editor; cameraman Simon Pass is one of two on site.

Fiona Bruce considers a balsa wood model of BBC Broadcasting House, one of the objects filmed for the Chenies Manor House Roadshow.

She relishes the interaction with the public. *"I love this big outside broadcast. There are not many programmes where so many members of the public come. They all have stories to tell and things wrapped up in their newspapers. I'm professionally nosey so this is the perfect job."* Of her skill in helping expert Philip Mould to identify the Van Dyck in 2013, she admits modestly *"I'll dine out on that for the rest of my life. It was just an extraordinary coming together of different factors at exactly the right moment. Philip is always going on about overpaint and condition so now I go 'Goodness, look at that overpaint and ooh, that needs a good clean'."*

Three thousand people turned up at Chenies (a record for the season) and it quickly became clear that the Antiques Roadshow is an exercise in queuing. You arrive at 9.30 and queue for reception, where you are greeted by your first level of expertise; your objects are assessed and you are given tickets for your treasures, maybe one for jewellery, one for paintings and one miscellaneous; you move on to each of those queues in turn. You may still be queuing, but once you have passed reception, you are in the throng with interesting interviews going on around you and you can earwig any conversation you like. If you are chosen for filming, you get tea and biscuits while you wait for make up (if you live close you may even have time to race home and smarten up, though either most come prepared for the cameras, just in case, or Buckinghamshire folk are just well turned out). As long as you arrive before 4.30 you will be seen. Twenty-four specialists have turned up so there are plenty of breaks, but this is a long tiring day which will not finish before 7.00pm. *"It's no good limiting how many items people bring"* explains Press Officer, Olwen Gillespie. *"It's always the last minute thing grabbed off the shelf that turns out to be the interesting one."*

For the BBC, this makes it an exercise in crowd control though with an invisible hand. *"It's like a campaign,"* says Hilary Kay (Miscellaneous). Plentiful purple-sashed stewards marshal and cajole visitors to well signposted specialists, who behave as if no one needs to rush.

The outside broadcast unit moves through several pre-planned locations.

"This show absolutely fits with my natural instincts. I'll keep doing it for as long as they keep asking me!"

The only slightly harassed figure is series editor Simon Shaw, who buzzes from expert to expert with a fierce expression of concentration under his panama. For the specialists, the point is to learn something new and hope for an elusive treasure and the prize is a filmed spot aired on the programme which will raise their profile. If something special turns up, Simon Shaw is summoned and adds object, owner and expert to the filming schedule. There's no pressure. Richard Price (Clocks) is almost dancing with excitement at the discovery of a rare early table clock, made in Augsburg in the 16th century. The owner, an attractive blonde in her twenties, is camera shy and passes up the opportunity to appear on the programme. Her decision is quietly accepted and, though the thrill of discovery is still palpable, the specialists move on to the next customer. Some are more popular with visitors than others and the old hands are well known. Favourites Paul Atterbury and Hilary Kay (Miscellaneous) and David Battie

(Ceramics) have been with the programme since the early days but the younger generation, Alastair Chandler (Clocks) or Justin Croft (Books) are catching up. Andy McConnell (Glass) recognises that the show is about performance and has the crowd roaring with tales of dowagers impersonated by clapping the lid of a Victorian scent bottle as if it talks. Of course, at any Roadshow many objects are neither interesting nor valuable but the specialists are courteous. *"Ha! Copies!"* declares Rupert Maas (Paintings) *"Sorry to be so rude. Had you very high hopes?"*

Hilary Kay (Miscellaneous) thrilled with a collection of Hornby trains in original boxes. Far left: Joanna Hardy (Jewellery) peers at a promising gemstone. Stewards (left) keep everyone cheerful.

So what brings people here? It turns out that the motivation is more varied than you might imagine and visitors fall into various types.

The Knowledge Seeker owns something unidentifiable. A couple who live in Church House bring a small wooden head and a bunch of massive iron keys found in the attic. The head is 17th century, worth £300 and the keys, only £30, and Hilary Kay scurries off for advice and learns that two of them are early 19th century latch lifters.

The Know-It-All wants to show off. They have researched their obscure object in such detail that, unprepared, no specialist could match their knowledge. *"You hear them as they retreat, declaring 'That man knows nothing!'"* laughs Clive Stewart Lockhart (Miscellaneous). *"There's no point bringing me things when they know what they are and what they are worth."*

The Expert just wants an intelligent conversation with a fellow enthusiast. A man in the queue has brought the first electric typewriter, a Blickensderfer of 1902, and admits that he probably knows more about early typewriters than anyone but wants to share a prized possession.

The Local comes because of the venue. At Chenies a visitor with a collection of miniature items had a relative who rented the house from the Duke of Bedford in the 1880s, another brings a Civil War document signed by Parliamentarian John Hampden whose son was killed in a skirmish at Chenies in 1642. Nearly all live within 40 miles and many had not previously visited or not visited for many years.

The Relative brings an object that celebrates the life of an ancestor. A bust of Thomas Tait, modernist architect of Unilever House, by Sir William Reid Dick allows his family a moment of pride. More than anything, people bring memorabilia from the First World War; embroideries, sketches, souvenirs, photographs of moustachioed forebears, documents, medals and diaries, and, most poignantly, a letter sent to a grandmother after the death of a soldier, *"I wish I had the courage to ask you to marry me..."*

The Hobbyist is an amateur collector with a love of auctions or car boot sales and time to spare. One has packed a Victorian painting, two 17th century carved panels and a Rodin bronze into a wheelbarrow; all reassuringly good investments.

The Fan just wants to be part of the programme and will search out an object to bring without really wanting an answer. *"It probably isn't amazing, I just thought I'd bring something along,"* explains a woman with her grandfather's presentation fob watch. After a brief consultation she reels away knowing when and where it was made, its serial number, details of its movement, its Birmingham-made engraved case and a value, £35. *"May I take a photograph of my husband with you?"*

The Expectant wants their object to have high value. Expectations are not always gratified. *"A Victorian tea caddy that would have fetched £800 a few years ago is now worth not more than £80."* explains Christopher Payne (Furniture). *"The cost of reupholstering this turned English mahogany chair of 1880 is higher than its value, maybe £200."*

The Valuer is often in the Jewellery queue. *"Of course, we never write anything down, but people do want to know the value for their insurance,"* says Joanna Hardy (Jewellery), peering at a 1950s sapphire ring. *"This was valued by Christies at £1200 but now it's not worth more than £600 or £800."*

So was there treasure at Chenies?

The flowers and bronze foliage of Dahlia David Howard compliment the warm diapered brickwork of the medieval central tower at Chenies.

www.hudsonsheritage.com

Summer sunshine makes waiting easier but the crowds were not daunted by the rain at Hillsborough Castle a week earlier.

So was there treasure at Chenies? Anyone who watched the programmes will know, but there was certainly one off-screen late in the evening. A woman took an exquisite porcelain box from a hand quilted container. *"An old lady gave this to my Gran and she gave it to me; my mum did the quilting."* David Battie (Ceramics) is delighted, *"A hand-painted snuff box, made in about 1740 in the Meissen factory and I have rarely seen one so good or in such good condition. It's worth £10,000 to £15,000. If only you'd come earlier."* The owner is speechless; her five hour wait forgotten in the shock.

Overall what is impressive about this show is the seamless organisation – plenty of stewards, water and shade provided – the unassailable cheerfulness and patience of everyone involved, the depth of pooled expert knowledge and the generosity and enthusiasm with which it is shared, and of course, the setting. A summer afternoon strolling in the cool shade of Elizabeth MacLeod Matthews' Physic Garden at Chenies combines history with beauty as only an English country house can do.

Chenies Manor House, Buckinghamshire (p.141)

Celebrating the best visitor experiences

Each year **Hudson's Heritage Awards** highlight the best places for visitors to go in the UK. Our independent judges are **Norman Hudson**, **Lucinda Lambton**, **Jeremy Musson** and **Simon Foster** who together bring several lifetimes of experience and knowledge in understanding and evaluating heritage places. **Loyd Grossman** presented the awards to last year's winners at Goldsmiths Hall in London at a gathering of owners, managers and heritage personalities.

Thanks to Peel Heritage for sponsoring the reception.

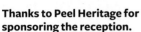

Best Family Day Out
Holkham Hall, Norfolk

Holkham is one of the great estates of Britain. In an area of extreme natural beauty, more activities have brought young families into the park and innovative exhibitions at all times of year have made the house more fun. Outside, you can now explore the park by bicycle, canoe, kayak or rowing boat or even by water zorbing! Inside events now have the 'wow' factor, with a snowy Forest and Gingerbread Room at Christmas, a giant Chocolate egg at Easter and spooky tours at Halloween. The local community, visiting children and adults of all ages now have new ways to enjoy the park, architecture and collections.

Holkham Hall, Norfolk (p.230)

Best Eating Out
Mount Stuart, Isle of Bute

Refreshments at Mount Stuart? You are spoilt for choice! The main visitor restaurant serves simple appealing dishes at good value in a glorious glass-walled contemporary building with far reaching views across the woodlands and gardens. There's an interesting coach party menu too. Or you can choose a traditional tea in a charming courtyard near the house (a clever conversion from a coalshed) or buy 'Food to Go' from the farm shop for your own picnic. There is private fine dining on offer as well as winter cooking workshops teaching skills like chutney and bread making. The focus is on local food, not just from producers on the Isle of Bute but from the kitchen garden - a visitor attraction in its own right. All this helps make Mount Stuart a destination at all times of year, just a short ferry ride down the coast from Glasgow.

Mount Stuart, Isle of Bute (p.341)

Best Shopping
sponsored by Spear's

SPEAR'S

Blenheim Palace, Oxfordshire

Blenheim Palace runs three separate shops, continuing an investment programme which started with the new East Courtyard Visitor Centre. The newest is The Children's Shop, selling pocket money toys, treats and fancy dress that will appeal to kids. Last year there was a shop selling high quality arts and crafts from the immediate surrounding area, this year transformed into a World War 1 shop. And of course there is an exemplary gift shop which sells a range of items including many carrying the Blenheim brand. The judges particularly liked Below Stairs, a new range of items inspired by the working lives of the household staff, so if you need the Valet's Shoe Polishing Kit or the Housemaid's Bannister Brush, you can now order it online and have it posted direct. *Blenheim Palace, Oxfordshire (p.159)*

Best New Discovery
Dunvegan Castle,
Isle of Skye

A Book of Correspondence, from the early 1800s until 1945, found in the Dunvegan Castle archive has led to a complete change of regime for cleaning and maintenance and helped visitors look under the skin of the castle. It revealed an old recipe for traditional lime mortar using local beach sand and lime from forgotten kilns on an island in the loch. It showed traditional alternatives to 20th century bleach and Brasso which had damaged the Castle linens and metalwares. A new programme of regular maintenance and environmentally conscious cleaning is now undertaken by retrained and reinvigorated staff, leading and supporting a new team of local volunteers. Visitors enjoy regular Conservation in Action days which have proved a popular way of sharing the secrets of keeping an ancient castle alive.
*Dunvegan Castle,
Isle of Skye (p.345)*

"A Book of Correspondence, has led to a complete change of regime for cleaning and maintenance"

Best Event
Houghton Hall, Norfolk, for *Houghton Revisited*

Houghton Hall retains, almost unchanged, the interiors designed by William Kent for Britain's first Prime Minister, Sir Robert Walpole in the 1720s. It has an outstanding collection of paintings, but this collection was once even richer; Sir Robert's art collection was considered the best in Europe by his contemporaries. After his death, many of the Old Masters were sold to Catherine the Great of Russia and they have been in the Hermitage Museum in St Petersburg ever since. Until last year, that is, when masterpieces by Van Dyck, Poussin, Rubens, Rembrandt, Velasquez and Murillo were hung once again in the rooms designed for them. This was an ambitious, world class exhibition which required vision, planning, negotiation with a major art institution and considerable personal investment by owner, Lord Cholmondeley. Nearly 120,000 people had a chance to step back in time to see this house exactly as it was in its heyday in the 1770s. It was the outstanding country house event of the year and probably of the decade.
Houghton Hall, Norfolk (p.231)

Best Accommodation
sponsored by Signpost Hotel Guide

Leeds Castle, Kent

Last year, Leeds Castle introduced a 'Knights' Glampsite', inspired by Henry VIII's procession to the Field of the Cloth of Gold in 1520 which stopped at this historic castle en route. Guests stay in double pavilions in jaunty stripes with civilised bathrooms, wood burning stoves and luxurious furnishings incorporating silk, wool and fur. The tents are named after Henry VIII's champions and this year a Knight's School gets everyone involved. It is camping certainly but more reminiscent of a top-of-the-range safari camp with a distinctly medieval flair. Knightly Glampers enjoy experiencing the castle after the general public have left and can opt for a barbecue or an evening dinner in the restaurant.
Leeds Castle, Kent (p.152)

![Hudson's Heritage Awards logo]

Best New Commission
sponsored by Smith & Williamson

Smith & Williamson

Hatfield House, Hertfordshire
for *Her Majesty the Queen's Jubilee Pageant, Looking West*

Here is a traditional piece of far sighted patronage by a great landowning family in the long tradition of their ancestors. It is a painting of the Queen's Jubilee Pageant on the Thames in June 2012, commissioned personally by the Marquess of Salisbury to commemorate this important national event. Lord Salisbury was Chairman of the Thames Diamond Jubilee Foundation which organised the pageant, which was itself in part inspired by a painting by Antonio Canaletto of *The Lord Mayor's Day on the Thames*, now hanging in Prague. Appropriately, Lord Salisbury commissioned a new painting of the Queen's Pageant from artist Nick Botting, who is well known for capturing the moment *en plein air* in the tradition

of the Impressionists. The painting is on public display at Hatfield House allowing visitors to share their memories of this great national event.
Hatfield House, Hertfordshire (p.228)

Best Commercial Innovation
sponsored by The Whetstone Group

Huntsham Court, Devon

Huntsham Court is a country house, but one that you can rent exclusively, just as if it were your home. The house has accommodation for 72 in 30 bedroom suites or you could have a party for 120 and arrange it any way you like. There are no in house services and no service charges, catering and housekeeping and so on is available if required from experienced local suppliers – or not, your choice. Gaps in the calendar are filled with charitable events on the same basis. This model, built on flexibility with no hidden charges, has allowed the owners to rescue this run down Victorian mansion, restore it, share it with others, generate income for the local community in a way that is very on trend. If you want to host the quintessential English country house party, this may be the place.

Best Hidden Gem
The Judge's Lodging, Presteigne, Powys

The Hidden Gem award is for a heritage attraction that just hasn't been noticed. The winner is a small rural museum with big ideas. This Victorian courthouse in a tiny Welsh border town recalls its grander past as the county town of Radnorshire. Despite the austere courtroom and cells, visitors are immediately immersed into the life of the 19th century judges and the household who lived here. Everything is touchable and the house is entirely lit by gas and oil lamps. The audio tour is engaging and the range of activities from napkin folding to jelly tasting is innovative and fun. There are free family fun days, dinners, recitals and plenty of theatre. Children especially like the guidebook full of 'Gross Facts' and school parties get to play 'Hunt the Toilet' and carry water up 41 stairs for the Judge's bath. This small charitable enterprise is independently attracting visitors into the area and the town, boosting the local economy and bringing its past back to life.

The Judge's Lodging, Presteigne, Powys (p.354)

Best Heritage Picnic Spot
Chatsworth House, Derbyshire

The winner of this award is nominated by a member of the general public. It is an award for a heritage site which is a special place to have a picnic. The winning picnic spot was nominated by Mrs Olwen Wright, who said of Chatsworth.... *"As we entered the parkland and got our first view of the House and its surrounds, our grandchildren, aged 9 and 14, who would never usually comment, both said 'Wow!' There is something for everybody, whatever their age or inclination on the Estate. So many beautiful designated picnic areas, and even a hut to buy picnic food if you decide on the spur of the moment! Nothing here is forgotten and it adds up to a memorable day."*
Chatsworth House, Derbyshire (p.244)

The 2015 Hudson's Heritage Awards will be announced on 3 March 2015 and presented by TV historian, Dan Snow. Go to www.hudsons-awards.co.uk for details of these and the 2016 awards.

Best Wedding Venue
The Carriage Rooms, Montalto Estate, County Down

Montalto is a Georgian estate in Northern Ireland, where the main house was nearly lost after a disastrous fire in 1984. Like many houses that host weddings, their business was limited by the size of the rooms in the main house. An ambitious restoration of a disused historic sawmill on the estate has provided a whole new dedicated location for wedding parties. The character of the mill has been carefully preserved and now offers rooms suitable for wedding ceremonies, receptions and evening parties with well-designed gardens and terraces. The Banquet Hall can seat up to 180 separate from the equally spacious bar and dance floor. The restoration of a collection of antique carriages has given the business a clear brand. All in all, a beautiful well planned wedding venue for large parties has been created out of an unpromising unused industrial building on an historic estate.

The Carriage Rooms, Montalto Estate, County Down (p.362)

Pick your *favourite picnic spot!*

© VISIT BRITAIN IMAGES

Win a fabulous *Hudson's* hamper and an invitation to the *Hudson's Heritage Awards*.

Take a picnic to any heritage site in the UK this year and you could win a gorgeous traditional hamper. All you need to do is nominate your favourite picnic spot. It might be a family picnic on a sunny summer afternoon or a picnic supper during a concert or theatre performance or even a place for a quick sandwich on a cycle ride. We want to know where is the best heritage picnic spot in the UK? Past winners have been Port Eliot *(see p.194)*, where the view from the picnic meadows leading down to the river Tiddy includes the arches of Brunel's towering viaduct, and Chatsworth House *(see p.244)* which has not only many places where you can spread your picnic rug in a fantastic setting but also the means to buy all the food you need for an impromptu picnic.

Send us a photograph (or up to 4) of your picnic place telling us where it is and describe why it is special to you in 150 words.

If yours is the winning entry you will receive a special Hudson's picnic hamper for 6, loaded with delicious goodies and an invitation for 2 to attend the presentation of Hudson's Heritage Awards, held each year in London. Your winning entry will also feature in next year's Hudson's Historic Houses & Gardens.

Winners and runners up will receive a free copy of Hudson's Historic Houses & Gardens 2016.

All entries received will be judged by our independent judging panel chaired by Norman Hudson, OBE. Details can be found at www.hudsons-awards.co.uk where you can also make your nomination online. Make sure you include your name, address, email address and telephone number. You can nominate somewhere by post to: Hudson's Best Heritage Picnic Award, 35 Thorpe Road, Peterborough PE3 6AG.

● The closing date for all entries is 30 September 2015.
● Winners will be advised by 1 January 2016.
● The judges' decision is final and no correspondence will be entered into.
● Hudson's reserves the right to reproduce all images provided for use in publicity materials.

Historic House Hotels of the National Trust

National Trust

Past, Present & Future Perfect

Hartwell House & Spa

Bodysgallen Hall & Spa

Middlethorpe Hall & Spa

The three Historic House Hotels which became part of the National Trust by donation in 2008 were each rescued from an uncertain future in the 1980's. They, with their gardens and parks, were restored and converted to hotels, combining historically accurate standards with the provision of traditional and up-to-date comfort for guests.

STAY IN AN HISTORIC HOUSE HOTEL OF THE NATIONAL TRUST...

...and enjoy not only the comfort of these restored houses, but also the very best of British hospitality, although well suited for their present role, guests should not expect them to be modern hotels like new built in town or country, however, very few allowances need to be made for the fact that the building is more than 300 year old.

Regional Directory

Holkham Park

Borders

South West Scotland, Dumfries & Galloway, Ayrshire &
The Isle of Arran

Edinburgh City, Edinburgh, Coast & Countryside

Greater Glasgow & The Clyde Valley

Tayside: Perthshire, Angus & Dundee & The Kingdom of Fife

West Highlands & Islands, Loch Lomond, Stirling & Trossachs

Grampian Highlands, Aberdeen & North East Coast

Highlands & Skye

We want to make Hudson's easy for you to use. Turn to our maps on pages 385 for all sites and another for Churches Conservation Trust properties on pages 407. Do check opening times before you visit. Many properties are open regularly, but others only occasionally and some may only open for weddings and special events.

Key to Symbols

i	Information
🛍	Shop
🌱	Plant Sales
🍸	Corporate Hospitality / Functions
♿	Suitability for the Disabled
☕	Refreshments / Cafe / Tearoom
🍴	Restaurant
🚶	Guided Tours
🎧	Audio Tours
P	Parking Available
🖼	Education - School Visits
🐕	Suitability for Dogs
🚫🐕	No Dogs
🏨	Accommodation
🔔	Civil Wedding Licence
❄	Open All Year
🎭	Special Events
€	Accept Euros
🏛	Member of the Historic Houses Association but does **not** give free access to Friends
🏛 Ⓕ	Member of the HHA giving free access under the HHA Friends Scheme
⛪	Property in the care of The Churches Conservation Trust
🌳	Property owned by National Trust
⊞	Property in the care of English Heritage
⚜	Property owned by The National Trust for Scotland
🏰	Property in the care of Historic Scotland
✿	Properties in the care of Cadw, the Welsh Government's historic environment service
◆	2014 Hudson's Heritage Awards Winner
◆	2014 Hudson's Heritage Awards Highly Commended

Kew Palace, Kew
©VisitEngland/Royal Botanic Gardens, Kew/A. McRobb

London

Everyone should visit the Tower of London and Windsor Castle, but don't overlook the many birthplace museums and smaller historic houses in Britain's vibrant capital.

London

Find stylish hotels with a personal welcome and good cuisine in London. More information on page 364.

- The Mayflower Hotel
- New Linden Hotel
- San Domenico House
- Searcys Roof Garden Rooms
- Twenty Nevern Square

London - England

© Clive Boursnell

■ Owner
Chiswick House and Gardens Trust and English Heritage

■ Address
Chiswick House
Burlington Lane
London
W4 2RP

■ Location
Map 19:C8
OS Ref. TQ210 775
Burlington Lane,
London W4 2RP.
Rail: ½m NE of Chiswick Station.
Underground: Turnham Green, ¾m.
Bus: 190, E3.

■ Contact
The Estate Office
Tel: 020 8742 3905

■ Opening Times
Gardens
7am - dusk all year round.
Chiswick House
28 February - 29 March.
Weekends only during the Camellia Show 10am-4pm.
30 March 2015 onwards.
Sun - Wed 10am - 5pm.
Check website for Winter 2015 closure.
Open Bank Holiday Mondays in the season.
Café
Open daily all year round from 9am.

■ Admission
Gardens
Entry	Free

House
Adult	£6.10
Conc.	£5.50
Child	£3.70
Family	£15.90
Discount for groups 11+	
EH Members	Free

Prices correct at time of press

Garden Tours & Group Bookings
Chiswick House
020 8995 0508.
Garden Tours and Camellia Show Group Bookings
020 8742 3905.

■ Special Events
Camellia Show 2015
28 February - 29 March.
Conservatory open daily 10am - 4pm.
There are year-round events from garden and family activities to open-air performances after dark - see www.chgt.org.uk.

Conference/Function
ROOM	Size	Max Cap
Chiswick House		150
Burlington Pavilion		350
The Conservatory		120
The Cafe		80

CHISWICK HOUSE AND GARDENS ⌗
www.chgt.org.uk

Chiswick House is a magnificent neo-Palladian villa set in 65 acres of beautiful historic gardens.

Chiswick House is internationally renowned as one of the first and finest English Palladian villas. Lord Burlington who designed and built the villa from 1725 – 1729, was inspired by the architecture and gardens of ancient Rome. The opulent interiors created by William Kent, display a rich collection of Old Master paintings.

The Grade 1 listed gardens surrounding Chiswick House have, at every turn, something to surprise and delight the visitor from the magnificent cedar trees to the beautiful Italianate gardens with their cascade, statues, temples, urns and obelisks. The gardens have been fully restored to their former glory, including the Conservatory, which houses the world famous Camellia collection in bloom during February and March.

There is also a children's play area and a modern café designed by award-winning architects Caruso St John. Open daily it offers seasonal breakfast and lunch menus, snacks, afternoon teas and refreshments.

Chiswick House once acted both as a gallery for Lord Burlington's fine art collection and as a glamorous party venue where he could entertain. Whether you are looking to host a wedding, exclusive private dinner, celebrate a special occasion or arrange a team building day, it is the ideal location. From a stylishly simple civil ceremony to an elaborate wedding reception, champagne celebration in the domed Conservatory, team building days in our Private Walled Gardens or a party in the Cafe. The House and Gardens are also a popular location for filming and photo shoots.

KEY FACTS

ⓘ WCs. Filming, plays, photographic shoots. Weddings, corporate and private events and party hire - please call 020 8742 2762 or events@chgt.org.uk or see website.

Private & corporate hospitality.

See website for disabled access.

Personal guided tours must be booked in advance.

House. (Downloadable tours-Garden).

Ⓟ Pay and display machines (approx. 60 bays).

Contact Estate Office.

Gardens except for clearly sign-posted dog-free and short lead only areas.

House.

© Clive Boursnell

© Richard Bryant

VISITOR INFORMATION

■ **Owner**
Historic Royal Palaces

■ **Address**
Kensington Gardens
London
W8 4PX

■ **Location**
Map 20:I8
OS Ref. TQ258 801
In Kensington Gardens.
Underground:
Queensway on Central
Line, High Street
Kensington on Circle &
District Line.

■ **Contact**
Tel: 0844 482 7777
**Venue Hire and
Corporate Hospitality:**
020 3166 6115
E-mail: kensingtonpalace
@hrp.org.uk

■ **Opening Times**
Nov-Feb: daily, 10am-5pm
(last admission 4pm).
Mar-Oct: daily, 10am-6pm
(last admission 5pm).
Closed 24-26 Dec.

■ **Admission**
Call 0844 482 7777 or visit
www.hrp.org.uk for more
information.

KENSINGTON PALACE

www.hrp.org.uk/kensingtonpalace

Home to royalty for over 300 years.

Discover stories from Queen Victoria's life in her own words, as queen, wife and mother in the Victoria Revealed exhibition, told through extracts from her own letters and diaries. Follow in the footsteps of Georgian courtiers in the sumptuous King's State Apartments which show some breathtaking examples of the work of architect and painter William Kent.

Plus, don't miss Fashion Rules, featuring rare and exquisite dresses from HM Queen Elizabeth II, Princess Margaret and Diana Princess of Wales. This elegant exhibition will provide a feast for the eyes and a nostalgic glance back at recent decades.

Explore the beautiful gardens, inspired by the famous lawns that existed in the 18th Century and enjoy a leisurely lunch or an indulgent afternoon tea in the splendour of Queen Anne's Orangery, once the setting for the most lavish of court entertainments.

KEY FACTS

Tel: 020 3166 6115.

Please book, 0844 482 7777.

VISITOR INFORMATION

◼ Address
Spencer House
27 St James's Place
London SW1A 1NR

◼ Location
Map 20:L8
OS Ref. TQ293 803
Central London:
off St James's Street,
overlooking Green Park.
Underground:
Green Park.

◼ Contact
Jane Rick, Director
Tel: 020 7514 1958
Fax: 020 7409 2952
Recorded Info Line:
020 7499 8620.
E-mail:
tours@spencerhouse.co.uk

◼ Opening Times
2015
Open on Sundays from:
10.30am-5.45pm.
Last tour 4.45pm.
Regular tours throughout
the day.
Max number on each tour
is 20.
Monday mornings: for
pre-booked groups only.
Group size: min 15-60.
Closed: January & August.
Open for private and
corporate hospitality except
during August.

◼ Admission
Adult: £12.00
Conc*:   £10.00
*Students, Members of the
V&A, Friends of the Royal
Academy, Tate Members
and senior citizens (only on
production of valid
identification), children
under 16. No children
under 10 admitted.
Prices include guided tour.

**For further information
please view the website:**
www.spencerhouse.co.uk
**or telephone the Tours
Administrator:** 020 7514
1958 (Mon-Fri only) or the
**Recorded Information
Line:** 020 7499 8620.

All images are copyright of
Spencer House Limited and
may not be used without
the permission of Spencer
House Limited.

Conference/Function

ROOM	Size	Max Cap
Receptions		400
Lunches & Dinners		126
Board Meetings		40
Theatre-style Meetings		100

The Great Room

SPENCER HOUSE
www.spencerhouse.co.uk

London's most magnificent 18th Century aristocratic private palace.

Spencer House, built 1756-66 for the first Earl Spencer, an ancestor of Diana, Princess of Wales (1961-97), is London's finest surviving 18th Century town house. The magnificent private palace has regained the full splendour of its late 18th Century appearance after a painstaking ten-year restoration programme.

Designed by John Vardy and James 'Athenian' Stuart, the nine State Rooms are amongst the first neo-classical interiors in Europe. Vardy's Palm Room, with its spectacular screen of gilded palm trees and arched fronds, is a unique Palladian set-piece, while the elegant mural decorations of Stuart's Painted Room

reflect the 18th Century passion for classical Greece and Rome. Stuart's superb gilded furniture has been returned to its original location in the Painted Room by courtesy of the V&A and English Heritage. Visitors can also see a fine collection of 18th Century paintings and furniture, specially assembled for the House, including five major Benjamin West paintings, graciously lent by Her Majesty The Queen.

The State Rooms are open to the public for viewing on Sundays. They are also available on a limited number of occasions each year for private and corporate entertaining during the rest of the week.

KEY FACTS

ℹ️ No photography inside House or Garden.

♿ House only, ramps and lifts. WC.

🚶 Obligatory. Comprehensive colour guidebook.

🐕 Guide Dogs only.

The Palm Room

The West Facade

SYON PARK 🏛ⓕ
www.syonpark.co.uk

London home of the Duke of Northumberland with magnificent Robert Adam interiors, 40-acres of gardens, including the spectacular Great Conservatory.

Described by John Betjeman as the 'Grand Architectural Walk', Syon House and its 200-acre park is the London home of the Duke of Northumberland, whose family, the Percys, have lived here for 400 years. Originally the site of a late medieval monastery, excavated by Channel 4's Time Team, Syon Park has a fascinating history. Catherine Howard was imprisoned at Syon before her execution, Lady Jane Grey was offered the crown whilst staying at Syon, and the 9th Earl of Northumberland was imprisoned in the Tower of London for 15 years because of his association with the Gunpowder Plot. The present house has Tudor origins but contains some of Robert Adam's finest interiors, which were commissioned by the 1st Duke in the 1760s. The private apartments and State bedrooms are available to view.

The house can be hired for filming and photo shoots subject to availability. Within the 'Capability' Brown landscaped park are 40 acres of gardens which contain the spectacular Great Conservatory designed by Charles Fowler in the 1820s. The House and Great Conservatory are available for corporate and private hire. The Northumberland Room in Syon House is an excellent venue for conferences, meetings, lunches and dinners (max 60). The State Apartments make a sumptuous setting for dinners, concerts, receptions, launches and wedding ceremonies (max 120). Marquees can be erected on the lawn adjacent to the house for balls and corporate events. The Great Conservatory is available for summer parties, launches, filming, photoshoots and wedding receptions (max 150).

KEY FACTS

- ⓘ No photography in the House.
- 🏪 Garden Centre.
- ⏲
- 🛗 WCs. House - Limited access . Gardens and Great Conservatory - fully accessible.
- 🍽 The Refectory in the Garden Centre.
- 🍴
- 🚶 By arrangement.
- Ⓟ Free parking.
- 🎓
- 🔔
- ♿ See website for details.

VISITOR INFORMATION

■ Owner
The Duke of Northumberland

■ Address
Syon House
Syon Park
Brentford
Middx
TW8 8JF

■ Location
Map 19:B8
OS Ref. TQ173 767
Between Brentford & Twickenham, off A4, A310 in SW London.
Sat Nav: TW7 6AZ
Public Transport:
Gunnersbury Station then bus 237 or 267. Brentford Rail, Ealing Broadway or Boston Manor Underground, then bus E8. Minicab companies available at the stations.
Air: Heathrow 8m.

■ Contact
Estate Office
Tel: 020 8560 0882
Fax: 020 8568 0936
E-mail:
info@syonpark.co.uk

■ Opening Times
Syon House:
18 Mar-1 Nov
Weds, Thurs, Suns and BHs 11am-5pm, last entry 4pm.

Gardens only:
16 Mar-1 Nov
Daily 10.30am-5pm, last entry at 4pm.
House, Gardens and Great Conservatory:
Closed from 2 Nov 2015-14 Mar 2016.

■ Admission
House, Gardens & Conservatory:
Adult	£12.00
Child	£5.00
Conc.	£10.50
Family (2+2)	£27.00

Booked groups (25+)
Adult	£10.50
Conc.	£9.50
School Group	£3.00

Gardens & Great Conservatory:
Adult	£7.00
Child	£3.50
Conc.	£5.50
Family (2+2)	£15.00
School Group	£2.00

Syon House Ventures reserves the right to alter opening times. Please phone or check website for up to date details and special events.

Conference/Function

ROOM	Size	Max Cap
Great Hall	50'x30'	120
Great Conservatory	60'x40'	150
Marquee		800

London - England

© Historic Royal Palaces

VISITOR INFORMATION

■ Owner
Historic Royal Palaces

■ Address
London
EC3N 4AB

■ Location
Map 20:P7
OS Ref. TQ336 806
Bus: 15, 42, 78, 100, RV1.
Underground: Tower Hill on Circle/District Line.
Docklands Light Railway: Tower Gateway Station.
Rail: Fenchurch Street Station and London Bridge Station.
Boat: From Embankment Pier, Westminster or Greenwich to Tower Pier.
London Eye to Tower of London Express.

■ Contact
Tel: 0844 482 7777
Venue Hire and Corporate Hospitality:
020 3166 6226
E-mail: visitorservices.tol @hrp.org.uk

■ Opening Times
Summer:
Mar-Oct, Tues-Sat
9am-5.30pm (last admission 5pm).
Mons & Suns
10am-5.30pm (last admission 5pm).
Winter:
Nov-Feb, Tues-Sat
9am-4.30pm (last admission 4pm).
Mons & Suns
10am-4.30pm (last admission 4pm).
Closed 24-26 Dec and 1 Jan.

■ Admission
Call 0844 482 7777 or visit www.hrp.org.uk for more information.

TOWER OF LONDON
www.hrp.org.uk/toweroflondon

The ancient stones reverberate with dark secrets, priceless jewels glint in fortified vaults and pampered ravens strut the grounds.

The Tower of London, founded by William the Conqueror in 1066-7, is one of the world's most famous fortresses, and one of Britain's most visited historic sites. Despite a grim reputation for a place of torture and death, there are so many more stories to be told about the Tower and its intriguing cast of characters.

This powerful and enduring symbol of the Norman Conquest has been enjoyed as a royal palace, served as an armoury and for over 600 years even housed a menagerie! Don't miss the re-presented Crown Jewels in the famous Jewel House, unlocking the story behind the 23,578 gems in the priceless royal jewels. Marvel at the Imperial State Crown and the largest diamond ever found and see the only treasure to escape destruction in 1649, after the Civil War. For centuries, this dazzling collection has featured in royal ceremonies, and it is still in use today.

Join Yeoman Warder tours to be entertained by captivating talks of pain, passion, treachery and torture at the Tower. Visit Tower Green and see the memorial to the people who died within the Tower walls. Find out why the last execution at the Tower was in 1941 and see how instruments of torture were used to extract 'confessions' from prisoners. Discover what life was like in the surprisingly luxurious Medieval Palace, and explore the stories of Henry II, Edward I and their courts at work.

See one of the Tower's most famous sights, the ravens. Legend has it Charles II believed that if the ravens were ever to leave the Tower, the fortress and the kingdom would fall. Step into 1000 years of history every day at the Tower of London.

KEY FACTS

- ℹ No Photography in Jewel house.
- ⬚
- ⬚ Tel: 020 3166 6226
- ⬚ WCs.
- ⬚ Licensed.
- ⬚ Yeoman Warder tours are free and leave front entrance every ½ hr.
- 🎧
- 🅿 None for cars. Coach parking nearby.
- ⬚ To book 0844 482 7777.
- ⬚
- ⬚
- ⬚

Yeoman Warders

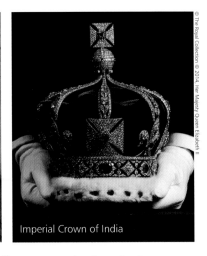
Imperial Crown of India

© The Royal Collection © 2014, Her Majesty Queen Elizabeth II

Register for news and special offers at **www.hudsonsheritage.com**

HAM HOUSE AND GARDEN ❧
HAM ST, RICHMOND-UPON-THAMES, SURREY TW10 7RS
www.nationaltrust.org.uk/ham-house

One of London's best kept secrets, this atmospheric Stuart mansion nestles on the banks of leafy Richmond-upon-Thames. It has remained virtually unchanged for 400 years and is internationally recognised for its superb collection of textiles, furniture and art which have remained in the house for centuries. Largely the vision of Elizabeth Murray, Countess of Dysart, who was deeply embroiled in the politics of the English Civil War and subsequent restoration of the monarchy, Ham House and Garden is an unusually complete survival of the 17th Century. It is reputed to be one of the most haunted houses in Britain.
Location: Map 19:B8. OS Ref TQ172 732. On S bank of the Thames, W of A307 at Petersham between Richmond and Kingston.

Owner: National Trust
Contact: The Property Administrator
Tel: 020 8940 1950
E-mail: hamhouse@nationaltrust.org.uk
Open: House and Garden opening times vary throughout the year, please see website for further details.
Admission: National Trust members free. Prices vary throughout the year, please see website for further details.
Key facts: ⓘ No flash photography. ▢ ⚲ ⊤ ⬣ WCs. ▦ ⬚ Licensed. ⚐ By arrangement. ⓟ Ltd for coaches. ▦ ⬚ Guide dogs only. ⚐ ⬚

HOUSES OF PARLIAMENT
WESTMINSTER, LONDON SW1A 0AA
www.parliament.uk/visiting

Inside one of London's most iconic buildings, tours of the Houses of Parliament offer visitors a unique combination of one thousand years of history, modern day politics, and stunning art and architecture.

Both audio and fully guided tours include the route taken by the Queen at the State Opening of Parliament; from The Queen's Robing Room, through the Royal Gallery and Prince's Chamber, and into the majestic Lords Chamber. Tours then move on to Central Lobby, Members' Lobby and one of the voting lobbies before entering the Commons Chamber, scene of many lively debates. Passing through St Stephen's Hall, the tours end in 900 year old Westminster Hall. Afternoon tea in the Terrace Pavilion can be added to some tours.
Location: Map 20:M8. OS Ref TQ303 795. Central London, 1km S of Trafalgar Square. Underground: Westminster. **Tel:** 020 7219 4114

Open: Sats throughout the year and on selected weekdays when Parliament is not sitting during holiday periods (including the summer, Christmas and Easter).
Admission: Audio tours: Adults £17.50, Concessions £15.00, Children 1 child free with each paying adult otherwise £7.00. Guided tours: Adults: £25.00, Concessions £20.00, Children £10.00. Concession prices apply to over 60s, students and members of the UK Armed Forces.
Key facts: ⓘ Searches, similar to those used in airports, are conducted on entry. Cameras cannot be used except in Westminster Hall. ▢ Jubilee Shop off Westminster Hall offers a range of books, gifts and souvenirs. ⬣ ▦ Jubilee Cafe serves a selection of light meals, and hot and cold drinks. ⚐ Guided tours - approx 100 mins, available in a number of languages. ⓘ Audio tours - approx 60 to 75 mins, available in a number of languages. ▦ Assistance dogs only. ⬚

© National Trust Images / Andrew Butler

OSTERLEY PARK AND HOUSE ❧
JERSEY ROAD, ISLEWORTH, LONDON TW7 4RB
www.nationaltrust.org.uk/osterley

Created in the late 18th Century by architect Robert Adam, Osterley is one of the last surviving country estates in London. From the tree lined driveway, spot the Charolais cattle and ponies lazing away the day. Just around the lake the magnificent House awaits; presented as it would have been in its 1780s heyday. Three floors of rooms, from the classical grandeur of the Entrance Hall to the contrasting servants' quarters. Spot the animals in the immaculately preserved tapestries in the state apartments and imagine sleeping in the eight poster bed, reserved for visits from the monarch. The grounds are perfect for picnics or leisurely strolls. Or relax in the serenity of the restored 18th Century pleasure grounds, full of herbaceous borders, roses and ornamental vegetable beds as well as the original Robert Adam summer house with its lemon trees and highly scented shrubs. **Location:** Map 19:C7. OS Ref TQ146 780. A4 between Hammersmith and Hounslow. Main gates at Thornbury & Jersey Road junction. SatNav: TW7 4RD. **Owner:** National Trust **Tel:** 020 8232 5050 **E-mail:** osterley@nationaltrust.org.uk

Open: Gardens & Café open all year, 10-5pm (or dusk if earlier). House* & Shop open 28 Feb-29 Mar 12-4pm; 30 Mar-27 Sep 11-5pm; 28 Sep-1 Nov 12-4pm. Shop open w/e only from 7 Nov-13 Dec, House open w/e only from 5-13 Dec. Park & car park open 7am-7pm all year. Whole property (aside from Park) closed 25 & 26 Dec. * House: Mon & Tues 'behind-the-scenes' guided tours & only basement floor open. **Admission:** *House & Garden: Adult £11.00, Child £5.50, Family £27.50. Groups (15+) £8.40. Garden: Adult £4.80, Child £2.40, Family £12. *includes voluntary 10% Gift Aid donation. Car Park: £5.00, free to NT Members. Park and grounds: Free. **Key facts:** ℹ No flash photography inside House. 🛍 Wide range of goods, second-hand bookshop and plant sales. ⊤ Rooms available, contact for info. ♿ WCs. 🍴 Seasonal menus, freshly baked cakes & cream teas. Family friendly. Kids' lunchboxes. 🍴 🅕 By arrangement. 🎧 Audio-visual guides. 🅿 Limited for coaches. 🎓 Schools programme, contact for info. 🦮 Guide dogs only. 💒 Civil Weddings ceremonys & receptions, contact for info. ❋ Park, gardens & cafe open all year (closed 25 & 26 Dec). ☗

Houses of Parliament - Lords Chamber

SUTTON HOUSE ❧
2 & 4 HOMERTON HIGH STREET, HACKNEY, LONDON E9 6JQ
www.nationaltrust.org.uk/suttonhouse

A rare example of a Tudor red-brick house, built 1535 by Sir Ralph Sadleir, Principal Secretary of State for Henry VIII, with 18th Century alterations and later additions. Restoration revealed 16th Century detail, even in rooms of later periods. Notable features include original linenfold panelling and 17th Century wall paintings. Peel back the layers of time in this Hackney home and discover some unexpected occupants. Open Georgian Panels to reveal Tudor arches or see the squatters' artwork. Delve into family treasure chests or experience the sights and smells of a Tudor Kitchen. New garden for 2015; the Breaker Yard revealing the site's industrial past as a car breaker's yard with upcycled vehicles used for growing plants, play and ice-creams.
Location: Map 20:P3. OS Ref TQ352 851. At the corner of Isabella Road and Homerton High St.
Owner: National Trust **Contact:** House and Gardens Manager

Tel: 020 8986 2264 **E-mail:** suttonhouse@nationaltrust.org.uk
Open: 5 Feb-20 Dec, Wed-Sun, 12pm-5pm. Open daily in August. Open BH Mons and Good Friday. Property regularly used by local community groups – rooms always open as advertised, but call if you would like to visit during a quiet time. Occasional 'Museum Lates' opening.
Key facts: ▣ NT Gift Shop & secondhand book shop. ⊤ From lectures & talks to team building & workshops, our barn area provides you with privacy, while our adjoining café can provide you with refreshments. ▣ Ground floor only. WC. ▣ Open all year round and everyday in the summer, indulge in a cream tea served on vintage crockery in our tearoom. ▣ Guided Tours are held at weekends. Please call ahead for times. ▣ ▣ Assistance dogs only. ▣ From Feb to Dec, whether you're looking for a ceremony only, or an all day reception, enjoy a perfect wedding day at Sutton House. ▣

18 STAFFORD TERRACE
18 Stafford Terrace, London W8 7BH
www.rbkc.gov.uk/museums

From 1875, 18 Stafford Terrace was the home of Punch cartoonist Edward Linley Sambourne, his wife Marion, their two children and live-in servants. Originally decorated by the Sambournes in keeping with fashionable Aesthetic principles, the interiors evolved into wonderfully eclectic artistic statements within the confines of a typical middle-class home. **Location:** Map 20:I8. OS Ref TQ252 794. Parallel to Kensington High St, between Phillimore Gardens & Argyll Rd.
Owner: The Royal Borough of Kensington & Chelsea **Contact:** Curatorial staff
Tel: 020 7602 3316 **E-mail:** museums@rbkc.gov.uk
Open: Mid Sep-Mid Jun. Visits are by guided tours only; Weds 11.15am, 2.15pm, Sats and Suns 11.15am, 1pm, 2.15pm, 3.30pm (weekend afternoon tours are costumed). **Admission:** Adult £8.00, Concession £6.00, Child (under 18yrs) £3.00. Groups (12+) £9.50pp. Joint group (12+) guided tour with Leighton House Museum £17.00pp. **Key facts:** ⓘ No photography. ▣ ▣ Obligatory. ▣ None. ▣ ▣ Guide dogs only. ▣

575 WANDSWORTH ROAD ❧
Lambeth, London SW8 3JD
www.nationaltrust.org.uk/575wandsworthroad

The hand-carved fretwork interior of this modest, early 19th Century, terraced house is enthralling and inspiring. Created by Khadambi Asalache, a Kenyan-born poet, novelist, philosopher of mathematics and British civil servant, who, over 20 years, turned his home into a work of art. Prompted initially by the need to disguise persistent damp he embellished almost every wall, ceiling and door in the house with fretwork patterns and motifs, The house stands as he left it, with his painted decoration on walls, doors and floors and with rooms furnished with his handmade fretwork furniture and carefully arranged collections of objects.
Location: Map 20:L12. OS Ref 176:292761. 220 Yards from Wandsworth Road Overground Station
Tel: 020 7720 9459
E-mail: 575wandsworthroad@nationaltrust.org.uk
Open: Sun 1 Mar-Sun 1 Nov, Wed evening, Fri, Sat & Sun.
Admission: By guided tour only, booking essential as placed are limited.

BANQUETING HOUSE
Whitehall, London SW1A 2ER
www.hrp.org.uk/banquetinghouse

This revolutionary structure was the first in England to be built in a Palladian style. It was designed by Inigo Jones for James I, and work finished in 1622. Intended for the splendour and exuberance of court masques, the Banqueting House is probably most famous for one real life drama: the execution of Charles I which took place here in 1649. One of Charles's last sights as he walked to his death was the magnificent ceiling painted by Peter Paul Rubens in 1630-4.
Location: Map 20:M8. OS Ref TQ302 80. Located on Whitehall in central London, the Banqueting House is a short walk from Westminster, Charing Cross and Embankment Underground and rail stations.
Owner: Historic Royal Palaces
Contact: Banqueting House Visitor Services **Tel:** 0844 482 7777
E-mail: banquetinghouse@hrp.org.uk
Open: Mon-Sun 10am-5pm. Last admission 4.15pm. Closed 24, 25 and 26 Dec and 1 Jan. Before visiting, please call 020 3166 6155/6154/6152.
Admission: Enquiry line 0844 482 7777.
Key facts: Video and audio guide.

DR JOHNSON'S HOUSE
17 Gough Square, London EC4A 3DE
www.drjohnsonshouse.org

Dr Johnson's House is a charming 300-year-old townhouse, nestled amongst a maze of courts and alleys in the historic City of London. Samuel Johnson, the writer and wit, lived and worked here during the eighteenth century, compiling his great 'Dictionary' in the Garret. Today, the House is open to the public with restored interiors and a wealth of original features. **Location:** Map 20:N7. OS Ref TQ313 812. North of Fleet Street. **Owner:** Dr Johnson's House Trust
Contact: The Curator **Tel:** 020 7353 3745
E-mail: curator@drjohnsonshouse.org
Open: 11am-5pm Oct-Apr. 11am-5.30pm May-Sep.
Admission: Adults £4.50, Conc. (over 60s, students, registered unemployed) £3.50, Child (up to 17) £1.50, Family £10.00. National Trust members discount.
Key facts: Small shop-books, gifts & souvenirs. Available for private events evenings & Suns. Many unavoidable steps. Pre-booked groups 10+. £2. Interpretation available in 10 languages. Disabled bays only in Gough Square & neighbouring streets. English & History workshops, tours/talks schools, A-level groups & universities. Check website for Christmas closures.

BUCKINGHAM PALACE
London SW1A 1AA
www.royalcollection.org.uk

Buckingham Palace serves as both the office and London residence of Her Majesty The Queen. During the summer, when the Palace is not being used in its official capacity, visitors can tour the nineteen spectacular State Rooms, which are furnished with some of the greatest treasures from the Royal Collection.
Location: Map 20:L8. OS Ref TQ291 796.
Underground: Green Park, Victoria, St James's Park.
Owner: Official Residence of Her Majesty The Queen
Contact: Ticket Sales and Information Office
Tel: +44 (0)20 7766 7300
E-mail: bookinginfo@royalcollection.org.uk
Open: Selected dates in the year.
Contact for details or visit website.
Admission: Visit www.royalcollection.org.uk for details.
Key facts: Assistance dogs welcome.

The Gallery at Strawberry Hill House

KENWOOD HOUSE ⌗
Hampstead Lane, London NW3 7JR
www.english-heritage.org.uk/kenwoodhouse

Set in tranquil parkland in fashionable Hampstead, with panoramic views over London, Kenwood has undergone an extensive programme of repairs with striking re-presentations of its fabulous interior and outstanding art collections. View the sumptuous Robert Adam rooms and admire famous paintings.
Location: Map 20:J1. OS Ref TQ270 874. M1/J2. Signed off A1.
Owner: English Heritage **Tel:** 020 8348 1286
E-mail: kenwood.house@english-heritage.org.uk
Open: Please visit www.english-heritage.org.uk for opening times, admission prices and the most up-to-date information.
Key facts: ⓘ WCs. Concerts, exhibitions, filming. No photography in house. ⬚ Ⓣ Exclusive private and corporate hospitality. ⬚ Ⓘ Available on request (in English). Please call for details. Ⓟ West Lodge car park (Pay & Display) on Hampstead Lane. Parking for the disabled. ⬚ ⬚ Guide dogs only. ✳ ⬚

SOMERSET HOUSE
Strand, London WC2R 1LA
www.somersethouse.org.uk

Somerset House is a spectacular neo-classical building in the heart of London. During summer 55 fountains dance in the courtyard, and in winter you can skate on London's favourite ice rink. Somerset House also hosts open-air concerts and films, contemporary art and design exhibitions, learning events and free guided tours. **Location:** Map 20:N7. OS Ref TQ308 809. Sitting between the Strand and the north bank of the River Thames. Entrances on Strand, Embankment and Waterloo Bridge.
Owner: Somerset House Trust
Contact: Visitor Communications
Tel: 020 7845 4600 **Fax:** 020 7836 7613 **E-mail:** info@somersethouse.org.uk
Open: For opening times, please see website.
Admission: For admission prices, please see website.
Key facts: ⬚ Ⓣ ⬚ WCs. ⬚ Licensed. Ⓘ Licensed. Ⓘ By arrangement. ⬚ ⬚ On leads. ⬚ ✳ ⬚

ST PAUL'S CATHEDRAL
St Paul's Churchyard, London EC4M 8AD
www.stpauls.co.uk

St Paul's Cathedral, with its famous dome, is England's architectural masterpiece and place of national celebration. Enter and explore the beauty of Christopher Wren's St Paul's; the cathedral floor, crypt and famous whispering, stone and golden galleries. Included are touch-screen multimedia guides, scheduled guided tours and the Oculus film experience. **Location:** Map 20:N7. OS Ref TQ321 812. Central London. **Owner:** Chapter of St Paul's Cathedral
Tel: 020 7246 8350 / 020 7246 8348 **Fax:** 020 7248 3104
E-mail: reception@stpaulscathedral.org.uk **Open:** Mon-Sat, 8.30am-4.30pm. Last admission for sightseeing 4pm. Once inside the cathedral, the galleries are open from 9.30am-4.15pm. **Admission:** Please contact us or view the website for up to date details of the admission prices as well as discounts for groups and online booking. **Key facts:** ⓘ No photography or videos permitted inside Cathedral. ⬚ Ⓣ ⬚ Wheelchair accessible throughout, except galleries. ⬚ Ⓘ Ⓘ Ⓟ None for cars, limited for coaches in surrounding area. ⬚ ⬚ Assistance dogs only. ⬚ ⬚

STRAWBERRY HILL 🏛
268 Waldegrave Road, Twickenham TW1 4ST
www.strawberryhillhouse.org.uk

Strawberry Hill is internationally famous as Britain's finest and first example of Georgian Gothic revival architecture. With the aid of a guide book written by Horace Walpole, Strawberry Hill's creator, visitors can enjoy this 'little gothic castle's' award-winning restored interiors and a unique collection of Renaissance painted glass. **Location:** Map 19:C8. OS Ref TQ158 722. Off A310 between Twickenham and Teddington.
Owner: Strawberry Hill Trust **Contact:** Laura Teale
Tel: 020 8744 1241 **E-mail:** enquiry@strawberryhillhouse.org.uk
Open: Strawberry Hill is open Sat through Wed 1 Mar-1 Nov 2015. Weekends 12pm-4pm (last entry). Mon, Tue, Wed 1.40pm-4pm (last entry). Closed Thu & Fri.
Admission: Adult £12.00, Under 16s free, please visit our website for the full list of concessions and discounts.
Key facts: ⬚ Ⓘ Ⓣ ⬚ WCs. ⬚ Licensed. Ⓘ By arrangement. Ⓟ Limited for cars. No coaches. ⬚ ⬚ Guide dogs only. ⬚ ⬚

BURGH HOUSE AND HAMPSTEAD MUSEUM
New End Square, Hampstead, London NW3 1LT

A grade 1 listed Queen Anne house located by Hampstead Heath in the picturesque cobbled streets of Hampstead village. Run by the Burgh House Trust, an independent self funding Charity. Burgh House is free to enter and home to Hampstead Museum, changing exhibitions and art shows, recitals, talks and events. Wedding licence, private hire and fully licensed café with beautiful Gertrude Jekyll garden terrace. Level access to the ground floor, accesable toilet and baby changing. **Location:** Map 20:J2. OS Ref TQ266 859. New End Square, E of Hampstead Underground station.
Owner: Burgh House Trust **Contact:** General Manager **Tel:** 020 7431 0144
Buttery cafe: 020 7794 3943 **E-mail:** info@burghhouse.org.uk
Website: www.burghhouse.org.uk **Open:** House and Museum: Wed-Fri & Sun 12-5pm. Buttery cafe: Wed-Fri 11am-5pm, Sat & Sun 9.30am-5.30pm.
Admission: Free. **Key facts:** 🖼 🖭 🖾 Suitable. WCs. 🖼 Licensed. 🍴 Licensed. 🖾 By arrangement. 🖼 By arrangement. 🐾 Dogs welcome. 🔺 🏵 🐾

HONEYWOOD MUSEUM
Honeywood Walk, Carshalton SM5 3NX

Local history museum in a 17th Century listed building, next to the picturesque Carshalton Ponds, containing displays on the history of the house and local area, plus a changing programme of exhibitions and events on a wide range of subjects. Special facilities for school visits. Attractive garden at rear.
Location: Map 19:D9. OS Ref TQ279 646. A232 approximately 4m W of Croydon.
Owner: London Borough of Sutton
Contact: The Curator **Tel:** 020 8770 4297
E-mail: honeywoodmuseum@sutton.gov.uk
Website: www.sutton.gov.uk / www.friendsofhoneywood.co.uk
Open: Wed-Fri, 11am-5pm. Sat, Sun & BH Mon, 10am-5pm. Tea room closes 4.30pm.
Admission: Free admission.
Key facts: 🖼 🖾 WCs. 🖭 🖾 By arrangement. 🅿 Limited. 🖼 🖾 Guide dogs only. 🏵 🐾

KEATS HOUSE
Keats Grove, Hampstead, London NW3 2RR

This Grade I listed Regency house is where the poet John Keats lived from 1818 to 1820. Here he wrote 'Ode to a Nightingale' and met and fell in love with Fanny Brawne. Suffering from tuberculosis, Keats left for Italy, where he died at the age of 25. Fanny wore his engagement ring until her death, and it is now displayed at the house. The museum runs regular poetry readings, talks and family events throughout the year. **Location:** Map 20:K3. OS Ref TQ272 856. Nearest Underground Belsize Park & Hampstead. **Owner:** City of London
Contact: The Manager **Tel:** 020 7332 3868
E-mail: keatshouse@cityoflondon.gov.uk **Website:** www.cityoflondon.gov.uk/keats **Open:** 1 Mar-31 Oct: Tue-Sun, 1pm-5pm; 1 Nov-28 Feb: Fri-Sun, 1pm-5pm. BH Mons. School parties and pre-booked groups by arrangement.
Admission: Adults £5.50, Conc. £3.50, Child 17 & under Free. Tickets valid for one year. **Key facts:** 🖼 🖾 Ground floor. Accessible toilet. 🖾 Regular tours at 3pm - check before visiting. 🅿 None. 🖼 🖾 Guide dogs only. 🐾

LITTLE HOLLAND HOUSE
40 Beeches Avenue, Carshalton SM5 3LW

Step back in time and visit the former home of Frank Dickinson (1874-1961) who dreamt of a house which would follow the ideals of Morris and Ruskin. Dickinson designed, built and furnished the house himself from 1902 onwards. The Grade II interior features handmade furniture, metalwork, carvings and paintings produced by Dickinson in an eclectic mix of the Arts and Crafts and Art Nouveau styles.
Location: Map 19:D9. OS Ref TQ275 634. On B278 1m S of junction with A232.
Owner: London Borough of Sutton **Contact:** Ms V Murphy
Tel: 020 8770 4781 **Fax:** 020 8770 4777
E-mail: valary.murphy@sutton.gov.uk **Website:** www.sutton.gov.uk
Open: First Sun of each month & BH Suns & Mons (excluding Christmas & New Year), 1.30pm-5.30pm.
Admission: Free. Groups by arrangement, £5.00pp (includes talk & guided tour).
Key facts: 🖾 No photography in house. 🖼 🖾 Partial. 🖾 By arrangement. 🖼 Guide dogs only. 🏵

PITZHANGER MANOR HOUSE & GALLERY
Walpole Park, Mattock Lane, Ealing W5 5EQ

Pitzhanger Manor House & Gallery comprises the Grade I listed Pitzhanger Manor-House, once owned and designed by revered British architect Sir John Soane (1800-1810), and Pitzhanger Manor Gallery, housed in the 1940s extension. Art and design exhibitions run throughout the year, supported by a programme of educational events. In 2015 the building will close for a major restoration project.
Location: Map 19:C7. OS Ref TQ176 805. Ealing, London.
Owner: London Borough of Ealing
Contact: Exhibition and Events Co-ordinator
Tel: 020 8567 1227 **Fax:** 020 8567 0595
E-mail: pitzhanger@ealing.gov.uk **Website:** www.pitzhanger.org.uk
Open: All year: Tue-Fri, 1-5pm. Sat, 11am-5pm. Summer Sundays: 1-5pm (May-Sep only). Closed Bank Holidays. **Admission:** Free.
Key facts: 🖾 See website. 🖾 Partial. 🖾 By arrangement. 🖼 🖼 🖾 🔺 🏵 🐾

WESTMINSTER CATHEDRAL
Victoria, London SW1P 1QW

The Roman Catholic Cathedral of the Archbishop of Westminster. Spectacular building in the Byzantine style, designed by J F Bentley, opened in 1903, famous for its mosaics, marble and music. Bell Tower viewing gallery has spectacular views across London. Exhibition displaying vestments, rare ecclesiastical objects and sacred relics. **Location:** Map 20:L9. OS Ref TQ293 791. Off Victoria Street, between Victoria Station and Westminster Abbey. **Owner:** Diocese of Westminster **Contact:** Revd Canon Christopher Tuckwell **Tel:** 020 7798 9055
Fax: 020 7798 9090 **Website:** www.westminstercathedral.org.uk
Open: All year: 7am-7pm. Please telephone for times at Easter & Christmas.
Admission: Free. Tower lift/viewing gallery charge: Adult £5.00 Family (2+4) £11.00 Conc. £2.50. Exhibition prices as those for viewing gallery. Telephone 020 7798 9028 for opening times of Tower and exhibition. The Cathedral was recently named a TripAdvisor 2014 Winner and awarded a Certificate of Excellence.
Key facts: 🖼 🖾 🖾 🖾 Booking required. 🖼 Worksheets & tours. 🖼 🏵

WHITEHALL
1 Malden Road, Cheam SM3 8QD

A Tudor timber-framed house, c1500, in the heart of Cheam Village. Interactive history room settings. Displays include the house and the people who lived here; Henry VIII's Nonsuch Palace - including stunning scale model; Cheam School and 'Dr. Syntax'. Changing exhibitions and special events throughout the year. Special facilities for school visits. Garden with medieval well. Homemade cakes in tearoom.
Location: Map 19:C9. OS Ref TQ242638. Approx. 2m S of A3 on A2043 just N of junction with A232.
Owner: London Borough of Sutton **Contact:** The Curator
Tel/Fax: 020 8643 1236 **E-mail:** whitehallmuseum@sutton.gov.uk
Website: www.sutton.gov.uk
Open: Wed-Fri, 2-5pm; Sat 10am-5pm; Sun & BH Mons, 2-5pm. Tearoom closes 4.30pm.
Admission: Free; Groups by arrangement £4.00pp (includes talk and tour).
Key facts: 🖼 🖾 Partial. 🖭 🖾 By arrangement. 🖼 🖼 Guide dogs only. 🏵 🐾

APSLEY HOUSE ⌗
Hyde Park Corner, London W1J 7NT

Apsley House, also known as No. 1 London, is the former residence of the first Duke of Wellington. **Location:** Map 20:L8. OS Ref TQ284 799.
Tel: 020 7499 5676 **Website:** www.english-heritage.org.uk/apsleyhouse
Open: Please visit www.english-heritage.org.uk for opening times, admission and the most up-to-date information.

OLD ROYAL NAVAL COLLEGE
King William Walk, Greenwich, London SE10 9NN

One of the most important ensembles in European Baroque architecture and the centrepiece of the Maritime Greenwich World Heritage site.
Location: Map 19:F7. OS Ref TQ383 778.
Tel: 020 8269 4747 **E-mail:** boxoffice@ornc.org **Website:** www.ornc.org
Open: Please see website for up to date opening and admission details.

2 WILLOW ROAD
2 Willow Road, Hampstead, London NW3 1TH
Tel: 020 7435 6166 **E-mail:** 2willowroad@nationaltrust.org.uk

7 HAMMERSMITH TERRACE
London W6 9TS
Tel: 020 8741 4104 **E-mail:** admin@emerywalker.org.uk

18 FOLGATE STREET
Spitalfields, East London E1 6BX
Tel: 020 7247 4013 **E-mail:** info@dennisevershouse.co.uk

CARLYLE'S HOUSE
24 Cheyne Row, Chelsea, London SW3 5HL
Tel: 020 7352 7087 **E-mail:** carlyleshouse@nationaltrust.org.uk

CHANDOS MAUSOLEUM
Whitchurch Lane, Little Stanmore, London HA8 6RB
Tel: 0845 303 2760 **E-mail:** central@thecct.org.uk

ELTHAM PALACE AND GARDENS
Eltham Palace, Court Yard, Eltham, London SE9 5QE
Tel: 020 8294 2548 **E-mail:** customers@english-heritage.org.uk

FENTON HOUSE
Hampstead Grove, London NW3 6SP
Tel: 020 7435 3471 **E-mail:** fentonhouse@nationaltrust.org.uk

FORTY HALL
Forty Hill, Enfield, Middlesex EN2 9HA
Tel: 020 8363 8196 **E-mail:** forty.hall@enfield.gov.uk

FULHAM PALACE & MUSEUM
Bishop's Avenue, Fulham, London SW6 6EA
Tel: 020 7736 3233 **E-mail:** admin@fulhampalace.org

GUNNERSBURY PARK & MUSEUM
Gunnersbury Park, London W3 8LQ
Tel: 020 8992 1612 **E-mail:** gp-museum@carillionservices.co.uk

HOGARTH'S HOUSE
Hogarth Lane, Great West Road, London W4 2QN
Tel: 020 8994 6757 **E-mail:** john.collins@carillionservices.co.uk

LEIGHTON HOUSE MUSEUM
12 Holland Park Road, London W14 8LZ
Tel: 020 7602 3316 **E-mail:** museums@rbkc.gov.uk

MARBLE HILL HOUSE
Richmond Road, Twickenham TW1 2NL
Tel: 020 8892 5115 **E-mail:** customers@english-heritage.org.uk

ST ANDREW'S CHURCH
Old Church Lane, Kingsbury, London NW9 8RU
Tel: 0845 303 2760 **E-mail:** central@thecct.org.uk

WELLINGTON ARCH
Hyde Park Corner, London W1J 7JZ
Tel: 020 7930 2726 **E-mail:** customers@english-heritage.org.uk

WILLIAM MORRIS GALLERY
Lloyd Park, Forest Road, Walthamstow, London E17 4PP
Tel: 020 8527 9782

Keats House

Gilbert White's House,
Hampshire

Firle Place, East Sussex

Berkshire
Buckinghamshire
Hampshire
Kent
Oxfordshire
Surrey
Sussex
Isle of Wight

South East

Proximity to the capital means a wealth of country houses in the rural hinterland with views of rolling hills and wooded valleys.

New Entries for 2015:

- Newhaven Fort
- Cobham Wood & Mausoleum
- Denmans Garden
- Boughton Monchelsea Place
- Stowe Gardens
- Gilbert White's House & Garden
- The Bodleian Library

Find stylish hotels with a personal welcome and good cuisine in the South East. More information on page 364.

- Deans Place Hotel
- Drakes Hotel
- Flackley Ash Hotel
- Hotel Una
- Mill House Hotel & Restaurant
- The Millstream Hotel
- Montagu Arms Hotel
- Powder Mills Hotel
- The Priory Bay Hotel
- The White Horse Hotel

SIGNPOST
SELECTED PREMIER HOTELS 2015

www.signpost.co.uk

DORNEY COURT 🏠Ⓕ
Nr. Windsor, Berkshire SL4 6QP
www.dorneycourt.co.uk

"One of the finest Tudor Manor Houses in England" - Country Life. Grade I listed and noted for its outstanding architectural and historical importance. Home of the Palmers since the early 16th Century, passing from father to son over thirteen generations. Highlights include the magnificent Great Hall, oak and lacquer furniture and artwork which spans the lifetime of the house. The stunning Old Coach House Barn with its landscaped courtyard provides a beautiful and flexible space for weddings as well as private and corporate events. **Location:** Map 3:G2. OS Ref SU926 791. 5 mins off M4/J7, 10mins from Windsor, 2m W of Eton.
Owner/Contact: Mr James Palmer
Tel: 01628 604638 **E-mail:** enquiries@dorneycourt.co.uk
Open: May BHs (4 & 5 May; 25 & 26 May) and every day in Aug. 1.30pm-5pm.
Admission: Adult: £8.00, Child (10yrs+) £5.00. OAPs: £7.50. Groups (10+): £7.50 when house is open to public. Private group rates at other times.
Key facts: ⓘ Film & photographic shoots. No stiletto heels. 🏵 Garden centre. 🔲 Wedding receptions. 🔲🔲 Licensed. 🔲 Licensed. 🔲 Obligatory. 🅿🔲 🔲 Guide dogs only. 🔲🔲🔲 €

WINDSOR CASTLE
Windsor, Berkshire SL4 1NJ
www.royalcollection.org.uk

Established in the 11th Century by William the Conqueror, Windsor Castle is the oldest and largest occupied castle in the world. Visitors can enjoy the magnificent State Apartments, Queen Mary's Dolls' House, changing exhibitions in the Drawings Gallery, and St George's Chapel. In winter months, the sumptuous Semi-State Rooms are also open to visitors.
Location: Map 3:G2. OS Ref SU969 770. M4/J6, M3/J3. 20m from central London. **Owner:** Official Residence of Her Majesty The Queen
Contact: Ticket Sales and Information Office
Tel: +44 (0)20 7766 7304 **E-mail:** bookinginfo@royalcollection.org.uk
Open: Please see website for opening times.
Admission: Visit www.royalcollection.org.uk for details.
Key facts: ⓘ Photography and filming (for private use only) is permitted in the Castle Precincts. 🔲 Most public areas are accessible for wheelchair-users, including the State Apartments. 🔲 Guided tours of the Castle Precincts are available at regular intervals throughout the day. 🔲🔲 Assistance dogs only.

ST THOMAS' CHURCH 🔲
East Shefford, Hungerford, Berkshire RG17 7EF

This simple little church, with pre-Norman origins, stands in an idyllic spot beside a water meadow next to the River Lambourn. Its village has long since vanished, but the spirit of the villagers shines through in the church's simple craftsmanship, glorious medieval wallpaintings and fabulous tombs.
The alabaster statue of local noble Sir Thomas Fettiplace lies alongside that of his wife and gives a rare glimpse of 15th Century fashion. Look out for the lovely Norman tub font, an early medieval tomb, and fragments of early stained glass.
Location: OS Ref SU391 747. 2 miles north east of M4 junction 14, off A338 (Wantage Road).
Website: www.visitchurches.org.uk
Open: Open daily.

Dorney Court

CHENIES MANOR HOUSE 🏠Ⓕ

www.cheniesmanorhouse.co.uk

The Manor House is in the picturesque village of Chenies and lies in the beautiful Chiltern Hills.

The picturesque village of Chenies lies in the beautiful Chiltern Hills. The Manor House is approached by a gravel drive leading past the church. Home of the MacLeod Matthews family, this 15th and 16th Century manor house with fortified tower is the original home of the Earls of Bedford, visited by Henry VIII and Elizabeth I. Elizabeth was a frequent visitor, first coming as an infant in 1534 and as Queen she visited on several occasions, once staying for six weeks. The Bedford Mausoleum is in the adjacent church. The house contains tapestries and furniture mainly of the 16th and 17th Centuries, hiding places and a collection of antique dolls. Art exhibitions are held throughout the season in the restored 16th Century pavilion. The Manor is surrounded by five acres of enchanting gardens which have been featured in many publications and on television. It is famed for the Spring display of tulips. From early June there is a succession of colour in the Tudor Sunken Garden, the White Garden, herbaceous borders and Fountain Court. The Physic Garden contains a wide selection of medicinal and culinary herbs. In the Parterre is an ancient oak and a complicated yew maze while the Kitchen Garden is in Victorian style with unusual vegetables and fruit. Attractive dried and fresh flower arrangements decorate the house. Winner of the Historic Houses Association and Christie's Garden of the Year Award, 2009.

KEY FACTS

Gardens only.

Delicious homemade teas in the Garden Room.

HUGHENDEN 🦌
HIGH WYCOMBE, BUCKINGHAMSHIRE HP14 4LA
www.nationaltrust.org.uk/hughenden

Amid rolling Chilterns countryside, discover the hideaway and colourful private life of Benjamin Disraeli, the most unlikely Victorian Prime Minister. Follow in his footsteps, stroll through his German forest, relax in his elegant garden and imagine dining with Queen Victoria in the atmospheric manor. Uncover the Second World War story of Operation Hillside, for which unconventional artists painted maps for bombing missions - including the famous Dambusters raid. Discover the story of the map makers in our basement exhibition. Outdoors, get tips for growing your own vegetables in our walled garden. Don't miss our ancient woodland, where you may spot red kites soaring overhead.

Location: Map 3:F1. OS Ref SU866 955. 1½ m N of High Wycombe on the W side of the A4128.

Owner: National Trust **Contact:** The Estate Office

Tel: 01494 755573 **Fax:** 01494 474284 **Infoline:** 01494 755565
E-mail: hughenden@nationaltrust.org.uk
Open: Garden, shop & restaurant: 1 Jan-14 Feb, daily, 10am-5pm, 15 Feb-31 Dec, daily, 10am-5pm, or dusk if earlier. Manor: 1 Jan-14 Feb, daily, 12pm-4pm, 15 Feb-31 Dec, daily, 11am-5pm, or dusk if earlier. Closed 24 and 25 Dec.
Admission: House & Garden: Adult £11.00, Child £5.50, Family £27.50. Garden only: Adult £4.50, Child £2.75, Family £12.00. Woodlands Free. Groups: Adult £9.00. Child £4.00. Free to NT Members. Includes a voluntary 10% donation but visitors can choose to pay the standard prices advised at the property.
Key facts: 🅿️ ♿ 🍴 Partial. WCs. 🛍️ 🍴 Daily. 🅿️ 🚌 🐕 Guide dogs only in the formal and walled gardens. ❋ ♿

NATIONAL TRUST STOWE 🦌
NEW INN FARM, BUCKINGHAM MK18 5EQ
www.nationaltrust.org.uk/stowe

A monumental day out. The scale and beauty of Stowe has attracted visitors for over 300 years. Picture-perfect views, winding paths, lakeside walks and temples create a timeless landscape, reflecting the changing seasons. Full of hidden meaning, the gardens were created as an earthly paradise, and still cast their spell today. Your visit starts at the New Inn visitor centre outside the gardens. This fusion of modern and restored 18th Century buildings was where visitors of the day were welcomed to Stowe. Stop by the light and airy cafe for delicious fresh food. The sheer size and space is perfect for those who love the outdoors and enjoy walking. A short walk or a ride in a buggy takes you into the gardens, where another world await.

Location: Map 7:B10. OS Ref SP681 364. Off A422 Buckingham - Banbury Rd. 3m NW of Buckingham. **Contact:** National Trust Stowe

Tel: 01280 817156 **Twitter:** @NTStowe **Facebook:** National Trust Stowe
E-mail: stowe@nationaltrust.org.uk
Open: Gardens, shop, café, parlour rooms. 7 days a week all year round, 10am-6pm or dusk if earlier. Landscape gardens closed 23 May but visitor centre, parkland, café and shop open. Last entry to the gardens is recommended 90 minutes before closing. Closed 25 Dec. House not National Trust, open for tours call infoline on 01494 755568. Parkland open all year dawn to dusk.
Admission: New Inn Visitor Centre - Free of charge. Gardens: Adult £11.00, Child £5.50, Family £27.50. Groups (15+) £9.50, Child £4.75. Free to NT members. House (not NT): call infoline for details, charge including members, admission payable at National Trust reception.
Key facts: 🅿️ ♿ 🍴 ♿ 🛍️ 🍴 🅿️ 🚌 🐕 🏠 ❋ ♿

Gardens at Chenies Manor House

WOTTON HOUSE
Wotton Underwood, Aylesbury
Buckinghamshire HP18 0SB

The Capability Brown Pleasure Grounds at Wotton, currently undergoing restoration, are related to the Stowe gardens, both belonging to the Grenville family when Brown laid out the Wotton grounds between 1750 and 1767. A series of man-made features on the 3 mile circuit include bridges, temples and statues.
Location: Map 7:B11. OS Ref 468576, 216168. Either A41 turn off Kingswood, or M40/J7 via Thame.
Owner/Contact: David Gladstone
Tel: 01844 238363
Fax: 01844 238380
E-mail: david.gladstone@which.net
Open: 1 Apr-2 Sep: Weds only, 2-5pm. Also: 6 Apr, 25 Apr, 25 May, 4 Jul and 22 Aug: 2-5pm.
Admission: Adult £6.00, Child Free, Conc. £3.00. Groups (max 25).
Key facts: 🔲 🖼 Obligatory.
🅿 Limited parking for coaches. 🐕 On leads.

CLIVEDEN 🌺
Taplow, Maidenhead SL6 0JA
Relax in grand style as you explore these stunning gardens, woodlands and Thames riverbank. Beautiful floral displays. **Location:** Map 3:F1. OS Ref SU915 851.
Tel: 01628 605069 **E-mail:** cliveden@nationaltrust.org.uk
Website: www.nationaltrust.org.uk/cliveden
Open: Please see website for up to date opening and admission details.

NETHER WINCHENDON HOUSE 🏠ⓕ
Nether Winchendon, Nr Thame, Buckinghamshire HP18 0DY
Mediaeval Manor Strawberry Hill Gothick. Home last Royal Governor Massachussetts. Continuous family occupation since 1559.
Location: Map 7:C11. **Tel:** 01844 290101 **Website:** www.nwhouse.co.uk
Open: 20 Apr-22 May & BHs 4 & 25 May & 31 Aug (not Sats or Sun 3 May & 24 May). 2.45, 3.45 & 4.45pm tours. **Admission:** £8.00, Art Fund £6.00, HHA Free, Conc. £5.00, not Sun or BH's. No conc to Art Fund or HHA when open for NGS.

WADDESDON MANOR 🏠 🌺
Waddesdon, Nr Aylesbury, Buckinghamshire HP18 0JH
Magnificent house and grounds in the style of a 19th Century French chateau. Built by Baron Ferdinand de Rothschild to display his superb collection of art treasures and entertain the fashionable world. **Location:** Map 7:C11. OS Ref SP740 169. **Tel:** 01296 653226 **Website:** www.nationaltrust.org.uk/waddesdon-manor **Open:** Please see website for up to date opening and admission details.

ASCOTT 🌺
Wing, Leighton Buzzard, Buckinghamshire LU7 0PR
www.ascottestate.co.uk

Originally a half-timbered Jacobean farmhouse, Ascott was bought in 1876 by the de Rothschild family and considerably transformed and enlarged. It now houses an exceptional collection of fine paintings, Oriental porcelain and English and French furniture. The extensive gardens are a mixture of the formal and natural.
Location: Map 7:D11. OS Ref SP891 230. ½m E of Wing, 2m SW of Leighton Buzzard, on A418. **Owner:** National Trust **Contact:** Estate Manager
Tel: 01296 688242 **Fax:** 01296 681904
E-mail: info@ascottestate.co.uk
Open: House & Garden: 24 Mar-3 May: Tue-Sun, 2-6pm. 5 May-9 Jul: Tue-Thu, 2-6pm. 14 July-13 Sep Tue-Sun, 2-6pm. Last admission 5pm. Open BH Mons.
Admission: House & Garden: Adult £10.00, Child £5.00. Garden only: £5.00, Child £2.50. No reduction for groups. Groups must book prior to visit.
NT members free, except NGS days, 4 May & 31 Aug, where normal admission fees apply.
Key facts: ℹ Wheelchairs available from the Entrance Kiosk. Mobility shuttle. 🚻 WCs in the National Trust car park only. 🅿 220 metres. Limited for coaches. 🐕

VISITOR INFORMATION

■ Owner
Lord Montagu

■ Address
Beaulieu
Hampshire
SO42 7ZN

■ Location
Map 3:C6
OS Ref. SU387 025
M27 to J2, A326, B3054
follow brown signs.
Bus: Local service within
the New Forest.
Rail: Station at
Brockenhurst 7m away.

■ Contact
John Montagu Building,
Beaulieu, Hants SO42 7ZN
Tel: 01590 612345
E-mail:
visit@beaulieu.co.uk

■ Opening Times
Summer Whitsun -
September Daily,
10am-6pm. Winter
October-Whitsun Daily,
10am-5pm Please check
website for exact dates.
Closed Christmas Day.

■ Admission
All year Individual rates
upon application. Groups
(15+) Rates upon
application.

■ Special Events
Boatjumble: 26 April
Spring Autojumble:
16-17 May
Truckmania: 24 – 25 May
**Custom & Hot Rod
Festival:** 21 June
Motorcycle Ride-In Day:
12 July
Supercar Showdown:
23 August (TBC)
**International
Autojumble:**
September (TBC)

All ticket enquiries to our
Special Events Booking
Office. Tel 01590 612888.

Conference/Function

ROOM	Size	Max Cap
Brabazon (x3)	40' x 40'	85 (x3)
Domus	69' x 27'	150
Palace House		60
Motor Museum		250

Palace House

BEAULIEU 🏛Ⓕ
www.beaulieu.co.uk

Beaulieu, at the heart of the New Forest, is home to Lord Montagu and features a range of heritage attractions.

Palace House
Home of the Montagu family since 1538, Palace House was built around the Great Gatehouse of Beaulieu Abbey. Explore this fantastic gothic styled Victorian country home as costumed guides give you a flavour of life `below stairs' and share with you the fascinating history of the house and the generations who have lived there.

Beaulieu Abbey & Exhibition
Founded on land gifted by King John to Cistercian monks in 1204, Beaulieu Abbey was largely destroyed during the Reformation. The conserved ruins demonstrate the scale of what was once a vast complex. One of the surviving buildings houses an exhibition on the history of the Abbey and the monks that lived and worked here.

The National Motor Museum
Over 250 vehicles tell the story of motoring in Britain from its pioneering origins to the present day. From the earliest motor carriages to classic family saloons, displays include historic sporting motors, modern rally cars, F1 racers, a rustic 1930's country garage and Wheels – a fascinating pod ride through motoring history.

Grounds & Gardens
Explore the informal Wilderness Garden, fragrant Victorian Flower Garden and the Victorian Kitchen Garden. Enjoy the Mill Pond walk through parkland woods and look out for the Rufus Memorial Cairn – to commemorate the death of King William Rufus who, evidence suggests, was killed by an arrow whilst hunting at Beaulieu in 1100.

KEY FACTS

ℹ️	Allow 4-5 hrs for visits. Helicopter landing point.
🏠	Palace House Kitchen Shop & Main Reception Shop.
🍷	Please see http://www.beaulieu.co.uk/hospitality
♿	WC. Wheelchairs in Visitor reception by prior booking.
☕	Part of the Brabazon Restuarant- sandwiches to cooked meals and tea & cold drinks.
🍴	Seats 250.
🚶	Attendants on duty.
🅿️	Unlimited. Free admission for coach drivers plus voucher.
👥	Professional staff available to assist.
🐕	In grounds, on leads only.
🏨	Please see http://www.beaulieu.co.uk/hospitality
❄️	Only closed Christmas Day

© Fergus Baird

AVINGTON PARK 🏠Ⓕ
WINCHESTER, HAMPSHIRE SO21 1DB
www.avingtonpark.co.uk

From the wrought iron gates and long avenue of limes, approach well tended lawns, bordering the river Itchen and the elegant Palladian facade. William Cobbett wrote of Avington Park that it was 'one of the prettiest places in the County' and indeed it is true today. Dating back to the 11th Century, and enlarged in 1670, the house enjoys magnificent painted and gilded state rooms overlooking lawns and parkland. Over the years Charles II and George IV stayed at various times. St Mary's, a fine Georgian church, may also be visited.
Location: Map 3:D4. OS Ref SU534 324. 4m NE of Winchester ½m S of B3047 in Itchen Abbas. **Owner/Contact:** Mrs S L Bullen

Tel: 01962 779260
E-mail: enquiries@avingtonpark.co.uk
Open: May-Sep: Suns & BH Mons plus Mons in Aug, 2.30-5.30pm. Last tour 4.30pm. Group visits welcome by appointment all year.
Admission: Adult £7.50, Child £3.00.
Key facts: ℹ️ Conferences, weddings, films, photoshoots, private parties, seminars, corporate events, exclusive use. 📷
Ⓟ Partial (ground floor only) and WC. 🅿️ Ⓕ Obligatory. Ⓟ
🐕 In grounds, on leads. Guide dogs only in house. 🅿️ By arrangement. ☑️

© John Anderson

© Gilbert White & The Oates Collections

EXBURY GARDENS & STEAM RAILWAY
Exbury, Southampton, Hampshire SO45 1AZ
www.exbury.co.uk

A tranquil 200-acre woodland garden world-famous for dazzling displays of rhododendrons, azaleas and camellias in spring. Summer brings hydrangeas and showpiece exotics heat up the Herbaceous Borders. The extensive tree collection ensures year-round interest and stunning autumn colour. A ride on the 1¼ mile steam railway will delight visitors of all ages.
Location: Map 3:D6. OS Ref SU425 005. 20 mins Junction 2, M27 west. 11m SE of Totton (A35) via A326 & B3054 & minor road. In the New Forest.
Owner: Exbury Gardens Ltd.
Contact: Estate Office
Tel: 023 8089 1203
Fax: 023 8089 9940
E-mail: info@exbury.co.uk
Open: Sat 14 Mar-Sun 8 Nov 2015, 10am-5.30pm last admission 4.30pm.
Admission: Please see website for up to date admission prices. Prices and opening dates subject to variations. Please visit www.exbury.co.uk.
Key facts: 🏪 Licensed. Ⓕ By arrangement. Ⓟ
🐕 In grounds, on short leads. 🅿️ ☑️

GILBERT WHITE & THE OATES COLLECTIONS
Gilbert Whites House, High St, Selborne, Alton GU34 3JH
www.gilbertwhiteshouse.org.uk

Gilbert White & The Oates Collections explores the lives of three explorers of the natural world. The historic house was the home of the 18th Century naturalist Gilbert White, and is surrounded by 25 acres of restored garden and parkland. The Oates Collections celebrates the lives of 19th Century explorer Frank Oates, and Captain Lawrence Oates who travelled with Scott on the ill-fated Terra Nova Expedition. **Location:** Map 3:E4. OS Ref SU741 336. Selborne is on the B3006 from Alton to the A3. **Tel:** 01420 511275
E-mail: info@gilbertwhiteshouse.org.uk **Open:** 1 Jan-15 Feb, Fri–Sun, 10.30am-4.30pm. 16 Feb–31 Mar, Tue–Sun, 10.30am-4.30pm. 1 Apr–31 Oct, Tue–Sun, 10.30am-5.15pm. 1 Nov–20 Dec, Tue–Sun, 10.30am-4.30pm. BH Suns & Mons Jul & Aug. **Admission:** Adult £9.50, Conc £8.50, Under 16 £4.00, Under 5 Free, Family Ticket (2A+3C) £24.50. Pre-booked group of 10 or more £7.50. Garden Only £7.50. **Key facts:** 🛍️ Gift shop, books, local produce & gifts. 🌱 A gardener's dream, buy plants from Gilbert White's garden. 🅿️ 🅿️ Suitable. Assistance provided. 🍽️ Elegantly restored dining room. Ⓟ Village car park 2 min walk. 🔬 Gilbert White Field Study Centre. 🐕 In grounds only. 🅿️ ☑️

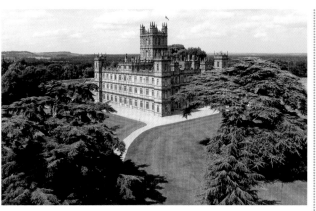

HIGHCLERE CASTLE, GARDENS & EGYPTIAN EXHIBITION 🏛️Ⓕ
Highclere Castle, Newbury, Berkshire RG20 9RN
www.highclerecastle.co.uk

This spectacular Victorian Castle is currently the setting for Downton Abbey. Visit the splendid State Rooms; admire the masculine opulence of the Library and the lovely south facing Drawing Room. Explore the Egyptian Exhibition in the Castle Cellars; the Antiquities Room and an amazing recreation of the discovery of Tutankhamun's tomb. Gardens inspired by Capability Brown including; Monk's Garden, Secret Garden and new Arboretum.

Location: Map 3:D3. OS Ref SU445 587. M4/J13 - A34 south. M3/J8 - A303 - A34 north. **Owner:** Earl of Carnarvon **Contact:** The Castle Office
Tel: 01635 253210 **Fax:** 01635 255315
E-mail: theoffice@highclerecastle.co.uk **Open:** 29 Mar-2 Apr; 4-12 Apr. 3-5 May; 24-26 May; 12 Jul-10 Sep (Sun-Thu). Information correct at time of publication.
Admission: Group Rates, Concessions, Family Tickets for Castle, Exhibition & Gardens; each element available separately, please check website for admission prices. **Key facts:** ◻ Ⓣ 🔲 Partial. WCs. 🍽 Licensed.
ⓘ By arrangement. 🅿 📷 🔲 Guide dogs only. 🏨 ♿

Houghton Lodge Gardens

HINTON AMPNER ☘
Bramdean, Alresford, Hampshire SO24 0LA
www.nationaltrust.org.uk/hinton-ampner

This elegant country manor and tranquil garden sit so harmoniously within the landscape that one cannot exist without the other. Enjoy the exquisite collection of ceramics and art and avenues of sculptured topiary leading to breathtaking views across the South Downs. With newly opened parkland, one can experience all Hinton Ampner has to offer.

Location: Map 3:E5. OS Ref SU597 275. M3/J9 or A3 on A272, 1m W of Bramdean. **Owner:** National Trust
Contact: Property office
Tel: 01962 771305
E-mail: hintonampner@nationaltrust.org.uk
Open: Gardens, Tearoom, Shop and Estate: 1 Jan-31 Dec, 10am-5pm. Winter exhibition: 27 Dec-8 Feb. House: 14 Feb-29 Nov, 5 Dec-20 Dec, 11am-4pm, Closed Christmas Eve and Christmas day.
Admission: Adult £10.30, Child £5.15, Family £25.50, Groups (15+) £7.80.
Key facts: ◻ ⓘ 🔲 WCs. 🍽 Licensed. ⓘ By arrangement. 🅿 Limited for coaches. 🐾 Dogs are welcome on parkland, estate and tea-room courtyard.

KING JOHN'S HOUSE & HERITAGE CENTRE
Church Street, Romsey, Hampshire SO51 8BT
www.kingjohnshouse.org.uk

Three historic buildings on one site: Medieval King John's House, containing 14th Century graffiti and rare bone floor, Tudor Cottage complete with traditional tea room and Victorian Heritage Centre with recreated shop and parlour. Beautiful period gardens, special events/exhibitions and children's activities. Gift shop and Tourist Information Centre. Receptions and private/corporate functions.

Location: Map 3:C5. OS Ref SU353 212. M27/J3. Opposite Romsey Abbey, next to Post Office. **Owner:** King John's House & Tudor Cottage Trust Ltd
Contact: Anne James **Tel:** 01794 512200 **E-mail:** annerhc@aol.com
Open: Mon-Sat, 10am-4pm. Limited opening on Sundays. Evenings also for pre-booked groups. Open all year except christmas week and occasional private bookings - check for details.
Admission: Adult £4.00, Child 50p, Conc. £3.00. Family & Season tickets.
Key facts: ◻ ⓘ Plant sale in May. Ⓣ 🔲 Partial. 🍽 Homemade cakes, cream teas & light lunches ⓘ By arrangement. 🅿 Off Latimer St, through King John's Garden. 📷 Reenactment days - Stone age to Victorian 🐾 Guide dogs only. 🏨 ♿

STRATFIELD SAYE HOUSE 🏛ⓕ
Stratfield Saye, Hampshire RG7 2BZ
www.stratfield-saye.co.uk

After the Duke of Wellington's victory against Napoleon at the Battle of Waterloo in 1815, the Duke chose Stratfield Saye as his country estate. The house contains many of the 1st Duke's possessions and is still occupied by his descendents being a family home rather than a museum.
Location: Map 3:E2. OS Ref SU700 615. Equidistant from Reading (M4/J11) & Basingstoke (M3/J6) 1½m W of the A33.
Owner: The Duke of Wellington
Contact: Estate Office
Tel: 01256 882694
Open: Thu 2-Mon 6 Apr. Thurs 30 Jul-Mon 24 Aug.
Admission: Weekends: Adult £12.00, Child £5.00, OAP/Student £11.00. Weekdays: Adult £10.00, Child £4.00, OAP/Student £9.00. Groups by arrangement only.
Key facts: 🅰 🚻 WC. 📷 📷 Obligatory. 🅿 🐕 Guide dogs only.

HOLY TRINITY CHURCH 🏛
Merepond Lane, Privett, Alton, Hampshire GU34 3PE

The spire of Holy Trinity soars high above the trees, visible for miles around in an idyllic corner of Hampshire. It is an extraordinary experience to find this lavishly decorated medieval-style church with Italian marble mosaic floors in such a rural location. Built in 1876-78, the church was funded by William Nicholson - a local benefactor and gin distiller - and designed by Gothic architect Sir Arthur Blomfield, later responsible for the Royal College of Music. Blomfield used the best craftsmen of the day to produce the magnificent stonework, mosaics and stained glass. The walls are made from warm-toned Ham Hill stone with bands of Bath stone. Marble mosaic floors run across the church and are particularly colourful in the chancel. At any time you can soak up the wonderful views all over Hampshire, but if you are lucky, you may even hear the lovely peal of eight bells ringing out across the countryside. **Location:** OS Ref SU677 270. 5 miles west from Petersfield, off A272. **Website:** www.visitchurches.org.uk **Open:** Open daily from 10am-3pm.

Stratfield Saye House

HOUGHTON LODGE GARDENS 🏛ⓕ
Stockbridge, Hampshire SO20 6LQ

An 18th Century Grade II* listed Gothic 'Cottage Orne' idyllically set above the tranquil River Test. Peaceful formal and informal gardens with fine trees. Chalk Cob walls enclose a traditional Kitchen Garden with themed Herb Garden, cutting meadow, espaliers, hydroponics and stunning orchid house with many rare varieties. 14 acres of picturesque countryside, meadow walks and 3 charming Alpacas. Tea House for refreshments and homemade cake. **Location:** Map 3:C4. OS Ref SU344 332. 1½m S of Stockbridge (A30) on minor road to Houghton village.
Owner: Captain Busk **Contact:** Sophie Busk **Tel:** 01264 810063
Marketing: Jo Andrews, 07591170720, jo@themarketing-collective.com.
E-mail: info@houghtonlodge.co.uk **Website:** www.houghtonlodge.co.uk
Open: 1 Mar-31 Oct, Thu-Tue, 10am-5pm. House tours - pre-booked groups.
Admission: Adult £6.50. Children £3.00. Coach Tours & Groups, any day by appointment - special rates if booked in advance. **Key facts:** 🅣 📷 Self Service. 📷 By arrangement. 🅿 Hard standing for 2 coaches. 🐕 On short leads. 🅰 📷

ST MARY'S CHURCH 🏛
Itchen Stoke, Alresford, Hampshire SO24 0QU

St Mary's was built in 1866 by Henry Conybeare for his brother, the Rector of the church, who felt the previous church was cold and damp. He himself bore most of the cost, with the parishioners contributing £50 towards the cost of the windows, as a mark of their regard for him. This dazzling and colourful Victorian jewel of a church overwhelms the senses - tall and imposing - especially as you approach it from the steep path from the road. Its design is clearly inspired by the soaring elegance of the 13th Century Sainte Chapelle in Paris, chapel of French kings. The church is a dazzling kaleidoscope of pattern and colour with the richly painted roof, the floor near the altar decorated with sparkling tiles and the pulpit displaying five panels filled with scrollwork and foliage. Best of all is the stained glass, especially in the west window. The elegant arched windows contain small pieces of clear red, blue and green glass in geometrical patterns. **Location:** OS Ref SU559 323. 6m E of Winchester, on B3047; 1.5m from Alresford. **Website:** www.visitchurches.org.uk **Open:** Open daily, 10am-4pm.

WINCHESTER CITY MILL 🌾
Bridge Street, Winchester SO23 9BH

Winchester City Mill is a working watermill dating back to at least Saxon times. Now fully restored by the National Trust, the City Mill is probably the oldest working watermill in the UK. Visitors can discover more about the mill's long and fascinating history as well as see the mill in action and learn how we produce traditional stone-ground wholemeal flour using the power of the River Itchen. **Location:** Map 3D:4. OS Ref SU486 293. M3/J9 & 10. City Bridge near King Alfred's statue. 15 min walk from station.
Owner: National Trust **Contact:** Anne Aldridge **Tel:** 01962 870057
E-mail: winchestercitymill@nationaltrust.org.uk
Website: www.nationaltrust.org.uk/winchestercitymill
Open: Open Daily: 1 Jan-15 Feb 10am-4pm, 16 Feb-1 Nov 10am-5pm, 2 Nov-24 Dec 10am-4pm, Closed 25-31 Dec.
Admission: Adults £4.40, Children £2.20, Family £11.00.
Key facts: 🅰 📷 🅣 📷 Obligatory. By arrangement. 🅿 Nearby public car park. 📷 📷 📷

BROADLANDS
Romsey, Hampshire SO51 9ZD

Broadlands is the historic home of the Brabourne family.
Location: Map 3:C5.
Tel: 01794 529750 **Website:** www.broadlandsestates.co.uk
Open: Jun to Sep. Please see our website for details.

MOTTISFONT 🌾
Mottisfont, Nr Romsey, Hampshire SO51 0LP

A romantic house and gallery, crafted from a medieval priory, set in beautiful riverside gardens. **Location:** Map 3:C5. OS Ref SU327 270.
Tel: 01794 340757 **E-mail:** mottisfont@nationaltrust.org.uk
Website: www.nationaltrust.org.uk/mottisfont
Open: Please see website for up to date opening and admission details.

VISITOR INFORMATION

■ Owner
Mr and Mrs D Kendrick

■ Address
Boughton Monchelsea
Nr Maidstone, Kent
ME17 4BU

■ Location
Map 4:K3
OS Ref. TQ772 499
On B2163, 5m from
M20/J8.
Rail: Maidstone or Marden
(+ Taxi)

■ Contact
Mrs Marice Kendrick
Tel: 01622 743120
E-mail:
mk@boughtonplace.co.uk

■ Opening Times
Not open to individual
visitors. Guided tours for
private groups of 15 - 50
persons available Tuesday
to Thursday by prior
arrangement only. Private
functions Monday to
Saturday 9am to 5pm;
corporate events 9am to
10.30pm. Outdoor event
site for large corporate
functions 8am - 11.30pm
any day.

■ Admission
**Gardens and Guided
House Tour**
£6.00 per person
Min 15 persons, max 50.
Venue hire : POA

■ Special Events
**July and August
dates TBC**
Open-air Theatre
Shakespeare's The Two
Gentlemen of Verona
Noel Coward's Hay Fever
Tickets from Hazlitt Arts
Centre, 01622 758611.

BOUGHTON MONCHELSEA PLACE
www.boughtonplace.co.uk

Tudor Manor House near Maidstone with spectacular panoramic views.

Boughton Monchelsea Place dates from the 1550s and is set in its own country estate just outside Maidstone. This Grade 1 listed building is privately owned and is still lived in as a family home.

From the lawns surrounding the house and from the new South Terrace there are wonderful views over the estate's private deer park, home to wild fallow deer for 500 years and surrounded by unspoilt Kent countryside as far as the eye can see. At the rear of the house is a pretty courtyard rose and herb garden with steps leading to the formal walled gardens and orchard. Beyond the courtyard an extensive range of Tudor barns and outbuildings surrounds the old stableyard.

Next door is the medieval church of St Peter, with its tranquil rose garden and ancient lych-gate. Tours of the church can be arranged in conjunction with tours of the house.

Internally, rooms vary in style, from Tudor to Georgian Gothic. There is a fine Jacobean staircase, some interesting stained glass windows and examples of wall panelling from various periods. Furnishings are mainly Victorian or later, with a few earlier pieces. The atmosphere is friendly and welcoming throughout.

The premises are licensed for civil marriage and partnership ceremonies, although evening receptions are not offered. Location work is welcome, as are group visits and many types of corporate, private and public function. All clients are guaranteed exclusive use of this prestigious venue.

KEY FACTS

⊤
♿ Unsuitable.
♨
🍴 Obligatory.
🅿
✂
♨
❄
♘

CHIDDINGSTONE CASTLE 🏛ⓕ
www.chiddingstonecastle.org.uk

Chiddingstone Castle is a hidden gem in the Garden of England; a unique house with fascinating artefacts and beautiful grounds.

Situated in an historic village in the heart of the idyllic Kentish Weald, Chiddingstone Castle has Tudor origins and delightful Victorian rooms. Lying between Sevenoaks and Tunbridge Wells, it is conveniently located close to the M25 (Junction 5 - Sevenoaks or Junction 6 - Oxted). We welcome individuals, families and groups - guided tours are available. There is ample parking available in the large car park. Delicious light lunches, homemade cakes and traditional cream teas can be enjoyed in the cosy Tea Room set in the Old Buttery or in the delightful sheltered courtyard. The Castle's Gift Shop can be found in the former Well Tower.

Set in 35 acres of informal gardens, including a lake, waterfall, rose garden and woodland, this attractive country house originates from the 1550s when High Street House, as the Castle was known, was home to the Streatfeild family. Several transformations have since taken place and the present building dates back to 1805 when Henry Streatfeild extended and remodelled his ancestral home in the 'castle style' which was then

fashionable. Rescued from creeping dereliction in 1955 by the gifted antiquary Denys Eyre Bower, the Castle became home to his amazing and varied collections - Japanese Samurai armour, swords and lacquer, Egyptian antiquities, Buddhist artefacts, Stuart paintings and Jacobite manuscripts. Visitors can also visit Bower's Study and learn of his eccentric and complicated life, which featured a notorious scandal.

Further exhibition rooms are open showing the Victorian history of the Castle - the Victorian Kitchen and Scullery and the fascinating Housekeeper's Room. From the Servants' Hall, visitors can climb the secret back stairs and discover the Servant's Bedroom in the attic – a real 'upstairs downstairs' experience!

In 2014 the Castle created a new Ancient Egyptian garden in the grounds to complement the antiquities found indoors; the 'Fields of Eternity' is a grass maze and treasure trail full of interesting discoveries - fun for Egyptologists of all ages!

VISITOR INFORMATION

▓ Owner
The Denys Eyre Bower Bequest, Registered Charitable Trust

▓ Address
Chiddingstone Castle
Nr Edenbridge
Kent
TN8 7AD

▓ Location
Map 19:G12
OS Ref. TQ497 452
10m from Tonbridge, Tunbridge Wells and Sevenoaks. 4m Edenbridge. Accessible from A21 and M25/J5. London 35m.
Bus: Enquiries: Tunbridge Wells TIC 01892 515675.
Rail: Tonbridge, Tunbridge Wells, Edenbridge then taxi. Penshurst then 2m walk.
Air: Gatwick 15m.

▓ Contact
Tel: 01892 870347
E-mail: events@ chiddingstonecastle.org.uk

▓ Opening Times
Sunday, Monday, Tuesday, Wednesday & Bank Holidays from 1st April until the end of October (check the website for any unforeseen alterations to this).

Times: 11am to 5pm. Last entry to house 4:15pm.

▓ Admission
Adults	£9.00
Children (5-13)	£4.00
Family (2 adults + 2 children or 1 adult + 3 children)	£23.50
Grounds and Tea Rooms	Free
Parking	£2.00

▓ Special Events
We have a series of event days - Egyptian and Japanese Days and the Country and Christmas Fairs. Please visit the website What's On page for more information.

KEY FACTS

ℹ️ Museum, weddings, business and private functions, scenic gardens and lake, picnics, fishing available.

🏬 Well stocked gift shop.

✸

🍸 Available for special events. Licensed for Civil Ceremonies. Wedding receptions.

♿ WCs.

🍰 Cream teas a speciality.

🍴

👤 By arrangement.

🅿️

🏫 We welcome visits from schools who wish to use the collections in connection with classroom work.

🐕 In grounds and Tea Room courtyard on leads.

VISITOR INFORMATION

■ **Owner**
English Heritage

■ **Address**
Dover Castle
Castle Hill
Dover
Kent
CT16 1HU

■ **Location**
Map 4:O4
OS Ref. TR325 419
Easy access from A2 and M20. Well signposted from Dover centre and east side of Dover. 2 hrs from central London.
Bus: 0870 6082608.
Rail: London St. Pancras Intl (fast train); London Victoria; London Charing Cross.

■ **Contact**
Visitor Operations Team
Tel: 01304 211067
E-mail: customers@ english-heritage.org.uk

■ **Opening Times**
Please visit www.english-heritage.org.uk for opening times, admission prices and the most up-to-date information.

■ **Special Events**
Please visit www.english-heritage.org.uk for the most up-to-date information on our exciting days out and events.

DOVER CASTLE ⊞
www.english-heritage.org.uk/dovercastle

Explore over 2,000 years of history at Dover Castle.

Immerse yourself in the medieval world and royal court of King Henry II as you climb the stairs into the Great Tower and meet the first of the many life like projected figures which will guide you round the six great recreated rooms and several lesser chambers of the palace. On special days throughout the year interact with costumed characters as they bring to life the colour and opulence of medieval life.

Take an adventurous journey into the White Cliffs as you tour the maze of Secret Wartime Tunnels. Children will love dressing up in wartime uniforms, exploring the tunnels, the interactive displays and virtual tour. Through sight, sound and smells, re-live the wartime drama of a wounded pilot fighting for his life. Discover what life would have been like during the dark and dramatic days of the Dunkirk evacuation with exciting audio-visual experiences. See the pivotal part the Secret Wartime Tunnels played in Operation Dynamo.

Above ground, enjoy magnificent views of the White Cliffs from Admiralty Lookout and explore the Fire Command Post, re-created as it would have appeared 90 years ago in the last days of the Great War. Also see a Roman Lighthouse and Anglo-Saxon church, as well as an intriguing network of medieval underground tunnels, fortifications and battlements.

Dover Castle was used as a film location for The Other Boleyn Girl starring Natalie Portman and Scarlett Johanssen and Zaffirelli's Hamlet amongst others.

KEY FACTS

ℹ	WCs. No flash photography within the Great Tower.
🛍	Two.
	Licensed.
🍴	Licensed.
🚶	Tour of tunnels. Last tour 1 hr before closing.
🅿	Ample.
🏫	Education centre. Pre-booking essential.
🐕	Dogs on leads only.
❄	
🛡	

Register for news and special offers at www.hudsonsheritage.com

HEVER CASTLE & GARDENS 🏚Ⓕ
www.hevercastle.co.uk

Experience 700 years of colourful history and spectacular award-winning gardens at the childhood home of Anne Boleyn.

Dating back to the 13th century, Hever Castle was once the childhood home of Anne Boleyn, second wife of Henry VIII and Mother of Elizabeth I and formed the unlikely backdrop to a sequence of tumultuous events that changed the course of Britain's history, monarchy and religion.

Its splendid panelled rooms contain fine furniture, tapestries, antiques and an important collection of Tudor portraits. Two beautifully illuminated prayer books on display in the Book of Hours Room belonged to Anne and bear her inscriptions and signature. One is believed to be the prayer book Anne took with her to her execution at the Tower.

The charming castle at Hever has a rich and varied history. Today much of what you see is the result of the remarkable efforts of a wealthy American, William Waldorf Astor, who used his fortune to restore and extend the Castle in the early 20th Century. A section of the Castle is dedicated to its more recent history, containing pictures and memorabilia relating to the Astor family and the Edwardian period.

The award-winning gardens are set in 125 acres of glorious grounds. Marvel at the Pompeiian wall and classical statuary in the Italian Garden; admire the giant topiary chess set and inhale the fragrance of over 4,000 rose bushes in the quintessential English Rose Garden. The Loggia, overlooking the 38-acre lake, is the perfect spot to relax before exploring the Tudor Garden, Blue Corner and Rhododendron Walk.

KEY FACTS

- ℹ️ Filming, residential conferences, Corporate hospitality and golf.
- 🎁 Gift, garden & book.
- 🍽️ Weddings, receptions and private banqueting.
- ♿ Partial. WCs.
- 🍴 Licensed.
- 🚶 By arrangement. Pre-booked tours in French, German, Dutch, Italian & Spanish (min 20).
- 🎧 English, French, German, Dutch, Russian & Chinese.
- 🅿️ Free parking.
- 🐕 Well behaved dogs on lead in grounds.
- 🛏️ Luxury B&B & Holiday Cottage in Astor Wing of the Castle.

VISITOR INFORMATION

⬛ Owner
Hever Castle Ltd

⬛ Address
Hever Castle
Hever
Edenbridge
Kent
TN8 7NG

⬛ Location
Map 19:G12
OS Ref. TQ476 450
See website for directions.

⬛ Contact
Tel: 01732 865224
Fax: 01732 866796
E-mail:
info@hevercastle.co.uk

⬛ Opening Times
14 Feb 2015–1 Jan 2016
Gardens open at 10.30am
Castle opens at 12 noon
Spring Season
14 Feb–22 Feb (Daily)
**25 Feb–29 Mar
(Wed-Sun)**
Last admission 3pm
Final exit 4.30pm
Main Season (Daily)
30 Mar–23 Oct
Last admission 4.30pm
Final exit 6pm
Winter Season
24 Oct–1 Nov (Daily)
**4 Nov–27 Nov
(Wed-Sun)**
Last admission 3.00pm
Final exit 4.30pm
**Christmas Tickets &
Winter Walks**
(See website for Christmas
information).

⬛ Admission
INDIVIDUAL
Castle & Gardens
Adult   £16.00
Senior   £14.00
Student   £13.50
Child   £9.00
Family   £42.50
Gardens only
Adult   £13.50
Senior   £12.00
Student   £11.50
Child   £8.50
Family   £37.00
GROUP (15+)
Adult   £12.65
Senior   £11.65
Student   £10.00
Child   £7.00
Gardens only
Adult   £10.65
Senior   £10.15
Student   £8.60
Child   £6.70

⬛ Special Events
An extensive events
programme. See website.

Conference/Function

ROOM	Size	Max Cap
Dining Hall	35' x 20'	70
Breakfast Rm	22' x 15'	12
Sitting Rm	24' x 20'	20
Pavilion	96' x 40'	250
Moat Restaurant	25' x 60'	75

VISITOR INFORMATION

■ **Owner**
Leeds Castle Foundation

■ **Address**
Leeds Castle
Maidstone, Kent
ME17 1PL

■ **Location**
Map 4:L3
OS Ref. TQ835 533
From London to A20/M20/
J8, 40m, 1 hr. 7m E of
Maidstone, ¼m S of A20.
Bus: Spot Travel operate a
shuttle bus from Bearsted
Train station in hire season.
Rail: South Eastern Trains,
London-Bearsted.
Air: Under 1 hr from Kent
International Airport &
London Gatwick airport.
Ferry: Under 1 hr from
Dover Channel Ports.

■ **Contact**
Tel: 01622 765400
Fax: 01622 735616
E-mail: enquiries@
leeds-castle.co.uk

■ **Opening Times**
Summer
1 Apr-30 Sep Daily,
10.30am-4.30pm (last
adm).
Winter
1 Oct-31 Mar Daily,
10.30am-3pm (last adm).

■ **Admission**
**Annual Tickets (prices
valid until 31 Mar 2015)**
Adults £24.00
Senior Citizens £21.00
Students £21.00
Visitors with
disabilities £21.00
Children (4-15yrs) £16.00
Infants (under 4yrs) Free

**Day Tickets (prices valid
until 31 Mar 2015)**
Adults £19.00
Senior Citizens £16.00
Students £16.00
Visitors with
disabilities £16.00
Children (4-15yrs) £11.00
Infants (under 4yrs) Free

Day Tickets can be
upgraded to Annual Tickets
for £5 per ticket on the day
of your visit at the Ticket
Office. Groups rates for
15+ available. Please see
website.

■ **Special Events**
Throughout the year. See
website for details.

Conference/Function

ROOM	Size	Max Cap
Fairfax Hall	19.8 x 6.7m	180
Garden House	9.8 x 5.2m	30
Terrace	8.9 x 15.4m	80
Castle Boardroom	9.7 x 4.8m	30
Castle Dining Rm	13.1 x 6.6m	70
Maiden's Tower	8 x 9m	120

LEEDS CASTLE
www.leeds-castle.com

"The Loveliest Castle in the World"

Set in 500 acres of beautiful Kent parkland, there's something to discover every day at "the loveliest castle in the world". The historic castle, glorious gardens, attractions and programme of events awaits visitors.

During its 900 year history, Leeds Castle has been a Norman stronghold, the private property of six of England's medieval Queens and a palace used by Henry VIII. In the 1930s the castle was a playground for the rich and famous, as Lady Baillie, the last private owner, entertained high society down from London for the weekends.

During your visit, the whole family will enjoy exploring the gardens and grounds, getting lost in the maze, watching a falconry display, riding on Elsie the Castle Land Train and crossing the Great Water on the Black Swan Ferry Boat. Children will love letting off steam in our Knights' Realm and Squires' Courtyard playgrounds.

After all that excitement, the Fairfax Restaurant offers an excellent choice of freshly prepared hot and cold dishes and Costa Coffee is now open in the Courtyard. For unusual, quality gifts and souvenirs, visit the two Leeds Castle shops before you leave.

Our golf course also has a fully stocked golf shop with advice from our PGA Professional.

KEY FACTS

ℹ️ Residential and day conferences, weddings, team building days, falconry, golf, croquet and helipad.

Banquets, meetings, seminars, presentations and conferences.

WCs.

Licensed.

Licensed.

Free parking.

Guide dogs only.

B&B, Holiday Cottages & Glamping.

Closed on 7/8 Nov & 25 Dec 2015.

Special events held throughout the year.

€

© David Sellman/Penshurst Place

© David Sellman/Penshurst Place

PENSHURST PLACE & GARDENS
www.penshurstplace.com

One of England's greatest family-owned historic houses with a history spanning nearly seven centuries.

In some ways time has stood still at Penshurst; the great House is still very much a medieval building with improvements and additions made over the centuries but without any substantial rebuilding. Its highlight is undoubtedly the medieval Baron's Hall, built in 1341, with its impressive 60ft-high chestnut-beamed roof. A marvellous mix of paintings, tapestries and furniture from the 15th, 16th and 17th Centuries can be seen throughout the House, including the helm carried in the state funeral procession to St Paul's Cathedral for the Elizabethan courtier and poet, Sir Philip Sidney, in 1587. This is now the family crest.

Gardens
The Gardens, first laid out in the 14th Century, have been developed over generations of the Sidney family, who first came to Penshurst in 1552. A twenty year restoration and re-planting programme undertaken by the 1st Viscount De L'Isle has ensured that they retain their historic splendour. He is commemorated with an Arboretum, planted in 1991.

The gardens are divided by a mile of yew hedges into 'rooms', each planted to give a succession of colour as the seasons change, with the completion of a major restoration project on the Jubilee Walk in 2012. There is also an Adventure Playground, Woodland Trail, Toy Museum and Garden Restaurant, with the Porcupine Pantry café and a Gift Shop open all year. A variety of events in the park and grounds take place throughout the year.

KEY FACTS

- Guidebook available to purchase. No photography in house.
- Gift Shop outside paid perimeter.
- Small plant centre.
- Conference and private banqueting facilities.
- Partial. Contact for details.
- Porcupine Pantry outside paid perimeter.
- Garden Restaurant in the grounds.
- Guided tours available by arrangement before the House opens to the public. Garden tours available 10.30am-4.30pm.
- Ample for cars and coaches.
- All year by appointment, discount rates, education room and teachers' packs.
- Guide dogs only.
- Wedding ceremonies and receptions.
- See opening times.
- See www.penshurstplace.com/whatson

VISITOR INFORMATION

Owner
Viscount De L'Isle MBE

Address
Penshurst
Nr Tonbridge
Kent
TN11 8DG

Location
Map 19:H12
OS Ref. TQ527 438
From London M25/J5 then A21 to Hildenborough, B2027 via Leigh; from Tunbridge Wells A26, B2176. Follow brown signs.
Bus: 231, 233 from Tunbridge Wells and Edenbridge.
Rail: Charing Cross/Waterloo East-Hildenborough, Tonbridge or Tunbridge Wells; then bus or taxi.

Contact
Tel: 01892 870307
Fax: 01892 870866
E-mail: enquiries@penshurstplace.com

Opening Times
House & Grounds:
14 Feb-29 Mar:
Sats & Suns only, 10.30am-6pm or dusk if earlier.
30 Mar-1 Nov:
Daily, 10.30am-6pm.
House
12 noon. Last entry 4pm.
Grounds
10.30am-6pm.
Last entry 5pm.
Shop & Porcupine Pantry
Open all year.
Winter
Open to Groups by appointment only.

Admission
For 2015 individual prices see website for details.
2015 Group prices:
(pre-booked 15+).
Freeflow.
Adult   £8.50
Child   £5.00
House Tours
Adult   £10.50
Child   £5.50
Garden Tours
(pre-booked 15+).
Adult   £10.50
Child   £5.50
House & Garden Tours
Adult   £17.00
Child (5-16 yrs)   £10.00
*under 5s Free.

Special Events
Weald of Kent Craft Show: First May Bank holiday and first weekend in September Friday – Sunday.
Glorious Gardens Week:
First week in June.
Please see www.penshurstplace.com/whatson.

CHARTWELL ❧
CHARTWELL, MAPLETON ROAD, WESTERHAM, KENT TN16 1PS
www.nationaltrust.org.uk/chartwell

Chartwell was the much-loved Churchill family home and the place from which Sir Winston drew inspiration from 1924 until the end of his life. The house is still much as it was when the family lived here with pictures, books and personal mementoes. The studio is home to the largest single collection of Churchill's paintings. The gardens reflect Churchill's love of the landscape and nature. The woodland estate offers family walks, trails, den building, a Canadian Camp, dormouse dens, bomb crater and opportunites to blow away cobwebs and stretch your legs and enjoy the spectacular views of Chartwell house. The Mulberry Room above the Landemare Café can be booked for meetings, weddings, conferences, lunches and dinners. **Location:** Map 19:F11. OS Ref TQ455515. 2m S of Westerham, forking left off B2026.
Owner: National Trust **Contact:** Visitor Experience Manager
Tel: 01732 868381 **Fax:** 01732 868193 **E-mail:** chartwell@nationaltrust.org.uk
Open: House: 28 Feb-1 Nov, Daily, 11am-5pm last entry 4.15pm. Garden, Shop,

Café, Exhibition, & Studio, everyday 1 Jan-31 Dec, times vary please call 01732 868381 for further details. The studio is closed in Jan, by tour only in Feb. The exhibition closes for short periods to change the display. All visitors require a timed ticket to visit the house, please obtain upon arrival at the Visitor Centre - places limited.
Admission: House, Garden & Studio: Adult £14.30, Child £7.15, Family £35.75. Garden, Exhibition, Studio & Winter season only: Adult £7.15, Child £3.60, Family £17.90. Gift Aid prices. Groups (15+) Adult £11.00, Child £5.50.
Key facts: ⓘ Conference, wedding & function facilities. ⬛ The shop stocks Churchill memorabilia, books, interesting ranges and has regular tastings of local produce. Gifts for all ages. ⬛ ⓣ The Mulberry room can accommodate up to 90 people. ⬛ Partial. WCs. ⬛ Licensed. Our popular café offers a selection of hot and cold meals and delicious desserts. ⓘ By arrangement. ⓟ Free for NT members, £3 for non-members. ⬛ ⬛ In grounds on leads. ⬛ ⬛ ⬛

Belmont House Gardens

BELMONT HOUSE & GARDENS 🏠ⓕ
Belmont Park, Throwley, Faversham, Kent ME13 0HH
www.belmont-house.org

Belmont is an elegant 18th Century house with views over the rolling Kentish North Downs. Its hidden gardens range from a Pinetum complete with grotto, a walled ornamental garden and a walled kitchen garden with Victorian greenhouses. Belmont also has the finest private collection of clocks in Britain to explore. **Location:** Map 4:M3. OS Ref TQ986 564. 4½m SSW of Faversham, off A251. **Owner:** Harris (Belmont) Charity **Tel:** 01795 890202 **E-mail:** administrator@belmont-house.org

Open: April-Sep. Wed tours 11am & 1pm, Sat tours 2.15pm & 3.15pm, Sun & BH Mon tours 2.15pm, 3pm & 3.45pm. Gardens open every day 10am-6pm or dusk if earlier. Groups Tue & Thu by appointment. Pre-booked specialist clock tours last Sat of the month (Apr-Sep). For special events and up to date information please visit our website.

Admission: House & Garden: Adult £8.00, Child (Under 12's free) £5.00, Conc. £7.00. Garden Only: Adult £5.00, Child (12-16yrs) £2.50, Conc. £4.00. Pre-booked Clock Tour £15.00. **Key facts:** ⓘ No photography in house. 回 🌱 Plants for sale in the Kitchen Garden. 🖼 🔲 Partial. WCs. 🍽 Tearoom open from 2pm on Sat & Sun for afternoon tea & cakes. Self-service Mon-Fri. 🎫 Obligatory. 🅿 Limited for coaches. 🐕 In the gardens, on lead only. ❀ Gardens. See opening times. 🎫

RESTORATION HOUSE 🏠ⓕ
17-19 CROW LANE, ROCHESTER, KENT ME1 1RF
www.restorationhouse.co.uk

Fabled city mansion deriving its name from the stay of Charles II on the eve of The Restoration. This complex ancient house has beautiful interiors with exceptional early paintwork related to decorative scheme 'run up' for Charles' visit. The house also inspired Dickens to create 'Miss Havisham' here. 'Interiors of rare historical resonance and poetry', Country Life. Fine English furniture and strong collection of English portraits (Mytens, Kneller, Dahl, Reynolds and several Gainsboroughs). Charming interlinked walled gardens and ongoing restoration of monumental Renaissance water garden. A private gem. 'There is no finer pre-Civil war town house in England than this' - Simon Jenkins, The Times. **Location:** MAP 4:K2 OS Ref TQ744 683. Historic centre of Rochester, off High Street, opposite the Vines Park.

THE GRANGE
St Augustine's Road, Ramsgate, Kent CT11 9NY
www.landmarktrust.org.uk

Augustus Pugin is regarded as being one of Britain's most influential architects and designers and to stay here in the home he designed for himself and his family offers a unique chance to step into his colourful and idiosyncratic world. **Location:** Map 4:O2. OS Ref TR377 643. **Owner:** The Landmark Trust **Tel:** 01628 825925 **E-mail:** bookings@landmarktrust.org.uk **Open:** Self-catering accommodation. Parts of house open Wed afternoons; there are 8 Open Days. **Admission:** Free, visits by appointment. Contact Catriona Blaker 01843 596401. **Key facts:** ⓘ This house was designed as a family home and it works as well today as it did in 1844. 🎫 🅿 🐕 🐕 🎫 🎫 🎫

Owner: R Tucker & J Wilmot **Contact:** Robert Tucker **Tel:** 01634 848520 **Email:** robert.tucker@restorationhouse.co.uk **Open:** 28 May – 25 Sep, Thu & Fri, 10am-5pm, plus Sats 30 May & 11 Jul 12-5pm. **Admission:** Adult £7.50 (includes 36 page illustrated guidebook), Child £3.75, Conc £6.50. Booked group (8+) tours: £8.50pp. **Tea Shop:** 1st, 2nd & 4th Thurs in month and other days by arrangement (see website for updates). **Key Facts:** ⓘ No stiletto heels. No photography in house. 🖼 Garden by appointment. 🎫 1st, 2nd & 4th Thurs in month & other days by arrangement. 🎫 By arrangement. 🅿 None. 🐕 Guide Dogs Only.

South East - England

IGHTHAM MOTE ✤
Mote Road, Ivy Hatch, Sevenoaks, Kent TN15 0NT
www.nationaltrust.org.uk/ighthammote

Moated manor dating from 1320, reflecting seven centuries of history, from the medieval Crypt to a 1960s Library. Owned by knights, courtiers to Henry VIII and society Victorians. Highlights include Great Hall, Drawing Room, Tudor painted ceiling, Grade 1 listed dog kennel and apartments of US donor.

Location: Map 19:H11. OS Ref TQ584 535. 6m E of Sevenoaks off A25. 2½m S of Ightham off A227. **Owner:** National Trust **Contact:** Administrator
Tel: 01732 810378 **Fax:** 01732 811029
E-mail: ighthammote@nationaltrust.org.uk
Open: Daily all year, excl 24 & 25 Dec. 10am-5pm or dusk if earlier. House: 11am, last entry half hour before closing. Some areas may be partially open during certain times of the year. See website for full details. **Admission:** Adult £12.00, Child £6.00, Family £30.00, Group rate £9.00 (15+). Reduced rates in winter - partial house & gardens open. *Includes voluntary donation, standard prices displayed at property. **Key facts:** ℹ No flash photography. Volunteer 8 seated electric buggy. ⌂ 🎁 🍴 ♿ WCs. 3 wheelchairs ground floor access only. Photograph album of upstairs. 🍽 Licensed. Outside patio area with views of house. 🎦 House tour £3.00pp. Garden tours with Head Gardener £5.00pp. 🅿 ▣ ✳ ☂

KNOLE ✤
Knole, Sevenoaks, Kent TN15 0RP
www.nationaltrust.org.uk/knole

Knole is vast, complex and full of hidden treasures. Originally an Archbishop's palace, the house passed through royal hands to the Sackville family – its inhabitants from 1603 to today. Knole is in the midst of a huge project to conserve and refurbish its remarkable rooms and collections, peeling back the layers of 600 years of history and sharing the work with visitors. This year, building works may affect some areas & refreshments are outdoors, in Kent's last remaining medieval deer park. **Location:** Map 19:H10. OS Ref TQ532 543. 25m SE of London. M25/ J5 (for A21). Off A225 at S end of High Street, Sevenoaks, opposite St Nicholas Church. For satnav use TN13 1HU. **Owner:** National Trust **Contact:** Property Manager **Tel:** 01732 462100 **E-mail:** knole@nationaltrust.org.uk
Open: Please see website. **Admission:** Please see website.
Key facts: ⌂ New Bookshop Café opens March 2015. ♿ Please ask us how we can help you visit Knole. WCs; steps with handrail to first floor showrooms. 🅿 Free to NT members. 🎦 Contact education officer.
🐕 In park & Green Court only, on leads. ✳ Car park and outdoor refreshments available all year except Dec 24 & 25. ☂

SISSINGHURST CASTLE ✤
Sissinghurst, Cranbrook, Kent TN17 2AB
www.nationaltrust.org.uk/sissinghurst

One of the world's most celebrated gardens and a sensory paradise of colour and beauty throughout the year. Vita Sackville-West, a Bloomsbury group member and her husband Sir Harold Nicolson created the garden around the surviving parts of an Elizabethan mansion. The original design still exists today with a series of garden rooms, intimate in scale and romantic in atmosphere. See the White Garden, Lime Walk, Tower with Vita's study and Cottage Garden.
Location: Map 4:L4. OS Ref TQ807 383. 1m E of Sissinghurst village.
Owner: National Trust **Contact:** The Administrator
Tel: 01580 710700 **E-mail:** sissinghurst@nationaltrust.org.uk
Open: Please see website for opening times and admission prices.
Key facts: ⌂ 🎁 🍴 ♿ 🍽 Licensed.
🅿 £2.00 per car. Book coaches in advance.
🐕 Gardens: Guide dogs only. Grounds: On leads.

GOODNESTONE PARK GARDENS 🏠®
Goodnestone Park, Nr Wingham, Canterbury, Kent CT3 1PL
Set in 14 acres. There is a woodland area with many fine trees and woodland shrubs; a large walled garden with roses, clematis and other herbaceous plants.
Location: Map 4:N3. OS Ref TR254 544. 8m Canterbury, 1½m E of B2046 - A2 to Wingham Road, signposted from this road. Postcode of Car Park: CT3 1PJ.
Contact: Francis Plumptre
Tel/Fax: 01304 840107
E-mail: enquiries@goodnestoneparkgardens.co.uk
Website: www.goodnestoneparkgardens.co.uk
Open: Suns only 22 Feb–29 Mar, 12pm-4pm. Main season Wed 1 Apr-Fri 25 Sep. Open Days Wed, Thu, Fri 11am-5pm & Suns 12pm-5pm. Oct, Suns only 12pm-4pm.
Admission: Adult £6.00, Child (6-16 yrs) £2.00, OAP £5.50, Family tickets (2+2) £14.00. Groups (20+) £5.50 out of opening hours £7.50.
Key facts: 🎁 ♿ Suitable. WCs. 🍽 Licensed.
🎦 Partial. By arrangement. 🅿 🐕 🏠 ☂

MOUNT EPHRAIM GARDENS 🏠®
Hernhill, Faversham, Kent ME13 9TX

In these enchanting 10 acres of Edwardian gardens, terraces of fragrant roses lead to a small lake and woodland area. A grass maze, unusual topiary, Japanese-style rock garden, arboretum, herbaceous border and many beautiful mature trees are other highlights. Peaceful, unspoilt atmosphere set in Kentish orchards with magnificent views over the Thames Estuary.
Location: Map 4:M3. OS Ref TR065 598. In Hernhill village, 1m from end of M2. Signed from A2 & A299. **Owner:** William Dawes & Family **Contact:** Lucy Dawes
Tel: 01227 751496 **E-mail:** info@mountephraimgardens.co.uk
Website: www.mountephraimgardens.co.uk
Open: Open Apr-end Sep: Wed, Thu, Fri, Sat & Sun, 11am-5pm and BH Mons. Groups Mar-Oct by arrangement.
Admission: Adult £6.00, Child (4-16) £2.50. Groups (10+): £5.00.
Key facts: ⌂ 🎁 🍴 ♿ Partial. WCs. 🍽 Licensed. 🍴 Licensed. 🎦 By arrangement. 🅿 ▣ 🐕 On leads. 🏠 Licensed for civil weddings inside and out. ☂

NURSTEAD COURT
**Nurstead Church Lane, Meopham
Kent DA13 9AD**

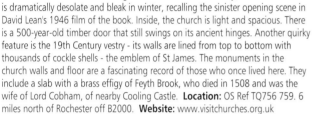

Nurstead Court is a Grade I listed manor house built in 1320 of timber-framed, crownposted construction, set in extensive gardens and parkland. The additional front part of the house was built in 1825. Licensed weddings are now held in the house with receptions and other functions in the garden marquee.

Location: Map 4:K2. OS Ref TQ642 685. Nurstead Church Lane is just off the A227 N of Meopham, 3m from Gravesend.
Owner/Contact: Mrs S Edmeades-Stearns **Tel:** 01474 812368 / 01474 812121.
E-mail: info@nursteadcourt.co.uk **Website:** www.nursteadcourt.co.uk
Open: Every Tue & Wed in Sep, and first Tue & Wed in Oct 2-5pm or all year round by arrangement.
Admission: Adult £5.00, Child £2.50, OAP/Student £4.00 Group (max 54): £4.00.
Key facts: ⊤ Weddings & functions catered for. ⎙ ▣ Licensed. ⌨ Obligatory, by arrangement. ℙ Limited for coaches. ▦ ▧ Guide Dogs only. ⧉ ❋

ST JAMES' CHURCH
Main Road, Cooling, Rochester, Kent ME3 8DG

Charles Dickens used the churchyard of St James as his inspiration in the opening chapter of Great Expectations, where the hero Pip meets Magwitch the convict. The site - on the Hoo Peninsula with marshes stretching north to the Thames estuary, is dramatically desolate and bleak in winter, recalling the sinister opening scene in David Lean's 1946 film of the book. Inside, the church is light and spacious. There is a 500-year-old timber door that still swings on its ancient hinges. Another quirky feature is the 19th Century vestry - its walls are lined from top to bottom with thousands of cockle shells - the emblem of St James. The monuments in the church walls and floor are a fascinating record of those who once lived here. They include a slab with a brass effigy of Feyth Brook, who died in 1508 and was the wife of Lord Cobham, of nearby Cooling Castle. **Location:** OS Ref TQ756 759. 6 miles north of Rochester off B2000. **Website:** www.visitchurches.org.uk
Open: Open daily from 10am-4pm.

Knole

ST MARY'S CHURCH
Manor House Lane, Capel-le-Ferne, Folkestone, Kent CT18 7EX

This lovely church is remote from the road and squats snugly on bleak downland above Folkestone. It has views across the channel, looking towards France. A single Norman window, with a little delicate wallpainting in the reveal, indicates its early origins; but most notable is a 14th Century three-arched stone rood-screen with, uniquely in England, an arched opening above for the rood itself. There are also ancient roof timbers, a small brass and a 13th Century piscina.
Location: OS Ref TR257 400. 2 miles north east of Folkestone off B2011.
Website: www.visitchurches.org.uk
Open: Open daily from 10am-4pm.

ST MICHAEL'S CHURCH
Old Church Lane, East Peckham, Tonbridge, Kent TN12 5NG

When the village moved down nearer to the river, St Michael's was left romantically sited on a hilltop among beeches, with glorious views over the Medway valley to the Weald. Originally Norman, the church seems to have expanded to its present size around 1300; the piers and arches are clearly 14th Century, the windows and south porch mainly 15th Century, and the shingled spirelet has an attractive weathervane dating from 1704. Inside there are fragments of ancient glass, a Royal Arms of George II and two centuries of memorials dedicated to the Twysden family. The churchyard has some lovely 18th Century headstones.
Location: OS Ref TQ661 522. 2m N of East Peckham, off B2016, black and white traffic sign on B2016.
Website: www.visitchurches.org.uk
Open: Open daily from 10am-4pm.

ST PETER'S CHURCH
Market Street, Sandwich, Kent CT13 9DA

St Peter's is the guardian of an ancient Sandwich tradition. Every day at 8pm, the curfew bell rings out, signalling that the townspeople should cover their fires to make them safe for the night. Much of today's building dates from 800 years ago, though it has been altered many times. The handsome tower with its distinctive onion dome top is a 17th Century addition - built by Flemish protestant refugees, in the style of their homeland churches. The present church dates from the late 13th/early 14th Centuries. The atmospheric crypt - open by arrangement - was once a charnel house where bones from the graveyard were stored to make room for new graves. **Location:** OS Ref TR331 580. In centre of town; identifiable by its onion dome on top of the tower; main door on Market Street.
Website: www.visitchurches.org.uk
Open: Open daily but occasionally closed at short notice for events; please telephone 01304 621554 in advance of your visit.

CHURCH OF ST THOMAS A BECKET
Church Lane, Capel, Tonbridge, Kent TN12 6SX

Becket himself is said to have preached in this small Norman Wealden church. The tower was partly rebuilt after a fire in 1639. Inside, the crown-post roof is striking and there are some interesting fittings. Most significant however, are the extensive medieval wallpaintings which cover most of the nave, depicting, amongst others, Cain and Abel and Christ's entry into Jerusalem.
Location: OS Ref TQ637 445. 4 miles east of Tonbridge off B2017. Large car park at rear of church.
Website: www.visitchurches.org.uk
Open: Open daily. 10am-4pm.

TONBRIDGE CASTLE

Tonbridge & Malling Borough Council, Castle Street, Tonbridge, Kent TN9 1BG

Standing in landscaped gardens overlooking the River Medway, Tonbridge Castle's mighty motte and bailey Gatehouse is among the finest in England. Experience the sights and sounds of the 13th Century as we bring them to life with interactive displays, dramatic special effects and personal audio tour. We take bookings for schools, paranormal groups, weddings and other ceremonies. **Location:** Map 19:H11. OS Ref TQ590 466. 5 mins walk from Tonbridge Train Station at the North end of Town. **Owner:** Tonbridge & Malling Borough Council **Contact:** Tina Levett- Gateway/Castle Manager **Tel:** 01732 770929 **E-mail:** tonbridge.castle@tmbc.gov.uk **Website:** www.tonbridgecastle.org **Open:** All year: Mon-Sat, 9am-5pm last tour 4pm. Suns & BHs, 10.30am-4pm last tour 3.30pm. **Admission:** 2014: Gatehouse - Adult £7.70, Child/Conc. £4.40. Family £21.00 max 2 adults. Includes audio tour. The grounds are free. **Key facts:** Toys, Maps etc. Some areas. Close by. Close by. By appointment. Grounds only.

COBHAM HALL

Cobham Hall, Cobham, Kent DA12 3BL

Magnificent Jacobean, Elizabethan manor house with Repton designed gardens set in 150 acres of parkland. **Location:** Map 4:K2. OS Ref TQ683 689.
Tel: 01474 823371 **Fax:** 01474 825902
E-mail: enquiries@cobhamhall.com **Website:** www.cobhamhall.com
Open: Specific days only. Check website or phone for details.
Admission: Adult £5.50, Conc. £4.50, Self-guided garden tour £2.50.

COBHAM WOOD AND MAUSOLEUM

Cobham DA12 3BS

Restored 18th Century mausoleum & ancient woodland.
Location: Map 4:K2. OS Ref 178:TQ6946. Via the M2 and A2. Exit A2 at Shorne/Cobham. **Tel:** 01732 810378 **E-mail:** cobham@nationaltrust.org.uk
Website: www.nationaltrust.org.uk/cobham-wood
Open: Woods open all year. Mausoleum see website for details.

DOWN HOUSE, THE HOME OF CHARLES DARWIN

Down House, Luxted Road, Downe, Kent BR6 7JT

It was here that Charles Darwin worked on his scientific theories and wrote On the Origin of Species by Means of Natural Selection. **Location:** Map 19:F9. OS Ref TQ431 611. **Tel:** 01689 859119 **Website:** www.english-heritage.org.uk/darwin
Open: Please see website for up to date opening and admission details.

LULLINGSTONE CASTLE & WORLD GARDEN

Lullingstone Castle, Eynsford, Kent DA4 0JA

Fine state rooms. Site for the World Garden of Plants. **Location:** Map 19:G9. OS Ref TQ530 644. 1m S Eynsford W side of A225. **Tel:** 01322 862114
Fax: 01322 862115 **E-mail:** info@lullingstonecastle.co.uk **Website:** www.lullingstonecastle.co.uk **Open:** Apr-Sep: Fris, Sats, Suns & BHs 12pm-5pm (House tour 2pm). Closed Good Friday. **Admission:** Adult £8.00, Child £4.00, OAP £6.50, Family £18.00, Groups (20+) £8.00pp plus £40 guide (Wed & Thu).

OWLETTS

The Street, Cobham, Gravesend DA12 3AP

Former home of the architect Sir Herbert Baker. Highlights include an impressive Carolean staircase, plasterwork ceiling and large kitchen garden.
Location: Map 4:K2. OS Ref TQ665687. 1m south of A2 at west end of village. Limited parking at property. Parking nearby in Cobham village.
Tel: 01732 810378 **E-mail:** owletts@nationaltrust.org.uk
Website: www.nationaltrust.org.uk/owletts **Open:** See website for details.

QUEX PARK

Quex Park, Birchington, Kent CT7 0BH

Fine Regency country house with beautiful gardens set in the heart of an historic estate. Powell Cotton Museum houses natural history specimens and cultural objects from Africa, Asia and the Far East. **Location:** Map 4:O2. OS Ref TR309 682. **Tel:** 01843 841119 **Website:** www.quexpark.co.uk
Open: Please see website for up to date opening and admission details.

RIVERHILL HIMALAYAN GARDENS

Sevenoaks, Kent TN15 0RR

Privately-owned historic gardens. Spectacular views, remarkable plant and tree collection, contemporary sculpture. Shop and Café. **Location:** Map 4:J3. OS Ref TQ541 522. 2m S of Sevenoaks on A225. **Tel:** 01732 459777
E-mail: sarah@riverhillgardens.co.uk **Website:** www.riverhillgardens.co.uk
Open: 14 Mar-13 Sep, Weds-Sun & BH Mons, 10.30am-5pm.
Admission: Adult £7.75, Child £5.75, Seniors £6.95.

ST JOHN'S JERUSALEM

Sutton-at-Hone, Dartford, Kent DA4 9HQ

13 Century chapel surrounded by a tranquil moated garden, once part of the former Commandery of the Knight's Hospitallers. **Location:** Map 4:J2. OS Ref TQ558703. 3 miles south of Dartford **Tel:** 01732 810378
E-mail: stjohnsjerusalem@nationaltrust.org.uk
Website: www.nationaltrust.org.uk/st-johns-jerusalem/
Open: See website for details. **Admission:** See website for details.

WALMER CASTLE AND GARDENS

Deal, Kent CT14 7LJ

A tudor fort transformed into an elegant stately home. Beautiful gardens including the Queen Mother's garden. **Location:** Map 4:O3. OS Ref TR378 501.
Tel: 01304 364288 **E-mail:** customers@english-heritage.org.uk
Website: www.english-heritage.org.uk/walmer
Open: Please see website for up to date opening and admission details.

Quex House

BLENHEIM PALACE 🏛Ⓕ ◆
www.blenheimpalace.com

Blenheim Palace is home to the 11th Duke and Duchess of Marlborough and the birthplace of Sir Winston Churchill.

Blenheim Palace was a gift from Queen Anne and a grateful nation to the 1st Duke of Marlborough for his great victory at the Battle of Blenheim in 1704. The Palace's design reflects this triumph, from the military details of the trophies on the colonnades to the scale of the heroic Grand Bridge. This dramatic effect harmonises perfectly with 'Capability' Brown's 2000 acres of landscaped parkland and Formal Gardens that surround the Palace.

A true masterpiece of Baroque architecture, Blenheim Palace delivers an awe-inspiring experience for visitors. From the imposing Great Hall to the beautifully intricate State Rooms, the Palace balances delicate detail with ambitious architecture on the grandest scale and is home to some of the finest collections of

antique furniture, tapestries, porcelain and painted ceilings in Europe.

As well as finding a host of historical monuments across the parkland, from the Column of Victory to the Temple of Diana, where Sir Winston Churchill proposed to his wife, there is the rose garden, secret garden and water terraces to be enjoyed.

Blenheim Palace is not only an iconic part of history, but also a living, changing experience with a wealth of sporting and cultural events, themed exhibitions and tours throughout the year.

Blenheim Palace is a timeless pleasure, a precious time, every time for its visitors.

KEY FACTS

- ℹ Filming, product launches, activity days. No photography inside the palace.
- 🏠 Four shops.
- ⊤ Corporate Hospitality includes weddings, receptions, dinners, meetings and corporate events.
- ♿ Suitable. WCs/lift.
- 🍴 Licensed.
- 🍴 Licensed.
- 🚶 Guided tours except Sundays.
- 🎧
- 🅿 Unlimited for cars and coaches.
- 🏫 Sandford Award holder since 1982. Teacher pre-visits welcome.
- 🐕 Dogs on leads, park only. Guide dogs welcome.
- 🔔
- ❄
- 🛡

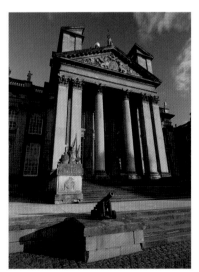

VISITOR INFORMATION

■ Owner
The Duke of Marlborough

■ Address
Blenheim Palace
Woodstock
OX20 1PX

■ Location
Map 7:A11
OS Ref. SO441 161
From London, M40, A44 (1½ hrs), 8m NW of Oxford. London 63m Birmingham 54m.
Bus: No.S3 from Oxford Station, Gloucester Green & Cornmarket.
Coach: From London (Victoria) to Oxford.
Rail: Oxford Station.
Air: Heathrow 60m. Birmingham 50m.

■ Contact
Visitor Information
Tel: 0800 8496500
E-mail: operations@ blenheimpalace.com

■ Opening Times
Sat 15 Feb - Sun 13 Dec 2015
Sat 15 Feb - Sun 2 Nov 2015 open daily.
Wed 4 Nov - Sun 13 Dec 2015 open Wed - Sun.

Palace and Pleasure Gardens
Open daily from 10.30am - 5.30pm (last admission 4.45pm).
The Formal Gardens open at 10am.

Park
Open daily from 9am - 6pm (last admission 4.45pm).

■ Admission
Palace, Park & Gardens

Adult	£22.00
Concessions	£17.30
Child*	£12.00
Family	£58.00

*(5-16 yrs)

Park & Gardens

Adult	£12.80
Concessions	£9.50
Child*	£6.60
Family	£33.50

*(5-16 yrs)

(Prices are subject to change)

Annual Pass Offer
Buy one day get 12 months free!

Discounts on group bookings (15+): contact group sales on 01993 815600 email groups@ blenheimpalace.com

■ **Owner**
Lord Saye & Sele

■ **Address**
Broughton Castle
Broughton
Nr Banbury
Oxfordshire
OX15 5EB

■ **Location**
Map 7:A10
OS Ref. SP418 382
Broughton Castle is 2½m SW of Banbury Cross on the B4035, Shipston-on-Stour - Banbury Road. Easily accessible from Stratford-on-Avon, Warwick, Oxford, Burford and the Cotswolds. M40/J11.
Rail: From London/ Birmingham to Banbury.

■ **Contact**
Manager, Mrs James
Tel: 01295 276070
E-mail: info@broughtoncastle.com

■ **Opening Times**
Summer
Easter Sun & Mon, 1 May-15 September Weds, Suns & BH Mons, 2-5pm. Also Thurs in July and August, 2-5pm. Last admission 4.30pm. Open all year on any day, at any time, for group bookings - by appointment only.

■ **Admission**
Adult	£9.00
Child (5-15yrs)	£5.00
OAP/Student	£8.00
Garden only	£5.00
Groups	
Adult	£9.00
OAP	£9.00
Child (5-10yrs)	£5.00
Child (11-15yrs)	£6.00
Garden only	£6.00

(There is a minimum charge for groups - please contact the manager for details)

BROUGHTON CASTLE 🏠Ⓕ
www.broughtoncastle.com

"About the most beautiful castle in all England...for sheer loveliness of the combination of water, woods and picturesque buildings." Sir Charles Oman (1898).

Broughton Castle is essentially a family home lived in by Lord and Lady Saye & Sele and their family. The original medieval Manor House, of which much remains today, was built in about 1300 by Sir John de Broughton. It stands on an island site surrounded by a 3 acre moat. The Castle was greatly enlarged between 1550 and 1600, at which time it was embellished with magnificent plaster ceilings, splendid panelling and fine fireplaces. In the 17th Century William, 8th Lord Saye & Sele, played a leading role in national affairs. He opposed Charles I's efforts to rule without Parliament and Broughton became a secret meeting place for the King's opponents. During the Civil War William raised a regiment and he and his four sons all fought at the nearby Battle of Edgehill. After

the battle the Castle was besieged and captured. Arms and armour from the Civil War and other periods are displayed in the Great Hall. Visitors may also see the gatehouse, gardens and park together with the nearby 14th Century Church of St Mary, in which there are many family tombs, memorials and hatchments.

Gardens

The garden area consists of mixed herbaceous and shrub borders containing many old roses. In addition, there is a formal walled garden with beds of roses surrounded by box hedging and lined by more mixed borders.

KEY FACTS

ⓘ Photography allowed in house.

📷

♿ Partial.

☕ Teas on Open Days. Groups may book morning coffee, light lunches and afternoon teas.

🚶 Available for booked groups.

🅿 Limited.

🐕 Guide dogs only in house. On leads in grounds.

❄ Open all year for groups.

VISITOR INFORMATION

■ **Owner**
The National Trust
(Administered on their
behalf by Lord Faringdon)

■ **Address**
Buscot Park
Faringdon
Oxfordshire
SN7 8BU

■ **Location**
Map 6:P12
OS Ref. SU239 973
Between Faringdon and
Lechlade on A417.
Bus: Stagecoach 65/66
Oxford to Swindon, alight
Faringdon; Stagecoach 64
Swindon to Carterton,
alight Lechlade.
Taxi: Faringdon or
Lechlade
Rail: Oxford or Swindon

■ **Contact**
The Estate Office
Tel: 01367 240786
Fax: 01367 241794
Info Line: 01367 240932
E-mail:
estbuscot@aol.com

■ **Opening Times**
**House, Grounds and
Tearoom:** 1 Apr-30 Sep,
Wed-Fri and BH's and
weekends as listed below,
2pm-6pm
(last entry to House 5pm,
Tearoom last orders
5.30pm).
Apr 4/5/6,18/19.
May 2/3/4, 09/10,
23/24/25.
Jun 13/14, 27/28.
Jul 11/12, 25/26.
Aug 8/9, 22/23, 29/30/31.
Sep 12/13, 26/27.
Grounds Only:
1 Apr-29 Sep, Mon-Tue,
2pm-6pm.

■ **Admission**
House & Grounds:
Adult   £10.00
Over 65s   £8.00
Child (5-15)   £5.00
Under 5 Free.
Grounds only:
Adult   £7.00
Over 65s   £5.00
Child (5-15)   £3.50
National Trust
members   Free
Groups: Advance booking
must be made with the
Estate Office.

BUSCOT PARK 🌿

www.buscotpark.com

One of Oxfordshire's best kept secrets.

Buscot Park is the home of the Henderson Family and the present Lord and Lady Faringdon, with their eldest son James and his wife Lucinda. They look after the property on behalf of the National Trust as well as the family collection of pictures, furniture, ceramics and objects d'art, known as the Faringdon Collection, which is displayed in the House.

Built between 1780 and 1783 for a local landowner, Edward Lovedon Townsend, the estate was purchased in 1889 by Lord Faringdon's great-grandfather, Alexander Henderson, a financier of exceptional skill and ability, who in 1916 was created the 1st Lord Faringdon. He greatly enlarged the House, commissioned Harold Peto to design the famous Italianate water garden, and

laid the foundations of the Faringdon Collection. Among his many purchases were Rembrandt's portrait of Pieter Six, Rossetti's portrait of Pandora, and Burne-Jones's famous series, The Legend of the Briar Rose.

His grandson and heir, Gavin Henderson, added considerably to the Collection, acquiring important furniture designed by Robert Adam and Thomas Hope, and was instrumental in returning the House to its late Eighteenth Century appearance.

The family, together with their fellow Trustees, continue to add to the Collection, to freshen its display, and to enliven the gardens and grounds for the continuing enjoyment of visitors.

KEY FACTS

- ℹ️ No photography in house.
- 🌱 A selection of plants and surplus kitchen garden produce available when in season.
- ♿ Partial. WCs, some ramps, motorised PMVs available – please contact Estate Office prior to visit for more information. Steps to House.
- 🍴 Homemade teas, ice cream, local cider, and honey available when house open.
- 🅿️ Ample for cars, 2 coach spaces.
- 🐕 Guide dogs only.

VISITOR INFORMATION

▓ Owner
The Lord & Lady Camoys

▓ Address
Stonor Park
Henley-On-Thames
Oxfordshire
RG9 6HF

▓ Location
Map 3:E1
OS Ref. SU743 893
1 hr from London, M4/
J8/9. A4130 to Henley-on-
Thames. A4130/B480 to
Stonor. On B480 NW of
Henley. M40/J6. B4009 to
Watlington. B480 to
Stonor.
Bus: None
Taxi: Henley on Thames
5m
Rail: Henley on Thames
5m, or Reading 9m
Air: Heathrow

▓ Contact
Jonathan White
Tel: 01491 638587
E-mail:
administrator@stonor.com

▓ Opening Times
5 April - 27 September
Sundays and BH Mondays.
Also Wednesdays and
Thursdays, June, July and
August only.

**Gardens, Chapel &
Tea Room**
12.00pm-5.30pm.

House & Giftshop
1.30pm-5.30pm. Last Entry
4.30pm.

Private Groups
20+ by arrangement
Tuesdays, Wednesdays and
Thursdays, April-
September.

▓ Admission
**House, Gardens &
Chapel**
Adults	£10.00
First Child (5-16)	£5.00
2 or more	
Children (5-16)	Free
Under 5s	Free

Gardens & Chapel
Adults	£5.00
First Child (5-16)	£2.50
2 or more	
Children (5-16)	Free
Under 5s	Free

Groups
Adults	£11.00
Child (5-16)	£5.50
Includes guided tour.

▓ Special Events
May 31
VW Owners' Rally.

July 12
Rare Plant Fair.

August 28-31
Chilterns Craft & Design
Show.

STONOR ▓ⓕ
www.stonor.com

Stonor - a story of continuity. The same family have lived here for over 850 years and have always been Roman Catholics.

Stonor has been home to the Stonor family for over 850 years and is now home to The Lord and Lady Camoys. The history of the house inevitably contributes to the atmosphere; unpretentious yet grand. A facade of warm brick with Georgian windows conceals older buildings dating back to the 12th Century and a 14th Century Catholic Chapel sits on the south east corner. Stonor nestles in a fold of the beautiful wooded Chiltern Hills with breathtaking views of the park where Fallow deer have grazed since medieval times.

It contains many family portraits, old Master drawings and paintings, Renaissance bronzes and tapestries, along with rare furniture and a collection of modern ceramics.

St Edmund Campion sought refuge at Stonor during the

Reformation and printed his famous pamphlet 'Ten Reasons', in secret, on a press installed in the roof space. A small exhibition celebrates his life and work.

Mass has been celebrated since medieval times in the Chapel. The stained glass windows were executed by Francis Eginton: installed in 1797. The Chapel decoration is that of the earliest Gothic Revival, begun in 1759, with additions in 1797. The Stations of the Cross were carved by Jozef Janas, a Polish prisoner of war in World War II and given to Stonor by Graham Greene in 1956.

The gardens offer outstanding views of the Park and valley and are especially beautiful in May and June, containing fine displays of daffodils, irises, peonies, lavenders and roses along with other herbaceous plants and shrubs.

KEY FACTS

ℹ️ No photography in house. Dogs on leads in the park at all times. Dogs not allowed in the formal gardens.

🏪 Small gift shop.

🍽️ Please contact the Administrator for further details.

♿ Partial.

🍴 Tea Room open from 12pm to 5pm. Group visits - all refreshments must be prebooked.

🚶 By arrangement. Minimum 20, maximum 55.

🅿️ 100yds away.

🎪 Please contact the Administrator for further details.

🐕 Guide dogs only.

💍

KINGSTON BAGPUIZE HOUSE 🏛Ⓕ
KINGSTON BAGPUIZE, ABINGDON, OXFORDSHIRE OX13 5AX
www.kbhevents.uk

This lovely family home dates from the 1660's and was remodelled in the early 1700's for the Blandy family. With English and French furniture in the elegant panelled rooms the entrance hall is dominated by a handsome cantilevered staircase. The house is surrounded by mature parkland and gardens notable for an interesting collection of cultivated plants which give year round interest including snowdrops in February, Magnolia and Fritillary in March and April, Wisteria, Cornus and roses in May and June, the herbaceous border and Albizia julibrissin in July and August, Colchicum and autumn colour from September. A raised terrace leads to the 18th Century panelled pavilion which looks over the gardens and towards the house. Venue for weddings and receptions.

Location: Map 7:A12. OS Ref SU408 981. In Kingston Bagpuize village, off A415 Abingdon to Witney road S of A415/A420 intersection. Abingdon 5m, Oxford 9m.

Owner: Mrs Francis Grant **Contact:** Virginia Grant

Tel: 01865 820259 **E-mail:** info@kbhevents.uk

Open: Gardens Only (Snowdrops): 1, 8, 15 & 22 Feb & 1 Mar. House & Gardens: 22-24 Mar. 19-21 Apr. 10-12, 24-26 & 31 May. 1-2 & 21-23 Jun. 12-14 Jul. 2-4 & 23-25 Aug. 6-8 & 14 & 15 Sep. All days 2-5pm. (Last entry to house 4pm). Free flow visits to ground floor of house.

Admission: House & Garden: Adult £7.50, Child (4-16) £4.50, Family (2+3) £20.00. Gardens: Adult £5.00, Child (4-16) £3.00. Season tickets available. Group rates 20+ by appointment weekdays throughout the year. NB: Please visit website to confirm before travelling as dates & times may be subject to change.

Key facts: ℹ No photography in house on open days. 🎁 Small selection of gifts in tea room. 🌿 Rare Plant Fair 24 May 2015 www.rareplantfair.co.uk 🅣 See website. 🚻 WCs. 🍰 Home made teas. ℹ Free flow visits to ground floor only on advertised open days. Guided tours for pre-booked groups only. 🅿 🐕 Guide dogs only. ♿ See website. ❄ ♥

Broughton Castle

MAPLEDURHAM HOUSE AND WATERMILL
MAPLEDURHAM, READING RG4 7TR
www.mapledurham.co.uk

Late 16th Century Elizabethan home of the Blount family. Original plaster ceilings, great oak staircase, fine collection of paintings and a private chapel in Strawberry Hill Gothick added in 1797. 15th Century watermill fully restored producing flour, semolina and bran. Hydro powered turbine producing green electricity added in 2011. Visitors may visit the Old Manor tea room where cream teas and cakes are served. A passenger boat service from nearby Caversham runs on open days.
Location: Map 3:E2. OS Ref SU670 767. N of River Thames. 4m NW of Reading, 1½ m W of A4074.
Owner: The Mapledurham Trust **Contact:** Mrs Lola Andrews

Tel: 0118 9723350 **Fax:** 0118 9724016
E-mail: enquiries@mapledurham.co.uk
Open: Easter-Sep: Sats, Suns & BHs, 2-5.30pm. Last admission 5pm. Midweek parties by arrangement only. Also Sun afternoons in Oct.
Admission: Please call 01189 723350 for details. Mapledurham Trust reserves the right to alter or amend opening times or prices without prior notification.
Key facts: Gift shop located in the watermill. Ideal venue for fairs, shows and wedding receptions. Partial. Tea room serving cream teas and cakes. Guides tours for midweek party visits.

ROUSHAM HOUSE
NR STEEPLE ASTON, BICESTER, OXFORDSHIRE OX25 4QX
www.rousham.org

Rousham represents the first stage of English landscape design and remains almost as William Kent (1685-1748) left it. One of the few gardens of this date to have escaped alteration. Includes Venus' Vale, Townesend's Building, seven-arched Praeneste, the Temple of the Mill and a sham ruin known as the 'Eyecatcher'. The house was built in 1635 by Sir Robert Dormer. Dont miss the walled garden with their herbaceous borders, small parterre, pigeon house and espalier apple trees. A fine herd of Longhorn cattle are to be seen in the park.
Excellent location for fashion, advertising, photography etc.
Location: Map 7:A10. OS Ref SP477 242. E of A4260, 12m N of Oxford, S of B4030, 7m W of Bicester.
Owner/Contact: Charles Cottrell-Dormer Esq

Tel: 01869 347110 / 07860 360407 **E-mail:** ccd@rousham.org
Open: Garden: All year: daily, 10am-4.30pm (last adm). House: Pre-booked groups, May-Sep (Mon-Thu).
Admission: Garden: £5.00. No children under 15yrs.
Key facts: Rousham is an ideal Oxfordshire venue for wedding receptions, offering a site to pitch a marquee together with acres of landscape and formal gardens that can be used for photographs and pre-reception drinks. We have also held some car rallies, The Bentley, MG and Aston Martin owners clubs have all held rallies at Rousham. These events are held in the park, immediately next to the house. Open access to the house and garden can be arranged. Partial.

BODLEIAN LIBRARY
Broad Street, Oxford OX1 3BG
www.bodleian.ox.ac.uk/whats-on/visit

A trip to Oxford is incomplete without a visit to the magnificent Divinity School (the first teaching room in the University) or a guided tour around the Library. See the oldest reading room, Duke Humfrey's Library dated 1488, or the iconic Radcliffe Camera. Groups are welcome but must book in advance.

The Bodleian is also licensed for civil weddings and available for corporate and private event hire. In March 2015, the grand atrium in the new Weston Library will also be available for events.

Location: Map 7:A12. OS Ref SP515 064.
Tel: 01865 277224 **Email:** events@bodleian.ox.ac.uk.
E-mail: tours@bodleian.ox.ac.uk
Open: 9am-5pm Mon-Sat, 11am-5pm Sun.
Key facts: ℹ First opened in 1488, the Bodleian is the 2nd largest library in the UK with over 11 million volumes. 🅿 🖥 The Divinity School, Convocation House and Blackwell Hall are available for events up to 450 guests. ☒ 🖥 Café opening in March 2015. ✍ 🅿 🏠 ❄

GREYS COURT ❧
Rotherfield Greys, Henley-On-Thames
Oxfordshire RG9 4PG
www.nationaltrust.org.uk/greys-court

This enchanting and intimate family home in a 16th Century mansion, is set amidst a patchwork of colourful walled gardens, courtyard buildings including a Tudor donkey wheel and medieval walls and towers. Beyond lies an estate and beech woodlands set in the rolling Chiltern Hills.

Location: Map 3:E1. OS Ref SU725 834.
3m W of Henley-on-Thames, E of B481.
Owner: National Trust **Contact:** Property Administrator
Tel: 01491 628529 **Infoline:** 01494 755564
E-mail: greyscourt@nationaltrust.org.uk
Open: 1 Jan-31 Dec. Garden, shop & tea room 10am-5pm. House 11am-5pm. Hourly tours Jan, Feb & Nov. Other months tours 11am & 12pm & then freeflow from 1pm. Closed: Sun 6 Sep & Christmas Eve & Day. Check website for details.
Admission: House & Garden: Adult £12:00, Child £6.00, Family £30.00. Groups (15+) must book in advance. Free to NT members. Prices include voluntary donation but visitors can choose to pay the standard prices displayed at the property and on the website.
Key facts: 🅿 ☒ Partial. 🖥 ✍ By arrangement. 🅿 Limited for coaches. 🐕

The Tower of Five Orders, main entrance to the Old Schools Quandrangle, Bodleian Library

MILTON MANOR HOUSE
Milton, Abingdon, Oxfordshire OX14 4EN

Dreamily beautiful mellow brick house, traditionally designed by Inigo Jones. Celebrated Gothick library and Catholic chapel. Lived in by family; pleasant relaxed and informal atmosphere. Park with fine old trees, stables, walled garden and woodland walk. Picknickers welcome. Free parking, refreshments and pony rides usually available.

Location: Map 3:D1. OS Ref SU485 924. Just off A34, village and house signposted, 9m S of Oxford, 15m N of Newbury. 3m from Abingdon & Didcot.
Owner: Anthony Mockler-Barrett Esq **Contact:** By email for weddings, special events etc florentinagifts@hotmail.co.uk or 020 899 32580. Please write to the administrator for group visits giving contact details & proposed dates & numbers.
Tel: 01235 831287 **Fax:** 01235 862321
Open: Easter Sun and BH Mon, 5/6 Apr; Sun 3 May & BH Mon 4 May; Sun 17 May to Sun 31 May; Sun 16 Aug to BH Mon 31 Aug. Guided tours of house 2pm, 3pm, 4pm. Groups by arrangement throughout year.
Admission: House and Gardens: Adult £8.00; Child (under 14) £2.00. Gardens and grounds only: Adult £4.00, Child (under 14) £1.00.
Key facts: ☒ Grounds. ✍ Obligatory. 🅿 Free. 🐕 Guide dogs only. 🏠 🖥

NUFFIELD PLACE 🌿
Huntercombe, Henley on Thames RG9 5RY
www.nationaltrust.org.uk/nuffield-place

The home of one of the most remarkable men of the 20th Century The time-capsule home of the philanthropist William Morris, Lord Nuffield, the founder of Morris Motor Cars and one of the richest men in the world. Lord Nuffield gave much of his wealth to good causes and his house reflects a relatively modest lifestyle. Lord and Lady Nuffield's personal possessions remain as they left them with the decor and furnishings intact, making it a perfect example of a complete 1930s country home. **Location:** Map 3:E1. OS Ref SU679 878. On the B4130 between Nettlebed and Wallingford

Owner: National Trust **Contact:** Property Administrator
Tel: 01491 641224
E-mail: nuffieldplace@nationaltrust.org.uk
Open: Mon-Sun, 2 Mar-1 Nov. Closed 26 Apr, 28 Jun & 9 Jul.
Admission: House & Garden: Adult £8.80, Child £4.40, Family £22.00. Free to NT members. Groups of 15+ must book in advance.
Key facts: 🖼 ♿ 🚻 Some uneven paths in garden, house ground floor accessible. 🍴 Intimate tearoom-light lunches, tea, coffee & cake. 🅿 ♿

WATERPERRY GARDENS
Waterperry, Nr Wheatley,
Oxfordshire OX33 1JZ
www.waterperrygardens.co.uk

Eight acres of beautiful ornamental gardens with a fascinating history. Established as a School of Horticulture for Ladies by Beatrix Havergal in 1932. Gardens feature a 200 foot long herbaceous border, formal knot and rose garden, riverside walk and herbaceous nursery stock beds. Estate - Plant Centre, Garden Shop, Gallery, Gift Barn, Museum, Teashop, House & Frescos. Events throughout the year and groups welcome. **Location:** Map 7:B12. OS Ref SP610 068. 4 miles from J8 & 8a of the M40. 6-7 miles from Oxford. **Contact:** Waterperry Gardens
Tel: 01844 339226 **Fax:** 01844 339883 **E-mail:** office@waterperrygardens.co.uk
Open: All year except 16-19 Jul 2015, 25, 26 & 31 Dec 2015 & 1-2 Jan 2016. Oct-Mar: 10am-5pm. Apr-Sep: 10am-5.30pm.
Admission: Jan free entry, Feb-Dec Adults £6.80, Children aged 16 and under free. Please see website for seasonal offers.
Key facts: 🖼 Gallery and Gift Barn. 🌱 Plant Centre and Garden Shop. 🚻 WCs. 🍴 Licensed Teashop. 🅣 By arrangement. 🅿 Limited for coaches. 🐕 Guide dogs only. (On leads.) ♿ 🚻

26A EAST ST HELEN STREET
Abingdon, Oxfordshire

One of the best preserved examples of a 15th Century dwelling in the area. Originally a Merchant's Hall House with later alterations, features include a remarkable domestic wall painting, an early oak ceiling, traceried windows and fireplaces.
Location: Map 7:A12. OS Ref SU497 969.
Owner: Oxford Preservation Trust
Contact: Mrs Debbie Dance
Tel: 01865 242918
E-mail: info@oxfordpreservation.org.uk
Website: www.oxfordpreservation.org.uk
Open: By prior appointment.
Admission: Small charge.

ARDINGTON HOUSE 🏠®
Wantage, Oxfordshire OX12 8QA

Ardington House is a beautiful early Georgian stately home nestled in the foot of the North Wessex Downs in Oxfordshire. Built in 1720, the House remains a private home to the Baring family, but is also open to the public on the dates below and is available for rent throughout the year for weddings, corporate events, private parties and film location work.
Location: Map 3:D1. OS Ref SU432 883. 12m S of Oxford, 12m N of Newbury, 21/2 m E of Wantage.
Owner: The Baring Family **Contact:** Charlotte Cross
Tel: 01235 821566 **E-mail:** info@ardingtonhouse.com
Website: www.ardingtonhouse.com
Open: Mon–Wed throughout May & Jun. Easter Mon and all BH Mons in Apr, May and Aug. Hours of access: 11am - 3pm. Last entry at 2.00pm.
Admission: £5.00 per person, concessions for HHA members.
Key facts: 🅣 Marquee available for weddings, parties, corporate events. 🅿 ♿

SULGRAVE MANOR
Manor Road, Sulgrave, Nr Banbury, Oxfordshire OX17 2SD

Built by Lawrence Washington, George Washington's five times great grandfather, in the mid-1500s. See original Tudor features on a house tour including the Great Hall and entrance porch. **Location:** Map 7:B10. OS Ref SP560 455.
Tel: 01295 760205 **Website:** www.sulgravemanor.org.uk
Open: Please see website for up to date opening and admission details.

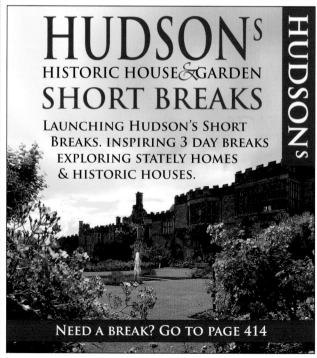

Clandon parterre view

© Matthew Batchelor

CLANDON PARK & 🍂 HATCHLANDS PARK

www.nationaltrust.org.uk/clandon-park & www.nationaltrust.org.uk/hatchlands-park

Two Georgian country houses set in beautiful grounds and just five minutes drive apart.

Clandon Park is a Palladian Mansion, built c1730 for the politically prominent Onslow family and notable for its magnificent Marble Hall. The only Maori meeting house in the UK can be found in the gardens, brought back from New Zealand by the 4th Earl of Onslow as a reminder of his time as Governor there. Displayed inside the house is a superb collection of 18th Century furniture, textiles and porcelain. During the First World War the house at Clandon Park was given over to the war effort and used as a military hospital. Today, Clandon Park's role in the war has been commemorated by the creation of a re-imagined WWI operating theatre in the Earl of Onslow's former dressing room.

Hatchlands Park was built in 1756 for Admiral Boscawen, hero of the Battle of Louisburg. The house is set in a beautiful 430-acre Repton park, with a variety of way-marked walks.
The woodlands are a haven for wildlife and there is a stunning bluebell wood in the spring. The house contains the Cobbe Collection of Old Master paintings and portraits and also the Cobbe Collection of keyboard instruments, the world's largest group of early keyboard instruments owned or played by famous composers such as Purcell, JC Bach, Mozart, Liszt, Chopin, Mahler and Elgar.

KEY FACTS

- ℹ️ No photography inside the houses.
- 📅 Clandon: Open as house plus 3 Nov-23 Dec, Tue-Thu & Suns, 12-4pm; Hatchlands: Open 1 Apr-1 Nov daily 10.30am-5.30pm.
- 🌱 Plant sales at Hatchlands.
- ♿ Please call for details.
- ☕ Hatchlands café- open as shop.
- 🍴 Clandon restaurant-open as shop.
- 🚻 Hatchlands Thursday. Clandon - by arrangement.
- 🎧 Available at Hatchlands.
- 🅿️ Free parking.
- 🎓
- 🐕 Clandon - Guide dogs only. Hatchlands - under close control in designated areas of parkland.
- 🛏️ Clandon only. Call 01483 222502.
- 🎪 Events throughout the year.

Hatchlands Park

© James Duffy

The Music Room at Hatchlands

© National Trust Images / Chris Lacey

VISITOR INFORMATION

Owner
Historic Royal Palaces

Address
Hampton Court Palace
Surrey
KT8 9AU

Location
Map 19:B9
OS Ref. TQ155 686
From M25/J15 or M25/J12
or M25/J10.
Rail: 30 minutes from
Waterloo, zone 6
travelcard
Boat: From Richmond,
Kingston or Runnymede

Contact
Historic Royal Palaces
Tel: 0844 482 7777
**Venue Hire and
Corporate Hospitailty:**
020 3166 6507.
E-mail:
hamptoncourt@hrp.org.uk

Opening Times
Mar-Oct: Daily,
10am-6pm
(last admission 5pm).
Nov-Feb: Daily,
10am-4.30pm (last
admission 3.30pm).
Closed 24-26 Dec.
Please always check
website before visiting for
full details.

Admission
Call 0844 482 7777 or visit
www.hrp.org.uk for more
information.

HAMPTON COURT PALACE
www.hrp.org.uk/hamptoncourtpalace

Discover the magnificence of this former royal residence, once home to the flamboyant King Henry VIII.

Marvel at the two distinct and contrasting Tudor and Baroque architectural styles and soak up the atmosphere in 60 acres of stunning gardens. Extended and developed in grand style in the 1520s by Henry VIII, the present day elegance and romance of the palace owes much to the Christopher Wren designed baroque buildings commissioned by William and Mary at the end of the 17th Century.

At the palace you are able to step back in time and relive some of the extraordinary moments in the life of Henry VIII and the Glorious Georgians. Try on a courtier gown and explore the

majestic environment where kings have entertained, celebrated and mourned. Marvel at the grandeur of the magnificent Great Hall and Great Watching Chamber, see the stunning vaulted ceiling of the Chapel Royal and explore the enormous kitchens, the most extensive surviving 16th Century kitchens in Europe today.

The palace is surrounded by formal gardens and sits in 60 acres of parkland gardens, including the 18th Century Privy Garden and world famous maze.

KEY FACTS

- [i] Information Centre.
- 📷
- ☎ 020 3166 6507.
- ♿ WCs.
- 🏪
- 🍽 Licensed.
- 🎧
- 🅿 Ample for cars, coach parking nearby.
- 🅿 Rates on request 0844 482 7777.
- 🐕 Guide dogs only.
- 🔔
- ❄
- 📹

POLESDEN LACEY ❧
GREAT BOOKHAM, NR DORKING, SURREY RH5 6BD
www.nationaltrust.org.uk/polesdenlacey

'This is a delicious house...' remarked Queen Elizabeth, the Queen Mother on her honeymoon at Polesden Lacey. This country retreat, with glorious views across the rolling Surrey Hills, was home to famous Edwardian hostess Mrs Greville, who entertained royalty and the celebrities of her time. The house has stunning interiors and contains a fabulous collection of art and ceramics.

The gardens offer something for every season, including climbing roses, herbaceous borders and a winter garden. There are four waymarked countryside walks around the estate.

Location: Map 19:B10. OS Ref TQ136 522. 5m NW of Dorking, 2m S of Great Bookham, off A246. **Owner:** National Trust

Tel: 01372 452048 **E-mail:** polesdenlacey@nationaltrust.org.uk

Open: Gardens, café & shops: daily from 10am-5pm (4pm in winter). Closed 10 Feb, 24 & 25 Dec. House: 1 Mar-2 Nov, daily 11am-5pm (weekday mornings entry by guided tour only). Jan, Feb & Nov house open for guided tours weekends only. Four weekends before Christmas house open for special event at additional charge for all visitors (inc NT members).

Admission: House & Grounds: Adults £13.75, Child £6.90, Family £34.70 Group (15+) £11.10. Grounds only: Adult £8.50, Child £4.30, Family £21.50, Group (15+) £6.85.

Key facts: ▢ ⌖ ⬓ Accessible toilets, catering & retail. Courtesy shuttle. Grounds mostly accessible. Free wheelchairs & powered mobility vehicles. Assistance dogs welcome. Hearing loops available. ▣ Hot & cold food, home-made cakes & drinks made from local seasonal produce.

⌖ House tours weekday mornings Mar-Nov, weekends in winter. Free garden tours. ▢ Gardens only. ▣ ▥ In the grounds (excluding formal gardens). ❋ Grounds only. ♥

Great Fosters - Parterres

GODDARDS
Abinger Common, Dorking, Surrey RH5 6TH
www.landmarktrust.org.uk

Goddards, a masterpiece of the Arts and Crafts movement, was built by architect, Edwin Lutyens in about 1900 and has a garden laid out by his friend and collaborator, Gertrude Jekyll.

Goddards is approached by deeply sunken lanes that are almost tunnels through the wooded landscape.

Location: Map 19:B12.

Owner: The Lutyens Trust, leased to The Landmark Trust

Tel: 01628 825925

E-mail: bookings@landmarktrust.org.uk

Open: Self-catering accommodation. Garden & house by appointment, Wed 2.30-5pm, Easter - end Oct. Tours on Weds afternoons. School visits by arrangement. **Admission:** £4.00 for Weds afternoon tours, contact Mrs Dorothy Baker, 01306 730871.

Key facts: Amid the many large, light-filled rooms a most elegant bowling alley waits for a strike. Tours on Weds afternoons. School visits by arrangement.

KEW PALACE
Kew Gardens, Kew, Richmond, Surrey TW9 3AB
www.hrp.org.uk/kewpalace

Kew Palace was built as a private house in 1631 but became a royal residence between 1729 and 1818. More like a home than a palace, the privacy and intimacy of this smallest of English royal palaces made it the favourite country retreat for King George III and his family in the late 18th Century. Don't miss the Royal Kitchens, the most perfectly preserved Georgian royal kitchens in existence. At weekends Queen Charlotte's Cottage is also open to visitors.

Location: Map 19:C7. OS Ref TQ188 776.193. A307. Junc A307 & A205 (1m Chiswick roundabout M4).

Owner: Historic Royal Palaces

Tel: 0844 482 7777

E-mail: kewpalace@hrp.org.uk

Open: Apr–Sep 10am-5.30pm. Last entry 5pm.

Admission: Free of charge but please note admission tickets to Kew Gardens must be purchased to gain access to Kew Palace (for gardens admission prices, please visit the Kew Gardens website).

Key facts: WCs.

PAINSHILL LANDSCAPE GARDEN
Portsmouth Road, Cobham, Surrey KT11 1JE
www.painshill.co.uk

Painshill is a beautiful 18th Century landscape garden. The 158 acre wonderland has something for everyone. Discover mystical follies, including the restored crystal Grotto (limited opening times), historic plantings, the John Bartram Heritage Collection of North American trees and shrubs (Plant Heritage) and spectacular views of Surrey. **Location:** Map 19:B9. OS Ref TQ 10228 6. M25/J10/A3 to London. W of Cobham on A245. Signposted.

Owner: Painshill Park Trust **Contact:** Visitor Operations Team

Tel: 01932 868113 **Fax:** 01932 868001

E-mail: info@painshill.co.uk

Open: All Year (Closed 25-26 Dec). Mar-Oct 10.30am-6pm or dusk (last entry 4.30pm). Nov-Feb 10.30am to 4pm or dusk (last entry 3pm).

Admission: Adult £7.70 Conc. £6.60, Child (5-16 yrs) £4.20, Family (2 Adults & 4 Children) £25.00, Under 5's & Disabled Carer: Free. Group rates available.

Key facts: Books, gifts, Painshill Sparkling Wine & Painshill Honey. WCs. Accessible route. Free pre-booked wheelchair loan. Pre-booked guided buggy tours. Licensed. Picnic area. Pre-book 10+ groups. Free. Coaches must book. Pre-book via Education Dept. On short leads.

GREAT FOSTERS
Stroude Road, Egham, Surrey TW20 9UR

Set amongst 50 acres of stunning gardens and parkland Great Fosters is a fine example of Elizabethan architecture and is now a luxury hotel and restaurant, The Estate Grill. Partake in afternoon tea by one of the fires or on the terrace in warmer months. Its past is evident in the mullioned windows, chimneys and brick finials, whilst the gardens include a Saxon moat, Japanese bridge, amphitheatre and knot garden designed by WH Romaine-Walker and Gilbert Jenkins.

Location: Map 3:G2. OS Ref TQ015 694. M25 J/13, follow signs to Egham and then brown historic signs for Great Fosters

Owner: The Sutcliffe family **Contact:** Amanda Dougans

Tel: 01784 433822 **Fax:** 01784 472455

E-mail: reception@greatfosters.co.uk

Website: www.greatfosters.co.uk

Open: All year. **Admission:** No charge.

Key facts: WCs. Licensed. Guide dogs only.

CHURCH OF ST PETER & ST PAUL
Albury Park, Albury, Guildford, Surrey GU5 9BB

This charming, ancient church dating from Saxon and Norman times, is a flint-walled gem, set amongst the trees of beautiful Albury Park above the River Tilling. Inside, you'll find a light, limewashed uncluttered interior with a stunning medieval wall painting of St Christopher and interesting monuments including a brass of John Weston who died in 1440 and an 18th Century shingled cupola over the tower. Another highlight is the South Chapel; remodelled by renowned Victorian architect A.W. Pugin, responsible for the interior of the Palace of Westminster. He used his rich and colourful style here to create a dazzling mortuary chapel for Albury Park's Drummond family - this is lavishly decorated, with stained glass, painted walls and ceiling, and a magnificent tiled floor. **Location:** OS Ref TQ063 479. 5m SE of Guildford off A248. Turn into minor road on sharp bend and then into private drive with lodge at entrance to Albury Park. Follow drive, fork left to church.

Website: www.visitchurches.org.uk **Open:** Open daily from 10am-5pm.

ARUNDEL CASTLE & GARDENS 🏛

www.arundelcastle.org

Ancient Castle, Stately Home, Gardens & The Collector Earl's Garden.

A thousand years of history is waiting to be discovered at Arundel Castle in West Sussex. Dating from the 11th Century, the Castle is both ancient fortification and stately home of the Dukes of Norfolk and Earls of Arundel.

Set high on a hill, this magnificent Castle commands stunning views across the River Arun and out to sea. Climb the Keep, explore the battlements, wander in the grounds and recently restored Victorian gardens and relax in the garden of the 14th Century Fitzalan Chapel.

In the 17th Century during the English Civil War the Castle suffered extensive damage. The process of structural restoration began in earnest in the 18th Century and continued up until 1900. The Castle was one of the first private residences to have electricity and central heating and had its own fire engine.

Inside the Castle over 20 sumptuously furnished rooms may be visited including the breathtaking Barons' Hall with 16th Century furniture; the Armoury with its fine collection of armour and weaponry, and the magnificent Gothic library entirely fitted out in carved Honduras mahogany. There are works of art by Van Dyck, Gainsborough, Canaletto and Mytens; tapestries; clocks; and personal possessions of Mary Queen of Scots including the gold rosary that she carried to her execution.

There are special event days throughout the season, including, Shakespeare in The Collector Earl's Garden, Arundel International Jousting & Medieval Tournament, and medieval re-enactments.

Do not miss the magnificent Collector Earl's Garden based on early 17th Century classical designs.

KEY FACTS

- 🛈 No photography or video recording inside the Castle.
- 🎁 Distinctive and exclusive gifts.
- 🚻 WCs.
- ☕ Licensed.
- 🍴 Licensed.
- 🚶 By prior arrangement. Tour time 1½-2 hrs. Tours available in various languages - please enquire.
- 🅿 Ample car and coach parking in town car park. Free admission and refreshment voucher for coach driver.
- 👪 Norman Motte & Keep, Armoury & Victorian bedrooms. Special rates for schoolchildren (aged 5-16) and teachers.
- 🐕 Registered Assistance dogs only.
- 💷 On special event days admission prices may vary.

VISITOR INFORMATION

■ Owner
The Goodwood Estate Co.Ltd. (Earl of March and Kinrara).

■ Address
Goodwood House
Goodwood
Chichester
West Sussex
PO18 0PX

■ Location
Map 3:F6
OS Ref. SU888 088
3½m NE of Chichester. A3 from London then A286 or A285. M27/A27 from Portsmouth or Brighton.
Rail: Chichester 3½m Arundel 9m.
Air: Heathrow 1½ hrs Gatwick ¾hr.

■ Contact
Assistant to the Curator
Tel: 01243 755012
Fax: 01243 755005
Recorded Info:
01243 755040.
Weddings:
01243 775537.
E-mail: curator@ goodwood.com or estatesalesofficeenquiries @goodwood.com

■ Opening Times
Summer
15 Mar-12 Oct: Most Suns and Mons, 1-5pm (last entry 4pm).
2-31 Aug: Sun-Thu, 1-5pm. Please check Recorded Info 01243 755040.
12 May and 1 Sep 2014: Connoisseurs' Days. Special tours for booked groups of 20+ only.
Closures
Closed for some special events and for the Festival of Speed and Revival Meeting. Please ring before travelling to check these dates and occasional extra closures.

■ Admission
House
Adult	£9.50
Young Person (12-18yrs)	£4.00
Child (under 12yrs)	Free
Family	£22.00

Booked Groups (20-60)
Open Day (am - by request only)	£12.00
Open Day (pm)	£9.00
Connoisseurs Day	£12.00

■ Special Events
73rd Members' Meeting Festival of Speed Glorious Goodwood Goodwood Revival Meeting
Please visit our website for up-to-date information.

Conference/Function
ROOM	Size	Max Cap
Ballroom	79' x 23'	180

GOODWOOD HOUSE 🏛Ⓕ
www.goodwood.com

Goodwood House, ancestral home of the Dukes of Richmond and Gordon with magnificent art collection.

Goodwood is one of England's finest sporting estates. At its heart lies Goodwood House, the ancestral home of the Dukes of Richmond and Gordon, direct descendants of King Charles II. Today, it is lived in by the present Duke's son and heir, the Earl of March and Kinrara, with his wife and family. Their home is open to the public on at least sixty days a year.

The art collection includes a magnificent group of British paintings from the Seventeenth and Eighteenth Centuries, such as the celebrated views of London by Canaletto and superb sporting scenes by George Stubbs. The rooms are filled with fine English and French furniture, Gobelins tapestries and Sèvres Porcelain. Special works of art are regularly rotated and displayed and the books can be viewed by written application to the Curator (there is a special charge for these viewings). The summer exhibition will celebrate 200 years since the Duchess of Richmond's Ball, given in Brussels just before the Battle of Waterloo.

Goodwood is also renowned for its entertaining, enjoying a reputation for excellence. Goodwood's own organic farm provides food for the table in the various restaurants on the estate. With internationally renowned horseracing and motor sport events, the finest downland golf course in the UK, its own aerodrome and hotel, Goodwood offers an extraordinarily rich sporting experience.

KEY FACTS

ℹ️ Conference and wedding facilities. No photography. Very well informed guides. Shell House optional extra on Connoisseurs' Days.

🚻 WCs.

🍴 Obligatory.

🅿️ Ample.

🐕 Guide dogs only.

🏨 Goodwood Hotel.

💍 Civil Wedding Licence. Telephone number for Weddings is 01243 775537 and email is estatesalesofficenquiries@goodwood.com.

GREAT DIXTER HOUSE & GARDENS 🏛Ⓕ

www.greatdixter.co.uk

A very special garden with a great deal of character, planted with flair, always something to see, whatever the season.

Great Dixter, built c1450, is the birthplace of the late Christopher Lloyd, gardening author. Its Great Hall is the largest medieval timberframed hall in the country, restored and enlarged for Christopher's father (1910-12). The house was largely designed by the architect, Sir Edwin Lutyens, who added a 16th Century house (moved from elsewhere) knitting the buildings together as a family home. The house retains much of the collections of furniture and other items put together by the Lloyds early in the 20th Century, with some notable modern additions by Christopher. The gardens feature a variety of topiary, ponds, wild meadow areas and the famous Long Border and Exotic Garden. Featured regularly in 'Country Life' from 1963, Christopher was asked to contribute a series of weekly articles as a practical gardener - he never missed an issue in 42 years. There is a specialist nursery which offers an array of unusual plants of the highest quality, many of which can be seen in the fabric of the gardens. Light refreshments are available in the gift shop as well as tools, books and gifts. The whole estate is 57 acres which includes ancient woodlands, meadows and ponds which have been consistently managed on a traditional basis. Coppicing the woodlands, for example, has provided pea sticks for plant supports and timber for fencing and repairs to the buildings. There is a Friends programme available throughout the year. Friends enjoy invitations to events and educational courses as well as regular newsletters.

KEY FACTS

- ℹ️ No photography in House.
- 🛍️
- ♿
- 🚶 Obligatory.
- 🅿️ Limited for coaches.
- ▦
- 🐕 Guide dogs only.
- ▣

VISITOR INFORMATION

▨ Owner
The Great Dixter Charitable Trust

▨ Address
Northiam
Rye
East Sussex
TN31 6PH

▨ Location
Map 4:L5
OS Ref. TQ817 251
Signposted off the A28 in Northiam.

▨ Contact
Perry Rodriguez
Tel: 01797 252878
E-mail: office@greatdixter.co.uk

▨ Opening Times
1 April-25 October:
Tue-Sun, House 2-5pm.
Garden 11am-5pm.
Specialist Nursery Opening times:
April-October
Mon-Fri, 9am-5pm.
Sat 9am-5pm.
Sun 10am-5pm.
November-End of March
Mon-Fri, 9am-12.30pm,
1.30-4.30pm.
Sat 9am-12.30pm.
Sun Closed.

▨ Admission
House & Garden   £10.00
Child   £3.50
Garden only   £8.00
Child   £2.50
A Gift Aid on admission scheme is in place.

▨ Special Events
Study days on a wide range of subjects available. Please check the website for details.

■ VISITOR INFORMATION

■ Owner
Lancing College
Chapel Trust

■ Address
Lancing
West Sussex
BN15 0RW

■ Location
Map 3:H6
OS Ref. TQ 196 067
North of the A27 between
Shoreham-by-Sea and
Lancing at the Coombes
Road/Shoreham Airport
traffic lights. Filter right if
coming from the east. Turn
off Coombes Road at sign
for Lancing College and
proceed to the top of
Lancing College drive. It is
usually possible to park
outside the Chapel.
Rail: Train to Shoreham-by
Sea or Lancing on the
London-Littlehampton and
Portsmouth line and
take a taxi.
Bus: The nearest bus
routes are Brighton and
Hove Buses 2A, Compass
Buses, 106 and
Coastliner 700.

■ Contact
The Verger
Tel: 01273 465949
Fax: 01273 464720
Enquiries may also be
made at the Porter's Lodge,
Lancing College
on 01273 452213.
E-mail: ahowat
@lancing.org.uk

■ Opening Times
10.00am to 4.00pm
Monday to Saturday;
12noon to 4.00pm on
Sunday. Every day of the
year except for Christmas
Day and Boxing Day.

■ Admission
Admission Free.
Donations are requested
for the Friends of
Lancing Chapel.
Visitors are asked to sign in
for security purposes as
they enter the Chapel.
The other College buildings
are not open to the public.

■ Special Events
Visitors can reserve seats
for Public Carol Services by
applying in writing to
Lancing College Chapel,
Lancing, West Sussex,
BN15 0RW with a
stamped, self-addressed
envelope.
Visitors wishing to attend
other services should
contact the Verger.

The glorious gothic architecture of Lancing College Chapel

LANCING COLLEGE CHAPEL
www.lancingcollege.co.uk

'I know of no more spectacular post-Reformation ecclesiastical building in the kingdom.' Evelyn Waugh, former pupil.

Lancing College Chapel is the place of worship for the community of Lancing College, the Central Minster of the Woodard Schools and a well-loved Sussex landmark. The Chapel stands prominently on the South Downs. The exterior, with its pinnacles and flying buttresses, is a testament to Victorian structural bravado. Designed by Herbert Carpenter in the 13th Century French gothic style, it is the fourth tallest ecclesiastical building in England.

The foundations were laid in 1868 and the atmospheric crypt came into use in 1875. The upper chapel was dedicated in 1911 but the west wall and rose window were added in the 1970s. There is now a plan to complete the building with a west porch. A beautiful war memorial cloister was built in the 1920s.

The interior is breathtaking. Soaring columns branch out into fan vaulting, perfectly proportioned arches and vast clerestory windows. There are stained glass windows by Comper and Dykes Bower and one commemorating former pupil Fr Trevor Huddleston made by Mel Howse in 2007. Behind the high altar are superb tapestries woven on the William Morris looms in the 1920s. The oak stall canopies are by Gilbert Scott. There are two organs (Walker 1914 and Frobenius 1986) with intricately carved oak cases.

The Chapel has a fascinating history which is still unfolding and it is a treasure house of ecclesiastical art. Lancing Chapel welcomes visitors both as an important heritage landmark and as a place of quiet reflection and prayer.

KEY FACTS

- ℹ Guide books, information leaflets & a DVD.
- Stall with guide books & postcards at entrance to the Chapel.
- The upper chapel (but not the crypt) is easily accessible for the disabled.
- Guided tours & brief talks about the Chapel can be booked with the Verger. Groups should be booked in advance.
- P It is usually possible to park very near the entrance to the Chapel.
- School & other educational groups are welcome & may request guided tours & other information.
- Guide dogs in Chapel. Dogs on leads in College grounds.
- ❄ Open all year except Christmas Day & Boxing Day.

Interior of Lancing College Chapel looking East

The splendid rose window and Walker organ

BATEMAN'S ❧

BATEMAN'S, BURWASH, ETCHINGHAM, EAST SUSSEX TN19 7DS

www.nationaltrust.org.uk/batemans

"A good and peaceable place" was how Rudyard Kipling described Bateman's, a beautiful Sussex sandstone manor house and garden where the Kiplings lived from 1902 - 1936. Originally built in 1634 this mellow house, with its little watermill, was a sanctuary to the most famous writer in the English speaking world. Set in the glorious landscape of the Sussex Weald, the house and gardens are kept much as they were in Kipling's time and visitors can discover a fascinating collection of mementos of Kipling's time in India and illustrations from his famous Jungle Book tales of Mowgli, Baloo and Shere Khan.

Location: Map 4:K5. OS Ref TQ671 238.
0.5 m S of Burwash off A265.
Owner: National Trust

Contact: The Administrator
Tel: 01435 882302
Fax: 01435 882811
E-mail: batemans@nationaltrust.org.uk
Open: 1 Jan-31 Dec: 7 days/week. House: 11am-5pm. Garden, shop and restaurant: 10am-5pm.
Admission: House & Garden: Adult £10.50, Child £5.25, Family £26.00 (2+3)*. Groups: Adult £8.10, Child £4.05, Family £20.10. *Gift Aid Prices, standard prices are available at property and on website.
Key facts: ⬚ ⬚ ⬚ ⬚ Partial. WCs. ⬚ ⬚ Limited for coaches. ⬚ ⬚ Guide dogs only. ⬚ Closed Christmas Eve and Christmas Day.

FIRLE PLACE ⬚ⓕ

FIRLE, LEWES, EAST SUSSEX BN8 6LP

www.firle.com

Firle Place has been the home of the Gage family for over 500 years. Set at the foot of the Sussex Downs within its own parkland, this unique house of Tudor origin was built of Caen stone by Sir John Gage, friend of Henry VIII. Remodelled in the 18th Century, the house contains a magnificent collection of Old Master paintings, fine English and European furniture and an impressive collection of Sèvres porcelain. Events: Events and wedding receptions can be held in the parkland throughout the year or in the Georgian Riding School from April to October. The Great Tudor Hall can, on occasion, be used for private dinners, with drinks on the Terrace or in the Billiard Room. Please contact the Estate Office for all event and wedding reception enquiries on 01273 858567 or visit the website for further information. Tea Room: Enjoy the licensed tea room and terrace with views over the garden and parkland, serving light lunches and afternoon tea using local produce from Firle Place gardens and the wider Firle Estate. **Location:** Map

4:J6. OS Ref TQ473 071. 4m SE of Lewes on A27 Brighton/Eastbourne Road.
Owner: The Rt Hon Viscount Gage
Tel: 01273 858307 House
Fax: 01273 858118 **Events:** 01273 858567
E-mail: enquiries@firle.com
Open: Jun–Sep, Sun–Thu, 2.00–4.30pm. Dates and times subject to change without prior notice. Tea Room open on House opening days only, from 12.00–4.30pm. Garden Open Days 25-26 Apr 2015.
Admission: Adult £8.50, Child £4.00, Conc. £7.50
Private Tours: Private group tours can be arranged by prior appointment. Please telephone 01273 858307 for details or visit the website.
Key facts: ⬚ No photography in house. ⬚ ⬚ ⬚ Ground floor & tea room. ⬚ Licensed. ⬚ ⬚ ⬚ In grounds on leads. ⬚

NYMANS ❧
HANDCROSS, HAYWARDS HEATH, WEST SUSSEX RH17 6EB
www.nationaltrust.org.uk/nymans

In the late 1800's Ludwig Messel bought the Nymans Estate in the Sussex High Weald to make a dream family home. Inspired by the wooded surroundings he created a garden with plants collected from around the world. Today it is still a garden lovers' home - a place to relax all year round in a peaceful country garden. The house was partially destroyed by fire in 1947 and romantic ruins of a fairytale gothic mansion remain. As well as a large shop and plant centre there is a café with seasonal food, year round activities, a small gallery and a bookshop.

Location: Map 4:I4. OS Ref SU187:TQ265 294. At Handcross on B2114, 12 miles south of Gatwick, just off London-Brighton M23.

Owner: National Trust **Contact:** Nymans
Tel: 01444 405250 **E-mail:** nymans@nationaltrust.org.uk

Open: Garden, woods, café, shop and garden centre, gallery in the House, and second hand bookshop: 1 Jan-28 Feb, daily, 10am-4pm. 1 Mar-31 Oct, daily, 10am-5pm. 1 Nov-31 Dec, daily, 10am-4pm. House open for special events only from 1 Nov-28 Feb. Closed 25 & 26 Dec. Last adm to Gallery 30mins before closing and for short periods during the year to change exhibitions. For more information and any other changes please check the website. **Admission:** Adult (Gift Aid prices) £12.20, Child £6.60, Family (2 Adults, 3 Children) £30.80, Family (1 adult, 3 Children) £19.00, Booked Groups (15+) Adult £10.50, Child £5.80.

Key facts: ⊡ ⚇ ⛾ ⊞ WC, some level paths. ⚇ Licensed. ⊞ Daily, free. Special interest tours for groups £2.50pp booked in advance. ⊡ ⚇ ⛾ Guide dogs only. ⛾ No dogs in garden. ⚇ ❄ Closed Christmas Day & Boxing Day. ⚇

Petworth House

PARHAM HOUSE & GARDENS ⓕ
PARHAM PARK, STORRINGTON, NR PULBOROUGH, WEST SUSSEX RH20 4HS
www.parhaminsussex.co.uk

One of the top twenty in Simon Jenkins's book 'England's Thousand Best Houses'. Idyllically set in the heart of a 17th Century deer park, below the South Downs, the house contains an important collection of needlework, paintings and furniture. The spectacular Long Gallery is the third longest in England. The award-winning gardens include a four acre walled garden with stunning herbaceous borders. Parham has always been a much-loved family home. Now owned by a charitable trust, the house is lived in by Lady Emma Barnard, her husband James and their family.

Location: Map 3:G5. OS Ref TQ060 143. Midway between Pulborough & Storrington on A283. Equidistant from A24 & A29. For SatNav please enter postcode RH20 4HR.

Owner: Parham Park Trust **Contact:** Parham Estate Office

Tel: 01903 742021
Fax: 01903 746557
Facebook: www.facebook.com/ParhamHouseAndGardens
Twitter: @parhaminsussex
E-mail: enquiries@parhaminsussex.co.uk
Open: Open 5 Apr – 25 Oct. Please see website or contact property for full opening dates and details.
Admission: Please contact property or see website for admission prices.
Key facts: ⓘ No flash photography in house. Disabled access in the gardens and ground floor of the house. Coffees, light lunches and afternoon teas are served on open days during the open season. Licensed. By arrangement. In grounds, on leads.

PETWORTH HOUSE & PARK
CHURCH STREET, PETWORTH, WEST SUSSEX GU28 0AE
www.nationaltrust.org.uk/petworth

Explore this majestic mansion and beautiful landscaped deer park, forever immortalised in JMW Turner's masterpieces. Unlock the intriguing family history and marvel at the internationally important picture collection, including works by Turner, Van Dyck, Reynolds and Blake together with ancient and Neo-classical sculpture. In contrast to the lavish House, venture 'below stairs' to discover the secrets of the Servants' Quarters. Stroll the Pleasure Grounds and enjoy breathtaking views, whatever the season.

Location: Map 3:G5. OS Ref SU976 218. In the centre of Petworth town (approach roads A272/A283/A285) Car park signposted.
Owner: National Trust
Contact: The Administration Office
Tel: 01798 342207
E-mail: petworth@nationaltrust.org.uk

Open: House: 14 Mar-4 Nov, Sat-Wed, 11am-5pm last admission 4:30pm, partially open on Thu-Fri for guided speciality tours only.
Pleasure Grounds, Restaurant, Coffee Shop & Gift Shop: 1 Jan-31 Dec, Sat-Sat, 10am-5pm or dusk; (closed 24 & 25 Dec).
Admission: House and Grounds Adult £14.00, Child (5-17yrs) £7.00, Family (2+3) £35.00 Groups (pre-booked) £11.20. Includes voluntary donation but visitors can choose to pay the standard prices displayed on the property.
Key facts: ⓘ Events & Exhibitions throughout the year. Baby feeding and changing facilities, highchairs, pushchairs admitted in House but no prams please. WCs. Licensed. Licensed. By arrangement. Audio House Tours. 700 meters from house. Coach parties alight at Church Lodge entrance, coaches then park in NT car park. Coaches must book in advance. Guide dogs only.

ST MARY'S HOUSE & GARDENS 🏠Ⓕ
BRAMBER, WEST SUSSEX BN44 3WE
www.stmarysbramber.co.uk

Enchanting medieval house, winner of Hudsons Heritage 'Best Restoration' award. Features in Simon Jenkins' book 'England's Thousand Best Houses'. Fine panelled interiors, including unique Elizabethan 'Painted Room'. Interesting family memorabilia. Rare Napoleonic collection. English costume-dolls.
Traditional cottage-style tea room. Five acres of grounds include formal gardens with amusing topiary, exceptional example of the Ginkgo biloba and the Victorian 'Secret' Garden. Original fruit-wall and pineapple pits, Rural Museum, Jubilee Rose Garden, Terracotta Garden, King's Garden, woodland walk and unusual circular Poetry Garden. New for 2015: Wildlife Water Garden with its island and dramatic waterfall. In the heart of the South Downs National Park, St. Mary's is a house of fascination, charm and friendliness.

Location: Map 3:H6. OS Ref TQ189 105. Bramber village off A283. From London 56m via M23/A23 or A24. Buses from Brighton, Shoreham and Worthing.
Owner: Mr Peter Thorogood MBE and Mr Roger Linton MBE
Tel: 01903 816205 **E-mail:** info@stmarysbramber.co.uk
Open: May-end Sep: Suns, Thus & BH Mons, 2-6pm. Last entry 5pm. Groups at other days and times by arrangement.
Admission: House & Gardens: Adult £9.00, Conc. £8.50, Child £4.00. Groups (25+) £9.00. Gardens only: Adult £6.00, Child £2.00, Groups £6.00.
Key facts: ⓘ No photography in house. 🖼 ♿ 🚻 🔲 Partial. 🖼 👤 Obligatory for groups (max 55). Visit time 2½-3 hrs. 🅿 20 cars or 2 coaches. 🖼 ✂ ⚓ ♿

SHEFFIELD PARK AND GARDEN 🌿
SHEFFIELD PARK, UCKFIELD, EAST SUSSEX TN22 3QX
www.nationaltrust.org.uk/sheffield-park-and-garden

The garden is a horticultural work of art formed through centuries of landscape design, with influences of 'Capability' Brown and Humphry Repton. Four lakes form the heart of the garden, with paths circulating through the glades and wooded areas surrounding them. Each owner has left their impression, which can still be seen today in the layout of the lakes, the construction of Pulham Falls, the planting of Palm Walk and the many different tree and shrub species from around the world. Our historic parkland forms a larger footprint for the Sheffield Park estate. Dating back several centuries, it has had many uses including a deer park and WWII camp, and is now grazed with livestock. (Please note house is privately owned). **Location:** Map 4:I5. OS Ref TQ415 240. Midway between East Grinstead and Lewes, 5m NW of Uckfield on E side of A275.
Owner: National Trust **Contact:** Property Office
Tel: 01825 790231 **Fax:** 01825 791264 **Alt tel:** 01825 790302

E-mail: sheffieldpark@nationaltrust.org.uk
Open: Garden/Shop/Tearoom: Open all year (closed Christmas Day). Please call 01825 790231 or visit our website for details of seasonal opening times. Parkland: Open all year, dawn to dusk.
Admission: For 2015 prices, please call 01825 790231 or visit our website. Groups discount available (15+ prebooked) NT, RHS Individual Members and Great British Heritage Pass holders Free. Discounts available in conjunction with the Bluebell Railway for groups. **Key facts:** ⓘ Garden: Accessibility dogs only. Parkland: Dogs allowed under close control. 🔲 Gifts, condiments, books, gardening accessories & outdoor wear. 🖼 Extensive, well-stocked plant sales area. ♿ Accessible route in garden. WCs in tearoom & reception. Mobility scooters & wheelchairs. ☕ Coach House tearoom. 👤 Tues & Thus 11am-12pm. 🅿 Coach parking area & accessible spaces. 🖼 🖼 ❄ 🖼

STANDEN ❧
WEST HOATHLY ROAD, EAST GRINSTEAD, WEST SUSSEX RH19 4NE
www.nationaltrust.org.uk/standen

Designed by Philip Webb in the 1890s for wealthy solicitor, James Beale, and his family, Standen is a family home with nationally important Arts & Crafts interiors, most famous for its Morris & Co. designs. The 12 acre hillside garden, is part of a 5 year project to restore lost features and conserve the historic plant collection. A licensed café serves seasonal dishes and Arts & Crafts inspired gifts are available in the shop. **Location:** Map 4:I4. OS Ref TQ389 356. 2m S of East Grinstead, signposted from B2110. **Owner:** National Trust **Contact:** Property Office **Tel:** 01342 323029 **Twitter & Facebook:** Search for StandenNT. **E-mail:** standen@nationaltrust.org.uk **Open:** 1 Jan–13 Feb: Mon-Sun, Garden, Café, Shop 10am-4pm (House 11am-3.30pm last entry at 3pm. Behind the scenes tours only Mon-Fri). 14 Feb-1 Nov: Mon-Sun, Garden, Café, Shop 10am-5pm (House 11am–4.30pm last entry

4pm). 2 Nov–31 Dec: Mon-Sun, Garden, Café, Shop 10am-4pm (House 11am–3.30pm last entry 3pm). * Access by guided tour only at certain times, please check website for full details. **Closed 24 and 25 Dec. **Admission:** House & Garden*: Adult £11.55, Child £5.80, Family £28.90. Pre-booked groups: £9.00 (min 15). *Includes voluntary donation but visitors can choose to pay the standard prices displayed on the property and on the website. **Key facts:** ℹ Year round events programme including contemporary art selling exhibitions, garden open days, lectures, demonstrations & school holiday children's activities. ▣ ▣ ▤ WCs. Wheelchairs available to borrow. ▣ Licensed. ⊞ Licensed. ▣ Guided tours available at certain times, check website for details. ▣ ▣ ▤ Dogs welcome in the gardens on short leads. ▣ Morris Apartment (Self-catering, sleeps 2+2) available to hire. ▣ Closed 24 & 25 Dec. ▣

BODIAM CASTLE ❧
Bodiam, Nr Robertsbridge, East Sussex TN32 5UA
www.nationaltrust.org.uk/bodiam-castle

Built in 1385 to defend the surrounding countryside and as a comfortable dwelling for a rich nobleman, Bodiam Castle is one of the finest examples of medieval architecture. The virtual completeness of its exterior makes it popular with adults, children and film crews alike. Inside, although a ruin, floors have been replaced in some of the towers and visitors can climb the spiral staircase to enjoy superb views from the battlements. Discover more of its intriguing past in an introductory film and new exhibition, and wander in the peacefully romantic Castle grounds. **Location:** Map 4:K5. OS Ref TQ785 256. 3m S of Hawkhurst, 2m E of A21 Hurst Green. **Owner:** National Trust **Contact:** The Property Manager **Tel:** 01580 830196 **E-mail:** bodiamcastle@nationaltrust.org.uk **Open:** Please see website for opening times and admisson prices. **Key facts:** ▣ ▤ Ground floor & grounds. ⊞ ▣ ▣ Teachers resources & education base. ▣ ▣

CHARLESTON
Charleston, Firle, Nr Lewes, East Sussex BN8 6LL
www.charleston.org.uk

Charleston, with its unique interiors and beautiful walled garden, was the home of artists Vanessa Bell and Duncan Grant from 1916 and the country meeting place of the Bloomsbury group. They decorated the house, painting walls, doors and furniture and filling the rooms with their own paintings and works by artists they admired, such as Picasso, Derain and Sickert. **Location:** Map 4:J6. OS Ref TQ490 069. 7 miles east of Lewes on A27 between Firle and Selmeston **Owner:** The Charleston Trust **Tel:** 01323 811626 **E-mail:** info@charleston.org.uk **Open:** Apr-Oct: Wed-Sat, guided tours from 1pm (12pm Jul-Sep) Last entry 5pm. Sun & BH Mon open 1-5.30pm. **Admission:** Please check website for full details of admission costs. **Key facts:** ℹ ▣ ▣ ⊞ ▤ ▣ ▣ Obligatory, except Sunday. ▣ ▣ ▣

CHICHESTER CATHEDRAL
Chichester, W Sussex PO19 1PX
www.chichestercathedral.org.uk

Ancient and modern, this magnificent 900 year old Cathedral has treasures from every age, from medieval stone carvings to world famous contemporary artworks. Open every day and all year with free entry. Free guided tours and special trails for children. Regular exhibitions, free weekly lunchtime concerts and a superb Cloisters Restaurant and Shop. A fascinating place to visit.

Location: Map 3:F6. OS Ref SU860 047. West Street, Chichester.
Contact: Visitor Services Officer
Tel: 01243 782595 **Fax:** 01243 812499
E-mail: visitors@chichestercathedral.org.uk
Open: Summer: 7.15am-7pm, Winter: 7.15am-6pm. Choral Evensong daily (except Wed).
Admission: Free entry. Donations greatly appreciated.
Key facts:

CLINTON LODGE GARDEN
Fletching, E Sussex TN22 3ST
www.clintonlodgegardens.co.uk

A formal but romantic garden around a Caroline and Georgian house, reflecting the gardening fashions throughout its history, particularly since the time of Sir Henry Clinton, one of Wellington's generals at Waterloo. Lawn and parkland, double blue and white herbaceous borders between yew and box hedges, a cloister walk swathed in white roses, clematis and geraniums, a Herb Garden where hedges of box envelop herbs, seats are of turf, paths of camomile. A Pear Walk bursts with alliums or lilies, a Potager of flowers for cutting, old roses surround a magnificent water feature by William Pye, and much more. Private groups by appointment.

Location: Map 4:I5. OS Ref TQ428 238. In centre of village behind tall yew and holly hedge. **Owner/Contact:** Lady Collum **Tel/Fax:** 01825 722952
E-mail: garden@clintonlodge.com
Open: NGS Open Days: Sun 27 Apr, Mon 15 Jun & Mon 3 Aug. Other days by appointment. **Admission:** NGS Entrance £5.00, Children Free.
Key facts: WCs. Partial. By arrangement. Limited. Guide dogs only.

GLYNDE PLACE
Glynde, East Sussex BN8 6SX
www.glyndeplace.co.uk

Glynde Place is a magnificent example of Elizabethan architecture commanding exceptionally fine views of the South Downs. Amongst the collections of 400 years of family living can be seen 17th and 18th Century portraits of the Trevors, furniture, embroidery and silver.

Location: Map 4:J5. OS Ref TQ456 092. Signposted off the A27, 4m SE of Lewes at top of village. Rail: Glynde is on the London/Eastbourne and Brighton/Eastbourne mainline railway. London 1½ hours by car, Gatwick 35 mins by car.
Contact: The Estate Office **Tel:** 01273 858224
E-mail: info@glynde.co.uk **Open:** May–Jun: Wed, Thu & Sun & BHs from 1-5pm. Aug: BH and preceding Sun from 1-5pm. Visits to the House are by guided tours only starting at 2pm, 3pm and 4pm. Group bookings by prior arrangement only.
Admission: House & Grounds: Adult £5.00, Children over 12yrs & Students £3.00, Children under 12 yrs free. **Key facts:** House, gardens & parkland available for corporate events. All visits to the House by guided tours only. Limited parking for coaches. Guide dogs only. A range of wedding options are available. Please contact the Estate Office for more information.

HAMMERWOOD PARK
East Grinstead, Sussex RH19 3QE
www.hammerwoodpark.co.uk

The best kept secret in Sussex, "untouched by a corporate plan". Built by White House architect Latrobe in Greek Revival style in 1792, left derelict by Led Zeppelin, painstakingly restored by the Pinnegar family over the last 30 years and brought to life with guided tours, concerts and filming.
Location: Map 4:J4. OS Ref TQ442 390. 3.5 m E of East Grinstead on A264 to Tunbridge Wells, 1m W of Holtye.
Owner: David and Anne-Noelle Pinnegar
Tel: 01342 850594 **E-mail:** antespam@gmail.com
Open: 1 Jun-end Sep: Wed, Sat & BH Mon, 2-5pm. Guided tour starts 2.05pm. Private groups: Easter-Jun. Coaches strictly by appointment. Small groups any time throughout the year by appointment.
Admission: House & Park: Adult £8.00, Child £2.00. Private viewing by arrangement.
Key facts: ⓘ Conferences. Helipad (see Pooley's - prior permission required). ⊤ ▦ ⓘ Obligatory. ▦ ▩ In grounds. ▦ B&B. ❄ ▨ €

PALLANT HOUSE GALLERY
9 North Pallant, Chichester, West Sussex PO19 1TJ
www.pallant.org.uk

A Grade I-listed Queen Anne townhouse and award-winning contemporary building housing one of the best collections of Modern British art in the UK. An innovative exhibition programme includes important international exhibitions and print shows. There is also an on-site cafe restaurant with courtyard garden and a first-class art bookshop.
Location: Map 3:F6. OS Ref SU861 047. City centre, SE of the Cross
Owner: Pallant House Gallery Trust **Contact:** Reception
Tel: 01243 774557 **E-mail:** info@pallant.org.uk
Open: Tue-Sat: 10am-5pm; Thu: 10am-8pm; Sun & BH; Mon: 11am-5pm Mon: Closed. **Admission:** Adult £9.50*, Child 6-16yrs £4.00 (Under 6's Free), Student £5.50, Family £22.00* (2 adults and up to 4 children), Friends Free, Groups £7.50 per person (booking required). Tues half price Adult Entry £4.75; Thus 5-8pm Free (excluding main exhibition). *Gift aid can be applied: voluntary donation (£1.00 per adult). **Key facts:** ⓘ No photography. ▢ ⊤ ⓛ WCs. ▦ ⓘ Licensed. ⓧ ▦ ▩ Guide dogs only. ❄ ▨

© Newhaven Fort

NEWHAVEN FORT
Fort Road, Newhaven, East Sussex, England BN9 9DS
www.newhavenfort.org.uk

This scheduled ancient monument tells the story of life in a Victorian Fortress and the on-site military museum demonstrates Newhaven Fort's role through two World Wars. Explore the echoing tunnels built into the chalk cliffs or enjoy the stunning views from the ramparts. Sit in our air raid shelter simulation and experience how it would have felt being caught in a real air-raid!
Location: Map 4:J6. OS Ref TQ449 002. Between Brighton & Eastbourne on A259 coast road & linked to Lewes on A27, via A26. Brown tourist signs on approach.
Owner: Lewes District Council **Tel:** 01273 517622 **Fax:** 01273 512059
E-mail: info@newhavenfort.org.uk **Open:** Every day from 1 Mar-31 Oct. Mar-Sep 10.30am-6pm, last adm at 5pm. Oct 10.30am-5pm, last adm at 4pm.
Admission: Adult £6.00. Senior/Conc £5.00. Child £4.00. Family (2 Adults & 2/3 Children) £18.70. Disabled Adult £3.25. Disabled Child Free. Carer £2.00.
Key facts: ▦ Small gift shop. ▧ Disabled parking. Shop, cafe & exhibits all accessible. ▦ Open daily throughout the season. ▣ Free parking. Height Barrier (1.8m) at entrance. Alternative parking spaces available via Fort Rise. ▦ Open all year round for school visits. ▨ On leads. ▨

SACKVILLE COLLEGE
High Street, East Grinstead, West Sussex RH19 3BX
www.sackvillecollege.org.uk

Built in 1609 for Robert Sackville, Earl of Dorset, as an almshouse and overnight accommodation for the Sackville family. Feel the Jacobean period come alive in the enchanting quadrangle, the chapel, banqueting hall with its fine hammerbeam roof and minstrels' gallery, the old common room and Warden's study where the carol "Good King Wenceslas" was composed. Chapel weddings by arrangement.
Location: Map 4:I4. OS Ref TQ397 380. A22 to East Grinstead, College in High Street (town centre).
Owner: Board of Trustees **Contact:** The Warden
Tel: 01342 323414
E-mail: admin@sackvillecollege.org.uk
Open: Mid Jun-Mid Sep, Wed to Sun afternoons, 2-5pm. Groups all year round, by arrangement. Pre-booked school visits welcome.
Admission: Adult £4.00, Child £1.00. Groups: (10-60) no discount.
Key facts: ⓘ Large public car park adjacent to entrance. ▢ ⓧ ⊤ ▧ Partial. ⓧ Obligatory. ▣ Chequer Mead car park nearby. ▦ Pre-booked school groups welcome. ▨ Guide dogs only. ▨

STANSTED PARK 🏛Ⓕ
Stansted Park, Rowlands Castle, Hampshire PO9 6DX
www.stanstedpark.co.uk

Stansted Park, on the South Downs, is a beautiful Edwardian house with ancient private chapel, with spectacular views south over the Solent. The state rooms are furnished as if the 10th Earl of Bessborough was still at home, and the amazing servants' quarters are jam-packed with old-fashioned things to see.
Location: Map 3:F5. OS Ref SU761 103. Follow brown heritage signs from A3(M) J2 Emsworth or A27 Havant **Owner:** Stansted Park Foundation
Contact: Reception **Tel:** 023 9241 2265 **Fax:** 023 9241 3773
E-mail: enquiry@stanstedpark.co.uk
Open: House: Apr-May: Sun & BHol 1-5pm. Jun-Sep: Sun-Wed 1-5pm (last adm. 4pm). Tea Room & Garden Centre: open every day. Maze: weekends and school holidays 11-4pm (Feb-Oct). Light Railway: weekends and Weds.
Admission: House & Chapel: Adult £7.00, Child (5-15yrs) £3.50, Conc. £6.00, Family (2+3) £18.00. Groups/educational visits by arrangement.
Key facts: 🏛 📷 Private & corporate hire. 🔲 Suitable. WCs. 📷 Licensed. 📷 By arrangement. 📷 📷 By arrangement. 🐕 Guide dogs only. 📷 ❄ Grounds. 📷

WILMINGTON PRIORY
Wilmington, Nr Eastbourne, East Sussex BN26 5SW
www.landmarktrust.org.uk

The Priory is part of an outstanding now mostly ruinous monastic site in the South Downs, combined with the comfort of rooms improved by the Georgians. This area was beloved by the Bloomsbury set whose influential houses are nearby; it close to Glyndebourne and a few miles from the sea.
Location: Map 3:F5. OS Ref TQ544 042.
Owner: Leased to the Landmark Trust by Sussex Archaeological Society
Tel: 01628 825925
E-mail: bookings@landmarktrust.org.uk
Open: Self-catering accommodation. 30 days Apr-Oct, contact for details.
Admission: Free on Open Days, visits by appointment.
Key facts: 📷 A vaulted medieval entrance porch leading off the large farmhouse kitchen makes an atmospheric summer dining room and the monastic ruins are yours to wander.
📷 📷 📷 📷 📷 ❄ 📷

UPPARK HOUSE & GARDEN 🌿
South Harting, Petersfield, West Sussex GU31 5QR
www.nationaltrust.org.uk/uppark

Admire the Georgian grandeur of Uppark from its stunning hilltop location on the South Downs. Discover the fascinating world of Sir Harry Fetherstonhaugh, Lady Emma Hamilton and the dairymaid who married her master. See the famous doll's house, Victorian servants' quarters, lovely garden and breathtaking views.
Location: Map 3:F5. OS Ref 197 SU775 177. In Between Petersfield & Chichester on B2146. **Owner:** National Trust **Contact:** The Property Office
Tel: 01730 825415 **Fax:** 01730 825873
E-mail: uppark@nationaltrust.org.uk
Open: Garden, café, shop: 7 Mar-31 Dec, 10am-5pm. Below stairs: 7 Mar-1 Nov, 11am-4:30pm; 7 Nov-31 Dec, 11am-3pm. House: 7 Mar-1 Nov, 12.30pm-4.30pm; 7 Nov-27 Dec, 12pm-3pm. Closed Christmas Eve and Christmas Day. **Admission:** Adult £11.00, Child (5-17yrs) £5.50, Family (2+3) £27.50. Garden only: Adult £6.60, Child £3.30. Gift Aid prices.
Key facts: 📷 No photography in the house. 📷 📷
🔲 WCs at carpark, in shop and in house. Lift to basement of house. 📷
📷 Available for hire. 📷 📷 Enabling dogs only. 📷

Pallant House Gallery

ARUNDEL CATHEDRAL
London Road, Arundel, West Sussex BN18 9AY

French Gothic Cathedral, church of the RC Diocese of Arundel and Brighton built by Henry, 15th Duke of Norfolk and opened 1873.

Location: Map 3:G6. OS Ref TQ015 072. Above junction of A27 and A284.
Contact: Rev. Canon T. Madeley
Tel: 01903 882297
Fax: 01903 885335
E-mail: aruncath1@aol.com
Website: www.arundelcathedral.org
Open: Summer: 9am-6pm. Winter: 9am-dusk. Tue, Wed, Fri, Sat: Mass 10am; Mon and Thu: Mass 8.30am (at Convent of Poor Clares, Crossbush); Sat: Vigil Mass 6.15pm (at Convent of Poor Clares, Crossbush); Sun: Masses 9.30am and 11.15am. Shop open in the summer, Mon-Fri, 10am-4pm and after services and on special occasions and otherwise on request.
Admission: Free.
Key facts: ⬚ ⓘ By arrangement. ✦

BORDE HILL GARDEN 🏛ⓔ
Borde Hill Lane, Haywards Heath, West Sussex, RH16 1XP

Botanical heritage and stunning landscapes make Borde Hill the perfect day out for horticulture enthusiasts, country lovers, and families. The Elizabethan House nestles in the centre of the formal garden which is set as outdoor 'rooms', including the Azalea, Rhododendron, Rose and Italian gardens.Themed events, gift shop, café, tea garden, restaurant, and gallery. Dog friendly. Quote 'Hudsons' for 20% off standard admission (excludes ticketed events). **Location:** Map 4:I5. OS Ref TQ323265. 1½ miles north of Haywards Heath, 20 mins N. of Brighton, or S. of Gatwick on A23 taking exit 10a via Balcombe & Cuckfield.
Contact: Aurelia Mandato **Tel:** 01444 450326 **E-mail:** info@bordehill.co.uk
Website: www.bordehill.co.uk **Open:** Please see website or call for details.
Admission: Adults £8.00, Conc. £7.50, Group £6.00, Child £5.00. Season Tickets.
Key facts: ⬚ ⓘ ⓣ ⬚ WCs. Maps. ⬚ Homemade food. ⬚ Award-winning. ⬚ Garden & House. ⓟ Free parking. ⬚ On leads. ⬚

COWDRAY HERITAGE TRUST 🏛ⓔ
River Ground Stables, Midhurst, West Sussex GU29 9AL

Cowdray is one of the most important survivals of a Tudor nobleman's house. Set within the stunning landscape of Cowdray Park, the house was partially destroyed by fire in 1793. Explore the Tudor Kitchen, Buck Hall, Chapel, Gatehouse, Vaulted Storeroom and Cellars, Visitor Centre and Shop.
Location: Map 3:F5. OS Ref TQ891 216. On the outskirts of Midhurst on A272.
Owner: Cowdray Heritage Trust **Contact:** The Manager
Tel: 01730 812423 **Visitor Centre Tel:** 01730 810781 (during opening hours only) **E-mail:** info@cowdray.org.uk **Website:** www.cowdray.org.uk
Open: Please check our website for opening times. Groups all year round by arrangement. **Admission:** Check website for details.
Key facts: ⬚ ⬚ Full level access, WCs, wheelchair available, limited disabled parking. ⓘ Free audio guides. Children's tour available. ⓟ In Midhurst by bus stand, a short walk along causeway. ⬚ Well behaved dogs on leads welcome.

HIGH BEECHES WOODLAND & WATER GARDEN 🏛ⓔ
High Beeches Lane, Handcross RH17 6HQ

A hidden gem in the High Weald of Sussex. There is much to see and appreciate throughout the seasons. Camellias, magnificent magnolias and hosts of daffodils in spring. In summer wander through glades carpeted with bluebells and surrounded by the colour of many azaleas and rhododendrons. The wildflower meadow is at its best in June and autumn brings a display of glorious autumn colour. **Location:** Map 4:I4. OS Ref TQ275 308. S side of B2110. 1m NE of Handcross **Owner:** High Beeches Gardens Conservation Trust (Reg. Charity 299134) **Contact:** Sarah Bray
Tel: 01444 400589 **E-mail:** gardens@highbeeches.com
Website: www.highbeeches.com **Open:** Apr-1 Nov: daily except Weds, 1-5pm (last adm. 4.30pm). Coaches/guided tours anytime, by appointment only.
Admission: Adult £7.00, Child (under 14yrs) Free. Group concessions (20+). Guided tours for groups £10pp. **Key facts:** ⬚ Partial. WCs. Tearoom fully accessible. ⬚ ⬚ Licensed. ⓘ By arrangement. ⓟ ⬚ Guide dogs only. ⬚ ⬚

CHURCH OF ST JOHN THE EVANGELIST 🔥
St John's Street, Chichester, West Sussex PO19 1UR

Built in 1812, the delightfully elegant design of St John's reflects the importance of the evangelical movement. Unusually, it was not built as a parish church, but was privately funded and run by trustees of the evangelical movement of the Church of England. Ministers were largely paid by the income from renting seats in the church. Pews in the upper gallery, where the rich sat apart from the lower orders, still have their own hire numbers. These originally had separate entrances so that those above could enter by different doorways from the poor who sat on benches below. The church is arranged rather like a theatre, with an impressive triple-decker pulpit taking centre stage with only a small chancel behind. **Location:** OS Ref SU864 046. In St John's Street, which leads off East Street. **Contact:** The Churches Conservation Trust on 0845 303 2760 (Mon-Fri)
Website: www.visitchurches.org.uk **Open:** Open daily from 10am-4pm.
Admission: Free entry - donations welcome.

ST PETER'S CHURCH 🔥
Preston Drove, Preston Park, Brighton BN1 6SD

This simple square-towered church, built from flint rubble, is 800-years old. It stands in the beautiful landscaped park of Preston Manor. Now all looks serene but in 1906 the church was damaged by fire and nearly lost its greatest treasures - its 14th Century wallpaintings. Although fragments, you can pick out the nativity with a bowl-shaped crib and the infant Jesus. The violent scene of Thomas Becket's murder in Canterbury is clearer - you can see one of the four knights, possibly William de Tracy, plunge his sword into Becket's head and you can see blood dripping from the hand of Edward Grim, Becket's chaplain, who was injured while trying to protect him. Sumptuous 20th Century restoration brought the church new life after the fire, and today the walls, windows and floors around the altar glow with a gorgeous mix of pattern and colour. **Location:** OS Ref TQ304 064. Immediately adjacent to Preston Manor which is at the northern tip of Preston Park on the A23 in Brighton. **Website:** www.visitchurches.org.uk
Open: Open daily, 11am-3pm and sometimes longer in the summer.

CHURCH OF THE HOLY SEPULCHRE 🔥
Church Park Lane, Warminghurst RH20 3AW

The setting of this 13th Century sandstone church is lovely but the building itself surpasses all expectations. The unspoilt 18th Century interior contains silvery oak pews, a clerk's desk, a triple-decker pulpit, a curved brace roof and an elegant three-arched wooden screen. Above the screen is a wonderful painting of the coat of arms of Queen Anne, with theatrical swags of painted drapery. On the walls are lovely memorials to the Shelley and Butler families. Look for the clerk's chair - it suggests that one of the past parish officials was very well fed!
Location: OS Ref TQ117 169. Off northern end of main street, just off A24.
Contact: The Churches Conservation Trust on 0845 303 2760 (Mon-Fri).
Website: www.visitchurches.org.uk
Open: Usually open daily, 10am-4pm; at other times keyholder nearby.
Admission: Free entry - donations welcome.
Key facts: ✦

DENMANS GARDEN
Denmans Lane, Fontwell, Denmans Lane BN18 0SU

Unique 4 acre garden, home of renowned garden designer John Brookes MBE. Plant centre and Café. **Location:** Map 3:G6. OS Ref SU944 070.
Tel: 01243 542808 **E-mail:** denmans@denmans-garden.co.uk
Website: www.denmans-garden.co.uk **Open:** 10am-4pm daily all year - check website for winter opening times. **Admission:** Adults £4.95, OAP £4.75.

THE ROYAL PAVILION
Brighton, East Sussex BN1 1EE

Universally acclaimed as one of the most exotically beautiful buildings in the British Isles, the Royal Pavilion is the former seaside residence of King George IV.
Location: Map 4:I6. OS Ref TQ312 041. **Tel:** 03000 290900 **E-mail:** visitor.services@brighton-hove.gov.uk **Website:** www.royalpavilion.org.uk
Open: Please see website for up to date opening and admission details.

VISITOR INFORMATION

■ **Owner**
English Heritage

■ **Address**
Osborne House
East Cowes
Isle of Wight
PO32 6JX

■ **Location**
Map 3:D6
OS Ref. SZ516 948
1 mile SE of East Cowes.
Ferry: Isle of Wight ferry
terminals. Red Funnel, East
Cowes 1½ miles Tel: 02380
334010. Wightlink,
Fishbourne 4 miles Tel:
0870 582 7744

■ **Contact**
The House Administrator
Tel: 01983 200022
**Venue Hire and
Hospitality Tel:** 01983
203055
E-mail:
customers@english-
heritage.org.uk

■ **Opening Times**
Please visit www.english-
heritage.org.uk for
opening times and prices
and the most up-to-date
information.

■ **Special Events**
There is an exciting events
programme available
throughout the year, for
further details please
contact the property or visit
the website.

Conference/Function

ROOM	Max Cap
Duchess of Kent Suite	Standing 70 Seated 30
Durbar Hall	Standing/Seated 40
Marquee	Large scale events possible
Upper Terrace	Standing 250
Victoria Hall	Standing 120 Seated 80

OSBORNE HOUSE ⊞
www.english-heritage.org.uk/osborne

Take an intimate glimpse into the family life of Britain's longest reigning monarch and the house Queen Victoria loved to call home.

Osborne House was a peaceful, seaside retreat of Queen Victoria, Prince Albert and their family. Step inside and marvel at the richness of the State Apartments including the lavish Indian Durbar Room.

The Queen died at the house in 1901 and many of the rooms have been preserved almost unaltered ever since. The nursery bedroom remains just as it was in the 1870s when Queen Victoria's first grandchildren came to stay.

Don't miss the Swiss Cottage, a charming chalet in the grounds built for teaching the royal children domestic skills. Enjoy the beautiful gardens with their stunning views over the Solent, the fruit and flower Victorian Walled Garden and Queen Victoria's private beach – now open to visitors for the first time.

Osborne hosts events throughout the year, and Queen Victoria's palace-by-the-sea offers both the superb coastal location and facilities for those who want to entertain on a grand scale in style.

KEY FACTS

Available for corporate and private hire. Suitable for filming, concerts, drama. No photography in the house.

Private and corporate hire.

WCs.

Nov-Mar for pre-booked guided tours only. Tours allow visitors to see the Royal Apartments and private rooms.

Ample.

Please book. Education room.

BASILDON PARK 🍂
Lower Basildon, Reading, Berkshire RG8 9NR
Tel: 0118 984 3040 **E-mail:** basildonpark@nationaltrust.org.uk

ST BARTHOLOMEW'S CHURCH 🏛
Lower Basildon, Reading, Berkshire RG8 9NH
Tel: 0845 303 2760 **E-mail:** central@thecct.org.uk

ST MARGARET'S CHURCH 🏛
Catmore, Newbury, Berkshire RG20 7HN
Tel: 0845 303 2760 **E-mail:** central@thecct.org.uk

ST MARY'S CHURCH 🏛
Ermin Street, Woodlands St Mary, Berkshire RG17 7SR
Tel: 0845 303 2760 **E-mail:** central@thecct.org.uk

THE SAVILL GARDEN
Windsor Great Park, Wick Lane, Windsor, Berkshire TW20 0UU
Tel: 01753 847518 **E-mail:** emma.twyman@thecrownestate.co.uk

CHURCH OF THE ASSUMPTION 🏛
Hartwell House, Hartwell, Aylesbury HP17 8NR
Tel: 0845 303 2760 **E-mail:** central@thecct.org.uk

CLAYDON HOUSE 🍂
Claydon House, Middle Claydon, Buckinghamshire MK18 2EY
Tel: 01296 730349 **E-mail:** claydon@nationaltrust.org.uk

ST LAWRENCE'S CHURCH 🏛
Broughton Village, Milton Keynes, Bucks MK10 9AA
Tel: 0845 303 2760 **E-mail:** central@thecct.org.uk

ST MARY'S CHURCH 🏛
Church End, Edlesborough, Dunstable, Bucks LU6 2EP
Tel: 0845 303 2760 **E-mail:** central@thecct.org.uk

ST MARY'S CHURCH 🏛
Fleet Marston, Aylesbury, Buckinghamshire HP18 0PZ
Tel: 0845 303 2760 **E-mail:** central@thecct.org.uk

ST MARY'S CHURCH 🏛
Church Road, Pitstone, Leighton Buzzard LU7 9HA
Tel: 0845 303 2760 **E-mail:** central@thecct.org.uk

WEST WYCOMBE PARK 🍂
West Wycombe, High Wycombe, Buckinghamshire HP14 3AJ
Tel: 01494 513569

ALL SAINTS' CHURCH 🏛
Little Somborne, Stockbridge, Hampshire SO20 6QT
Tel: 0845 303 2760 **E-mail:** central@thecct.org.uk

CHURCH OF ST JOHN THE BAPTIST 🏛
Upper Eldon, Stockbridge, Hampshire SO20 6QN
Tel: 0845 303 2760 **E-mail:** central@thecct.org.uk

CHURCH OF ST PETER AD VINCULA 🏛
Colemore, Alton, Hampshire GU34 3RX
Tel: 0845 303 2760 **E-mail:** central@thecct.org.uk

JANE AUSTEN'S HOUSE MUSEUM
Chawton, Alton, Hampshire GU34 1SD
Tel: 01420 83262 **E-mail:** enquiries@jahmusm.org.uk

ST MARY THE VIRGIN OLD CHURCH 🏛
Preston Candover, Basingstoke, Hampshire RG25 2EN
Tel: 0845 303 2760 **E-mail:** central@thecct.org.uk

ST MARY'S CHURCH 🏛
Church Lane, Hartley Wintney, Hook, Hampshire RG27 8EE
Tel: 0845 303 2760 **E-mail:** central@thecct.org.uk

ST MARY'S CHURCH 🏛
Ashley, Kings Somborne, Stockbridge, Hampshire SO20 6RJ
Tel: 0845 303 2760 **E-mail:** central@thecct.org.uk

ST NICHOLAS' CHURCH 🏛
Freefolk, Laverstoke, Whitchurch, Hampshire RG28 7NW
Tel: 0845 303 2760 **E-mail:** central@thecct.org.uk

SIR HAROLD HILLIER GARDENS
Jermyns Lane, Ampfield, Romsey, Hampshire SO51 0QA
Tel: 01794 369318 **E-mail:** info@hilliergardens.org.uk

THE VYNE 🍂
Sherborne St John, Basingstoke RG24 9HL
Tel: 01256 883858 **E-mail:** thevyne@nationaltrust.org.uk

WINCHESTER CATHEDRAL
9 The Close, Winchester SO23 9LS
Tel: 01962 857200 **E-mail:** visits@winchester-cathedral.org.uk

ALL SAINTS' CHURCH 🏛
Church Lane, West Stourmouth, Canterbury, Kent CT3 1HT
Tel: 0845 303 2760 **E-mail:** central@thecct.org.uk

CHILHAM CASTLE
Canterbury, Kent CT4 8DB
Tel: 01227 733100 **E-mail:** chilhamcastleinfo@gmail.com

CHURCH OF ST MARY THE VIRGIN 🏛
The Drove, Fordwich, Canterbury, Kent CT2 0DE
Tel: 0845 303 2760 **E-mail:** central@thecct.org.uk

DEAL CASTLE ⊞
Victoria Road, Deal, Kent CT14 7BA
Tel: 01304 372762 **E-mail:** customers@english-heritage.org.uk

EMMETTS GARDEN 🍂
Ide Hill, Sevenoaks, Kent TN14 6BA
Tel: 01732 750367 **E-mail:** emmetts@nationaltrust.org.uk

GREAT COMP GARDEN
Comp Lane, Platt, Borough Green, Kent TN15 8QS
Tel: 01732 886154 **E-mail:** info@greatcompgarden.co.uk

GROOMBRIDGE PLACE GARDENS
Groombridge, Tunbridge Wells, Kent TN3 9QG
Tel: 01892 861 444 **E-mail:** carrie@groombridge.co.uk

HALL PLACE & GARDENS 🏛
Bourne Road, Bexley, Kent DA5 1PQ
Tel: 01322 526574 **E-mail:** info@hallplace.org.uk

QUEBEC HOUSE 🍂
Westerham, Kent TN16 1TD
Tel: 01732 868381

Blenheim Palace, Oxfordshire

ST BENEDICT'S CHURCH ⋔
Paddlesworth Road, Paddlesworth, Snodland, Kent ME6 5DR
Tel: 0845 303 2760 **E-mail:** central@thecct.org.uk

ST CATHERINE'S CHURCH ⋔
Kingsdown, Sittingbourne, Kent ME9 0AS
Tel: 0845 303 2760 **E-mail:** central@thecct.org.uk

ST CLEMENT'S CHURCH ⋔
Knowlton Court, Knowlton, Canterbury, Kent CT3 1PT
Tel: 0845 303 2760 **E-mail:** central@thecct.org.uk

ST MARY'S CHURCH ⋔
Church Street, Lower Higham, Rochester, Kent ME3 7LS
Tel: 0845 303 2760 **E-mail:** central@thecct.org.uk

ST MARY'S CHURCH ⋔
Luddenham Court, Luddenham, Faversham, Kent ME13 0TH
Tel: 0845 303 2760 **E-mail:** central@thecct.org.uk

ST MARY'S CHURCH ⋔
Old Church Road, Burham, Rochester, Kent ME1 3XY
Tel: 0845 303 2760 **E-mail:** central@thecct.org.uk

ST MARY'S CHURCH ⋔
Strand Street, Sandwich, Kent CT13 9EU
Tel: 0845 303 2760 **E-mail:** central@thecct.org.uk

ST PETER'S CHURCH ⋔
The Street, Swingfield Street, Swingfield, Kent CT15 7HA
Tel: 0845 303 2760 **E-mail:** central@thecct.org.uk

SCOTNEY CASTLE ⚘
Lamberhurst, Tunbridge Wells, Kent TN3 8JN
Tel: 01892 893820 **E-mail:** scotneycastle@nationaltrust.org.uk

ALL SAINTS' CHURCH ⋔
Nuneham Park, Nuneham Courtenay, Oxfordshire OX44 9PQ
Tel: 0845 303 2760 **E-mail:** central@thecct.org.uk

ALL SAINTS' CHURCH ⋔
Castle Road, Shirburn, Oxford, Oxfordshire OX49 5DL
Tel: 0845 303 2760 **E-mail:** central@thecct.org.uk

CHASTLETON HOUSE ⚘
Chastleton, Nr Moreton-In-Marsh, Oxfordshire
Tel: 01608 674981 **E-mail:** chastleton@nationaltrust.org.uk

CHURCH OF ST JOHN THE BAPTIST ⋔
Mongewell, Wallingford, Oxfordshire OX10 8BU
Tel: 0845 303 2760 **E-mail:** central@thecct.org.uk

ST KATHERINE'S CHURCH ⋔
Chislehampton, Oxford, Oxfordshire OX44 7XF
Tel: 0845 303 2760 **E-mail:** central@thecct.org.uk

ST MARY'S CHURCH ⋔
Newnham Murren, Wallingford, Oxfordshire OX10 8BW
Tel: 0845 303 2760 **E-mail:** central@thecct.org.uk

ST PETER'S CHURCH ⋔
Thames Street, Wallingford, Oxfordshire OX10 0BH
Tel: 0845 303 2760 **E-mail:** central@thecct.org.uk

CLAREMONT LANDSCAPE GARDEN ⚘
Portsmouth Road, Esher, Surrey KT10 9JG
Tel: 01372 467806 **E-mail:** claremont@nationaltrust.org.uk

LOSELEY PARK ⛫ⓕ
Events Office, Loseley Park, Guildford, Surrey GU3 1HS
Tel: 01483 304440 **E-mail:** enquiries @loseleypark.co.uk

RHS GARDEN WISLEY
Nr Woking, Surrey GU23 6QB
Tel: 0845 260 9000

ST GEORGE'S CHURCH ⋔
Esher Park Avenue, Esher, Surrey KT10 9PX
Tel: 0845 303 2760 **E-mail:** central@thecct.org.uk

CHURCH OF ST MARY MAGDALENE ⋔
Ford Road, Tortington, Arundel, West Sussex BN18 0FD
Tel: 0845 303 2760 **E-mail:** central@thecct.org.uk

CHURCH OF ST MARY THE VIRGIN ⋔
North Stoke, Arundel, West Sussex BN18 9LS
Tel: 0845 303 2760 **E-mail:** central@thecct.org.uk

HASTINGS CASTLE
Castle Hill Road, West Hill, Hastings, East Sussex TN34 3AR
Tel: 01424 444412 **E-mail:** bookings@discoverhastings.co.uk

LEWES PRIORY
Town Hall, High Street, Lewes, East Sussex BN7 2QS
Tel: 01273 486185 **E-mail:** enquiries@lewespriory.org.uk

MICHELHAM PRIORY ⛫
Upper Dicker, Hailsham, East Sussex BN27 3QS
Tel: 01323 844224 **E-mail:** adminmich@sussexpast.co.uk

PASHLEY MANOR GARDENS ⛫ⓕ
Pashley Manor, Ticehurst, Wadhurst, East Sussex TN5 7HE
Tel: 01580 200888 **E-mail:** info@pashleymanorgardens.com

PRESTON MANOR
Preston Drove, Brighton, East Sussex BN1 6SD
Tel: 03000 290900 **E-mail:** visitor.services@brighton-hove.gov.uk

ST ANDREW'S CHURCH ⋔
Waterloo Street, Hove, East Sussex BN3 1AQ
Tel: 0845 303 2760 **E-mail:** central@thecct.org.uk

ST BOTOLPH'S CHURCH ⋔
Annington Road, Botolphs, West Sussex BN44 3WB
Tel: 0845 303 2760 **E-mail:** central@thecct.org.uk

ST WILFRID'S CHURCH ⋔
Rectory Lane, Church Norton, Selsey, West Sussex PO20 9DT
Tel: 0845 303 2760 **E-mail:** central@thecct.org.uk

WEST DEAN COLLEGE & GARDENS ⛫
West Dean, Chichester, West Sussex PO18 0RX
Tel: Gardens: 01243 818210 **E-mail:** enquiries@westdean.org.uk

NUNWELL HOUSE & GARDENS ⛫
Coach Lane, Brading, Isle Of Wight PO36 0JQ
Tel: 01983 407240 **E-mail:** info@nunwellhouse.co.uk

Powderham Castle,
Devon

The Peto Garden at Iford Manor, Wiltshire

Channel Islands
Cornwall
Devon
Dorset
Gloucestershire
Somerset
Wiltshire

South West

While the coast and countryside of the West Country draws many eager visitors, the South Western counties offer some of our most unexpected country houses and outstanding gardens.

New Entries for 2015:
- Hemerdon House
- Owlpen Manor
- Sausmarez Manor

Gloucester-shire

Wiltshire

Somerset

Devon

Dorset

Cornwall

Channel Islands

Find stylish hotels with a personal welcome and good cuisine in the South West. More information on page 364.

- Alexandra Hotel
- The Berry Head Hotel
- Bridge House Hotel
- Budock Vean Hotel
- The Cottage Hotel
- Dart Marina Hotel & Spa
- Grasmere House Hotel
- Hannafore Point Hotel
- Ilsington Country House Hotel
- The Inn at Fossebridge

- Langdon Court Country House Hotel
- The Moorings Hotel
- Mortons House Hotel
- The Pear Tree at Purton
- Plantation House Hotel
- Plumber Manor
- The Queens Arms
- Trevalsa Court Country House Hotel
- The White Hart Royal Hotel

SIGNPOST
SELECTED PREMIER HOTELS 2015

www.signpost.co.uk

189

South West - England

SAUSMAREZ MANOR
SAINT MARTIN, GUERNSEY, CHANNEL ISLANDS GY4 6SG
www.sausmarezmanor.co.uk www.artparks.co.uk

A delightful Manor to tour, crammed with history of the family since C1220 with the façade built at the bequest of one of the first Governors of New York. It is regarded as the finest example of Queen Anne Colonial Architecture, voted the Best private Attraction in 2013 by the Visitors to Guernsey. The Wild Subtropical Garden, with its collection of Exotica, Bamboos, Lilies, Brugmansias, Camellias, Banana & Palm trees and Tree Ferns & tender plants draws people worldwide as does the changing selection of sculptures spread throughout. Also the ride on train, 9 hole Par 3, the Copper Smithy Tearoom, Craft shop & Saturday Farmers' Country Market.

Location: Map 2:O11. 2m S of St Peter Port, clearly signposted.
Owner/Contact: Peter de Sausmarez
Tel: 01481 235571 / 01481 235655.
E-mail: sausmarezmanor@cwgsy.net
Open: Daily Apr-Oct, 10am-5pm.
Admission: House £7.00, Subtropical Gardens/Sculpture Park £6.00, P&P £6.00, Train £2.00, everything else free. Check website for concessions.
Key facts: 🖰 🖸 🕇 🖤 🖾 Guided tours of House Easter-Oct. 🅿 🖩 🖾 Guide dogs only. 🖸 2 holiday flats available. 🔺 🌐 🖾 €

© EHPL / Skyscan

VISITOR INFORMATION

■ **Owner**
English Heritage

■ **Address**
Tintagel
Cornwall
PL34 0HE

■ **Location**
Map 1:F7
**OS Ref. Landranger
Sheet 200 SX048 891**
On Tintagel Head, ½m
along uneven track from
Tintagel.

■ **Contact**
Visitor Operations Team
Tel: 01840 770328
E-mail: tintagel.castle@
english-heritage.org.uk

■ **Opening Times**
Please visit the website for
opening times, admission
prices and the most up-to-
date information.

■ **Special Events**
There is an exciting events
programme available
throughout the year, for
further details please
contact the property or visit
the website.

TINTAGEL CASTLE ▦

www.english-heritage.org.uk/tintagel

Tintagel Castle is a magical day with its wonderful location, set high on the rugged North Cornwall coast.

Steeped in legend and mystery; said to be the birthplace of King Arthur, you can still visit the nearby Merlin's Cave. The castle also features in the tale of Tristan and Isolde.

Joined to the mainland by a narrow neck of land, Tintagel Island faces the full force of the Atlantic. On the mainland, the remains of the medieval castle represent only one phase in a long history of occupation.

The remains of the 13th Century castle are breathtaking. Steep stone steps, stout walls and rugged windswept cliff edges encircle the Great Hall, where Richard Earl of Cornwall once feasted.

KEY FACTS

 WC. Video film shown about the Legend of Arthur.

 No vehicles. Parking (not EH) in village only.

Dogs on leads only.

© English Heritage

© English Heritage

BOCONNOC 🏛
THE ESTATE OFFICE, BOCONNOC, LOSTWITHIEL, CORNWALL PL22 0RG
www.boconnoc.com

Boconnoc House the winner of the 2012 HHA/Sotheby's Award for Restoration and the Georgian Group Award was bought with the proceeds of the Pitt Diamond in 1717. Three Prime Ministers, a history of duels and the architect Sir John Soane play a part in the story of this unique estate. The beautiful woodland garden, the Georgian Bath House, Soane Stable Yard, 15th Century Church and naturesque landscape tempt the explorer. The Boconnoc Music Award for ensembles from the Royal College of Music, the Cornwall Spring Flower Show and fairy-tale weddings are part of Boconnoc today, in between filming, fashion shoots, corporate days and private parties. Groups by appointment (15-150).
Location: Map 1:G8. OS Ref 148 605. A38 from Plymouth, Liskeard or from Bodmin to Dobwalls, then A390 to East Taphouse and follow signs.
Owner: Anthony Fortescue Esq. **Contact:** Sam Cox

Tel: 01208 872507
Fax: 01208 873836
E-mail: info@boconnoc.com
Open: Garden: 3, 10 & 17 May: Suns 2-5pm. Special Events: 28 Feb VOTWO Glow in the Park Run, 28 & 29 Mar CGS Spring Flower Show, 17 May Dog Show, 20 & 21 Jun Endurance GB Ride, Jul Boconnoc Music Award, 24-26 Jul Steam Fair. Group bookings daily by appointment.
Admission: House: £5.00, Garden: £5.00. Children under 12yrs free.
Key facts: 🖻 🔳 Conferences. 🔲 Partial. 🖥 Licensed. 🚹 By arrangement. 🅿 🔳 🔳 In grounds, on leads. 🔳 19 doubles (13 en suite). Holiday and residential houses to let. 🔳 Church or Civil ceremony. 🔳 🔳

CAERHAYS CASTLE & GARDEN 🏛ⓕ
CAERHAYS, GORRAN, ST AUSTELL, CORNWALL PL26 6LY
www.caerhays.co.uk

One of the very few Nash built castles still left standing - situated within approximately 120 acres of informal woodland gardens created by J C Williams, who sponsored plant hunting expeditions to China at the turn of the century. As well as guided tours of the house from March to June visitors will see some of the magnificent selection of plants brought back by the intrepid plant hunters of the early 1900s these include not only a national collection of magnolias but a wide range of rhododendrons and the camellias which Caerhays and the Williams familly are associated with worldwide.
Location: Map 1:F9. OS Ref SW972 415. S coast of Cornwall - between Mevagissey and Portloe. 9m SW of St Austell.
Owner: F J Williams Esq **Contact:** Lucinda Rimmington
Tel: 01872 501310 **Fax:** 01872 501870 **E-mail:** enquiries@caerhays.co.uk
Open: House: 23 Mar-19 Jun: Mon-Fri only (including BHs), tours 11.30am,

1.00pm and 2.30pm, booking recommended. Gardens: 16 Feb-21 Jun: daily (including BHs), 10am-5pm (last admission 4pm).
Caerhays Summer Fete – Sun 21 Jun.
Admission: House: £8.00. Gardens: £8.00. House & Gardens: £13.00. Group tours: £9.50 by arrangement. Groups please contact Estate Office.
Key facts: 🚹 No photography in house. 🖻 Selling a range of Caerhays products & many other garden orientated gifts. 🔳 Located beside entrance point. 🔳 The Georgian Hall is available for hire for meetings. 🔳 🖥 The Magnolia Tea Rooms serve a wide range of foods using locally sourced produce. 🚹 Obligatory. By arrangement. 🅿 Limited for large coaches. 🔳 🔳 On leads. 🔳 Caerhays has a selection of 5 * properties available for hire for self-catering holidays. 🔳 Weddings can be held at The Vean or the Coastguard's Lookout. Please visit www.caerhays.co.uk for more information. 🔳

Register for news and special offers at **www.hudsonsheritage.com**

PRIDEAUX PLACE ⓕ
PADSTOW, CORNWALL PL28 8RP

www.prideauxplace.co.uk

Tucked away above the busy port of Padstow, the home of the Prideaux family for over 400 years, is surrounded by gardens and wooded grounds overlooking a deer park and the Camel estuary to the moors beyond. The house still retains its 'E' shape Elizabethan front and contains fine paintings and furniture. Now a major international film location, this family home is one of the brightest jewels in Cornwall's crown. The historic garden is undergoing major restoration work and offers some of the best views in the county. A cornucopia of Cornish history under one roof.

Location: Map 1:E8. OS Ref SW913 756. 5m from A39 Newquay/Wadebridge link road. Signposted by Historic House signs.

Owner/Contact: Peter Prideaux-Brune Esq
Tel: 01841 532411 **Fax:** 01841 532945 **E-mail:** office@prideauxplace.co.uk
Open: Easter Sun 5 Apr to Thu 9 Apr. Sun 10 May to Thu 8 Oct. Grounds & Tearoom: 12.30-5pm. House Tours: 1.30-4pm (last tour).
Admission: House & Grounds: Adult £8.50, Child £2.00.
Grounds only: Adult £4.00, Child £1.00. Groups (15+) discounts apply.
Key facts: ℹ Open air theatre, open air concerts, car rallies, art exhibitions, charity events. ◻ ⊤ By arrangement. ⅃ Partial. Ground floor & grounds. ⬛ Fully licensed. Ⓡ Obligatory. Ⓟ ■ By arrangement. ⬛ On leads. ⁑ By arrangement. ⬛

ST MICHAEL'S MOUNT ⚜
MARAZION, NR PENZANCE, CORNWALL TR17 0HS

www.stmichaelsmount.co.uk / www.nationaltrust.org.uk

This beautiful island has become an icon for Cornwall and has magnificent views of Mount's Bay from its summit. There the church and castle, whose origins date from the 12th Century, have at various times acted as a Benedictine priory, a place of pilgrimage, a fortress, a mansion house and now a magnet for visitors from all over the world. Following the Civil War, the island was acquired by the St Aubyn family who still live in the castle today alongside a 30-strong community of islanders. **Location:** Map 1:C10. OS Ref SW515 300. 3 miles East of Penzance.
Owner: National Trust **Contact:** Charlotte Somers, St Aubyn Estates, King's Road, Marazion, Cornwall TR17 OEL
Tel: 01736 710507 (710265 tide information)
E-mail: enquiries@stmichaelsmount.co.uk
Open: Castle: 15 Mar-1 Nov, Sun-Fri, 10.30am-5pm (29 Jun–31 Aug,

10.30am-5.30pm). Ticket Office closes 45 mins before closing times.
Gardens: 20 Apr-1 Jul Mon-Fri; 2 Jul-28 Aug Thu & Fri; 3 Sep-25 Sep Thu & Fri, 10.30am-5pm (5.30pm Jul & Aug).
Admission: Castle: Adult £8.50, Child (under 17) £4.00, Family £21.00, 1 Adult Family £12.50. Booked Groups: £7.50. Garden: Adult £5.50, Child £2.50.
Combined Castle & Garden: Adult £11.50, Child £5.50, Family £28.50, 1 Adult Family £17.00.
Key facts: ℹ Parking on mainland (not NT). Dogs not permitted in the castle or gardens. For a full events calendar throughout the season, please check the website. ◻ ⬛ ⅃ Partial. WCs. ⬛ Licensed. ⊞ Licensed. Ⓡ By arrangement. Tel for details. Ⓟ On mainland, including coach parking (not NT.) ■
⬛ Guide dogs only. ⁑ ⬛

© Pencarrow

PENCARROW 🏠Ⓕ
Washaway, Bodmin, Cornwall PL30 3AG
www.pencarrow.co.uk

Owned, loved and lived in by the family. Georgian house and Grade II* listed gardens. Superb collection of portraits, furniture and porcelain. Marked walks through 50 acres of beautiful formal and woodland gardens, Victorian rockery, Italian garden, over 700 different varieties of rhododendrons, lake, Iron Age hill fort and icehouse.

Location: Map 1:F8. OS Ref SX040 711. Between Bodmin and Wadebridge. 4m NW of Bodmin off A389 & B3266 at Washaway.

Owner: Molesworth-St Aubyn family **Contact:** Administrator

Tel: 01208 841369 **Fax:** 01208 841722 **E-mail:** info@pencarrow.co.uk

Open: House: 29 Mar–1 Oct 2015, Sun-Thu, 11am-4pm (guided tour only - last tour of the House at 3pm). Café & shop 11am-5pm. (House, cafe and shop closed Fridays and Saturdays.) Gardens: 1 Mar-31 Oct, Daily, 10am-5.30pm.

Admission: House & Garden: Adult £10.50, Conc. £9.50, Child (5-16 years) £5.00. Grounds only: Adult £5.50, Conc. £5.00, Child (5-16 years) £2.50. Discounted family tickets and group rates available.

Key facts: ℹ️ Cafe, Gift and plant shop, small children's play area. 📷 🎁 🍴 ♿ 🐾 🎟 Obligatory. 🅿 Free. 🚌 🐕 In grounds. 🔺 🎗

PORT ELIOT HOUSE & GARDENS 🏠Ⓕ
St. Germans, Saltash, Cornwall PL12 5ND
www.porteliot.co.uk

Port Eliot is an ancient, hidden gem, set in stunning fairytale grounds which nestle beside a secret estuary in South East Cornwall. It has the rare distinction of being a Grade I Listed house, park and gardens. This is due in part to the work of Sir John Soane, who worked his magic on the house and Humphrey Repton, who created the park and garden. Explore the treasures in the house. Gaze at masterpieces by Reynolds and Van Dyck. Decipher the Lenkiewicz Round Room Riddle Mural. Still a family home, you will be beguiled by the warm atmosphere.

Location: Map 1:H8. OS Ref SX359 578. Situated in the village of St Germans on B3249 in SE Cornwall. **Owner:** The Earl of St Germans

Contact: Port Eliot Estate Office **Tel:** 01503 230211 **E-mail:** info@porteliot.co.uk

Open: 1 Mar 2015 to 28 Jun 2015 except Fri & 6th & 7th June, 2pm-6pm (last admission 5pm). Tea Rooms available. **Admission:** House & Garden: Adult £8.00, Student/Senior/Group (20+)/Visitors arriving by public transport £7.00, Children £4.00. Family £20.00. Grounds only: Adult £5.00, Children £2.00. **Key facts:** ℹ️ No photography. ♿ Suitable. WCs. 🖥 www.thelonggallery.co.uk 01503 230753. 🎟 🎗 By arrangement. 🅿 🚌 🐕 In grounds. Guide dogs only in house. 🔺 🎗

ST ANTHONY'S CHURCH 🏠
St Anthony-in-Roseland, Portscatho, Truro, Cornwall TR2 5EZ

Behind the turreted ancestral home of the Spry family, and looking across the creek to St Mawes, St Anthony-in-Roseland is unusual in that it still has its original medieval cruciform plan, despite being extensively restored in the 19th Century.

During the 12th Century, much of the land at St Anthony was owned by the Augustinian Priory at Plympton, Devon; it was during this time that the Prior established the church here. By the 19th Century the chancel was in ruins. Samuel Spry, the MP for Bodmin, employed his cousin, the Revd Clement Carlyon, to oversee the restoration of the church. Carlyon, an amateur architect, rebuilt the chancel and installed the wooden roofs, floor tiles and stained glass. He also designed many of the furnishings, including the chunky pulpit and pews, some of which he may have carved himself. **Location:** OS Ref SW855 320. 20m SW of St Austell, off A3078; opposite St Mawes & 4m S of Gerrans.
Website: www.visitchurches.org.uk **Open:** Open daily.

TREWITHEN 🏠Ⓕ
Grampound Road, Near Truro, Cornwall TR2 4DD

Trewithen is an historic estate near Truro, Cornwall. Owned and lived in by the same family for 300 years, it is both private home and national treasure. The woodland gardens are outstanding with 24 champion trees and famously rare and highly prized plants. The garden is one of only 30 International Camellia Society Gardens of Excellence in the world and is also RHS recommended. Tours of the house prove equally memorable. **Location:** Map 1:E9. OS Ref SW914 524. Grampound Road, near Truro, Cornwall. **Owner:** A M J Galsworthy

Contact: The Estate Office **Tel:** 01726 883647 **Fax:** 01726 882301

E-mail: info@trewithengardens.co.uk **Website:** www.trewithengardens.co.uk

Open: House & Gardens: Mar-Jun. House open Mon & Tue afternoons, including Aug BH Mon. Please contact us or visit website for further opening times.

Admission: Adult £8.50, Children U12 Free. Combined entry & group rates also available. Please contact us or visit website for more information.

Key facts: ℹ️ No photography in house. 📷 🎁 ♿ WCs. 🖥 🎟 By arrangement. 🅿 🐕 On leads.

LANHYDROCK 🌿
Lanhydrock, Bodmin, Cornwall PL30 5AD

Lanhydrock is the grandest house in Cornwall, set in a glorious landscape of gardens, parkland and woods overlooking the valley of the River Fowey.
Location: Map 1:F8. OS Ref SX085 636. **Tel:** 01208 265950
E-mail: lanhydrock@nationaltrust.org.uk **Website:** www.nationaltrust.org.uk/lanhydrock **Open:** Please see website for most up to date times and prices.

LAWRENCE HOUSE MUSEUM 🌿
9 Castle Street, Launceston, Cornwall PL15 8BA

Fine Georgian House used as a 'little jewel' of a museum and Mayor's Parlour.
Location: Map 1:H7. OS Ref SX330 848. Launceston **Tel:** 01566 773277
E-mail: lawrencehousemuseum@yahoo.co.uk
Website: www.lawrencehousemuseum.org **Open:** Apr-Oct Mon-Fri. 10.30am-4.30pm. Last entry 4.00pm. Occasional Sats. Open BHs.
Admission: Free - Donations welcomed.

© Dave Lacker

St Michael's Mount

CLOVELLY
www.clovelly.co.uk

Most visitors consider Clovelly to be unique. Whatever your view, it is a world of difference not to be missed.

From Elizabethan days until today, Clovelly village has been in private ownership, which has helped preserve its original character. The main traffic-free street known as 'up-a-long' and 'down-a-long', tumbles its cobbled way down to the tiny harbour, which is protected by an ancient stone breakwater. It is a descent through flower-strewn cottages broken only by little passageways and winding lanes that lead off to offer the prospect of more picturesque treasures.

At the top of the cliffs you will find the Visitor Centre in which there is a range of gift shops, a café and an audio-visual theatre where visitors are treated to a history of the village. Just beyond the centre there is the Stable Yard with a pottery and silk workshop. The steep cobbled village street is traffic-free and donkeys and sledges are the only means of transport.

The New Inn, halfway down the street, is 400 years old and the Red Lion is right on the quay. Both inns have long histories and an atmosphere rarely found in our modern world. Together with wonderful sea views, the effect is a perfect maritime experience. There are also stunning coastal and woodland walks along the cliff tops.

Next to the C13th parish church of All Saints, you can visit Clovelly Court Garden. It is a classic example of a lovingly restored Victorian walled kitchen garden and includes magnificent lean-to glasshouses sheltering Mediterranean fruits.

Access to the village is restricted to pedestrians only via the Visitor Centre with a Land Rover taxi service to and from the harbour (Easter to October) for which there is a small charge.

KEY FACTS

 Rubber soled, low heel shoes are recommended.

🛍️

✻

♿ Partial.

☕ Licensed.

🍴 Licensed.

🧑 By arrangement.

🅿️ P

🏛️

🐕 On leads.

🛏️ 24 double, 1 single, all en suite.

💒 Civil Wedding Licence.

❄️

❆

VISITOR INFORMATION

■ Owner
The Hon. John Rous

■ Address
Clovelly
Nr Bideford
N Devon
EX39 5TA

■ Location
Map 1:H5
OS Ref. SS248 319
On A39 10 miles W of Bideford, 15 miles E of Bude. Turn off at 'Clovelly Cross' roundabout and follow signs to car park.
Bus: From Bideford.
Rail: Barnstaple 19 miles.
Air: Exeter & Plymouth Airport both 50 miles.

■ Contact
Visitor Centre
Tel: 01237 431781
E-mail: visitorcentre@ clovelly.co.uk

■ Opening Times
High season:
9am-6pm.
Low season:
10am-4.30pm.

■ Admission
Adult	£6.75
Child (7-16yrs)	£4.25
(Under 7yrs)	Free
Family (2+2)	£17.75
Group Rates (20+)	
Adult	£5.50
Child	£3.75

The entrance fee covers parking, admission to the audio-visual film. Fisherman's Cottage, Kingsley Museum, Clovelly Court Gardens, and contributes to the ongoing maintenance of the village to preserve its timeless charm and magic.
Prices correct at time of going to press.

■ Special Events
May
Celebration of Ales & Ciders
June
Seaweed Festival
July
Clovelly Maritime Festival
Woolsery Agricultural Show
Lundy Row
August
Lifeboat Day
Clovelly Gig Regatta
September
Lobster & Crab Feast
November
Clovelly Herring Festival
December
Christmas Lights

GREAT FULFORD
DUNSFORD, NR. EXETER, DEVON EX6 7AJ
www.greatfulford.co.uk

On a hill overlooking a lake and set in a landscaped park Great Fulford has been the home of the Fulford family since at least the 12th Century. The current house reflects the financial ups and downs of the family over the centuries, with a major rebuilding and enlargement taking place in 1530 and again in 1580 while in 1690 the house, which had been badly damaged in the Civil War, was fully restored. Internally then there is a stunning suite of Great Rooms which include a superb Great Hall replete with some of the finest surviving examples of early Tudor carved panelling as well as a William & Mary period Great Staircase which leads to the recently restored Great Drawing Room or Ballroom. Other rooms in the house are in the 'gothic' taste having been remodelled, as was the exterior, by James Wyatt in 1805.

Location: Map 2:J7. OS Ref SX790 917. In centre of Devon. 10m W of Exeter. South of A30 between villages of Cheriton Bishop and Dunsford.
Owner/Contact: Francis Fulford
Tel: 01647 24205 **Fax:** 01647 24401
E-mail: francis@greatfulford.co.uk
Open: All year by appointment for parties or groups containing a minimum of 10 persons, alternatively individuals can book tours on prearranged dates via www.invitationtoview.co.uk.
Admission: £9.00 per person.
Key facts: ⊤ ☏ ⓘ Obligatory.
🅿 🎄 🛏 🖼 🔺 ❄

HARTLAND ABBEY 🏚ⓕ
HARTLAND ABBEY, NR BIDEFORD, NORTH DEVON EX39 6DT
www.hartlandabbey.com

Built in 1160, Hartland Abbey is a hidden gem on the stunning North Devon coast. Passing down generations from the Dissolution to the present day it remains a welcoming family home full of fascination: architecture from 1160 to 1850 by Meadows and Sir George Gilbert Scott; murals, important paintings and furniture, porcelain, early photographs and documents, family memorabilia and changing exhibitions. Family links to characters such as Sir Walter Raleigh, Rev William Stukeley, Pocohontas, Haile Sellasie. Woodland gardens and walks lead to the Jekyll designed Bog Garden and Fernery, restored 18thC Walled Gardens brimming with flowers, fruit and vegetables, the Summerhouse, Gazebo and the beach at Blackpool Mill, film location for 'Sense and Sensibility'. Beautiful daffodils, bluebells and tulips in spring. Delicious homemade food in The Old Kitchens. Only 1 mile to Hartland Quay. For Special Events see website.
Location: Map 1:G5. OS Ref SS240 249. 15m W of Bideford, 15m N of Bude off

A39 between Hartland and Hartland Quay on B3248.
Owner: Sir Hugh Stucley Bt **Contact:** Theresa Seligmann
Tel: 01237441496/234 / 01884 860225 **E-mail:** ha_admin@btconnect.com
Open: House, Gardens, Grounds & Beachwalk 29 Mar–4 Oct, Sun-Thu 11–5pm. (House 2–5pm). Last adm 4.30pm. Tea Room, Light lunches and cream teas 11am–5pm. **Admission:** House, Gardens, Grounds & Beachwalk: Adult £11.50, OAP £10.50, Child (5–15ys) £5.00, Under 5 Free, Registered disabled £8.50, Family (2+2) £28.00. Gardens, Grounds, Beachwalk & Exhibition: Adult £7.50, OAP £7.00, Child (5–15ys) £4.00, Under 5 Free, Registered disabled £4.50, Family (2+2) £20.00. Groups and coaches: Concessions 20+. Open at other dates and times. Booking essential. Large car park adjacent to the house.
Key facts: ⊙ ⓘ ⊤ Wedding receptions. ⓛ Partial. WC. ☏ ⓘ By arrangement. 🐕 In grounds, on leads. 🔺 ♨

Register for news and special offers at **www.hudsonsheritage.com**

POWDERHAM CASTLE 🏛ⓕ
KENTON, NR EXETER, DEVON EX6 8JQ
www.powderham.co.uk

Powderham Castle is the magnificent 600 year old family home of the 18th Earl and Countess of Devon. The Castle, a grade 1 listed building since 1952, is set amidst a 200 acre Deer Park with breathtaking views across the Exe Estuary. Set in beautiful grounds, Powderham Castle is open to visitors from April to October and is available all year round to hire for private functions. Visitors can enjoy the impressive architecture and fine interiors of the Castle on entertaining guided tours which run frequently throughout the day. The Courtenay Cafe offers a selection of home cooked food. Gift shop, plant centre and an extensive calendar of events creates a wonderful day out.

Location: Map 2:K7. OS Ref SX965 832. 6m SW of Exeter, 4m S M5/J30. Access from A379 in Kenton village.

Owner: The Earl of Devon **Contact:** Mr Simon Fishwick - Estate Director

Tel: 01626 890243 **Fax:** 01626 890729
E-mail: castle@powderham.co.uk
Open: Apr-Oct 2015. Please visit our website for specific dates and times. Woodland Garden and Belvedere close on 1 Aug 2015.
Admission: Please visit Powderham Castle website for admission prices.
Key facts: ⓘ Available for private hire, including corporate events, all year round. Powderham Castle is licenced for Marriages and Civil Partnerships and has accommodation for 18 guests within the Castle. 🖥 📶 📺 ⑤ Partial. WCs. 🖥 Licensed. 🍽 Licensed. 🎟 Obligatory. Included. 1hr. 🅿 Free. ⬛ Victorian Learning Programme - suitable for Key Stage 1 and 2 - An excellent learning resource to supplement children's learning outside of the classroom. 🐕 Guide dogs only. 🚗 🔼 ⬇

CADHAY 🏛ⓕ
Ottery St Mary, Devon EX11 1QT
www.cadhay.org.uk

Cadhay is approached by an avenue of lime-trees, and stands in an extensive garden, with herbaceous borders and yew hedges, with excellent views over the original medieval fish ponds. The main part of the house was built in about 1550 by John Haydon who had married the de Cadhay heiress. He retained the Great Hall of an earlier house, of which the fine timber roof (about 1420-1460) can be seen. An Elizabethan Long Gallery was added by John's successor at the end of the 16th Century, forming a unique courtyard with statues of Sovereigns on each side, described by Sir Simon Jenkins as one of the 'Treasures of Devon'.

Location: Map 2:L6. OS Ref SY090 962. 1m NW of Ottery St Mary. From W take A30 and exit at Pattesons Cross, follow signs for Fairmile and then Cadhay. From E, exit at the Iron Bridge and follow signs as above.

Owner: Mr R Thistlethwayte **Contact:** Jayne Covell **Tel:** 01404 813511
Open: May-Sep, Fri 2pm-5pm. Also: late May + Summer BH Sat-Sun-Mon. Last tour 4pm. **Admission:** House (Guided tour) and Gardens: Adult £7.00, Child £3.00. Gardens Only: Adults £3.00, Child £1.00. Parties of 15+ by prior arrangement. **Key facts:** 📶 ⑤ Ground floor & grounds. 🖥 🎟 Obligatory. 🅿 🐕 Guide dogs only. 🚗 🔼

CASTLE HILL GARDENS 🏛
Castle Hill, Filleigh, Barnstaple, Devon EX32 0RQ
www.castlehilldevon.co.uk

Set in the rolling hills of Devon, Castle Hill Gardens provides a tranquil and beautiful setting. Stroll through the spectacular gardens, dotted with mystical temples, follies, statues, vistas and a sham castle.The path through the Woodland Gardens, filled with flowering shrubs, leads you down to the river, the magical Satyr's temple and Ugley Bridge. Newly restored 18th Century Holwell Temple and special Memorial Plantation.

Location: Map 2:I14. OS Ref SS661 362. A361, take B3226 to South Molton. Follow brown signs to Castle Hill.

Owner: The Earl and Countess of Arran **Contact:** Michelle White
Tel: 01598 760421 / 01598 760336 Ext 1 **Fax:** 01598 760457
E-mail: gardens@castlehill-devon.com
Open: Daily except Sats Apr-Sep 11am-5pm. Oct-Mar 11am-dusk. Refreshments are only available outside from Apr to Sep. Groups and coach parties are welcome at all times by prior arrangement.
Admission: Adults £6.00, Senior citizens £5.50, Family £15.00, Children 5-15 £2.50, Under 5's Free, Groups (20+) £5.00. **Key facts:** 📺 ⑤ Partial. WCs. 🎟 By arrangement. 🅿 Free parking. 🐕 🐕 On leads. 🔼 ❋ Daily except Sats. ⬇

FURSDON HOUSE 🏛Ⓕ
Cadbury, Nr Thorverton, Exeter, Devon EX5 5JS
www.fursdon.co.uk

Fursdon House is at the heart of a small estate where the family has lived for over 750 years. Set within a hilly and wooded landscape the gardens and grounds are attractive with walled and open areas with far reaching views. Family memorabilia with fine costume and textiles are displayed on informal guided tours. Two spacious apartments and a restored Victorian cottage offer stylish holiday accommodation.

Location: Map 2:K6. OS Ref SS922 046. By car- Off A3072 between Bickleigh & Crediton. 9m N of Exeter signposted through Thorverton from A396 Exeter to Tiverton road **Owner:** Mr E D Fursdon **Contact:** Mrs C Fursdon
Tel: 01392 860860 **Fax:** 01392 860126
E-mail: admin@fursdon.co.uk
Open: Garden & Tea Room, Wed, Sun and BH Mons from Easter to end Sep 2pm-5pm; House open for tours BH Mons & Wed & Sun in Jun, Jul & Aug 2.30pm & 3.30pm.
Admission: House and Garden Adult £8.00, Child Free. Garden only £4.00.
Key facts: ⓘ Conferences. No photography or video. 🍴 🖥 🎦 Obligatory. 🅿 Limited for coaches. 🐕 Dogs on leads are allowed in the gardens 🏠 Self-catering.

HEMERDON HOUSE 🏛
Hemerdon House, Plympton, Devon PL7 5BZ
www.hemerdonhouse.co.uk

Situated in the beautiful South Hams area of Devon, and set in its own parkland, Hemerdon House was built in the late 18th Century by the ancestors of the current owners. Members of the family offer guided tours of the interior on certain days of the year and visitors are also welcome to explore the grounds on those days. The house contains a wealth of local history, with naval and military mementos, paintings, furniture, china and silver collected by the family through many generations. **Location:** Map 2:I9. The house is situated between the villages of Hemerdon and Sparkwell. SatNav instructions may be misleading at the very last stage of the journey, so please note the directions given on our website.
Contact: Sukey Woollcombe-Morris **Tel:** 07704 708416
E-mail: hemerdon.house@gmail.com **Open:** Check our website for 2015 dates.
Admission: Entrance fee £7.50, HHA members and children under 12 no charge.
Key facts: ⓘ Parties of 6 or more please contact us in advance; parties of 10 or more by prior arrangement only. ♿ Wheelchair access to part of the house and grounds, but please see website for details. 🎦 Two tours of approximately 1 hour 15 minutes each, starting at 2.15pm and 4pm - last entry at 4pm. 🅿 Free parking. 🐕 Dogs on leads are permitted in the grounds while the house is open.

Tiverton Castle

SHILSTONE 🏛
Modbury, Devon PL21 0TW
www.shilstonedevon.co.uk

Shilstone is a Georgian house in the heart of the Devon countryside overlooking an important historical landscape. Recently restored, the house is now a private home and romantic wedding venue with beautiful elevations and exquisite detail that make it comfortable in its site, and timeless in its design.

Location: Map 2:J9. OS Ref SX674 536.
Owner: Lucy and Sebastian Fenwick
Contact: Abigail Gray
Tel: 01548830888
E-mail: abi@shilstonedevon.co.uk
Open: By appointment only.
Admission: £12.00 per person, minimum 4 people.
Key facts: 🚃 🛆 Unsuitable. 🍽 Must pre-book. 🛏 Must pre-book. 🎥 Obligatory. 🅿 Ample parking and can accomodate up to 24 seat coaches. 🍴 🐕 Guide dogs only. 🛎 ✕ 🎗 €

DOWNES 🏛
Crediton, Devon EX17 3PL

Downes is a Palladian Mansion dating originally from 1692. The former home of General Sir Redvers Buller, the house contains a large number of items relating to his military campaigns. The property is now predominantly a family home with elegant rooms hung with family portraits, and a striking main staircase.

Location: Map 2:K6. OS Ref SX852 997. Approx 1m from Crediton town centre.
Owner: Trustees of the Downes Estate Settlement
Contact: Darren & Eva Tate
Tel: 01363 775142 **E-mail:** darren@downesestate.co.uk
Website: www.downesestate.co.uk
Open: Mons & Tues 6 Apr-14 Jul & BH 31 Aug & 1 Sep. Tours 2.15pm. Group bookings (15+) by prior appointment.
Admission: Adults £7.50, Children (5-16 years) £3.75, Groups (over 15) £6.00 each for Adults or £3.00 each for Children (Groups must be pre booked).
Key facts: 🚃 🛆 Partial. 🎥 Obligatory. 🅿 Limited. 🎗

ST MARTIN'S CHURCH 🏛
Cathedral Close, Exeter, Devon EX1 1EZ

One of the oldest buildings in the city, consecrated a year before the Norman Conquest, St Martin's was once one of six churches clustered in the cathedral's shadow. It is one of the most important and complete churches in the centre of Exeter, having escaped both Victorian refurnishing and the Second World War bombings. The first church on this site was consecrated on 6th July 1065 by Bishop Leofric, the same bishop who founded the cathedral in Exeter. The roughcast exterior of red volcanic stone with bright, white Beer stone windows makes it look a little bit like a fancy gingerbread house. Inside, it is simple and full of light. On the gallery is painted the arms of the city and of Bishop Trelawny, a local hero in Cornwall, who was imprisoned for libel by James II. There are also several magnificent monuments in the church including one of Philip Hooper (a benefactor who donated the reredos) splendidly bewigged, he kneels at a prayer desk with a skull and pile of books. **Location:** OS Ref SX922 926. Cathedral Close **Website:** www.visitchurches.org.uk **Open:** Mon-Fri: 9.30am-4.30pm. Sat: 10am-5pm.

SAND 🏛ⓔ
Sidbury, Sidmouth EX10 0QN

Sand is one of East Devon's hidden gems. The beautiful valley garden extends to 6 acres and is the setting for the lived-in Tudor house, the 15th Century Hall House, and the 16th Century Summer House. The family, under whose unbroken ownership the property has remained since 1560, provide guided house tours.
Location: Map 2:L7. OS Ref SY146 925. Well signed, 400 yards off A375 between Honiton and Sidmouth. **Contact:** Mr & Mrs Huyshe-Shires
Tel: 01395 597230 **E-mail:** info@SandSidbury.co.uk
Website: www.SandSidbury.co.uk
Open: Suns & Mons in Jun and BH Suns & Mons. Other dates see website. Open 2-6pm. Groups by appointment.
Admission: House & Garden: Adult £7.00, Child/Student £1.00. Garden only: Adult £3.00, accompanied Child (under 16) Free.
Key facts: 🛈 No photography in house. 🛆 Partial. 🎥 Obligatory. 🅿 Limited. 🐕 On leads. 🎗

TIVERTON CASTLE 🏛ⓔ
Park Hill, Tiverton EX16 6RP

Part Grade I Listed, part Scheduled Ancient Monument, few buildings evoke such immediate feeling of history. Originally built 1106, later alterations. Home of medieval Earls of Devon & Princess Katherine Plantagenet. Fun for children, try on Civil War armour; ghost stories, secret passages, medieval loos, beautiful walled gardens. Interesting furniture, pictures. Comfortable holiday accommodation.
Location: Map 2:K5. OS Ref SS954 130. Just N of Tiverton town centre.
Owner: Mr and Mrs A K Gordon **Contact:** Mrs A Gordon
Tel: 01884 253200 **Fax:** 01884 254200 **Alt tel:** 01884 255200.
E-mail: info@tivertoncastle.com **Website:** www.tivertoncastle.com
Open: Easter-end Oct: Sun, Thu, BH Mon, 2.30-5.30pm. Last admission 5pm. Open to groups (12+) by prior arrangement at any time.
Admission: Adult £7.00; Child 7-16yrs £3.00, under 7 Free; Garden only £2.00.
Key facts: 🎥 🚃 🛆 Partial. 🎥 By arrangement. 🅿 Limited for coaches. 🍴 🐕 Guide dogs only. ✕ 🎗 5 properties

A LA RONDE 🏵
Summer Lane, Exmouth, Devon EX8 5BD

A unique sixteen sided house, completed c1796. Built for two spinster cousins, Jane and Mary Parminter, on their return from a grand tour of Europe.
Location: Map 2:L7. OS Ref SY004 834. 2m N of Exmouth on A376.
Tel: 01395 265514 **E-mail:** alaronde@nationaltrust.org.uk
Website: www.nationaltrust.org.uk/a-la-ronde
Open: Please see website for up to date opening and admission details.

CASTLE DROGO 🏵
Drewsteignton, Nr Exeter EX6 6PB

Extraordinary granite and oak castle which combines the comforts of the 20th Century with the grandeur of a Baronial castle. **Location:** Map 2:J7. OS Ref SX724 902. **Tel:** 01647 433306 **E-mail:** castledrogo@nationaltrust.org.uk
Website: www.nationaltrust.org.uk/castle-drogo
Open: Please see website for up to date opening and admission details.

GREENWAY 🏵
Greenway Road, Galmpton, nr Brixham, Devon TQ5 0ES

Greenway house and garden: 'the loveliest place in the world'. Take this extraordinary glimpse into the beloved holiday home of the famous author Agatha Christie. **Location:** Map 2:K8. OS Ref SX876 548. **Tel:** 01803 842382
E-mail: greenway@nationaltrust.org.uk **Website:** www.nationaltrust.org.uk/greenway **Open:** Please see website for up to date opening and admission details.

VISITOR INFORMATION

■ **Owner**
Mr & Mrs Patrick Cooke

■ **Address**
Athelhampton
Dorchester
Dorset
DT2 7LG

■ **Location**
Map 2:P6
OS Ref. SY771 942
Athelhampton House is
located just 5 miles East of
Dorchester, between
Puddletown and Tolupddle
villages.
Follow the brown tourist
signs for Athelhampton
from the A35.

■ **Contact**
Owen Davies or Laura
Pitman
Tel: 01305 848363
E-mail: enquiry
@athelhampton.co.uk

■ **Opening Times**
1 Mar-1 Nov, Sun, Mon,
Tue, Wed, Thurs,
10am-5pm. Closed every
Fri & Sat (also open every
Sunday throughout the
Winter months).

■ **Admission**
House & Gardens:
Adult   £13.00
Senior   £11.00
Child (under 16)   £3.00
Disabled/Student   £8.00
Gardens Only Ticket   £8.00
Please contact us for group
booking rates and
hospitality
some Fridays may be
available by appointment.

■ **Special Events**
Spring Flower Festival.
MG Car Rally.
Car Auction.
Christmas Food Event.
Outdoor Theatre.
Traditional Village Fete.

Athelhampton has a
thriving Conference and
Wedding business and
offers exclusive use for
Wedding parties and
private functions on Fridays
and Saturdays throughout
the year.

Please see contact us by
phone or visit our website
for more information.

Conference/Function

ROOM	Size	Max Cap
Long Hall	13mx6m	80
Conservatory	16mx11m	120
Media Suite/ Cinema	fixed seating	75
Great Hall	12mx8m	82

ATHELHAMPTON HOUSE 🏛Ⓕ & GARDENS
www.athelhampton.co.uk

One of the finest 15th Century Houses in England nestled in the heart of the picturesque Piddle Valley in the famous Hardy county of rural Dorset.

Home to the Cooke family, this House dates from 1485 and is a magnificent example of early Tudor architecture. Sir William Martyn was granted a licence by Henry VII to enclose 160 acres of deer park and to build the fortified manor. His great hall, with a roof of curved brace timbers and an oriel window with fine heraldic glass is now one of the finest examples from this period. In 1891 Alfred Carte de Lafontaine (the then owner of Athelhampton) commissioned the building of the formal gardens.

The Grade 1 listed gardens which have won the HHA 'Garden of the Year' award surround the main house, with Elizabethan style ham stone courts. The famous 30 feet high yew pyramids dominate the Great Court and the 15th Century Dovecote is still home to a colony of beautiful white fantail doves. Water forms a

recurring theme with pools, fountains and the River Piddle. The House has an array of fine furniture from Jacobean to Victorian periods. The west wing gallery hosts an exhibition of paintings and sketches by the Russian Artist, Marevna (1892 - 1984). The collection of her works, painted mainly in the cubist style, includes pieces painted throughout her lifetime including her travels, life in Paris, her time whilst she lived at Athelhampton during the 1940's and 50's and her final years in Ealing.

New for 2015, the kitchen garden will be opened for the first time in a generation. The garden had been lost to the wild and over the next few years it will be lovingly restored to its former glory, providing our thriving restaurant and pub with fresh and seasonal produce, as well as enhancing our visitor experience.

KEY FACTS

ℹ️ www.athelhampton.co.uk

🏬 Books, food, DVDs, gifts & souvenirs.

✳️ Plants for sale from the gift shop.

🍷 By arrangement, for a range of activities and catering.

♿ Limited access to upper floors.

☕ Coffee, lunches & afternoon tea.

🍴 The Topiary: Home-cooked lunches, morning coffee and afternoon tea, The Long Hall: Sunday Carvery.

🚶 Guided tours by arrangement. Free guidebook loan.

🅿️ Free car and coach parking.

🏫 Educational staff to assist available.

🐕 On leads, grounds only.

🛏️ Delightful holiday cottage on the estate, sleeps 6 in 3 en-suite bedrooms.

🔔 Civil wedding ceremonies inc open air.

❄️ Open all year round on a Sunday.

🎭 Open air theatre.

SHERBORNE CASTLE & GARDENS 🏛Ⓕ
NEW ROAD, SHERBORNE, DORSET DT9 5NR
www.sherbornecastle.com

Built by Sir Walter Raleigh in 1594, Sherborne Castle has been the home of the Digby family since 1617. Prince William of Orange was entertained here in 1688, and George III visited in 1789. Splendid interiors and collections of art, furniture and porcelain are on view in the Castle. Lancelot 'Capability' Brown created the 50 acre lake in 1753 and gave Sherborne the very latest in landscape gardening, with magnificent vistas of the surrounding parklands. Today, over 30 acres of beautiful lakeside gardens and grounds are open for public viewing.

Location: Map 2:O5. OS Ref ST649 164. 4m SE of Sherborne town centre. Follow brown signs from A30 or A352. ½m S of the Old Castle.
Owner: Mr & Mrs John Wingfield Digby

Contact: Robert B. Smith
Tel: 01935 812072 Ext 2 **Fax:** 01935 816727
E-mail: enquiries@sherbornecastle.com
Open: 1 Apr-31 Oct 2015. Castle, Gardens, Gift Shop and Tearoom; daily except Mon and Fri, 11am-4:30pm (last adm). BH Mons 11am-4:30pm (last adm).
Admission: Castle & Gardens: Adult £11.00, Senior £10.00, Child Free (max 4 per adult). Gardens Only: Adult/Senior: £6.00, Child Free (max 4 per adult). Groups 15+ Castle & Gardens: Adult Free Flow tour £8.50, Child Free Flow tour £3.50. Castle Private Viewing (before 11am): Adult £12.00, Child £6.00.
Key facts: 🏠 ⊤ 🚻 WCs. 🅿 🍴 🎫 By arrangement. 🅿 🏠 🖼 On leads. 🏠 🎥

CLAVELL TOWER
Kimmeridge, near Wareham, Dorset BH20 5PE
www.landmarktrust.org.uk

This four storey, circular tower stands high on the cliff overlooking one of the most striking bays on the Dorset coast. Built in 1830 its location has captivated many including writers like Hardy and PD James.
Location: Map 2:A7. OS Ref SY915 796.
Owner: The Landmark Trust
Tel: 01628 825925
E-mail: bookings@landmarktrust.org.uk
Open: Self-catering accommodation. Two Open Days per year. Other visits by appointment. **Admission:** Free on Open Days and visits by appointment.
Key facts: ℹ A four storey tower with each room on a different floor. The bedroom, on the first floor, has a door onto a balcony that encircles the whole building. 🅿 🖼 🖼 ❄ 🎥

HIGHCLIFFE CASTLE 🏛Ⓕ
Highcliffe-On-Sea, Christchurch BH23 4LE
www.highcliffecastle.co.uk

Built in the 1830s in the Romantic/Picturesque style. Although no longer with its rich interiors, the Castle now houses a Heritage Centre & Gift Shop providing a unique setting for exhibitions and events. Licenced for civil weddings. Available for ceremonies, receptions, banquets and corporate use. Cliff-top grounds. Access to Christchurch Coastal Path and beach.
Location: Map 3:B6. OS Ref SZ200 930. Off the A337 Lymington Road, between Christchurch and Highcliffe-on-Sea. **Owner:** Christchurch Borough Council
Contact: David Hopkins **Tel:** 01425 278807 **Fax:** 01425 280423
E-mail: enquiries@highcliffecastle.co.uk **Open:** 1 Feb-23 Dec: daily, 11am-5pm. Last adm 4.30pm (4pm Fri/Sat). Grounds: All year: daily from 7am. Tearooms daily (except Christmas Day). Coaches by appointment. **Admission:** Adult £3.45, accompanied U16 free. Group (10+) rates available. Guided tour (including non-public areas): Adult £5.85. Grounds: Free *Prices correct at time of going to press.
Key facts: 🏠 Aladdin's Cave of gifts & cards. ⊤ Wedding receptions. 🖼 🍴 Open daily except Xmas Day. 🎫 Public Tours 11am Sun. 2pm Tue & Thu. Private tours any day (by arrangement). 🅿 Limited. Charges 1 Apr-30 Sep. 🖼 By arrangement. 🖼 On leads in grounds, may be off-lead on beach. 🏠 Romantic & Picturesque, just perfect. ❄ Check for room closures before visiting. 🎥

LULWORTH CASTLE & PARK 🏠F
East Lulworth, Wareham, Dorset BH20 5QS
www.lulworth.com

Impressive C17th Castle & historically important C18th Chapel set in extensive parkland, with views towards the Jurassic Coast. Built as a hunting lodge to entertain Royalty, the Castle was destroyed by fire in 1929. Since then it has been externally restored and internally consolidated by English Heritage. The Castle provides informative displays & exhibitions on its history.
Location: Map 3:A7. OS Ref ST853 822. In E Lulworth off B3070, 3m NE of Lulworth Cove. **Owner:** The Weld Estate **Tel:** 0845 4501054
Fax: 01929 40563 **E-mail:** enquiries@lulworth.com
Open: Castle & Park: All year, Sun-Fri. Opening dates & times may vary throughout the year, check website or call before visiting. Last admission to Castle is 1hr before closing. **Admission:** Pay & Display parking £3.00, allowing access to Park walks, Play & Picnic areas. Admission applies for Castle & Chapel - please see website www.lulworth.com. EH & HHA members Free. **Key facts:** 🎵 Concerts, corporate & private hire/events, weddings by arrangement. 🚻 WCs. Lift access to Upper Ground floor. 📷 Obligatory. By arrangement. 🅿️ 🚻 🐕 Guide dogs only. ▲ ✳ 🏷

MINTERNE GARDENS 🏠F
Minterne Magna, Nr Dorchester, Dorset DT2 7AU
www.minterne.co.uk

Landscaped in the manner of 'Capability' Brown, Minterne's unique garden has been described by Simon Jenkins as 'a corner of paradise.' 20 wild, woodland acres of magnolias, rhododendrons and azaleas providing new vistas at each turn, with small lakes, streams and cascades. Private House tours, dinners, corporate seminars, wedding and events. As seen on BBC Gardeners' World. Voted one of the ten Prettiest Gardens in England by The Times.
Location: Map 2:O6. OS Ref ST660 042. On A352 Dorchester/Sherborne Rd, 2m N of Cerne Abbas.
Owner/Contact: The Hon Mr & Mrs Henry Digby
Tel: 01300 341370
E-mail: enquiries@minterne.co.uk
Open: Mid Feb-9 Nov: daily, 10am-6pm.
Admission: Adult £5.00, accompanied children free. Free to RHS members.
Key facts: 🎵 ♿ Unsuitable. 📷 By arrangement. 🅿️ Free. Picnic tables in car park. 🐕 In grounds on leads. ▲

© Justin Barton

MAPPERTON 🏠F
Beaminster, Dorset DT8 3NR
www.mapperton.com

'The Nation's Finest Manor House'- Country Life. Jacobean manor, All Saints Church, stables and dovecote overlooking an Italianate garden, orangery, topiary and borders, descending to ponds and arboretum. A unique valley garden in an Area of Outstanding Natural Beauty with fine views of Dorset hills and woodlands.
Location: Map 2:N6. OS Ref SY503 997. 1m S of B3163, 2m NE of B3066, 2m SE Beaminster, 5m NE Bridport. **Owner/Contact:** The Earl & Countess of Sandwich
Tel: 01308 862645 **Fax:** 01308 861082 **E-mail:** office@mapperton.com
Open: House: 6 Jul-7 Aug (Mon-Fri) plus 4 May & 25 May, timed tours 2-4.30pm, booking advisable. Garden & Church: 1 Mar-31 Oct: daily (exc Sat) 11am-5pm. Café: 1 Apr-30 Sep: daily (exc. Sat) 11am-5.00pm, 01308 863 348.
Admission: Gardens: Adult £6.00, Child (under 18yrs) £3.00, under 5yrs free. House: £6.00. Group tours by appointment. House and Gardens combined £10.00 for groups over 20. **Key facts:** 🏠 🎁 🎵 ♿ Partial. WCs. 🍴 Licensed. 📷 By arrangement. 🅿️ Limited for coaches. 🚻 🐕 Guide dogs only. ▲ 🏷

ST GILES HOUSE 🏠
Wimborne St Giles, Dorset BH21 5NA
www.shaftesburyestates.com

Beautiful secluded setting in unspoilt Dorset, famous for the Grand Shaftesbury Run in May. Home of the Earls of Shaftesbury, the 17th Century house, gardens and landscape are under restoration.
Events held in the parkland, designed by Henry Flitcroft, in the summer months; the house is available for bespoke events. The Grand Shaftesbury Run is half marathon or 10km run or 1km fun run through the pleasure grounds and woodland.
Location: Map 3:A5. OS Ref SU031119.
In Wimborne St Giles, 4mls SE of A354, past almshouses and church.
Owner: The Earl of Shaftesbury
Tel: 01725 517214
E-mail: office@shaftesburyestates.com
Open: By appointment for groups and for bespoke events.
Key facts: 🎵 🐕 ▲ 🏷

WOLFETON HOUSE 🏠Ⓕ
Nr Dorchester, Dorset DT2 9QN

A fine medieval and Elizabethan manor house lying in the water-meadows near the confluence of the rivers Cerne and Frome. It was embellished around 1580 and has splendid plaster ceilings, fireplaces and panelling. To be seen are the Great Hall, Stairs and Chamber, Parlour, Dining Room, Chapel and Cyder House.

Location: Map 2:O6. OS Ref SY678 921. 1½m from Dorchester on the A37 towards Yeovil. Indicated by Historic House signs.
Owner: Capt N T L L T Thimbleby
Contact: The Steward
Tel: 01305 263500
E-mail: kthimbleby.wolfeton@gmail.com
Open: Jun-end Sep: Mon, Wed & Thu, 2-5pm. Groups by appointment throughout the year.
Admission: £7.00
Key facts: ℹ Catering for groups by prior arrangement. 🎦 By arrangement. ♿ 📷 By arrangement. 🅿 Limited for coaches. 🔲 ⛔ ❄

CHURCH OF OUR LADY & ST IGNATIUS
North Chideock, Bridport, Dorset DT6 6LF

Built by Charles Weld of Chideock Manor in 1872 in Italian Romanesque style, it is a gem of English Catholicism and the Shrine of the Dorset Martyrs. Early 19th Century wall paintings in original barn-chapel (priest's sacristy) can be seen by arrangement. A museum of local history & village life displayed in adjoining cloister.

Location: Map 2:A7. OS Ref SY090 786. A35 to Chideock, turn into N Rd & ¼mile on right
Owner: The Weld Family Trust **Contact:** Mrs G Martelli
Tel: 01308 488348 **E-mail:** amyasmartelli40@hotmail.com
Website: www.chideockmartyrschurch.org.uk
Open: All year: 10am-4pm.
Admission: Donations welcome.
Key facts: ♿ Partial. 🅿 Limited for coaches. 🔲 🐕 Guide dogs only ❄

EDMONDSHAM HOUSE & GARDENS 🏠Ⓕ
Cranborne, Wimborne, Dorset BH21 5RE

Charming blend of Tudor and Georgian architecture with interesting contents. Organic walled garden, 6 acre garden with unusual trees and spring bulbs. 12th Century church nearby.

Location: Map 3:A5. OS Ref SU062 116. Off B3081 between Cranborne and Verwood, NW from Ringwood 9m, Wimborne 9m.
Owner/Contact: Mrs Julia E Smith
Tel: 01725 517207
Open: House & Gardens all BH Mons, Weds in Apr & Oct only, 2-5pm. Gardens Apr-Oct Suns & Weds 2-5pm. Groups by arrangement (max 50).
Admission: House & Garden: Adult £5.00, Child £1.00 (under 5yrs free). Garden only: Adult £2.50, Child 50p (under 5yrs free).
Key facts: 🎦 ♿ Partial. WCs. 🍴 Only Weds Apr & Oct. 📷 Obligatory. 🅿 Limited. 🔲 🐕 Guide dogs only. 🏠

HIGHER MELCOMBE 🏠
Melcombe Bingham, Dorchester, Dorset DT2 7PB

Consists of the surviving wing of a 16th Century house with its attached domestic chapel. A fine plaster ceiling and linenfold panelling. Conducted tours by owner.
Location: Map 2:P6. OS Ref ST749 024. 1km W of Melcombe Bingham.
Owner/Contact: Mr M C Woodhouse
Tel: 01258 880251
Website: www.highermelcombemanor.co.uk
Open: May-Sep by appointment.
Admission: Adult £2.00 (takings go to charity).
Key facts: ♿ Unsuitable. 📷 By written appointment only. 🅿 Limited. 🐕 Guide dogs only.

ST GEORGE'S CHURCH ⛪
Reforne, Wide Street, Portland, Dorset DT5 2JP

Vast and solitary, St George's is one of the most magnificent 18th Century churches in Dorset. It rises from the rocky, treeless and dramatic peninsula of Portland and is the masterwork of a local mason named Thomas Gilbert who supplied the Portland stone used to build St Paul's Cathedral. The interior is fabulously preserved with its lectern, pulpit, box pews and galleries all surviving. It is a 'preacher's church' with all the seating facing the twin pulpits - one for reading 'the Word' (scripture), the other for lengthy sermons. The sprawling churchyard is a treasure trove of fabulous headstones and memorials that tell tales of murder, piracy and adventure in a gloriously atmospheric setting. There are inscriptions to Mary Way and William Lano, who were shot and killed in 1803 by a press gang, and Joseph Trevitt, an assistant warder at Portland Prison who was murdered by a convict in 1869. **Location:** OS Ref SY686 720. Easton, Isle of Portland. Parking nearby. **Website:** www.visitchurches.org.uk
Open: 10am-5pm until Oct. 10am-3pm Winter Months.

SANDFORD ORCAS MANOR HOUSE
Sandford Orcas, Sherborne, Dorset DT9 4SB

Tudor manor house with gatehouse, fine panelling, furniture, pictures. Terraced gardens with topiary and herb garden. Personal conducted tour by owner.
Location: Map 2:O5. OS Ref ST623 210. 2½m N of Sherborne, Dorset 4m S of A303 at Sparkford. Entrance next to church.
Owner/Contact: Sir Mervyn Medlycott Bt
Tel: 01963 220206
Open: Easter Mon, 10am-5pm. May & Jul-Sep: Suns & Mons, 2-5pm.
Admission: Adult £5.00, Child £2.50. Groups (10+): Adult £4.00, Child £2.00.
Key facts: ♿ Unsuitable. 📷 Obligatory. 🅿 Parking available. 🐕 In grounds, on leads.

KINGSTON LACY 🏛
Kingston Lacy, Wimborne Minster, Dorset BH21 4EA

Explore this elegant country mansion, built to resemble an Italian Palace, and discover an outstanding collection of fine works of art.
Location: Map 3:A6. OS Ref ST980 019. **Tel:** 01202 883402
E-mail: kingstonlacy@nationaltrust.org.uk **Website:** www.nationaltrust.org.uk/kingston-lacy **Open:** Please see website for up to date opening and admission

---

STOCK GAYLARD HOUSE 🏠Ⓕ
Stock Gaylard, Sturminster Newton, Dorset DT10 2BG

Georgian house overlooking an ancient deer park with parish church of St Barnabas in garden. **Location:** Map 2:P5. OS Ref ST722 130. 1m S junction A357 & A3030 Lydlinch Common. **Tel:** 01963 23215
E-mail: langmeadj@stockgaylard.com **Website:** www.stockgaylard.com
Open: 25 Apr-4 May: 22-30 Jun and 22-30 Sep: 2-5pm. Groups by appointment.
Admission: Adult £5.00.

■ **Owner**
Mr David Lowsley- Williams

■ **Address**
Chavenage House
Chavenage
Tetbury
Gloucestershire
GL8 8XP

■ **Location**
Map 3:A1
OS Ref. ST872 952
Less than 20m from M4/ J16/17 or 18. 1¾m NW of Tetbury between the B4014 & A4135. Signed from Tetbury. Less than 15m from M5/J13 or 14. Signed from A46 (Stroud-Bath road).
Taxi: The Pink Cab 07960 036003
Rail: Kemble Station 7m.
Air: Bristol 35m. Birmingham 70m. Grass airstrip on farm.

■ **Contact**
Caroline Lowsley-Williams
Tel: 01666 502329
Fax: 01666 504696
E-mail: info@chavenage.com

■ **Opening Times**
Summer
May-September
Thur, Sun, 2-5pm. Last admission 4pm. Also Easter Sun, Mon & BH Mons.

NB. Will open on any day and at other times by prior arrangement for groups.

Winter
October-March
By appointment only for groups.

■ **Admission**
Guided Tours are inclusive in the following prices.
Summer
Adult   £8.00
Child (5-16 yrs)   £4.00
Winter
Groups only (any date or time) Rates by arrangement.

Conference/Function

ROOM	Size	Max Cap
Ballroom	70' x 30'	120
Oak Room	25 'x 20'	30

CHAVENAGE HOUSE 🏚Ⓕ
www.chavenage.com

The Elizabethan Manor Chavenage House, a TV/Film location is still a family home, offers unique experiences, with history, ghosts and more.

Chavenage is a wonderful Elizabethan house of mellow grey Cotswold stone and tiles which contains much of interest for the discerning visitor. The approach aspect of Chavenage is virtually as it was left by Edward Stephens in 1576. Only two families have owned Chavenage; the present owners since 1891 and the Stephens family before them. A Colonel Nathaniel Stephens, MP for Gloucestershire during the Civil War was cursed for supporting Cromwell, giving rise to legends of weird happenings at Chavenage since that time.

There are many interesting rooms housing tapestries, fine furniture, pictures and relics of the Cromwellian period. Of particular note are the Main Hall, where a contemporary screen forms a minstrels' gallery and two tapestry rooms where it is said Cromwell was lodged.

Recently Chavenage has been used as a location for TV and film productions: credits include, Barry Lyndon, the Hercule Poirot story The Mysterious Affair at Styles, The House of Elliot, Casualty, Cider with Rosie, Jeremy Musson's The Curious House Guest; Dracula, Lark Rise to Candleford; Bonekickers; Tess of the D'Urbervilles and Channel 4 historical drama New Worlds. Scenes from the upcoming 'Wolf Hall' were shot at Chavenage recently. **STOP PRESS Chavenage is set to feature as Trenwith House in the new adaptation of 'Poldark' STOP PRESS ***. Chavenage is the ideal attraction for those wishing an intimate, personal tour, usually conducted by the owner or his family, or for groups wanting a change from large establishments. Meals for pre-arranged groups have proved hugely popular. It also provides a charming venue for wedding receptions, small conferences and other functions.

KEY FACTS

ℹ️ Suitable for filming, photography, corporate entertainment, activity days, seminars, receptions & product launches. No photography inside house.

🎭 Occasional.

☕ Corporate entertaining. Private drinks parties, lunches, dinners, anniversary parties & wedding receptions.

♿ Partial. WCs.

🚐

👤 By owner. Large groups given a talk prior to viewing. Couriers/group leaders should arrange tour format prior to visit.

🅿️ Up to 100 cars. 2-3 coaches (by appointment). Coaches access from A46 (signposted) or from Tetbury via B4014, enter back gates for parking area.

🪑 Chairs can be arranged for lecturing.

🍽️

❄️ Out of season - only by appointment.

Register for news and special offers at **www.hudsonsheritage.com**

VISITOR INFORMATION

■ **Owner**
Elizabeth, Lady Ashcombe and family

■ **Address**
Sudeley Castle & Gardens
The Cotswolds
Gloucestershire
GL54 5JD

■ **Location**
Map 6:O10
OS Ref. SP032 277
8m NE of Cheltenham, at Winchcombe off B4632. From Bristol or Birmingham M5/J9. Take A46 then B4077 towards Stow-on-the-Wold.
Bus: Castleways to Winchcombe.
Rail: Cheltenham Station 8m.
Air: Birmingham or Bristol 45m.

■ **Contact**
Visitor Centre
Tel: 01242 604 244
Fax: 01242 602 959
Estate Office:
01242 602 308.
E-mail:
enquiries@sudeley.org.uk

■ **Opening Times**
Sudeley Castle & Gardens is open daily from 16th March to 1st November 2015; 10am to 5pm. Events planned throughout the season - check the website or call for details.

■ **Admission**
2015 Admission Prices:
Adult   £14.00
Concessions   £13.00
Child (5-15yrs)   £5.00
Family (2 adults +
3 children)   £35.00
Children under 5   Free
Members of the Historic
Houses Association   Free

Season Tickets:
Adult   £20.00
Child (5–15 years)   £10.00
Family (2 adults,
3 children)   £50.00

■ **Special Events**
Special events throughout the season. See www.sudeleycastle.co.uk, Facebook.com/SudeleyCastle and Twitter @SudeleyCastle.

SUDELEY CASTLE & GARDENS 🏛ⓕ
www.sudeleycastle.co.uk

A must-see on any visit to The Cotswolds, Sudeley Castle & Gardens is the only private castle in England to have a queen – Katherine Parr – buried within the grounds.

Located only eight miles from the picturesque Broadway, Sudeley Castle & Gardens has played an important role in England's history, boasting royal connections that stretch back over 1,000 years - and is now a much-loved family home with award-winning gardens.

Inside, the castle contains many fascinating treasures from ancient Roman times to the present day. Outside, the castle is surrounded by award-winning gardens and a breathtaking 1,200 acre estate.

It is also the only private castle in England to have a queen buried within the grounds. The last of Henry VIII's six wives, Katherine Parr lived and died in the castle. She is now entombed in a beautiful 15th Century church found within the award-winning gardens.

Sudeley Castle's magnificent gardens are world-renowned, providing variety and colour from spring through to autumn. The centrepiece is the Queens Garden, so named because four of England's queens – Anne Boleyn, Katherine Parr, Lady Jane Grey and Elizabeth I – once admired the hundreds of varieties of roses found in the garden.

An owlery, pheasantry, adventure playground with picnic area, gift shop and Terrace Café in the banqueting hall complete the perfect day out.

KEY FACTS

ℹ️ www.sudeleycastle.co.uk 01242 604244.

📷 Open daily 16 March - 1 November 2015.

🌱 Plant sales at the Visitor Centre.

⏏ Weddings & Events.

♿ Partial. WCs.

☕ Light lunches, afternoon tea, cakes, snacks, tea, coffee & soft drinks.

🍴 Licensed.

🗝 By arrangement. Call the Estate Office.

Ⓟ Ample parking.

🏫 Contact Estate Office for schools materials.

🐕 Guide dogs only.

🏠 Country Cottages.

🔔 The family's Private Library situated within the family's apartments is available for civil ceremonies & civil partnerships.

♛ See website.

Conference/Function

ROOM	Size	Max Cap
Chandos Hall		60
Banqueting Hall + Pavilion		100
Marquee		Unlimited
Long Room		80
Library		50

FRAMPTON COURT, THE ORANGERY AND FRAMPTON MANOR 🏛
FRAMPTON ON SEVERN, GLOUCESTERSHIRE GL2 7EP

www.framptoncourtestate.co.uk

The Cliffords have lived in Frampton since the 11th Century. Grade I listed Frampton Court, built in 1731 & currently run as a luxury B&B, has a superb panelled interior containing historic furniture, china & 19th Century 'Frampton Flora' watercolours. The 18th Century 'Strawberry Hill' gothic Orangery sits, breath-takingly, at the end of a Dutch ornamental canal in the grounds of The Court & is now a self-catering holiday house. The striking 16th Century Frampton Manor is said to be the birthplace of 'Fair Rosamund' Clifford, mistress of Henry II; its walled garden is a plantsman's delight & the magnificent neighbouring 16th Century Wool Barn has been dated to around 1550 & is one of the most impressive timber-framed buildings of its type.

Location: Map 6:M12. OS Ref SO 748080. 2 miles west of J13 of the M5. Follow the A38 south from the M5 & then the Perryway (B4071) to Frampton.

Owner: Mr & Mrs Rollo Clifford **Contact:** Janie Clifford for tour enquiries
Tel: 01452 740268 - or to enquire about accommodation / hosting an event or wedding, please call 01452 740698. **E-mail:** events@framptoncourtestate.co.uk
Open: Frampton Court & Frampton Manor by appointment for groups (10+). Frampton Manor Garden: Mon & Fri 2.30-5pm, 27 Apr to 3 Aug 2015.
Admission: Frampton Court: House & Garden £10.00. Frampton Manor: House, Garden & Wool Barn £10.00. Garden only £5.00. Wool Barn only £3.00. Packages available. Frampton Country Fair 13 Sep 2015.
Key facts: ℹ Filming, Parkland for hire. 🌱 Pan Global Plants in The Orangery's walled garden. 🔽 Wedding receptions. 👓 Partial. WCs. 🍽 For pre-booked groups. 🎭 Usually by family members. 🅿 ❌ ♿ B&B at Frampton Court: 01452 740267. Self-catering at The Orangery: 01452 740698. ❂ By arrangement. 👤

Sudeley Castle Gardens

Register for news and special offers at **www.hudsonsheritage.com**

RODMARTON MANOR 🏠ⓕ
CIRENCESTER, GLOUCESTERSHIRE GL7 6PF

www.rodmarton-manor.co.uk

A Cotswold Arts and Crafts house, one of the last great country houses to be built in the traditional way, containing beautiful furniture, ironwork, china and needlework specially made for the house. The large garden complements the architecture and contains many areas of great beauty and character including the magnificent herbaceous borders, topiary, roses, rockery and kitchen garden. Available as a film location and for small functions.

Location: Map 6:N12. OS Ref ST934 977.
Off A433 between Cirencester and Tetbury.
Owner: Mr Simon Biddulph
Contact: John & Sarah Biddulph
Tel: 01285 841442 **E-mail:** enquiries@rodmarton-manor.co.uk

Open: House & Garden: Easter Mon, May-Sep; Weds, Sats & BHs, 2-5pm (not guided tours). Garden (snowdrops): 1, 8, 12 & 15 Feb: from 1.30pm. Guided tours of the house (approx. 1hr) may be booked for groups (15+) all year (min group charge £120). Groups (5+) may book guided or unguided tours of the garden at other times.
Admission: House & Garden: £8.00, Child (5-15yrs) £4.00. Garden only: £5.00, Child (5-15yrs) £1.00. Guided tour of Garden: Entry fee plus £40.00 per group.
Key facts: ⓘ Colour guidebook & postcards on sale. Available for filming. No photography in house. WCs in garden. ♿ Garden & ground floor.
☕ Open days & groups by appointment. 🅵 By arrangement. 🅿 🚽
🐕 Guide dogs only. ❋

STANWAY HOUSE & WATER GARDEN 🏠ⓕ
STANWAY, CHELTENHAM, GLOS GL54 5PQ

www.stanwayfountain.co.uk

'As perfect and pretty a Cotswold manor house as anyone is likely to see' (Fodor's Great Britain 1998 guidebook). Stanway's beautiful architecture, furniture, parkland and village are complemented by the restored 18th Century water garden and the magnificent fountain, 300 feet, making it the tallest garden and gravity fountain in the world. Teas available. Beer for sale. Wedding reception venue.
The Watermill in Church Stanway, now fully restored as a working flour mill, was recently re-opened by HRH The Prince of Wales. Its massive 24-foot overshot waterwheel, 8th largest waterwheel in England, drives traditional machinery, to produce stoneground Cotswold flour.

Location: Map 6:O10. OS Ref SP061 323. N of Winchcombe, just off B4077.

Owner: The Earl of Wemyss and March
Contact: Debbie Lewis
Tel: 01386 584528
Fax: 01386 584688
E-mail: stanwayhse@btconnect.com
Open: House & Garden: Jun-Aug: Tue & Thu, 2-5pm. Private tours by arrangement at other times.
Admission: Please see website for up to date admission prices.
Key facts: ⓘ Film & photographic location. 🖼
🍽 Wedding receptions.
☕ 🅵 By arrangement. 🅿 🐕 In grounds on leads. ❋

KIFTSGATE COURT GARDENS 🏠ⓕ
Chipping Campden, Gloucestershire GL55 6LN
www.kiftsgate.co.uk

Magnificently situated garden on the edge of the Cotswold escarpment with views towards the Malvern Hills. Many unusual shrubs and plants including tree peonies, abutilons, specie and old-fashioned roses.
Winner HHA/Christie's Garden of the Year Award 2003.
Location: Map 6:O9. OS Ref SP173 430. 4m NE of Chipping Campden. ¼ m W of Hidcote Garden.
Owner: Mr and Mrs J G Chambers
Contact: Mr J G Chambers
Tel: 01386 438777
E-mail: info@kiftsgate.co.uk
Open: May, Jun, Jul, Sat-Wed, 12 noon-6pm. Aug, Sat-Wed, 2pm-6pm. Apr & Sep, Sun, Mon & Wed, 2pm-6pm.
Admission: Adult: £8.00, Child £2.50. Groups (20+) £7.00.
Key facts: 🎥 ♿ Partial. 🍽 🅿 Limited for coaches. 🐕 Guide dogs only.

PAINSWICK ROCOCO GARDEN 🏠ⓕ
Painswick, Gloucestershire GL6 6TH
www.rococogarden.org.uk

Painswick Rococo Garden is set in a hidden Cotswold valley. It allows you to step back into the sensual early 18th Century, when gardens were becoming theatrical and romantic backdrops for entertaining guests. Our restaurant serves a delicious range of homemade cakes and light meals using products grown here or from local producers.
Location: Map 6:M11. OS Ref SO864 106. 1½m NW of Painswick on B4073.
Owner: Painswick Rococo Garden Trust
Contact: P R Moir
Tel: 01452 813204
E-mail: info@rococogarden.org.uk
Open: 10 Jan-31 Oct: daily 11am-5pm.
Admission: Adult £7.00, Child £3.50, OAP £6.00. Family (2+2) £18.00. Free introductory talk for pre-booked groups (20+).
Key facts: 🎥 ♿ Partial. WCs. 🍽 Licensed. 🍴 Licensed. 🎓 By arrangement. 🅿 🍽 🐕 On leads. 🏠 ✳ ♿

OWLPEN MANOR
Uley, Nr Dursley, Gloucestershire GL11 5BZ
www.owlpen.com

The romantic Tudor manor house stands in a picturesque valley setting with church, courthouse and mill. Stuart terraced gardens with magnificent yew topiary. Unique painted cloths, and family and Arts and Crafts collections. "By far the finest small manor house in all of England"— Prof Francis Comstock. "Owlpen, in Gloucestershire: ah, what a dream is there!"— Vita Sackville-West.
Location: Map 6:M12. OS Ref ST800 983. One mile east of Uley, off the B4066.
Owner: Sir Nicholas and Lady Mander **Contact:** Bella Wadsworth
Tel: 01453 860261 **E-mail:** sales@owlpen.com
Open: The house will be open by appointment only for groups of 15 people or more. Apr-Oct, Mon-Fri.
Admission: Cream tea £26.00 per person including a tour of the house and gardens. Or, a 2 course lunch for £36.00 per person including a tour of the house and gardens.
Key facts: ℹ Accessible by coach only via Uley Village. 🎓 Usually by owner. 🅿 At top of drive. ✳ 🛏 9 Self catering holiday cottages. ♿

SEZINCOTE 🏠ⓕ
Moreton-In-Marsh, Gloucestershire GL56 9AW
www.sezincote.co.uk

Exotic oriental water garden by Repton and Daniell. Large semi-circular orangery. House by S P Cockerell in Indian style was the inspiration for Brighton Pavilion.
Location: Map 6:P10. OS Ref SP183 324. 2 miles west of Moreton-in-Marsh on the A44 opposite entrance to Batsford Arboretum.
Contact: Dr E Peake
Tel: 01386 700444
E-mail: enquiries@sezincote.co.uk
Open: Garden: Thurs, Fris & BH Mons, 2-6pm except Dec. House: As above May-Sep. Teas in Orangery when house open.
Admission: House: Adult £10.00 (guided tour). Garden: Adult £5.00, Child £1.50 (under 5yrs Free). Groups welcomed weekdays, please contact for details.
Key facts: ℹ Please see our website for up to date events and special openings. ♿ For full information for disabled visitors please email enquiries@sezincote.co.uk. 🍽 🎓 Obligatory. 🐕 Guide dogs only. 🏠 Weddings. ✳ ♿

NEWARK PARK ❦
Ozleworth, Wotton-Under-Edge, Gloucestershire GL12 7PZ

Newark Park is a Tudor hunting lodge which has been extended, converted and restored over 450 years into a fascinating home. The house has eclectic collections and exhibitions, and the garden provides space to play and contemplate, with spectacular views over the Cotswolds. Our beautiful estate offers several walks through woods and glades, really showcasing the changing seasons.
Location: Map 2:P1. OS Ref 172. ST786 934. Not far from M5 jcts 13 & 14. Off A4135 Tetbury/Dursley road, follow signs for Newark Park. **Owner:** National Trust
Tel: 01453 842644 **E-mail:** newarkpark@nationaltrust.org.uk
Website: www.nationaltrust.org.uk/newark-park **Open:** Open Wed-Sun & BHs (closed Mon & Tue). 18-22 Feb, 5 & 6 Dec & 12 & 13 Dec: 11am-4pm.
4 Mar-1 Nov: 11am-5pm. Last entry 30 mins before closing (dusk if earlier).
Admission: Adult £8.40, Child £4.20, Family £21.00.
Key facts: ◻ ◻ ◻ Ground floor. ◻ ◻ ◻ On leads. ◻ Holiday cottage ◻

BATSFORD ARBORETUM
Batsford, Moreton-in-Marsh, Gloucestershire GL56 9QB

Batsford is home to one of the finest botanical collections in the country. At 56 acres in size, Batsford is an intimate and romantic place to visit.
Location: Map 6:O10. OS Ref SP186 338. Please use GL56 9AD for Satnav.
Tel: 01386 701441 **E-mail:** arboretum@batsfordfoundation.co.uk
Website: www.batsarb.co.uk
Open: Please see website for up to date opening and admission details.

BOURTON HOUSE GARDEN
Bourton-on-the-Hill, Gloucestershire GL56 9AE

An award-winning three acre garden featuring wide herbaceous borders with stunning plant and colour combinations.
Location: Map 6:P10. OS Ref SP180 324. **Tel:** 01386 700754
E-mail: info@bourtonhouse.com **Website:** www.bourtonhouse.com
Open: Please see website for up to date opening and admission details.

CHEDWORTH ROMAN VILLA ❦
Yanworth, Cheltenham, Gloucestershire GL54 3LJ

One of the best preserved Roman sites in Britain set in beautiful Cotswold countryside. **Location:** Map 6:N11. OS Ref SP05 6136. **Tel:** 01242 890256
E-mail: chedworth@nationaltrust.org.uk **Website:** www.nationaltrust.org.uk/chedworth **Open:** Daily 15 Feb-30 Nov. Café and gift shop.
Admission: NT Members Free. Gift Aid (Standard in brackets): £9.90 (£9.00), Child £4.95 (£4.50), Family £24.75 (£22.50). Groups (15+) £8.00, Child £4.00.

Owlpen Manor

DYRHAM PARK ❦
Dyrham, Nr Bath, Gloucestershire SN14 8ER

Spectacular late 17th Century mansion, garden and deer park. Inside the impressive mansion discover fascinating interiors little changed in 300 years.
Location: Map 2:P2. OS Ref ST741 757. **Tel:** 0117 937 2501
E-mail: dyrhampark@nationaltrust.org.uk **Website:** www.nationaltrust.org.uk/dyrham-park **Open:** Please see website for up to date details.

HAILES ABBEY ⌗
Nr Winchcombe, Cheltenham, Gloucestershire GL54 5PB

Cloister arches and extensive excavated remains in lovely surroundings of an abbey founded by Richard, Earl of Cornwall, in 1246. **Location:** Map 6:O10. OS Ref SP050 300. **Tel:** 01242 602398 **E-mail:** customers@english-heritage.org.uk
Website: www.english-heritage.org.uk/hailes
Open: Please see website for up to date opening and admission details.

HIDCOTE MANOR GARDEN ❦
Hidcote Bartrim, Nr Chipping Campden, Gloucs GL55 6LR

One of the most delightful gardens in England, created in the early 20th Century by the great horticulturist Major Lawrence Johnston.
Location: Map 6:O10. OS Ref SP176 429. **Tel:** 01386 438333
E-mail: hidcote@nationaltrust.org.uk **Website:** www.nationaltrust.org.uk/hidcote
Open: Please see website for up to date opening and admission details.

WHITTINGTON COURT ◻ⓕ
Cheltenham, Gloucestershire GL54 4HF

Elizabethan & Jacobean manor house with church
Location: Map 6:N11. OS Ref SP014 206. 4m E of Cheltenham on N side of A40.
Tel: 01242 820556 **E-mail:** jstringer@whittingtoncourt.co.uk
Open: 4-19 Apr & 15-31 Aug: 2-5pm.
Admission: Adult £5.00/Child £1.00/OAP £4.00.

CHURCH OF ST JOHN THE BAPTIST ◻
Broad Street, Bristol, Bristol BS1 2EZ

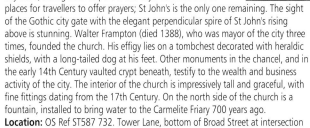

In the 12th Century there were five churches built into Bristol's city walls, acting both as part of the city's defences and as places for travellers to offer prayers; St John's is the only one remaining. The sight of the Gothic city gate with the elegant perpendicular spire of St John's rising above is stunning. Walter Frampton (died 1388), who was mayor of the city three times, founded the church. His effigy lies on a tombchest decorated with heraldic shields, with a long-tailed dog at his feet. Other monuments in the chancel, and in the early 14th Century vaulted crypt beneath, testify to the wealth and business activity of the city. The interior of the church is impressively tall and graceful, with fine fittings dating from the 17th Century. On the north side of the church is a fountain, installed to bring water to the Carmelite Friary 700 years ago.
Location: OS Ref ST587 732. Tower Lane, bottom of Broad Street at intersection with Nelson Street. **Website:** www.visitchurches.org.uk **Open:** Church opened regularly, but please call the Bristol office on 0117 9291766 before you visit.

CHURCH OF ST THOMAS THE MARTYR ◻
Thomas Lane, Bristol BS1 6JG

Located in Bristol city centre, this handsome late 18th Century church was designed in 1789 by local architect and carver, James Allen, to replace a medieval church deemed unsafe for use. Allen retained the 15th Century west tower of the old church, intending it to be 'raised and modernised' in a classical fashion, but the plan was never carried out and the church is an unusual-but pleasing-blend of both periods. There is a fine ring of eight bells, all cast by local founders from 15th-19th Century. At the east end is a reredos of 1716 and at the west a gallery of 1728-32, both transferred from the previous church. On the north side of the chancel is a superb 18th Century organ case. Some of the other furnishings are 18th Century, but most date from the 1896 restoration by H Roumieu Gough. They are excellently designed and all contribute to one of the best church interiors in Bristol. **Location:** OS Ref ST591 727. St Thomas Street, to SW of Bristol Bridge nr intersection of Redcliff St & Victoria St. **Website:** www.visitchurches.org.uk **Open:** Mon-Fri, 9:30am-5pm.

Glastonbury Abbey, Somerset

GLASTONBURY ABBEY
Magdalene Street, Glastonbury BA6 9EL
www.glastonburyabbey.com

A hidden jewel in the heart of Somerset, Glastonbury Abbey is traditionally associated with the earliest days of Christianity in Britain. It is also the resting place for three Saxon kings and the legendary King Arthur. Open 364 days a year. Events held throughout the year - check out the website or follow on Twitter @glastonburyabbe.

Location: Map 2:N4. OS Ref ST499 388. 50 yds from the Market Cross, in centre of Glastonbury. M5/J23, A39, follow signs to Glastonbury; M4/J18 to Bath, A367 to Shepton Mallet and A361 to Glastonbury; M3/J8 A303 and head for Glastonbury. **Owner:** Glastonbury Abbey Estate

Tel: 01458 832267 **Fax:** 01458 836117 **E-mail:** info@glastonburyabbey.com

Open: Daily except Christmas Day. Nov-Feb 9am-4pm. Mar-May 9am-6pm. Jun-Aug 9am-8pm. Sep-Oct 9am-6pm. **Admission:** Adult £7.60*, Child (5-15) £4.75, Conc £6.60*, Family (2+3) £19.60*. *Gift Aid admission price.

Key facts: ⓘ 🅰 ▣ Summer. 🎦 Mar-Oct (groups pre-book Nov-Feb). 🅿 Pay & display car parks nearby. 🏫 Primary to University, RE, History, tailormade workshops & activities 01458 8361103. 🐕 On leads. ✳ Except Xmas Day. ♿

ROBIN HOOD'S HUT
Halswell, Goathurst, Somerset TA5 2EW
www.landmarktrust.org.uk

An 18th Century garden building with two faces, a rustic cottage and an elegant pavillion.

Location: Map 2:M4. OS Ref ST255 333.

Owner: The Landmark Trust

Tel: 01628 825925

E-mail: bookings@landmarktrust.org.uk

Open: Self-catering accommodation. 6 Open Days per year, visits by appointment.

Admission: Free on Open Days and visits by appointment.

Key facts: ⓘ You may dine al fresco beneath the elegant canopy of the umbrello whilst admiring the fine views. The bathroom is housed in a separate building a few metres away from the bedroom door.

🅿 🐕 ▣ ✳ ♿

FAIRFIELD
Stogursey, Bridgwater, Somerset TA5 1PU

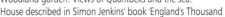
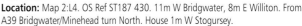

Elizabethan and medieval house. Occupied by the same family (Acland-Hoods and their ancestors) for over 800 years. Woodland garden. Views of Quantocks and the sea. House described in Simon Jenkins' book 'England's Thousand Best Houses'.

Location: Map 2:L4. OS Ref ST187 430. 11m W Bridgwater, 8m E Williton. From A39 Bridgwater/Minehead turn North. House 1m W Stogursey.

Tel: 01278 732251

Open: 6 Apr-25 May, 3-10 Jun Wed, Thu, Fri & BH Mon. Guided house tours at 2.30 & 3.30pm. Garden also open.

Admission: £6.00 in aid of Stogursey Church. Advisable to contact to confirm dates.

Key facts: ⓘ No inside photography. 🅰 🎦 Obligatory. 🅿 No coach parking. 🐕 Guide dogs only.

DODINGTON HALL
Nr Nether Stowey, Bridgwater, Somerset TA5 1LF

Small Tudor manor house on the lower slopes of the Quantocks. Great Hall with oak roof. Semi-formal garden with roses and shrubs.

Location: Map 2:L4. OS Ref ST172 405. ½m from A39, 11m W of Bridgwater, 7m E of Williton. **Tel:** 01278 741400 **Open:** 1-11 Jun, 2-5pm.

Admission: Donations to Dodington Church. No coach parking.

KENTSFORD
Washford, Watchet, Somerset TA23 0JD

Location: Map 2:L4. OS Ref ST058 426.

Tel: 01984 632309 **E-mail:** wyndhamest@btconnect.com

Open: Please contact for details.

Admission: Please contact for details.

MONTACUTE HOUSE 🦌
Montacute, Somerset TA15 6XP

A glittering Elizabethan house, adorned with elegant chimneys, carved parapets and other Renaissance features. **Location:** Map 2:N5. OS Ref ST499 172.

Tel: 01935 823289 **E-mail:** montacute@nationaltrust.org.uk

Website: www.nationaltrust.org.uk/montacute-house

Open: Please see website for most up to date times and prices.

ORCHARD WYNDHAM 🏠
Williton, Taunton, Somerset TA4 4HH

English manor house. Family home for 700 years encapsulating continuous building and alteration from the 14th to the 20th Century.

Location: Map 2:L4. OS Ref ST072 400. 1m from A39 at Williton.

Tel: 01984 632309 **E-mail:** wyndhamest@btconnect.com

Open: Please telephone for details. **Admission:** Please telephone for details.

PRIOR PARK LANDSCAPE GARDEN 🦌
Ralph Allen Drive, Bath BA2 5AH

Beautiful and intimate 18th Century landscape garden created by Bath entrepreneur Ralph Allen with advice from Alexander Pope and 'Capability' Brown. **Location:** Map 2:P3. OS Ref ST762 628. **Tel:** 01225 833422

E-mail: priorpark@nationaltrust.org.uk **Website:** www.nationaltrust.org.uk/prior-park **Open:** Please see website for up to date opening and admission details.

TYNTESFIELD 🦌
Wraxall, North Somerset BS48 1NX

Extraordinary Victorian Estate. The House is a Gothic revival extravaganza with surrounding formal gardens, kitchen garden and extensive woodland.

Location: Map 2:N2. OS Ref ST506715. **Tel:** 0844 800 4966

E-mail: tyntesfield@nationaltrust.org.uk **Website:** www.nationaltrust.org.uk/tyntesfield **Open:** Please see website for up to date opening and admission details.

WILTON HOUSE 🏠Ⓕ
WILTON, SALISBURY SP2 0BJ
www.wiltonhouse.com

Wilton House has been the Earl of Pembroke's ancestral home for 460 years. Inigo Jones and John Webb rebuilt the house in the Palladian style after the 1647 fire whilst further alterations were made by James Wyatt from 1801. Recipient of the 2010 HHA/Sotheby's Restoration Award, the chief architectural features are the 17th Century state apartments (Single and Double Cube rooms), and the 19th Century cloisters. The House contains one of the finest art collections in Europe and is set in magnificent landscaped parkland featuring the Palladian Bridge. A large adventure playground provides hours of fun for younger visitors.

Location: Map 3:B4. OS Ref SU099 311. 3m W of Salisbury along the A36.
Owner: The Earl of Pembroke **Contact:** The Estate Office
Tel: 01722 746714 **Fax:** 01722 744447 **E-mail:** tourism@wiltonhouse.com
Open: House: 3 Apr-6 Apr inclusive, 2 May-31 Aug Sun-Thu plus BH Sats, 11.30am-5pm, last admission 4.30pm. *Please check website for up to date information. Grounds: 29 Mar-12 Apr, 2 May–13 Sep Sun-Thu plus BH Sats, 11.00am-5.30pm. Private groups at other times by arrangement.

Admission: House & Grounds*: Adult £14.50, Child (5-15) £7.50, Concession £11.75, Family £36.00 *includes admission to Dining & South Ante Rooms when open. Grounds: Adult £6.00, Child (5-15) £4.50, Concession £5.75, Family £17.00. Group Admission: Adult £12.50, Child £6.00, Concession £9.75. Guided Tour: £8.00. Exhibitions: "Cecil Beaton at Wilton". An exhibition of photographs from The Cecil Beaton Studio Archive at Sotheby's: Lord Pembroke's Classic Car Collection, in the Old Riding School.

Key facts: ⓘ Film location, equestrian events, antiques fairs, vehicle rallies. No photography in house. 🗓 Open 7 days a week during the season. ♿ WCs. 🍴 Licensed. 🍽 Licensed. 🎟 By arrangement. £8.00. French, German and Spanish. 🅿 200 cars & 12 coaches. Free coach parking. Group rates (min 15), drivers' meal voucher. 🎓 National Curriculum KS1/2. Sandford Award Winner 2002 & 2008. 🐕 Guide dogs only. 🔺 🔻

The Merchant's House

South West - England

CORSHAM COURT 🏛Ⓕ
Corsham, Wiltshire SN13 0BZ
www.corsham-court.co.uk

Corsham Court is a splendid Elizabethan house dating from 1582. An internationally renowned collection of Old Masters hangs in the magnificent Picture Gallery and suite of State Rooms. Delightful gardens and parkland, designed by Brown and Repton, surround the Court.

Location: Map 3:A2. OS Ref ST874 706. Signposted from the A4, approx. 4m W of Chippenham. **Owner:** J Methuen-Campbell Esq **Contact:** The Curator **Tel:** 01249 712214 01249 701610.
E-mail: staterooms@corsham-court.co.uk
Open: Spring/Summer 20 Mar-30 Sep. Daily, except Mon & Fri but inc BHs 2-5.30pm. Last adm 5pm. Winter 1 Oct-19 Mar (closed Dec) w/e only 2-4.30pm. Last adm 4pm. Throughout year by appointment for groups.
Admission: Adult £10, Child (5-15yrs) £5, Family (2 adults & 2 children) £25. Garden only Adult £5, Child (5-15yrs) £2.50. **Key facts:** ⓘ No photography in house. 🎁 Guide books, postcards, etc at cash desk. ♿ Platform lift & WC. 🚻 Max 45. If requested the owner may meet the group. Morning tours preferred. Ⓟ 120yds from house. Coaches may park in Church Square. Coach parties must book in advance. ⬛ Available: rate negotiable. A guide will be provided. 🐕 ❄

LYDIARD PARK 🏛
Lydiard Tregoze, Swindon, Wiltshire SN5 3PA
www.lydiardpark.org.uk

Lydiard Park is the ancestral home of the Viscounts Bolingbroke. The Palladian house contains original family furnishings and portraits, exceptional plasterwork and rare 17th Century window. The Georgian ornamental Walled Garden has beautiful seasonal displays of flowers and unique garden features. Exceptional monuments, including the Golden Cavalier, in the church.

Location: Map 3:B1. OS Ref SU104 848. 4m W of Swindon, 1½m N M4/J16. **Owner:** Swindon Borough Council **Contact:** Lydiard Park Manager **Tel:** 01793 466664 **E-mail:** lydiardpark@swindon.gov.uk
Open: House & Walled Garden: Tue to Sun 11am-5pm (Feb-Nov). Tue to Sun 11am-4pm (Dec-Mar). Open BH Mons. Grounds: All day, closing at dusk.
Admission: House & Walled Garden: Adult £4.70, Senior Citizen £4.20, Child £2.30. Family ticket (2 adults & 2 children) £12. Under 5's Free.
Key facts: ⓘ No photography in house. 🎁 Small gift shop. 🎫 Selection seasonal plants available to buy. ♿ Designated parking. WCs. ☕ Forest Cafe open all year, Coach House Tea Rooms closed winter. 🚻 By arrangement. Ⓟ Free parking, limit parking for coaches. ⬛ Full programme of school sessions linked to National Curriculum. 🐕 In grounds only. ❄ ⬤

IFORD MANOR: THE PETO GARDEN 🏛Ⓕ
Lower Westwood, Bradford-on-Avon, Wiltshire BA15 2BA
www.ifordmanor.co.uk

Unique Grade-1 Italian-style garden set on a romantic hillside above the River Frome. Designed by Edwardian architect Harold Peto, who lived at Iford from 1899-1933, the garden features terraces, colonnades, cloisters, casita, statuary, evergreen planting and magnificent rural views. Winner of the 1998 HHA/Christie's Garden of the Year Award. **Location:** Map 2:P3. OS Ref ST800 589. 7m SE of Bath via A36, signposted Iford. 2m SW of Bradford-on-Avon via B3109 and Lower Westwood. Coaches must call in advance for directions.
Owner: Mrs E A J Cartwright-Hignett **Contact:** Mr William Cartwright-Hignett **Tel:** 01225 863146 **E-mail:** info@ifordmanor.co.uk
Open: Apr-Sep: Tue-Thu, Sat, Sun & BH Mons, 2-5pm. Oct: Sun only, 2-5pm. Tearoom at weekends May-Sep. Children under 10yrs preferred weekdays only for safety reasons. **Admission:** Adult £5.50, Conc. £5.00. Groups (10+) welcome for exclusive use outside normal opening hours, strictly by appointment.
Key facts: ⓘ No professional photography without permission. 🎁 ♿ Partial. WCs. ☕ Housekeeper's Tearoom open at weekends 2:30-5pm; 'tea and biscuits' on weekdays. 🚻 Subject to availability for groups booked in advance. Ⓟ Limited for coaches. 🐕 On leads. ⬤

THE MERCHANT'S HOUSE
132 High Street, Marlborough, Wiltshire SN8 1HN
www.themerchantshouse.co.uk

The House of Thomas Bayly was built in 1653 following the Great Fire of Marlborough. It is a fine timber and brick building, with panelled interiors, original wall paintings and a commanding oak staircase. Its position on Marlborough's lively High Street is a reminder that it was both the shop and the home of a prosperous puritan family. The ongoing restoration by the Merchant's House Trust makes the House a special and unusual place to visit.

Location: Map 3:B2. OS Ref SU188 691. N side of High Street, near Town Hall.
Owner: Marlborough Town Council, leased to The Merchant's House (Marlborough) Trust
Contact: Sophie Costard
Tel: 01672 511491
E-mail: admin@merchantshousetrust.co.uk
Open: Apr-end Oct Tue, Fri and Sat, guided tours 10.30am, 12noon, 1.30pm and 3pm. Group bookings by application.
Admission: Adult £6.00, Child £1.00.
Key facts: ⓘ Photography only by arrangement. 🎁 ♿ 🚻

MOMPESSON HOUSE 🏛
Cathedral Close, Salisbury, Wiltshire SP1 2EL
www.nationaltrust.org.uk

Elegant, spacious house in the Cathedral Close, built 1701. Featured in award-winning film Sense and Sensibility. Magnificent plasterwork and fine oak staircase. Good period furniture and the Turnbull collection of 18th Century drinking glasses. The delightful walled garden has a pergola and traditional herbaceous borders. Garden Tea Room serves light refreshments. For 2015, an exhibition entitled 'Sense and Sensibility Revisited: Did Jane Austen know the Portman Sisters of Mompesson House?'. **Location:** Map 3:B4. OS Ref SU142 297. On N side of Choristers' Green in Cathedral Close, near High Street Gate.
Owner: National Trust **Contact:** The Property Manager
Tel: 01722 335659 **Fax:** 01722 321559 **Infoline:** 01722 420980
E-mail: mompessonhouse@nationaltrust.org.uk
Open: 14 Mar-1 Nov: Sat-Wed, 11am-5pm. Last admission 4.30pm. Open Good Fri. **Admission:** *Adult £6.50, Child £3.30, Family (2+3) £16.40, Groups £5.30. Garden only: £1.00. Tearoom vouchers when arriving by public transport.
*Includes voluntary donation, visitors can pay standard prices.
Key facts: ▢ ⛭ WCs. ▣ ⛭ By arrangement. ▣ ⛭ Guide dogs only. ⛭

CHURCH OF ST JOHN
THE BAPTIST ⛪
Inglesham, Swindon, Wiltshire SN6 7RD
This exquisitely beautiful and fascinating 13th Century church stands on a gentle rise of land above waterside meadows near the Thames. Pioneering Victorian designer William Morris oversaw St John's restoration in the 19th Century. An amazing series of paintings, from the 13th-19th Century cover the walls, often with one painted over another. While it is not always easy to puzzle out the subjects, you can see 15th Century angels above the chancel arch, an early 14th Century doom on the east wall of the north aisle and several 19th Century texts. There is an unusual and powerful Saxon stone carving of the Madonna and Child set in the south wall. The woodwork of the roofs, the 15th Century screens and the 17th and 18th Century pulpit and box pews are all original to the church, and their arrangement is still much as it would have been in Oliver Cromwell's time.
Location: OS Ref SU205 984. 1 mile south of Lechlade, off A361.
Website: www.visitchurches.org.uk **Open:** Open daily.

BOWOOD HOUSE & GARDENS 🏛
Calne, Wiltshire SN11 0LZ
The House is set in one of the most beautiful parks in England. Over 2,000 acres of gardens and grounds were landscaped by 'Capability' Brown between 1762 and 1768. **Location:** Map 3:A2. OS Ref ST974 700. **Tel:** 01249 812102
E-mail: houseandgardens@bowood.org **Website:** www.bowood.org
Open: Please see website for up to date opening and admission details.

LACOCK ABBEY 🏛
Lacock, Nr Chippenham, Wiltshire SN15 2LG
Founded in 1232 and coverted to a country house in c1540, once home to William Henry Fox Talbot. **Location:** Map 3:A2. OS Ref ST919 684. **Tel:** 01249 730459
E-mail: lacockabbey@nationaltrust.org.uk
Website: www.nationaltrust.org.uk/lacock
Open: Please see website for up to date opening and admission details.

LONGLEAT 🏛
Longleat, Warminster, Wiltshire BA12 7NW
Longleat House is widely regarded as one of the best examples of high Elizabethan architecture in Britain. **Location:** Map 2:P4. OS Ref ST809 430.
Tel: 01985 844328 **E-mail:** sales@longleat.co.uk
Website: www.longleat.co.uk **Open:** Please see www.longleat.co.uk to confirm opening dates and times.

NEWHOUSE 🏛
Redlynch, Salisbury, Wiltshire SP5 2NX
A brick, Jacobean 'Trinity' House, c1609, with two Georgian wings and a basically Georgian interior. **Location:** Map 3:B5. OS Ref SU218 214. 9m S of Salisbury between A36 & A338. **Tel:** 01725 510055
E-mail: events@newhouseestate.co.uk **Website:** www.newhouseestate.co.uk
Open: 2 Mar-9 Apr, Mon-Fri & 25 Aug: 2-5pm. **Admission:** Adult £5.00, Child £3.00, Conc. £5.00. Groups (15+): Adult £4.00, Child £3.00, Conc. £4.00.

NORRINGTON MANOR
Alvediston, Salisbury, Wiltshire SP5 5LL
Built in 1377 it has been altered and added to in every century since, with the exception of the 18th Century. **Location:** Map 3:AS. OS Ref ST966 237. Signposted to N of Berwick St John and Alvediston road (half way between the two villages). **Tel:** 01722 780 259 **Open:** By appointment in writing.
Admission: A donation to the local churches is asked for.

Bowood House

ANTONY HOUSE & GARDEN ❧
Torpoint, Cornwall PL11 2QA
Tel: 01752 812191 **E-mail:** antony@nationaltrust.org.uk

COTEHELE ❧
Saint Dominick, Saltash, Cornwall PL12 6TA
Tel: 01579 351346 **E-mail:** cothele@nationaltrust.org.uk

THE LOST GARDENS OF HELIGAN
Pentewan, St Austall, Cornwall PL26 6EN
Tel: 01726 845100 **E-mail:** info@heligan.com

MOUNT EDGCUMBE HOUSE & COUNTRY PARK
Cremyll, Torpoint, Cornwall PL10 1HZ
Tel: 01752 822236

PENDENNIS CASTLE ⌗
Falmouth, Cornwall TR11 4LP
Tel: 01326 316594 **E-mail:** pendennis.castle@english-heritage.org.uk

TREBAH GARDEN ▥
Mawnan Smith, Nr Falmouth, Cornwall TR11 5JZ
Tel: 01326 252200 **E-mail:** mail@trebah-garden.co.uk

TRELISSICK GARDEN ❧
Feock, Truro, Cornwall TR3 6QL
Tel: 01872 862090 **E-mail:** trelissick@nationaltrust.org.uk

TRERICE ❧
Kestle Mill, Nr Newquay, Cornwall TR8 4PG
Tel: 01637 875404 **E-mail:** trerice@

ARLINGTON COURT ❧
Nr Barnstaple, North Devon EX31 4LP
Tel: 01271 850296 **E-mail:** arlingtoncourt@nationaltrust.org.uk

BUCKLAND ABBEY ❧
The National Trust, Yelverton, Devon PL20 6EY
Tel: 01822 853607 **E-mail:** bucklandabbey@nationaltrust.org.uk

CHURCH OF ST MICHAEL & ALL ANGELS ⌖
Tavistock Road, Princetown, Yelverton, Devon PL20 6RE
Tel: 0845 303 2760 **E-mail:** central@thecct.org.uk

CH. OF ST PETER THE POOR FISHERMAN ⌖
Stoke Beach, Noss Mayo, Revelstoke, Plymouth PL8 1HE
Tel: 0845 303 2760 **E-mail:** central@thecct.org.uk

COLETON FISHACRE ❧
Brownstone Road, Kingswear, Dartmouth TQ6 0EQ
Tel: 01803 842382 **E-mail:** coletonfishacre@nationaltrust.org.uk

COMPTON CASTLE ❧
Marldon, Paighton TQ3 1TA
Tel: 01803 843235 **E-mail:** compton@nationaltrust.org.uk

HOLY TRINITY CHURCH ⌖
Torbryan Hill, Torbryan, Newton Abbot, Devon TQ12 5UR
Tel: 0845 303 2760 **E-mail:** central@thecct.org.uk

KILLERTON ❧
Broadclyst, Exeter EX5 3LE
Tel: 01392 881345 **E-mail:** killerton@nationaltrust.org.uk

KNIGHTSHAYES ❧
Bolham, Tiverton, Devon EX16 7RQ
Tel: 01884 254665 **E-mail:** knightshayes@nationaltrust.org.uk

RHS GARDEN ROSEMOOR
Great Torrington, Devon EX38 8PH
Tel: 01805 624067 **E-mail:** rosemooradmin@rhs.org.uk

ST JAMES' CHURCH ⌖
Luffincott, Tetcott, Holsworthy, Devon EX22 6RB
Tel: 0845 303 2760 **E-mail:** central@thecct.org.uk

ST MARY'S CHURCH ⌖
North Huish, South Brent, Devon TQ10 9NQ
Tel: 0845 303 2760 **E-mail:** central@thecct.org.uk

ST NONNA'S CHURCH ⌖
Bradstone, Tavistock, Devon PL19 0QS
Tel: 0845 303 2760 **E-mail:** central@thecct.org.uk

ST PETER'S CHURCH ⌖
Satterleigh, Umberleigh, Devon EX37 9DJ
Tel: 0845 303 2760 **E-mail:** central@thecct.org.uk

ST PETROCK'S CHURCH ⌖
Church Lane, Parracombe, Barnstaple, Devon EX31 4RJ
Tel: 0845 303 2760 **E-mail:** central@thecct.org.uk

SALTRAM ❧
Plympton, Plymouth, Devon PL7 1UH
Tel: 01752 333500 **E-mail:** saltram@nationaltrust.org.uk

ABBOTSBURY SUBTROPICAL GARDENS ▥℗
Abbotsbury, Weymouth, Dorset DT3 4LA
Tel: 01305 871387 **E-mail:** info@abbotsbury- tourism.co.uk

ALL SAINTS' CHURCH ⌖
Nether Cerne, Dorchester, Dorset DT2 7AJ
Tel: 0845 303 2760 **E-mail:** central@thecct.org.uk

THE CHURCH (NO DEDICATION) ⌖
Whitcombe, Dorchester, Dorset DT2 8NY
Tel: 0845 303 2760 **E-mail:** central@thecct.org.uk

CORFE CASTLE ❧
Wareham, Dorset BH20 5EZ
Tel: 01929 477 062 **E-mail:** corfecastle@nationaltrust.org.uk

FORDE ABBEY & GARDENS ▥℗
Forde Abbey, Chard, Somerset TA20 4LU
Tel: 01460 221290 **E-mail:** info@fordeabbey.co.uk

HOLY TRINITY OLD CHURCH ⌖
Old Church Road, Bothenhampton, Bridport, Dorset DT6 4BP
Tel: 0845 303 2760 **E-mail:** central@thecct.org.uk

ST ANDREW'S CHURCH ⌖
Off Marsh Lane, Winterborne Tomson, Dorset DT11 9HA
Tel: 0845 303 2760 **E-mail:** central@thecct.org.uk

ST CUTHBERT OLD CHANCEL ⌖
London Road, Oborne, Sherborne, Dorset DT9 4JY
Tel: 0845 303 2760 **E-mail:** central@thecct.org.uk

ST EDWOLD'S CHURCH
Stockwood, Evershot, Dorchester, Dorset DT2 0NG
Tel: 0845 303 2760 **E-mail:** central@thecct.org.uk

ALL SAINTS' CHURCH
Shorncote, Cirencester, Gloucestershire GL7 6DE
Tel: 0845 303 2760 **E-mail:** central@thecct.org.uk

CHURCH OF ST NICHOLAS OF MYRA
Ozleworth, Wotton-Under-Edge, Gloucestershire GL12 7QA
Tel: 0845 303 2760 **E-mail:** central@thecct.org.uk

KELMSCOTT MANOR
Kelmscott, Nr Lechlade, Gloucestershire GL7 3HJ
Tel: 01367 252486 **E-mail:** admin@kelmscottmanor.org.uk

ST ARILD'S CHURCH
Oldbury-on-the-Hill, Badminton, Gloucestershire GL9 1EA
Tel: 0845 303 2760 **E-mail:** central@thecct.org.uk

ST MARY'S CHURCH
Little Washbourne, Tewkesbury, Gloucestershire GL20 8NQ
Tel: 0845 303 2760 **E-mail:** central@thecct.org.uk

ST MARY'S CHURCH
Shipton Sollars, Cheltenham, Gloucestershire GL54 4HU
Tel: 0845 303 2760 **E-mail:** central@thecct.org.uk

ST MICHAEL & ST MARTIN'S CHURCH
Eastleach Martin, Cirencester, Gloucestershire GL7 3NN
Tel: 0845 303 2760 **E-mail:** central@thecct.org.uk

ST NICHOLAS' CHURCH
Broadway, Saintbury, Gloucestershire WR12 7PX
Tel: 0845 303 2760 **E-mail:** central@thecct.org.uk

ST NICHOLAS' CHURCH
Westgate Street, Gloucester, Gloucestershire GL1 2PG
Tel: 0845 303 2760 **E-mail:** central@thecct.org.uk

ST OSWALD'S TOWER
Lassington Lane, Highnam, Gloucester GL2 8DH
Tel: 0845 303 2760 **E-mail:** central@thecct.org.uk

ST SWITHUN'S CHURCH
Stroud Road, Brookthorpe, Gloucester GL4 0UJ
Tel: 0845 303 2760 **E-mail:** central@thecct.org.uk

ST PAUL'S CHURCH
Portland Square, Bristol BS2 8SJ
Tel: 0845 303 2760 **E-mail:** central@thecct.org.uk

ALL SAINTS' CHURCH
The Hill, Langport, Somerset TA10 9QF
Tel: 0845 303 2760 **E-mail:** central@thecct.org.uk

ALL SAINTS' CHURCH
Otterhampton, Bridgwater, Somerset TA5 2PT
Tel: 0845 303 2760 **E-mail:** central@thecct.org.uk

THE AMERICAN MUSEUM & GARDENS
Claverton Manor, Bath BA2 7BD
Tel: 01225 460503 **E-mail:** info@americanmuseum.org

Clovelly

ASSEMBLY ROOMS
Bennett Street, Bath BA1 2QH
Tel: 01225 477785 **E-mail:** costume_enquiries@bathnes.gov.uk

CHURCH OF ST MARTIN OF TOURS 🏛
Silverdown Hill, Elworthy, Taunton, Somerset TA4 3PY
Tel: 0845 303 2760 **E-mail:** central@thecct.org.uk

CHURCH OF ST THOMAS A BECKET 🏛
Old Road, Pensford, Bristol, Somerset BS39 4AL
Tel: 0845 303 2760 **E-mail:** central@thecct.org.uk

CHURCH OF THE BLESSED VIRGIN MARY 🏛
Chapel Hill, Emborough, Wells, Somerset BA3 4SG
Tel: 0845 303 2760 **E-mail:** central@thecct.org.uk

COTHAY MANOR & GARDENS
Greenham, Wellington, Somerset TA21 0JR
Tel: 01823 672283 **E-mail:** cothaymanor@btinternet.com

DUNSTER CASTLE 🌿
Dunster, Nr Minehead, Somerset TA24 6SL
Tel: 01643 821314 **E-mail:** dunstercastle@nationaltrust.org.uk

HOLY SAVIOUR'S CHURCH 🏛
Puxton, Hewish, Weston-Super-Mare, Somerset BS24 6TF
Tel: 0845 303 2760 **E-mail:** central@thecct.org.uk

ROMAN BATHS
Roman Baths, Abbey Church Yard, Bath BA1 1LZ
Tel: 01225 477785 **E-mail:** romanbaths_bookings@bathnes.gov.uk

ST ANDREW'S CHURCH 🏛
Roman Road, Northover, Yeovil, Somerset BA22 8JR
Tel: 0845 303 2760 **E-mail:** central@thecct.org.uk

ST ANDREW'S CHURCH 🏛
Holcombe, Radstock, Somerset BA3 5ES
Tel: 0845 303 2760 **E-mail:** central@thecct.org.uk

ST JAMES' CHURCH 🏛
Cameley, Temple Cloud, Bristol, Somerset BS39 5AH
Tel: 0845 303 2760 **E-mail:** central@thecct.org.uk

ST MARY'S CHURCH 🏛
Church Lane, Seavington, Ilminster, Somerset TA19 0QP
Tel: 0845 303 2760 **E-mail:** central@thecct.org.uk

ST MARY'S CHURCH 🏛
Owl Street Lane, Stocklinch Ottersey, Ilminster TA19 9JN
Tel: 0845 303 2760 **E-mail:** central@thecct.org.uk

ST NICHOLAS' CHURCH 🏛
Uphill Way, Uphill, Weston-Super-Mare, Somerset BS23 4TN
Tel: 0845 303 2760 **E-mail:** central@thecct.org.uk

ST NICHOLAS' CHURCH 🏛
Brockley, Backwell, Somerset BS48 3AU
Tel: 0845 303 2760 **E-mail:** central@thecct.org.uk

ST THOMAS' CHURCH 🏛
Thurlbear, Taunton, Somerset TA3 5BW
Tel: 0845 303 2760 **E-mail:** central@thecct.org.uk

ALL SAINTS' CHURCH 🏛
Alton Priors, Salisbury, Wiltshire SN8 4LB
Tel: 0845 303 2760 **E-mail:** central@thecct.org.uk

ALL SAINTS' CHURCH 🏛
Idmiston, Salisbury, Wiltshire SP4 0AU
Tel: 0845 303 2760 **E-mail:** central@thecct.org.uk

ALL SAINTS' CHURCH 🏛
Leigh, Cricklade, Wiltshire SN6 6QY
Tel: 0845 303 2760 **E-mail:** central@thecct.org.uk

BORBACH CHANTRY 🏛
Off Rectory Hill, West Dean, Salisbury, Wiltshire SP5 1JJ
Tel: 0845 303 2760 **E-mail:** central@thecct.org.uk

CHURCH OF ST MARGARET OF ANTIOCH 🏛
Leigh Delamere, Chippenham, Wiltshire SN14 6JZ
Tel: 0845 303 2760 **E-mail:** central@thecct.org.uk

CHURCH OF ST MARY & ST LAWRENCE 🏛
Stratford Tony, Salisbury, Wiltshire SP5 4AT
Tel: 0845 303 2760 **E-mail:** central@thecct.org.uk

ST ANDREW'S CHURCH 🏛
Rollestone Road, Rollestone, Salisbury, Wiltshire SP3 4HG
Tel: 0845 303 2760 **E-mail:** central@thecct.org.uk

ST GEORGE'S CHURCH 🏛
Orcheston, Salisbury, Wiltshire SP3 4HL
Tel: 0845 303 2760 **E-mail:** central@thecct.org.uk

ST GILES' CHURCH 🏛
Imber, Warminster, Wiltshire
Tel: 0845 303 2760 **E-mail:** central@thecct.org.uk

ST LEONARD'S CHURCH 🏛
Duck Street, Sutton Veny, Warminster, Wiltshire BA12 7AL
Tel: 0845 303 2760 **E-mail:** central@thecct.org.uk

ST MARY'S CHURCH 🏛
Shipton Road, South Tidworth, Tidworth, Wiltshire SP9 7ST
Tel: 0845 303 2760 **E-mail:** central@thecct.org.uk

ST MARY'S CHURCH 🏛
Old Dilton, Westbury, Wiltshire BA13 4DB
Tel: 0845 303 2760 **E-mail:** central@thecct.org.uk

ST MARY'S CHURCH 🏛
Maddington, Shrewton, Salisbury, Wiltshire SP3 4JE
Tel: 0845 303 2760 **E-mail:** central@thecct.org.uk

ST MARY'S CHURCH, WILTON 🏛
Wilton, Salisbury, Wiltshire SP2 0HQ
Tel: 0845 303 2760 **E-mail:** central@thecct.org.uk

ST PETER'S CHURCH 🏛
Everleigh, Marlborough, Wiltshire SN8 3HD
Tel: 0845 303 2760 **E-mail:** central@thecct.org.uk

STOURHEAD 🌿
Stourton, Nr Warminster BA12 6QD
Tel: 01747 841152 **E-mail:** stourhead@nationaltrust.org.uk

Holkham Hall, Norfolk

Bedfordshire
Cambridgeshire
Essex
Hertfordshire
Norfolk
Suffolk

East of England

Norfolk

Cambridgeshire

Suffolk

Bedford-shire

Hertford-shire

Essex

Between Norwich, once England's second city, and London, still its first, the flat lands and big skies of East Anglia shelter medieval castles, ancient moated manor houses and some of Britain's greatest country estates.

New Entries for 2015:
• Bruisyard Hall
• Somerleyton Hall and Gardens
• The Munnings Collection at Castle House

219

VISITOR INFORMATION

■ Owner
The Duke and Duchess of Bedford & The Trustees of the Bedford Estates

■ Address
Woburn
Bedfordshire
MK17 9WA

■ Location
Map 7:D10
OS Ref. SP965 325
Signposted from M1 J12/J13 and A4012. Easy access from A5 via Hockliffe, follow signs to Woburn village.
Rail: London Euston to Leighton Buzzard, Bletchley/Milton Keynes. Kings Cross Thameslink to Flitwick.
Air: Luton 14m. Heathrow 39m.
Please note there is no public transport to Woburn Abbey.

■ Contact
Woburn Abbey
Tel: 01525 290333
E-mail:
admissions@woburn.co.uk

■ Opening Times
Woburn Abbey, Gardens and Deer Park.
Please telephone or visit our website for details.

■ Admission
Please telephone or visit our website for details.
Group rates available.

■ Special Events
Events in 2015 include:
The Woburn Abbey Garden Show 27th and 28th June. Classic car shows. Outdoor theatre performances. Horticulture study days. Luminaries Woburnensis (Abbey Gardens illuminated after dark). Children's activities during school holidays. Maze is open on Bank Holidays.

Conference/Function

ROOM	Size	Max Cap
Sculpture Gallery	128' x 24'	300 Gallery 250 (sit-down)
Lantern Rm	44' x 21'	60
Howland Rm	58' x 21'	50
Russell Rm	34' x 21'	30

WOBURN ABBEY AND GARDENS 🏛Ⓕ ◆
www.woburnabbey.co.uk

Visit the home of Afternoon Tea to enjoy priceless treasures, uncover fascinating stories, and explore the beautiful gardens.

Set in a 3,000 acre deer park with nine free roaming species of deer, Woburn Abbey has been the home of the Russell Family for nearly 400 years, and is now home to the 15th Duke of Bedford and his family.

Touring the house reveals centuries of the family's stories and English history over three floors including the State Rooms, gold and silver vaults and porcelain display in the crypt. The stunning art collection includes over 250 pictures by artists such as Rembrandt, Gainsborough, Reynolds, Van Dyck and even Queen Victoria.

The Abbey also houses the largest private collection of Venetian views by Canaletto (pictured). The English tradition of Afternoon

Tea was reportedly popularised by Duchess Anna Maria, wife of the 7th Duke, who entertained her friends in the Abbey.

Explore the 28 acres of gardens and enjoy elegant horticultural designs, woodland glades, ponds and architectural features; much of which were the inspiration of Humphry Repton who contributed to their design. The restoration of Repton's original Pleasure Grounds from 200 years ago continues today with the rockery and Children's Garden recently recreated.

Woburn Abbey provides a magnificent backdrop for a myriad of events throughout the year which, in 2015, includes classic car shows, sport events, open air theatre and the annual Woburn Abbey Garden Show (27th and 28th June 2015).

KEY FACTS

ⓘ Suitable for tv/film location, fashion shows, product launches, company 'days out'. No photography in House.

� Conferences, exhibitions, banqueting, luncheons, dinners.

♿ Very limited access in the house. Good access in the gardens.

☕ Licensed Tea Room. Serves food, hot and cold drinks, and afternoon tea.

🍴 By arrangement.

🎧 Guide book and audio guide available (additional charge).

🅿 Free parking

🚉 Please telephone for details.

🐕 Except assistance dogs in Gardens only.

Register for news and special offers at **www.hudsonsheritage.com**

MOGGERHANGER PARK ⓘⓕ
Park Road, Moggerhanger, Bedfordshire MK44 3RW
www.moggerhangerpark.com

Award Winning Georgian Grade I listed Country House designed by Sir John Soane, recently restored, in 33 acres of Humphry Repton designed parkland and woodland. Moggerhanger House has 3 executive conference suites and 2 function rooms, making an ideal venue for conferences, promotions, corporate entertainment, family functions and weddings. Bed and breakfast accommodation available in our beautifully refurbished bedrooms.

Location: Map 7:E9. OS Ref TL048 475. On A603, 3m from A1 at Sandy, 6m from Bedford. **Owner:** Moggerhanger House Preservation Trust
Contact: Reception
Tel: 01767 641007
E-mail: enquiries@moggerhangerpark.com
Open: House Tours: See website or telephone for current information. Grounds, Woodland Café and Exhibition Room: Open all year.
Admission: Please telephone 01767 641007.
Key facts: ⓘ No smoking. 🚻 🅃 ♿ WCs, ramp, lift. 🍴 Licensed. 🎫 By arrangement. 🅿 🅱 🐾 On leads. 🛏 21 bedrooms. ❄ ♥

QUEEN ANNE'S SUMMERHOUSE
Shuttleworth, Old Warden, Bedfordshire SG18 9DU
www.landmarktrust.org.uk

Hidden in a pine wood on the edge of the Shuttleworth estate is this intriguing folly with high quality 18th Century brickwork. Inside is the most elegant bedsit and a staircase in which one of the turrets winds up to the roof terrace or down to the vaulted basement, now a bathroom, where the servants once prepared refreshments. Surrounded by the flora and fauna of beautiful woodland, this is a magical spot.

Location: Map 7:E10.
Owner: The Landmark Trust
Tel: 01628 825925
E-mail: bookings@landmarktrust.org.uk
Open: Self-catering accommodation. Visits by appointment.
Admission: Free for visits by appointment.
Key facts: ⓘ A bedsit with kitchen, dining, sitting and sleeping on the ground floor. A spiral staircase leads down to the bathroom.
🅿 🐾
🛏 ❄ ♥

TURVEY HOUSE ⓘⓕ
Turvey, Bedfordshire MK43 8EL

A neo-classical house set in picturesque parkland bordering the River Great Ouse. The principal rooms contain a fine collection of 18th and 19th Century English and Continental furniture, pictures, porcelain, objets d'art and books. Walled Garden.
Location: Map 7:D9. OS Ref SP939 528.
Between Bedford and Northampton on A428.
Owner: The Hanbury Family
Contact: Daniel Hanbury
Tel: 01234 881244
E-mail: danielhanbury@hotmail.com
Open: 21 Feb, 18 and 21 Mar, 1, 4, 15, 18 and 29 Apr, 2, 4, 13, 16, 25, 27 and 30 May, 10, 13, 24 and 27 Jun 8, 11, 22 and 25 Jul, 5, 8, 19, 22 and 31 Aug. Last admission 4.30pm.
Admission: Adult £6.00, Child £3.00.
Key facts: ⓘ No photography in house. ♿ 🎫 Obligatory. 🅿 Ample for cars, none for coaches. ❄

SWISS GARDEN
Old Warden Park, Bedfordshire SG18 9EP

The Swiss Garden is a late Regency garden created between 1820 and 1835 by the third Lord Ongley and is an outstanding example of the Swiss picturesque.
Location: Map 7:E10. OS Ref TL150 447.
Tel: 01767 627927 **Website:** www.theswissgarden.org
Open: Please see website for up to date opening and admission details.

WREST PARK ⌗
Silsoe, Luton, Bedfordshire MK45 4HS

Take a stroll through three centuries of landscape design at Wrest Park.
Location: Map 7:E10. OS Ref 153. TL093 356.
Tel: 01525 860000 **E-mail:** customers@english-heritage.org.uk
Website: www.english-heritage.org.uk/wrest
Open: Please see website for up to date opening and admission details.

Woburn Abbey Gardens

East of England

ELTON HALL 🏛ⓕ
Nr Peterborough PE8 6SH
www.eltonhall.com

Elton Hall is a fascinating mixture of styles and every room contains treasures – magnificent furniture and fine paintings from early 15th Century Old Masters to the remarkable 19th Century work of Alma Tadema and Millais. Great British artists are well represented by Gainsborough, Constable and Reynolds
Location: Map 7:E7. OS Ref TL091 930. Close to A1 in the village of Elton, off A605 Peterborough - Oundle Road.
Owner: Sir William Proby Bt, CBE
Contact: Caroline Heath
Tel: 01832 280468 **E-mail:** events@eltonhall.com
Open: 2pm-5pm: May: Last May BH, Sun & Mon. Jun & Jul: Wed, Thu. Aug: Wed, Thu, Sun & BH Mon. Private groups by arrangement daily Apr-Sep.
Admission: House & Garden: Adult £9.00, Conc. £8.00. Garden only: Adult £6.50, Conc. £6.00. Accompanied children under 16 Free.
Key facts: ⓘ No photography in house. ◻ 🎁 📷 ⅃ Garden suitable. 🍴 ⅃ Obligatory. 🅿 🚆 Guide dogs in gardens only. ⓘ

KIMBOLTON CASTLE
Kimbolton, Huntingdon, Cambridgeshire PE28 0EA
www.kimbolton.cambs.sch.uk/thecastle

Vanbrugh and Hawksmoor's 18th Century adaptation of 13th Century fortified house. Katherine of Aragon's last residence. Tudor remains still visible. Courtyard by Henry Bell of Kings Lynn. Outstanding Pellegrini murals. Gatehouse by Robert Adam. Home of Earls and Dukes of Manchester, 1615-1950. Family portraits in State Rooms. Now Kimbolton School.
Location: Map 7:E8. OS Ref TL101 676. 7m NW of St Neots on B645.
Owner: Governors of Kimbolton School
Contact: Mrs N Butler
Tel: 01480 860505 **Fax:** 01480 861763
Open: 1 Mar & 1 Nov 2015, 1-4pm.
Admission: Adult £5.00, Child £2.50, OAP £4.00. Groups by arrangement throughout the year, including evenings, special rates apply.
Key facts: 📷 ⅃ Unsuitable. 🍴 ⅃ By arrangement. 🅿 🚆 🚆 On leads. In grounds only. ⓘ

ISLAND HALL 🏛
Godmanchester, Cambridgeshire PE29 2BA
www.islandhall.com

An important mid 18th Century mansion of great charm, owned and restored by an award-winning interior designer. This family home has lovely Georgian rooms, with fine period detail, and interesting possessions relating to the owners' ancestors since their first occupation of the house in 1800. A tranquil riverside setting with formal gardens and ornamental island forming part of the grounds in an area of Best Landscape. Octavia Hill wrote 'This is the loveliest, dearest old house, I never was in such a one before.'
Location: Map 7:F8. OS Ref TL244 706. Centre of Godmanchester, Post Street next to free car park. 1m S of Huntingdon, 15m NW of Cambridge A14.
Owner: Mr Christopher & Lady Linda Vane Percy **Contact:** Mr C Vane Percy
Tel: Groups 01480 459676. Individuals via Invitation to View 01206 573948.
E-mail: enquire@islandhall.com
Open: Groups by arrangement: All year round. Individuals via Invitation to View.
Admission: Groups (40+) £8.00 per person, (30+) £8.50 and Parties under 20 a minimum charge of £180.
Key facts: 📷 See website for more details. 🍴 Home made teas. ⅃ 🚆 🏛 ⓘ ✳

THE MANOR, HEMINGFORD GREY 🏛
Norman Court, High Street, Hemingford Grey, Cambridgeshire PE28 9BN
www.greenknowe.co.uk

Built about 1130 and one of the two oldest continuously inhabited houses in Britain. Made famous as 'Green Knowe' by the author Lucy M Boston. The internationally known patchwork collection sewn by her is also shown. Four acre garden, laid out by Lucy Boston, surrounded by moat, with topiary, old roses, award winning irises and herbaceous borders. **Location:** Map 7:F8. OS Ref TL290 706. A14, 3m SE of Huntingdon. 12m NW of Cambridge. Access via small gate on riverside. **Owner:** Mrs D S Boston **Contact:** Diana Boston
Tel: 01480 463134 **E-mail:** diana_boston@hotmail.com
Open: House: All year (except May), to individuals or groups by prior arrangement. May guided tours daily at 2pm (booking advisable). Garden: All year, daily, 11am-5pm (4pm in winter). **Admission:** House & Garden: Adult £7.00, Child £2.00, OAP £5.50, Family £18.00. Garden only. See website.
Key facts: ⓘ No photography in house. ◻ 🎁 ⅃ Partial. 🍴 The Garden Room, High Street. 🍺 The Cock Pub, High Street. ⅃ Obligatory. 🅿 Cars: Disabled plus a few spaces if none in High Street. Coaches: Nearby. 🚆 🚆 ✳ 🎦

PECKOVER HOUSE & GARDEN ✵ ◆
North Brink, Wisbech, Cambridgeshire PE13 1JR
www.nationaltrust.org.uk/peckover

Peckover House is an oasis hidden away in an urban environment. A classic Georgian merchant's townhouse, it was lived in by the Peckover family for 150 years and reflects their Quaker lifestyle. The house is open over three floors, including the basement service area and our Banking Wing. The gardens are outstanding - two acres of sensory delight, complete with summerhouses, Orangery, over 60 varieties of rose and specimen trees.
Location: Map 7:G6. OS Ref TF458 097. N bank of River Nene, Wisbech B1441.
Owner: National Trust **Contact:** The Property Secretary
Tel: 01945 583463 **Fax:** 01945 587904 **E-mail:** peckover@nationaltrust.org.uk
Open: We are open on varying days between 10 Jan-1 Nov 2015. See website or call for full opening information. **Admission:** Adult £7.85, Child £3.95, Family £19.65. NT members free. Groups discount: (min 15 people) book in advance with Property Secretary. See website for full admission prices. **Key facts:** ⓘ PMV available for loan in grounds. Free garden tours & Behind the Scenes tours on selected days. ▢ 🔄 🔲 🔲 Partial. WCs. 🔲 Licensed. 🔲 By arrangement. 🅿 Signposted. 🔲 🔲 Guide dogs only. 🔲 www.nationaltrustcottages.co.uk 🔲 🔲

ALL SAINTS' CHURCH ⛪
Jesus Lane, Cambridge CB5 8BP

All Saints' stands opposite the gates of Jesus College in the heart of Cambridge, its pale stone spire a prominent city landmark. It was built in the 1860s to the plans of the famous 19th Century architect G.F. Bodley and is a triumph of Victorian art and design. Light gleams through stained-glass windows, designed by leading Arts and Crafts artists, including William Morris, Edward Burne-Jones and Ford Madox Brown. What's more, almost every surface has painted, stencilled or gilded decoration. Pomegranates burst with seeds; flowers run riot over the walls. There is a glorious painting of Christ, Mary and St John, with throngs of angels. The north aisle features three fine windows by C.E. Kempe and Co (1891-1923) together with glass by Douglas Strachan.
Location: OS Ref TL453 587. In Jesus Lane opposite Jesus College, 250 yards from roundabout on A1303 at south end of Victoria Avenue. **Contact:** Please call The Churches Conservation Trust on 0845 303 2760 (Mon-Fri, 9am–5pm).
Website: www.visitchurches.org.uk **Open:** Open daily.

ST PETER'S CHURCH ⛪
Castle Hill, Cambridge CB3 0AJ

Originally built in the 11th Century, this tiny, tall-spired St Peter's is tucked away in a quiet corner of Cambridge with ancient trees in the churchyard. Traces of its Saxon past survive in the form of two carved doorways and the stone font, decorated with four mermen grasping their split tails. Mermen may have an ancient link to St Peter, patron saint of fishermen. There is a charming weathervane outside with the initials AP on it; these are said to be those of Andrew Perne, an 18th Century Dean of Ely. With the homely domestic architecture of the neighbouring houses, including Kettle's Yard Museum next door, and the quaint buildings of the Cambridge Folk Museum nearby, this corner of Cambridge has an almost rural feel, in contrast to the grandeur of the city's more famous sights. **Location:** OS Ref TL445 592. In centre of Cambridge, off Castle Street. **Website:** www.visitchurches.org.uk
Open: Tues - Sun, 11.00am - 5.00pm & Mon 9am -12pm. At other times key is available from Kettle's Yard Gallery.

ANGLESEY ABBEY, GARDENS & LODE MILL ✵
Quy Road, Lode, Cambridgeshire CB25 9EJ
A passion for tradition and style inspired one man to transform a run-down country house and desolate landscape.
Location: Map 7:G9. OS Ref TL533 622. 6m NE of Cambridge on B1102, signs from A14 jct35. **Tel:** 01223 810080 **E-mail:** angleseyabbey@nationaltrust.org.uk
Website: www.nationaltrust.org.uk/angleseyabbey
Open: Please see website for up to date opening and admission details.

WIMPOLE ESTATE ✵
Arrington, Royston, Cambridgeshire SG8 0BW
A unique working estate still guided by the seasons, an impressive mansion at its heart with beautiful interiors by Gibbs, Flitcroft and Soane.
Location: Map 7:F9. OS Ref 154, TL336 510. **Tel:** 01223 206000
E-mail: wimpolehall@nationaltrust.org.uk **Website:** www.nationaltrust.org.uk/wimpole-estate **Open:** Please see website for up to date details.

Peckover House Gardens

VISITOR INFORMATION

■ **Owner**
English Heritage

■ **Address**
Audley End House
Audley End
Saffron Walden
Essex
CB11 4JF

■ **Location**
Map 7:G10
OS Ref. TL525 382
1m W of Saffron Walden
on B1383, M11/J8 & J10.
Rail: Audley End 1¼ m.

■ **Contact**
Visitor Operations Team
Tel: 01799 522842
E-mail: customers@
english-heritage.org.uk

■ **Opening Times**
Please visit www.english-heritage.org.uk for opening times, admission prices and the most up-to-date information.

■ **Special Events**
There is an exciting events programme available throughout the year, for further details please contact the property or visit the website.

AUDLEY END ⊞

www.english-heritage.org.uk/audleyend

One of England's finest country houses, Audley End is also a mansion with a difference. Enjoy a great day out.

Experience the daily routine of a Victorian stable yard as it is brought to life. Complete with resident horses and a costumed groom, the stables experience includes an exhibition where you can find out about the workers who lived on the estate in the 1880s, the tack house and the Audley End fire engine. There is also a children's play area and Café which are ideal for family visitors.

Every great house needed an army of servants and the restored Victorian Service Wing shows a world 'below stairs' that was never intended to be seen. Immerse yourself in the past as you visit the kitchen, scullery, pantry and laundries with film projections, introductory wall displays and even original food from the era.

The cook, Mrs Crocombe, and her staff can regularly be seen trying out new recipes and going about their chores.

Audley End House is itself a magnificent house, built to entertain royalty. Among the highlights is a stunning art collection including works by Masters Holbein, Lely and Canaletto. Its pastoral parkland is designed by 'Capability' Brown and there is an impressive formal garden to discover. Don't miss the working Organic Kitchen Garden with its glasshouses and vinery growing original Victorian varieties of fruit and vegetables. Audley End also boasts Cambridge Lodge a two storey detached holiday cottage. The sitting room enjoys magnificent views of the grounds of Audley End House.

KEY FACTS

ℹ️ Open air concerts and other events. WCs.

🛍️ Service Yard and Coach House Shops.

👟 By arrangement for groups.

🅿️ Coaches to book in advance. Free entry for coach drivers and tour guides.

🐕 Dogs on leads only.

VISITOR INFORMATION

■ **Owner**
National Trust

■ **Address**
25 West Street
Coggeshall
Near Colchester
Essex
C06 1NS

■ **Location**
Map 8:I11
OS Ref. TL848 225
On West Street, parking
available nearby or at The
Grange Barn (also NT), a
five minute walk away.

■ **Contact**
The Manager
Tel: 01376 561305
E-mail: paycockes
@nationaltrust.org.uk

■ **Opening Times**
25 March - 1 November:
11am-5pm (last admission
4.30pm) Wed-Sun and BH
Mons.

■ **Admission**
Adults   £5.50
Children: £2.50
National Trust
Members   Free
Joint discount tickets
available with
The Grange Barn.

PAYCOCKE'S HOUSE & GARDEN 🌿

www.nationaltrust.org.uk/paycockes

"One of the most attractive half-timbered houses of England" - Nikolaus Pevsner

A magnificent half-timbered Tudor wool merchant's house with a beautiful and tranquil arts-and-crafts style cottage garden. Visitors can follow the changing fortunes of the house over its five hundred year history as it went from riches to rags and discover how it was saved from demolition and restored to its former glory as one of the earliest buildings saved by the National Trust.

Thomas Paycocke was an affluent merchant whose home reflected the wealth of the wool industry in Coggeshall. The House passed to the Buxton family, descendents of Paycocke but after the decline of the wool trade it saw harder times passing through different hands and uses and by the Nineteenth Century was used as tenements and a haulier's store and office and threatened with dereliction. In 1904 it was bought by Noel Buxton, a descendent of the family who owned the House from the late Sixteenth Century. He began a twenty year renovation of the building to restore it to how he thought it might have looked in 1509 when it was built. During this time it was lived in by friends and relatives of Buxton including Conrad Noel the 'red' vicar of Thaxted and composer Gustav Holst. Buxton bequeathed Paycocke's to the National Trust on his death in 1924. The House has a charming Coffee Shop and relaxing garden.

KEY FACTS

Cream tea, coffee and cake offer.

At The Coggeshall Grange Barn.

Guide dogs only in Garden.

Coffee Shop

Study

BRENTWOOD CATHEDRAL
INGRAVE ROAD, BRENTWOOD, ESSEX CM15 8AT

The new (1991) Roman Catholic classical Cathedral Church of St Mary and St Helen incorporates part of the original Victorian church. Designed by classical architect Quinlan Terry with roundels by Raphael Maklouf. Architecturally, the inspiration is early Italian Renaissance crossed with the English Baroque of Christopher Wren. The north elevation consists of nine bays divided by Doric pilasters. This is broken by a half-circular portico. The Kentish ragstone walls have a rustic look, which contrasts with the smooth Portland stone of the capitals and column bases. Inside is an arcade of Tuscan arches with central altar with the lantern above.

Location: Map 4:J1. OS Ref TQ596 938. A12 & M25/J28. Centre of Brentwood, opposite Brentwood School.
Owner: Diocese of Brentwood
Tel: 01277 232266
E-mail: bishop@dioceseofbrentwood.org
Open: All year, daily.
Admission: Free.
Key facts: ⬇ Suitable. 🅿 Limited. None for coaches. ⬚ ⬚

COPPED HALL
Crown Hill, Epping, Essex CM16 5HS
www.coppedhalltrust.org.uk

Mid 18th Century Palladian mansion under restoration. Situated on ridge overlooking landscaped park. Ancillary buildings including stables and racquets court. Former elaborate gardens being rescued from abandonment. Large 18th Century walled kitchen garden - adjacent to site of 16th Century mansion where 'A Midsummer Night's Dream' was first performed. Ideal film location.
Location: Map 7:G12. OS Ref TL433 016. 4m SW of Epping, N of M25.
Owner: The Copped Hall Trust
Contact: Alan Cox
Tel: 020 7267 1679
E-mail: coxalan1@aol.com
Open: Ticketed events and special open days. See website for dates. Private tours by appointment.
Admission: Open Days £8.00. Guided Tour Days £8.00. Gardens Only £5.00.
Key facts: ⬚ ⬚ ⬇ Partial. ⬚ ⬚ 🅿 ⬚ ⬚ In grounds on leads. ⬚ ⬚

© Peter Gamble

Copped Hall

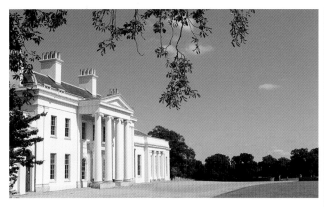

HYLANDS ESTATE
Hylands Park, London Road, Chelmsford CM2 8WQ
www.chelmsford.gov.uk/hylands

Hylands House is a beautiful Grade II* listed building, set in 574 acres of historic landscaped parkland. Built c1730, the original house was a Queen Anne style mansion. Subsequent owners modernised and enlarged the property. The Stables Visitor Centre, incorporates a Gift Shop, Café, Artist Studios and a second-hand bookshop.

Location: Map 7:H12. OS Ref TL681 054. 2m SW of Chelmsford. Signposted on A414 from J15 off A12
Owner: Chelmsford City Council
Contact: Ceri Lowen
Tel: 01245 605500
E-mail: hylands@chelmsford.gov.uk
Open: House: Suns & Mons, 10am-5pm Apr-Sep, Stable Visitor Centre & Park: Daily. Guided Tours, Talks and Walks are available by arrangement.
Admission: House: Adult £3.80, Conc. £2.80, Accompanied Children under 16 Free. Visitor Stables Centre and Park: Free.
Key facts: Visitor Centre. Daily. By arrangement. By arrangement. In grounds. Guide dogs only in house.

INGATESTONE HALL
Hall Lane, Ingatestone, Essex CM4 9NR
www.ingatestonehall.com

16th Century mansion, with 11 acres of grounds (formal garden and wild walk), built by Sir William Petre, Secretary of State to four Tudor monarchs, which has remained in his family ever since. Furniture, portraits and memorabilia accumulated over the centuries - and two Priests' hiding places.

Location: Map 7:H12. OS Ref TQ654 986. Off A12 between Brentwood & Chelmsford. From London end of Ingatestone High St., take Station Lane, cross level crossing and continue for ½ mile.
Owner: The Lord Petre **Contact:** Lord Petre
Tel/Fax: 01277 353010 **Additional Contact:** Mrs Gina Cordwell.
E-mail: house@ingatestonehall.co.uk
Open: 5 Apr-27 Sep: Wed, Suns & BH Mons (not Weds in Jun), 12noon-5pm.
Admission: Adult £6.00, Child £2.50 (under 5yrs Free), Conc. £5.00. (Groups of 20+ booked in advance: Adult £5.00, Child £1.50, Conc. £4.00).
Key facts: No photography in house. No dogs (except guide dogs). Partial. WCs. Available out of normal hours by arrangement. Free parking. Guide dogs only.

Paycocke's

ST MARTIN'S CHURCH
West Stockwell Street, Colchester, Essex CO1 1HN
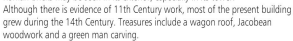
St Martin's lies southeast of Colchester Town Hall, a spectacular medieval survivor with a massive truncated tower. Many reused Roman bricks may be seen in its exterior, especially in its tower. Although there is evidence of 11th Century work, most of the present building grew during the 14th Century. Treasures include a wagon roof, Jacobean woodwork and a green man carving.
Location: OS Ref TL996 255. West Stockwell Street - turn off the High Street at the Town Hall, church found on the right.
Website: www.visitchurches.org.uk
Open: Open daily, 10.00am - 4.00pm.

CHURCH OF ST MARY THE VIRGIN
Off Church Road, Burton End, Stansted Mountfitchet, Essex CM24 8UB
This medieval church, with parts dating from the 1100s, has a bold brick tower and stands next to the grounds of Stansted Hall in a peaceful setting despite the nearby motorway and airport. It contains two exceptional 17th Century tomb figures - wasp-waisted Hester Salusbury in her hunting clothes and her father, Sir Thomas Middleton.
Location: OS Ref TL521 242. 3 miles north east of Bishop's Stortford off B1383; follow signs to 'Norman Castle and The House on the Hill Toy Museum' in village centre and then keep right on Church Road, after 0.8 miles you pass the school on your right, church shortly afterwards down lane on your left.
Website: www.visitchurches.org.uk
Open: Open daily 11am-3pm.

THE MUNNINGS ART MUSEUM
Castle House, Castle Hill, Dedham, Essex CO7 6AZ
Paintings by Sir Alfred Munnings (1878-1959) **Location:** Map 8:J10. OS Ref TM060 328. Approximately ¾m from the village centre on the corner of East Lane.
Tel: 01206 322127 **E-mail:** enquiries@munningsmuseum.org.uk
Website: www.munningsmuseum.org.uk
Open: 1 Apr-31 Oct 2015, Wed-Sun & BH Mons, 2-5pm.
Admission: £6.50, Conc £5.00, Child £1.00.

East of England

■ Owner
The 7th Marquess of Salisbury

■ Address
Hatfield House
Hatfield
Hertfordshire
AL9 5NQ

■ Location
Map 7:F11
OS Ref. TL237 084
21 miles north of London, M25 Jct 23, A1(M) Jct 4. Pedestrian Entrance directly opposite Hatfield Railway Station.
Bus: Nearest stop at Hatfield Station, also regular buses from surrounding towns.
Rail: Kings Cross to Hatfield 25mins. Station is opposite entrance to Park. Underground links to main line at Finsbury Park.

■ Contact
Visitors Department
Tel: 01707 287010
E-mail: visitors@hatfield-house.co.uk

■ Opening Times
House
4 April to 30 September 2015 Wed-Sun & BH 11-4.30pm (last admission 3.30pm).
Garden, Park, Farm, Shops and Restaurant
Tues-Sun & BH 10am to 5.30pm.

■ Admission
House, Park and West Garden:
Adults £16.00
Seniors £15.00
Children £8.00
Group rates available.
East Garden:
(Wednesday only) £4.00 per person.

West Garden and Park only:
Adults £10.00
Seniors £9.00
Children £6.00
Group rates available.

■ Special Events
There are a number of events held throughout the year, pleasee see the website for more details.

Conference/Function

ROOM	Size	Max Cap
The Old Palace	112' x 33'	280
Riding School Conference Centre	100' x 40'	170

HATFIELD HOUSE ◆ ✦
www.hatfield-house.co.uk

Over 400 years of culture, history and entertainment.

Hatfield House is the home of the 7th Marquess and Marchioness of Salisbury and their family. The Estate has been in the Cecil family for over 400 years. Superb examples of Jacobean craftsmanship can be seen throughout the House.

In 1611, Robert Cecil, 1st Earl of Salisbury built his fine Jacobean House adjoining the site of the Old Palace of Hatfield. The House was splendidly decorated for entertaining the Royal Court, with State Rooms rich in paintings, fine furniture and tapestries.

Superb examples of Jacobean craftsmanship can be seen throughout Hatfield House such as the Grand Staircase with its fine carving and the rare stained glass window in the private chapel. Displayed throughout the House are many historic mementos collected over the centuries by the Cecils, one of England's foremost political families.

The garden at Hatfield House dates from the early 17th Century when Robert Cecil employed John Tradescant the Elder to collect plants for his new home. Tradescant was sent to Europe where he found and brought back trees, bulbs, plants and fruit trees, which had never previously been grown in England.

In the Park, an oak tree marks the place where the young Princess Elizabeth first heard of her accession to the throne. Visitors can enjoy extensive walks in the park, following trails through the woods and along the Broadwater. The Veteran Tree Trail also provides the opportunity to learn more about our ancient oaks.

KEY FACTS

- ℹ️ No flash photography in house. Tours of Old Palace when building is not in use.
- 🏠 Newly refurbished Stable Yard home to variety of independent retailers & Hatfield House Gift Shop.
- 🍸 Weddings, Banquets & Conferences venue & catering. Tel 01707 262055.
- ♿ All floors of House accessible via lift.
- 🍽️ The Coach House Restaurant. Morning coffee, afternoon tea, Cakes, hot & cold Lunches. Tel: 01707 262030.
- 👥 Group tours by arrangement, please call 07107 287052.
- 🎧 Audio tours of House.
- 🅿️ Free.
- 🏫 Living History Schools programme.
- 🐕 On leads. Park only.

KNEBWORTH HOUSE 🏛️Ⓕ
Knebworth, Hertfordshire SG1 2AX
www.knebworthhouse.com

Originally a Tudor manor house, rebuilt in gothic style in 1843. Contains rooms in various styles, which include a Jacobean banqueting hall. Home of the Lytton family since 1490. Set in 250 acres of parkland, the historic formal gardens cover 28 acres and include a dinosaur trail and walled vegetable garden. Events programme throughout the year. Knebworth is well known for its rock concerts and as a popular TV/feature film location.
Location: Map 7:E11. Direct access off the A1(M) J7 Stevenage, SG1 2AX, 28m N of London, 15m N of M25/J23 **Contact:** The Estate Office
Tel: 01438 812661 **E-mail:** info@knebworthhouse.com
Open: Mar-Sep, check website for open dates and times. Open all year for events, corporate and social functions.
Admission: Adults: £12.50, Child*/Conc: £12.00, Family (4): £44.00. *4-16 yrs, under 4s Free. HHA members free on non-event days.
Key facts: ⓘ 🏠 🎁 🍴 🔲 ☕ 🎥 Admission generally by guided tour. 🅿️
🖼️ See the Education section at www.knebworthhouse.com.
🐾 Welcome in the Park on leads only. 🔆 ♿

BENINGTON LORDSHIP GARDENS 🏛️Ⓕ
Stevenage, Hertfordshire SG2 7BS

7 acre garden overlooking lakes in a timeless setting. Features include Norman keep and moat, Queen Anne manor house, James Pulham folly, formal rose garden, renowned herbaceous borders, walled vegetable garden, grass tennis court and verandah. Spectacular display of snowdrops in February. Location work welcome. **Location:** Map 7:F11. OS Ref TL296 236. In village of Benington next to the church. 4m E of Stevenage.
Owner: Mr R R A Bott **Contact:** Mr or Mrs R R A Bott **Tel:** 01438 869668
E-mail: garden@beningtonlordship.co.uk
Website: www.beningtonlordship.co.uk
Open: Snowdrops 7 Feb-1 Mar 2015 daily 12-4pm, Easter and May BH Suns & Mons 12-4pm, NGS Sunday 14 June 12-5pm, Chilli Festival August bank holiday weekend 10-5pm (admission £7.50).
Admission: Adult £5.00, Conc £4.00, Child under 12 Free.
Key facts: 📷 February only. 🔲 Partial. ☕ 🎥 By arrangement. 🅿️ Limited. 🐾 ♿

GORHAMBURY 🏛️Ⓕ
St Albans, Hertfordshire AL3 6AH

Late 18th Century house by Sir Robert Taylor. Family portraits from 15th-21st Centuries.
Location: Map 7:E11. 2m W of St Albans. Access via private drive off A4147 at St Albans. For SatNav please enter AL3 6AE for unlocked entrance to estate at Roman Theatre.
Owner: Gorhambury Estates Co Ltd
Contact: The Administrator
Tel: 01727 854051
Open: May-Sep: Thurs, 2-5pm (last entry 4pm).
Admission: House: Adult £8.00, Senior £7.00, Child £5.00 including guided tour. Special groups by arrangement (Thu am preferred).
Key facts: ⓘ No photography. 🔲 Partial. 🎥 Obligatory. 🅿️ 🐾

Knebworth House

VISITOR INFORMATION

■ Owner
Trustees of the Holkham Estate. Home of the Coke Family.

■ Address
Holkham Estate Office
Wells-next-the-Sea
Norfolk
NR23 1AB

■ Location
Map 8:14
OS Ref. TF885 428
London 120m Norwich 35m King's Lynn 30m.
Bus: King's Lynn to Cromer Coasthopper route.
Coach: Access south gates only, follow brown/white signs 'Holkham Hall Coaches'.
Rail: Norwich 35m. King's Lynn 30m.
Air: Norwich Airport 32m.

■ Contact
Marketing Manager
Laurane Herrieven
Tel: 01328 710227
Fax: 01328 711707
E-mail: enquiries@holkham.co.uk

■ Opening Times
Hall: 29 Mar-31 Oct 12-4pm, Sun, Mon, Thur, plus Good Fri and Easter Sat. NB. Chapel, Libraries and Strangers' Wing form part of private accommodation, open at the family's discretion.
Walled Gardens, Gift Shop, Café & Woodland Play Area: 29 Mar-31 Oct 10am-5pm, every day.

■ Admission
Hall & Walled Gardens:
Adult	£12.00
Child (5-16yrs)	£6.00
Family (2 adults and up to 3 children)	£33.00

Walled Gardens Only:
Adult	£2.50
Child (5-16yrs)	£1.00

Car Parking:
Per day	£2.50

Redeembale in shop or café on £10+ purchases
Groups: (20+) 10% discount, free parking, organiser free entry, coach driver's refreshment voucher.
Private Guided Tours:
Min 12 people, price per person £20.00.
Cycle Hire: See www.cyclenorfolk.co.uk
Lake Activities: See www.norfolkadventure.co.uk.

■ Special Events
Grounds for corporate events, shows, rallies, product launches, filming and weddings.

HOLKHAM HALL
www.holkham.co.uk

A breathtaking Palladian house with an outstanding art collection, panoramic landscapes and the best beach in England.

Holkham is a special place where a stunning coastal landscape meets one of England's great agricultural estates. At the heart of this thriving 25,000 acre estate on the north Norfolk coast stands Holkham Hall, an elegant 18th Century Palladian style house, based on designs by William Kent and built by Thomas Coke the 1st Earl of Leicester. The house remains privately owned and is home to Thomas Coke's descendants.

The Marble Hall is a spectacular introduction to this imposing building, with its 50ft pressed plaster dome ceiling and walls of English alabaster, not marble as its name implies. Stairs lead to magnificent state rooms displaying superb collections of ancient statuary, original furniture, tapestries and paintings by Rubens, Van Dyck, Claude, Gaspar Poussin and Gainsborough.

Surrounded by parkland, discover the wildlife and landscape with nature trails, cycle and boat hire. Or visit the 18th century walled gardens to see the ongoing restoration project to sensitively restore the 6.5 acres of gardens to their former glory. Families with young children will enjoy the woodland adventure play area with its tree house, high-level walkways and zip wire. Locally sourced produce can be found in the gift shop and café.

At the north entrance to the park lies Holkham village with the estate-owned inn, The Victoria, a selection of shops and the entrance to the award-winning Holkham beach and national nature reserve, renowned for its endless golden sands and panoramic vista; a haven for wildlife, walkers and anyone seeking to connect with the uplifting power of nature.

KEY FACTS

- **ⓘ** Photography allowed. Stair climbing machine in hall offers access for most manual wheelchairs. Shop/café will be relocated for 2015 to make way for major refurbishment project in the courtyard.
- Gift shop in the park. Local produce.
- In gift shop.
- Hall and grounds.
- WC in park. Full access statement on Holkham website.
- Café in the park. Licensed. Local produce.
- Licensed. The Victoria, Holkham village.
- Private guided tours by arrangement.
- **P** Ample. Parking charge.
- Education programme on request.
- Guide dogs only in hall.
- Civil ceremonies and partnerships.
- Full events programme throughout year.

Register for news and special offers at **www.hudsonsheritage.com**

HOUGHTON HALL 🏛ⓕ ❖
HOUGHTON, KING'S LYNN, NORFOLK PE31 6UE
www.houghtonhall.com

Houghton Hall is one of the finest examples of Palladian architecture in England. Built in the 18th Century by Sir Robert Walpole, Britain's first prime minister. Original designs by James Gibbs & Colen Campbell, interior decoration by William Kent. The House has been restored to its former grandeur, containing many of its original furnishings. Award-winning 5-acre walled garden divided into 'rooms'. Stunning 120 yard double-sided herbaceous borders, formal rose garden with over 150 varieties, mixed kitchen garden, fountains and statues. Unique Model Soldier Collection, over 20,000 models arranged in various battle formations. Contemporary Sculptures in the Gardens.

Location: Map 8:15. OS Ref TF792 287. 13m E of King's Lynn, 10m W of Fakenham 1½m N of A148.

Owner: The Marquess of Cholmondeley
Contact: Susan Cleaver
Tel: 01485 528569
Fax: 01485 528167
E-mail: info@houghtonhall.com
Admission: See website for opening times/prices/booking details. www.houghtonhall.com.
Key facts: 🅿 🚻 ♿ WCs. Allocated parking near the House. ▣ Licensed. 🍴 Licensed. 🎫 By arrangement. 🅿 🐕 On leads.

OXBURGH HALL ❀
OXBOROUGH, KING'S LYNN, NORFOLK PE33 9PS
www.nationaltrust.org.uk/oxburgh-hall

A romantic, moated manor house built by the Bedingfeld family in the 15th Century, they have lived here ever since. Inside, the family's Catholic history is revealed, complete with a secret priest's hole. See the astonishing needlework by Mary, Queen of Scots, original medieval documents and royal letters, and reproduction costumes of King Henry VII and Elizabeth of York, who stayed at Oxburgh in 1487. Outside, enjoy panoramic views from the gatehouse roof, explore the Victorian parterre and woodland trails. The late winter drifts of snowdrops are not to be missed.

Location: Map 8:16. OS Ref TF742 012. At Oxborough, 7m SW of Swaffham on S side of Stoke Ferry road.

Owner: National Trust **Contact:** The Property Administrator
Tel: 01366 328258 **Fax:** 01366 328066

E-mail: oxburghhall@nationaltrust.org.uk
Open: Garden, Shop, Tea Room: 3 Jan-8 Feb, 11am-4pm; 14 Feb-13 Mar, 10.30am-4pm. House: 14 Feb-13 Mar, 12pm-3pm. Whole Property: 14 Mar-2 Oct, 11am-5pm (Gates open 10.30am). House: 3 Oct-1 Nov, 11am-4pm. Garden, Shop, Tea Room: 3 Oct-1 Nov, 10.30am-5pm; 2 Nov-20 Dec, 11am-4pm.
Admission: House & Garden: (Gift Aid in brackets) Adult £8.90 (£9.80), Child £4.45 (£4.90), Family £22.25 (£24.50). Garden & Estate: Adult £4.90 (£5.40), Child £2.45 (£2.70), Family £12.75 (£13.50). Groups (booked in advance): House & Garden: Adult £8, Child £4. Garden & Estate: Adult £4.40, Child £2.20.
Key facts: ℹ Free garden tours daily. Souvenir guides, gift shop, second-hand bookshop. 🅿 🚻 🍴 ♿ WCs. ▣ Licensed. 🎫 By arrangement. 🅿 Limited for coaches. 🔲 🐕 Guide dogs only. ❄ ▾

HINDRINGHAM HALL AND GARDENS 🏛
Blacksmiths Lane, Hindringham, Norfolk NR21 0QA
www.hindringhamhall.org

House: Beautiful Tudor Manor House surrounded by 12th Century moat. A scheduled Ancient Monument, along with the adjacent 3 acres of fishponds. Gardens: Four acres of peaceful gardens within and without the moat surrounding the house. Working walled vegetable garden, herb parterre, daffodil walk, bluebell and cyclamen copse, stream garden, bog garden, herbaceous borders, autumn border, victorian nut tunnel, rose and clematis pergolas.

Location: Map 8:J4. Turn off the A148 halfway between Fakenham & Holt signposted Hindringham & follow brown signs.
Owner/Contact: Mr & Mrs Charles Tucker **Tel:** 01328 878226
E-mail: info@hindringhamhall.org **Open:** House: 4 times a year for a 2 hr guided history tour. Groups on other days by arrangement. 01328 878226. Gardens and tearoom: Suns and/or Weds Mar-Oct. See website www.hindringhamhall.org for dates and times. **Admission:** House: Tour £17.50 including refreshments. Garden: Adults £6.00, Children under 15 Free. **Key facts:** 🛈 Many plants for sale from seeds & cuttings from the gardens. 🚫 No hills or steps but some gravel paths. 🍵 Teas, coffee and other beverages and cakes. 🅿 ✖ 3 detached holiday cottages within the grounds each with their own garden- sleep 2 and 4.

CASTLE RISING CASTLE
Castle Rising, King's Lynn, Norfolk PE31 6AH
www.castlerising.co.uk

Possibly the finest mid-12th Century Keep in England: it was built as a grand and elaborate palace. It was home to Queen Isabella, grandmother of the Black Prince. Still in good condition, the Keep is surrounded by massive ramparts up to 120 feet high. Picnic area, adjacent tearoom. Audio tour.
Location: Map 7:H5. OS Ref TF666 246.
Located 4m NE of King's Lynn off A149.
Owner: Lord Howard **Contact:** The Custodian
Tel: 01553 631330
Fax: 01533 631724
Open: 1 Apr-1 Nov: daily, 10am-6pm (closes at dusk if earlier in Oct). 2 Nov-31 Mar: Wed-Sun, 10am-4pm. Closed 24-26 Dec.
Admission: Adult £4.00, Child £2.50, Conc. £3.30, Family £12.00. 15% discount for groups (11+). Opening times and prices are subject to change.
Key facts: 🛈 Picnic area. 🔲 🚫 Suitable. 🔲 🅿 ❄

Holkham Hall

RAVENINGHAM GARDENS 🏛ⓕ
Raveningham, Norwich, Norfolk NR14 6NS
www.raveningham.com

Superb herbaceous borders, 19th Century walled kitchen garden, Victorian glasshouse, herb garden, rose garden, contemporary sculptures, 14th Century church in a glorious parkland setting.
Location: Map 8:L7. OS Ref TM399 965. Between Norwich & Lowestoft off A146 then B1136.
Owner: Sir Nicholas Bacon Bt
Contact: Barbara Linsley
Tel: 01508 548480
Fax: 01508 548958
E-mail: barbara@raveningham.com
Open: Tue, Wed and Thu from Apr to end Aug. Special 2 week openings for snowdrops, agapanthus, rose and Autumn weeks - see website for full details.
Admission: Adult £4.00, Child (under 16yrs) Free, OAP £3.50.
Groups by prior arrangement.
Key facts: 🍵 Tea room, drinks and cakes only. 🅿
🐕 Well behaved dogs on leads welcome. 🐕

BLICKLING ESTATE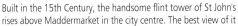
Blickling, Norwich, Norfolk NR11 6NF

For four centuries, the Blickling Estate has been home to many, from the Boleyn family to the RAF, stationed here during the Second World War. Cooks and butlers, gardeners and scullery maids have all made their mark on this beautiful country estate and you can follow in their footsteps. Built in the early C17th, it boasts one of England's finest Jacobean houses, famed for its important book collection. Explore the spectacular 55 acre gardens and enjoy the tranquillity of a ramble around the lake and parkland. **Location:** Map 8:K5. 1½m NW of Aylsham on B1354. Signposted off A140 Norwich (14m) to Cromer. **Owner:** National Trust **Tel:** 01263 738030 **E-mail:** blickling@nationaltrust.org.uk **Website:** www.nationaltrust.org.uk/blickling **Open:** Please see website or contact us for up to date information. **Admission:** NT members free. Please see website or contact us for up to date admission prices.

Key facts: 🛈 📷 🎨 📺 ♿ 🍴 👶 🅿 🍽 🛏 🐾 ❄ 🎗

CHURCH OF ST JOHN MADDERMARKET 🏛
Maddermarket, Norwich, Norfolk NR2 1DS

Built in the 15th Century, the handsome flint tower of St John's rises above Maddermarket in the city centre. The best view of it is from the north, where its tower stands over Maddermarket Alley, affording one of the city's most attractive townscapes. It is believed that an original chancel may have been demolished as part of a road-widening scheme when Queen Elizabeth I came to visit Norwich. It survived a gas explosion in 1876 during a choir practice that stunned the rector, singed the choirboys and shattered windows. Today's stained-glass windows are Victorian; 20th Century replacements which flood the church with light. The church's interior is filled with marvellous monuments, from elegant plaques to detailed little figures in Tudor dress. All around are rich furnishings - part of an interesting and eccentric collection assembled by William Busby (rector from 1898 to 1923). **Location:** OS Ref TG229 087. In centre of Norwich off Pottergate. **Website:** www.visitchurches.org.uk **Open:** Regularly throughout the week. Please check website for times.

ST MARGARET'S CHURCH 🏛
**Church Lane, Hales, Norwich
Norfolk NR14 6QL**

St Margaret's, with its round tower and thatched roof, is a church from another time, standing in an isolated setting, as if still in its 12th Century Norman world. The magnificent carved doorway with bands of richly carved patterns zigzags, stars and rosettes over the arch is breathtaking; there is another similar doorway, though less richly carved, in the south wall. Inside the church is simple and rustic. Medieval faces painted on the walls peer out from across the centuries - look for St Christopher carrying Christ and St James, holding his pilgrim's staff, with a delicate band of twining foliage. The 500-year-old font is carved with angels, lions and roses - and there are memorials in the brick floor.
Location: OS Ref TM384 962. 12 miles south east of Norwich, east of the A146 after Loddon bypass.
Website: www.visitchurches.org.uk **Open:** Open daily.

CHURCH OF ST MICHAEL THE ARCHANGEL 🏛
Booton, Norwich, Norfolk NR10 4NZ

This amazingly decorative and extraordinary church was the creation of eccentric clergyman Reverend Whitwell Elwin; a descendant of Pocahontas of Hiawatha fame. Elwin not only raised the funds for the building, he also designed it. Some of his models can be identified; the west doorway was inspired by Glastonbury Abbey, for example, but the slender twin towers which soar over the wide East Anglian landscape and central pinnacle, seem to have sprung solely from his imagination. Inside, he filled his fairy-tale creation with angels modelled on the rector's young female friends. The wooden carved angels holding up the roof are the work of James Minns, a well-known master-carver whose carving of a bull's head is still the emblem on Colman's Mustard. You may love the church; you may be outraged by it, but you cannot remain unmoved by such an exuberant oddity. **Location:** OS Ref TG123 224. 12 m NW of Norwich, off B1145 SE of Reepham & SW of Cawston. **Website:** www.visitchurches.org.uk **Open:** Daily, 9am-4pm (winter), 10am-5pm (summer).

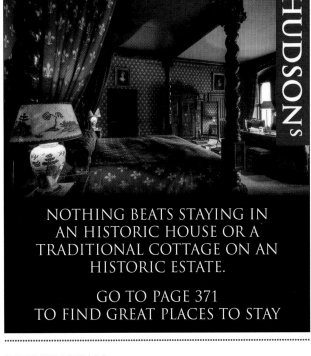

SANDRINGHAM
The Estate Office, Sandringham, Norfolk PE35 6EN

Sandringham House, the Norfolk retreat of Her Majesty The Queen, is set in 60 acres of beautiful gardens. The main ground floor rooms used by The Royal Family, still maintained in the Edwardian style, are open to the public, as well as the fascinating Museum and the charming parish church.
Location: Map 7:H5. OS Ref TF695 287. 8m NE of King's Lynn on B1440 off A148. **Owner:** H M The Queen
Contact: The Public Enterprises Manager
Tel: 01485 545408 **Fax:** 01485 541571 **E-mail:** visits@sandringhamestate.co.uk
Website: www.sandringhamestate.co.uk
Open: 4 Apr - late Jul & early Aug - 1 Nov.
Admission: House, Museum & Gardens, Adult £13.50, Child £6.50, Conc. £11.50. Museum & Gardens, Adult £9.00, Child £4.50, Conc. £8.00.
Key facts: 🛈 No photography in house. 📷 🏪 Plant Centre. 📺 Visitor Centre only. ♿ WCs. 🍴 Licensed. 🍴 Licensed. 🎭 By arrangement. Private evening tours. 🅿 Ample. 🐕 Guide dogs only. 🎗

WALSINGHAM ABBEY GROUNDS & THE SHIREHALL MUSEUM 🏛
Common Place, Walsingham, Norfolk NR22 6BP

Ruins of the medieval Augustinian Priory and place of pilgrimage. Peaceful gardens with spectacular naturalised snowdrops throughout 18 acres of woods in February. Visitor entry is at The Shirehall Museum, a preserved Georgian Courthouse, now a museum where you can discover more of Walsingham's unique history since 1061. **Location:** Map 8:J4. OS Ref TF934 367. About 4 miles N of Fakenham, on the B1105. Coaches please follow route marked. **Owner:** Walsingham Estate Company **Tel:** 01328 820510 **Website:** www.walsinghamabbey.com **Open:** Grounds & Museum: 31 Jan-1 Mar, Mon-Sun, 10am-4pm. Mar, Sat & Sun, 11am-4pm. 30 Mar-1 Nov, Mon-Sun, 11am-4pm. Grounds only: Nov-end Jan, Mon-Fri, 11am-1pm & 2pm-4pm. Mar, Mon-Fri, 11am-1pm & 2pm-4pm. Grounds only entry at The Estate Office, adjacent to The Shirehall Museum.
Admission: Adult £4.00, Child 6-16 £2.50. Under 6 free.
Key facts: 🛈 Local tourism. 📷 Gift shop. 🏪 Feb snowdrops. ♿ Partial access. 🍴 In village. 🍴 🎭 By arrangement. 🅿 In village. 🐕 Dogs on leads. ❄ 🎗

CLIFTON HOUSE
Queen Street, King's Lynn PE30 1HT

Magnificent Grade 1 listed merchant's house. Elizabethan watch-tower, 14th Century vaulted cellars. **Location:** Map 7:H5. OS Ref TF615 198.
E-mail: anna@kingstaithe.com **Website:** www.cliftonhouse.org.uk
Open: Sat 18 Jul & Sun 19 Jul 2015 11am-4pm. Pre-booked guided tours throughout the year through www.invitationtoview.co.uk.
Admission: Adult: £3.50.

VISITOR INFORMATION

■ **Owner**
Paul Rous

■ **Address**
Bruisyard Hall
Bruisyard
Saxmundham
Woodbridge
IP17 2EJ

■ **Location**
Map 8:L9
OS Ref. TM33 4662
By Car: Bruisyard Hall is located 5 minutes off the the B1119 between the A12 and Framlingham. The closest main towns are Framlingham and Saxmundham. From the A12 heading along the B1119 through Rendham village, turn right on the sharp corner between the Church and the White Horse pub. At the end of the road, turn right and then take the first left. You will see Bruisyard Hall and Barn on the right hand side of the road.

By train: Our nearest train station is Saxmundham from where there are connections to Liverpool Street once an hour via Ipswich. If you wish we can arrange for a taxi to collect you from the station, a 10 minute drive to Bruisyard Hall. We advise that you book in advance as there are no waiting taxi ranks.

Sat Nav: Our address is Bruisyard Hall, Bruisyard, Saxmundham, Suffolk IP17 2EJ.

■ **Contact**
Tel: 01728 639000
E-mail: info@ bruisyardhall.co.uk

■ **Opening Times**
Open all year round for family stays, B&B's and weddings. Viewings by appointment only.

Bruisyard Hall in spring

BRUISYARD HALL
www.bruisyardhall.co.uk

Beautiful country manor hall steeped in history.

Dating back to 1354, the Hall combines traditional elegance with modern luxuries. Whilst the Hall exudes history and elegance with three sizeable reception rooms (perfect both for formal entertaining or curling up with your favourite book), practical needs like WIFI, a games room packed with entertainment for all ages, and a large dining room are all at guests' disposal.

The Bruisyard Hall team will help create your perfect countryside escape, offering additional touches such as scrumptious Suffolk afternoon tea in the drawing room, a day's shooting, or a private car from wherever you are, direct to the door of Bruisyard Hall. Simply get in touch and we'll make all the necessary arrangements for you.

The Hall accommodates up to 20 guests, with an additional 2 rooms available in the adjacent Bruisyard Barn, enabling you to have up to 24 guests stay on the estate. The Barn also functions as an event venue in itself – the Medieval Hall, Banqueting Hall and Minstrels Gallery can be adapted to fulfil your every entertainment need, whatever the occasion.

KEY FACTS

 Private tours can be arranged.

 There are 20 spaces available at the hall.

 Dogs are allowed downstairs in the hall.

 The Hall accommodates up to 20 guests, with an additional 2 rooms available in the adjacent Bruisyard Barn, enabling you to have up to 24 guests stay on the estate.

License for 30 guests at the hall.

Bruisyard Hall

Clock Tower and Card Table

LAVENHAM: THE GUILDHALL OF CORPUS CHRISTI ❧
THE MARKET PLACE, LAVENHAM, SUDBURY CO10 9QZ
www.nationaltrust.org.uk

Once one of the wealthiest towns in Tudor England, Lavenham oozes charm and character. The rich clothiers who thrived here left a legacy of buildings that now make up the streets of crooked timber-framed houses that are so beloved of visitors today.

With its timber-framed houses and magnificent church, a visit to picturesque Lavenham is a step back in time. The Sixteenth Century Guildhall is the ideal place to begin with its exhibitions on local history bringing to life the fascinating stories behind this remarkable village.

Once you have explored the Guildhall and sampled some home-made fare in our tearoom, why not visit some of the unique shops and galleries in the village. Lavenham truly has something for everyone.

Location: Map 8:J9. OS Ref OS155, TL915 942. 6m NNE of Sudbury. Village centre. A1141 & B1071.
Owner: National Trust **Contact:** Jane Gosling
Tel: 01787 247646
E-mail: lavenhamguildhall@nationaltrust.org.uk
Open: Guildhall, shop & tearoom: 17 Jan-1 Mar, Sat & Sun, 11am-4pm. 2 Mar-1 Nov, Mon-Sun, 11am-5pm. 5 Nov-20 Dec, Thu-Sun, 11am-4pm. Parts of the building may be closed occasionally for community use.
Admission: Adult £6.50, Child £3.25, Family £16.25, Groups £4.95. School parties by arrangement.
Key facts: 🖼 🎁 ☕ 📷 By arrangement. 🐕 ♿

Bruisyard Barn - Banqueting hall

FRESTON TOWER
Nr Ipswich, Suffolk IP9 1AD
www.landmarktrust.org.uk

Freston Tower is a six-storey Tudor folly that looks out over the River Orwell. There is a single room on each floor with the sitting room at the top to take advantage of the unrivalled views.

Location: Map 8:K9. OS Ref TM177 397.
Owner: The Landmark Trust
Tel: 01628 825925
E-mail: bookings@landmarktrust.org.uk
Open: Self-catering accommodation. Open Days on 8 days per year, other visits by appointment.
Admission: Free on Open Days and visits by appointment.
Key facts: ⓘ Six storeys joined by a steep spiral staircase. There is a room on each floor and a roof terrace. 🅿 ⊞ ⊞ ⊠ ⊡

HELMINGHAM HALL GARDENS 🏠 Ⓕ
Helmingham, Suffolk IP14 6EF
www.helmingham.com

Grade 1 listed gardens, redesigned by Lady Tollemache (a Chelsea Gold Medallist) set in a 400 acre deer park surrounding a moated Tudor Hall.

Visitors are enchanted by the stunning herbaceous borders, the walled kitchen garden, herb, knot, rose and wild gardens. A delicious range of local food is served in the Coach House Tearooms and the Stable Shops offer a wide range of local produce, plants, garden accessories and local crafts.

Coach bookings warmly welcomed. There are a variety of events throughout the season including The Festival of Classic & Sports Cars and Suffolk Dog Day.

Location: Map 8:K9. OS Ref TM190 578. B1077, 9m N of Ipswich, 5m S of Debenham. **Owner:** The Lord & Lady Tollemache **Contact:** Events Office
Tel: 01473 890799 **E-mail:** events@helmingham.com
Open: Gardens only 3 May-20 Sep 2015 (12-5pm Tue, Wed, Thu, Sun and all Bank Holidays).
Admission: Adults £7.00, Child (5-15yrs) £3.50. Groups (30+) £6.00.
Key facts: ⊡ ⊞ ⊤ ⊠ WCs. ⊡ Licensed. Ⓕ By arrangement. 🅿 ⊞ Pre-booking required. ⊞ Dogs on leads only. ⊡ ⊡

GAINSBOROUGH'S HOUSE
46 Gainsborough St, Sudbury, Suffolk CO10 2EU
www.gainsborough.org

Gainsborough's House is the childhood home of Thomas Gainsborough RA (1727-1788) and displays an outstanding collection of his paintings, drawings and prints. A varied programme of temporary exhibitions is also shown throughout the year. The historic house dates back to the 16th Century and has an attractive walled garden. **Location:** Map 8:I10. OS Ref TL872 413. 46 Gainsborough St, Sudbury town centre. **Owner:** Gainsborough's House Society
Contact: Liz Cooper **Tel:** 01787 372958 **Fax:** 01787 376991
E-mail: mail@gainsborough.org
Open: All year: Mon-Sat, 10am-5pm; Suns 11am-5pm. Closed: Good Friday and Christmas to New Year. **Admission:** Please telephone 01787 372958 for details of admission charges or go to our website www.gainsborough.org.
Key facts: ⓘ No photography in the Exhibition Gallery. ⊡ The new shop offers a range of themes based on the heritage of Gainsborough and the Georgian period. ⊞ A small selection of plants from Gainsborough's Garden are available for sale. ⊠ Suitable WCs. Ⓕ By arrangement. ⊞ ⊞ Guide dogs only. ⊞

Helmingham Hall

ICKWORTH HOUSE, PARKLAND, WOODLAND & GARDENS ❧
Horringer, Bury St Edmunds, Suffolk IP29 5QE
www.nationaltrust.org.uk/ickworth

A touch of classical Italy brought to Suffolk. Enjoy an entertaining day at this idiosyncratic and beautiful country estate. The grand Rotunda is filled with treasures collected by the Hervey family and sits in tranquil, landscaped parkland with waymarked walks and cycle routes. Discover one of the earliest Italianate gardens in England. Experience 1930's life in the newly restored Servants' basement. **Location:** Map 8:19. OS Ref TL816 611. In Horringer, 3m SW of Bury St Edmunds on W side of A143. **Owner:** The National Trust **Contact:** Property Administrator **Tel:** 01284 735270 **E-mail:** ickworth@nationaltrust.org.uk **Open:** House: 13 Mar-1 Nov, Thu-Tue, 11am-4pm (Tours only until 12noon, last entry 3pm). Parkland & Gardens: Daily dawn-dusk all year. Shop & Restaurant: Daily 10.30am-5pm. Closed Christmas Day. **Admission:** Gift Aid Admission: House, Park & Gardens £14.00, Child £7.00, Family £35.00. Groups (15+) £11.00pp. **Key facts:** ▣ 🏵 Mar-Nov. 🔲 Lift in main house. Mobility scooters available. West Wing drop off point. 🖰 🍴 🅵 🅿 Car park with parking for coaches. 🐕 Assistance dogs only in Italianate gardens. 🏠 Holiday cottages. ❋ ⚘

OTLEY HALL
Hall Lane, Otley, Suffolk IP6 9PA
www.otleyhall.co.uk

Stunning medieval Moated Hall (Grade I) frequently described as 'one of England's loveliest houses'. Noted for its richly carved beams, superb linenfold panelling and 16th Century wall paintings. The unique 10-acre gardens include historically accurate Tudor re-creations and were voted among the top 10 gardens to visit in Great Britain.
Location: Map 8:K9. OS Ref TM207 563. 7m N of Ipswich, off the B1079.
Owner: Dr Ian & Reverend Catherine Beaumont
Contact: Karen Gwynne - Vince
Tel: 01473 890264
Fax: 01473 890803 **E-mail:** events@otleyhall.co.uk
Open: Open Gardens every Wed May-Sep. 11am-5pm. £3.00 entrance, café serving light lunches and afternoon tea also open every Wed May-Sep. The House and grounds are available for wedding ceremonies and receptions where we offer exclusive access to the venue on the wedding day. For more information please visit our website. **Admission:** By appointment only.
Key facts: 🍴 🔲 Partial. 🍷 Licensed. 🅵 By arrangement. 🅿 🏠 ❋ ⚘

SOMERLEYTON HALL & GARDENS 🏛ℱ
Somerleyton, Lowestoft, Suffolk NR32 5QQ
www.somerleyton.co.uk

Originally Jacobean, re-modelled in 1844 to a magnificent Anglo-Italian styled stately home featuring beautiful architecture, sumptuous state rooms and ornate sculptures. 12 acres of beautiful gardens, include the famous yew hedge maze, 300ft pergola, Vulliamy tower clock, Paxton glasshouses, restored Nestfield's parterre and new white sunken garden. Tea rooms with homemade cakes.
Location: Map 8:M7. OS Ref TM493 977. 5m NW of Lowestoft on B1074, 7m SW of Great Yarmouth off A143.
Owner: Lord and Lady Somerleyton **Contact:** Clare
Tel: 08712 224244 (office) **Fax:** 01502 732143 **Twitter:** @SomerleytonHall.
Facebook: facebook.com/SomerleytonHall. **E-mail:** info@somerleyton.co.uk
Open: Please visit www.somerleyton.co.uk or call the estate office for opening dates, events and admission prices. **Key facts:** ⓘ No photography in house. ▣ 🏵 🍴 Receptions/functions/conferences/weddings. 🔲 Suitable. WCs. Partial disabled access. 🖰 🅵 Obligatory. 🅿 🏠 🐕 Guide dogs only. 🐾 🏠 ⚘

FLATFORD BRIDGE COTTAGE
Flatford, East Bergholt, Suffolk CO7 6UL

In the heart of the beautiful Dedham Vale, the hamlet of Flatford is the location for some of John Constable's most famous paintings. Discover more about the work of John Constable in our exhibition, explore Bridge Cottage then relax in our riverside tea room and gift shop. Note: No public entry inside Flatford Mill.
Location: Map 8:J10. OS Ref TM076 332. On N bank of Stour, 1m S of East Bergholt B1070. **Owner:** National Trust **Contact:** Visitor Services
Tel: 01206 298260 **E-mail:** flatfordbridgecottage@nationaltrust.org.uk
Website: www.nationaltrust.org.uk **Open:** 3 Jan–1 Mar, 10:30–3:30, Sat & Sun; 4 Mar–29 Mar, 10:30–5, Wed-Sun; 30 Mar–26 Apr, 10:30–5, open all week; 27 Apr–4 Oct, 10:30–5:30, open all week; 5 Oct–1 Nov, 10:30–5, open all week; 4 Nov–20 Dec, 10:30–3:30, Wed-Sun. Parking £3.50.
Key facts: Parking free for NT members. WCs. Licensed. Charge applies. Limited parking for coaches, advanced booking recommended. Please be aware that between the car park and Bridge Cottage is a flight of steps.

HAUGHLEY PARK
Stowmarket, Suffolk IP14 3JY

Grade 1 listed red-brick manor house of 1620 set in gardens, park and woodland. Original five-gabled east front, north wing rebuilt in Georgian style, 1820. Varied six acre gardens including walled kitchen garden. Way-marked woodland walks. 17th Century barn bookable for Weddings, Meetings etc.
Location: Map 8:J8. OS Ref TM005 618. Signed from J47a and J48 on A14.
Owner: Mr & Mrs Robert Williams
Contact: Barn Office
Tel: 01359 240701 **E-mail:** info@haughleyparkbarn.co.uk
Website: www.haughleyparkbarn.co.uk
Open: Garden only: May-Sep: Tues, 2-5.30pm. For Bluebell Sunday and Weird & Wonderful Wood dates, see website.
Admission: Garden: £4.00 Child under 16 Free.
Key facts: Picnics allowed. Bluebell Sun. WCs. By arrangement. Limited for coaches. On leads.

ST EDMUNDSBURY CATHEDRAL
Angel Hill, Bury St Edmunds, Suffolk IP33 1LS

The striking Millennium Tower, completed in 2005, is the crowning glory of St Edmundsbury Cathedral. Further enhanced with the stunning vaulted ceiling in 2010, the 150ft Lantern Tower, along with new chapels, cloisters and North Transept, completes nearly fifty years of development in a style never likely to be repeated.
Location: Map 8:I8. OS Ref TL857 642. Bury St Edmunds town centre.
Owner: The Church of England **Contact:** Sarah Friswell
Tel: 01284 748720
E-mail: pr.manager@stedscathedral.org
Website: www.stedscathedral.co.uk
Open: All year: daily 8.30am-6pm.
Admission: Donations invited.
Key facts: Open daily. Open Mon-Sat. 11.30am.

ST MARY'S CHURCH
St Mary's Street, Bungay, Suffolk NR35 1AX

The graceful and elegant tower of this grand church, with its tall pinnacles, stands 33.5 metres high. If you look up as you approach you can see intriguing carved heads under the parapet of the north aisle. Built in the late 15th Century as part of the church of the Benedictine priory, St Mary's remained the parish church after the priory was closed by Henry VIII in 1536.
Inside, the church is flooded with light from the plain glass windows, especially the west window and has an amazing display of tracery design in its upper half. The splendid carvings on the roof bosses include angels, a lion, two-headed eagles and a splendid bat. Look out for a wooden dole-cupboard near the entrance which was given by the curate in 1675 where bread was left for collection by the poor - it has religious worthies and a perky rat carved on it. There is also a fine 17th Century carved Flemish panel of the Resurrection in the War Memorial Chapel.
Location: OS Ref TM337 898. In Bungay town centre.
Website: www.visitchurches.org.uk **Open:** Open daily.

ST MARY'S CHURCH
Churchway, Redgrave, Diss, Suffolk IP22 1RJ

Five centuries of parishioners have worshipped at St Mary's, a vast country church set in open fields. Everything is on a grand scale: the east window is stunning, with glorious stained-glass images of saints and angels. The collection of hatchments and monuments is of national importance. Tombs have life-size statues in elaborate 17th Century fashions and there are 13 hatchments - wood and canvas coats of arms - more than any other church in Suffolk. The north-east brick vestry is a rare survival from the 16th Century, and a wander round the churchyard reveals many 18th Century gravestones, some with little carved skulls peeping over the top.
Location: OS Ref TM057 782. 4 miles west of Diss, off B1113; 1 mile from village centre. **Website:** www.visitchurches.org.uk
Open: Please see website for latest opening times.

ST PETER'S CHURCH
Church Lane, Claydon, Ipswich, Suffolk IP6 0EQ

On a commanding site above the Gipping Valley, St Peter's was commissioned by eccentric High Church rector, George Drury. It is stunning, full of vibrant stained glass and extravagant carvings. Drury himself was responsible for the design of the stained glass in the east and west windows and he may also have carved some of the stonework. The surviving 19th Century fittings are all of high quality and also bear the stamp of Father Drury's personality.
Location: OS Ref TM137 499. 4 miles north west of Ipswich, off A14.
Website: www.visitchurches.org.uk
Open: Open daily.

CECIL HIGGINS ART GALLERY
Castle Lane, Bedford MK40 3RP
Tel: 01234 718618 **E-mail:** thehiggins@bedford.gov.uk

CHURCH OF ST MARGARET OF ANTIOCH ⋔
Melchbourne Road, Knotting, Bedfordshire MK44 1AF
Tel: 0845 303 2760 **E-mail:** central@thecct.org.uk

ST DENY'S CHURCH ⋔
Little Barford, St Neots, Bedfordshire PE19 6YE
Tel: 0845 303 2760 **E-mail:** central@thecct.org.uk

ST GEORGE'S CHURCH ⋔
Edworth, Biggleswade, Bedfordshire SG18 8QX
Tel: 0845 303 2760 **E-mail:** central@thecct.org.uk

ST MARY'S CHURCH ⋔
Lower Gravenhurst, Gravenhurst, Bedfordshire MK45 4JR
Tel: 0845 303 2760 **E-mail:** central@thecct.org.uk

ST MARY'S CHURCH ⋔
Potsgrove, Milton Keynes, Bedfordshire MK17 9HG
Tel: 0845 303 2760 **E-mail:** central@thecct.org.uk

ST MICHAEL'S CHURCH ⋔
Farndish, Wellingborough, Bedfordshire NN29 7HJ
Tel: 0845 303 2760 **E-mail:** central@thecct.org.uk

ALL SAINTS' CHURCH ⋔
Church Lane, Conington, Peterborough, Cambs PE7 3QA
Tel: 0845 303 2760 **E-mail:** central@thecct.org.uk

CHURCH OF ST CYRIAC & ST JULITTA ⋔
High Street, Swaffham Prior, Cambridge CB25 0LD
Tel: 0845 303 2760 **E-mail:** central@thecct.org.uk

CHURCH OF ST JOHN THE BAPTIST ⋔
Main Road, Parson Drove, Wisbech, Cambridgeshire PE13 4LF
Tel: 0845 303 2760 **E-mail:** central@thecct.org.uk

ST ANDREW'S CHURCH ⋔
Steeple Gidding, Huntingdon, Cambridgeshire PE28 5RG
Tel: 0845 303 2760 **E-mail:** central@thecct.org.uk

ST JOHN'S CHURCH ⋔
Green Street, Duxford, Cambridge, Cambridgeshire CB22 4RG
Tel: 0845 303 2760 **E-mail:** central@thecct.org.uk

ST MARGARET'S CHURCH ⋔
High Street, Abbotsley, St Neots, Cambridgeshire PE19 6UJ
Tel: 0845 303 2760 **E-mail:** central@thecct.org.uk

ST MICHAEL'S CHURCH ⋔
Longstanton, Cambridge, Cambridgeshire CB24 3BZ
Tel: 0845 303 2760 **E-mail:** central@thecct.org.uk

ST PETER'S CHURCH ⋔
High Street, Offord D'Arcy, St Neots, Cambs PE19 5RH
Tel: 0845 303 2760 **E-mail:** central@thecct.org.uk

ALL SAINTS' CHURCH ⋔
East Horndon, Brentwood, Essex CM13 3LL
Tel: 0845 303 2760 **E-mail:** central@thecct.org.uk

CHURCH OF ST MARY THE VIRGIN ⋔
Barlon Road, Little Bromley, Manningtree, Essex CO11 2PP
Tel: 0845 303 2760 **E-mail:** central@thecct.org.uk

HOLY TRINITY CHURCH ⋔
Trinity Street, Halstead, Essex CO9 1JH
Tel: 0845 303 2760 **E-mail:** central@thecct.org.uk

LAYER MARNEY TOWER ▥ⓕ
Nr Colchester, Essex CO5 9US
Tel: 01206 330784 **E-mail:** info@

RHS HYDE HALL
Creephedge Lane, Rettendon, Chelmsford, Essex CM3 8ET
Tel: 0845 265 8071 **E-mail:** hydehall@rhs.org.uk

ST LEONARD-AT-THE-HYTHE CHURCH ⋔
Hythe Hill, Colchester, Essex CO1 2NP
Tel: 0845 303 2760 **E-mail:** central@thecct.org.uk

ST MARY'S CHURCH ⋔
Chickney, Broxted, Dunmow, Essex CM6 2BY
Tel: 0845 303 2760 **E-mail:** central@thecct.org.uk

ST MARY'S CHURCH ⋔
Hall Road, West Bergholt, Colchester, Essex CO6 3DU
Tel: 0845 303 2760 **E-mail:** central@thecct.org.uk

ASHRIDGE GARDENS ▥ⓕ
Berkhamsted, Hertfordshire HP4 1NS
Tel: 01442 843491 **E-mail:** reception@

CHURCH OF ST MARY THE VIRGIN ⋔
Little Hormead, Buntingford, Hertfordshire SG9 0LS
Tel: 0845 303 2760 **E-mail:** central@thecct.org.uk

OXHEY CHAPEL ⋔
Gosforth Lane, South Oxhey, Watford, Herts WD19 7AX
Tel: 0845 303 2760 **E-mail:** central@thecct.org.uk

ST ANDREW'S CHURCH ⋔
Rectory Close, Buckland, Buntingford, Hertfordshire SG9 0PT
Tel: 0845 303 2760 **E-mail:** central@thecct.org.uk

ST JAMES' CHURCH ⋔
Roydon Road, Stanstead Abbotts, Ware, Herts SG12 8JZ
Tel: 0845 303 2760 **E-mail:** central@thecct.org.uk

ALL SAINTS' CHURCH ⋔
West Harling, Thetford, Norfolk NR16 2SE
Tel: 0845 303 2760 **E-mail:** central@thecct.org.uk

ALL SAINTS' CHURCH ⋔
Thurgarton, Norwich, Norfolk NR11 7HT
Tel: 0845 303 2760 **E-mail:** central@thecct.org.uk

CHURCH OF ST JOHN THE BAPTIST ⋔
Hellington Hill, Hellington, Norwich, Norfolk NR14 7BS
Tel: 0845 303 2760 **E-mail:** central@thecct.org.uk

FELBRIGG HALL ⚘
Felbrigg, Norwich, Norfolk NR11 8PR
Tel: 01263 837444 **E-mail:** felbrigg@nationaltrust.org.uk

Elton Hall, Cambridgeshire

ST AUGUSTINE'S CHURCH 🏛
St Augustine's Street, Norwich, Norfolk NR3 3BY
Tel: 0845 303 2760 **E-mail:** central@thecct.org.uk

ST FAITH'S CHURCH 🏛
Little Witchingham, Norwich, Norfolk NR9 5PA
Tel: 0845 303 2760 **E-mail:** central@thecct.org.uk

ST GEORGE'S CHURCH 🏛
Shimpling, Diss, Norfolk IP21 4UF
Tel: 0845 303 2760 **E-mail:** central@thecct.org.uk

ST GREGORY'S CHURCH 🏛
Norton Road, Heckingham, Norwich, Norfolk NR14 6QT
Tel: 0845 303 2760 **E-mail:** central@thecct.org.uk

ST LAURENCE'S CHURCH 🏛
St. Benedict's Street, Norwich, Norfolk NR2 3PE
Tel: 0845 303 2760 **E-mail:** central@thecct.org.uk

ST MARY'S BELL TOWER 🏛
School Road, West Walton, Wisbech, Norfolk PE14 7ET
Tel: 0845 303 2760 **E-mail:** central@thecct.org.uk

ST MARY'S CHURCH 🏛
Islington Green, Tilney, King's Lynn, Norfolk PE34 4SB
Tel: 0845 303 2760 **E-mail:** central@thecct.org.uk

ST MARY'S CHURCH 🏛
Reedham Road, Moulton, Norwich, Norfolk NR13 3NW
Tel: 0845 303 2760 **E-mail:** central@thecct.org.uk

ST MARY'S CHURCH 🏛
Boughton Long Road, Barton Bendish, Norfolk PE33 9DN
Tel: 0845 303 2760 **E-mail:** central@thecct.org.uk

ST MARY'S CHURCH 🏛
Church Street, East Bradenham, Thetford, Norfolk IP25 7QL
Tel: 0845 303 2760 **E-mail:** central@thecct.org.uk

ST MARY'S CHURCH 🏛
East Ruston, Norwich, Norfolk NR12 9HN
Tel: 0845 303 2760 **E-mail:** central@thecct.org.uk

ST MICHAEL'S CHURCH 🏛
Church Lane, Coston, Norwich, Norfolk NR9 4DT
Tel: 0845 303 2760 **E-mail:** central@thecct.org.uk

ST NICHOLAS' CHAPEL 🏛
St Ann's Street, King's Lynn, Norfolk PE30 1NH
Tel: 0845 303 2760 **E-mail:** central@thecct.org.uk

ST NICHOLAS' CHURCH 🏛
School Road, Buckenham, Norwich, Norfolk NR13 4HN
Tel: 0845 303 2760 **E-mail:** central@thecct.org.uk

ST PETER'S CHURCH 🏛
North Barningham, Norwich, Norfolk NR11 7LB
Tel: 0845 303 2760 **E-mail:** central@thecct.org.uk

ALL SAINTS' CHURCH 🏛
Little Wenham, Ipswich, Suffolk CO7 6PU
Tel: 0845 303 2760 **E-mail:** central@thecct.org.uk

ALL SAINTS' CHURCH 🏛
Church Road, Newton Green, Sudbury, Suffolk CO10 0QP
Tel: 0845 303 2760 **E-mail:** central@thecct.org.uk

ALL SAINTS' CHURCH 🏛
The Street, Icklingham, Bury St Edmunds, Suffolk IP28 6PL
Tel: 0845 303 2760 **E-mail:** central@thecct.org.uk

ALL SAINTS' CHURCH 🏛
Ellough, Beccles, Suffolk NR34 7TR
Tel: 0845 303 2760 **E-mail:** central@thecct.org.uk

ALL SAINTS' CHURCH 🏛
Wordwell, Bury St Edmunds, Suffolk IP28 6UN
Tel: 0845 303 2760 **E-mail:** central@thecct.org.uk

CHURCH OF ST JOHN THE BAPTIST 🏛
Stanton, Bury St Edmunds, Suffolk IP31 2XD
Tel: 0845 303 2760 **E-mail:** central@thecct.org.uk

CHURCH OF ST MARY THE VIRGIN 🏛
Church Lane, Stonham Parva, Stowmarket, Suffolk IP14 5JL
Tel: 0845 303 2760 **E-mail:** central@thecct.org.uk

CHURCH OF ST MARY-AT-THE-QUAY 🏛
Foundation Street, Ipswich, Suffolk IP4 1BU
Tel: 0845 303 2760 **E-mail:** central@thecct.org.uk

FRAMLINGHAM CASTLE ⌗
Framlingham, Suffolk IP13 9BP
Tel: 0870 333 1181 **E-mail:** customers@english-heritage.org.uk

MELFORD HALL ❦
Long Melford, Sudbury, Suffolk CO10 9AA
Tel: 01787 379228 **E-mail:** melford@nationaltrust.org.uk

ST ANDREW'S CHURCH 🏛
Covehithe, Lowestoft, Suffolk NR34 7JW
Tel: 0845 303 2760 **E-mail:** central@thecct.org.uk

ST ANDREW'S CHURCH 🏛
Sapiston, Thetford, Suffolk IP31 1RY
Tel: 0845 303 2760 **E-mail:** central@thecct.org.uk

ST MARY'S CHURCH 🏛
Washbrook, Ipswich, Suffolk IP8 3HQ
Tel: 0845 303 2760 **E-mail:** central@thecct.org.uk

ST MARY'S CHURCH 🏛
Rickinghall Superior, Diss, Suffolk IP22 1EZ
Tel: 0845 303 2760 **E-mail:** central@thecct.org.uk

ST MARY'S CHURCH 🏛
Akenham, Ipswich, Suffolk IP1 6TQ
Tel: 0845 303 2760 **E-mail:** central@thecct.org.uk

ST MARY'S CHURCH 🏛
Badley, Ipswich, Suffolk IP6 8RU
Tel: 0845 303 2760 **E-mail:** central@thecct.org.uk

ST PETER'S CHURCH 🏛
Market Square, Sudbury, Suffolk CO10 2TP
Tel: 0845 303 2760 **E-mail:** central@thecct.org.uk

Tissington Hall, Derbyshire

Grimsthorpe Castle, Lincolnshire

East Midlands

Derbyshire
Leicestershire &
Rutland
Lincolnshire
Northamptonshire
Nottinghamshire

Derby-shire
Nottingham-shire
Lincolnshire
Leicestershire & Rutland
Northampton-shire

The heartlands of agricultural England generated wealth for the builders of some of the country's most magnificent castles and stately homes.

New Entries for 2015:
• The Welbeck Estate & the Harley Gallery
• Tissington Hall
• Lincoln Castle
• Gainsborough Old Hall

**Find stylish hotels with a personal welcome and good cuisine in the East Midlands.
More information on page 364.**

- Barnsdale Lodge Hotel
- Biggin Hall Hotel
- The Cavendish Hotel
- Langar Hall
- Losehill House Hotel & Spa
- The Manners Arms
- The Talbot Hotel
- Washingborough Hall Hotel
- Whittlebury Hall Hotel & Spa

SIGNPOST
SELECTED PREMIER HOTELS 2015

www.signpost.co.uk

■ **Owner**
Chatsworth House Trust

■ **Address**
Chatsworth
Bakewell
Derbyshire
DE45 1PP

■ **Location**
Map 6:P2
OS Ref. **SK260 703**
From London 3 hrs M1/
J29, signposted via
Chesterfield. 3m E of
Bakewell, off B6012,10m
W of Chesterfield.
Rail: Chesterfield Station,
11m
Bus: Chesterfield - Baslow
1½m

■ **Contact**
The Booking Office
Tel: 01246 565430
Fax: 01246 583536
E-mail:
visit@chatsworth.org

■ **Opening Times**
House, garden and farmyard:
Open daily from 28 March 2015.

The farmyard and adventure playground will open for half term, 7 – 22 February.

The Stables gift shops, restaurants and the Chatsworth Estate Farm Shop are open every day from 2 January 2015.

■ **Admission**
The admission prices for the house, garden and farmyard are listed on our website at www.chatsworth.org. Online tickets available.

Conference/Function

ROOM	Size	Max Cap
Hartington Rm		80
Burlington Rm		80
Racing Rm		22

CHATSWORTH ◆
www.chatsworth.org

The home to the duke and duchess of Devonshire is one of the Country's greatest treasure houses.

The house is renowned for the quality of its art, landscape and hospitality. Home of the Cavendish family since the 1550s, it has evolved through the centuries to reflect the tastes, passions and interests of succeeding generations. Today Chatsworth contains works of art that span 4000 years, from ancient Roman and Egyptian sculpture, and masterpieces by Rembrandt, Reynolds and Veronese, to work by outstanding modern artists, including Lucian Freud, Edmund de Waal and David Nash. The garden is famous for its rich history, historic and modern waterworks and sculptures, the Victorian rock garden and the maze. Younger visitors also enjoy the farmyard and adventure playground and the 1000 acre park is open every day.

In 2015 we will be hosting a number of exciting events including our annual Horse Trials, concerts in the garden, Country Fair, bonfire and fireworks and Christmas market; and from early November the lower floors of the house will be transformed for Christmas.

In addition to our busy events programme, we will be hosting a number of special exhibitions included with admission. We are excited to be showcasing the best in contemporary seat design with headline exhibition 'Make Yourself Comfortable', as well as joining forces with Nottingham Contemporary, Derby Museums, and the Harley Foundation to create a 'Grand Tour' of Nottinghamshire and Derbyshire's cultural history and landscape. In the autumn we play host to Sotheby's Beyond Limits sculpture exhibition in the garden, as well as our rolling programme showcasing Old Master Drawings in the house.

KEY FACTS

- 5 gift shops and Farm shop.
- Available for conferences and private functions. Contact Catering.
- WCs.
- Licensed.
- Licensed.
- Small charge for daily tours. Groups pre-book.
- Handheld and audio guides available to hire in English.
- Cars 100 yds, Coaches drop off at house.
- Guided tours, packs, and self guiding materials. Free preliminary visit.
- Dogs on leads only.
- Holiday cottages.

HADDON HALL 🏛Ⓕ
www.haddonhall.co.uk

Haddon Hall sits on a rocky outcrop above the River Wye near the market town of Bakewell, looking much as it would have done in Tudor times.

There has been a dwelling here since the 11th Century but the house we see today dates mainly from the late 14th Century with major additions in the following 200 years and some alterations in the early 17th Century including the creation of the Long Gallery. William the Conqueror's illegitimate son Peverel, and his descendants, held Haddon for 100 years before it passed to the Vernon family. In the late 16th Century the estate passed through marriage to the Manners family, in whose possession it has remained ever since. When the Dukedom of Rutland was conferred on the Manners family in 1703, they moved to Belvoir Castle, and Haddon was left deserted for 200 years. This was Haddon's saving grace as the Hall thus escaped the major architectural changes of the 18th and 19th Centuries ready for the great restoration at the beginning of the 20th Century by the 9th

Duke of Rutland. Henry VIII's elder brother Arthur, who was a frequent guest of the Vernons, would be quite familiar with the house as it stands today. Haddon Hall is a popular location for film and television productions. Recent filming includes 'Pride and Prejudice', and both the BBC dramatization of 'Jane Eyre' and the 2011 feature film 'Jane Eyre' in which Haddon Hall doubled as Mr Rochester's Thornfield.

Gardens
Magnificent terraced gardens, adorned with roses, clematis and beautiful herbaceous borders, providing colour and scent throughout spring, summer and autumn. Fountain Terrace re-designed by award winning garden designer, Arne Maynard.

KEY FACTS

- ℹ️ Ideal film location due to authentic & genuine architecture requiring little alteration. Suitable locations also on Estate.
- 🏪 Gatehouse Gift Shop, local & specially selected souvenirs, gifts, cards & plants.
- 🚻 WCs.
- ♿
- 🍴 Licensed.
- 🚶 Special tours £15pp min. 10. 7 days notice.
- 🅿️ Ample. 450yds from house. £2/car.
- 🎭 Tours of the house bring alive Haddon Hall of old. Costume room also available, very popular!
- 🐕 Assistance dogs only.
- 💒 Licensed for civil ceremonies.
- 🎗️

VISITOR INFORMATION

■ Owner
Lord Edward Manners

■ Address
Estate Office
Haddon Hall
Bakewell
Derbyshire
DE45 1LA

■ Location
Map 6:P2
OS Ref. SK234 663
From London 3 hrs
Sheffield ½hr Manchester
1 hr Haddon is on the E
side of A6 1½m S of
Bakewell. M1/J29.
Bus: Chesterfield Bakewell.
Rail: Chesterfield Station,
12m.

■ Contact
Vikki Kastenbauer Stronge
Tel: 01629 812855
E-mail:
info@haddonhall.co.uk

■ Opening Times
Easter: 28th March - 6th
April 12noon-5 pm.
April: Saturday, Sunday &
Monday.
May - September:
Open daily (except 30th &
31st May).
October: Saturday,
Sunday & Monday.
Opening times:
12 noon-5 pm (last
admission 4 pm).
Christmas: 8th - 19th
December (opening times
10.30 am-4 pm (last
admission 3.30pm).
Please note: Haddon Hall
is closed during January,
February and November.

■ Admission

Adult	£12.00
Conc./ Student	£11.00
Child (5-15yrs)	£6.00
Family (2+3)	£35.00
Regular Visitor Pass	£49.00

Groups (15+)

Adult	£10.50
Conc./Student	£9.50
Guided tour	£15.00
Parking	£2.00

Due to age and nature of Haddon, there are many uneven floors and steps within the house and gardens and this should be borne in mind when visiting. Please telephone in advance for further information and to hear about the assistance we can give. Further accessibility information can also be found on our website.

■ Special Events
Regular programme of special events - check website. Weddings - Up to 100 in Long Gallery or 35 in our cosy Parlour. Terrace hire for pre-reception drinks & canapes.

East Midlands - England

VISITOR INFORMATION

■ Owner
Welbeck Estates Company Limited

■ Address
Welbeck Abbey
Welbeck
Worksop
Nottinghamshire
S80 3LL

■ Location
Map 7:B2
OS Ref. SK 56328 74286
From the M1 – leave the motorway at Junction 30 and follow brown signs for Welbeck.
From the A1 – leave the A1 at Worksop and follow brown signs to Welbeck.

The car park entrance is marked on the A60 with a brown sign for The Harley Gallery.

■ Contact
The Harley Gallery
Tel: 01909 501700
E-mail:
info@harleygallery.co.uk

■ Opening Times
Tours run twice daily during August, at 10.15am and 2.30pm.
The maximum number on each tour is 20.
Please always check the website before visiting for full details.

■ Admission
£16.50 per person.

Welbeck Abbey

WELBECK ABBEY 🏛
www.welbeck.co.uk

Home to the Cavendish-Bentinck family from 1607 to the present.

The Welbeck Estate covers some 15,000 acres, nestled between Sherwood Forest & Clumber Park. At its heart lies Welbeck Abbey, a stately home which dates back to 1153 when it was founded as a Premonstratensian monastery.

Welbeck was acquired by Charles Cavendish, Bess of Hardwick's third son, in 1607. Over the next four centuries, the family at Welbeck would collect artworks, commission architecture and combine family names, with, unusually, three females in succession inheriting the Estate. This line of descent includes marriages with the Dukedom of Newcastle, Earldom of Oxford and the Dukedom of Portland, each bringing additional wealth, status and power to Welbeck.

Welbeck Abbey's architecture has evolved as it has passed through the generations. Visitors to the Abbey can see some of these additions, including the Countess of Oxford's soaring plasterwork ceiling in the Gothic Hall, and the Duchess of Portland's State

Rooms remodelled by Sir Ernest George, c. 1905. The State Rooms are decorated with objects and artworks from The Portland Collection; an internationally significant collection which includes one of the largest privately owned collections of British portraits. Works on show at Welbeck Abbey include pieces by Sir Peter Lely, John Wootton and Sir Joshua Reynolds.

Welbeck Abbey's State Rooms are open to the public during August for guided tours, which depart from The Harley Gallery by mini bus. Tours last approximately an hour and a half. Visitors are advised that there are no toilet facilities or seating on the tour. Toilets, refreshments, shopping and exhibitions can be found at The Harley Gallery.

The Harley Foundation and Gallery was set up by Ivy, Duchess of Portland in 1977, to 'encourage creativity in all of us'. The Harley Gallery shows a programme of contemporary exhibitions, alongside displays from The Portland Collection.

KEY FACTS

- ℹ️ No photography. No bags.
- 🛍 The Harley Shop
- ♿ By prior arrangement. Ground floor only.
- ☕ The Harley Café
- 🚶 Obligatory.
- 🅿 Free parking. Please park at The Harley Gallery.

The Swan Drawing Room

The Gobelin Tapestries

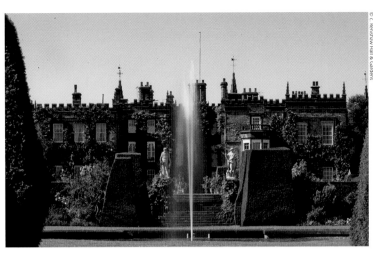

RENISHAW HALL AND GARDENS 🏛Ⓕ
RENISHAW, NR SHEFFIELD, DERBYSHIRE S21 3WB
www.renishaw-hall.co.uk

Renishaw Hall and Gardens have been home to the Sitwell family for over 400 years. Its present owner, Alexandra, welcomes you. Renishaw Hall is set in eight acres of Italianate gardens, designed by Sir George Sitwell featuring statues, yew hedges, beautiful herbaceous borders and ornamental ponds. Mature woodlands and lakes offer wonderful walks. The hall offers an intriguing insight into the Sitwell family's history, with a fascinating collection of paintings including work by John Piper. The hall & gardens are open for group and public tours, see website for details. The Gallery Café, shop and museum are in the stables. Tours of the vineyard are available throughout the season. The hall & gardens can be hired for film and photo shoots. **Location:** Map 7:A2. OS Ref SK435 786. On A6135, 3m from M1/J30, located between Sheffield and Chesterfield.
Owner: Mrs Hayward **Contact:** The Operations Manager **Tel:** 01246 432310 **Fax:** 01246 430760 **E-mail:** enquiries@renishaw-hall.co.uk **Open:** 2015: 27

Mar-27 Sep. Gardens open Wed-Sun & BH Mons, 10.30am-4.30pm. Hall open to public on Fridays throughout season 1pm or 2.30pm & weekends in Aug, pre-booking advisable for guided tours. Hall, garden & vineyard tours available throughout year for private groups & coach tours, by appointment only.
Admission: HHA /RHS members free entry to Gardens. Guided Hall Tours £6.50. Discounts for coach/group bookings over 25 people. Parking £1.00. Non member entry Gardens Adults £6.50, Concessions £5.50, Children £3.25, under 5s free. Non member Guided Hall Tour Adults £12.75, Concessions £11.75.
Key facts: ℹ️ Gallery Café, Gift Shop, WC available during garden opening. 📷 🌿 Plant sales by Handley Rose Nursery available at the visitor centre. 🇹 ♿ Partial. WCs. 🍽 Licensed. 📷 By arrangement throughout season for groups & on Fridays to public. 🅿️ £1 per car for the day. 🐕 On leads. ♠ The stunning Red Dining Room can be hired for up to 70 guests for a civil ceremony. 💒

Haddon Hall

CATTON HALL 🏛Ⓕ
Catton, Walton-On-Trent, South Derbyshire DE12 8LN
www.catton-hall.com

Catton, built in 1745, has been in the hands of the same family since 1405 and is still lived in by the Neilsons as their private home. This gives the house a unique, relaxed and friendly atmosphere, with its spacious reception rooms, comfortable bedrooms and delicious food and wine. Catton is centrally located for residential or non-residential business meetings/seminars, product launches and team-building activities, as well as for accommodation for those visiting Birmingham, the NEC, the Belfry - or just for a weekend celebration of family and friends. The acres of parkland alongside the River Trent are ideal for all types of corporate and public events. **Location:** Map 6:P5. OS Ref SK20 6153. Between Lichfield & Burton-on-Trent (8m from each). Birmingham NEC 20m.
Owner/Contact: Robin & Katie Neilson
Tel: 01283 716311 **E-mail:** r.neilson@catton-hall.com
Open: By prior arrangement all year, for corporate hospitality, shooting parties, or private groups. Guided tours at 2pm BH Mons, and all Mons in Aug.
Key facts: ℹ️ Conference facilities. 🇹 By arrangement. ♿ 📷 By arrangement. 🛏 4 x four posters, 5 twin, all en suite. 💒

MELBOURNE HALL & GARDENS 🏛ⓕ
Melbourne, Derbyshire DE73 8EN
www.melbournehall.com

This beautiful house of history, in its picturesque poolside setting, was once the home of Victorian Prime Minister William Lamb. The fine gardens, in the French formal style, contain Robert Bakewell's intricate wrought iron arbour and a fascinating yew tunnel. Upstairs rooms available to view by appointment.
Location: Map 7:A5. OS Ref SK389 249. 8m S of Derby. From London, exit M1/J24. **Owner:** Lord & Lady Ralph Kerr **Contact:** Mrs Gill Weston
Tel: 01332 862502 **Fax:** 01332 862263
E-mail: melbhall@globalnet.co.uk
Open: Hall: Aug only (not first 3 Mons) 2-5pm. Last admission 4.15pm. Gardens: 1 Apr-30 Sep: Weds, Sats, Suns, BH Mons, 1.30-5.30pm. Additional open days possible in Aug. Additional days in Aug whenever the Hall is open.
Admission: Please see website or telephone for up to date admission charges.
Key facts: ℹ️ No photography in house. 📷 Visitor centre shops, hospice shop, gift shop, antiques, jewellery, cakes, furniture restorer.
♿ Partial. WCs. ☕ Melbourne Hall Tea room. 🎫 Obligatory in house Tue-Sat.
🅿️ Limited. No coach parking. 🐕 Guide dogs only. ✉️

TISSINGTON HALL 🏛ⓕ
Ashbourne, Derbyshire DE6 1RA
www.tissingtonhall.co.uk

Tissington Hall stands at the centre of its estate, built in 1609 by Francis FitzHerbert it still remains in the family. The Hall is open on published days. Private group tours, functions and weddings are welcome all year-round, all of which can enjoy the fabulous gardens and 5 acre arboretum.
Location: Map 6:P3. OS Ref SK175 524. 4m N of Ashbourne off A515 towards Buxton. **Owner:** Sir Richard FitzHerbert Bt
Tel: 01335 352200 **E-mail:** events@tissingtonhall.co.uk
Open: 6-10 Apr; 4 & 5 May; 18, 19 & 20 May; 25-28 May; 3-31 Aug (closed 13 Aug 2015) Mon-Thu. 12-3pm (last tour 2.30pm). Group visits & special tours welcome throughout the year by prior arrangement. NB Tissington Village open throughout the year.
Admission: Hall & Gardens: Adult £10.00, Child (10-16yrs) £5.00, Conc. £9.00. Gardens only: Adult £5.00, Child £2.50, Conc. £4.00. Group Visits welcome throughout the year at prior arrangement.
Key facts: ℹ️ No photography in house. 📷 🎫 ☕ Licensed. 🍴 🎫 Obligatory.
🅿️ Limited. 🐕 Guide dogs only. ✉️

ALL SAINTS' CHURCH 🏛
Kedleston Hall, Kedleston, Quarndon, Derbyshire DE22 5JH

All Saints' church is all that remains of the medieval village of Kedleston, razed in 1759 by Sir Nathaniel Curzon to make way for the magnificent Kedleston Hall. Today, the hall is a beautiful National Trust property and you can easily combine a trip to both attractions at once. The Curzon family has lived at Kedleston for 700 years and their stunning memorials - created by several famous designers including Robert Adam - fill the church. The grandest was erected in 1909, commissioned by Lord Curzon, Viceroy of India, for his wife Mary. A dazzling marble tomb - with lifesize figures and watching angels - floats on a sea of green translucent quartz in its own little chapel with superb stained glass windows. **Location:** OS Ref SK313 404. From Ashbourne on the A52, follow brown National Trust signs to Kedleston Hall. **Contact:** The Churches Conservation Trust 0845 303 2760 (Mon-Fri) **Tel:** 0845 303 2760 **E-mail:** north@thecct.org.uk **Website:** www.visitchurches.org.uk **Open:** 26 Mar-30 Oct: Mon-Wed and on w/e, 11am to 5pm. **Admission:** Free.

HARDWICK ESTATE 🌿
Doe Lea, Chesterfield, Derbyshire S44 5QJ

One of the most splendid houses in England. Built by the extraordinary Bess of Hardwick in the 1590's, and unaltered, yet its huge windows and high ceilings make it feel strikingly modern. Rich tapestries, plaster friezes and alabaster fireplaces colour the rooms. Walled courtyards enclose fine gardens, orchards and a herb garden. The Parkland has circular walks, fishing ponds and rare breed animals. **Location:** Map 7:A3. OS Ref OS120 SK456 651. 7½m NW of Mansfield, 9½m SE of Chesterfield: approach from M1/J29 via A6175 From M1/J29 take A6175, signposted to Clay Cross then first left and left again to Stainsby Mill. **Owner:** National Trust **Contact:** Support Service Assistant
Tel: 01246 850430 **Fax:** 01246 858424 **Shop/Restaurant:** 01246 858409 **E-mail:** hardwickhall@nationaltrust.org.uk **Website:** www.nationaltrust.org.uk/hardwick **Open:** Please see website or contact us for up-to-date information.
Admission: Please see website or contact us for up-to-date information.
Key facts: ℹ️ 📷 🎫 ♿ Partial. WCs. ☕ 🍴 Licensed. 🎫 By arrangement.
🅿️ Limited for coaches. 🐕 Guide dogs only. ✉️

BOLSOVER CASTLE 🏰
Castle Street, Bolsover, Derbyshire S44 6PR

An enchanting and romantic spectacle, situated high on a wooded hilltop dominating the surrounding landscape. **Location:** Map 7:A2. OS Ref OS120, SK471 707. **Tel:** 01246 822844 **E-mail:** customers@english-heritage.org.uk
Website: www.english-heritage.org.uk/bolsover
Open: Please visit wesbite for opening times and the most up-to-date information.

KEDLESTON HALL 🌿
Kedleston Hall, Derby DE22 5JH

Kedleston Hall boasts the most complete and least altered sequence of Robert Adam interiors in England. Take in the 18th Century pleasure grounds and 800 acre park. **Location:** Map 6:P4. OS Ref SK312 403. **Tel:** 01332 842191
E-mail: kedlestonhall@nationaltrust.org.uk **Website:** www.nationaltrust.org.uk/kedleston **Open:** Please see website for up to date opening and admission details.

Renishaw Hall

STANFORD HALL ⓕ
STANFORD HALL, LUTTERWORTH, LEICESTERSHIRE LE17 6DH
www.stanfordhall.co.uk

Stanford has been the home of the Cave family, ancestors of the present owner. since 1430. In the 1690s, Sir Roger Cave commissioned the Smiths of Warwick to pull down the old Manor House and build the present Hall. Throughout the house are portraits of the family and examples of furtniture and objects which they collected over the centuries. There is also a collection of Royal Stuart portriats. The Hall and Stables are set in an attractive Park on the banks of Shakespeare's Avon. There is a walled Rose Garden and an early ha-ha.

Location: Map 7:B7. OS Ref SP587 793. M1/J18 6m, M1/J19 (from/to the N only) 2m, M6 exit/access at A14/M1(N)J19 2m, A14 2m. Historic House signs.
Owner: Mr & Mrs N Fothergill **Contact:** Nick Fothergill
Tel: 01788 860250 **E-mail:** enquiries@stanfordhall.co.uk
Open: Special 3 week Easter opening – Mon 23 Mar-Sun 12 Apr 2015. Open other days in conjunction with park events and bank holidays.

See our website or telephone for details. House open any weekday or weekday evening for pre-booked groups.
Admission: House & Grounds: Adult £8.00, Child (5-15 yrs) £2.50. Private group tours (20+): Adult £8.50, Child £2.50.
Special admission prices will apply on event days.
Key facts: ⓘ Craft centre (event days and Bank Hols). Corporate days, clay pigeon shoots, filming, photography, small conferences, accommodation. Parkland, helicopter landing area, lecture room, Stables Tearoom. Caravan site. ⓘ Ⓣ Lunches, dinners & wedding receptions. ⓛ Partial. WCs. ⓦ Stables Tearoom. Ⓘ Tour time: ¾ hr in groups of approx 25.
ⓟ 1,000 cars and 6-8 coaches. Free meals for coach drivers, coach parking on gravel in front of house. ⓦ ⓗ Dogs on leads only.
ⓔ Accommodation available. Group bookings only. ⓔ

■ Owner
Burghley House
Preservation Trust Ltd

■ Address
House Manager
Stamford
Lincolnshire
PE9 3JY

■ Location
Map 7:E7
OS Ref. TF048 062
Burghley House is 1m SE of
Stamford. From London,
A1 2hrs. Visitors entrance
is on B1443.
Rail: London -
Peterborough 1hr (East
Coast mainline). Stamford
Station 12mins, regular
service from Peterborough.
Taxi: Direct line 01780
481481

■ Contact
The House Manager
Tel: 01780 752451
Fax: 01780 480125
E-mail:
burghley@burghley.co.uk

■ Opening Times
House & Gardens:
14 March-1 November
(closed 3-6 September).
Open daily (House closed
on Fridays), 11am-5pm,
(last admission 4.30pm).

■ Admission
House & Gardens
Adult	£15.00*
Child (3-15yrs)	£7.50*
Conc.	£13.20*
Family	£42.00*

Groups (20+)
Adult	£11.80
School (up to 15yrs)	£6.70

Gardens only
Adult	£9.00*
Child (3-15yrs)	£6.00*
Conc.	£7.50*
Family	£29.00*

*Includes a voluntary Gift
Aid donation but visitors
can choose to pay the
standard prices displayed
on our website.

■ Special Events
South Gardens Opening
14 March-12 April (11-12
April National Gardens
Scheme).
Battle Proms Concert
4 July.
**The Burghley Horse
Trials**
3-6 September.
Burghley Flower Festival
3-11 October (closed Friday
9 October).

Conference/Function

ROOM	Size	Max Cap
Great Hall	70' x 30'	160
Orangery	100' x 20'	120
Summer House	17.5' x 17.5'	25

BURGHLEY HOUSE 🏠Ⓕ
www.burghley.co.uk

Burghley House, home of the Cecil family for over 400 years is one of England's Greatest Elizabethan Houses.

Burghley was built between 1555 and 1587 by William Cecil, later Lord Burghley, principal adviser and Lord High Treasurer to Queen Elizabeth. During the 17th and 18th Centuries, the House was transformed by John 5th Earl of Exeter and Brownlow, the 9th Earl; travelling to the cultural centres of Europe and employing many of the foremost craftsmen of their day. Burghley contains one of the largest private collections of Italian art, unique examples of Chinese and Japanese porcelain and superb items of 18th Century furniture. Principal artists and craftsmen of the period are to be found at Burghley: Antonio Verrio, Grinling Gibbons and Louis Laguerre all made major contributions to the beautiful interiors.

Park and Gardens
The house is set in a 300-acre deer park landscaped by 'Capability' Brown. A lake was created by him and delightful avenues of mature trees feature largely in his design. The park is home to a large herd of Fallow deer, established in the 16th Century. The Garden of Surprises is a modern oasis of flowing water and fountains, statues, and obelisks. The contemporary Sculpture Garden was reclaimed from 'Capability' Brown's lost lower gardens in 1994 and is dedicated to exhibiting innovative sculptures. The private gardens around the house are open from mid-March to mid-April for the display of spring bulbs.

KEY FACTS

ℹ️ Suitable for a variety of events, large park, golf course, helicopter landing area, cricket pitch. No photography in house.

🛗
♿ WCs.
🛍 Licensed.
🍴 Licensed.
🚶 By Arrangement.
🎧
🅿️ Ample. Free refreshments for coach drivers.
🚶 Welcome. Guide provided.
🐕 Guide dogs only.
🔔 Civil Wedding Licence.

GRIMSTHORPE CASTLE, PARK AND GARDENS 🏰ⓕ
GRIMSTHORPE, BOURNE, LINCOLNSHIRE PE10 0LZ
www.grimsthorpe.co.uk

Building styles from 13 Century. North Front is Vanbrugh's last major work. State Rooms and picture galleries including tapestries, furniture and paintings. Interesting collection of thrones, fabrics and objects from the old House of Lords, associated with the family's hereditary Office of Lord Great Chamberlain. 3,000 acre park with lakes, ancient woods, walking and cycle trail, hire shop. Extensive gardens including unusual ornamental kitchen garden. Groups can explore the park in their own coach by booking a one-hour, escorted park tour. Tailor-made group visits available on request including Head Gardener tour and 'How Grimsthorpe Works' day. **Location:** Map 7:D5. OS Ref TF040 230. 4m NW of Bourne on A151, 8m E of Colsterworth Junction of A1. **Owner:** Grimsthorpe & Drummond Castle Trust Ltd. A Charity registered in England, Wales & Scotland

SCO39364. **Contact:** Ray Biggs **Tel:** 01778 591205
E-mail: ray@grimsthorpe.co.uk
Open: Castle - Apr & May: Sun, Thu & BH Mons. Jun-Sep: Sun-Thu inclusive. 12-4pm (last admission 3pm). Park & Gardens - same days as Castle, 11am-6pm (last admission 5pm). Groups: Apr-Sep: by arrangement.
Admission: Castle, Park & Garden: Adult £10.50, Child £4.00, Conc. £9.50, Family (2+3) £25.00. Park & Gardens: Adult £5.50, Child £2.00, Conc. £4.50, Family (2+3) £13.00. Group rates on application.
Key facts: ⓘ No photography in house. 📷 🅣 Conferences (up to 40), inc catering. ♿ WCs. 🍽 Light lunches 12-2.30. Afternoon tea service. Closes 5pm. 📷 Obligatory except Suns & BH Mons. 🅟 Ample. 🚶 🐕 Dogs on leads only. 🅥

AUBOURN HALL 🏰
Lincoln LN5 9DZ
www.aubournhall.co.uk

Nine acres of lawns and floral borders surround this homely Jacobean manor house. The Rose and Prairie Gardens and the Turf Maze, Dell Garden and Stumpery all add to the fascination of this much loved family home. Guided tours are available throughout the season. We are excited to announce Aubourn Hall Gardens are now available as a Wedding Reception Venue, we can provide a stunning setting for your bespoke marquee wedding celebrations.
Location: Map 7:D3. OS Ref SK928 628. 6m SW of Lincoln. 2m SE of A46.
Owner: Mr & Mrs Christopher Nevile **Contact:** Vanessa Sparkes, Estate Office
Tel: 01522 788224 **Fax:** 01522 788199
E-mail: estate.office@aubournhall.co.uk
Open: Garden open for Events, Groups and Garden visits from May-Sep. Please contact the Estate Office or go to our website www.aubournhall.co.uk for details.
Admission: Adults £4.50. Children Free.
Key facts: 📷 ♿ Partial. WCs. 🍽
📷 By arrangement. 🅟 Limited for coaches. 🐕 Guide dogs only.

AYSCOUGHFEE HALL MUSEUM & GARDENS
Churchgate, Spalding, Lincolnshire PE11 2RA
www.ayscoughfee.org

Ayscoughfee Hall, a magnificent grade I listed building, was built in the 1450s. The Hall is set in extensive landscaped grounds which include amongst other features a memorial designed by Edwin Lutyens. The Museum features the history of the Hall, the people who lived there and the surrounding Fens.
Location: Map 7:F5. OS Ref TF249 223. E bank of the River Welland, 5 mins walk from Spalding town centre.
Owner: South Holland District Council **Contact:** Museum Officer
Tel: 01775 764555
E-mail: museum@sholland.gov.uk
Open: Hall 10.30am-4pm Wed-Sun (open on BH Mon), closed over Christmas period. Gardens 8am until dusk
Admission: Free.
Key facts: ⓘ Photography allowed. 📷 Small shop in Hall. 🅣 Email for info. ♿ WCs, lift. 🍽 Open 7 days a week. 📷 By arrangement. 📷 🚶 Email for info. 🐕 Guide dogs only. 🏠 Email for info. 🏵 Closed at Christmas 🅥

DODDINGTON HALL & GARDENS 🏠ⓕ
Lincoln LN6 4RU
www.doddingtonhall.com

Romantic Smythson house standing today as it was built in 1595. Still a family home. Georgian interior with fascinating collection of porcelain, paintings and textiles. Five acres of wild and walled formal gardens plus kitchen garden provide colour and interest year-round. Award-winning Farm Shop, Café & Restaurant. Country Clothing, Farrow & Ball and India Jane Interiors Store.
Location: Map 7:D2. OS Ref SK900 710. 5m W of Lincoln on the B1190, signposted off the A46 and B1190. **Owner:** Mr & Mrs J J C Birch
Contact: The Estate Office **Tel:** 01522 812510
E-mail: info@doddingtonhall.com **Open:** Gardens Only: From 15 Feb-5 Apr & throughout Oct. Suns only, 11am-4pm. Last admission 3.30pm. House & Gardens: 5 Apr-27 Sep, Suns, Weds and BH Mons. 1-5pm (Gardens open at 11am) Last admission 4.15pm. **Admission:** Gardens only: Adult £6.00, Child £3.00. House & Gardens: Adult £10, Child £4.75. U4 free. Family & Season Tickets available. Group visits (guided tours for 20+) £10 per head. **Key facts:** ⓘ Photography permitted, no flash. No stilettos. 🛍 Farm Shop - Doddington & local produce. 🍴 Seasonal. 📅 🖼 Virtual tour. Garden accessible -mixed surface. 🍽 Open 7 days. Breakfast, lunches and teas. No booking. 🍴 Open 7 days and Fri/Sat eve. 🎭 By arrangement. 📷 🅿 🖼 Workshops for KS1/2. 🖼 Guide dogs only. 🏠🔔❄🐾

GAINSBOROUGH OLD HALL
Parnell Street, Gainsborough, Lincolnshire DN21 2NB
www.gainsboroughholdhall.com

Gainsborough Old Hall is one of the country's best preserved Medieval Manor houses, and offers a fascinating insight into bygone days of medieval splendour. The house was built by Sir Thomas Burgh as the manor to his estate in Gainsborough, not only as a family home, but also as a symbol of his wealth and status. The Burgh family entertained both Richard III and Henry VIII.
Location: Map 7:C1. OS Ref SK813 900. In centre of Gainsborough, opposite library. **Owner:** English Heritage **Contact:** Lincolnshire County Council
Tel: 01427 677348 / 01522 782040.
E-mail: gainsboroughholdhall@lincolnshire.gov.uk
Open: 1 Mar-31 Oct, Mon-Fri, 10am-5pm, Sat-Sun 11am-5pm. 1 Nov-28 Feb, Mon-Fri, 10am-4pm, Sat 11am-4pm, Sun closed. 20 Dec-3 Jan closed.
Admission: Admission charge applies. **Key facts:** ⓘ 📷 Our shop has something to tempt everyone from craftware by local artisans to bespoke jewellery. 🍴 Medieval Style Banquets for up to 130 guests. 🍽 Highly commended in last year's Select Lincolnshire Awards. 🎭 Costumed tour guide for groups visits. 📷 Award winning multimedia tours. 🖼 Sandford Award winning Education programme. ❄🏠 www.gainsboroughweddings.co.uk ❄🐾

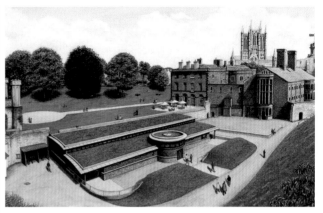

LINCOLN CASTLE
Castle Hill, Lincoln LN1 3AA
www.lincolnshire.gov.uk/castle

From April 2015 Three Attractions One Castle: Medieval Wall Walk - Victorian Prison - Magna Carta Vault 1000 years of history where it happened.
Location: Map 7:D2. OS Ref SK976 718. Set next to Lincoln Cathedral in the Historic Quarter of the city. Follow signs from A1 Newark or A15 North and South.
Owner: Lincolnshire County Council **Contact:** Lincoln Castle
Tel: 01522 511068 **E-mail:** lincoln_castle@lincolnshire.gov.uk
Open: From 1 Apr 2015. 10am-5pm Apr-Sep. 10am-4pm Oct-Mar. Closed 24-26 Dec & 31 Dec-1 Jan.
Admission: Adults £12.00, Conc £9.60, Child 5 & over £7.20, Under 5's free. Walk, Prison & Vault included. Entry to the Castle grounds, shop and café are free.
Key facts: ⓘ Events through the year. Some events will have seperate admission prices. 📷 Set within the Prison with a range to suit all pockets. 🍴 Tailor made packages. 🖼 Accessible including part of the Medieval Wall. 🍽 Set within the Prison and licenced. 🎭 A variety of tours available. 🎧 Audio tour inlcuded in admission price. 🖼 Please contact us for education visits. 🐾 Assistance dogs only. ❄ Closed 24-26 Dec & 31 Dec-1 Jan.

ALL SAINTS' CHURCH ⛪
Old Church Lane, Great Steeping, Spilsby, Lincolnshire PE23 5PR

Built in 1748, this riverside church stands proudly on lush marshland. It is surrounded by a complex and undisturbed medieval field system, revealed by aerial photography.
Its distinctively Georgian design is elegant yet simple - essentially a nave topped with an attractive wooden bell turret.
Location: OS Ref TF434 639. 3 miles south east of Spilsby, off the B1195.
Contact: Please call The Churches Conservation Trust on 0845 303 2760 (Monday-Friday, 9am–5pm) **Tel:** 0845 303 2760
E-mail: north@thecct.org.uk
Website: www.visitchurches.org.uk
Open: Open daily - please check website for details.
Admission: Free entry - donations welcome.
Key facts: 🖼 🖼 ❄

ALL SAINTS' CHURCH ⛪
Thacker Bank, Theddlethorpe, Louth, Lincolnshire LN12 1PE

A 14th to 15th Century church with Norman origins, All Saints is known as the Cathedral of the Marsh - a testament to its impressive length and spacious light-filled interior, as well as the quality of the interior carvings.
Despite its lonely grandeur, the outside of the church has a colourful appearance as the local north Lincolnshire Greens and is patched with brick and limestone.
Location: OS Ref TF464 882.
7 miles east of Louth, off A1031.
Contact: Please call The Churches Conservation Trust on 0845 303 2760 (Mon-Fri, 9am–5pm) **E-mail:** north@thecct.org.uk
Website: www.visitchurches.org.uk
Open: Keyholder nearby. **Admission:** Free entry - donations welcome.
Key facts: 🖼 ❄

FULBECK MANOR

Fulbeck, Grantham, Lincolnshire NG32 3JN

Built c1580. 400 years of Fane family portraits. Open by written appointment. Guided tours by owner approximately 1¼ hours. Tearooms at Craft Centre, 100 yards, for light lunches and teas.
Location: Map 7:D3. OS Ref SK947 505. 11m N of Grantham. 15m S of Lincoln on A607. Brown signs to Craft Centre & Tearooms and Stables.
Owner/Contact: Mr Julian Francis Fane
Tel: 01400 272231
E-mail: fane@fulbeck.co.uk
Open: By written appointment.
Admission: Adult £7.00. Groups (10+) £6.00.
Key facts: ⓘ No photography. Partial. WCs. Obligatory. Ample for cars. Limited for coaches. Guide dogs only.

MARSTON HALL

Marston, Grantham NG32 2HQ

The ancient home of the Thorold family. The building contains Norman, Plantaganet, Tudor and Georgian elements through to the modern day. Marston Hall is undergoing continuous restoration some of which may be disruptive. Please telephone in advance of intended visits.
Location: Map 7:D4. OS Ref SK893 437. 5m N of Grantham and 1m E of A1.
Owner/Contact: J R Thorold
Tel: 07812 356237
Fax: 0208 7892857
E-mail: johnthorold@aol.com
Open: 24, 25 & 26 Jan, 20, 21 & 22 Mar, 3, 4, 5, 6 & 7 Apr, 1, 2, 3, 4, 23, 24 and 25 May, 13, 14 & 15 Jun, 4, 5, 6 & 7 Jul, 29, 30 & 31 Aug.
Admission: Adult £4.00, Child £1.50. Groups must book.
Key facts: ⓘ No photography.

ST BENEDICT'S CHURCH

Church Lane, Haltham-on-Bain, Horncastle, Lincolnshire LN9 6JF

A lovely Norman church, with a stunning decorated east window and a beautifully simple interior. Look out for the 17th Century pulpit and the unusual Norman carving above the south doorway. There are also old pews with carved ends in various directions facing the 17th Century pulpit, a screen adapted as a family pew, Royal Arms of Charles I and lovely old tiled floors. The wooden-fenced churchyard is filled with wildflowers in spring.
Location: OS Ref TF246 638. 4 miles south of Horncastle, on A153.
Contact: The Churches Conservation Trust on 0845 303 2760 (Mon-Fri)
Website: www.visitchurches.org.uk
Open: Open daily.
Admission: Free - donations welcome.

ST MICHAEL'S CHURCH

Burwell, Louth, Lincolnshire LN11 8PR

The brick-and-greensand church tower of St Michael's can be seen on a hillside above the main road and the church has great views over gently rolling countryside.
The walls show clear signs of alterations over the centuries: there was once a south aisle and the near windowless north wall may have been adjacent to monastic buildings.
Prominent inside is the exquisite Norman chancel arch with carved capitals; above it, a medieval wallpainting depicts a crowned head. There is also a 17th Century pulpit and some interesting monuments.
Location: OS Ref TF356 797.
5 miles south of Louth on A16.
Contact: The Churches Conservation Trust on 0845 303 2760 (Mon-Fri)
Website: www.visitchurches.org.uk
Open: Open daily. **Admission:** Free - donations welcome.

ST PETER'S CHURCH

South Somercotes, Louth
Lincolnshire LN11 7BW

This 13th Century church has a tall, slender spire, which for centuries has guided sailors along the Lincolnshire coast, giving the church the nickname of 'The Queen of the Marsh'.
The building is mainly 13th Century, but the tower and spire were added somewhat later, and many windows were inserted in the 15th Century. Its spacious interior contains a superb 15th Century font carved with the instruments of the Passion.
Location: OS Ref TF416 938. 8 miles north east of Louth, off A1013.
Contact: The Churches Conservation Trust on 0845 303 2760 (Mon-Fri)
Website: www.visitchurches.org.uk
Open: Open daily. **Admission:** Free - donations welcome.

ARABELLA AUFRERE TEMPLE

Brocklesby Park, Grimsby, Lincolnshire DN41 8PN
Garden Temple of ashlar and red brick with coupled doric columns.
Location: Map 11:E12. OS Ref TA139 112. Off A18 in Great Limber Village.
Tel: 01469 560214 **E-mail:** office@brocklesby.co.uk
Open: 1 Apr–31 Aug: viewable from permissive paths through Mausoleum Woods at all reasonable times. **Admission:** None.

BELTON HOUSE

Grantham, Lincolnshire NG32 2LS
Begun for Sir John Brownlow in 1685, Belton was certainly designed to impress and across its 300 year history, each generation of the Brownlows left their creative mark. **Location:** Map 7:D4. OS Ref SK929 395.
Tel: 01476 566116 **E-mail:** belton@nationaltrust.org.uk
Website: www.nationaltrust.org.uk/belton-house
Open: Please see website for up to date opening and admission details.

BROCKLESBY MAUSOLEUM

Brocklesby Park, Grimsby, Lincolnshire DN41 8PN
Family Mausoleum designed by James Wyatt and built between 1787 and 1794.
Location: Map 11:E12. OS Ref TA139 112. Off A18 in Great Limber Village.
Tel: 01469 560214 **E-mail:** office@brocklesby.co.uk
Open: By prior arrangement with Estate Office.
Admission: Modest admission charge for interior.

LEADENHAM HOUSE

Leadenham House, Lincolnshire LN5 0PU
Late Eighteenth Century house in park setting. **Location:** Map 7:D3. OS Ref SK949 518. Entrance on A17 Leadenham bypass (between Newark and Sleaford).
Tel: 01400 273256 **E-mail:** leadenhamhouse@googlemail.com
Open: 30, 31 Mar; 1, 2; 7-10; 13-17; 20-24; 28-30 Apr; 11-15 May; Spring & Aug Bank Hols. **Admission:** £5.00. Please ring door bell.
Groups by prior arrangement only.

SCAWBY HALL

Brigg, N. Lincolnshire DN20 9LX
Early Jacobean manor house. WW1 Centenary exhibit.
Location: Map 11:D12. OS Ref SE966 058. **Tel:** 01652 654 272
E-mail: info@scawbyhall.com **Website:** www.scawbyhall.com
Open: Tours conducted between 1.30-4.30pm, May 25-26, Jun 13-21, Jul 4-10 and Aug 20-31. **Admission:** Adults: £8.00, Concessions: £6.50, Child (under 16): £4.00, Child (under 5): Free, Family: £18.50.

VISITOR INFORMATION

■ Owner
Mr and Mrs Robert Brudenell

■ Address
Deene Park
Corby
Northamptonshire
NN17 3EW

■ Location
Map 7:D7
OS Ref. SP950 929
6m NE of Corby off A43.
From London via M1/J15
then A43, or via A1, A14,
A43 - 2 hrs. From
Birmingham via M6, A14,
A43, 90 mins.
Rail: Corby Station 10 mins
and Kettering Station
20mins.

■ Contact
The Administrator
Tel: 01780 450278
Fax: 01780 450282
E-mail:
admin@deenepark.com

■ Opening Times
Apr: Sun 5 & BH Mon 6.
May: Suns 3, 10, 17, 24,
31, BH Mons 4, 25.
Jun: Suns 7, 14, 21, 28.
Jul: Suns 5, 12, 19, 26.
Aug: Suns 2, 9, 16, 23,
30, BH Mon 31.
Sep: Weds 2, 9, 16, 23,
30.

Gardens & tearoom
12pm-5pm. House 2-5pm,
last adm 4pm. Tea Room
open for light lunches until
2pm and afternoon tea
from 2pm-5pm.

■ Admission
Public Open Days
House & Gardens
Adult	£9.00
Conc.	£8.00
Child (5-16yrs)	£5.00

Under 5 free with an adult.
Gardens only:
Adult & Conc.	£6.00
Child (5-16yrs)	£3.00

Under 5 free with an adult.

Groups (20+)
by arrangement:
Tue-Thu, Suns	£9.00
(Min 20	£180.00)

Under 5 free with an adult.

■ Special Events
Please visit our website for
full details of our special
events.

DEENE PARK 🏛Ⓕ
www.deenepark.com

Home of the Brudenell family since 1514, this sixteenth century house incorporates a medieval manor with important Georgian additions.

Seat of the 7th Earl of Cardigan who led the charge of the Light Brigade at Balaklava in 1854, today the house is the home of Mr and Mrs Robert Brudenell and their son William. The rooms on show are regularly used by their family and friends. It has grown in size as generations have made their own mark through the years, providing the visitor with an interesting yet complementary mixture of styles. There is a considerable collection of family portraits and possessions, including memorabilia from the Crimean War.

The gardens are mainly to the south and west of the house and include long borders, old-fashioned roses and specimen trees. Close to the house there is a parterre designed by David Hicks in the 1990s. The topiary teapots, inspired by the finial on the Millenium obelisk, form a fine feature as they mature.

Open parkland lies across water from the terraced gardens providing enchanting vistas in many directions. The more energetic visitor can discover these during a rewarding walk in the tranquil surroundings. As well as the flora, there is also a diversity of bird life ranging from red kites to kingfishers and black swans to little grebes. On public open days home-made scones and cakes are available in the Old Kitchen and souvenirs can be found in the Courtyard Gift Shop. Group visits are available at anytime by prior arrangement, with booked lunch and dinners available.

KEY FACTS

- ℹ️ No photography in house. No large bags.
- 🛍️ Shop.
- 🍽️ Including buffets, lunches and dinners by arrangement.
- ♿ Partial. Visitors may alight at the entrance, access to ground floor & garden.
- 💷 Special rates for groups, bookings can be made in advance, menus on request.
- 🍴 In house dining by arrangement.
- 🚶 Available for group visits by arrangement (approx 90 mins).
- 🅿️ Unlimited for cars, space for 2 coaches 10 yds from house.
- 🐕 In car park only.
- 🏛️ Conference facilities by arrangement.
- ❄️ Winter opening by arrangement only.
- 🎥 Suitable for events, filming and lectures. See website.

ALTHORP 🏠Ⓕ
NORTHAMPTON NN7 4HQ
www.spencerofalthorp.com

Althorp House was built in 1508, by the Spencers, for the Spencers, and that is how it has remained for over 500 years. Today, Althorp contains one of the finest private collections of art, furniture and ceramics in the world, including numerous paintings by Rubens, Reynolds, Stubbs, Gainsborough and Van Dyck. Visitors can enjoy the extensive Grounds and the Arboretum, the new Spencer Exhibition and Café in the Stables, as well as viewing the House by guided tour.

Location: Map 7:C9. OS Ref SP682 652. From the M1, 7 miles from J16 and 10 miles from J18. Situated on A428 Northampton - Rugby. Rail: 5 miles from Northampton station and 14 miles from Rugby station. Sat nav postcode: NN7 4HQ. **Owner:** The Rt Hon The 9th Earl Spencer **Contact:** Althorp
Tel: 01604 770107 **E-mail:** mail@althorp.com
Open: 1pm-5pm, with last adm 4pm, on the following dates in 2015: May: Sun 3, Mon 4, Sun 10, Sun 17, Sun 24, Mon 25, Sun 31. Jun: Sun 7, Thur 11-Sat 13

for the Althorp Literary Festival, Sun 14, Sun 21, Sun 28. Jul: Sun 12, Sun 19, Fri 24-Fri 31. Aug: Sat 1-Mon 31 (open at 12pm Aug only). Sep: Sun 6, Sun 13, Sun 20, Sun 27. For more information about events at Althorp, please visit our website: www.spencerofalthorp.com
Admission: Grounds, Exhibition and guided tour. Adults £18.50, Conc £16.00, 5-16 years £11.00, 0-4 years and HHA Friends free entry. Please call 01604 770107 or email groups@althorp.com to pre-book coach parties & group visits.
Key facts: ℹ No indoor photography with still or video cameras. 📷 🍵 ♿ House and Estate accessible to wheelchairs, except the first floor of the House. ☕ The Stables Cafe serves a wide selection of drinks, cakes, sandwiches and snacks. 👤 Althorp is available to view by guided tour only, departing frequently throughout afternoon. 🅿 Free parking with a 5/10 minute walk to the House. Disabled parking available. 🐕 Guide dogs only. 🏨 🛏

COTTESBROOKE HALL & GARDENS 🏠Ⓕ
COTTESBROOKE, NORTHAMPTONSHIRE NN6 8PF
www.cottesbrooke.co.uk

Dating from 1702 the Hall's beauty is matched by the magnificence of the gardens and the excellence of the picture, furniture and porcelain collections. The Woolavington collection of sporting pictures is possibly the finest of its type in Europe and includes paintings by Stubbs, Ben Marshall and artists renowned for works of this genre. Portraits, bronzes, 18th Century English and French furniture and fine porcelain are among the treasures.

The formal gardens are continually being updated and developed by influential designers. The Wild Gardens, a short walk across the Park, are planted along the course of a stream.

Location: Map 7:B8. OS Ref SP711 739. 10m N of Northampton near Creaton on A5199 (formerly A50). Signed from Junction 1 on the A14.

Owner: Mr & Mrs A R Macdonald-Buchanan
Contact: The Administrator
Tel: 01604 505808 **Fax:** 01604 505619
E-mail: welcome@cottesbrooke.co.uk
Open: May-end of Sep. May & Jun: Wed & Thu, 2-5.30pm. Jul-Sep: Thu, 2-5.30pm. Open BH Mons (May-Sep), 2-5.30pm.
The first open day is Wed 6 May 2015.
Admission: House & Gardens: Adult £8.00, Child £4.50, Conc £7.00. Gardens only: Adult £5.50, Child £3.50, Conc £5.00. Group & private bookings by arrangement.
Key facts: ℹ No large bags or photography in house. Filming & outside events. 🍵 ♿ Partial. WCs. 🍴 👤 Hall guided tours obligatory. 🅿 🛏 🐕 Guide dogs only. 🛏

HOLDENBY HOUSE 🏛Ⓕ
HOLDENBY HOUSE, NORTHAMPTON NN6 8DJ
www.holdenby.com

Once the largest private house in England and subsequently the palace of James I and prison of Charles I, Holdenby has recently been seen in the BBC's acclaimed adaptation of 'Great Expectations'. Its suite of elegant state rooms overlooking beautiful Grade I listed gardens and rolling countryside make it an enchanting and ever popular venue for weddings. Its combination of grandeur and intimacy make it a magnificent location for corporate dinners, parties and meetings, while the spacious grounds have accommodated many large events, from Civil War battles and concerts to The Northamptonshire Food Show. Ask about visiting Holdenby's remarkable Falconry Centre and special interest days in the Garden in addition to the normal Sunday openings.

Location: Map 7:B8. OS Ref SP693 681. M1/J15a.

7m NW of Northampton off A428 & A5199.
Owner: James Lowther
Contact: Gilly Wrathall, Commercial Manager
Tel: 01604 770074 **Fax:** 01604 770962
E-mail: gilly@holdenby.com
Open: Gardens and Tearoom open: Apr-Sep; Suns & BH Mons; 1-5pm.
Admission: Adult £5.00, Child £3.50, Conc. £4.50, Family (2+3) £15.00; Different prices on event days. Groups must book.
Key facts: ⓘ Children's play area. 🍴🍵♿🎁 Victorian Kitchen Tearoom serving homemade Cream Teas and cakes. 🎟 Obligatory, by arrangement. 🅿 Limited for coaches. 🏆 6 times Sandford Award Winner. 🐕 On leads. ▲ ♿

KELMARSH HALL AND GARDENS 🏛Ⓕ
KELMARSH, NORTHAMPTON NN6 9LY
www.kelmarsh.com

Built in the Palladian style to a James Gibbs design, 18th Century Kelmarsh Hall is set in beautiful gardens with views over the surrounding parkland. The former home of society decorator, Nancy Lancaster, Kelmarsh still reflects the essence of her panache and flair. Within the Hall is the Croome Exhibition, showcasing furniture and paintings on loan from Croome Court in Worcestershire. The award-winning gardens include a formal terrace, horse chestnut avenues, rose gardens and the historic walled kitchen garden. Kelmarsh Hall, gardens and parkland can be hired exclusively for weddings, corporate events and private parties.

Location: Map 7:C8. OS Ref SP736 795. 1/3 m N of A14-A508 jct 2. Rail & Bus: Mkt Harborough.

Owner: The Kelmarsh Trust
Tel/Fax: 01604 686543
E-mail: enquiries@kelmarsh.com
Open: Please refer to website at www.kelmarsh.com for exact 2015 opening times. The seasons runs from Apr to Sep.
Admission: House tour with garden admission: Adult £8.00, Concessions available. Gardens only: Adult £6.00, Concessions and Family tickets available. Garden season tickets available. Visit website for all pricing details.
Key facts: 🍴🎁🍵 Suitable for corporate events & functions. ♿ WCs. 🍷 Licensed. 🍴 🎟 Obligatory. 🅿 🏛 🐕 On leads. ▲ ♿ €

LAMPORT HALL & GARDENS 🏠Ⓕ
LAMPORT HALL, NORTHAMPTONSHIRE NN6 9HD
www.lamporthall.co.uk

Lamport Hall contains an outstanding collection of furniture and paintings accumulated over 400 years by the Isham family, including works acquired on the Grand Tour in the 1670s. The west front is by John Webb and the Smiths of Warwick. Surrounded by beautiful parkland, the 10-acre gardens are world famous as the home of the first garden gnome, and there are fascinating examples of changes in garden design across the centuries. 2015 sees a major new exhibition in the Edwardian stable block, with the Museum of Rural Life an added attraction. Group visits very welcome.

Location: Map 7:C8. OS Ref SP759 745. Entrance on A508. Midway between Northampton and Market Harborough, 3m S of A14 J2.
Owner: Lamport Hall Preservation Trust
Contact: Executive Director

Tel: 01604 686272 **Fax:** 01604 686224
E-mail: admin@lamporthall.co.uk
Open: Open every Wed & Thu from Easter Sun to 11 Oct (guided house tours at 2.15 and 3pm; free-flow around gardens). Also open most BH Sun/Mon (free-flow). Private tours at other times by arrangement. Please check website for opening times and prices.
Admission: House & Garden: Adult £8.50, Senior £8.00, Child (11-18) £3.00. Gardens Only: Adult £5.00, Senior £4.50, Child (11-18) £2.50. Private groups: House and gardens £8.50, Gardens only £5.00. Minimum charges apply.
Key facts: ⓘ No photography in house. Available for filming. 🅃 🄻 Partial. WCs. 🍽 Licensed. 🎦 Obligatory other than Fair Days. 🅿 Limited for coaches. 🐕 Guide dogs only. 🛏 ✳ Groups only. ♿

ROCKINGHAM CASTLE 🏠Ⓕ
ROCKINGHAM, MARKET HARBOROUGH, LEICESTERSHIRE LE16 8TH
www.rockinghamcastle.com

Rockingham Castle stands on the edge of an escarpment giving dramatic views over five counties and the Welland Valley below. Built by William the Conqueror, the Castle was a royal residence for 450 years. In the 16th Century Henry VIII granted it to Edward Watson and for 450 years it has remained a family home. The predominantly Tudor building, within Norman walls, has architecture, furniture and works of art from practically every century. Surrounding the Castle are 18 acres of gardens following the foot print of the medieval castle. The 400 year old 'Elephant Hedge' bisects the formal terraced gardens.

Location: Map 7:D7. OS Ref SP867 913. 1m N of Corby on A6003. 9m E of Market Harborough. 14m SW of Stamford on A427.
Owner: James Saunders Watson **Contact:** Laurie Prashad, Operations Manager
Tel: 01536 770240 **Fax:** 01536 771692

E-mail: estateoffice@rockinghamcastle.com **Open:** Easter Sun, 5 Apr-end of May, Suns & BH Mons. Jun-Sep, Tues, Suns & BH Mons. Open noon-5pm. Grounds open at noon. Castle opens at 1pm. Last entry 4.30pm.
Admission: House & Gardens: Adults £10.50, Children (5-16 years) £6.00, Family (2+2) £27.00. Grounds only: (Incl. Gardens, Salvin's Tower, Gift Shop & Licensed Tea Room) Adult or Child £6.00 (Not when special events held in grounds). Groups: (min 20) Adults £10.50 (on open days), Adults £12.00 (private guided tour), Children (5-16 years) £5.00. School groups: (min 20) Adult £10.50, Children £5.00 (1 Adult free with 15 Children). Groups/school parties on most days by arrangement.
Key facts: ⓘ No photography in Castle. 🄘 🅃 🄻 Partial. WCs. 🍽 Licensed. 🍴 Licensed. 🎦 By arrangement. 🄾 🅿 Limited for coaches. 🐕 🐾 On leads. 🛏

HADDONSTONE SHOW GARDENS
The Forge House, Church Lane, East Haddon
Northampton NN6 8DB
www.haddonstone.com

See Haddonstone's classic garden ornaments in the beautiful setting of the walled manor gardens including: planters, fountains, statues, bird baths, sundials and balustrades - even an orangery, gothic grotto and other follies. As featured on BBC Gardeners' World. New features include a statue walk, contemporary garden and wildflower meadow. Gastro pub nearby.

Location: Map 7:B8. OS Ref SP667 682. 7m North West of Northampton off A428. Located in centre of village opposite school. Signposted.
Owner: Haddonstone Ltd **Contact:** Simon Scott, Marketing Director
Tel: 01604 770711 **Fax:** 01604 770027 **E-mail:** info@haddonstone.co.uk
Open: Mon-Fri, 9am-5.30pm. Closed weekends, BHs and Christmas period. Check press or Haddonstone website for details of NGS weekend openings and Sat openings in Summer months. **Admission:** Free (except NGS weekends). Groups by appointment only. Not suitable for coach parties.
Key facts: ⓘ No photography without permission. 📷 ♿ Almost all areas of garden accessible. 🖼 By arrangement. 🅿 Limited. 🐕 Guide dogs only. ❄ 🏳 €

78 DERNGATE: THE CHARLES RENNIE MACKINTOSH HOUSE & GALLERIES
82 Derngate, Northampton NN1 1UH

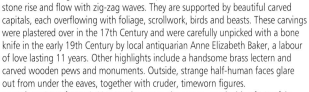

Northamptonshire's Award Winning House and Galleries. 78 Derngate was remodelled by the world-famous architect and designer, Charles Rennie Mackintosh, in his iconic modernist style. Free entry to the Gallery, café, gift and craft shop. Style, inspiration and innovation, truly is a must-see venue.
Location: Map 7:C9. OS Ref SP759 603. In the heart of Northampton close to The Royal & Derngate Theatres. **Owner:** 78 Derngate Northampton Trust
Contact: House Manager **Tel:** 01604 603407 **E-mail:** info@78derngate.org.uk
Website: www.78derngate.org.uk **Open:** 1 Feb-20 Dec 2015, Tue-Sun & BH Mons: 10am-5pm. Group and school bookings are also available.
Admission: Please visit the website for the current entry prices.
Key facts: ⓘ 📷 🍴 ♿ WCs. We offer partial mobility access. 🍽 Licensed. 🖼 Guided tours subject to availability, booking advised. 🅿 🐕 Guide dogs only. 🏳

ST PETER'S CHURCH 🏛
Marefair, Northampton NN1 1SR

St Peter's stands in a pretty grass churchyard in Northampton town centre, beside the buried remains of a Saxon palace. This 900-year-old Norman church is filled with glorious carved treasures. Inside, great Norman arches of plain and banded stone rise and flow with zig-zag waves. They are supported by beautiful carved capitals, each overflowing with foliage, scrollwork, birds and beasts. These carvings were plastered over in the 17th Century and were carefully unpicked with a bone knife in the early 19th Century by local antiquarian Anne Elizabeth Baker, a labour of love lasting 11 years. Other highlights include a handsome brass lectern and carved wooden pews and monuments. Outside, strange half-human faces glare out from under the eaves, together with cruder, timeworn figures.
Location: OS Ref SP749 603. Northampton city centre, south side of Marefair adjoining St. Peter's Way/Marefair junction. **Website:** www.visitchurches.org.uk
Open: Please check website for latest opening times.

SOUTHWICK HALL 🏠ⓕ
Southwick, Nr Oundle, Peterborough PE8 5BL

Well off the beaten track, Southwick Hall- a family home for 700 years- offers a friendly and informal welcome. Featuring an unusual variety of family and local village artefacts and with building alterations and additions throughout its history, the house vividly illustrates the development of the English Manor House.
Location: Map 7:E7. OS Ref TL022 921. 3m N of Oundle, 4m E of Bulwick.
Owner: Christopher Capron
Contact: G Bucknill
Tel: 01832 274064 **E-mail:** southwickhall@hotmail.co.uk
Website: www.southwickhall.co.uk
Open: BH Mons: 6 Apr, 25 May, 31 Aug & Sun 13 Sep under Heritage Open Day scheme all 2-5pm; last admission 4.30pm.
Admission: House & Grounds: Adult £7.00, Child £3.50.
Key facts: ♿ Partial. 🍽 🖼 Groups welcome by arrangement. 🅿 ♿

BOUGHTON HOUSE 🏠ⓕ
Kettering, Northamptonshire NN14 1BJ

Boughton is a Tudor manor house transformed into a vision of Louis XIV's Versailles. The house displays a staggering collection of fine art.
Location: Map 7:D8. OS Ref SP900 815.
Tel: 01536 515731 **E-mail:** blht@boughtonhouse.co.uk
Website: www.boughtonhouse.co.uk
Open: Please see website for up to date opening and admission details.

RUSHTON TRIANGULAR LODGE ⌗
Rushton, Kettering, Northamptonshire NN14 1RP

Triangular building constructed between 1593 and 1597. The number 3, symbolising the Holy Trinity is apparent everywhere.
Location: Map 7:C7. OS Ref SP825 830. **Tel:** 01536 710761
Website: www.english-heritage.org.uk/rushton
Open: Please see website for up to date opening and admission details.

STOKE PARK PAVILIONS
Stoke Bruerne, Towcester, Northamptonshire NN12 7RZ

The two pavilions, dated c1630 and attributed to Inigo Jones, formed part of one of the first Palladian country houses built in England. They have extensive gardens and overlook parkland. **Location:** Map 7:C10. OS Ref SP740 488. 7m S of Northampton. **Tel:** 01604 862329 **Open:** Aug: daily, 3-6pm. Other times by appointment only. **Admission:** Adult £3.00, Child £1.50.

WAKEFIELD LODGE 🏠
Potterspury, Northamptonshire NN12 7QX

Georgian hunting lodge with deer park. **Location:** Map 7:C10. OS Ref SP739 425. 4m S of Towcester on A5. Take signs to farm shop for directions. **Tel:** 01327 811395 **Open:** House: 16 Apr-29 May: Mon-Fri (closed BHs), 12 noon-4pm. Appointments by telephone. Access walk open Apr & May. **Admission:** £5.00.

WESTON HALL 🏠
Towcester, Northamptonshire NN12 8PU

A Queen Anne Northamptonshire manor house with an interesting collection associated with the literary Sitwell family.
Location: Map 7:B10. OS Ref SP592 469. 5 miles W of Towcester **Tel:** 07710 523879 **E-mail:** george@endven.com **Open:** Most weekends by appointment. **Admission:** £8.00. Free on Open Days.

Haddonstone Show Gardens

MR STRAW'S HOUSE
5-7 Blyth Grove, Worksop S81 0JG

Discover how a grocer's family lived in a Midlands market town in their extraordinary home, virtually unchanged since 1923 and full of treasured possessions and ordinary household objects. Pre-booked groups welcome. Free car park. Small shop with souvenirs, books and plants. Coffee area, picnic tables in garden. Braille and large print guide. Assistance dogs welcome. Several flights of steep stairs in both houses, steps to access house, garden and WC.

Location: Map 7:B4. OS Ref SK592802. On small private road off B6045 Blyth Road, south of Bassetlaw Hospital entrance. **Owner:** National Trust
Tel: 01909 482380 **E-mail:** mrstrawshouse@nationaltrust.org.uk
Website: www.nationaltrust.org.uk/mrstrawshouse
Open: 3 Mar-31 Oct 2015, Tue-Sat 11am-5pm (last adm 4pm). Closed Good Friday. Entry by pre-booked timed ticket only - please telephone to book.
Admission: Adult £7.45/£6.75, Child £3.75/£3.35, Family £18.65/£16.80, Groups (15+) £6.00. **Key facts:** ⓟ Free parking.

MILTON MAUSOLEUM 🏛
Markham Clinton, Newark, Nottinghamshire NG22 0PJ

Completed in 1833, this splendid classical building with its domed tower was designed by Sir Robert Smirke for the 4th Duke of Newcastle as a mausoleum for his wife. The nave is separated from the mausoleum by an elegant Ionic reredos screen. Inside there are some stunning marble effigies.

Location: OS Ref SK715 730. 1 mile NW of Tuxford off A1 & B1164; access via country lane to West Markham, off B1164. Take High Street and Milton Road; mausoleum adjoins Milton Road before village.
Contact: The Churches Conservation Trust on 0845 303 2760 (Mon-Fri)
Website: www.visitchurches.org.uk
Open: 1 May-30 Sep: 2nd & 4th Sun of each month, 2.30pm-4.30pm.
Admission: Free - donations welcome.

PAPPLEWICK HALL 🏛
Papplewick, Nottinghamshire NG15 8FE

A beautiful classic Georgian house, built of Mansfield stone, set in parkland, with woodland garden laid out in the 18th Century. The house is notable for its very fine plasterwork, and elegant staircase. Grade I listed.

Location: Map 7:B4. OS Ref SK548 518. Halfway between Nottingham & Mansfield, 3m E of M1/J27. A608 & A611 towards Hucknall. Then A6011 to Papplewick and B683 N for ½m.
Owner/Contact: Mr J R Godwin-Austen **Tel:** 0115 9632623
E-mail: mail@papplewickhall.co.uk
Website: www.papplewickhall.co.uk
Open: 1st, 3rd & 5th Wed in each month 2-5pm, and by appointment.
Admission: Adult £5.00. Groups (10+): £4.00.
Key facts: ⓘ No photography. 🎟 Obligatory. ⓟ Limited for coaches. 🐕 In grounds on leads. 🌸

CALKE ABBEY ❧
Ticknall, Derbyshire DE73 7LE
Tel: 01332 863822 **E-mail:** calkeabbey@nationaltrust.org.uk

ST MICHAEL'S CHURCH 🏛
Rectory Lane, Stretton-en-le-Field, Swadlincote DE12 8AF
Tel: 0845 303 2760 **E-mail:** central@thecct.org.uk

ST WERBURGH'S CHURCH 🏛
Friar Gate, Derby, Derbyshire DE1 1UZ
Tel: 0845 303 2760 **E-mail:** central@thecct.org.uk

ALL SAINTS' CHURCH 🏛
Highcross Street, Leicester, Leicestershire LE1 4PH
Tel: 0845 303 2760 **E-mail:** central@thecct.org.uk

CHURCH OF ST MARY MAGDELENE 🏛
Stapleford Park, Stapleford, Melton Mowbray, Leics LE14 2EF
Tel: 0845 303 2760 **E-mail:** central@thecct.org.uk

CHURCH OF ST MICHAEL & ALL ANGELS 🏛
Main Street, Edmondthorpe, Melton Mowbray, Leics LE14 2JU
Tel: 0845 303 2760 **E-mail:** central@thecct.org.uk

HOLY CROSS CHURCH 🏛
Burley-on-the-Hill, Burley, Oakham, Rutland LE15 7SU
Tel: 0845 303 2760 **E-mail:** central@thecct.org.uk

QUENBY HALL
Hungarton, Leicestershire LE7 9JF
Tel: 0116 2595224 **E-mail:** enquiries@quenbyhall.co.uk

ST MARY'S CHURCH 🏛
Saxby Road, Garthorpe, Melton Mowbray, Leics LE14 2RS
Tel: 0845 303 2760 **E-mail:** central@thecct.org.uk

ST PETER'S CHURCH 🏛
Main Street, Allexton, Oakham, Leicestershire LE15 9AB
Tel: 0845 303 2760 **E-mail:** central@thecct.org.uk

STAUNTON HAROLD HALL 🏛
Staunton Harold, Ashby de la Zouch, Leicestershire LE65 1RT
Tel: 01332 862 599 **E-mail:** rowan@stauntonharoldhall.co.uk

WITHCOTE CHAPEL 🏛
Oakham Road, Withcote, Oakham, Leicestershire LE15 8DP
Tel: 0845 303 2760 **E-mail:** central@thecct.org.uk

ALL SAINTS' CHURCH 🏛
Haugham, Louth, Lincolnshire LN11 8PU
Tel: 0845 303 2760 **E-mail:** central@thecct.org.uk

ALL SAINTS' CHURCH 🏛
Saltfleetby, Louth, Lincolnshire LN11 7TU
Tel: 0845 303 2760 **E-mail:** central@thecct.org.uk

CHURCH OF ST JOHN THE BAPTIST 🏛
High Street, Burringham, Scunthorpe, Lincolnshire DN17 3LY
Tel: 0845 303 2760 **E-mail:** central@thecct.org.uk

CHURCH OF ST JOHN THE BAPTIST 🏛
Main Road, Yarborough, Louth, Lincolnshire LN11 0PN
Tel: 0845 303 2760 **E-mail:** central@thecct.org.uk

EASTON WALLED GARDENS 🏛ⓔ
Easton, Grantham, Lincolnshire NG33 5AP
Tel: 01476 530063 **E-mail:** info@eastonwalledgardens.co.uk

ELSHAM HALL GARDENS & COUNTRY PARK 🏛ⓔ
Elsham Hall, Brigg, Lincolnshire DN20 0QZ
Tel: 01652 688698 **E-mail:** enquiries@elshamhall.co.uk

GUNBY HALL ❧
Gunby Hall, Spilsby, Lincolnshire PE23 5SL
Tel: 01754 890102 **E-mail:** gunbyhall@nationaltrust.org.uk

ST ANDREW'S CHURCH 🏛
Main Street, Ufford, Nr Stamford, Lincolnshire PE9 3BH
Tel: 0845 303 2760 **E-mail:** central@thecct.org.uk

ST ANDREW'S CHURCH 🏛
Redbourne, Gainsborough, Lincolnshire DN21 4QN
Tel: 0845 303 2760 **E-mail:** central@thecct.org.uk

ST BOTOLPH'S CHURCH 🏛
Skidbrooke, Louth, Lincolnshire LN11 7DQ
Tel: 0845 303 2760 **E-mail:** central@thecct.org.uk

ST HELEN'S CHURCH 🏛
Watery Lane, Little Cawthorpe, Louth, Lincolnshire LN11 8LZ
Tel: 0845 303 2760 **E-mail:** central@thecct.org.uk

ST JOHN'S CHURCH 🏛
St John's Street, Stamford, Lincolnshire PE9 2DB
Tel: 0845 303 2760 **E-mail:** central@thecct.org.uk

ST LAWRENCE'S CHURCH 🏛
Snarford, Market Rasen, Lincolnshire LN8 3SL
Tel: 0845 303 2760 **E-mail:** central@thecct.org.uk

ST MARTIN'S CHURCH 🏛
Church Lane, Waithe, Grimsby, Lincolnshire DN36 5PR
Tel: 0845 303 2760 **E-mail:** central@thecct.org.uk

ST MARY'S CHURCH 🏛
Church Lane, Alvingham, Louth, Lincolnshire LN11 0QD
Tel: 0845 303 2760 **E-mail:** central@thecct.org.uk

ST MARY'S CHURCH 🏛
Church Hill, Barnetby-Le-Wold, Barnetby, Lincs DN38 6JL
Tel: 0845 303 2760 **E-mail:** central@thecct.org.uk

ST NICHOLAS' CHURCH 🏛
Normanton-on-Cliffe, Grantham, Lincolnshire NG32 3BH
Tel: 0845 303 2760 **E-mail:** central@thecct.org.uk

ST PETER'S CHURCH 🏛
Main Street, Normanby-by-Spital, Lincoln LN8 2HF
Tel: 0845 303 2760 **E-mail:** central@thecct.org.uk

ST PETER'S CHURCH 🏛
Kingerby, Market Rasen, Lincolnshire LN8 3PU
Tel: 0845 303 2760 **E-mail:** central@thecct.org.uk

ALL SAINTS' CHURCH 🏛
Thorpe Rd, Aldwincle, Kettering, Northamptonshire NN14 3EA
Tel: 0845 303 2760 **E-mail:** central@thecct.org.uk

ALL SAINTS' CHURCH 🪧
Holdenby Rd, Holdenby, Northamptonshire NN6 8DJ
Tel: 0845 303 2760 **E-mail:** central@thecct.org.uk

CANONS ASHBY ❦
Canons Ashby, Daventry, Northamptonshire NN11 3SD
Tel: 01327 861900 **E-mail:** canonsashby@nationaltrust.org.uk

CHURCH OF ST PETER & ST PAUL 🪧
Preston Deanery, Northampton, Northamptonshire NN7 2DX
Tel: 0845 303 2760 **E-mail:** central@thecct.org.uk

HOLY TRINITY CHURCH 🪧
Main Street, Blatherwycke, Stamford, Northants PE8 6YW
Tel: 0845 303 2760 **E-mail:** central@thecct.org.uk

KIRBY HALL ⌗
Deene, Corby, Northamptonshire NN17 3EN
Tel: 01536 203230 **E-mail:** customers@english-heritage.org.uk

ST ANDREW'S CHURCH 🪧
Grafton Road, Cranford, Kettering, Northants NN14 4AD
Tel: 0845 303 2760 **E-mail:** central@thecct.org.uk

ST BARTHOLEMEW'S CHURCH 🪧
Furtho, Old Stratford, Milton Keynes, Northants MK19 6NR
Tel: 0845 303 2760 **E-mail:** central@thecct.org.uk

ST MICHAEL'S CHURCH 🪧
Upton Lane, Upton, Northampton NN5 4UX
Tel: 0845 303 2760 **E-mail:** central@thecct.org.uk

ST PETER'S CHURCH 🪧
Deene, Corby, Northamptonshire NN17 3EJ
Tel: 0845 303 2760 **E-mail:** central@thecct.org.uk

CHURCH OF ST MARTIN OF TOURS 🪧
Gainsborough Road, Saundby, East Retford, Notts DN22 9ER
Tel: 0845 303 2760 **E-mail:** central@thecct.org.uk

CLUMBER PARK ❦
Clumber Park, Worksop, Nottinghamshire S80 3AZ
Tel: 01909 544917 **E-mail:** clumberpark@nationaltrust.org.uk

ELSTON CHAPEL 🪧
Old Chapel Lane, Elston, Newark, Nottinghamshire NG23 5NY
Tel: 0845 303 2760 **E-mail:** central@thecct.org.uk

HOLME PIERREPONT HALL 🏛Ⓟ
Holme Pierrepont, Nr Nottingham NG12 2LD
Tel: 0115 933 2371

ST MICHAEL'S CHURCH 🪧
Cotham, Newark, Nottinghamshire NG23 5JS
Tel: 0845 303 2760 **E-mail:** central@thecct.org.uk

ST NICHOLAS' CHURCH 🪧
Littleborough Road, Littleborough, Retford, Notts DN22 0HD
Tel: 0845 303 2760 **E-mail:** central@thecct.org.uk

ST WILFRID'S CHURCH 🪧
Holme Lane, Low Marnham, Tuxford, Notts NG23 6SL
Tel: 0845 303 2760 **E-mail:** central@thecct.org.uk

© Mark Hibbert

Burghley House

Weston Park, Shropshire

Herefordshire
Shropshire
Staffordshire
Warwickshire
West Midlands
Worcestershire

Heart of England

Stafford-shire

Shropshire

West Midlands

Worcester-shire   Warwick-shire

Herefordshire

Often undervalued by visitors, the Heart of England protects exciting heritage places both on the Stratford-on-Avon to Warwick tourist trail and in its more remote corners.

New Entries for 2015:
- Stoneleigh Abbey
- Charlecote Park
- Heath House
- Ludlow Castle
- Bewdley Museum

263

EASTNOR CASTLE 🏛ⓕ ✦
EASTNOR CASTLE, NR LEDBURY, HEREFORDSHIRE HR8 1RL
www.eastnorcastle.com

Eastnor Castle was built 200 years ago by John, 1st Earl Somers, and is an example of Norman Revival. Standing at the southern end of the Malvern Hills, the castle is still a family home. The inside is dramatic: a 60' high Hall leads to the State Rooms, including the Pugin Gothic Drawing Room and an Italian-style Library, each with a view of the lake. There is a collection of mature specimen trees in the grounds, with a maze, tree trail, children's adventure playground, Burma Bridge tree top walkway, junior assault course and full-size-play Land Rover. Exclusive use offered for weddings, private and corporate events.
Location: Map 6:M10. OS Ref SO735 368. 2m SE of Ledbury on A438 Tewkesbury road. M50/J2 & from Ledbury take the A449/A438. Tewkesbury 20 mins, Malvern 20 mins, Hereford 25 mins, Cheltenham 30 mins, B'ham 1 hr.
Owner: Mr J Hervey-Bathurst **Contact:** Castle Office
Tel: 01531 633160 **Fax:** 01531 631776 **E-mail:** enquiries@eastnorcastle.com

Open: Easter weekend Fri 3, Sat 4, Sun 5 & BH Mon 6 Apr. May BH Weekends Sun 3, BH Mon 4 & Sun 24, BH Mon 25 May. Aug BH Weekend Sun 30 & BH Mon 31 Aug. Every Sun from 31 May–27 Sep. Sun-Thu from 19 Jul–27 Aug.
Admission: Castle & Grounds: Adult £10.00, Child (3-15yrs) £6.50, Family (2+3) £26.50. Grounds Only: Adult £6.50, Child (3-15yrs) £4.50, Family (2+3) £17.50, Groups (20+) Guided £11.50, Self-guided £8.50, Schools £7.00 Groups (40+) Guided £11.00, Self-guided £8.25.
Key facts: ⓘ Corporate events - off-road driving, team building, private dinners, exclusive hire, visitor events. 🖼 Gift shop open on visitor open days.
🎦 Product launches, TV & feature films, concerts & charities. ♿ Wheelchair stairclimber to main state rooms. 🍽 Licensed. 🎟 Pre-booked on Mons & Tues all year, Self-Guided on normal opening hours. 🅿 Ample 10-200 yds from Castle.
🚹 Guides available. 🐕 Dogs on leads. 🏨 Exclusive use accommodation. 🛏 ♿

Hergest Croft Gardens

HERGEST CROFT GARDENS 🏠Ⓕ
Kington, Herefordshire HR5 3EG
www.hergest.co.uk

Garden for all seasons; from bulbs to spectacular autumn colour, including spring and summer borders, roses, azaleas and an old-fashioned kitchen garden growing unusual vegetables. Brightly coloured rhododendrons 30ft high grow in Park Wood. Over 60 champion trees set in 70 acres of spectacular countryside of the Welsh Marches. **Location:** Map 6:J9. OS Ref SO281 565. Follow brown tourist signs along A44 to Rhayader. **Owner:** Mr E J Banks **Contact:** Mrs Melanie Lloyd **Tel:** 01544 230160 **E-mail:** gardens@hergest.co.uk
Open: Mar: Sats & Suns. Daily from 28 Mar-1 Nov: daily, 12 noon-5.30pm. Season tickets and groups by arrangement throughout year. Flower Fair, Mon 4 May 10.30am-5.30pm. Plant Fair, 12 Oct 10.30am-4.30pm. See website for all other events. **Admission:** Adult £6.00, Child (under 16yrs) Free. Pre-booked groups (20+) £5.00 per person. Pre-booked group with guided tour (20+) £7.50 per person. Season ticket £25.00 each. **Key facts:** ⌂ Containing interesting gifts. 🌿 Rare & unusual plants. ♿ Limited disabled access, special disabled route & WC. ☕ 🍴 Ridgeway Catering supply homemade light lunches, cakes and teas in the old dining room. 🎫 Pre- booked. 🅿 🐕 Dogs on leads welcome. 🏠 Haywood Cabin - available through website. ❄ Seasonal. ♥

KINNERSLEY CASTLE
Kinnersley, Herefordshire HR3 6QF

Marches castle renovated around 1580. Still a family home. Available for fashion shoots, small scale weddings/celebrations. Fine plasterwork solar ceiling. Organic gardens with specimen trees including one of Britain's largest gingkos.
Location: Map 6:K9. OS Ref SO3460 4950. A4112 Leominster to Brecon road, castle drive behind Kinnersley village sign on left.
Owner/Contact: Katherina Garratt-Adams
Tel: 01544 327407
E-mail: katherina@kinnersley.com
Website: www.kinnersleycastle.co.uk
Open: See website for dates and wedding information.
Admission: Adult £5.50. Child £2.00. Concs. & Groups over 8: £4.50.
Key facts: ⓘ No indoor photography. Coach parties by arrangement throughout year. ♿ Unsuitable. 🎫 Obligatory. 🅿

OLD SUFTON
Mordiford, Hereford HR1 4EJ

A 16th Century manor house which was altered and remodelled in the 18th and 19th Centuries and again in this Century. The original home of the Hereford family (see Sufton Court) who have held the manor since the 12th Century.
Location: Map 6:L10. OS Ref SO575 384. Mordiford, off B4224 Mordiford - Dormington road.
Owner: Trustees of Sufton Heritage Trust
Contact: Mr & Mrs J N Hereford
Tel: 01432 870268/01432 850328.
E-mail: james@sufton.co.uk
Open: By written appointment to Sufton Court or by fax or email.
Admission: Adult £5.00, Child 50p.
Key facts: ♿ Partial. 🎫 Obligatory. 🅿
🏫 Small school groups. No special facilities. ❄ ❄

SUFTON COURT 🏠Ⓕ
Mordiford, Hereford HR1 4LU
Sufton Court is a small Palladian mansion house. Built in 1788 by James Wyatt for James Hereford. The park was laid out by Humphry Repton whose 'red book' still survives. The house stands above the rivers Wye and Lugg giving impressive views towards the mountains of Wales.
Location: Map 6:L10. OS Ref SO574 379. Mordiford, off B4224 on Mordiford-Dormington road.
Owner: J N Hereford **Contact:** Mr & Mrs J N Hereford
Tel: 01432 870268/01432 850328
E-mail: james@sufton.co.uk
Open: 12-25 May & 18-31 Aug: 2-5pm. Guided tours: 2, 3 and 4pm.
Admission: Adult £5.00, Child 50p.
Key facts: 🎫 Obligatory. 🅿 Only small coaches.
🏫 Small school groups. No special facilities. 🐕 In grounds, on leads.

LANGSTONE COURT 🏠
Llangarron, Ross on Wye, Herefordshire HR9 6NR
Mostly late 17th Century house with older parts. Interesting staircases, panelling and ceilings. **Location:** Map 6:L11. OS Ref SO534 221. Ross on Wye 5m, Llangarron 1m. **Tel:** 01989 770254 **E-mail:** richard.jones@langstone-court.org.uk **Website:** www.langstone-court.org.uk **Open:** 2nd Mon & Tue Jan-Dec, 1st Mon & Tue in Jun: 11am-2.30pm, also spring & summer BHs. **Admission:** Free.

VISITOR INFORMATION

■ Owner
The Earl of Powis & The Trustees of the Powis Estates

■ Address
Castle Square
Ludlow
Shropshire
SY8 1AY

■ Location
Map 6:L8
OS Ref. SO509 745
Shrewsbury 28m, Hereford 26m. A49 centre of Ludlow.

■ Contact
Sonja Belchere (Custodian)
Tel: 01584 874465
E-mail:
info@ludlowcastle.com

■ Opening Times
Weekends Only:
January - 3rd Monday in February

7 Days a week:
October - March
10am - 4pm

April - September
10am-5pm

Closed Christmas Day.
Please see website for alterations and planned closures.

■ Admission
Please see our website for up to date admission charges.

■ Special Events
Please visit our website for special events.

LUDLOW CASTLE
www.ludlowcastle.com

The finest of medieval ruined castles.

Ludlow Castle is one the finest medieval ruins in the glorious Shropshire countryside at the heart of the superb bustling black and white town of Ludlow. It was described as 'being in the perfection of decay, all the fine courts, royal apartments, halls and rooms of state lie opened, abandoned and falling down' by Daniel Defoe.

The castle was firstly a Norman fortress and extended over the centuries to become a fortified Royal Palace built to hold back the unconquered Welsh. It passed through the families of de Lacy and Mortimer to Richard Plantaganet, Duke of York. It became Crown property in 1461 and remained a royal castle for the next 350 years, during which time the Council of the Marches was formed with responsibility for the Government of Wales and the border

counties. Abandoned in 1689 the castle quickly fell into ruin.

Since 1811 the castle has been owned by the Earls of Powis who have allowed this magnificent historical monument to be opened to the public. Today the castle is home to Ludlow's major festivals and open all year with the exception of Christmas Day.

In 2007 Castle House was completed to provide, The Tea Room, described as a real hidden gem, with waitress service, renowned for traditional English Teas and home-made cakes. Three 4 and 5* self catering apartments within the castle walls, well equipped with all mod cons. The Function Rooms are available for parties, wedding receptions, civil ceremonies and wakes.

KEY FACTS

- Partial. WCs.
- Licensed.
- By arrangement.
-
- Welcome throughout Castle, Tea Rooms and the Sir Henry Sidney Apartment.
- Three 4-5* self catering apartments.
- Civil ceremonies and receptions.

WESTON PARK

www.weston-park.com

Weston Park is a magnificent Stately Home and Parkland situated on the Shropshire/Staffordshire border.

The former home of the Earls of Bradford, the House, Park and Gardens is now owned and maintained by the Weston Park Foundation, an independent charitable trust.

Built in 1671, by Lady Elizabeth Wilbraham, this warm and welcoming house boasts internationally important paintings including works by Van Dyck, Gainsborough and Stubbs; furniture and objets d'art, providing enjoyment for all visitors.

Step outside to enjoy the 1,000 acres of glorious Parkland, take one of a variety of woodland and wildlife walks, all landscaped by the legendary 'Capability' Brown in the 18th Century.

With the exciting Woodland Adventure Playground, Orchard, Deer Park and Miniature Railway, there is plenty to keep children entertained.

Over in the Granary Grill & Deli you can enjoy home cooked seasonal dishes, light bites, freshly brewed coffee and homemade cakes and pastries. The Deli's shelves are stocked with an excellent range of delicious food and drink. Upstairs the Granary Art Gallery stages a series of exciting changing exhibitions throughout the year. (The Granary Grill & Deli and Art Gallery are open all year round. Free Entry).

The House can be hired on an exclusive use basis for business meetings, entertaining, weddings, celebrations and private parties.

KEY FACTS

- ⓘ Interior photography by prior arrangement only.
- Granary Deli & Cafe is open all year round. (Closed on Mondays)
- ⊤ Full event organisation service. Residential parties, special dinners, wedding receptions.
- ♿
- The Granary Deli & Cafe serves coffee, homemade cakes and light bites.
- ⑪ Granary Grill. Licensed.
- 🚶 By arrangement.
- Ⓟ Ample free parking.
- Award-winning educational programme available during all academic terms. Private themed visits aligned with both National Curriculum and QCA targets.
- In grounds. On leads.
- Weston Park offers 28 delightful bedrooms with bathrooms (26 doubles and 2 singles). 17 en suite.

VISITOR INFORMATION

■ Owner
The Weston Park Foundation

■ Address
Weston Park
Weston-Under-Lizard
Nr Shifnal
Shropshire
TF11 8LE

■ Location
Map 6:N6
OS Ref. SJ808 107
Birmingham 40 mins. Manchester 1 hr. Motorway access M6/J12 or M54/J3 and via the M6 Toll road J11A. House situated on A5 at Weston-under-Lizard.
Rail: Nearest Railway Stations: Wolverhampton, Stafford or Telford.
Air: Birmingham, West Midlands, Manchester.

■ Contact
Kate Thomas
Tel: 01952 852100
E-mail: enquiries@ weston-park.com

■ Opening Times
Open daily from Saturday 23rd May to Sunday 6th September (Except 19th - 26th August inc.) House is closed on Saturdays. Granary Deli & Cafe and Art Gallery. Free entry and open all year round (Deli is closed on Mondays). Granary Grill open daily all year round for lunch. Dates are correct at the time of going to print.

■ Admission
Park & Gardens:
Adult	£5.50
Child (3-14yrs)	£3.50
Family (2+3/1+4)	£23.00
OAP	£5.00
House admission +	£3.00

Groups (Parks & Gardens):
Adult	£4.00
Child (3-14yrs)	£3.00
OAP	£4.00
House admission +	£2.00

Granary Deli & Cafe and Art Gallery
Free entry and open all year round.

Granary Grill
Open daily, all year round, for lunch.
Prices are correct at the time of going to print.

Conference/Function

ROOM	Size	Max Cap
Dining Rm	52' x 23'	90
Orangery	56'1"x 22'4'	120
Music Rm	55' x 17'	60
The Hayloft	32' x 22'	40
Doncaster	49' x 18'7'	80

STOKESAY COURT 🏛
Onibury, Craven Arms, Shropshire SY7 9BD
www.stokesaycourt.com

Unspoilt and secluded, Stokesay Court is an imposing late Victorian mansion with Jacobean style façade, magnificent interiors and extensive grounds containing a grotto, woodland and interconnected pools. Set in the rolling green landscape of South Shropshire near Ludlow, the house and grounds featured as the Tallis Estate in award winning film 'Atonement'. During WW1 Stokesay Court played an important role as a military hospital and additional rooms and displays bring this history to life. **Location:** Map 6:K7. OS Ref SO444 786. A49 Between Ludlow and Craven Arms. **Owner/Contact:** Ms Caroline Magnus
Tel: 01584 856238
E-mail: info@stokesaycourt.com
Open: Guided tours Apr-Oct for booked groups (20+). Groups (up to 60) can be accommodated by arrangement. Tours for individuals take place on dates advertised on website. Booking essential.
Admission: Please check website for up to date admission prices.
Key facts: ℹ No stilettos. No photography in house. 🚽 ♿ Partial. WCs. ▣ 📷 Obligatory. 🅿 ▣ 🔲 Dogs on leads - gardens only. 📷

UPTON CRESSETT HALL 🏛
Bridgnorth, Shropshire WV16 6UH
www.uptoncressetthall.co.uk

Moated romantic Grade 1 Elizabethan manor with a magnificent Gatehouse and Norman church set in 5 acre gardens near Bridgnorth. Winner of 'Best Hidden Gem' at the Hudson's Awards, visitors include the eldest 'Prince in the Tower' on his fateful journey from Ludlow to the Tower in 1483, Prince Rupert during the Civil War and Margaret Thatcher. Home-made cakes and teas served in Medieval Pavilion. Exotic peacocks and fowl.
Location: Map 6:M7. OS Ref OS506 592. Bridgnorth 4 miles. Ludlow 17 miles.
Owner: William Cash **Contact:** The Administrator **Tel:** Office 01746 714616
E-mail: enquiries@uptoncressett.co.uk **Open:** Group tours all year by appointment. See website for public opening times, Apr-Sep.
Admission: Group tours £10.00p inc. tea & cake. Min tour 10 people, max 45. Individual admission: Hall, gardens & tour: Adult £7.50. Child (up to 10 yrs) free. Please note: we are not members of the HHA Friends' Scheme.
Key facts: ℹ No large coaches due to narrow lane. Max coach size: 26 seater. New public toilets. ▣ 🚽 🔲 Pre-booked lunches/teas for groups. 🅿 ▣ 🔲 On leads. ▣ Gatehouse, www.ruralretreats.co.uk. ⊗ Church of St Michael. 📷 €

Ludlow Castle Cafe

HODNET HALL GARDENS
Hodnet, Market Drayton, Shropshire TF9 3NN

Over 60 acres of brilliant coloured flowers, magnificent forest trees, sweeping lawns and a chain of ornamental pools which run tranquilly along the cultivated garden valley to provide a natural habitat for waterfowl and other wildlife. No matter what the season, visitors will always find something fresh and interesting to ensure an enjoyable outing.
Location: Map 6:L5. OS Ref SJ613 286. 12m NE of Shrewsbury on A53; M6/J15, M54/J3. **Owner:** Sir Algernon and the Hon Lady-Percy
Contact: Secretary
Tel: 01630 685786 **Fax:** 01630 685853
E-mail: secretary@heber-percy.freeserve.co.uk
Website: www.hodnethallgardens.org
Open: Every Sun and BH Mon from Sun 5 Apr-Sun 27 Sep, 12pm-5pm.
Please see our website for details of our up and coming special days and events.
Admission: Adult £6.50. Children £3.00.
Key facts: Partial. WCs. On leads.

LONGNER HALL
Uffington, Shrewsbury, Shropshire SY4 4TG

Designed by John Nash in 1803, Longner Hall is a Tudor Gothic style house set in a park landscaped by Humphry Repton. The home of one family for over 700 years. Longner's principal rooms are adorned with plaster fan vaulting and stained glass.
Location: Map 6:L6. OS Ref SJ529 110. 4m SE of Shrewsbury on Uffington road, ¼m off B4380, Atcham.
Owner: Mr R L Burton **Contact:** Mrs R L Burton
Tel: 01743 709215
Open: Apr-Sep: Tues & BH Mons, 2-5pm. Tours at 2pm & 3.30pm. Groups at any time by arrangement.
Admission: Adult £5.00, Child/OAP £3.00.
Key facts: No photography in house. Partial. Obligatory. Limited for coaches. By arrangement. Guide dogs only.

ST ANDREW'S CHURCH
Wroxeter, Shropshire SY5 6PH

St Andrew's is built on the Roman site of Viroconium and the evidence for the ancient town is everywhere. The gateposts are made from two Roman columns; the walls contain massive Roman stones; and the huge font is made from an inverted Roman column base. The interior dates mostly from the 17th and 18th Centuries, with some excellent woodwork in the box pews, pulpit and altar rails. Inside the church are three wonderful 16th Century alabaster tombs - each has a life-size, and eerily life-like, painted figure lying in repose.
Location: OS Ref SJ564 083. 4m SE of Shrewsbury on B4380. Church in village past Wroxeter Hotel.
Contact: The Churches Conservation Trust on 0845 303 2760 (Mon-Fri)
Website: www.visitchurches.org.uk **Open:** Open daily.
Admission: Free - donations welcome.
Key facts: By arrangement.

CHURCH OF ST MARY THE VIRGIN
St Mary's Street, Dogpole, Shrewsbury, Shropshire SY1 1DX

The spire of St Mary's is one of the tallest in England - for over 500 years it has dominated the skyline of Shrewsbury's old town. The church is now the only complete medieval church in Shrewsbury. It dates from Saxon times and has beautiful additions from the 12th Century onwards. Inside, the atmosphere is peaceful with the soaring stone arches giving way to the church's great treasure - its glorious stained glass, including the world-famous 14th Century 'Jesse window' filled with figures of Old Testament kings and prophets. Scenes from the life of St Bernard shows him ridding flies from an abbey, riding a mule and curing the sick. No other church in the country has a collection to equal it.
Location: OS Ref SJ494 126. Off St Mary's Street in the town centre.
Contact: The Churches Conservation Trust on 0845 303 2760 (Mon-Fri).
Website: www.visitchurches.org.uk **Open:** Mon-Sat, 10am-4pm.
Admission: Free entry - donations welcome. **Key facts:**

COUND HALL
Cound, Shropshire SY5 6AH

Queen Anne red brick Hall.
Location: Map 6:L6. OS Ref ST560 053.
Tel: 01743 761721 **Fax:** 01743 761722
Open: Mon 19 Oct–Fri 23 Oct 2015, 10am-4pm.
Admission: Adult £4.50, Child £2.30, Conc. £3.40, Family £11.30.

DUDMASTON ESTATE
Quatt, Bridgnorth, Shropshire WV15 6QN

Enchanted wooded parkland, sweeping gardens and a house with a surprise, Dudmaston is something unexpected in the Shropshire countryside.
Location: Map 6:M7. OS Ref SO748 888. **Tel:** 01746 780866
E-mail: dudmaston@nationaltrust.org.uk **Website:** www.nationaltrust.org.uk/dudmaston-estate **Open:** Please see website for up to date details.

SHIPTON HALL
Much Wenlock, Shropshire TF13 6JZ

Elizabethan house with Georgian extensions. Fine plasterwork and panelling. Gardens, church and dovecote. **Location:** Map 6:L7. OS Ref SO563 918. 6 miles from Much Wenlock on B4378 towards Craven Arms, close to junction with B4368 **Tel:** 01746 785225 **E-mail:** mjanebishop@hotmail.co.uk **Open:** Easter-end Sep: Thu, 2.30-5.30pm. BH Suns/Mons, 2.30-5.30pm. Groups 20+ by arrangement.
Admission: Adult £6.00, Child (under 14yrs) £3.00.

Stokesay Court - Drawing Room

CHILLINGTON HALL ⓗⒻ
CODSALL WOOD, WOLVERHAMPTON, STAFFORDSHIRE WV8 1RE
www.chillingtonhall.co.uk

Home of the Giffards since 1178. Third house on the site. The present house was built during the 18th Century, firstly by the architect Francis Smith of Warwick adding the South Wing to the Tudor House in 1724 and then completed by John Soane in 1786 replacing the Tudor House in its entirety. Parkland laid out by 'Capability' Brown in the 1760s with additional work by James Paine and possibly Robert Woods. Chillington was the winner of the HHA/Sotheby's Restoration Award 2009 for work done on Soane's magnificent Saloon. Brown's great showpiece The Pool with its follies can be seen by those who want more than a stroll in the garden.

Location: Map 6:N6. OS Ref SJ864 067.
2m S of Brewood off A449. 4m NW of M54/J2.

Owner: Mr & Mrs J W Giffard **Contact:** Estate Office
Tel: 01902 850236 **E-mail:** info@chillingtonhall.com
Open: House: 2pm-4pm (last entry 3.30pm). 5 Apr-9 Apr; 3 May-7 May; 24 May-26 May; 1 Jun-4 Jun; 3 Aug-6 Aug; 10 Aug-13 Aug; 17 Aug-20 Aug. Grounds: as house. Parties at other times by prior arrangement.
Admission: Adult £8.00, Child £4.00. Grounds only: half price.
Key facts: ⓘ Available for Civil Ceremonies, private business functions and special occasions. The 18th Century Stableblock and Model Farm has a meeting room/educational facility. ⓣ ⓢ WCs.
ⓕ Obligatory. ⓟ ▣ ▦ In grounds. ▲ Licensed for up to 130 guests for the ceremony in the Grand Saloon.

WHITMORE HALL 🏚️Ⓕ
Whitmore, Newcastle-Under-Lyme ST5 5HW

Whitmore Hall is a Grade I listed building, designated as a house of outstanding architectural and historical interest. Parts of the hall date back to a much earlier period and for 900 years has been the seat of the Cavenagh-Mainwarings, who are direct descendants of the original Norman owners. The hall has beautifully proportioned light rooms and has recently been refurbished; it is in fine order. There are good family portraits to be seen with a continuous line dating from 1624 to the present day. The park encompasses an early Victorian summer house and the outstanding and rare Elizabethan stables.

Location: Map 6:M4. OS Ref SJ811 413. On A53 Newcastle-Market Drayton Road, 3m from M6/J15.
Owner/Contact: Mr Guy Cavenagh-Mainwaring
Tel: 01782 680478 or for wedding/events 01782 680868
E-mail: whitmore.hall@yahoo.com
Open: 1 May-31 Aug: Tues and Weds, 2pm-5pm (last tour 4.30pm).
Admission: Adult £5.00, Child 50p.
Key facts: 🖼 Ground floor and grounds.
🍴 Afternoon teas for booked groups (15+), May-Aug. 🅿 Ample. 🐾

CASTERNE HALL 🏚️Ⓕ
Ilam, Nr Ashbourne, Derbyshire DE6 2BA

Panelled manor house in own grounds in stunning Peak District location above the Manifold Valley. A seat of the Hurt family for 500 years. Georgian front, 17th Century and medieval rear. Finalist in 'Country Life' magazine's 'England's Favourite House' competition. Featured in 5 films including 'The Hound of the Baskervilles' and 'Hercule Poirot'. **Location:** Map 6:O3. OS Ref SK123 523. Leave Ilam north towards Stanshope. First left turning, signed 'Castern', & continue past No Through Road sign up steep hill. **Owner/Contact:** Charles Hurt **Tel:** 01335 310489
E-mail: mail@casterne.co.uk **Website:** www.casterne.co.uk **Open:** 18-22 May, 1-12 Jun, 24 Jun-10 Jul: weekdays only for tour at 3pm only. Groups of 10+ by arrangement all year. Teas & refreshments by arrangement. **Admission:** £6.50.
Key facts: ℹ️ Silver service & candlelit lunches & dinners for parties of 12-22 by prior arrangement. 📧 Focus groups & corporate events welcomed. 🖼 Partial. Ground floor only. 📷 Obligatory. 45 min tour. 🅿 Limited for coaches. ■ 🐾 Guide dogs only. 🛏 B&B by prior arrangement. 🔺 Licensed. Civil ceremonies & marriages in Hall or Drawing Room. Wedding parties welcomed. ❋ €

THE HEATH HOUSE 🏚️
Tean, Stoke-On-Trent, Staffordshire ST10 4HA

Set in rolling parkland with fine formal gardens, Heath House is an early Victorian mansion built 1836-1840 in the Tudor style for John Burton Philips. The original collection of paintings and chattels remains intact. Ground floor rooms only available to view. **Location:** Map 6:O4. OS Ref SK030 392. A522 off A50 at Uttoxeter 5m W, at Lower Tean turn right.
Owner: Mr Ben & Justin Philips
Contact: Mr Justin Philips
Tel: 01538 722212
E-mail: justin@theheathhouse.co.uk
Website: www.theheathhouse.co.uk
Open: Good Fri, Easter Mon, 2 May, 6-15 May, 24 May, 1-12 , 15 Jun, 31 Aug. 2-6pm. Last entry 5pm. Please telephone in advance.
Admission: £6.50. No Conc. No reductions for groups.
Key facts: ℹ️ 📧 🖼 WCs. 🅿 ⬛

BIDDULPH GRANGE GARDEN 🌿
Grange Road, Biddulph, Staffordshire ST8 7SD

This amazing Victorian garden was created by James Bateman for his collection of plants from around the world. **Location:** Map 6:N3. OS Ref SJ891 592.
Tel: 01782 517999 **E-mail:** biddulphgrange@nationaltrust.org.uk
Website: www.nationaltrust.org.uk/biddulph-grange-garden
Open: Please see website for up to date opening and admission details.

SHUGBOROUGH ESTATE 🌿
Milford, Stafford, Staffordshire ST17 0XB

Rare survival of a complete estate, with all major buildings including mansion house, servants' quarters, model farm and walled garden. **Location:** Map 6:N5. OS Ref SJ990 215. **Tel:** 0845 459 8900 **E-mail:** shugborough@ nationaltrust.org.uk **Website:** www.nationaltrust.org.uk/shugborough-estate
Open: Please see website for up to date opening and admission details.

Biddulph Grange Garden

Heart of England

VISITOR INFORMATION

■ **Owner**
The Viscount Daventry

■ **Address**
Arbury Hall
Nuneaton
Warwickshire
CV10 7PT

■ **Location**
Map 6:P7
OS Ref. SP335 893
London, M1, M6/J3 (A444 to Nuneaton), 2m SW of Nuneaton. 1m W of A444. Nuneaton 5 mins. Birmingham City Centre 20 mins. London 2 hrs, Coventry 20 mins.
Bus/Coach: Nuneaton Station 3m.
Air: Birmingham International 17m.

■ **Contact**
Events Secretary
Tel: 024 7638 2804
Fax: 024 7664 1147
E-mail:
info@arburyestate.co.uk

■ **Opening Times**
Hall & Gardens open on Bank Holiday weekends only (Sunday & Monday) Easter - August from 1pm to 6pm. Last guided tour of the Hall 4.30pm. Groups/Parties (25+) by arrangement.

■ **Admission**
Hall & Gardens
Adult	£8.50
Child (up to 14 yrs)	£4.50
Family (2+2)	£20.00

Gardens Only
Adult	£5.50
Child (up to 14 yrs.)	£4.00

Conference/Function

ROOM	Size	Max Cap
Dining Room	35' x 28'	120
Saloon	35' x 30'	70
Room 3	48' x 11'	40
Stables Tearooms	31' x 18'	80

ARBURY HALL 🏠Ⓕ
www.arburyestate.co.uk

Arbury Hall, original Elizabethan mansion house, Gothicised in the 18th Century surrounded by stunning gardens and parkland.

Arbury Hall has been the seat of the Newdegate family for over 450 years and is the ancestral home of Viscount Daventry. This Tudor/Elizabethan House was Gothicised by Sir Roger Newdegate in the 18th Century and is regarded as the 'Gothic Gem' of the Midlands. The principal rooms, with their soaring fan vaulted ceilings and plunging pendants and filigree tracery, stand as a most breathtaking and complete example of early Gothic Revival architecture and provide a unique and fascinating venue for corporate entertaining, product launches, fashion shoots and activity days. Exclusive use of this historic Hall, its gardens and parkland is offered to clients. The Hall stands in the middle of beautiful parkland with landscaped gardens of rolling lawns, lakes and winding wooded walks. Spring flowers are profuse and in June rhododendrons, azaleas and giant wisteria provide a beautiful environment for the visitor. George Eliot, the novelist, was born on the estate and Arbury Hall and Sir Roger Newdegate were immortalised in her book 'Scenes of Clerical Life'.

KEY FACTS

ℹ️ Corporate hospitality, film location, small conferences, product launches and promotions, marquee functions, let day shooting. No cameras or video recorders indoors.

🛍️ Small selection of souvenir gifts.

🍽️ Exclusive lunches and dinners for corporate parties in dining room, max. 50, buffets 80.

♿ Partial, WCs.

☕ Stables Tearooms (on first floor) open from 1pm.

🚶 Obligatory. Tour time: 50min.

🅿️ 200 cars and 3 coaches 250 yards from house. Follow tourist signs. Approach map available for coach drivers.

🐕 Dogs on leads only. Guide dogs only.

SHAKESPEARE'S FAMILY HOMES
www.shakespeare.org.uk

Discover Shakespeare's family homes, farm and gardens in Stratford-upon-Avon, plus hidden gem, Harvard House.

Shakespeare's Birthplace - Where the story began
Explore the extraordinary story of William and the house he was born and grew up in. Our fascinating guides will captivate you with tales of his father's business ventures. Take centre stage and bring his works to life with our costumed troupe, Shakespeare Aloud!

Mary Arden's Farm - A working Tudor farm
Visit the family farm where Shakespeare's mother grew up. Experience the sights, sounds and smells of a working Tudor farm and follow our resident Tudors as they work. Meet rare breed animals, enjoy archery and falconry, or explore the nature trails and playground. Don't miss our free events throughout the school holidays.

Anne Hathaway's Cottage - Love and marriage
Follow young Shakespeare's footsteps to the Cottage where he courted an older woman. Our guides will bring this Tudor love story to life in its original setting. Explore nine acres of beautiful cottage gardens, woodland walks and sculpture trail. Enjoy refreshments in the newly refurbished Cottage Garden Cafe.

Harvard House - Stratford's hidden gem
Built during Shakespeare's lifetime by the wealthy Thomas Rogers it is one of Stratford-upon-Avon's most striking Elizabethan houses. Explore this unique three-story town house and its fascinating story, and admire the fine exterior oak carvings, 16th Century stained glass and painted panels. Also, see exciting plans for a proposed major redevelopment of New Place, the final home of Shakespeare, due to reopen in 2016.

Hall's Croft - Daughter and Granddaughter
The elegant Tudor home of Shakespeare's daughter Susanna and her husband Dr John Hall. Stroll round the walled garden planted with fragrant herbs used in Dr Hall's remedies. Unwind in the cafe or browse hand crafted local gifts in The Arter gift shop.

VISITOR INFORMATION

■ Owner
The Shakespeare Birthplace Trust

■ Address
Henley Street
Stratford-upon-Avon
CV37 6QW

■ Location
Map 6:P9
OS Ref.
Birthplace: SP201 552
Harvard: SP201 549
Hall's Croft: SP200 546
Hathaway's: SP185 547
Arden's: SP166 582
2 hrs from London 45 mins from Birmingham by car. 4m from M40/J15 and well signed from all approaches.
Rail: Direct service from London (Marylebone).

■ Contact
The Shakespeare Birthplace Trust
Tel: 01789 204016 (General Enquiries)
Tel: 01789 201806 (Group Visits).
E-mail:
info@shakespeare.org.uk
groups@shakespeare.org.uk

■ Opening Times
The Shakespeare houses are open daily throughout the year except Christmas Day and Boxing Day (Shakespeare's Birthplace is open on Boxing Day). Mary Arden's Farm closes for Winter from November to March.

Opening times vary throughout the year. Please see www.shakespeare.org.uk for up to date information.

■ Admission
Visit the website for full details on ticket prices.

You can enjoy 12 months free admission with every pass as tickets to the Shakespeare Houses are valid for a year with unlimited entry. Pay for a day and take the whole year to explore!

Multi-house passes also include a visit to Shakespeare's grave at Holy Trinity Church.

Visit the website for further details
www.shakespeare.org.uk.

KEY FACTS

- ℹ City Sightseeing bus tour connecting town houses with Anne Hathaway's Cottage and Mary Arden's Farm. No photography inside houses.
- Gifts available.
- Plants for sale at Anne Hathaway's Cottage.
- Available, tel for details.
- Partial. WCs.
- Shakespeare's Birthplace, Mary Arden's Farm, Anne Hathaway's Cottage, Hall's Croft.
- By special arrangement.
- **P** Free coach terminal for groups drop off and pick up at Birthplace. Max stay 30 mins. Parking at Mary Arden's Farm. Pay & display parking at Anne Hathaway's Cottage.
- Available for all houses. For information 01789 201804.
- Guide dogs only.
- Please check for full details.
- Please check website for details.

CHARLECOTE PARK ✤
WELLESBOURNE, WARWICK, WARWICKSHIRE CV35 9ER

www.nationaltrust.org.uk/charlecote-park

Protected by the Rivers Dene & Avon and by its distinctive cleft-oak paling fencing Charlecote Park presents a picture of peace and repose. Generations of the Lucy family have left their mark on the property. The house holds surprising treasures from early editions of Shakespeare to an impressive Beckford table. The Tudor Gatehouse draws visitors from park to court walking in the same processional footsteps as Queen Elizabeth 1. The outbuildings consist of a Laundry, Brew House, Carriage House & Stables. The gardens present a riot of colour throughout the year. The family's continued presence adds an intriguing dimension for visitors as they picnic, play and wander through the parkland watched by the Jacob sheep & fallow deer.

Location: Map 6:P9. OS Ref OS151, SP263 564. 1m W of Wellesbourne, 5m E of Stratford-upon-Avon. Exit 15 from M40 (Take A429 marked Stow & follow brown NT signs). **Owner:** National Trust **Contact:** Property Office

Tel: 01789 470277 **Fax:** 01789 470544
E-mail: charlecotepark@nationaltrust.org.uk
Open: Park, gardens, outbuildings, shop & tea room open daily 10.30am-5.30pm. Closing at 4pm in winter or dusk if earlier. House 14 Feb-27 Mar, 12-3.30pm (Closed Wed), 28 Mar-1 Nov, 11am-4.30pm (Closed Wed), 7 Nov-20 Dec 12-3.30pm Sat and Sun only. Tea Room serves full menu when house open & light meals at all other times. Whole property closed 27, 28 & 29 Jan and 23, 24 & 25 Dec. Last admission ½ hour before closing.
Admission: House, Garden & Park Gift Aid (Standard): Adult £11.10 (£10.05), Child £5.50 (£5.00), Family £27.50 (£25.00). Garden and Park only: Adult £7.50 (£6.80), Child £3.75 (£3.40), Family £18.75 (£17.00). House, Garden & Park Winter: Adult £7.50 (£6.80), Child £3.75 (£3.40) Family £18.75 (£17.00).
Key facts: 🛈 🖻 ♿ 🐕 🎁 Ⓟ 🗾 ❄ ☕

Charlecote Park

LORD LEYCESTER HOSPITAL

HIGH STREET, WARWICK CV34 4BH

www.lordleycester.com

This magnificent range of 14th and 15th Century half-timbered buildings was adapted into almshouses by Robert Dudley, Earl of Leycester, in 1571. The Hospital still provides homes for ex-Servicemen and their wives. The Guildhall, Great Hall, chantry Chapel, Brethren's Kitchen and galleried Courtyard are still in everyday use. The regimental museum of the Queen's Own Hussars is housed here. The historic Master's Garden was featured in BBC TV's Gardener's World, and the Hospital buildings in many productions including, most recently, 'Dr Who' and David Dimbleby's 'How We Built Britain'.

Location: Map 6:P8. OS Ref 280 468. 1m N of M40/J15 on the A429 in town centre. Rail: 10 minutes walk from Warwick Station.

Owner: The Governors
Contact: The Master
Tel: 01926 491422
Open: All year: Tue-Sun & BHs (except Good Fri & 25 Dec), 10am-5pm (4pm in winter). Garden: Apr-Sep: 10am-4.30pm.
Admission: Adult £5.90, Child £4.90, Conc. £5.40. Garden only £2.00.
Key facts: Partial. WCs.
By arrangement.
Limited for cars. No coaches.
Guide dogs only.

ASTLEY CASTLE

Nuneaton, Warwickshire CV10 7QS

www.landmarktrust.org.uk

Groundbreaking modern accommodation has been inserted within the ruined walls of this ancient moated site to combine the thrill of modern architecture with the atmosphere of an ancient place. Large glass walls now frame views of medieval stonework and the adjacent church and surrounding countryside.

Location: Map 7:A7. OS Ref SP310 894.
Owner: The Landmark Trust
Tel: 01628 825925
E-mail: bookings@landmarktrust.org.uk
Open: Self-catering accommodation. Part of grounds open Mon and Fri, 8 Open Days per year, contact office.
Admission: Free on Open Days and visits by appointment.
Key facts: The living accommodation is on the first floor and the bedrooms and bathrooms on the ground floor. A lift enables easy access for all.

COMPTON VERNEY

Compton Verney, Warwickshire CV35 9HZ

www.comptonverney.org.uk

Set within a Grade I listed mansion remodelled by Robert Adam in the 1760s, Compton Verney offers a unique art gallery experience. Relax and explore the 120 acres of 'Capability' Brown landscaped parkland, discover a collection of internationally significant art, enjoy free tours and a programme of popular events.

Location: Map 7:A9. OS Ref SP312 529. 9m E of Stratford-upon-Avon, 10 mins from M40/J12, on B4086 between Wellesbourne and Kineton. Rail: nearest station is Banbury or Leamington Spa. Air: Nearest airport Birmingham International.
Owner: Compton Verney House Trust **Contact:** Ticketing Desk
Tel: 01926 645500 **Fax:** 01926 645501
Ticket Desk hours: 11am-4.30pm Tue-Sun. **E-mail:** info@comptonverney.org.uk
Open: 14 Mar -13 Dec 2015, Tue-Sun and BH Mons, 11am-5pm. Last entry to Gallery 4.30pm. Groups welcome, please book in advance.
Admission: Please call for details. Group discounts are available.
Key facts: Photography is not permitted in some areas of the Gallery. WCs. and access throughout the building on all floors. Licensed. Licensed and waitress service. By arrangement. Ample. Guide dogs only.

HILL CLOSE GARDENS
Bread and Meat Close, Warwick CV34 6HF
www.hillclosegardens.com

Sixteen hedged Victorian gardens overlooking Warwick racecourse with delightful listed brick summerhouses. Created by tradespeople to escape the congestion and pollution of the town. Spring bulbs, old varieties of soft fruit and vegetables, unusual fruit trees and extensive herbaceous borders. Glasshouse for tender plants. Plant, produce and gift sales. Cafe serving lunches and teas at weekends and Bank Holidays in summer. Teas and snacks all year. Events throughout the year listed on website **Location:** Map 6:P8. M40 Junction 15 Follow A429 & signs for racecourse, enter main racecourse gate off Friars Street. Bear right to entrance to Gardens. **Owner:** Hill Close Gardens Trust **Contact:** Centre Manager
Tel: 01926 493 339 **E-mail:** centremanager@hcgt.org.uk
Open: Apr-Oct Gardens every day 11am-5pm. Café Sat & Sun & BH Mons. Nov-Mar Gardens Mon-Fri 11am-4pm. Teas & snacks available during all opening times. Closed Xmas-New Year. Check website for details.
Admission: Adults £3.50, Child £1.00 (to include garden trail). Under 5s free.
Key facts: ▣ Gifts, cards, jam. ▣ Plants produce. ▣ Centre for hire. ▣ Access, toilet & parking. ▣ Drinks, cakes. Quiche, soup, teacakes, scones. ▣ On request. ▣ 2 hours free. ▣ On request. ▣ Assistance only. ▣ Weekdays in winter. ▣

ALL SAINTS' CHURCH ▣
Billesley, Stratford Upon Avon, Warwickshire B49 6NF

All Saints rises from a lovely wooded churchyard in the hamlet of Billesley near Stratford-upon-Avon. From its approach through an avenue of limes, it looks like a Georgian country church but its origins actually go back 1,000 years. Tradition has it that William Shakespeare married Anne Hathaway here in 1582. In 1692, Bernard Whalley rebuilt the church to create a fashionable classical addition to his Billesley estate, however remains of the early church survive, in particular two spectacular 12th Century stone carvings on the east wall of the vestry. One shows a soldier in a kilt, a snake, a dragon and a bird, all surrounded by wonderfully twisted foliage. The other is part of a stone cross on which is a carved figure of Christ.
Location: OS Ref SP148 568. 4 miles W of Stratford-upon-Avon, off A46. Follow signs to Billesley & Billesley Manor Hotel. **Contact:** The Churches Conservation Trust on 0845 303 2760 (Mon-Fri) **Website:** www.visitchurches.org.uk
Open: Open daily. **Admission:** Free entry - donations welcome.

HONINGTON HALL ▣
Shipston-On-Stour, Warwickshire CV36 5AA

This fine Caroline manor house was built in the early 1680s for Henry Parker in mellow brickwork, stone quoins and window dressings. Modified in 1751 when an octagonal saloon was inserted. The interior was also lavishly restored around this time and contains exceptional mid-Georgian plasterwork. Set in 15 acres of grounds.
Location: Map 6:P9. OS Ref SP261 427. 10m S of Stratford-upon-Avon. 1½m N of Shipston-on-Stour. Take A3400 towards Stratford, then signed right to Honington.
Owner/Contact: Benjamin Wiggin Esq
Tel: 01608 661434 **Fax:** 01608 663717
E-mail: bhew@honingtonhall.plus.com
Open: By appointment for groups (10+).
Admission: Email for details.
Key facts: ▣ Obligatory. ▣

Birmingham Botanical Gardens

STONELEIGH ABBEY
Kenilworth, Warwickshire CV8 2LF

A Cistercian monastery converted into a stately home. Stoneleigh hosted Jane Austen and Queen Victoria. **Location:** Map 6:P8. OS Ref SP320 712.
Tel: 01926 858535 **E-mail:** enquire@stoneleighabbey.org
Website: www.stoneleighabbey.org **Open:** Good Fri-31 Oct. Guided tour only - times on website. Grounds 11am-5pm. **Admission:** House & Grounds Adult £8.00, Child £3.50, EH member £6.50. Grounds £3.50. Under 5 and carers Free.

WARWICK CASTLE
Warwick CV34 4QU

Over 1000 years of jaw-dropping history, where ancient myths and spell-binding tales will set your imagination alight. Meet history face to face and be prepared to participate fully in Castle life. **Location:** Map 6:P8. OS Ref SP283 647.
Tel: 01926 495 421 **E-mail:** customer.information@warwick-castle.com
Website: www.warwick-castle.com **Open:** Please visit our website for details.

WINTERBOURNE HOUSE AND GARDEN 🏛ⓕ
University of Birmingham, 58 Edgbaston Park Road, Birmingham B15 2RT

www.winterbourne.org.uk

Winterbourne is set in 7 acres of botanic garden, just minutes from Birmingham city centre. Ground and first floor exhibition spaces tell the history of the previous owners and the garden has a beautiful Japanese bridge, tea house and walled garden, all designed in the Arts and Crafts style. A terrace tea room overlooks the garden where afternoon tea, hot lunches and refreshments are served every day. **Location:** Map 6:O7. OS Ref SP052 839. Just off the A38 in Selly Oak, Birmingham. **Owner:** The University of Birmingham **Tel:** 0121 414 3003 **E-mail:** enquiries@winterbourne.org.uk **Open:** Jan-Mar/Nov-Dec 10am-4pm weekdays, 11am-4pm weekends Apr-Oct 10am-5.30pm weekdays, 11am-5.30pm weekends. Closed over Christmas period. **Admission:** Adult £5.50, Conc £4.50, Family £16.00. Group prices on request. **Key facts:** 🛈 Organised professional photography must be notified to management & will incur a charge. 🖼 Garden-inspired gifts, guidebooks, secondhand books & greetings cards. 🌿 Quality plants for sale, many home-grown species. 🎪 Conference facilities on site. 🚾 WCs. 🍽 Licensed. 🍴 Licensed. 🎫 Pre-booked. 🅿 🚌 🐕 Guide dogs only. ❄ ♿

BIRMINGHAM BOTANICAL GARDENS
Westbourne Road, Edgbaston, Birmingham B15 3TR

15 acres of beautiful historic landscaped gardens with 7000 shrubs, plants and trees. Four glasshouses, Roses and Alpines, Woodland and Rhododendron Walks, Rock Pool, Herbaceous Borders, Japanese Garden. Children's playground, aviaries, gallery, bandstand, tearoom giftshop, parking.
Location: Map 6:O7. OS Ref SP048 855. 2m W of city centre. Follow signs to Edgbaston then brown tourist signs. **Owner:** Birmingham Botanical & Horticultural Society **Contact:** Kim Hill **Tel:** 0121 454 1860
Fax: 0121 454 7835 **E-mail:** Kim@birminghambotanicalgardens.org.uk
Website: www.birminghambotanicalgardens.org.uk
Open: Daily: 10am-dusk. Closed Christmas Day and Boxing Day. Refer to website for details - www.birminghambotanicalgardens.org.uk **Admission:** Adult £7.00, Family £22.00. Groups, Conc. £4.75, Children under 5 free.
Key facts: 🖼 🌿 🎪 🚾 🍽 🎫 On application. 🅿 🚌 🐕 Guide dogs only. ♿ ❄ Not 25/26 Dec. ♿

CASTLE BROMWICH HALL GARDENS 🏛
Chester Road, Castle Bromwich, Birmingham B36 9BT

A unique survival of English formal garden design of the late 17th and early 18th Century – containing plants of the period and a holly maze making them one of the most important historic gardens in the country.
Location: Map 6:O6. OS Ref SP141 899. Off B4114, 5m E of Birmingham City Centre, 1 mile from M6/J5 exit N only.
Owner: Castle Bromwich Hall & Gardens Trust **Contact:** Sue Brain
Tel: 0121 749 4100 **E-mail:** admin@cbhgt.org.uk **Website:** www.cbhgt.org.uk
Open: 1 Apr-31 Oct: Tues-Thurs, 11am-4pm. Sat, Sun BH Mon 12.30-4.30pm. 1 Nov-31 Mar: Tues-Thur 11am-3pm.
Admission: Summer: Adults £4.50, Concs £4.00, Child £1.00. Winter: All Adults £4.00, Child £1.00.
Key facts: 🖼 🌿 ♿ WCs. 🍽 🎫 By arrangement. 🅿 Limited for coaches. 🚌 🐕 On leads. ❄ ♿

BADDESLEY CLINTON 🌿
Rising Lane, Baddesley Clinton, Warwickshire B93 0DQ

A 500 year old moated medieval manor house with hidden secrets!
Location: Map 6:P8. OS Ref SP199 715. **Tel:** 01564 783294
E-mail: baddesleyclinton@nationaltrust.org.uk
Website: www.nationaltrust.org.uk/baddesley-clinton
Open: Please see website for up to date opening and admission details.

WIGHTWICK MANOR & GARDENS 🌿
Wightwick Bank, Wolverhampton, West Midlands WV6 8EE

Wightwick is in every way an idyllic time capsule of Victorian nostalgia for medieval England. Step back in time and visit the family home that's also the world's most unlikely art gallery. **Location:** Map 6:N6. OS Ref SO869 985.
Tel: 01902 761400 **E-mail:** wightwickmanor@nationaltrust.org.uk
Website: www.nationaltrust.org.uk/wightwickmanor **Open:** Please see website.

Winterbourne House

CROOME
NEAR HIGH GREEN, WORCESTERSHIRE WR8 9DW
www.nationaltrust.org.uk/croome

Expect the unexpected. Step into what remains of a secret wartime air base, now our visitor centre, where thousands of people lived and worked in the 1940s. Walk through a masterpiece in landscape design, which is 'Capability' Brown's first. Over the past 17 years we have restored what was once a lost and overgrown parkland and we're continuing this work today. At the heart of the park, see Croome Court transform from a house of faded beauty with major repair work continuing this year. Explore the work for yourself and get up close to the action every day. Find stories of loss and survival and experience a unique country house. **Location:** Map 6:N9. OS Ref SO878 448. Approximately 10 miles south of Worcester. Leave M5 motorway at Junction 7 and follow B4084 towards Pershore. Alternatively, access from the A38. Follow Brown Signs.

Owner: National Trust **Contact:** House Manager
Tel: 01905 371006 **Fax:** 01905 371090
E-mail: croome@nationaltrust.org.uk
Open: See National Trust website for full opening times. Park, Restaurant & Shop open every day except 24 & 25 Dec. House open every day except Tues throughout the year.
Admission: House and Park: £11.00, Child £5.50, Family £27.50. Groups (15+) £9.00, Child £4.00. Park only: £7.50, Child £3.75, Family £18.75. Groups (15+) £6.00, Child £3.00. Gift Aid prices quoted.
Key facts: ⬚ ⬚ ⬚ ⬚ WCs. ⬚ Licensed. ⬚ Licensed. ⬚ By arrangement. P ⬚ ⬚ On leads. ⬚ ⬚

HARVINGTON HALL ⬚⬚
HARVINGTON, KIDDERMINSTER, WORCESTERSHIRE DY10 4LR
www.harvingtonhall.com

Harvington Hall is a moated, medieval and Elizabethan manor house. Many of the rooms have their original Elizabethan wall paintings and the Hall contains the finest series of priest hides in the country. During the 19th Century it was stripped of furniture and panelling and the shell was left almost derelict but is now restored. The Hall has walled gardens surrounded by a moat, a gift shop and a tea room serving morning coffees, light lunches and afternoon teas. A programme of events throughout the year including outdoor plays and music, candlelight tours and a pilgrimage is available.
On many weekends the Hall is enhanced by Living History events when the Hall's re-enactment group depict one of the many significant periods throughout its long history.
Location: Map 6:N8. OS Ref SO877 745. On minor road, ½m NE of A450/A448

crossroads at Mustow Green. 3m SE of Kidderminster.
Owner: Roman Catholic Archdiocese of Birmingham
Contact: The Hall Manager **Tel:** 01562 777846 **Fax:** 01562 777190
E-mail: harvingtonhall@btconnect.com
Open: Mar: Sats & Suns; Apr-Oct: Wed-Sun & BH Mons (closed Good Fri), 11.30am-4pm. Also open throughout the year for pre-booked groups and schools. Occasionally the Hall may be closed for a private function, please ring for up to date information.
Admission: Adult £8.50, Child (5-16) £5.50, OAP £7.50, Family (2 adults & 3 children) £24.00, Garden and Malt House Visitor Centre: £3.50.
Key facts: ⬚ ⬚ ⬚ P Partial. WCs. ⬚ ⬚ ⬚ P Limited for coaches. ⬚ ⬚ Guide dogs only. ⬚

BEWDLEY MUSEUM
12 Load Street, Bewdley, Worcestershire DY12 2AE
www.bewdleymuseum.co.uk

Situated in the delightful Georgian town of Bewdley this unique museum can be enjoyed by the whole family. Beautiful gardens, imaginative displays, a café with fresh local produce. Exhibitions, events and plenty of activities for children. The Tourist Information Centre is based on site at the entrance to the museum.
Location: Map 6:M8. OS Ref SO786 753. 4 miles to the west of Kidderminster on the B1490 in the centre of Bewdley. Two public car parks are within walking distance. **Owner:** Wyre Forest District Council **Contact:** Alison Bakr
Tel: 0845 603 5699 **E-mail:** Alison.bakr@wyreforestdc.gov.uk
Open: Mar-Oct 10am-4.30pm. Nov and Dec 11am-3pm. Fri, Sat and Sun. Café and access to the gardens Mar-Dec. **Admission:** Free.
Key facts: ▢ Situation at the entrance to the museum. ▢ Situated in the herb garden. ▢ Private events and functions are held on site. ▢ Full access on site. ▢ Shambles café set in the museum. ▢ Serving hot and cold drinks, snacks, lightbites, hot meals and alcohol. ▢ Guided tours and walks. ▢ Blitz and evacuation, river and rail plus bespoke programmes. ▢ Welcome on site. ▢ Wedding receptions and parties held in the museum and gardens. ▢

LITTLE MALVERN COURT 🏛ⓔ
Nr Malvern, Worcestershire WR14 4JN
Prior's Hall, associated rooms and cells, c1489. Former Benedictine Monastery. Oak-framed roof, 5 bays. Library, collection of religious vestments and relics. Embroideries and paintings. Gardens: 10 acres of former monastic grounds with spring bulbs, blossom, old fashioned roses and shrubs.
Access to Hall only by flight of steps. **Location:** Map 6:M9. OS Ref SO769 403. 3m S of Great Malvern on Upton-on-Severn Road (A4104).
Owner: Trustees of the late T M Berington **Contact:** Mrs T M Berington
Tel: 01684 892988 **Fax:** 01684 893057
E-mail: littlemalverncourt@hotmail.com **Website:** www.littlemalverncourt.co.uk
Open: 15 Apr until 23 Jul, Weds & Thus, 2.15-5pm, last admission 4.00pm. Open for NGS Sunday 22 Mar & Mon 4 May. Please note that the house is closed on Jun 3 & 4. Garden open as usual. **Admission:** House & Garden - Adult £7.00, Child £2.00. Garden only - Adult £6.00, Child £1.00. Groups by prior arrangement.
Key facts: ▢ ▢ Garden (partial). ▢ House only. 🅿 ▢

MADRESFIELD COURT
Madresfield, Malvern WR13 5AJ
Elizabethan and Victorian house with medieval origins. Fine contents. Extensive gardens and arboretum.
Location: Map 6:M9. OS Ref SO808 472. 6m SW of Worcester. 1½ m SE of A449. 2m NE of Malvern.
Owner: The Trustees of Madresfield Estate
Contact: Mrs Wendy Carruthers
Tel: 01684 573614 **E-mail:** madresfield@btconnect.com
Open: Guided tours on specific dates between Apr and Sep. Numbers are restricted and prior booking is essential to avoid disappointment.
Admission: £12.00.
Key facts: ▢ WCs. ▢ Obligatory. ▢ Dogs in grounds only.

ST LAWRENCE'S CHURCH 🏛
Market Place, Evesham WR11 4BG

St Lawrence, the parish church of All Saints' and the great Perpendicular bell tower of the Abbey at Evesham together form a spectacular architectural group. This large and imposing church is of Norman foundation, though it now appears entirely Perpendicular, having been rebuilt in the 16th Century. It fell into ruin in the 18th Century but was rescued and restored again by the local architect H Eginton in 1836. Outside, the east end has a great six-light window with elaborate tracery. Inside, the early 16th Century chantry chapel of St Clement has richly panelled arches and a beautiful fan vaulted ceiling. The windows contain fabulous glass by many of the major stained glass artists of the last 150 years.
Location: OS Ref SP037 436. Evesham town centre; from A4184 Abbey Road, take Vine Street & Market Place; from B4035 Waterside, turn left into Bridge St, shopping centre multi storey car park; church next to parish church
Website: www.visitchurches.org.uk
Open: Summer: Daily, 9.30am-4.30pm. Winter: 9.30am-3.30pm.

CHURCH OF ST MARY MAGDELENE 🏛
Croome Park, Croome D'Abitot, Worcester Worcestershire WR8 9DW

The original church at Croome was demolished by the 6th Earl of Coventry when he decided to replace his adjacent Jacobean house in the 1750s. His new house and park were designed and laid out by Capability Brown, as was the church. The views out to the Malvern Hills on a clear day are spectacular. The interiors of both house and church are attributed to Robert Adam and were completed in 1763. Built by some of the finest craftsmen in England, every detail has been considered, from pretty plaster mouldings to handsome carved pews - the church is a perfect fantasy of the period, with elegant Gothic windows and plasterwork, pulpit, communion rails, commandments and creed boards.
Location: OS Ref SO 886 450. 4m W of Pershore off A38 & A44; follow National Trust signs to Croome Park. Parking at National Trust car park. Access to church via visitor centre. **Website:** www.visitchurches.org.uk **Open:** Open when Croome Park is open. For detailed opening times, see the Croome Park website.

THE TUDOR HOUSE MUSEUM
16 Church Street, Upton-upon-Severn, Worcestershire WR8 0HT
Exhibits of Upton past and present, local pottery and "Staffordshire Blue".
Location: Map 6:N10. OS Ref SO852 406. Centre of Upton-upon-Severn, 7miles SE of Malvern by B4211.
Owner: Tudor House Museum Trust
Tel: 01684 438820 **E-mail:** lavendertudor@talktalk.net
Open: Apr to Oct. Tue to Sun and BH afternoons. 2pm to 5pm.
Key facts: ▢ Garden and ground floor only. ▢ Prebooked. ▢

BROADWAY TOWER
Middle Hill, Broadway, Worcestershire WR12 7LB
Broadway Tower was the brainchild of the great 18th Century landscape designer, Capability Brown. His vision was carried out for George William 6th and completed in 1798. **Location:** Map 6:O10. OS Ref SP120 363. **Tel:** 01386 852390
E-mail: info@broadwaytower.co.uk **Website:** www.broadwaytower.co.uk
Open: Please see website for up to date opening and admission details.

SNOWSHILL MANOR ⚘
Snowshill, Broadway WR12 7JU
Cotswold manor house with stunning garden, packed with extraordinary treasures collected over a life time by Charles Wade. **Location:** Map 6:O10. OS Ref SP096 339. **Tel:** 01386 852410 **E-mail:** snowshillmanor@nationaltrust.org.uk
Website: www.nationaltrust.org.uk/snowshill-manor
Open: Please see website for up to date opening and admission details.

BERRINGTON HALL ❦
Nr Leominster, Herefordshire HR6 0DW
Tel: 01568 615721 E-mail: berrington@nationaltrust.org.uk

BROCKHAMPTON ESTATE ❦
Bringsty, Nr Bromyard WR6 5TB
Tel: 01885 488099 E-mail: brockhampton@nationaltrust.org.uk

GOODRICH CASTLE ⌗
Ross-On-Wye, Herefordshire HR9 6HY
Tel: 01600 890538 E-mail: customers@english-heritage.org.uk

HELLENS 🏠
Much Marcle, Ledbury, Herefordshire HR8 2LY
Tel: 01531 660504

CHURCH OF ST COSMAS & ST DAMIAN ⛪
Stretford, Leominster, Herefordshire HR6 9DG
Tel: 0845 303 2760 E-mail: central@thecct.org.uk

CHURCH OF ST JOHN THE BAPTIST ⛪
Llanrothal, Monmouth, Herefordshire NP25 5QJ
Tel: 0845 303 2760 E-mail: central@thecct.org.uk

ST BARTHOLEMEW'S CHURCH ⛪
Richards Castle, Nr Ludlow, Herefordshire SY8 4ET
Tel: 0845 303 2760 E-mail: central@thecct.org.uk

ST CUTHBERT'S CHURCH ⛪
Church Road, Holme Lacy, Hereford, Herefordshire HR2 6LX
Tel: 0845 303 2760 E-mail: central@thecct.org.uk

ST MARY'S CHURCH ⛪
Wormsley, Hereford, Herefordshire HR4 8LY
Tel: 0845 303 2760 E-mail: central@thecct.org.uk

ATTINGHAM PARK ❦
Atcham, Shrewsbury, Shropshire SY4 4TP
Tel: 01743 708170/162 E-mail: attingham@nationaltrust.org.uk

CHURCH OF ST MARY MAGDELENE ⛪
Battlefield, Shrewsbury, Shropshire SY1 1DX
Tel: 0845 303 2760 E-mail: central@thecct.org.uk

HAWKSTONE HALL & GARDENS
Marchamley, Shrewsbury, Shropshire SY4 5LG
Tel: 01630 685242 E-mail: hawkhall@aol.com

MAWLEY HALL
Cleobury Mortimer DY14 8PN
Tel: 0208 298 0429 E-mail: rsharp@mawley.com

MUCH WENLOCK PRIORY ⌗
Much Wenlock, Shropshire TF13 6HS
Tel: 01952 727466 E-mail: customers@english-heritage.org.uk

ST JAMES' CHURCH ⛪
Off Stirchley Road, Stirchley Village, Telford, Shrops TF3 1DY
Tel: 0845 303 2760 E-mail: central@thecct.org.uk

ST LEONARD'S CHURCH ⛪
Linley, Barrow, Shropshire TF12 5JU
Tel: 0845 303 2760 E-mail: central@thecct.org.uk

ST LEONARD'S CHURCH ⛪
St Leonards Close, Bridgnorth, Shropshire WV16 4EJ
Tel: 0845 303 2760 E-mail: central@thecct.org.uk

ST MARTIN'S CHURCH ⛪
Preston Gubbals, Shrewsbury, Shropshire SY4 3AN
Tel: 0845 303 2760 E-mail: central@thecct.org.uk

ST MICHAEL'S CHURCH ⛪
Upton Cressett, Bridgnorth, Shropshire WV16 6UH
Tel: 0845 303 2760 E-mail: central@thecct.org.uk

ST PETER'S CHURCH ⛪
Adderley Road, Adderley, Market Drayton, Shropshire TF9 3TD
Tel: 0845 303 2760 E-mail: central@thecct.org.uk

STOKESAY CASTLE ⌗
Nr Craven Arms, Shropshire SY7 9AH
Tel: 01588 672544 E-mail: customers@english-heritage.org.uk

TALBOT CHAPEL ⛪
Longford Road, Longford, Newport, Shropshire TF10 8LR
Tel: 0845 303 2760 E-mail: central@thecct.org.uk

WROXETER ROMAN CITY ⌗
Wroxeter, Shrewsbury, Shropshire SY5 6PH
Tel: 01743 761330 E-mail: customers@english-heritage.org.uk

BOSCOBEL HOUSE & THE ROYAL OAK ⌗
Bishop's Wood, Brewood, Staffordshire ST19 9AR
Tel: 01902 850244 E-mail: customers@english-heritage.org.uk

ERASMUS DARWIN HOUSE
Beacon Street, Lichfield, Staffordshire WS13 7AD
Tel: 01543 306260 E-mail: enquiries@erasmusdarwin.org

MOSELEY OLD HALL ❦
Moseley Old Hall Lane, Wolverhampton WV10 7HY
Tel: 01902 782808 E-mail: moseleyoldhall@nationaltrust.org.uk

ST MARY'S CHURCH ⛪
Patshull Hall, Burnhill Green, Wolverhampton WV6 7HY
Tel: 0845 303 2760 E-mail: central@thecct.org.uk

SANDON HALL 🏠
Sandon, Staffordshire ST18 OBZ
Tel: 01889 508004 E-mail: info@sandonhall.co.uk

THE TRENTHAM ESTATE
Stone Road, Trentham, Staffordshire ST4 8AX
Tel: 01782 646646 E-mail: enquiry@trentham.co.uk

BAGOTS CASTLE
Bagots Castle, Church Road, Baginton CV8 3AR
Tel: 07786 438711 E-mail: delia@bagotscastle.org.uk

CHURCH OF ST JOHN THE BAPTIST ⛪
Avon Dassett, Southam, Warwickshire CV47 2AH
Tel: 0845 303 2760 E-mail: central@thecct.org.uk

CHURCH OF ST MICHAEL & ALL ANGELS ⛪
Brownsover Lane, Brownsover, Rugby, Warwicks CV21 1HY
Tel: 0845 303 2760 E-mail: central@thecct.org.uk

COUGHTON COURT 🏠ⓕ🌿
Alcester, Warwickshire B49 5JA
Tel: 01789 400777 **E-mail:** coughtoncourt@nationaltrust.org.uk

FARNBOROUGH HALL 🌿
Banbury OX17 1DU
Tel: 01295 690002 **E-mail:** farnboroughhall@nationaltrust.org.uk

KENILWORTH CASTLE & GARDEN ⌗
Kenilworth, Warwickshire CV8 1NE
Tel: 01926 852 078 **E-mail:** customers@english-heritage.org.uk

PACKWOOD HOUSE 🌿
Lapworth, Solihull B94 6AT
Tel: 01564 783294 **E-mail:** packwood@nationaltrust.org.uk

ST PETER'S CHURCH 🏛
Wolfhamcote, Rugby, Warwickshire CV23 8AR
Tel: 0845 303 2760 **E-mail:** central@thecct.org.uk

UPTON HOUSE & GARDENS 🌿
Upton, Near Banbury, Warwickshire OX15 6HT
Tel: 01295 670266 **E-mail:** uptonhouse@nationaltrust.org.uk

BACK TO BACKS 🌿
55-63 Hurst Street, Birmingham, West Midlands B5 4TE
E-mail: backtobacks@nationaltrust.org.uk

HAGLEY HALL
Hall Lane, Hagley, Nr. Stourbridge, Worcestershire DY9 9LG
Tel: 01562 882408 **E-mail:** joycepurnell@hagleyhall.com

ALL SAINTS' CHURCH 🏛
Spetchley, Worcester, Worcestershire WR5 1RS
Tel: 0845 303 2760 **E-mail:** central@thecct.org.uk

CHURCH OF ST JOHN THE BAPTIST 🏛
Church Road, Strensham, Pershore, Worcestershire WR8 9LW
Tel: 0845 303 2760 **E-mail:** central@thecct.org.uk

HANBURY HALL 🌿
Droitwich, Worcestershire WR9 7EA
Tel: 01527 821214 **E-mail:** hanburyhall@nationaltrust.org.uk

ST BARTHOLEMEW'S CHURCH 🏛
Lower Sapey, Worcester, Worcestershire WR6 6HE
Tel: 0845 303 2760 **E-mail:** central@thecct.org.uk

ST MICHAEL'S CHURCH 🏛
Edwards Lane, Churchill, Worcester, Worcestershire WR7 4QE
Tel: 0845 303 2760 **E-mail:** central@thecct.org.uk

ST SWITHUN'S CHURCH 🏛
Church Street, Worcester, Worcestershire WR1 2RH
Tel: 0845 303 2760 **E-mail:** central@thecct.org.uk

SPETCHLEY PARK GARDENS 🏠ⓕ
Spetchley Park, Worcester WR5 1RS
Tel: 01453 810303 **E-mail:** hb@spetchleygardens.co.uk

WITLEY COURT & GARDENS ⌗
Great Witley, Worcestershire WR6 6JT
Tel: 01299 896636 **E-mail:** customers@english-heritage.org.uk

© Compton Verney

Compton Verney

Nunnington Hall, North Yorkshire
©National Trust Images

Burton Constable Hall,
East Yorkshire

East Yorkshire
North Yorkshire
South Yorkshire
West Yorkshire

Yorkshire & The Humber

Yorkshire

Great houses and gardens founded on agricultural trading and industrial riches surround the historic county town and regional capital of York.

New Entries for 2015:
• Nunnington Hall

Find stylish hotels with a personal welcome and good cuisine in Yorkshire & The Humber. More information on page 364.

- The Blue Bell Inn
- The Coniston Hotel & Country Estate
- Lastingham Grange

- Raithwaite Estate
- Sportsman's Arms Hotel & Restaurant
- The Traddock

WASSAND HALL
SEATON, HULL, EAST YORKSHIRE HU11 5RJ
www.wassand.co.uk

Fine Regency house 1815 by Thomas Cundy the Elder. Beautifully restored walled gardens, woodland walks, Parks and vistas over Hornsea Mere, part of the Estate since 1580. The Estate was purchased circa 1520 by Dame Jane Constable and has remained in the family to the present day, Mr Rupert Russell being the great nephew of the late Lady Strickland-Constable.

The house contains a fine collection of 18/19th Century paintings, English and Continental silver, furniture and porcelain. Wassand is very much a family home and retains a very friendly atmosphere. Homemade afternoon teas are served in the conservatory on Open Days.

Location: Map 11:F9. OS Ref TA174 460. On the B1244 Seaton-Hornsea Road. Approximately 2m from Hornsea.

Owner/Contact: R E O Russell - Resident Trustee
Tel/Fax: 01964 534488 **E-mail:** reorussell@lineone.net
Open: 22-25 May (May 25 Vintage Car Rally TBC); 4-8, 19-23 Jun; 10, 11 & 12 Jul (12 East Yorkshire youth Wind band concert), 24-31 Jul; (Sat 1 Aug Closed) 2 & 3, & 28-31 Aug.
Admission: Hall & Gardens: Adult £6.00, OAP £5.50, Child (11-15yrs) £3.00, Child (under 10) Free. Hall: Adult £4.00, OAP £3.50, Child (11-15yrs) £1.50, Child (under 10) Free. Grounds & Garden: Adult £4.00, OAP £3.50, Child (11-15yrs) £1.50, Child (under 10) Free. Guided tours and groups by arrangment - POA.
Key facts: ⬚ Limited. ⬚ ⬚ By arrangement. ⬚ Ample for cars, limited for coaches. ⬚ In grounds, on leads.

BURTON CONSTABLE ⬚Ⓕ
Skirlaugh, East Yorkshire HU11 4LN
www.burtonconstable.com

This truly hidden gem has 30 rooms filled with fine furniture, paintings, sculpture and a Cabinet of Curiosities. Explore our magnificent parkland, and newly restored 18th century stables with a Carriage House, Tack Rooms, Clock Tower, Stable Lad's Bedchamber, Stable Master's Sitting Room and not forgetting Moby Dick, the skeleton of a 58' sperm whale.

Location: Map 11:E10. OS Ref TA 193 369. Beverley 14m, Hull 10m. Signed from Skirlaugh. **Owner:** Burton Constable Foundation **Contact:** Mrs Helen Dewson
Tel: 01964 562400 **E-mail:** enquiries@burtonconstable.com
Open: Easter Sat to 25 Oct: Sat-Thu inclusive (every day in Jul & Aug). Christmas Opening 21 Nov to 13 Dec. Tea Room, Grounds, Stables, & Gift Shop 11am-5pm. Hall: 12noon-5pm, 11am-4pm Christmas, (last adm 1 hour before closing).
Admission: Adult £8.75, Child £4.50, OAP £8.25, Family £22.00 (2 adults & 4 children). Prices include 10% Gift Aid. **Key facts:** ⬚ Photography. ⬚ Small gift shop. ⬚ Seminars/meetings. ⬚ Mostly accessible. ⬚ Stables Tea Room. ⬚ A variety of tours can be arranged in advance of your visit. ⬚ Ample free parking. ⬚ Indoor and outdoor. ⬚ On leads in grounds. Guide dogs only in the hall. ⬚

BURTON AGNES HALL & GARDENS ⬚Ⓕ
Driffield, East Yorkshire YO25 4NB

Built in 1598 Burton Agnes Hall is a magnificent example of Elizabethan architecture filled with treasures collected over four centuries. Lawns and topiary bushes surround the Hall and an award winning garden contains a maze, potager, giant games, jungle garden and three thousand plant species. There is a woodland walk; picnic and children's play area.

Location: Map 11:E9. OS Ref TA103 633. Off A614 between Driffield and Bridlington. **Owner:** Burton Agnes Hall Preservation Trust Ltd
Contact: Mr Simon Cunliffe-Lister **Tel:** 01262 490324
Fax: 01262 490513 **E-mail:** office@burtonagnes.com
Website: www.burtonagnes.com **Open:** 1 Apr-31 Oct 11am-5pm. 14 Nov-23 Dec 11am-5pm. **Admission:** Hall & Gardens: Adult £9.00, OAP £8.50, Child £4.50, Under 5's Free. Gardens only, Adult £6.00, OAP £5.50, Child £3.50.
Key facts: ⬚ Gift Shop and home and garden shop. ⬚ ⬚ ⬚ WCs. ⬚ Licensed. ⬚ Licensed. ⬚ ⬚ ⬚ Dogs on leads only. ⬚

SLEDMERE HOUSE ⬚Ⓕ
Sledmere, Driffield, East Yorkshire YO25 3XG

At the heart of the Yorkshire Wolds, Sledmere House exudes 18th Century elegance with each room containing decorative plasterwork by Joseph Rose Junior.
Location: Map 11:D9. OS Ref SE931 648. **Tel:** 01377 236637
E-mail: info@sledmerehouse.com **Website:** www.sledmerehouse.com
Open: Please see website for up to date opening and admission details.

CASTLE HOWARD 🏛ⓕ
www.castlehoward.co.uk

Designed by Sir John Vanbrugh in 1699 Castle Howard is undoubtedly one of Britain's finest private residences.

Built for Charles Howard the 3rd Earl of Carlisle, Castle Howard remains home to the Howard family. Its dramatic interiors - with impressive painted and gilded dome - contain world-renowned collections including furniture, porcelain, sculpture and paintings; all gathered by succeeding generations. In each room friendly and knowledgeable guides will share with you the stories of the family and their influence in shaping the fortunes of Castle Howard.

The High South apartments, so tragically destroyed by fire in 1940, are now open to the public. During the 2008 film remake of Brideshead Revisited, the once bare shell was transformed into a film set and remains so today. An accompanying exhibition tells the story of the great fire of 1940 and how Evelyn Waugh's novel came to be filmed, not just once, but twice at Castle Howard.

Designed on a monumental scale, the breathtaking grounds reflect the grandeur of the house. With statues, lakes, temples and fountains, memorable sights include The Temple of the Four Winds, the Mausoleum and New River Bridge. Garden enthusiasts will enjoy the 18th Century Walled Garden with its collection of roses and ornamental vegetable garden. While Ray Wood, the woodland garden widely acknowledged as a 'rare botanical jewel', features a unique collection of trees, shrubs, rhododendrons, magnolias and azaleas.

Attractions include a changing programme of exhibitions and family events, plus free outdoor tours and illustrated children's trail. There is also an adventure playground, summer boat trips on the Great Lake (weather permitting), and a choice of cafés and shops, including garden centre, farm shop and gift shops.

KEY FACTS

- **ⓘ** Photography allowed.
- **🍸** Licensed for civil weddings.
- **♿** Access to all areas except High South, Exhibition Wing and Chapel.
- **☕** Choice of four Cafés.
- **🚶** Guides in each room.
- **P** Free parking.
- **🏫** School parties welcome.
- **🐕** Dogs welcome.
- **⛺** Camping and caravanning.
- **❄** Gardens, shops and cafés open all year.
- **👪** Full programme for all the family.

Yorkshire & The Humber - England

VISITOR INFORMATION

■ Address
Skipton Castle
Skipton
North Yorkshire
BD23 1AW

■ Location
Map 10:09
OS Ref. SD992 520
In the centre of Skipton, at the N end of High Street. Skipton is 20m W of Harrogate on the A59 and 26m NW of Leeds on A65.
Rail: Regular services from Leeds & Bradford.

■ Contact
Judith Parker
Tel: 01756 792442
Fax: 01756 796100
E-mail: info@ skiptoncastle.co.uk

■ Opening Times
All year
(closed 25 December)
Mon-Sat 10am-6pm
Suns 12 noon-6pm
(October-February 4pm).

■ Admission
Adult	£7.50
Child (0-4yrs)	Free
Child (5-17yrs)	£4.70
OAP	£6.60
Student (with ID)	£6.60
Family (2+3)	£24.20

Groups (15+)	
Adult	£6.40
Child (0-17yrs)	£4.70

Includes illustrated tour sheet in a choice of ten languages, plus free badge for children.

Groups welcome - Coach parking and guides available for pre-booked groups at no extra charge.

■ Special Events
Historical Re-enactments. Plays. Art Exhibitions. For up-to-date information and coming events, see our website www.skiptoncastle.co.uk.

Conference/Function
Room	Size	Max Cap
Oak Room		30
Granary		100

SKIPTON CASTLE
www.skiptoncastle.co.uk

Skipton Castle, over 900 years old, one of the best preserved, most complete medieval castles in England.

Guardian of the gateway to the Yorkshire Dales for over 900 years, this unique fortress is one of the most complete, well-preserved medieval castles in England. Standing on a 40-metre high crag, fully-roofed Skipton Castle was founded around 1090 by Robert de Romille, one of William the Conqueror's Barons, as a fortress in the dangerous northern reaches of the kingdom.

Owned by King Edward I and Edward II, from 1310 it became the stronghold of the Clifford Lords withstanding successive raids by marauding Scots. During the Civil War it was the last Royalist bastion in the North, yielding only after a three-year siege in 1645. 'Slighted' under the orders of Cromwell, the castle was skillfully restored by the redoubtable Lady Anne Clifford and today visitors can climb from the depths of the Dungeon to the top of the Watch Tower, explore the Banqueting Hall, Kitchens, the Bedchamber and even the Privy!

Every period has left its mark, from the Norman entrance and the medieval towers, to the beautiful Tudor courtyard with the great yew tree planted by Lady Anne in 1659.

In the grounds visitors can see the Tudor wing built as a royal wedding present for Lady Eleanor Brandon, niece of Henry VIII, the beautiful Shell Room decorated in the 1620s with shells and Jamaican coral and the ancient medieval chapel of St. John the Evangelist. The Chapel Terrace, with its delightful picnic area, has fine views over the woods and Skipton's lively market town.

KEY FACTS

ℹ	Fully roofed. Photography allowed for personal use only.
	Specialist books, cards, gifts. Online shop.
	Unusual plants grown in grounds.
	Corporate hospitality. Wedding ceremonies. Champagne receptions.
♿	Unsuitable.
	Licensed. Open all year.
⑂	Licensed. Open all year.
	By arrangement.
P	Large public coach and car park nearby.
	Tour guides, educational rooms and teachers packs available.
	Dogs on leads only.
	Civil Wedding Licence. Max 80 guests.
❋	Open all year except 25th December.

FOUNTAINS ABBEY & STUDLEY ROYAL ✤
RIPON, NORTH YORKSHIRE HG4 3DY
www.nationaltrust.org.uk/fountainsabbey

Come and discover for yourself why Fountains Abbey & Studley Royal is a World Heritage Site. Experience the beauty, history and tranquillity of this inspirational place in the heart of the beautiful North Yorkshire countryside. Explore the spectacular ruin of a 12th Century Cistercian Abbey, one of the best surviving examples of a Georgian Water Garden, Elizabethan Manor House, Monastic Watermill and Medieval Deer Park home to over 500 wild deer.

Enjoy exhibitions, guided tours, family activities and wildlife walks throughout the year. **Location:** Map 10:P8. OS Ref SE275 700. Abbey entrance: 4m W of Ripon off B6265. 8m W of A1.

Owner: National Trust

Contact: The National Trust

Tel: 01765 608888

E-mail: fountainsabbey@nationaltrust.org.uk

Open: Apr-Sep Daily: 10am-5pm. Oct-Mar Daily: 10am-4pm or dusk if earlier. Closed 24/25 Dec, & Fri from Nov-Jan. Deer Park: All year, daily during daylight. Closed 24/25 Dec.

Admission: Adult £12.10, Child (5-16yrs) £6.05, Family £30.25, Groups (15+) Adult £9.90, Groups (31+) Adult £9.60. Group discount applicable with prior booking. Telephone in advance, 01765 643197.

NT, EH Members & Under 5s Free. Group visits and disabled visitors, please telephone in advance.

Includes voluntary donation, visitors can choose to pay standard prices displayed at property and website. Does not apply to group prices.

Key facts: ℹ️ Events held throughout the year. Exhibitions. Seminar facilities. The Abbey is owned by English Heritage. St Mary's Church is owned by English Heritage and managed by the National Trust.

🏬 Two shops. 🍴 🍽 Dinners. ♿ WCs. 🍷 Licensed. 🍴 Licensed.

🎫 Free, but seasonal. Groups (please book on 01765 643197), please use Visitor Centre entrance.

🎧 Audio tour £2.00. 🅿️ Drivers must book groups. 🐕 Dogs on leads only.

🏰 Fountains Hall, an Elizabethan Mansion is an ideal setting for weddings. For details or a Wedding pack tel: 01765 643198. ❄ ♥

KIPLIN HALL AND GARDENS 🏛️Ⓕ ✦
NR SCORTON, RICHMOND, NORTH YORKSHIRE DL10 6AT
www.kiplinhall.co.uk

This Jacobean country seat of the founder of Maryland, George Calvert is an award-winning historic house and garden. 'Gothic' wing added in the 1820s and redesigned in 1887 by W.E. Nesfield. This intriguing property is now furnished as a comfortable Victorian home with an eclectic mix of previous owners' furniture, paintings, portraits and personalia, including many Arts and Crafts items. Numerous original paintings from 16th–19th Centuries include works by Beuckelaer, Carlevarijs, Kauffman, Lady Waterford and Watts. Ornamental Gardens, productive Walled Garden, woodland/lakeside walks. Award-winning tea room. Children's Play Ship, garden games, dipping-pond.

2015 Exhibition – Charting Chipeling – The Archaeology of the Kiplin Estate.

Location: Map 11:A7. OS Ref SE274 976. Midway between Richmond &

Northallerton, 5 miles east of A1, on B6271 Scorton – Northallerton road.

Owner: Kiplin Hall CIO **Tel:** 01748 818178 **E-mail:** info@kiplinhall.co.uk

Open: Gardens and Tea Room: Sun, Mon, Tue & Wed from 1 Feb until 28 Oct, 10am–5pm (4pm Feb & March). Also Good Fri & Easter Sat. Hall: Good Fri & Easter Sat 3 & 4 Apr and then Sun, Mon, Tue & Wed from 5 Apr, 2pm–5pm until 28 Oct. Christmas: Fri–Sun 4–6 and 11–13 Dec, 10am–4pm.

Admission: Hall/Gardens/Grounds: Adult £8.30, Conc. £7.30, Child £4.30, Family (2+3) £24.50. Gardens/Grounds only: Adult £5.30, Conc. £4.30, Child £2.30, Family (2+3) £14.50.

Key facts: ℹ️ Special Events - see website for details.

🏬 🍴 🍽 ♿ Partial. WCs. 🍷 🎫 By arrangement. 🅿️ 🐕 In grounds only. ♥

MARKENFIELD HALL 🏠Ⓕ
NR RIPON, NORTH YORKSHIRE HG4 3AD
www.markenfield.com

"This wonderfully little-altered building is the most complete surviving example of the medium-sized 14th century country house in England" John Martin Robinson The Architecture of Northern England. Tucked privately away down a mile-long winding drive, Markenfield is one of the most astonishing and romantic of Yorkshire's medieval houses: fortified, completely moated, and still privately owned. Winner of the HHA and Sotheby's Finest Restoration Award 2008.
Location: Map 10:P8. OS Ref SE294 672. Access from W side of A61. 2½ miles S of the Ripon bypass.

Owner: Mr Ian & Lady Deirdre Curteis **Contact:** The Administrator
Tel: 01765 692303 **Fax:** 01765 607195 **E-mail:** info@markenfield.com
Open: Open 2 - 17 May and 13 - 28 Jun daily 2pm - 5pm. Last entry 4:30pm. Groups bookings can be accepted all year round by appointment.
Admission: Prices £5.00 Adult, £4.00 conc. Booked groups £6.00 per person for a guided tour (min charge £100).
Key facts: ⓘ 📷 🎁 🍽 🚻 ♿ Partial. Wheelchair access to the ground floor only. 🅿 🔴 🐾 Dogs in grounds only. 🏠 ♿

© Peter Packer

NEWBY HALL & GARDENS 🏠Ⓕ
NEWBY HALL, RIPON, NORTH YORKSHIRE HG4 5AE
www.newbyhall.com

Designed under the guidance of Sir Christopher Wren, this graceful country house, home to the Compton family, epitomises the Georgian 'Age of Elegance'. Its beautifully restored interior presents Robert Adam at his best and houses rare Gobelins tapestries and one of the UK's largest private collections of classical statuary. The award winning gardens, created in the early 1920s boast one of Europe's longest double herbaceous borders and are of interest to specialist and amateur gardeners alike. Newby also offers a large, thoughtfully designed Adventure Garden for children, a miniature railway, excellent restaurant, shop and plant centre. Events: 10 May - Spring Plant Fair, 6 & 7 Jun - Tractor Fest, 19 Jul - Historic Vehicle Rally.
Location: Map 11:A8. OS Ref SE348 675. Midway between London and Edinburgh, 4m W of A1(M), towards Ripon. From north use J49, from south use J48 and follow brown tourist signs. 40 mins from York, 30 mins from Harrogate.
Owner: Mr Richard Compton **Contact:** The Administrator
Tel: 01423 322583 opt 3 **Fax:** 01423 324452

E-mail: info@newbyhall.com
Open: Summer- House*, 1 Apr-27 Sep. Apr, May, Jun & Sep: Tue-Sun & BH Mons; Jul-Aug: Daily. See website for tour times. *Areas of the House can be closed to the public from time to time, please check website for details. Garden, dates as House, 11am-5.30pm. last admission 5pm. Winter, Oct-end Mar closed.
Admission: See website for 2015 prices.
Key facts: ⓘ Allow a full day for viewing house and gardens. Suitable for filming and for special events. No indoor photography. 📷 'The Shop @ Newby Hall' - Modern British Art and Craftsmanship. Quality toys. 🌱 Quality plants available, reflecting the contents of the garden. 🍽 Wedding receptions & special functions. Licensed for civil ceremonies. ♿ Suitable. WCs. Parking. Electric and manual wheelchairs available - booking essential. 🍴 Licensed. 🍴 Licensed. ⓘ Obligatory. 🅿 Ample. Hard standing for coaches. 🔴 Welcome. Rates on request. Woodland discovery walk, adventure gardens and train rides. 🐾 Guide/hearing dogs only in Gardens/Woodland. Dog exercise area. 🏠 House licensed. ♿

NUNNINGTON HALL
NUNNINGTON, NORTH YORKSHIRE YO62 5UY
www.nationaltrust.org.uk/nunnington-hall

Picturesque Yorkshire manor house with organic garden and exciting exhibitions. Enjoy the atmosphere of this beautiful Yorkshire manor house, nestled on the quiet banks of the River Rye. Explore the period rooms whilst hearing the Hall's many tales and discover one of the world's finest collections of miniature rooms in the attic. Famed for its picturesque location, organic walled garden with spring-flowering meadows, flamboyant resident peacocks and a changing programme of exclusive and high profile art and photography exhibitions, Nunnington Hall offers something for everyone to enjoy.

Location: Map 11:C8. OS Ref SE669 793. In Ryedale, 4½ m SE of Helmsley, 1½ m N of B1257. **Owner:** National Trust **Contact:** The Property Manager

Tel: 01439 748283 **E-mail:** nunningtonhall@nationaltrust.org.uk
Open: 14 Feb-1 Nov, daily except Mons, 11am-5pm. 7 Nov-13 Dec, Sats & Suns, 11am-4pm. Last adm. 30min before closing. BH Mons & Mons in school holidays.
Admission: Adult £8.25, Child (under 17) £4.15, Family £20.65, Groups (15+) £6.75. National Trust Members Free. *includes voluntary donation but visitors can choose to pay standard prices displayed at the property and on website.
Key facts: A newly expanded shop for 2015 with an increased array of wonderful souvenirs and gifts. Ground floor and grounds. WC. Waitress service in our beautiful tea-room, serving local and seasonal produce. Guide dogs only in the hall. Dogs on a lead in the gardens.

BOLTON CASTLE
Bolton Castle, Nr Leyburn, North Yorkshire DL8 4ET
www.boltoncastle.co.uk

Bolton is one of the country's best preserved medieval castles. Completed in 1399, its scars bear testament to over 600 years of fascinating history, including Mary Queen of Scots' imprisonment and a Civil War siege. Enjoy our magnificent falconry experience, fascinating archery demonstrations and exciting Wild Boar feeding time. Explore our beautiful medieval gardens and maze and visit our wonderful tea room serving homemade and locally sourced light lunches, cakes and refreshments. **Location:** Map 10:07. OS Ref SE034 918. Approx 6m W of Leyburn. 1m NW of Redmire **Owner:** Lord Bolton **Contact:** Katie Boggis
Tel: 01969 623981 **E-mail:** info@boltoncastle.co.uk
Open: Open daily 10am-5pm from mid Feb - to the end of Oct (10am-4pm in Feb/Mar). Please note we may close early on occasional Sat/Sun due to weddings. Please check in advance.
Admission: Castle and Garden: Adults: £8.50, Conc/Child: £7.00, Family: £30.00.
Key facts: Group discounts and guided tours available when booked in advance. Gift and souvenir shop. Audio Visual App available. Parking fee is refundable. No Dogs.

BROUGHTON HALL ESTATE
Skipton, Yorkshire BD23 3AE
www.broughtonhall.co.uk

Broughton Hall Estate has been nurtured by the Tempest Family for over 900 years. Guests can exclusively hire any one of the three exquisite venues from contemporary Utopia, luxury holiday retreat Eden and the stately home itself, available all year round for residential stays, celebrations and corporate events. Our sister estate offers similar hospitality packages: Aldourie Castle Estate, Loch Ness, Scotland www.aldouriecastle.co.uk.
Location: Map 10:N9. OS Ref SD943 507. On A59, 2m W of Skipton.
Owner: The Tempest Family **Contact:** The Estate Office
Tel: 01756 799608 **Fax:** 01756 700357 **Email:** info@broughtonhall.co.uk
E-mail: tempest@broughtonhall.co.uk
Open: Show rounds by prior arrangement. **Admission:** P.O.A
Key facts: Meetings & Events space in the Hall or Utopia. Licensed. Licensed. By arrangement. Ample car parking onsite. Available only at short notice & depending on availability. Broughton Hall, Utopia, Eden, Higher Scarcliffe. 15 luxury en suite bedrooms sleeping 29 guests. Please enquire for Christmas & New Year packages.

CONSTABLE BURTON HALL GARDENS 🏛ⓕ
Leyburn, North Yorkshire DL8 5LJ
www.constableburton.com

A delightful terraced woodland garden of lilies, ferns, hardy shrubs, roses and wild flowers surrounds this beautiful Palladian house designed by John Carr. Garden trails and herbaceous borders and stream garden with large architectural plants and reflection ponds. Stunning seasonal displays of snowdrops and daffodils. An annual Tulip Festival takes place over the early May Bank Holiday weekend. Group tours of the House and Gardens are invited by prior arrangement.
Location: Map 10:P7. OS Ref SE164 913.
3m E of Leyburn off the A684.
Owner/Contact: M C A Wyvill Esq
Tel: 01677 450428 **Fax:** 01677 450622
E-mail: gardens@constableburton.com
Open: Garden open season 2015: Sat 21 Mar-Sun 27 Sep. Tulip Festival: Sat 2, Sun 3 & Mon 4 May. Please consult website for exceptional closures for private events. **Admission:** Adult £4.00, Child (5-16yrs) 50p, OAP £3.00.
Key facts: 🍴 🔲 WCs. 🎦 🅿 Limited for coaches. 🐕 On leads only. ♿

FAIRFAX HOUSE 🏛ⓕ
Fairfax House, Castlegate, York, North Yorkshire YO1 9RN
www.fairfaxhouse.co.uk

Containing a superb collection of 18th Century furniture, clocks, paintings and decorative arts, Fairfax House reveals the elegance of city living in Georgian York.
Location: Map 11:B9. OS Ref SE605 515. In the centre of York between Castle Museum and Jorvik Centre.
Owner: York Civic Trust **Contact:** Hannah Phillip
Tel: 01904 655543 **Fax:** 01904 652262
E-mail: info@fairfaxhouse.co.uk
Open: Closed 24, 25 & 26 Dec & 1 Jan-6 Feb. 7 Feb-31 Dec, Mons: Guided tours only (11am and 2pm), Tue-Sat & BHs: 10am-5pm. Sun: 11-3.30pm. Last admission half an hour before stated closing times.
Admission: Adult £6.00, Conc. £5.00, Children under 16 Free with full paying adult. Groups from £4.50 pp (min 10 persons).
Key facts: 🔲 Suitable for filming. No photography in house. 📷 🍴 The dining facilities can accommodate up to 30 people (min of 15). 🔲 Partial. 🎦 By arrangement. 🎧 🅿 🐕 Guide dogs only. ❋ ♿

DUNCOMBE PARK 🏛ⓕ
Helmsley, North Yorkshire YO62 5EB
www.duncombepark.com

The sweeping grass terraces, towering veteran trees, and classical temples are described by historian Christopher Hussey as 'the most spectacularly beautiful among English landscape conceptions of the 18th Century'. Beside superb views over the Rye valley, visitors will discover woodland walks, ornamental parterres, and a 'secret garden' at the Conservatory.
Location: Map 11:B7. OS Ref SE604 830. Entrance just off Helmsley Market Square, signed off A170 Thirsk-Scarborough road.
Owner/Contact: Hon Jake Duncombe
Tel: 01439 770213 **Fax:** 01439 771114 **E-mail:** info@duncombepark.com
Open: Garden Only: 7 Apr-31 Aug, Sun-Fri, 10:30am-5pm. The garden may close for private events and functions - please check website for information.
Admission: Gardens & Parkland: Adult £5.00, Conc £4.50, Child (5-16yrs) £3.00, Child (0-5yrs) Free, Groups (15+) £4.00, Group guided tour £5.00. Parkland: Adult £1.00, Child (0-16yrs) Free.
Key facts: 🔲 Wedding receptions, conferences, corporate hospitality, country walks, nature reserve, orienteering, film location, product launches, vehicle rallies. 🍴 Banqueting facilities. 📷 🎦 For 15+ groups only. 🅿 🐕 🏠 ♿

THE FORBIDDEN CORNER LTD
Tupgill Park Estate, Coverham, Nr Middleham
North Yorkshire DL8 4TJ
www.theforbiddencorner.co.uk

A unique labyrinth of tunnels, chambers, follies and surprises created in a four acre garden in the heart of the Yorkshire dales. The Temple of the Underworld, The Eye of the Needle, a large pyramid made of translucent glass paths and passageways that lead nowhere. Extraordinary statues at every turn. A day out with a difference that will challenge and delight children and adults of all ages.
Location: Map 10:07. OS Ref SE094 866. A6108 to Middleham, situated 2½ miles west of Middleham on the Coverham Lane. **Owner:** Colin R Armstrong CMG, OBE **Contact:** John or Wendy Reeves **Tel:** 01969 640638
Fax: 01969 640687 **E-mail:** forbiddencorner@gmail.com
Open: 1 Apr-2 Nov daily, then every Sun until Christmas. Mon-Sat 12-6pm. Suns & BHs 10am-6pm (or dusk if earlier). **Admission:** See www.theforbiddencorner.co.uk for up to date info & prices.
Key facts: 🔲 📷 Gifts & mementoes. 🔲 Partial. WCs. Ramps into shop. ☕ Own blend coffee, locally sourced food & award winning pies & teas. 🅿 Limited spaces for coaches. 🎦 Special rates (see our website). 🐕 Guide dogs only. 🏠 Self catering cottages all year. Free day pass with all stays. ❋

HOVINGHAM HALL 🏠ⓕ
Hovingham, York, North Yorkshire YO62 4LU
www.hovingham.co.uk

Attractive Palladian family home, designed and built by Thomas Worsley. The childhood home of Katharine Worsley, Duchess of Kent. It is entered through a huge riding school and has beautiful rooms with collections of pictures and furniture. The house has attractive gardens with magnificent Yew hedges and cricket ground.

Location: Map 11:C8. OS Ref SE666 756. 18m N of York on Malton/Helmsley Road (B1257). **Owner:** Sir William Worsley
Contact: The Estate Office
Tel: 01653 628771 **Fax:** 01653 628668
E-mail: office@hovingham.co.uk
Open: 1-28 Jun inclusive 12.30pm-4.30pm; Guided tours only (last tour at 3.30pm); Tea Room open daily 1pm-4pm.
Admission: Adult £9.50, Concessions £9.00, Child £4.00, Gardens only £5.00.
Key facts: ⓘ No photography permitted in the Hall. 🍵 🚻 Ground floor only. 📷 Tea room open daily 1pm-4pm, 1 Jun to 28 Jun inc. 👣 Obligatory. 🅿 Limited. None for coaches. 🐕 Dogs not permitted, with the exception of assistance dogs.

NEWBURGH PRIORY
Coxwold, York, North Yorkshire YO61 4AS
www.newburghpriory.co.uk

Home to the Earls of Fauconberg and the Wombwell family the house was built in 1145 with alterations in 1538 and 1720 and contains the tomb of Oliver Cromwell. The beautiful grounds contain a lake, water garden, walled garden, amazing topiary yews and woodland walks set against the White Horse.

Location: Map 11:B8. OS Ref SE541 764.
4m E of A19, 18m N of York, ½ m E of Coxwold.
Owner/Contact: Stephen Wombwell **Tel:** 01347 868372
E-mail: estateoffice@newburghpriory.co.uk
Open: 1 Apr-28 Jun, Wed & Sun. BH Mon 25 May & 31 Aug. Gardens 2-6pm, House 2.30-4.45pm. Tours every ½ hour. Bus parties by prior arrangement. Special tours of private apartments Wed 1, 8, 15, 22 & 29 Apr, £5.00pp.
Admission: House & Gardens: Adult £6.00, Child £2.00.
Gardens only: Adult £3.00, Child Free.
Key facts: ⓘ No photography in house. 🍵 🚻 Partial. 📷 👣 Obligatory. 🅿 Limited for coaches. 🐕 In grounds, on leads. 💍 And wedding receptions. 🎗

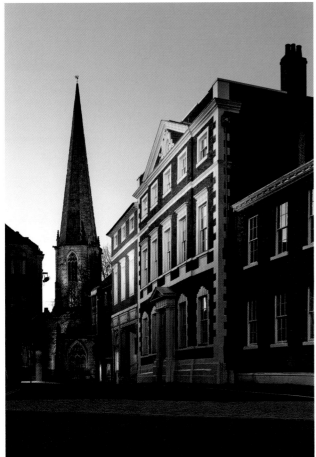

Fairfax House

SCAMPSTON WALLED GARDEN 🏠ⓕ
Scampston Hall, Malton, North Yorkshire YO17 8NG
www.scampston.co.uk/gardens

A contemporary garden with striking perennial meadow planting that explodes with colour in the summer. Created by acclaimed designer and plantsman, Piet Oudolf, the garden also contains traditional spring/autumn borders and a green "silent garden". The dramatic use of grasses, bulbs and unusual shrubs extend the season. Newly opened in 2015 is a Victorian conservatory with exhibitions, educational space and a programme of events.

Location: Map 11:D8. OS Ref SE865 755. 5m E of Malton, off A64.
Owner: Christopher Legard **Contact:** Anne Ainsley
Tel: 01944 759111 **E-mail:** info@scampston.co.uk
Open: 3 Apr-1 Nov, Tue-Sun plus BH Mons 10am-5pm, last adm. 4.30pm.
Admission: Adult £7.00, Child (5-16) £3.50, Under 5s Free. Groups (15+) welcome by arrangement. **Key facts:** ⓘ Spring Plant Fair 31 May. Please see website for exhibitions and events. 📷 👣 Plant sales area specialising in plants growing in the garden. 🍵 Restaurant and Conservatory available for corporate events. 🚻 Suitable. WCs. 📷 Serving light lunches and refreshments throughout the day. 🍴 Licensed. 🅿 Free parking. 🐕 💍 🎗

SION HILL 🏛

Kirby Wiske, Thirsk, North Yorkshire YO7 4EU

www.sionhillhall.co.uk

Sion Hill was designed in 1912 by the renowned York architect Walter H Brierley, 'the Lutyens of the North', receiving an award from the Royal Institute of British Architects as being of 'outstanding architectural merit'.

The house is furnished with a fine collection of antique furniture, paintings ceramics and clocks.

Location: Map 11:A7. OS Ref SE373 844. 6m S of Northallerton off A167. 4m W of Thirsk. **Owner:** H W Mawer Trust

Contact: R M Mallaby - Trustee

Tel: 01845 587206 **E-mail:** sionhill@btconnect.com

Open: Group visits only, available througout the year. Please contact the house for booking arrangements.

Admission: £12.00 per person to include guided tour of the house, tea/coffee and biscuits, followed by a leisurely stroll around the gardens.

Key facts: 🛈 No photography in the house. 🔲 Partial. WC. 🎦 By arrangement. 🅿 Ample for cars and coaches. 🐕 Guide dogs only.

STOCKELD PARK 🏛

Off the A661, Wetherby, North Yorkshire LS22 4AN

www.stockeldpark.co.uk

A gracious Palladian mansion by James Paine (1763), featuring a magnificent cantilevered staircase in the central oval hall. Surrounded by beautiful gardens and set in 18th Century landscaped parkland at the heart of a 2000 acre estate. Popular for filming and photography. In 2012 Stockeld Park was winner of Hudsons Best Family Day Out for its Adventure attraction, with interactive, imaginative play indoor and out and famous Enchanted forest.

Location: Map 11:A9. OS Ref SE376 497. York 12m, Harrogate 5m, Leeds 12m.

Owner: Mr and Mrs P G F Grant **Contact:** Mr P Grant

Tel: 01937 586101 **Fax:** 01937 580084 **E-mail:** office@stockeldpark.co.uk

Open: House: Privately booked events and tours only. Contact Estate Office 01937 586101. Please see web for further opening of the adventure site and special events www.stockeldpark.co.uk. Please note we are open throughout all the local school holidays. **Admission:** Prices on application.

Key facts: 🛍 Fantastic seasonal gift emporium filled with gift ideas. 🎪 Private event & Wedding enquiries welcome. 🍴 Home made & Local, Fully Licensed. 🎦 Groups, Tours and Groups welcome by appointment. 🅿 Free Parking 🏫 Schools welcome by appointment. 🐕 🍷

ASKE HALL 🏛

Richmond, North Yorkshire DL10 5HJ

Tours limited to 15 people per tour. Booking advisable and ID will be required (passport, driving licence etc). For further details contact Mandy Blenkiron. A predominantly Georgian collection of paintings, furniture and porcelain in house which has been the seat of the Dundas family since 1763.

Location: Map 10:P6. OS Ref NZ179 035. 4m SW of A1 at Scotch Corner, 2m from the A66, on the B6274.

Owner: Earl of Ronaldshay

Contact: Mandy Blenkiron

Tel: 01748 822000

E-mail: mandy.blenkiron@aske.co.uk

Website: www.aske.co.uk

Open: Thu 10 & Fri 11 Sep 2015 (Heritage Open Days). Tours at 10.00, 11.00 & 12.00.

Admission: Free.

Key facts: 🔲 Partial. 🎦 Obligatory. 🅿 Limited. 🐕

BROCKFIELD HALL 🏛ⓔ

Warthill, York YO19 5XJ

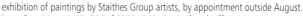

Georgian house (1804) by Peter Atkinson for Benjamin Agar Esq. Mrs. Wood's father was Lord Martin Fitzalan Howard, son of Lady Beaumont of Carlton Towers, Selby. Brockfield has portraits of her Stapleton family. There is a permanent exhibition of paintings by Staithes Group artists, by appointment outside August.

Location: Map 11:C9. OS Ref SE664 550. 5m E of York off A166 or A64.

Owner: Mr & Mrs Simon Wood **Contact:** Simon Wood

Tel: 01904 489362

E-mail: simon@brockfieldhall.co.uk

Website: www.brockfieldhall.co.uk

Open: Spring BH Mon (25 May). Daily in Aug from 1pm to 5pm except Mons but including BH Mon. On all the above days there will be three conducted tours by the owner at 1pm, 2.30pm and 4pm.

Admission: Adult £7.00.

Key facts: 🛈 No photography inside house. 🎦 By arrangement. 🅿

CHURCH OF CHRIST THE CONSOLER 🏛

Newby Hall, Skelton-cum-Newby, Ripon HG4 5AE

With its colourful and vibrant interior, this Victorian church seems the very celebration of life, yet it stands as a testament to tragedy. It is a memorial to Frederick Vyner who, age 23, was captured and murdered by brigands in 1870. His mother used the money collected for his ransom to commission celebrated architect William Burges to design this church at her home at Newby Hall. Standing surrounded by beech trees, the impressive exterior, with its lofty spire, pinnacles and fine rose window is matched by a wonderfully rich interior featuring stained glass, fine marble and gilded mosaics.

Location: OS Ref SE360 679. 4m SE of Ripon, off B6265; follow brown signs to Newby Hall. **Contact:** The Churches Conservation Trust on 0845 303 2760 (Mon-Fri, 9am–5pm) **E-mail:** north@thecct.org.uk **Website:** www.visitchurches.org.uk

Open: Open daily. **Admission:** Free entry - donations welcome.

Key facts: 🅿 🐕 ♿

HOLY TRINITY CHURCH 🏛

Low Lane, Wensley, Leyburn, North Yorkshire DL8 4HX

Built on 8th Century Saxon foundations, this 13th Century church sits on the bank of the river Ure at the eastern end of picturesque Wensleydale. Inside, its rich history is all around, with good examples of medieval wallpaintings, fine Flemish brasses and a 15th Century reliquary, which is claimed to have once held the relics of St Agatha. Sit and marvel at the sumptuous richness of the Scrope family pew (who were local landowners) and imagine life as the Lord or Lady of nearby Bolton Castle.

Location: OS Ref SE092 895. 2 miles south of Leyburn, on A684.

Contact: The Churches Conservation Trust on 0845 303 2760 (Mon to Fri)

Website: www.visitchurches.org.uk

Open: Open daily.

Admission: Free entry - donations welcome.

Key facts: 🐕 ♿

HOLY TRINITY CHURCH
Coverham, Leyburn, North Yorkshire DL8 4RN

Few churches can compare with the stunning setting of Holy Trinity, lying low in the valley of the River Cover in the Dales and offering a haven for walkers and many other visitors. This was an early Christian site and nearby are the few remains of Coverham Abbey. The handsome stone church has a large churchyard filled with interesting monuments and tombs. The building is of 13th Century origin and has a calm, light interior. The tower is 16th Century and many fittings date from the Victorian period.

Location: OS Ref SE 104 864. 4 miles south of Leyburn.
Contact: The Churches Conservation Trust on 0845 303 2760 (Mon-Fri).
Website: www.visitchurches.org.uk
Open: Open daily.
Admission: Free - donations welcome.

ST MARY'S CHURCH
**Lead, Saxton, Tadcaster,
North Yorkshire LS24 9QN**

Since being rescued by a group of walkers in 1931, St Mary's has been known as the Ramblers' Church. The repairs made then are recorded on the back of the church door. The church stands alone in the middle of a field filled with the bumps and furrows of earthworks that indicate the site of a medieval manor house. Nearby is Towton, the site of the War of the Roses battle, believed to be bloodiest in English history, which brought the wars to an end in 1461. 10,000 men are said to have been killed, and Cock Beck, the little stream that you cross to get to St Mary's, is said to have run red with blood. You can find monuments to crusading knights in the church. Despite its awesome history, St Mary's is a peaceful place.

Location: OS Ref SE 464 369. 5 miles S of Tadcaster. Off B1217; church in a field opposite the Crooked Billet pub.
Contact: The Churches Conservation Trust on 0845 303 2760 (Mon-Fri)
Website: www.visitchurches.org.uk **Open:** Daily. **Admission:** Free.

HOLY TRINITY CHURCH
70 Goodramgate, York YO1 7LF

Holy Trinity has the air of a hidden treasure. It stands in a small, secluded, leafy churchyard with the Minster towering behind, tucked away behind Goodramgate. To visit, you pass through an 18th Century archway tacked on to buildings that served as artisans' workshops in the 14th Century. Light filters through the windows, illuminating honey-coloured stone. The east window especially has marvellous stained glass, donated in the early 1470s by the Reverend John Walker, rector of the church. On sunny days, transient gems of coloured light are scattered on the walls, and medieval faces stare out from the windows. The building dates chiefly from the 15th Century, but has features from its foundation in the 12th Century right up to the 19th Century. The box pews, unique in York, are exceptionally fine.

Location: OS Ref SE605 522. York city centre, off Goodramgate; King's Square and Shambles 200 yards. **Website:** www.visitchurches.org.uk
Open: Sun & Mon, 12pm-4pm; Tue-Sat 10am-4pm. **Admission:** Free.

ST PETER'S CHURCH
**Church Lane, Wintringham, Malton, North
Yorkshire YO17 8HU**

This beautiful and peaceful church, with an elegant spire, was built from the Norman period to the 15th Century. The oldest part of the church is the Norman chancel with its priest's door and corbel table; the nave and west tower are of the 14th Century, although externally the tower has crenellated parapets and perpendicular tracery of the 15th Century. The graveyard is filled with 18th and 19th Century monuments to the former inhabitants of this sleepy village. The church is full of interesting furnishings including Jacobean bench pews, medieval carvings and stained glass. Look carefully and you might also find green men, mythical beasts and sword markings.

Location: OS Ref SE887 731. 11 miles east of Malton, off the A64.
Contact: The Churches Conservation Trust on 0845 303 2760 (Mon-Fri)
Website: www.visitchurches.org.uk
Open: Open daily. **Admission:** Free - donations welcome.

NORTON CONYERS
Nr Ripon, North Yorkshire HG4 5EQ

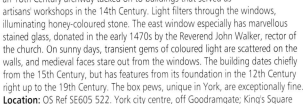

Visited by Charlotte Brontë, Norton Conyers, an original of 'Thornfield Hall', has belonged to the Grahams since 1624. The mid-18th Century walled garden retains its original design. Herbaceous borders flanked by yew hedges lead to central pavilion. House won the 2014 HHA/Sotheby's Restoration Award.

Location: Map 11:A8. OS Ref SF319 763. 4m NW of Ripon. 3 ½ m from the A1.
Owner: Sir James and Lady Graham **Contact:** The Administrator
Tel/Fax: 01765 640333 **E-mail:** visits@nortonconyers.org.uk
Website: www.nortonconyers.org.uk/www.weddingsatnortonconyers.co.uk
Open: Garden: All BH Suns & Mons, and Mons 7 Jun–23 Aug, 2-5pm. Also Mons & Thus throughout the year 10-4pm – please check during winter months. Wedding receptions by arrangement. **Admission:** Free (donations welcome), except for charity days & group bookings. House: (pre-bookings only) 19-26 Jul, 2-5 pm. See our website. **Key facts:** Pavilion is available for functions: seats up to 25. Partial. WC. By arrangement. Dogs on leads only.

SUTTON PARK
Sutton-On-The-Forest, N. Yorkshire YO61 1DP

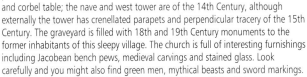

The Yorkshire home of Sir Reginald and Lady Sheffield. Early Georgian architecture. Magnificent plasterwork by Cortese. Rich collection of 18th Century furniture. Award winning gardens attract enthusiasts from home and abroad. Tranquil Caravan and Camping Club CL Site also available for Rallies. Woodland Walk. Tearooms. **Location:** Map 11:B9. OS Ref SE583 646. 8miles N of York on B1363 York-Helmsley Road follow brown signs **Contact:** Administrator
Tel: 01347 810249 **Fax:** 01347 811251 **E-mail:** suttonpark@statelyhome.co.uk
Website: www.statelyhome.co.uk **Open:** Private parties all year by appointment (min. charge for 15). Gardens: 11am-5pm 1 May-28 Jun inc. House: from 1pm 25 May Spring BH Mon, then Mon 1 Jun-Sun 28 Jun inc. 31 Aug Summer BH Mon. Heritage Days 10 & 11 Sep. For House tour times & admission prices see website for details. **Key facts:** No photography. Flower Power Fairs www.flowerpowerfairs.co.uk Partial. WCs. Licensed. Obligatory. Limited for coaches. Woodland Walk only.

PLUMPTON ROCKS
**Plumpton, Knaresborough
North Yorkshire HG5 8NA**

Grade II* listed garden extending to over 30 acres including an idyllic lake, dramatic millstone grit rock formation, romantic woodland walks winding through bluebells and rhododendrons. Declared by English Heritage to be of outstanding interest. Painted by Turner. Described by Queen Mary as 'Heaven on earth'.

Location: Map 11:A9. OS Ref SE353 535. Between Harrogate and Wetherby on A661, 1m SE of A661 junction with Harrogate southern bypass.
Owner/Contact: Robert de Plumpton Hunter
Tel: 01289 382322
Website: www.plumptonrocks.com
Open: Mar-Oct: Sat, Sun & BHs, 11am-6pm.
Admission: Adult £3.50, Child/OAP £2.50. (Prices subject to change).
Key facts: Unsuitable. Limited for coaches. In grounds, on leads.

RIEVAULX TERRACE & TEMPLES
The National Trust, Rievaulx, North Yorkshire YO62 5LJ

One of Yorkshire's finest 18th Century landscape gardens, containing two temples. Take in views from the terrace over the Cistercian ruin of Rievaulx Abbey.
Location: Map 11:B7. OS Ref SE579 848. **Tel:** 01723 870423
E-mail: nunningtonhall@nationaltrust.org.uk **Website:** www.nationaltrust.org.uk/rievaulx-terrace **Open:** Please see website for up to date details.

TREASURER'S HOUSE
Minster Yard, York, North Yorkshire YO1 7JL

Named after the Treasurer of York Minster, the house is not all that it first seems! The size and splendour and contents of the house are a constant surprise.
Location: Map 11:B9. OS Ref SE604 523. **Tel:** 01904 624247
Website: www.nationaltrust.org.uk/treasurers-house-york
Open: Please see website for up to date opening and admission details.

BRODSWORTH HALL & GARDENS ⌗
BRODSWORTH, NR DONCASTER, YORKSHIRE DN5 7XJ
www.english-heritage.org.uk/brodsworthhall

Time really does stand still at Brodsworth Hall. Inside this beautiful Victorian country house almost everything has been left exactly as it was when it was still a family home. Possessions that took more than 130 years to gather together, from the grandest piece of furniture to family mementoes, are still in their original places. The beautiful grounds, a collection of grand gardens in miniature, have been restored to their full Victorian splendour, and feature a colourful array of seasonal displays. With an adventure playground and cosy tearoom, Brodsworth Hall has everything you need for a family day out.

Location: Map 11:B12. OS Ref SE506 070. In Brodsworth, 5m NW of Doncaster off A635. Use A1(M)/J37.

Owner: English Heritage

Contact: Visitor Operations Team
Tel: 01302 722598
E-mail: customers@english-heritage.org.uk
Open: Please visit www.english-heritage.org.uk for the most up-to-date opening times and admission prices.
Key facts: ⓘ Exhibitions about the family, the servants and the gardens. WCs. No Cameras (house only). 🖾 🎁 🖾
🅺 Groups must book. Booked coach parties: 10am-1pm.
🅿 220 cars and 3 coaches. Free.
🎦 Education Centre. ♿
♿ Gardens, Tearoom and Servants' Wing only. ♿

HOLY TRINITY CHURCH ⋔
Main Street, Wentworth, Rotherham, South Yorkshire S62 7TX

This atmospheric, partly ruined building started life as a church in the 15th Century but was converted to a mausoleum in 1877 after a new church was commissioned. Today, only the chancel and north chapel remain intact. In the chancel, brass and stone memorials and alabaster effigies from the 16th and 17th Centuries trace the powerful Wentworth family. These include one to the Earl of Strafford, a supporter of the Crown who was beheaded on Tower Hill just before the Civil War, and Charles Watson-Wentworth, the 2nd Marquis of Rockingham, who helped to negotiate an end to the American War of Independence. Wentworth estate workers and villagers rest in the churchyard, including the 17 year old Chow Kwang Tseay from China, baptised John Dennis Blonde, and thought to have been rescued from 'HMS Blonde' and brought to Rotherham in 1847 as a 14 year old.

Location: OS Ref SK384 983. 5 miles NW of Rotherham, on B6090.
Website: www.visitchurches.org.uk **Open:** Open daily. **Admission:** Free.

Brodsworth Hall

Harewood House from the South-West

HAREWOOD HOUSE & GARDENS 🏛

www.harewood.org

Harewood is one of the finest Treasure Houses of England, in the setting of Yorkshire's most beautiful landscape.

From the moment you arrive, Harewood captures your imagination and feeds your curiosity. It's a place filled with culture and heritage, which continues to develop and thrive today.

Built 1759 – 1772, Harewood House is the seat of the Earl and Countess of Harewood. The magnificent Georgian building has remained within the Lascelles family since its construction and has retained much of its original splendour. Designed by renowned Georgian architect John Carr, furnished by Thomas Chippendale and with interiors by Robert Adam, Harewood House offers visitors the chance to unearth striking, original features and experience the grandeur of one of Yorkshire's finest county houses.

In each room, our friendly guides are on hand to offer insights into the history and detail of the House, including the extensive art collections. From El Greco, JMW Turner, and Joshua Reynolds to Epstein, Sidney Nolan and Gaudier-Brzeska, there is a diverse range on offer, spanning centuries of patronage. Visitors can relax and be inspired by the cultural richness of the House.

Like the building, the landscape was painstakingly created by the finest craftsman. With a 32 acre lake and rolling hills, views from the formal Italian Terrace are not to be missed. Wander through the rows of neat box hedging filled with perfumed flowers and gaze across at the "Capability" Brown designed vistas.

With over 100 acres of grounds and gardens to explore, from the informal Himalayan Garden which bursts into life in May, to the traditional south facing borders which are at their best in October, visitors won't be disappointed. From green fingered experts to lovers of the outdoors, the gardens are a wonderful place to while-away a lazy afternoon.

But that's not all! There are exhibitions of contemporary art, an award-winning educational department, renowned Bird Garden home to exotic penguins, flamingos and parrots, an Adventure Playground and a selection of popular cafes. Whether you want to visit the House and its awe-inspiring collections, see the latest exhibitions, or enjoy the Gardens and countryside, Harewood will provide a day of discovery.

VISITOR INFORMATION

■ Owner
The Earl and Countess of Harewood

■ Address
Harewood House
Harewood
Leeds
West Yorkshire
LS17 9LG

■ Location
Map 10:P10
OS Ref. SE311 446
A1 N or S to Wetherby.
A659 via Collingham,
Harewood is on A61
between Leeds and
Harrogate. Easily reached
from A1, M1, M62 and
M18. 40 mins from York,
20 mins from centre of
Leeds or Harrogate.
Bus: No. 36 from Leeds or
Harrogate.
Rail: London Kings Cross
to Leeds/Harrogate 2hrs 20
mins. Leeds/Harrogate
Station 7m.
Air: Leeds Bradford
Airport 9m.

■ Contact
Harewood House
Tel: 0113 2181010
E-mail:
info@harewood.org

■ Opening Times
House, Gardens, Grounds,
Bird Garden, Courtyard and
Bookshop open from April
to November 2015. Please
see website or call our
team for details.

■ Admission
Please see website.

Conference/Function
Private venue hire available.

KEY FACTS

- ℹ Please see website for further information.
- 🎁 Homeware, gifts, souvenirs, postcards and publications.
- 🌿 Seasonal vegetable stall May - September.
- ▼ Fine Dining in House & private venue hire available.
- ♿ WCs. No access to State Rooms for electric wheelchairs. Courtesy wheelchair.
- ☕ Terrace Café. Licensed.
- 🍴 Courtyard Café & Restaurant. Licensed.
- 🚶 Guided tours by arrangement.
- 🅿 Free. Designated for blue badge holders.
- 🎓 Sandford Award for Education. School parties welcome.
- 🐕 On leads. Service dogs welcome except in Bird Garden.
- 💒 Wedding venue hire available.

Gallery, Harewood House

The Terrace

OAKWELL HALL & RED HOUSE
OAKWELL HALL, NUTTER LANE, BIRSTALL WF17 9LG / RED HOUSE, OXFORD RD, GOMERSAL BD19 4JP
www.kirklees.gov.uk/museums

Visit two stunning West Yorkshire Historic Houses located less than a mile apart! Both have unique Brontë connections and featured in Charlotte Brontë's novel Shirley. Both have gorgeous award-winning period gardens to explore.

Oakwell Hall is an atmospheric Elizabethan manor house with important Civil War connections, displayed as the C17th home of the Batt family. Wander through the fine oak panelled Great Hall, decorative Parlours and evocative Kitchens. Surrounded by award winning Country Park and C17th gardens; Cafe, Play Area, Nature Trail, Arboretum & Shop.

Red House is a delightful former woollen cloth merchant's home set in enchanting 1830s gardens. From elegant Parlour to stone-flagged Kitchens, each room brings you closer to the 1830s, when Charlotte Brontë visited her friend, early feminist Mary Taylor, here. Restored Garden with scented old roses, period flowers and tree shaded lawns. Bronte & local history exhibitions. Shop.

Pre-booked Group Visits; Weddings & Venue Hire; Events & Schools programme.
Location: Map 10:P11. M62 Jct 26 take A58 towards Leeds, turn right on A651. M62 Jct 27 take A62 towards Huddersfield. Follow brown tourist signs.
Owner: Kirklees Council **Contact:** Oakwell Hall
Tel: 01924 326240. Red House 01274 335100
E-mail: oakwell.hall@kirklees.gov.uk; red.house@kirklees.gov.uk
Open: Summer opening: 1 Mar-31 Oct: Tue-Thu 11am-5pm; Sat & Sun 12noon-5 pm. Winter opening: 1 Nov-end Feb: Tue-Thu 11am-4pm Sat-Sun 12noon-4pm Closed Mon & Fri.
Admission: At each house: Adult £2.50, Child £1.00, Family £6.00 (2 adults+4 children). 'Tourist Ticket' (entry to both houses in a day): Adult £4.00, Child £1.50, Family £10.00, 'Annual Tickets' also available.
Key facts: ⓘ ⎙ ⊤ ⬥ Tel for access details. ☕ Ⓟ ▣ ✂ ⬥ ❄ ♨

LOTHERTON HALL ESTATE
Aberford, Leeds, West Yorkshire LS25 3EB
www.leeds.gov.uk/lothertonhall

Explore this Edwardian country estate with extensive grounds, historic house, deer park, gardens and children's playgrounds. Discover the stories of this fantastic country home, once the home of the Gascoigne family; housing a wonderful collection of fine and decorative arts, as well as a new dedicated Fashion Gallery due to open in March 2015. From the bird garden, to the woodland play area and to stunning nature trails, this historic estate really has got something for everyone.
Location: Map 11:B10. OS Ref SE450 360.
Owner: Leeds City Council **Contact:** Visitor Services
Tel: 0113 3782959
E-mail: lotherton.hall@leeds.gov.uk
Open: Please check the website or call 0113 3782959 for seasonal opening and admission prices.
Admission: Please check the website for current admission prices.
Key facts: ⓘ We welcome group visits, please call to arrange your day out. ▣ ⬥ New lift due to be installed March 2015. ☕ Ⓟ ▣ ✂ ♨

TEMPLE NEWSAM ESTATE
Temple Newsam Road, Leeds LS15 OAE
www.leeds.gov.uk/templenewsamhouse

One of the great country houses of England, this Tudor-Jacobean mansion was the birthplace of Lord Darnley, husband of Mary Queen of Scots. Rich in beautifully restored interiors, the House depicts 500 years of history through its paintings, Chippendale furniture, textiles, silver and ceramics. Temple Newsam sits within 1500 acres of stunning Capability Brown parkland with formal and wooded gardens as well as national plant collections.
Location: Map 10:P10. OS Ref SE358 321. 4m E of city centre B6159 or 2m from M1 junction 46. 4 miles from city centre.
Owner: Leeds City Council **Contact:** Visitor Services **Tel:** 0113 3367460
E-mail: temple.newsam.house@leeds.gov.uk **Open:** Please check the website or call 0113 3367460 for seasonal opening times and admission prices.
Admission: Please check the website or call 0113 3367460 for seasonal opening times and admission prices.
Key facts: ⓘ We welcome group visits, please call to arrange your day out. ⎙ ⊤ ⬥ ☕ ⎘ Obligatory. ▣ Ⓟ ▣ ✂ ♨

YORK GATE GARDEN
Back Church Lane, Adel, Leeds LS16 8DW
www.yorkgate.org.uk

Inspirational one acre garden widely recognised as one of Britain's finest small gardens. A series of smaller gardens with different themes and in contrasting styles are linked by a succession of delightful vistas. Striking architectural features play a key role throughout the garden which is noted for its exquisite planting details and Arts and Crafts features.

Location: Map 10:P10. OS Ref 275 403.
2¼m SE of Bramhope, just off A660.
Owner: Perennial **Contact:** The Garden Co-ordinator **Tel:** 0113 267 8240
Open: 1 Apr to 30 Sep, Sun to Thu and BH Mons, 1:30pm-4:30pm.
Evenings: Weds 10, 17 & 24 Jun, 6:30-9:00pm.
Admission: Standard admission £5.00. Gift Aid admission £5.50. Children (16 & under) Free. Annual Friends Membership £25.00 per annum.
Please phone for group prices.
Key facts: ⓘ Please park opposite church in Church Lane. Groups welcome by appointment (see website or phone for details). ▣ ⚤ ▣ ⬚ By arrangement. ⬚ Guide dogs only.

ALL SAINTS' CHURCH ⋔
Harewood Park, Harewood, Leeds, West Yorkshire LS17 9LG

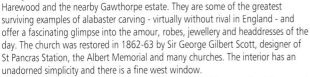

Nestling in the grounds of Harewood House, All Saints' dates from the 15th Century. It is remarkable for six pairs of effigies, dating from 1419 to 1510, commemorating the owners of Harewood and the nearby Gawthorpe estate. They are some of the greatest surviving examples of alabaster carving - virtually without rival in England - and offer a fascinating glimpse into the amour, robes, jewellery and headdresses of the day. The church was restored in 1862-63 by Sir George Gilbert Scott, designer of St Pancras Station, the Albert Memorial and many churches. The interior has an unadorned simplicity and there is a fine west window.
Location: OS Ref SE314 451. 7 miles N of Leeds off A61 in grounds of Harewood House. **Contact:** The Churches Conservation Trust on 0845 303 2760 (Mon-Fri) **Website:** www.visitchurches.org.uk **Open:** Apr-Oct daily from 10am-6pm; other times call Harewood Office on 0113 218 1010 in advance. **Admission:** Free entry - donations welcome. **Key facts:** ▣ Harewood House. ℗ ⬚

CHURCH OF ST JOHN
THE EVANGELIST ⋔
23 New Briggate, Leeds LS2 8JD

Built in 1632-34, St John's is the oldest church in Leeds city centre. The glory of the church lies in its magnificent Jacobean (Carolian) fittings, particularly the superb wooden screen decorated with flowers, hearts and grotesque heads of humans and animals. There is more lovely carving on the wall panels, pews and pulpit. Brightly painted angels play instruments in the roof. The church building was entirely funded by wealthy merchant and Royalist John Harrison, who also paid for the grammar school and almshouses nearby. Harrison's benevolent spirit still pervades the church and a series of stained-glass windows depicts his good works. One of the windows shows an apocryphal tale in which Harrison presents King Charles, imprisoned in Leeds, with a tankard of gold coins disguised as a draught of ale. **Location:** OS Ref SE302 338. In Mark Lane, off New Briggate. **Contact:** The Churches Conservation Trust on 0845 303 2760 (Mon-Fri) **Website:** www.visitchurches.org.uk
Open: Tue-Sat, 11am-3pm. **Key facts:** ⊞

LEDSTON HALL
Hall Lane, Ledston, Castleford, West Yorkshire WF10 2BB
17th Century mansion with some earlier work, lawned grounds.
Location: Map 11:A11. OS Ref SE437 289. 2m N of Castleford, off A656.
Tel: 01423 707830 **Fax:** 01423 521373 **E-mail:** joe.robinson@carterjonas.co.uk
Website: www.whelerfoundation.co.uk **Open:** Exterior only: May-Aug: Mon-Fri, 9am-4pm. Other days by appointment. **Admission:** Free.

NOSTELL PRIORY & PARKLAND ⚘
Doncaster Road, Wakefield, West Yorkshire WF4 1QE
One of Yorkshire's jewels, an architectural treasure by James Paine with later additions by Robert Adam. **Location:** Map 11:A11. OS Ref SE403 175.
Tel: 01924 863892 **E-mail:** nostellpriory@nationaltrust.org.uk
Website: www.nationaltrust.org.uk/nostell-priory
Open: Please see website for up to date opening and admission details.

York Gate Garden

Burton Constable, Yorkshire

SEWERBY HALL AND GARDENS
Church Lane, Sewerby, Bridlington YO15 1EA
Tel: 01262 673769 **E-mail:** sewerby.hall@eastriding.gov.uk

ALL SAINTS' CHURCH 🛐
Skelton-in-Cleveland, Saltburn-By-The-Sea TS12 2HQ
Tel: 0845 303 2760 **E-mail:** central@thecct.org.uk

ALLERTON PARK
Allerton Park, Knaresborough, North Yorkshire HG5 0SE
Tel: 01423 330927

BOLTON ABBEY
Skipton, North Yorkshire BD23 6EX
Tel: 01756 718009 **E-mail:** tourism@boltonabbey.com

CHURCH OF ST JOHN THE BAPTIST 🛐
Stanwick, Richmond, North Yorkshire DL11 7RT
Tel: 0845 303 2760 **E-mail:** central@thecct.org.uk

JERVAULX ABBEY
Ripon, North Yorkshire HG4 4PH
Tel: 01677 460226

MANSION HOUSE
St Helen's Square, York YO1 9QL
E-mail: mansionhouse@york.gov.uk

RHS GARDEN HARLOW CARR
Crag Lane, Harrogate, North Yorkshire HG3 1QB
Tel: 01423 565418 **E-mail:** harlowcarr@rhs.org.uk

RIEVAULX ABBEY ⌗
Rievaulx, Nr Helmsley, N. Yorkshire YO62 5LB
Tel: 01439 798228 **E-mail:** rievaulx.abbey@english-heritage.org.uk

RIPLEY CASTLE 🏠ℝ
Ripley, Harrogate, North Yorkshire HG3 3AY
Tel: 01423 770152 **E-mail:** enquiries@ripleycastle.co.uk

RIPON CATHEDRAL
Ripon, North Yorkshire HG4 1QR
Tel: 01765 602072

ST ANDREW'S CHURCH 🛐
East Heslerton, Malton, North Yorkshire YO17 8RN
Tel: 0845 303 2760 **E-mail:** central@thecct.org.uk

ST LAWRENCE'S TOWER 🛐
Hull Road, York, North Yorkshire YO10 3BN
Tel: 0845 303 2760 **E-mail:** central@thecct.org.uk

ST MARTIN'S CHURCH 🛐
Whenby, York, North Yorkshire YO61 4SE
Tel: 0845 303 2760 **E-mail:** central@thecct.org.uk

ST MARTIN'S CHURCH 🛐
Allerton Park, Knaresborough, North Yorkshire HG5 0SE
Tel: 0845 303 2760 **E-mail:** central@thecct.org.uk

ST MARY'S CHURCH 🛐
Birdforth, Thirsk, North Yorkshire YO61 4NW
Tel: 0845 303 2760 **E-mail:** central@thecct.org.uk

ST MARY'S CHURCH 🛐
Roecliffe, Ripon, North Yorkshire YO51 9LZ
Tel: 0845 303 2760 **E-mail:** central@thecct.org.uk

ST MARY'S CHURCH 🛐
Stainburn, Harrogate, North Yorkshire LS21 2LW
Tel: 0845 303 2760 **E-mail:** central@thecct.org.uk

ST MICHAEL'S CHURCH 🛐
Oak Road, Cowthorpe, Wetherby, North Yorkshire LS22 5EZ
Tel: 0845 303 2760 **E-mail:** central@thecct.org.uk

ST STEPHEN'S CHURCH 🛐
Robin Hood's Bay, Fylingdales, Whitby, N. Yorkshire YO22 4PN
Tel: 0845 303 2760 **E-mail:** central@thecct.org.uk

SHANDY HALL
Coxwold, Thirsk, North Yorkshire YO61 4AD
Tel: 01347 868465 **E-mail:** shandyhall@dial.pipex.com

THORP PERROW ARBORETUM
Bedale, North Yorkshire DL8 2PR
Tel: 01677 425323 **E-mail:** enquiries@thorpperrow.com

WHITBY ABBEY ⌗
Whitby, North Yorkshire YO22 4JT
Tel: 01947 603568 **E-mail:** customers@english-heritage.org.uk

CHURCH OF ST JOHN THE EVANGELIST 🛐
Cadeby, Doncaster, South Yorkshire DN5 7SW
Tel: 0845 303 2760 **E-mail:** central@thecct.org.uk

ST JOHN'S CHURCH 🛐
St John's Road, Throapham, Sheffield, South Yorks S25 1YL
Tel: 0845 303 2760 **E-mail:** central@thecct.org.uk

ST OSWALD'S CHURCH 🛐
Kirk Sandall Old Village, Doncaster, South Yorkshire DN3 1RA
Tel: 0845 303 2760 **E-mail:** central@thecct.org.uk

ST PETER'S CHURCH 🛐
Old Edlington, Doncaster, South Yorkshire DN12 1PZ
Tel: 0845 303 2760 **E-mail:** central@thecct.org.uk

ST STEPHEN'S CHURCH 🛐
North Dean Road, Copley, Halifax, West Yorkshire HX4 8QA
Tel: 0845 303 2760 **E-mail:** central@thecct.org.uk

WENTWORTH WOODHOUSE 🏠ℝ
Wentworth, South Yorkshire S62 7TQ
Tel: 01226 351161 or 01226 749639 **E-mail:** tours@wentworth

BRAMHAM PARK
The Estate Office, Bramham Park, Bramham LS23 6ND
Tel: 01937 846000 **E-mail:** enquiries@bramhampark.co.uk

EAST RIDDLESDEN HALL 🦌
Bradford Road, Riddlesden, Keighley, W. Yorkshire BD20 5EL
Tel: 01535 607075 **E-mail:** eastriddlesden@nationaltrust.org.uk

PONTEFRACT CASTLE
Castle Chain, Pontefract, West Yorkshire WF8 1QH
Tel: 01977 723 440 **E-mail:** castles@wakefield.gov.uk

Askham Hall, Cumbria

Blackwell, the Arts &
Crafts House, Cumbria

Cheshire
Cumbria
Lancashire
Manchester
Merseyside

North West

First fashionable in the 18th century, the Lake District still draws visitors, not least for its surviving castles, historic houses and gardens distinct from the black and white architecture of Lancashire.

New Entries for 2015:
- Lancaster Castle
- Askham Hall
- Ness Botanic Gardens
- Mirehouse Historic House and Gardens
- Abbot Hall Art Gallery
- Blackwell, The Arts & Craft House
- The Beatrix Potter Gallery, Hawkshead

VISITOR INFORMATION

■ Owner
Sir William and Lady Bromley-Davenport

■ Address
Capesthorne Hall
Siddington
Macclesfield
Cheshire
SK11 9JY

■ Location
Map 6:N2
OS Ref. SJ840 727
5m W of Macclesfield.
30 mins S of Manchester
on A34. Near M6, M60
and M62.
Rail: Macclesfield 5m
(2 hrs from London).
Air: Manchester
International 20 mins.

■ Contact
Christine Mountney
Hall Manager
Tel: 01625 861221
Fax: 01625 861619
E-mail: info@
capesthorne.com

■ Opening Times
Summer:
April-Oct Suns,
Mons & BHs.
Hall:
1.30-4pm.
Last admission 3.30pm.
Gardens & Chapel:
12 noon-5pm. Groups
welcome by appointment.

■ Admission
Sundays & BHs
Hall, Gardens & Chapel
Adult	£9.00
Child (5-16 yrs)	£5.00
Senior	£8.00
Family	£25.00

Sundays
Gardens & Chapel only
Adult	£6.50
Child (5-16 yrs)	£3.00
Senior	£5.50

Mondays Only
Park, Gardens & Chapel
Per Car	£10.00

Hall Entrance
Per person	£3.00

Discounts available for
groups and private tours.

**Caravan Park 4* AA
Rated
Open March to October
inclusive**

■ Special Events
Please visit
www.capesthorne.com.

CAPESTHORNE HALL ⛨Ⓕ
www.capesthorne.com

A spectacular venue for weddings, corporate functions, celebrations, park events or simply a fabulous day out.

Capesthorne Hall, set in 100 acres of picturesque Cheshire parkland, has been touched by nearly 1,000 years of English history - Roman legions passed across it, titled Norman families hunted on it and, during the Civil War, a Royalist ancestress helped Charles II to escape after the Battle of Worcester.

The Jacobean-style Hall has a fascinating collection of fine art, marble sculptures, furniture and tapestries. Originally designed by the Smiths of Warwick it was built between 1719 and 1732.

It was altered by Blore in 1837 and partially rebuilt by Salvin in 1861 following a disastrous fire.

The present Squire is Sir William Bromley-Davenport, whose ancestors have owned the estate since Domesday times when they were appointed custodians of the Royal Forest of Macclesfield.

In the grounds near the family Chapel the 18th Century Italian Milanese Gates open onto the herbaceous borders and maples which line the beautiful lakeside gardens. But amid the natural spectacle and woodland walks, Capesthorne still offers glimpses of its man-made past ... the remains of the Ice House, the Old Boat House and the curious Swallow Hole.

The hall can be hired for corporate occasions and family celebrations including Civil Wedding ceremonies and receptions.

KEY FACTS

ⓘ Available for corporate functions, meetings, product launches, promotions, exhibitions, seminars, activity days, still photography, clay shooting and garden parties.

🍽 Catering can be provided for groups (full menus on request). Function rooms available for corporate hospitality, meetings and other special events. The 'Butler's Pantry' serves light refreshments.

♿ Partial. WC.

🚶 Guided tours avaiable for pre-booked parties (except Sundays).

🅿 100 cars/20 coaches on hard-standing and unlimited in park, 50 yds from house.

🏕 Caravan Park 4* AA Rated, open March to October inclusive.

🔔 Licensed for Civil weddings.

🔔 Concerts, antique, craft and game fairs, car shows and triathalons.

© Peter Corcoran

NESS BOTANIC GARDENS

www.nessgardens.org.uk

"Welcome friend and welcome stranger, welcome one and welcome all" Arthur Kilpin Bulley, founder of Ness Gardens.

Ness Botanic Gardens is a beautiful 64 acre garden situated on the Dee Estuary in South Wirral. Its illustrious history is linked to the wealth, philanthropy and passion for plant-hunting of its creator AK Bulley.

From the start, Bulley shared his garden with his neighbours, and today's visitors can enjoy its relaxed and informal layout - so a visit to Ness feels more like strolling round the extensive grounds of a wealthy friend than a trip to a university botanic garden!

The diversity of different areas within the Gardens – deciduous woodlands, wildflower meadows, stunning herbaceous borders, a delightful potager, orchard, rock garden, terraces, water gardens, specimen lawns, pine wood – give Ness genuine year-round interest.

During February the snowdrop collections carpets the Gardens, attracting visitors from far afield to see over 60 varieties. In March it is the turn of the Crocus Lawn to star, early pale yellow narcissi peppering drifts of hundreds of thousands of pale purple crocus. In spring the visitors flock to see the thousands of flowering trees and shrubs at their peak right across the Gardens and particularly in the Water Gardens and Rock Garden.

During high summer the Gardens are simply superb. Then with the onset of autumn, the changing colours of the leaves set the Garden views ablaze. The Gardens have twice been the venue for BBC Radio 4's Gardeners' Question Time annual Summer Garden Party – attracting record audiences of thousands on both occasions and turning what was a niche occasion into a flagship event.

KEY FACTS

- Inspiring & high quality products for home & garden, indulgent treats.
- Seeds, plants & tools, vegetable produce from Ness's own Potager.
- We offer a unique mix of modern conference facilities in peaceful and inspiring surroundings. (Meetings Industry Accredited).
- Access for wheelchairs is shown on our visitor map.
- The Garden Kitchen café open daily from 9.30. The Garden Kiosk in summer.
- Group parties of 10 or more - Guide free when requested at time of booking.
- Free. 8 extra wide disabled bays.
- For Early Years and KS1-KS3 groups.
- Assistance & Guide dogs only.
- Please contact our Wedding Coordinator for our brochure.
- Please check our website for our events programme.

© Steve Godfrey

© Peter Corcoran

ADLINGTON HALL 🏛ⓕ
ADLINGTON HALL, MACCLESFIELD, CHESHIRE SK10 4LF
www.adlingtonhall.com

Adlington Hall, home of the Leghs from 1315 built on the site of a Hunting Lodge in the Forest of Macclesfield in 1040. Two oaks, part of the original building, remain rooted in the ground supporting the east end of the Great Hall. Between the trees in the Great Hall stands an organ built by 'Father' Bernard Smith. Played on by Handel.

The Gardens laid out over many centuries include a Lime walk planted 1688, Regency rockery surrounding the Shell Cottage. The Wilderness, a Rococo styled landscape garden containing the chinoserie T'Ing House, Pagoda bridge and classical Temple to Diana.

Location: Map 6:N2. OS Ref SJ905 804. 5m N of Macclesfield, A523,13m S of Manchester. London 178m.

Owner: Mrs C J C Legh

Tel: 01625 827595 **Fax:** 01625 820797
E-mail: enquiries@adlingtonhall.com
Open: Suns (closed Sun 2 Aug 2015) and BH Mons in May between Sun Apr 12 and Sun 4 Oct (inclusive), 2pm-5pm. Plant Hunter's Fair 10 May. NGS Open Day 7 Jun. **Admission:** House & Gardens: Adult £9.00, Child £5.00, Student £5.00, Gardens only: Adult £6.00, Child Free, Student Free, Groups of 20+ £8.50.
Key facts: ℹ️ Suitable for corporate events, product launches, business meetings, conferences, concerts, fashion shows, garden parties, rallies, filming and weddings. 🍽 The Great Hall and Dining Room are available for corporate entertaining. Catering can be arranged. ♿ WCs.
🍵 Tea room open on Hall open days 👤 By arrangement. 🅿 For 100 cars and 4 coaches, 100 yds from Hall. 🐕 On leads. 🛏🔲♿

CHOLMONDELEY CASTLE GARDEN 🏛ⓕ
MALPAS, CHESHIRE SY14 8AH
www.cholmondeleycastle.com

Cholmondeley Castle Garden is said by many to be among the most romantically beautiful gardens they have seen. Even the wild orchids, daisies and buttercups take on an aura of glamour in this beautifully landscaped setting with extensive ornamental gardens dominated by a romantic Castle built in 1801 of local sandstone. Visitors can enjoy the tranquil Temple Water Garden, Ruin Water Garden, memorial mosaic designed by Maggy Howarth, Rose garden and many mixed borders. Lakeside walk, picnic area, children's play areas and adventure den, farm animals including llamas and alpacas. Tea Room.

Location: Map 6:L3. OS Ref SJ540 515. Off A41 Chester/Whitchurch Rd. & A49 Whitchurch/ Tarporley Road. 7m N of Whitchurch.

Owner: Lavinia, Dowager Marchioness of Cholmondeley.
Contact: The Secretary **Tel:** 01829 720383 **Fax:** 01829 720877
E-mail: dilys@cholmondeleycastle.co.uk
Open: 29 Mar-27 Sep Wed, Thu, Sun and Bank Holidays 11am-5pm (last entry 4:30pm). Oct-Suns only for Autumn Tints.
(Castle open for groups only, by pre-arrangement, on limited days).
Admission: Adult £6.00, Child £3.00 (reduction for groups to gardens of 25+). For special events and variations to opening dates please refer to our website www.cholmondeleycastle.com.
Key facts: ℹ️ 🔲♿ Partial. WCs. 🍽🅿🐕 On leads. ♿

LYME PARK, HOUSE & GARDEN ❧
DISLEY, STOCKPORT, CHESHIRE SK12 2NR
www.nationaltrust.org.uk/lymepark

At Lyme there is a painting called 'The Servants' Ball', created at the height of the Edwardian age. It captures Lyme's golden era of family celebrations and hunting parties. Experience Lyme's last hoorah by dressing in Edwardian finery, re-enacting a play on the family stage and exploring newly opened rooms. Be inspired by lavish interiors, discover beautiful treasures and relax in stunning gardens. Enjoy a unique visit, experiencing a vanished age and decide for yourself… would life ever be the same again?

Location: Map 6:N2. OS Ref SJ965 825. Off the A6 at Disley. 6½m SE of Stockport. M60 J1.
Owner: National Trust **Contact:** The Visitor Experience Manager
Tel: 01663 762023 **Fax:** 01663 765035

Open: House: 16 Feb-1 Nov, 11am-5pm (last entry 4pm), Mon, Tue, Fri-Sun. Garden: 16 Feb-1 Nov, 11am-5pm (last entry 4.30pm), Mon-Sun. Please call for winter opening times.
Admission: House & Gardens:* Adult £11.00, Child £5.50, Family £25.00. Park: Car £7.00, Coach £25.00. NT members free. *includes a voluntary donation but visitors can choose to pay the standard prices.
Key facts: ⓘ Restricted photography in house. ⬚ ⬚ ⊤ ⬚ ⬚ Licensed. ⅆ Licensed. ⅀ Ⓟ Limited for coaches. ⬚ ⬚ Guide dogs only. ⬚ East Lodge. A beautiful Edwardian cottage built in 1904, with two bedrooms, sleeps 4 (one double, one twin), dogs welcome. Enjoy spectacular views of Manchester and the Peak District. Guests have access to Lyme Hall and Gardens. ✳ ♥

PEOVER HALL & GARDENS ⓘⒻ
OVER PEOVER, KNUTSFORD WA16 9HW
www.peoverhall.com

A Grade 2* listed Elizabethan family house dating from 1585. Situated within some 500 acres of landscaped 18th Century parkland with formal gardens designed between 1890-1900 that include a series of "garden rooms" filled with clipped box, lily ponds, Romanesque loggia, warm brick walls, unusual doors, secret passageways, beautiful topiary work, herb and walled gardens. The grounds of the Hall house working stables, estate cottages and the parish church of St Laurence which, contains two Mainwaring Chapels. The architectural jewel Grade I listed Carolean stables built in 1654, with richly carved stalls and original Tuscan columns and strap work.

Location: Map 6:M2. OS Ref SJ772 734. 4m S of Knutsford off A50 at Whipping

Stocks Inn. Further directions on website, satnav leads down an unsuitable road.
Owner: Mr R Brooks **Contact:** Mr I Shepherd
Tel: Mr I Shepherd: 01565 724220
Peover Estate Office: 01565 724220
E-mail: bookings@peoverhall.com
Open: 2015 May-Aug, Tue & Thu afternoons. Stables & Gardens open between 2-5pm. Tours of Peover Hall at 2.30pm & 3.30pm.
Admission: House, Stables & Gardens £6.00, Stables & Gardens only £4.00. Children under 16 years free of charge.
Key facts: ⬚ ⅀ Obligatory. ✳

TABLEY HOUSE

TABLEY HOUSE, TABLEY LANE, KNUTSFORD, CHESHIRE WA16 0HB

www.tableyhouse.co.uk

The finest Palladian House in the North West, Tabley a Grade I listing, was designed by John Carr of York for the Leicester family. It contains one of the first collections of English paintings, including works of art by Turner, Reynolds, Lawrence, Lely and Dobson. Furniture by Chippendale, Bullock and Gillow and fascinating family memorabilia adorn the rooms. Fine plasterwork by Thomas Oliver and carving by Daniel Shillito and Mathew Bertram. Interesting Tea Room and 17th Century Chapel adjoin, including Burne-Jones window.

Location: Map 6:M2. OS Ref SJ725 777. M6/J19, A556 S on to A5033. 2m W of Knutsford. **Owner:** The University of Manchester **Contact:** The Administrator **Tel:** 01565 750151 **E-mail:** tableyhouse@btconnect.com

Open: House: Apr-end Oct: Thu-Sun & BHs, 1-5pm. Last admission at 4.30pm. Tea Room open from 12noon to 5pm. (Tea Room Tel: 01565 651199).

Admission: Adult £5.00. Child/Student £1.50. Groups by arrangement.

Key facts: No photography in galleries. No stilleto heels. Slippers can be provided. Suitable for drinks receptions and presentations for up to 100 people. Call the office before arriving to arrange for lift entrance to be opened. Serving light lunches, afternoon teas. refreshments and homemade cakes. By arrangement, also available outside normal opening hours, guides provided at no extra charge. Free. Suitable for post 16 students. Guide dogs only. Civil Wedding and Partnerships Licence. Naming Ceremonies & Renewal of Vows.

DORFOLD HALL

Acton, Nr Nantwich, Cheshire CW5 8LD

Jacobean country house built in 1616 for Ralph Wilbraham. Family home of Mr & Mrs Richard Roundell.

Beautiful plaster ceilings and oak panelling. Attractive woodland gardens and summer herbaceous borders.

Location: Map 6:L3. OS Ref SJ634 525.
1m W of Nantwich on the A534 Nantwich-Wrexham road.
Owner/Contact: Richard Roundell
Tel: 01270 625245
Fax: 01270 628723
E-mail: dorfoldhall@btconnect.com
Open: Apr-Oct: Tue only and BH Mons, 2-5pm.
Admission: Adult £7.00, Child £3.00.
Key facts: Obligatory.
Limited. Narrow gates with low arch prevent coaches.

DUNHAM MASSEY IS THE STAMFORD MILITARY HOSPITAL

Altrincham, Cheshire WA14 4SJ

www.nationaltrust.org.uk/dunhammassey

During the First World War, Dunham Massey Hall - a Georgian house, set in a magnificent deer park - was transformed into a military hospital, becoming a sanctuary from the trenches for almost 300 soldiers. 2015 provides a second chance to discover what life was like for the patients and how the war changed everything for those who lived and worked at Dunham. Then take a stroll in one of the North's great gardens, which includes Britain's largest winter garden and a stunning rose garden **Location:** Map 6:M1. OS Ref SJ735 874. 3m SW of Altrincham off A56. M6/J19. M56/J7. Station Altrincham (Train & Metro) 3m.

Owner: National Trust **Contact:** Visitor Services **Tel:** 0161 941 1025 **E-mail:** dunhammassey@nationaltrust.org.uk **Open:** Please see website.

Admission: House & Garden: £13.50, Child £6.70, Family £33.70. Groups (15+) £11, Child £5.50. Garden only: £8.40, Child £4.20, Family £21. Groups (15+) £6.40, Child £3.20. Parking: Cars £6, Motorbikes £1.50, Coaches £20.

Key facts: Photography permitted, no flash or tripods. Large gift shop selling homewares & local produce. Plant sales area; seasonal bulbs & ornamental plants. Good access to most of property. Indoor & outdoor seating, range of light meals & snacks. Licensed. £6. Free to NT members. Dedicated walking area in North Park. Garden, shop & cafe.

GAWSWORTH HALL
Macclesfield, Cheshire SK11 9RN
www.gawsworthhall.com

Fully lived-in Tudor half-timbered manor house with Tilting Ground. Former home of Mary Fitton, Maid of Honour at the Court of Queen Elizabeth I, and the supposed 'Dark Lady' of Shakespeare's sonnets. Fine pictures, sculpture, furniture and beautiful grounds adjoining a medieval church. Garden Theatre performances take place in the Hall courtyard in July and August.

Location: Map 6:N2. OS Ref SJ892 697. 3m S of Macclesfield on the A536 Congleton to Macclesfield road.
Owner: Mr and Mrs T Richards **Contact:** Mr J Richards
Tel: 01260 223456
E-mail: gawsworthhall@btinternet.com
Open: See www.gawsworthhall.com.
Admission: Adult £7.50, Child £3.50. Groups (20+) £6.00.
Key facts: ◻ ◱ Partial. WCs. ◉ Licensed. ⍨ Licensed. ⍟ Guided tours by arrangement. �ⓟ ⌂ In grounds. ⌺ ⌆

RODE HALL ⌂ⓕ
Church Lane, Scholar Green, Cheshire ST7 3QP
www.rodehall.co.uk

Rode Hall stands in a Repton landscape and the extensive gardens include a woodland garden, formal rose garden designed by Nesfield in 1860 and a stunning two acre walled kitchen garden. Rode Pool also has its own herony on Birthday Island and the icehouse in the park is well worth a visit.

Location: Map 6:M3. OS Ref SJ819 573. 5m SW of Congleton between the A34 and A50. Kidsgrove railway station 2m NW of Kidsgrove.
Owner/Contact: Sir Richard Baker Wilbraham Bt
Tel: 01270 873237 **E-mail:** enquiries@rodehall.co.uk
Open: 1 Apr-30 Sep, Wed only. Gardens 12-5pm, House 2-5pm.
The gardens are also open alongside the monthly farmers' market on the first Sat of every month, (exc Jan) 9.30am-1pm. Snowdrop Walks 7 Feb-8 Mar daily 11am-4pm (exc Mons).
Admission: House & Garden: Adult £7.00, Conc £6.00 Children under 16 free. Garden only & Snowdrop walks: Adult £4.00. Children under 16 free. Tickets can now be bought on our website.
Key facts: ◻ ◲ ◉ Cream teas. ⍟ ⓟ ⌂ On leads.

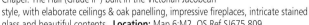

ARLEY HALL & GARDENS ⌂ⓕ
Northwich, Cheshire CW9 6NA

Arley has been a cherished family home owned for over 550 years. Renowned features include the double herbaceous border, pleached Lime Avenues, Ilex Columns, Cruck Barn and Chapel. The Hall (Grade II*) built in the Victorian Jacobean style, with elaborate ceilings & oak panelling, impressive fireplaces, intricate stained glass and beautiful contents. **Location:** Map 6:M2. OS Ref SJ675 809.
Owner: Viscount & Viscountess Ashbrook **Contact:** Helen Robinson - Marketing
Tel: 01565 777353 **E-mail:** reception@arleyhallandgardens.com
Website: www.arleyhallandgardens.com
Open: Gardens: 1 Mar-31 Oct, Mon-Sun 11am-5pm. The Hall: 1 Mar-27 Oct, Sun, Tues & BHs 12noon-5pm. **Admission:** Gardens: Adult £7.50, Children (5-12yrs) £3.00, Senior £7.00, Family (2+2) £18.00. Hall & Gardens: Adult £10.00, Child (5-12yrs) £4.00, Senior £9.00, Family (2+2) £25.00. Group rates are available please visit the website. **Key facts:** ⓘ Weddings & Corp. ◻ ◱ ⍨ ◲ WCs. ⍨ Licensed. ⍟ ⓟ Free. ◉ ⌂ Dogs on leads only.

TATTON PARK ⌘
Knutsford, Cheshire WA16 6QN

A complete historic estate with 1,000 acres of deer park, 200 year old 50 acre gardens and Tudor Old Hall. The neo-classical mansion houses one of the finest library collections in the National Trust. Families enjoy the working rare breed farm. Stableyard shopping and dining includes specialty shops, Stables restaurant and Gardener's Cottage tea room. Over 100 events take place each year. A perfect day out! **Location:** Map 6:M2. OS Ref SJ745 815. From M56/J7 follow signs. From M6/J19, signed on A56 & A50. **Owner:** National Trust (Managed by Cheshire East Council) **Tel:** 01625 374400/01625 374435 **E-mail:** tatton@cheshireeast.gov.uk **Website:** www.tattonpark.org.uk **Open:** Every day except Mons in low season. Attraction times vary. See website or call 01625 374400 for all opening times. **Admission:** See website or call 01625 374400.
Key facts: ⓘ ◻ ◱ ◲ Dinners, dances, weddings & conferences. ◉ ⍨ Licensed. ⍟ By arrangement. ⓟ Charge applies. See website, 200-300 yds. Meal vouchers for coach drivers. ◉ Please book. ⌂ In grounds. ◰ ⌆ ✳ ⌺ €

BEESTON CASTLE ⊞
Chapel Lane, Beeston, Tarporley, Cheshire CW6 9TX

Standing majestically on a sheer rocky crag, Beeston offers perhaps the most stunning views of any castle in England. **Location:** Map 6:L3. OS Ref SJ537 593.
Tel: 01829 260464 **Website:** www.english-heritage.org.uk/beeston
Open: Please visit www.english-heritage.org.uk/beeston for opening times, admission prices and the most up-to-date information.

Peover Hall

KIRKLINTON HALL AND GARDENS 🏛ⓕ
KIRKLINTON HALL, KIRKLINTON, CARLISLE CA6 6BB
www.kirklintonhall.co.uk

Adjacent to the 12th Century de Boyville stronghold, Kirklinton Hall is said to have been built from its stone. Begun in the 1670's, extended in the 1870's and ruined in the 1970's, the Hall has been a Restoration Great House, an RAF base, a school, a gangsters' gambling den and worse. Walk in the footsteps of Norman Knights, Cavalier Commanders, Victorian Plutocrats and the Kray twins. Now, Kirklinton Hall and its Gardens are being restored by the Boyle family to its former glory, a painstaking and fascinating process. It is also the official home of SlowFood Cumbria and is available for weddings and events. 'Spectacularly sinister ruin' - Pevsners Buildings of England.

Location: Map 10:K3. OS Ref NY433672. 6 miles north east of M6 junction 44, follow A7 towards Longtown. At Blackford turn right following sign to Kirklinton 5 miles. Stay on road and follow Brown Signs.

Owner: Mr and Mrs Christopher Boyle **Contact:** Alice Doyne or Ilona Boyle
Tel: 01697 748850 **Fax:** 01697 748472 **Facebook:** Kirklinton Hall.
Twitter: @kirklintonhall. **E-mail:** info@kirklintonhall.co.uk
Open: Open 1 Apr-30 Sep, 12-5 weekdays and Suns. Sats for Public or Private Events, Contact Alice Doyne. Available for Wedding Receptions.
Admission: Admission £4.00 Adults, £1.00 Children under 16. Free to HHA and MyCumbria Card Holders.
Key facts: 🖼 Postcards, David Austen Roses Books & Hudson's Heritage. 🌸 Specialising in David Austin Roses & Rare Rhododendrons. 🚻 Disabled Loo, Contact Alice for more information. ☕ Tea, coffee, cake, ice cream biscuits & soft drinks. 🍴 By arrangement for groups. 🅿 Free Car parking. 📷 Contact Alice Doyne. 🐕 On leads. 🏨 B&B at nearby Mallsgate Hall - contact Alice Doyne. 🛏

Kirklinton Hall

LEVENS HALL 🏛ⓕ
LEVENS HALL, KENDAL, CUMBRIA LA8 0PD
www.levenshall.co.uk

Levens Hall is an Elizabethan mansion built around a 13th Century pele tower. The much loved home of the Bagot family, with fine panelling, plasterwork, Cordova leather wall coverings, paintings by Rubens, Lely and Cuyp, the earliest English patchwork and Wellingtoniana combine with other beautiful objects to form a fascinating collection. The world famous Topiary Gardens were laid out by Monsieur Beaumont from 1694 and his design has remained largely unchanged to this day. Over 90 individual pieces of topiary, some over nine metres high, massive beech hedges and colourful seasonal bedding provide a magnificent visual impact.

Location: Map 10:L7. OS Ref SD495 851. 5m S of Kendal on the A6. Exit M6/J36.

Owner: C H Bagot **Contact:** The Administrator **Tel:** 015395 60321
Fax: 015395 60669 **E-mail:** houseopening@levenshall.co.uk
Open: 5 Apr-8 Oct Sun-Thu (closed Fri & Sat). Garden, Tea Room, Gift Shop & Plant Centre 10am-5pm. House 12 noon-4.30pm (last entry 4pm). Groups (20+) please book.
Winner of 'Cumbria Tourism Small Visitor Attraction of the Year 2013'
Admission: House & Gardens or Gardens Only. Please see www.levenshall.co.uk for full details, special offers & current events. Group Rates on application.
Key facts: ⓘ No indoor photography. 🖻 Gift shop. ♿ Partial. WCs. ● Licensed. 🍽 Licensed. 🎥 By arrangement. Ⓟ Free on-site parking. ⬛ 🐕 Assistance dogs only. ▲

MUNCASTER CASTLE GARDENS & OWL CENTRE 🏛ⓕ
MUNCASTER CASTLE, RAVENGLASS, CUMBRIA CA18 1RQ
www.muncaster.co.uk

The Large Visitor Attraction Silver winner at the 2012 Visit England Awards, Muncaster was described by Ruskin as Heaven's Gate. The many acres of Grade II* woodland gardens are famous for rhododendrons and breathtaking views of the Lake District fells. The Castle is a treasure trove of paintings, silver, embroideries and more. Muncaster hosts wonderful weddings, dinners and family celebrations. B&B is available in the "Coachman's Quarters". The World Owl Centre reveals a thrilling insight into these magical and mysterious creatures. Enjoy the Meet the Birds display and Heron Happy Hour. MeadowVole Maze, playground, gift shop, café & church. Special events throughout the year include the Muncaster Festival, Summer of Fun, Halloween Week, Christmas at the Castle and more. See www.muncaster.co.uk for details.

Location: Map 10:J7. OS Ref SD103 965. See our website for details. A595 1 mile south of Ravenglass. SatNav CA18 1RD.

Owner: Mrs Iona Frost Pennington
Contact: Reception
Tel: 01229 717614 **E-mail:** info@muncaster.co.uk
Open: Full Season: last Sun in Mar-last Sun in Oct, Gardens & World Owl Centre open daily 10.30am-6pm (dusk if earlier), Castle open Sun-Fri 12-4.30pm. Winter Season: 11am-4pm (dusk if earlier), Castle open reduced hours, please see website or call for details. Closed in Jan. Open for groups, conferences and weddings by appointment. See website or call for more details.
Admission: Please see www.muncaster.co.uk for details.
Key facts: ⓘ Church. Film location. 🖻 🎁 🍴 Wedding receptions and private parties. ♿ WCs. ● Licensed. 🍽 Licensed. 🎥 Private Castle and Garden Tours. 🎧 Individual audio tour. Ⓟ Free Parking. Central Coach parking. ⬛ Conservation and Owl tours available. 🐕 Dogs on leads only. ▤ ▲ ▨

ABBOT HALL ART GALLERY
Abbot Hall, Kendal, Cumbria LA9 5AL
www.abbothall.org.uk

Abbot Hall Art Gallery is housed in one of Kendal's most important buildings, a Grade I listed villa, on the banks of the River Kent. The galleries offer two floors of light-filled spaces in which to see art. The Gallery holds an impressive collection of 18th, 19th and 20th Century British art. The Gallery also hosts an ambitious temporary exhibition programme. **Location:** Map 10:L7. OS Ref SD517921. 10 min drive from M6 J36. Follow signs to south Kendal & then for Abbot Hall. Nearest train stations: main line, Oxenholme, the Lake District, local line, Kendal. **Owner/Contact:** Lakeland Arts **Tel:** 01539 722464 **E-mail:** info@abbothall.org.uk **Open:** Mon-Sat, 10.30am-5pm (4pm Nov-Feb). 16 Jan 2015-14 Feb 2016. Closed 24, 25, 26 Dec & 1 Jan. **Admission:** Adult £7.00 (without donation £6.35). Adult during Canaletto exhibition £9.00 (£8.15). Joint Gallery & Museum £9.00 (£8.60). Joint Gallery & Museum during Canaletto exhibition £10.00 (£9.00). Children & students free, 50% discount for National Art Pass. **Key facts:** ▣ The Gallery Shop is packed with books on art & culture, artists' prints & materials. ◉ Serving a menu of freshly prepared sandwiches & locally produced soups, quiches & cakes. ℙ Pay & display parking on site. ▣ See our website for details. ❋ See opening times.

ASKHAM HALL AND GARDENS
Askham, Penrith, Cumbria CA10 2PF
www.askhamhall.co.uk

Meander through the beautiful gardens, visit the animals and enjoy lunch in the Kitchen Garden Café. Askham Hall is grade I listed, dating back to the late 1200s. It has recently been transformed from a stately family home into a stylish retreat also with a restaurant, 12 luxurious bedrooms and a wedding barn. **Location:** Map 10:L5. OS Ref NY514237. Askham Hall in Cumbria is situated in a quiet and picturesque village within easy access (about ten minutes drive) from Penrith and junction 40 of the M6. Follow the brown tourist signs. **Tel:** 01931 712350 **E-mail:** enquiries@askhamhall.co.uk **Open:** Gardens and café: Every day except Sat. 10am to 5pm in high season, reduced hours and times in low season. Restaurant and accommodation: Tue- Sat for dinner and overnight stays. **Admission:** Entry to the gardens and animals: Adult £5.50, children are free. **Key facts:** ℹ http://www.askhamhall.co.uk/gardens-and-cafe/ ▣ ▣ ◉ Free to enter. ⦿ ▣ Groups, by arrangement. ℙ Free. ▣ Permitted in café but not gardens. ▣ ▲ ▣

Gardens at Hutton In The Forest

BLACKWELL, THE ARTS & CRAFTS HOUSE
Bowness-on-Windermere, Cumbria LA23 3JT
www.blackwell.org.uk

Blackwell, completed in 1900, is the largest and most important surviving example of work by architect Mackay Hugh Baillie Scott. Designed as a holiday retreat for Sir Edward Holt, the house survives in a truly remarkable state of preservation retaining many original decorative features. Visitors are encouraged to sit and soak up the atmosphere in Blackwell's fireplace inglenooks and are free to enjoy the house as it was originally intended, without roped-off areas. The period rooms are furnished with Arts & Crafts furniture and decorative arts, which are complemented by exhibitions of historical applied arts and contemporary craft. **Location:** Map 10:K7. OS Ref SD401945. 1.5 m S of Bowness just off the A5074 on the B5360. **Owner:** Lakeland Arts **Contact:** Blackwell **Tel:** 015394 46139 **E-mail:** info@blackwell.org.uk **Open:** Daily 10.30am-5pm (4pm Nov-Feb). 16 Jan-31 Dec 2015. Closed 25 & 26 Dec. **Admission:** Adult £8.50 (without donation £7.70), Children & Students free, 50% discount for National Art Pass. **Key facts:** ▣ Shop stocks contemporary craft by leading craft-makers selected for its quality & beauty. ▣ WCs. ◉ Café menu emphasises quality & the handmade, reflecting the philosophy of Arts & Crafts Movement. ℙ Free for cars, coaches by appointment. ▣ See website. ▣ Guide dogs only. ❋

DALEMAIN MANSION & GARDENS 🏛
Penrith, Cumbria CA11 0HB
www.dalemain.com

A fine mixture of Mediaeval, Tudor & early Georgian architecture. Lived in by the same family since 1679 and home to the International Marmalade Festival. Award winning gardens, richly planted with unusual combinations of flowers and shrubs. Highlights include the Rose Walk, Ancient Apple Trees, Tudor Knot Garden, Blue Himalayan Poppies, Earth Sculpture and Stumpery.
Location: Map 10:L5. OS Ref NY477 269. On A592 1m S of A66. 4m SW of Penrith. London, M1, M6/J40. Edinburgh, A73, M74, M6/J40.
Owner: Robert Hasell-McCosh Esq **Contact:** Jennifer Little - Administrator
Tel: 017684 86450 **Fax:** 017684 86223 **E-mail:** admin@dalemain.com
Open: 29 Mar-29 Oct: Gardens, Tearoom & Gift Shop: Sun-Thu 10.30am-5pm (4pm in Oct). House 11.15am-4pm (3pm in Oct). Groups (12+) please book.
Admission: House & Gardens or Gardens Only. Please see www.dalemain.com for details. Group Prices on application. **Key facts:** ℹ No photography in house. Moorings available on Ullswater. Phone for event enquiries. ⬜ 🚻 🍽 ♿ Partial. WCs. 🐕 🍴 Licensed. 🎦 1hr tours. German and French translations. Garden tour for groups extra. 🅿 50 yds. Free. ⬛ 🐕 Guide dogs only. 🐾

HOLKER HALL & GARDENS 🏛ⓕ
Cark-In-Cartmel, Grange-Over-Sands, Cumbria LA11 7PL
www.holker.co.uk

Holker is the family home of the Cavendish family, set amongst beautiful countryside surrounding the Lake District. Steeped in history, this magnificent Victorian Mansion of neo-Elizabethan Gothic style was largely re-built in the 1870's following a fire, but origins date back to the 1600's. The glorious gardens, café, food hall & gift shop complete the visitor experience.
Location: Map 10:K8. From Motorway M6/J36, Signed Barrow A590.
Owner: Cavendish Family **Contact:** Jillian Rouse
Tel: 015395 58328 **Fax:** 015395 58378 **E-mail:** info@holker.co.uk
Open: Hall: 28 Mar-1 Nov, Wed-Sun & BH Mons (closed Mon & Tue), 11am-4pm. Gardens: 10.30am-5pm. Cafe, Food Hall & Gift Shop: 28 Mar-23 Dec from 10.30am, Wed-Sun & BH Mons. **Admission:** Hall & Gardens: Adult £12.00, Child FOC. Gardens only: Adult £8.00, Child FOC. Hall only: Adults £7.50, Child FOC. Group Rates (10+) Hall & Gardens: Adult £8.00 Gardens only: Adult £5.50.
Key facts: ℹ No photography in house. 🏪 Food Hall. 🍴 🍽 ♿ 🐕 🚻 🎦 For groups, by arrangement. 🅿 75 yds from Hall. ⬛ 🐕 Dogs on leads (in park). 🐾

HUTTON-IN-THE-FOREST 🏛ⓕ
Hutton-in-the-Forest, Penrith, Cumbria CA11 9TH
www.hutton-in-the-forest.co.uk

The home of Lord Inglewood's family since 1605. Built around a medieval pele tower with 17th, 18th and 19th Century additions. Fine collections of furniture, paintings, ceramics and tapestries.
Outstanding grounds with terraces, topiary, walled garden, dovecote and woodland walk through magnificent specimen trees.
Location: Map 10:L5. OS Ref NY460 358. 6m NW of Penrith & 2m from M6 Jct 41 on B5305. **Owner:** Lord Inglewood **Contact:** Pamela Davidson
Tel: 017684 84449 **E-mail:** info@hutton-in-the-forest.co.uk
Open: House: 29 Mar-3 Oct. Weds, Thus, Suns and BH Mons, 12.30-4pm. Tearoom as House 11am-4.30pm. Gardens & Grounds: 29 Mar-1 Nov, daily except Sat, 11am-5pm.
Admission: Please see website or phone for details.
Key facts: ℹ Picnic area. 🏪 Gift stall selling locally made crafts and produce. 🌱 Small selection of beautiful plants grown by our Head Gardener. 🍴 By arrangement. ♿ Partial. WCs. 🐕 Licensed. 🎦 Guided tours available. 🅿 ⬛ 🐕 Dogs welcome on leads. 🐾

THE BEATRIX POTTER GALLERY 🌿
Main Street, Hawkshead, Ambleside LA22 0NS

This quirky 17th Century building, once the office of Beatrix Potter's husband, is now home to the National Trust's collection of original Beatrix Potter artwork. By popular demand, our 'On Holiday with Beatrix Potter' exhibition has been extended. With new exhibits featuring classic illustrations alongside rarely seen gems, it makes a great visit for Beatrix Potter fans of any age. Children can enjoy the interactive touch-screens, test themselves against the Gallery quiz or curl up with a good book in our cosy reading corner. Nearby Hill Top is a must visit too, for Beatrix Potter fans. **Location:** Map 10:K7. OS Ref SD35 1982. Take the B5286 from Ambleside (4 miles); or the B5285 from Coniston (5 miles). Park in Hawkshead village, Gallery located next to the Red Lion Inn. **Owner:** National Trust
Tel: 015394 36355 / 015349 41456. **E-mail:** beatrixpottergallery@ nationaltrust.org.uk **Website:** www.nationaltrust.org.uk/beatrix-potter-gallery
Open: Check website for details. **Admission:** Free for National Trust members. Check website for full details. **Key facts:** 🏪

BRANTWOOD 🏛
Coniston, Cumbria LA21 8AD

Brantwood, the former home of John Ruskin, is the most beautifully situated house in the Lake District. Filled with many fine paintings, beautiful furniture and Ruskin's personal treasures it retains the special feeling of being a much loved home. Explore Brantwood's estate and gardens or experience contemporary art in the Severn Studio. Enjoy a vibrant programme of events and exhibitions.
Location: Map 10:K7. OS Ref SD312 959. 2½m from Coniston village on the E side of Coniston Water. **Owner:** The Brantwood Trust **Contact:** Rachel Litten
Tel: 01539 441396 **Fax:** 01539 441263 **E-mail:** enquiries@brantwood.org.uk
Website: www.brantwood.org.uk **Open:** Mid Mar-Mid Nov: daily, 10.30am-5.00pm. Mid Nov-Mid Mar: Wed-Sun, 10.30am-4.00pm. **Admission:** House & Garden: (inc. gift aid) Adult £7.95, Students £6.30, Children Free. Gardens only: Adult £5.50, Student £4.50. **Key facts:** ℹ No photography in house. 🏪 Specialist book titles, crafts & gifts. 🍴 Rooms for business hire. ♿ Ground floor only. 🐕 🍽 Licensed. 🎦 By arrangement. 🅿 Limited for coaches. ⬛ Activities for schools. 🐕 In grounds, on leads. 🏠 Self catering accommodation. 🏠 ❄ 🐾

MIREHOUSE 🏠ⓕ
Keswick, Cumbria CA12 4QE

Melvyn Bragg described Mirehouse as 'Manor from Heaven'. Set in stunning landscape, Mirehouse is a literary house linked with Tennyson and Wordsworth. Live piano music and children's history trail in house. Natural playgrounds, serene bee garden and lakeside walk.

Location: Map 10:J5. OS Ref NY235 284. Beside A591, 3½m N of Keswick. Good bus service. **Owner:** James Fryer-Spedding
Contact: Janaki Spedding
Tel: 017687 72287 **E-mail:** info@mirehouse.com
Website: www.mirehouse.com
Open: Please see website for up to date opening times and admission prices.
Key facts: ⓘ No photography in house. 🔲 📷 ⓘ By arrangement. 🅿 🔲 🐾 On leads in grounds.

CARLISLE CASTLE ⌗
Carlisle, Cumbria CA3 8UR

Standing proudly in the city it has dominated for nine centuries, Carlisle Castle was a constantly updated working fortress until well within living memory.
Location: Map 10:K3. OS Ref NY396 562. **Tel:** 01228 591922 **E-mail:** customers@english-heritage.org.uk **Website:** www.english-heritage.org.uk/carlisle **Open:** Please see website for up to date opening and admission details.

LANERCOST PRIORY ⌗
Lanercost, Brampton, Cumbria CA8 2HQ

This Augustian Priory was founded c1166. The east end of the noble 13th Century church survives to its full height. **Location:** Map 10:L3. OS Ref NY556 637.
Tel: 01697 73030 **E-mail:** customers@english-heritage.org.uk
Website: www.english-heritage.org.uk/lanercost
Open: Please see website for up to date opening and admission details.

Browsholme Hall

LEIGHTON HALL 🏠ⓕ
CARNFORTH, LANCASHIRE LA5 9ST
www.leightonhall.co.uk

Leighton Hall's setting, in a bowl of parkland against a backdrop of the Lakeland Fells, can deservedly be described as spectacular. Nestled in 1,550 acres of lush grounds, this romantic, Gothic house is the lived-in home of the famous Gillow furniture making family.
Boasting priceless pieces of Gillow furniture, pictures, clocks, silver and objéts d'art, Leightons' informal guided tours appeal to all ages. Outside the Hall are woodland walks, an abundant 19th Century walled garden, herbaceous borders and roses, a fragrant herb patch and an ornamental vegetable plot. Birds of prey are flown every day at 3:30pm (weather permitting). Finally, visit Leighton's charming tea rooms for a quintessential English afternoon tea.
Location: Map 10:L8. OS Ref SD494 744. 9m N of Lancaster, 10m S of Kendal, 3m N of Carnforth. 1½ m W of A6. 3m from M6/A6/J35, signed from J35A.

Owner: Richard Gillow Reynolds Esq
Contact: Mrs C S Reynolds
Tel: 01524 734474 **Fax:** 01524 720357
Additional Contact: Mrs Lucy Arthurs
E-mail: info@leightonhall.co.uk
Open: May-Sep, Tue-Fri (also BH Sun and Mon, Sun in Aug) 2-5pm.
Pre-booked groups (25+) all year by arrangement. Group rates.
Admission: Adult £7.75, OAP/Student £6.95, Child (5 - 12 years) £4.95, Family (2 adults and up to 3 children) £24.50, Grounds only £4.50.
Key facts: ⓘ No photography in house. 🔲📷🚽🔲 Partial. WCs. 📷ⓘ🅿 Free and ample parking. 🔲 3 themed packages available covering the new cross curriculum. 🐾 On leads, on the parkland only. 🔲🔲

BROWSHOLME HALL 🏛
Clitheroe, Lancashire BB7 3DE
www.browsholme.com

Built in 1507 and the ancestral Home of the Parker Family, Browsholme is the oldest surviving home in Lancashire. This remarkable Tudor Hall has a major collection of oak furniture, portraits, glass, arms and armour. In 2010 an 18th Century 'tithe barn' was restored for refreshments, concerts, theatre, events and weddings.

Location: Map 10:M10. OS Ref SD683 452. 5m NW of Clitheroe off B6243.
Owner: The Parker Family
Contact: Catherine Turner - Administrator
Tel: 01254 827160
E-mail: info@browsholme.com
Open: Gardens & Tearoom 11am–4.30pm. Hall tours 1pm. Every Wed May to Sep. First Sun in each month May to Sep. Spring & Aug BH Mons. Booked parties & groups welcome at other times, inc Christmas (7-11 Dec), by prior arrangement.
Admission: See website for full details.
Key facts: 🖼 🍴 📷 🅿 🍽 🚻 Guide dogs only. 🏠 🛏

LANCASTER CASTLE
Shire Hall, Castle Parade, Lancaster, Lancashire LA1 1YJ
www.lancastercastle.com

Situated on a hill fortified by the Romans, Lancaster Castle is one of the most iconic buildings in the north-west of England. For over 800 years its primary function has been associated with law and order, serving as both a court and prison, and throughout this period it has witnessed some of the most famous and infamous trials in English history, including those of the Lancashire Witches.

Location: Map 10:L9. OS Ref SD473 618. In centre of Lancaster, roughly 250yds from train station & signposted from jcts 33 & 34 M6. Bus station 10 min walk.
Owner: The Duchy of Lancaster; tours by Lancashire County Council.
Contact: Information Desk **Tel:** 01524 64998 **E-mail:** lancastercastle @lancashire.gov.uk **Open:** 7 days/week (not Christmas/New Year) 9.30am-5pm. Guided tours 10am-4pm (1 Nov-28 Feb, 10am-3pm). **Admission:** Adults £8.00, Conc. £6.50, Family £20.00 (2+2 or 1+3). Accompanying Carers Free. Under 16s must be accompanied by adult. Xplorer Ticket deals. **Key facts:** ℹ️ No photography. 🛍 Quality souvenirs, Royal Collection items. 🎪 Corporate events; please contact. 🛗 Tour not suitable. Access to courtyard, shop & café. 🍽 NICE @ The Castle. 01524 848525. francesca@lancastercastle.com. 📷 📍 Tours for school parties of all ages, please contact. 🐕 Assistance dogs only. 🛏

HOGHTON TOWER 🏛ⓡ
Hoghton, Preston, Lancashire PR5 0SH

Visit award-winning Hoghton Tower. Join a tour of the staterooms to learn about the history of the house. Stroll through the walled gardens. Kids love the family tours, dungeons and dolls houses. Browse the shop and finish with an afternoon tea. Luxury accommodation available. Private and school tours welcome. Venue for private parties and weddings.

Location: Map 10:L11. OS Ref SD622 264. M65/J3. Midway between Preston & Blackburn on A675. **Owner:** Hoghton Tower Preservation Trust
Contact: Office **Tel:** 01254 852986
E-mail: mail@hoghtontower.co.uk **Website:** www.hoghtontower.co.uk
Open: May-Sep Sun to Thu. Oct limited tour times. BH Suns & Mons except Christmas & New Year. House open every Farmers Market Sunday. Group visits by appointment all year. Check website for variations. **Admission:** Please check website. **Key facts:** 🛍 Gift ideas. 🎪 Conferences. 🍰 Homemade cakes. 📷 Obligatory. 🅿 🍽 Prebook only. 🐕 Assis dog only. 🏠 Self-catering. 🏠 🛏

ASTLEY HALL, COACH HOUSE AND PARK 🏛
Astley Hall, Astley Park, Off Hallgate, Chorley PR7 1NP
Astley Hall "the most exhilarating house in Lancashire" (Simon Jenkins).
Location: Map 10:L11. OS Ref SD574 183. Jct 8 on M61. Signposted from A6
Tel: 01257 515151 **E-mail:** astley.hall@chorley.gov.uk
Website: www.chorley.gov.uk/astleyhall
Open: See website. **Admission:** Free admission.

MANCHESTER CATHEDRAL
Victoria Street, Manchester M3 1SX
Manchester Cathedral Grade I listed masterpiece. **Location:** Map 6:N1. OS Ref SJ838 988. **Tel:** 0161 833 2220 **Fax:** 0161 839 6218
E-mail: office@manchestercathedral.org
Website: www.manchestercathedral.org **Open:** Every day of the year, from 9am; various closing times. Please check the website. **Admission:** Donations welcome.

MEOLS HALL 🏛ⓡ
Churchtown, Southport, Merseyside PR9 7LZ
17th Century house with subsequent additions. Interesting collection of pictures and furniture. Tithe Barn available for wedding ceremonies and receptions all year.
Location: Map 10:K11. OS Ref SD365 184. 3m NE of Southport town centre in Churchtown. SE of A565.
Owner: The Hesketh Family
Contact: Pamela Whelan
Tel: 01704 228326 **Fax:** 01704 507185
E-mail: events@meolshall.com
Website: www.meolshall.com
Open: May BH Monday: 4 and 25 May and from 20 Aug-14 Sep.
Admission: Adult £4.00, Child £1.00. Groups welcome but Afternoon Tea is only available for bookings of 25+.
Key facts: 🎪 Wedding ceremonies and receptions available in the Tithe Barn. 🛍 🍴 🅿 🚻 🏠 🛏

Hoghton Tower

CHRIST CHURCH 🏛
Bridge Street, Macclesfield, Cheshire SK11 6EG
Tel: 0845 303 2760 **E-mail:** central@thecct.org.uk

LITTLE MORETON HALL 🌿
Congleton, Cheshire CW12 4SD
Tel: 01260 272018 **E-mail:** littlemoretonhall@nationaltrust.org.uk

ST MARY'S CHURCH 🏛
Thornton Green Lane, Thornton-le-Moors, Chester CH2 4HU
Tel: 0845 303 2760 **E-mail:** central@thecct.org.uk

ALLAN BANK 🌿
Grasmere, Cumbria LA22 9QZ
Tel: 015394 35143 **E-mail:** allanbank@nationaltrust.org.uk

DOVE COTTAGE & WORDSWORTH MUSEUM
Grasmere, Cumbria LA22 9SH
Tel: 01539 435544 **E-mail:** enquiries@wordsworth.org.uk

HILL TOP 🌿
Near Sawrey, Hawkshead, Ambleside, Cumbria LA22 0LF
Tel: 015394 36269 **E-mail:** hilltop@nationaltrust.org.uk

LOWTHER CASTLE & GARDENS TRUST
Lowther Castle, Penrith, Cumbria CA10 2HG
Tel: 01931 712192

NAWORTH CASTLE
Naworth Castle Estate, Brampton, Cumbria CA8 2HF
Tel: 016977 3229. **E-mail:** office@naworth.co.uk

OLD CHANCEL 🏛
Ireby, Cockermouth, Cumbria CA7 1HD
Tel: 0845 303 2760 **E-mail:** central@thecct.org.uk

RYDAL MOUNT & GARDENS
Rydal, Cumbria LA22 9LU
Tel: 01539 433002 **E-mail:** info@rydalmount.co.uk

ST GREGORY'S CHURCH 🏛
Marthwaite, Vale of Lune, Sedbergh, Cumbria LA10 5ED
Tel: 0845 303 2760 **E-mail:** central@thecct.org.uk

ST NINIAN'S CHURCH 🏛
Brougham, Penrith, Cumbria CA10 2AD
Tel: 0845 303 2760 **E-mail:** central@thecct.org.uk

SIZERGH CASTLE AND GARDEN 🌿
Sizergh, Kendal, Cumbria LA8 8AE
Tel: 015395 60951 **E-mail:** sizergh@nationaltrust.org.uk

STOTT PARK BOBBIN MILL ⌗
Colton, Ulverston, Cumbria LA12 8AX
Tel: 01539 531087 **E-mail:** stott.park@english-heritage.org.uk

TOWNEND 🌿
Troutbeck, Windermere, Cumbria LA23 1LB
Tel: 015394 32628 **E-mail:** townend@nationaltrust.org.uk

TULLIE HOUSE MUSEUM & ART GALLERY
Castle Street, Carlisle, Cumbria CA3 8TP
Tel: 01228 618718 **E-mail:** enquiries@tulliehouse.org

WORDSWORTH HOUSE AND GARDEN 🌿
Main Street, Cockermouth, Cumbria CA13 9RX
Tel: 01900 820884 **E-mail:** wordsworthhouse@nationaltrust.org.uk

ALL SOULS' CHURCH 🏛
Astley Street, Bolton, Lancashire BL1 8EH
Tel: 0845 303 2760 **E-mail:** central@thecct.org.uk

CHRIST CHURCH 🏛
Heaton Norris, Stockport, Lancashire SK4 2LJ
Tel: 0845 303 2760 **E-mail:** central@thecct.org.uk

CHURCH OF ST JOHN THE BAPTIST 🏛
School Lane, Pilling, Lancaster, Lancashire PR3 6HD
Tel: 0845 303 2760 **E-mail:** central@thecct.org.uk

CHURCH OF ST JOHN THE EVANGELIST 🏛
North Road, Lancaster, Lancashire LA1 1PA
Tel: 0845 303 2760 **E-mail:** central@thecct.org.uk

GAWTHORPE HALL 🌿
Padiham, Nr Burnley, Lancashire BB12 8UA
Tel: 01282 771004 **E-mail:** gawthorpehall@nationaltrust.org.uk

HOLY TRINITY CHURCH 🏛
Mount Pleasant, Blackburn, Lancashire BB1 5DQ
Tel: 0845 303 2760 **E-mail:** central@thecct.org.uk

RUFFORD OLD HALL 🌿
Rufford, Nr Ormskirk, Lancashire L40 1SG
Tel: 01704 821254 **E-mail:** ruffordoldhall@nationaltrust.org.uk

ST LEONARD'S CHURCH 🏛
Old Langho Road, Old Langho, Blackburn, Lancs BB6 8AW
Tel: 0845 303 2760 **E-mail:** central@thecct.org.uk

ST MARY'S CHURCH 🏛
Tarleton, Preston, Lancashire PR4 6HJ
Tel: 0845 303 2760 **E-mail:** central@thecct.org.uk

ST THOMAS' CHURCH 🏛
Heights Lane, Friarmere, Oldham, Lancashire OL3 5TU
Tel: 0845 303 2760 **E-mail:** central@thecct.org.uk

SMITHILLS HALL
Smithills Dean Road, Bolton BL7 7NP
Tel: 01204 332377 **E-mail:** historichalls@bolton.gov.uk

HEATON HALL
Heaton Park, Prestwich, Manchester M25 9WL
Tel: 0161 235 8815

ST GEORGE'S CHURCH 🏛
Manchester Road, Carrington, Greater Manchester M31 4AG
Tel: 0845 303 2760 **E-mail:** central@thecct.org.uk

ST WERBURGH'S CHURCH 🏛
Church Green, Warburton, Warrington WA13 9SS
Tel: 0845 303 2760 **E-mail:** central@thecct.org.uk

CHRIST CHURCH 🏛
Waterloo Road, Waterloo, Liverpool, Merseyside L22 1RF
Tel: 0845 303 2760 **E-mail:** central@thecct.org.uk

Cholmondeley Castle, Cheshire

Lady Waterford Hall, Northumberland

North East

Coast and castles, mansions built with fortunes founded on coal, the North East is becoming increasingly popular for holidaymakers seeking out its distinctive history, culture and countryside.

New Entries for 2015:
• Lady Waterford Hall
• The Castle Keep

Northumberland

Tyne & Wear

Co. Durham

Find stylish hotels with a personal welcome and good cuisine in the North East. More information on page 364.

• Waren House Hotel

SIGNPOST
SELECTED PREMIER HOTELS 2015

VISITOR INFORMATION

■ Owner
Auckland Castle Trust

■ Address
Market Place
Bishop Auckland
County Durham
DL14 7NR

■ Location
Map 10:P5
OS Ref. NZ213 302
From the Southbound A1, take junction 61 (Bowburn Interchange) sign posted Bishop Auckland (A688), 10 miles. From the Northbound A1 take junction 60 (Bradbury Interchange) sign posted Bishop Auckland, 8 miles. Darlington train station approx. 14 miles. Durham train station approx. 13 miles. Newcastle International Airport approx. 40 miles. Durham Tees Valley Airport approx. 20 miles.

Situated just off the Market Place in Bishop Auckland town centre.

■ Contact
Contact Visitor Services for opening times, group bookings, admissions etc.
Tel: 01388 743750
E-mail: enquiries@ aucklandcastle.org

■ Opening Times
31st March - 31st October 2015
Open daily (except Tuesday) from 10.30am to 3.30pm (last adm). Dates correct at time of publication, please check website for alterations.

■ Admission
Adults £8.00
Children under 16 Free

Those who take part in our short visitors survey will receive a 50% discount on admissions.

■ Special Events
Auckland Castle has a varied events programme running throughout each open season. To be kept up to date, please visit our website and subscribe to our mailing list or view the events listing.

Conference/Function
The Castle is available for private events ranging from initmate dinners to weddings and large outdoor events. Please contact our Events Team who will be happy to assist with your enquiry.

Auckland Castle

AUCKLAND CASTLE
www.aucklandcastle.org

Home to the Bishop of Durham for over 900 years and now fully open to the public, Auckland Castle is one of the best preserved medieval Bishops' palaces in Europe.

Following the Norman Conquest and the subsequent Harrying of the North, the Bishop of Durham was granted exceptional powers to act as a political and military leader. With Auckland Castle as his seat of power in North-East England, the King allowed him to raise taxes, mint coins, and hold his own parliaments. Such royal privileges made the Bishop of Durham the second most powerful man in the country – ruling the area between the Tyne and the Tees. Wealth, power, and influence flowed through Auckland Castle and left us the treasure that we invite you to explore. Our state rooms include The Long Dining Room, remodelled by Bishop Trevor (1752-71) and home to the thirteen paintings of Jacob and his Twelve Sons by Fransisco de Zurbarán (1598-1664).

Our other impressive state apartments house an exhibition exploring power and religion in Renaissance and Tudor England, the centrepiece of which is the recently rediscovered Paradise State Bed of Henry VII & Elizabeth of York. Also on display are key examples of Counter Reformation religious art, which contextualise and compliment the Zurbaráns, including paintings by Giovanni Bilivert, Lubin Baugin and Jusepe Ribera. St Peter's Chapel, widely acknowledged as the largest private chapel in Europe, is a fine example of the influence of Bishop Cosin with its stained glass, angels, Flemish reredos and the retable with imagery of the Instruments of the Passion. Our beautiful gardens and expansive parkland are a pleasure to explore, at the heart of which is a splendid Deer House folly.

KEY FACTS

- We have a gift shop on site stocking a range of locally sourced items.

- Auckland Castle is available for private hire, please visit the private hire section of our website or contact our Events Team.

- We have a cafe on site providing light lunches, afternoon tea and a range of hot and cold beverages.

- Guided tours take place twice a day - please see the Visiting Us section of our website or contact Visitor Services on 01388 743750 for details.

- Auckland Castle has an active education programme and works with many schools accross County Durham and the wider region. Please contact our Education and Outreach Team on 01388 743750 for more details or visit our website.

- Guide Dogs Only. Dog walkers welcome in the Bishop's Park.

St Peter's Chapel

The Deer House, Bishop's Park

RABY CASTLE 🏰Ⓕ
RABY CASTLE, STAINDROP, DARLINGTON, CO. DURHAM DL2 3AH
www.rabycastle.com

Raby Castle is surrounded by a large deer park, with two lakes and a beautiful walled garden with formal lawns, yew hedges and an ornamental pond. It was built by the mighty Nevill family in the 14th Century, and has been home to Lord Barnard's family since 1626. Highlights include the vast Barons' Hall, where it is reputed 700 knights gathered to plot the doomed 'Rising of the North' rebellion, and the stunning Octagon Drawing Room. With Meissen porcelain, fine furniture and paintings by Munnings, Reynolds, Van Dyck, Batoni, Teniers, Amigoni and Vernet. Also in the grounds is the 18th Century Stable block with impressive horse-drawn carriage collection, and a delightfully converted Gift Shop and Tearooms, and woodland play area.

Location: Map 10:O5. OS Ref NZ129 218. On A688, 1m N of Staindrop. 8m NE of Barnard Castle, 12m WNW of Darlington.
Owner: The Lord Barnard **Contact:** Castle Admin Office
Tel: 01833 660202 **E-mail:** admin@rabycastle.com

Open: Castle: Easter weekend Sat, Sun, Mon. May & Jun, Sun-Wed. Jul & Aug, Daily except Sats, Sep Sun-Wed. 1pm-4.30pm.
Park & Gardens: As Castle, 11am-5.00pm.
Admission: Castle, Park & Gardens: Adult £10.00, Child (5-15yrs) £4.50, Conc. £9.00, Family discounts available. Groups (12+): Adult £7.50. Park & Gardens: Adult £6.00, Child £2.50, Conc. £5.00. Groups (12+) Adult £4.50. Season Tickets available. Private Group Guided Tours (20+)* Adult £8.50 *Please book in advance. **Key facts:** ⓘ No photography or video filming is permitted inside. Colour guidebook on sale. 🖼 Gift Shop. ⬜ Limited access to Castle interior. Accessible WCs, designated parking, free wheelchair loan. ☕ Tearoom. 🎟 Castle Tours available on certain dates. 🅿 Ample car parking on grass and coach parking on hard standing. 🏫 Schools by arrangement, £4 a head. 🐕 Dogs welcome on leads in deer park only. No dogs are allowed in the Walled Gardens or inside buildings. ♿

Raby Castle

BINCHESTER ROMAN FORT
Bishop Auckland, Co. Durham
www.durham.gov.uk/archaeology

Displayed remains consist of part of commanding officer's house with attached baths-suite which includes one of best preserved examples of a hypocaust (underfloor heating) in whole of Britain. New excavations - both inside fort and in the civil settlement - can be visited weekdays beginning June until end of August. Programme of re-enactment events throughout season; for details see www.durham.gov.uk/archaeology.
Location: Map 10:P5. OS Ref NZ210 312. 1½m N of Bishop Auckland, signposted from A690 Durham-Crook and from A688 Spennymoor-Bishop Auckland roads.
Owner: Durham County Council **Contact:** Archaeology Section
Tel: 01388 663089 / 03000 267013 (outside opening hours).
Open: Every day, Easter Sat to end Sep 11am-5pm; Jul & Aug 10am-4.30pm.
Admission: Adult £3.00, Concession £2.00, Children £1.50, Under 4 Free.
Key facts: ⓘ ⬚ Publications and souvenirs for sale. Ⓟ Coaches should approach the fort from lane (Wear Chare) off Bishop Auckland market-place.
▦ School visits and activitiy days by arrangement. ⊠ Assistance dogs only. ♿

DURHAM CATHEDRAL
Durham DH1 3EH
www.durhamcathedral.co.uk

A World Heritage Site. Norman architecture. Burial place of St Cuthbert and the Venerable Bede.
Location: Map 10:P4. OS Ref NZ274 422. Durham City Centre.
Contact: The Cathedral Office
Tel: 0191 3864266
E-mail: enquiries@durhamcathedral.co.uk
Open: Daily 7.30am-6pm (8pm Summer), with Services three times daily.
Admission: Free, donations very welcome. Groups contact visits@durhamcathedral.co.uk www.facebook.com/DurhamCathedral
Key facts: ⓘ ⬚ Ⓣ ▣ Partial. ▦ ⑪ ⑂
Ⓟ Limited disabled, public parking nearby.
▦ ⊠ Guide dogs only. ❋ ♿

THE BOWES MUSEUM
Barnard Castle, County Durham DL12 8NP
www.thebowesmuseum.org.uk

Set in beautiful grounds, the newly transformed Museum houses fine art, fashion and textiles, ceramics and furniture. The iconic Silver Swan musical automation performs daily at 2pm. A rolling exhibition programme is complemented by varied indoor and outdoor events, the acclaimed Café Bowes and a high quality gift shop. Tranquil gardens and woodland walks add to the enjoyment. **Location:** Map 10:O6. OS Ref NZ055 163. Situated on Newgate in Barnard Castle. Just off the A66 in the heart of the North Pennines. **Tel:** 01833 690606 **Fax:** 01833 637163
E-mail: info@thebowesmuseum.org.uk **Open:** 10.00-5.00 daily. Closed only 25 & 26 Dec & 1 Jan. **Admission:** Adults £9.50, Conc. £8.50, 6 month pass £14.00. Admission to all exhibitions included. Accompanied children Free (U16). Accompanying carers Free. Free access to Café Bowes, Shop & Grounds.
Key facts: ⬚ Souvenirs & gifts. Open daily 10.00-4.45. Ⓣ hire@thebowes museum.org.uk. ▣ Access to all areas. ▦ Locally produced seasonal menu, speciality teas, coffees & wines. Mon-Sat 9.00-4.30, Sun 10.00-4.30. ⑂ Available via group visits or selected days in Summer. ⓘ Children's Audio available. Ⓟ Ample free parking & coach & accessible parking bays. ▦ education@thebowes museum.org.uk. ⊠ Except guide dogs. ▦ hire@thebowesmuseum.org.uk. ❋

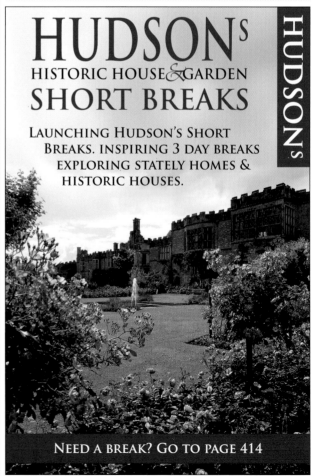

ALNWICK CASTLE 🏠Ⓕ
www.alnwickcastle.com

Home to the Duke of Northumberland's family, the Percys, for over 700 years; Alnwick Castle offers history on a grand scale.

Alnwick Castle's remarkable history is brimming with drama, intrigue, and extraordinary people; from a gunpowder plotter and visionary collectors, to decadent hosts and medieval England's most celebrated knight: Harry Hotspur.

Combining magnificent medieval architecture with sumptuous Italianate State Rooms, Alnwick Castle is one of the UK's most significant heritage destinations. In recent years it has also taken starring roles in a number of film and television productions, featuring as a location for ITV's Downton Abbey and as Hogwarts School of Witchcraft and Wizardry in the Harry Potter films.

With a history beginning in the Norman Age, Alnwick Castle was originally built as a border defence, before eventually being transformed from a fortification into a family home for the first Duke and Duchess of Northumberland in the 1760s.

The castle's State Rooms were later recreated by the 4th Duke in the lavish Italian Renaissance style that we see today, now boasting one of the country's finest private collections of art and furniture.

This remarkable collection includes works by Canaletto, Titian, Van Dyck, Turner, and Dobson; an extensive gallery of Meissen, Chelsea, and Paris porcelain; and the priceless Cucci cabinets, originally created for Louis XIV of France.

Alnwick Castle aims to create a vibrant and engaging heritage experience for families, with opportunities aplenty for children to get hands-on with history in the Knight's Quest arena, with dressing up, swordplay, medieval crafts and games.

KEY FACTS

- ℹ️ Storage available for suitcases. Photography is not permitted in the State Rooms.
- 🛍️ Gift Shop open daily.
- 🍽️ Team-building, banqueting, dinner dances. Call 01665 511 086.
- ♿ Accessible WCs. Free wheelchair and mobility scooter hire available. Limited access in areas.
- 🍷 Licensed.
- 🚶 Free daily tours of the State Rooms and grounds.
- 🅿️ Coach parking also available.
- Ⓟ Workshops, activities and discounted admission available. Call 01665 511 184.
- 🐕 Assistance dogs only.
- 🔔 Wedding ceremonies and receptions. Call 01665 511 086.
- 📺 See website for details.

VISITOR INFORMATION

■ Owner
His Grace The Duke of Northumberland

■ Address
Alnwick Castle
Alnwick
Northumberland
NE66 1NQ

■ Location
Well signposted less than a mile off A1; 35 miles north of Newcastle and 80 miles south of Edinburgh.
Bus: Regular bus services to Alnwick from around the region
Rail: 4 miles from Alnmouth Station (3.5 hours from London King's Cross)
Air: 34 miles from Newcastle Airport
Sea: 37 miles from North Sea ferry terminal

■ Contact
Tel: 01665 511 100
Group bookings: 01665 511 184.
Media & filming: 01665 511 794.
E-mail: info@alnwickcastle.com

■ Opening Times
27th March - 28th October 2015
10.00am-5.30pm (last admission 4.15pm).

State Rooms are open 11.00am-5.00pm (last admission 4.30pm, Chapel closes at 3.00pm).

Check alnwickcastle.com for up-to-date opening dates and times.

■ Admission
Adult: £14.50
Concession: £12.00
Child (5-16yrs): £7.50
Family (2+up to 4): £38.00
(2014 prices shown, subject to change).
Tickets can be validated for unlimited free visits for 12 months, at no extra cost (see website for T&Cs)
Discounted rates available for groups of 14 or more.

■ Special Events
Daily events include guided tours of the State Rooms and grounds, Knight's Quest activities, and broomstick training. Seasonal events include knights tournaments, falconry displays, jester performances, and visits from skilled artisans. See website for details.

Conference/Function

Venue	Size	Max cap
Guest Hall	100' x 30'	300
Hulne Abbey	varies	500

VISITOR INFORMATION

■ Owner
Sir Humphry Wakefield Bt

■ Address
Chillingham Castle
Northumberland
NE66 5NJ

■ Location
Map 14:L11
OS Ref. NU062 258
45m N of Newcastle
between A697 & A1.
2m S of B6348 at
Chatton.6m SE of Wooler.
Rail: Alnmouth or Berwick.

■ Contact
The Administrator
Tel: 01668 215359
E-mail:
enquiries@chillingham-
castle.com

■ Opening Times
Summer
Castle, Garden & Tearoom
Easter-31 October. Closed
Sats, 12 noon-5pm.
Winter
October-April. Groups &
Coach Tours any time by
appointment.
All function activities
available.

■ Admission
Adult	£9.50
Children	£5.50
Conc.	£8.50
Family Ticket	£23.00

(2 adults and 3 children
under 15)

CHILLINGHAM CASTLE 🏚Ⓕ
www.chillingham-castle.com

20 Minutes from seaside or mountains. 4 stars in Simon Jenkins' 'Thousand Best Houses' and the very first of The Independent's '50 Best Castles in Britain & Ireland'.

This remarkable and very private castle has been continuously owned by just one family line since the 1200's. A visit from Edward I in 1298 was followed by many other Royal visits right down through this century. See Chillingham's alarming dungeons as well as active restoration in the Great Halls and State Rooms which are gradually brought back to life with tapestries, arms and armour. We even have a very real torture chamber.

The 1100s stronghold became a fortified castle in 1344, see the original Royal Licence to Crenellate on view. Wrapped in the nation's history Chillingham also occupied a strategic position during Northumberland's bloody border feuds being a resting place to many royal visitors. Tudor days saw additions but the underlying medievalism remains. 18th and 19th Centuries saw decorative extravagances including Capability Brown lakes and grounds with gardens laid out by Sir Jeffrey Wyatville, fresh from his triumphs at Windsor Castle. Prehistoric Wild Cattle roam the park beyond more rare than mountain gorilla (a separate tour) and never miss the family tomb in the church.

Gardens
With romantic grounds, the castle commands breathtaking views of the surrounding countryside. As you walk to the lake you will see, according to season, drifts of snowdrops, daffodils or bluebells and an astonishing display of rhododendrons. This emphasises the restrained formality of the Elizabethan topiary garden, with its intricately clipped hedges of box and yew. Lawns, the formal gardens and woodland walks are all fully open to the public.

KEY FACTS

 Corporate entertainment, lunches, drinks, dinners, wedding ceremonies and receptions.

 By arrangement.

 Avoid Lilburn route, coach parties welcome by prior arrangement. Limited for coaches.

 Guide dogs only.

Self catering apartments.

BAMBURGH CASTLE 🏰ⓕ
Bamburgh, Northumberland NE69 7DF
www.bamburghcastle.com

These formidable stone walls have witnessed dark tales of royal rebellion, bloody battles, spellbinding legends and millionaire benefactors. With fourteen public rooms and over 3000 artefacts, including arms and armour, porcelain, furniture and artwork. The Armstrong and Aviation artefacts Museum houses artefacts spanning both World Wars as well as others relating to Lord Armstrongs ship building empire on the Tyne.
Location: Map 14:M10. OS Ref NU184 351. 42m N of Newcastle-upon-Tyne. 20m S of Berwick-upon-Tweed. 6m E of Belford by B1342 from A1 at Belford.
Owner: Francis Watson-Armstrong **Contact:** Chris Calvert, Director
Tel: 01668 214208 **E-mail:** administrator@bamburghcastle.com
Open: 7 Feb-1 Nov 2015, 10am-5pm. Last admission 4pm. 2 Nov 2015-5 Feb 2016, Weekends only, 11am-4.30pm. Last admission 3.30pm.
Admission: Adult £10.50, Senior £10.00, Child (5-16 yrs) £5.00, Family (2 adults and up to 3 dependants under 18) £25.00. For group rates & bookings please call 01668 214 208. **Key facts:** ⓘ No flash photography in the State Rooms. ▢ WCs. ▦ Licensed. ⓕ By arrangement at any time, min charge out of hours £150. ▢ 🅿 100 cars, coaches park on tarmac drive at entrance. ▦ Welcome. Guide provided if requested. ⌂ Guide dogs only. ✖ ▦ ▦

THE ALNWICK GARDEN
Denwick Lane, Alnwick, Northumberland NE66 1YU
www.alnwickgarden.com

One of the world's most contemporary gardens, The Alnwick Garden combines provocative and traditional landscapes in the heart of Northumberland. Featuring Europe's largest wooden treehouse, a Poison Garden and Bamboo Labyrinth, The Garden also offers an expansive rose garden, climbing clematis and honeysuckle, as well as interactive water features and stunning ornamental garden.
Location: Map 14:M11. OS Ref NU192 132. Just off the A1 at Alnwick, Northumberland. **Owner:** The Alnwick Garden Trust
Tel: 01665 511350
E-mail: info@alnwickgarden.com
Open: Apr-Oct 10am-6pm. Nov-Mar 12pm-6pm.
Admission: Please check website for details.
Key facts: ▢ ▦ ▱ ▱ WCs. ▦ ▦ Licensed. ⓕ By arrangement. 🅿 Cars & coaches. ▦ ⌂ Assistance dogs only. ▦ ✖ ▦

The Alnwick Garden

CRAGSIDE 🍃
Rothbury, Morpeth, Northumberland NE65 7PX
www.nationaltrust.org.uk/cragside

Revolutionary home of Lord Armstrong, Victorian inventor and landscape genius, Cragside sits on a rocky crag high above the Debdon Burn. Crammed with ingenious gadgets, it was the first house in the world to be lit with hydro-electricity.
Location: Map 14:L12. OS Ref NU073 022. ½m NE of Rothbury on B6341.
Owner: National Trust
Contact: Assistant to General Manager
Tel: 01669 620333
E-mail: cragside@nationaltrust.org.uk
Open: Please see website for opening times and admission prices.
Admission: Please note: payment by cash only at the admission point (to maintain speed of entry). Credit/debit cards can be used for purchases in the shop. Includes a voluntary donation but visitors can choose to pay the standard prices displayed at the property and on the website.
Key facts: ▢ ▦ ▱ ▦ Licensed. ▦ 🅿 ▦ ⌂ Dogs on leads only. ▦

LADY WATERFORD HALL & GALLERY
Ford, Berwick-Upon-Tweed TD15 2QA
www.ford-and-etal.co.uk

In the heart of Ford & Etal Estates, an agricultural estate in North Northumberland, this 'must see venue' is a real hidden gem. Built as a school in 1860, the building houses a unique collection of magnificent watercolour murals (1861-1883) and smaller original paintings & sketches by Louisa Waterford, one of the most gifted female artists of the 19thC. The fascinating story of Louisa's life & work is depicted through interpretation & film. Quizzes & games are offered for children to enjoy. **Location:** Map 14:K10. OS Ref NT945 374. On B6354, 9m from Berwick-upon-Tweed, midway between Newcastle-upon-Tyne and Edinburgh, close to A1 & A697. **Owner:** Ford & Etal Estates/Lady Waterford Hall Trust
Contact: Dorien Irving **Tel:** 07790 457580 /01890 820338
E-mail: tourism@ford-and-etal.co.uk **Open:** 11am-5pm daily (times may vary slightly early & late season), late Mar until early Nov - check website for details.
Admission: Adult £3.00, Conc/Child £2.50, Family £8.00. U-5's Free. Discount for pre-booked groups. **Key facts:** ℹ May occasionally be closed for private functions - please phone before travelling. 🖼 🛒 All at ground floor level. WC not suitable for wheelchairs. 🍴 Adjacent hall. 🅿 Free. 🐕 Guide dogs only.

BELSAY HALL, CASTLE & GARDENS ⌗
Belsay, Nr Morpeth, Northumberland NE20 0DX
Belsay has something for everyone. A fine medieval castle, which was later extended to include a magnificent Jacobean mansion.
Location: Map 10:O2. OS Ref OS87, NZ086 785.
Tel: 01661 881636 **Website:** www.english-heritage.org.uk/belsay
Open: Please visit www.english-heritage.org.uk/belsay for opening times, admission prices and the most up-to-date information.

CHIPCHASE CASTLE 🏠ⓔ
Wark, Hexham, Northumberland NE48 3NT
The Castle overlooks the River North Tyne and is set in formal and informal gardens. **Location:** Map 10:N2. 10m NW of Hexham via A6079 to Chollerton. 2m SE of Wark. **Tel:** 01434 230203 **E-mail:** info@chipchasecastle.com
Website: www.chipchasecastle.com **Open:** Castle: 1-28 Jun, 2-5pm daily. Gardens & Nursery: Easter-31 Aug, Thu-Sun Incl. & BH Mon, 10am-5pm.
Admission: Castle £6.00, Garden £4.00, concessions available. Nursery Free.

DUNSTANBURGH CASTLE 🌿 ⌗
Dunstanburgh Road, Craster, Northumberland NE66 3TT
Reached by a beautiful coastal walk, this 14th Century castle rivals any castle of its day. **Location:** Map 14:M11. OS Ref NU257 200. 8m NE of Alnwick.
Tel: 01665 576231 **Website:** www.english-heritage.org.uk/dunstanburghcastle
Open: Please visit www.english-heritage.org.uk for opening times, admission prices and the most up-to-date information.

LINDISFARNE CASTLE 🌿
Holy Island, Berwick-Upon-Tweed, Northumberland TD15 2SH
Built in 1550 to protect Holy Island harbour from attack, the castle was restored and converted into a private house for Edward Hudson in 1903.
Location: Map 14:L10. OS Ref NU136 417. **Tel:** 01289 389244
E-mail: lindisfarne@nationaltrust.org.uk **Website:** www.nationaltrust.org.uk/lindisfarne-castle **Open:** Please see website for most up to date details.

PRESTON TOWER 🏠ⓔ
Chathill, Northumberland NE67 5DH
Built by Sir Robert Harbottle in 1392.
Location: Map 14:M11. OS Ref NU185 253. Follow Historic Property signs on A1 7m N of Alnwick. **Tel:** 07966 150216 **Website:** www.prestontower.co.uk
Open: All year daily, 10am-6pm, or dusk, whichever is earlier.
Admission: Adult £2.00, Child 50p, Concessions £1.50. Groups £1.50.

WALLINGTON 🌿
Cambo, Morpeth, Northumberland NE61 4AR
Impressive, yet friendly, house with a magnificent interior and fine collections. Home to many generations of the unconventional Trevelyan family.
Location: Map 10:O2. OS Ref NZ030 843. **Tel:** 01670 773600
E-mail: wallington@nationaltrust.org.uk **Website:** www.nationaltrust.org.uk/wallington **Open:** Please see website for up to date details.

NEWCASTLE CASTLE
St Nicholas Street, Castle Garth, Newcastle, Tyne & Wear NE1 1RQ
Steeped in nearly 1000 years of history, the Castle was the reason Newcastle upon Tyne got its name. Originally built during the reign of Henry II as a defensive stronghold, it has been used as a Tudor prison and was besieged by the Scots during the English Civil War. This fine medieval Castle has seen it all!
Location: Map 14:L12. OS Ref NZ250638. The Castle Keep is a 5 min walk from Central Station, located just off St Nicholas Street. The postcode is NE1 1RQ for SatNav. **Owner:** Newcastle City Council, run by Heart of the City Partnership
Contact: General Manager **Tel:** 0191 230 6300
E-mail: info@newcastlecastle.co.uk **Website:** www.newcastlecastle.co.uk
Open: Daily 10am-5pm (last admission 4:15pm). Check website for Christmas opening times. **Admission:** Check website for admission prices.
Key facts: 🖼 🍴 🎁 🅿 Pay-and-display parking in Castle Garth adjacent to the Vermont Hotel. 🍴 ♿

GIBSIDE 🌿
Nr Rowlands Gill, Burnopfield, Newcastle upon Tyne NE16 6BG
Gibside is an 18th Century 'forest' landscape garden, created by wealthy coal baron George Bowes. **Location:** Map 10:P3. OS Ref NZ172 584. **Tel:** 01207 541820
E-mail: gibside@nationaltrust.org.uk **Website:** www.nationaltrust.org.uk/gibside
Open: Please see website for up to date opening and admission details.

Lady Waterford Hall - Fountain, Ford Village

BARNARD CASTLE

Nr Galgate, Barnard Castle, Durham DL12 8PR
Tel: 01833 638212 **E-mail:** barnard.castle@english-heritage.org.uk

BEAMISH, THE LIVING MUSEUM

Beamish Museum, Beamish, County Durham DH9 0RG
Tel: 0191 370 4000 **E-mail:** museum@beamish.org.uk

ROKEBY PARK

Barnard Castle, County Durham DL12 9RZ
Tel: 01609 748612 **E-mail:** admin@rokebypark.com

ST ANDREW'S CHURCH

Kiln Pit Hill, Shotley, Consett, County Durham DH8 9SJ
Tel: 0845 303 2760 **E-mail:** central@thecct.org.uk

CHERRYBURN

Station Bank, Mickley, Stocksfield, Northumberland NE43 7DD
Tel: 01661 843276 **E-mail:** cherryburn@nationaltrust.org.uk

ETAL CASTLE

Cornhill-On-Tweed, Northumberland TD12 4TN
Tel: 01890 820332 **E-mail:** customers@english-heritage.org.uk

MELDON PARK

Morpeth, Northumberland NE61 3SW
Tel: 01670 772341 **E-mail:** michelle@flyingfox.co.uk/james@flying-fox.co.uk

NORHAM CASTLE

Norham, Northumberland TD15 2JY
Tel: 01289 304493 **E-mail:** customers@english-heritage.org.uk

ST ANDREW'S CHURCH

Bywell, Stocksfield, Northumberland NE43 7AD
Tel: 0845 303 2760 **E-mail:** central@thecct.org.uk

SEATON DELAVAL HALL

The Avenue, Seaton Sluice, Northumberland NE26 4QR
Tel: 0191 237 9100 **E-mail:** seatondelavalhall@nationaltrust.org.uk

WARKWORTH CASTLE

Warkworth, Alnwick, Northumberland NE65 0UJ
Tel: 01665 711423 **E-mail:** warkworth.castle@english-heritage.org.uk

HOLY TRINITY CHURCH

Church Street East, Sunderland, Tyne & Wear SR1 2BB
Tel: 0845 303 2760 **E-mail:** central@thecct.org.uk

ST STEPHEN'S CHURCH

Brunel Terrace, Low Elswick, Newcastle-Upon-Tyne NE4 7NL
Tel: 0845 303 2760 **E-mail:** central@thecct.org.uk

SEGEDUNUM ROMAN FORT, BATHS & MUSEUM

Buddle Street, Wallsend NE28 6HR
Tel: 01912 772169 **E-mail:** caireen.butler@twmuseums.org.uk

TYNEMOUTH CASTLE AND PRIORY

Tynemouth, Tyne & Wear NE30 4BZ
Tel: 01912 691215 **E-mail:** customers@english-heritage.org.uk

WASHINGTON OLD HALL

The Avenue, Washington Village, Tyne & Wear NE38 7LE
Tel: 0191 416 6879 **E-mail:** washington.oldhall@nationaltrust.org.uk

Alnwick Castle - Inner Courtyard

Eilean Donan Castle,
Kyle of Lochalsh
©David Win

Stirling Castle, Stirling
©Historic Scotland

Borders ■

South West Scotland, ▨
Dumfries & Galloway, Ayrshire
& The Isle of Arran

Edinburgh ▨
City, Coast & Countryside

Greater Glasgow ☐
Glasgow & The Clyde Valley

Tayside ■
Perthshire, Angus, Dundee,
& The Kingdom of Fife

West Highlands & Islands, ▨
Loch Lomond, Stirling & Trossachs

Grampian Highlands, ☐
Aberdeen & North East Coast

Highlands & Skye ▨

Scotland

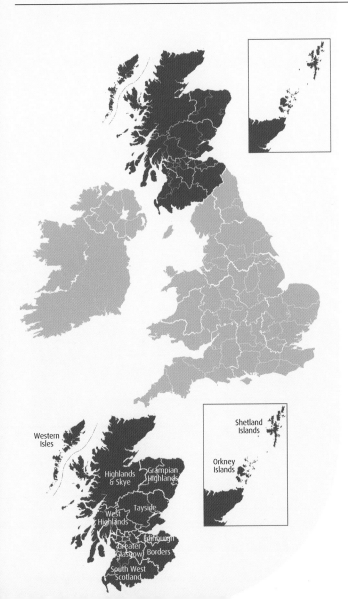

With attention focussed on Scotland by last year's independence debate, now is the time to explore the history, architecture and gardens of this remarkable region.

New Entries for 2015:
• Thirlestane Castle
• Sorn Castle

327

■ **Owner**
The Lord Palmer

■ **Address**
Manderston
Duns
Berwickshire
Scotland
TD11 3PP

■ **Location**
Map 14:K9
OS Ref. NT810 544
From Edinburgh 47m, 1hr.
1½m E of Duns on A6105.
Bus: 400yds.
Rail: Berwick Station 12m.
Airport: Edinburgh or
Newcastle both 60m or
80mins.

■ **Contact**
The Lord Palmer
Tel: 01361 883450
Fax: 01361 882010
Secretary: 01361 882636
E-mail:
palmer@manderston.co.uk

■ **Opening Times**
Summer 2015
7 May–27 September,
Thurs and Sun only.
Gardens and tearoom
open 11.30am.
House opens 1.30–5pm;
last entry 4.15pm. BH
Mons, late May and late
August. Groups welcome
all year by appointment.

Winter
Group visits welcome by
appointment.

■ **Admission**
House & Grounds
(Open Days)
Adult   £10.00
Child (under 12yrs)   Free
Groups (15+)   £9.50
Grounds only   £6.00
Open any other day by
appointment.

Conference/Function

ROOM	Size	Max Cap
Dining Rm	22' x 35'	100
Ballroom	34' x 21'	150
Drawing Rm	35' x 21'	150

MANDERSTON 🏠Ⓕ
www.manderston.co.uk

Manderston, together with its magnificent stables, stunning marble dairy and 56 acres of immaculate gardens, forms quite a unique ensemble.

Manderston is the supreme country house of Edwardian Scotland: the swansong of its era. Manderston, as it is today, is a product of the best craftsmanship and highest domestic sophistication the Edwardian era had to offer and was completely rebuilt between 1903 and 1905.

Visitors are able to see not only the sumptuous State rooms and bedrooms, decorated in the Adam manner, but also all original domestic offices, in a truly 'upstairs downstairs' atmosphere.

Manderston boasts a unique and recently restored silver staircase. There is a special museum with a nostalgic display of valuable tins made by Huntly and Palmer from 1868 to the present day. Winner of the AA/NPI Bronze Award UK 1994.

Gardens
Outside, the magnificence continues and the combination of formal gardens and picturesque landscapes is a major attraction unique amongst Scottish houses. The stables, still in use, have been described by Horse and Hound as 'probably the finest in all the wide world'. The Marble Dairy and its unusual tower, built to look like a Border Keep, enjoys commanding views. Manderston is often used as a film location but can also cater for corporate events. It is also an ideal retreat for business groups and think-tank weekends. Manderston also lends itself very well to fashion shows, air displays, archery, clay pigeon shooting, equestrian events, garden parties, shows, rallies, filming, product launches and marathons. Two airstrips for light aircraft, approx. 5m, grand piano, billiard table, pheasant shoots, sea angling, salmon fishing, stabling, cricket pitch, tennis court, lake.

KEY FACTS

ⓘ No photography in house.

📷

🍸 Available. Buffets, lunches and dinners. Wedding receptions.

♿ Special parking available outside the house.

☕ Snaffles Tearoom - home made lunches, teas, cakes and tray bakes. Can be booked in advance, menus on request.

🚶 Included. Available in French. Guides in rooms. If requested, the owner may meet groups. Tour time 1¼ hrs.

🅿 400 cars 125yds from house, 30 coaches 5yds from house. Appreciated if group fees are paid by one person.

🏫 Welcome. Guide can be provided. Biscuit Tin Museum of particular interest.

🐕 Grounds only, on leads.

🛏 6 twin, 4 double.

❄

ABBOTSFORD
HOME OF SIR WALTER SCOTT 🏛Ⓕ
The Abbotsford Trust, Abbotsford, Melrose, Roxburghshire TD6 9BQ
www.scottsabbotsford.com

Abbotsford, the home world renowned author & poet Sir Walter Scott built on the banks of the River Tweed within the beautiful landscape of the Scottish Borders. Stunning state of the art visitor centre with restaurant, gift shop & free to access Exhibition on the Life & Legacy of Sir Walter Scott. Luxury accommodation in the Hope Scott Wing, beautiful gardens, woodland play trail, riverside & estate walks.
Location: Map 14:I10. OS Ref NT508 342. 2 miles from Melrose & Galashiels. Edinburgh 35 miles, Glasgow & Newcastle approx 70 miles. Major routes: A1, A68 and A7. **Owner:** The Abbotsford Trust **Contact:** Beverley Rutherford
Tel: 01896 752043 **Fax:** 01896 752916
E-mail: enquiries@scottsabbotsford.co.uk
Open: Visitors Centre: 1 Mar-30 Sep, 10am-5pm. 1 Oct-28 Feb, 10am-4pm. House & Gardens: 1 Mar-30 Sep 10am-5pm, 1 Oct-30 Nov, 10am-4pm.
Admission: House & Gardens: £8.75, £7.50 Conc, £4.50 U17 (free for 5 years and under). Gardens only: £3.50, £2.50 Conc & U17, Group rates available.
Key facts: ⓘ ◉ Ⓣ 🔳 ⬤ Licensed. 🎦 House only. ◉ In house. 🅿 🔳 🔳 On leads except formal areas. 🔳 Hope Scott Wing. 🔳 ✳ Visitor Centre only. ☉

FLOORS CASTLE 🏛Ⓕ
Kelso, The Scottish Borders TD5 7SF
www.floorscastle.com

Explore the spectacular state rooms with outstanding collections of paintings, tapestries and furniture. Find hidden treasures like the collections of porcelain and oriental ceramics. Enjoy the picturesque grounds and gardens including the beautiful walled gardens. Stop at the Courtyard Café and enjoy a morning coffee or delicious lunch. For special events, please check our website www.floorscastle.com. **Location:** Map 14:J10. OS Ref NT711 347. From South A68, A698. From North A68, A697/9 In Kelso follow signs.
Owner: His Grace the Duke of Roxburghe
Contact: Beverley Rutherford
Tel: 01573 223333 **Fax:** 01573 226056
E-mail: brutherford@floorscastle.com
Open: 3–6 Apr then 1 May-25 Oct 2015.
Admission: Adult £8.50, Child (5–16yrs) £4.50, OAP/Student £7.50, Family £22.50, Under 5yrs Free.
Key facts: ⓘ Dogs must be kept on leads and under control at all times. Photography is not permitted within the Castle. ◉ 🔳 Ⓣ Exclusive lunches and dinners. 🔳 Partial. WCs. ⬤ Licensed. 🔳 🎦 By arrangement. 🅿 Cars and coaches. 🔳 🔳 Dogs on leads only. 🔳 ☉

Abbotsford

MELLERSTAIN HOUSE & GARDENS 🏛Ⓕ
Mellerstain, Gordon, Berwickshire TD3 6LG
www.mellerstain.com

Discover the story of Mellerstain and experience one of Scotland's finest stately homes. Located in the heart of the Scottish Borders and built in the 18th Century, Mellerstain is a unique example of William and Robert Adam design presenting a complete picture as it would have been some 240 yrs ago. Admire the classical perfection of this 'wonderful Adam house'. View the fine art (incl paintings by Aikman, Gainsborough, Ramsay, Van Dyck), embroidery, china and furniture collections. Relax in acres of parkland with prize winning gardens and lakeside/woodland walks. Picnic as the children have fun in the playground. Enjoy lunch or afternoon tea in the Courtyard Coffee Shop. Stay in our holiday cottages in an idyllic Scottish Borders location. **Location:** Map 14:J10. OS Ref NT648 392. From Edinburgh A68 to Earlston, turn left 5m, signed.
Owner: The Mellerstain Trust **Contact:** The Trust Administrator
Tel: 01573 410225 **Fax:** 01573 410636 **E-mail:** enquiries@mellerstain.com
Open: Easter weekend (4 days), May/Jun/Jul/Aug/Sep on Fri, Sat, Sun, Mon. House: 12.30-5pm. Last ticket 4.15pm. Coffee shop and gardens: 11.30am-5pm.
Admission: See our website or call us. **Key facts:** ℹ️ No photography or video cameras in the house. 🎥 ☕ ♿ 🎬 By arrangement. 🅿️ Onsite parking for vehicles and coaches. 🚌 🐕 Dogs on leads only. Guide dogs only in the house. 🏨 🏛 ♿

THIRLESTANE CASTLE 🏛
Lauder, Berwickshire TD2 6RU
www.thirlestanecastle.co.uk

Thirlestane Castle was the ancient seat of the Earls and Duke of Lauderdale and is still home to the Maitlands. Thirlestane has exquisite 17th Century plasterwork ceilings, a fine portrait collection, historic toys, kitchens and country life exhibitions. Facilities include free parking, Café, adventure playground, and woodland picnic tables.
Location: Map 14:I9. OS Ref NT540 473. Off A68 at Lauder, 28miles S of Edinburgh.
Owner: Thirlestane Castle Trust **Tel:** 01578 722430
E-mail: admin@thirlestanecastle.co.uk
Open: Please check website for 2015 opening program.
Admission: Castle and Grounds: Adults: £8.00, Children: £3.50, Senior Citizens: £6.50, Family: 2+3 £20. Grounds: Adult: £3.00, Children: £1.50, Group Castle & Grounds £7.00. Grounds Only: Adults: £3.00, Children: £1.50
Key facts: ℹ️ Woodland walk, children's adventure playground, country life display area. 🎥 ☕ ♿ Suitable. 🎬 🎬 By arrangement. 🅿️ Cars and coaches. 🚌 🏨 🏛 Double, ensuite. 🏛

TRAQUAIR HOUSE 🏛Ⓕ
Innerleithen, Peeblesshire EH44 6PW
www.traquair.co.uk

Dating back to 1107, Traquair was originally a hunting lodge for the kings and queens of Scotland. Later a refuge for Catholic priests in times of terror the Stuarts of Traquair supported Mary Queen of Scots and the Jacobite cause. Today, Traquair is a unique piece of living history.
Location: Map 13:H10. OS Ref NY330 354. On B709 near junction with A72. Edinburgh 1hr, Glasgow 1½ hrs, Carlisle 1½ hrs.
Owner/Contact: Catherine Maxwell Stuart, 21st Lady of Traquair
Tel: 01896 830323 **Fax:** 01896 830639 **E-mail:** enquiries@traquair.co.uk
Open: 5 Apr-31 Oct (11am–5pm & 11am-4pm in Oct).
Weekends only in Nov (11am-3pm).
Admission: House & Grounds: Adult £8.50; Child £4.25; Senior £7.50, Family £23 (2+3). Groups (20+): Adult £7.50; Child £3.50; Senior £6.50. Grounds only: Adults £4.00. Conc £3.00. Guide Book £4.50.
Key facts: ℹ️ No photography in house. 🛍 Brewery & Gift Shop. 🎫 Tours, Ale Tastings & Dinners available. ♿ 🍽 Licensed. 🎬 🅿️ Coaches; please book. 🚌 🐕 In grounds on leads. 🏨 Three spacious double en suite bedrooms furnished with antique furniture. 🏛 Please contact for more information. ♨

MERTOUN GARDENS 🏛Ⓕ
St. Boswells, Melrose, Roxburghshire TD6 0EA
26 acres of beautiful grounds. Walled garden and well preserved circular dovecot.
Location: Map 14:J10. OS Ref NT617 318. **Tel:** 01835 823236
Fax: 01835 822474 **E-mail:** mertoun@live.co.uk
Website: www.mertoungardens.co.uk **Open:** Apr-Sep, Fri-Mon 2-6pm. Last Admission 5.30pm. **Admission:** Adults £4.00, Conc. £3.00, Child Free.

Floors Castle Gardens

DUMFRIES HOUSE 🏛Ⓕ

www.dumfries-house.org.uk

A Georgian Gem, nesting within 2,000 acres of scenic Ayrshire countryside in south-west Scotland.

Commissioned by William Crichton Dalrymple, the 5th Earl of Dumfries, the House was designed by renowned 18th Century architect brothers John, Robert and James Adam and built between 1754 and 1759.

Recognised as one of the Adam brothers' masterpieces it remained unseen by the public since it was built 250 years ago until it opened its doors as a visitor attraction in June 2008. The former home of the Marquesses of Bute, it was saved for the nation at the eleventh hour by a consortium of organisations and individuals brought together by HRH The Prince Charles, Duke of Rothesay.

The house holds the most important collection of works from Thomas Chippendale's 'Director' period. It is widely recognised that Scotland was a testing ground for Thomas Chippendale's early rococo furniture and the Dumfries House collection is regarded as his key project in this area.

Dumfries House also holds the most comprehensive range of pieces by Edinburgh furniture makers Alexander Peter, William Mathie and Francis Brodie. Indeed, the Scottish furniture together with the Chippendale collection is of outstanding worldwide historical significance.

KEY FACTS

ℹ️ Pre-booking of tours is recommended (Online at www.dumfries-house.org.uk or via the Booking Line 01290 421742). Tour times may vary.

🖼️
🍴
♿ Stairlift. WCs. 1 wheelchair per tour.
🎧
🚶 Obligatory.
🅿️ Cars ample. Coaches ample.
🚌
🐕 On leads in grounds only. Guide dogs only in the house.
🔔 Minister license for weddings.
❄️ Grounds only.
📷

VISITOR INFORMATION

■ Owner
The Great Steward of Scotland's Dumfries House Trust

■ Address
Dumfries House
Cumnock
East Ayrshire
Scotland
KA18 2NJ

■ Location
Map 13:C11
OS Ref. NS539 200
Car: Cumnock, East Ayrshire. Sat Nav KA18 2LN. Visitors Entrance on Barony Road (B7036)
Rail: Auchinleck
Air: Prestwick

■ Contact
Visitor Services Tel: 01290 427975
Tel: Booking Line 01290 425959
Fax: 01290 425464
E-mail: info@dumfries-house.org.uk

■ Opening Times
Summer season:
Apr - Oct (inclusive)
7 days/week 10.00am to 4.00pm (check website for Sat openings)
Guided tours at frequent intervals
Winter season:
Nov - Mar (inclusive)
Sat and Sun 11.00am to 2.00pm
Please note: The House is closed for Christmas and New Year
Please be advised that you should call the Booking Line on 01290 421742 or go onto www.dumfries-house.org.uk to confirm any House closures before your visit.

■ Admission
Ticket Price for the House Tour
Adults £9.00
Child (5-16 yrs) £4.00
Children under 5 Free
Historic Scotland Members 25% discount
Art Fund Members Free
Grand Tour
Adults £13.00
Child (5-16 yrs) £4.00
Children under 5 Free
Art Fund Members 50% discount
Art Tour
Wednesday Only £13.00
Art Fund Members 50% discount.

■ Special Events
Special Events information available at www.dumfries-house.org.uk.
House available for private functions and corporate events.

■ VISITOR INFORMATION

■ Owner
Jamie McIntyre

■ Address
Sorn
Mauchline
Ayrshire
KA5 6HR

■ Location
Map 13:C10
OS Ref. NS545 270

From Glasgow
From the M77 follow signs for Kilmarnock/Prestwick Airport. At Junction 6, take the A77 exit to Galston. Turn right at T Junction. Travel straight on at roundabout and turn left just after traffic lights onto B7037, there is a small sign post for Sorn. Continue on road for 7 miles until you reach a T Junction, the castle gates are across the road.

From the South
From the M6 North, keep right at the fork, signposted for The North, Lancaster, The Lakes. Continue onto M74. At Junction 12 take the A70 exit Edinburgh/Ayr, at the roundabout take the first exit, continue on this road for 14 miles. 1 mile before Muirkirk turn right on the B743 signposted Sorn. Continue 7 miles until you reach the village of Sorn, at the T Junction turn left, through the village and out past the 30mph sign. The castle gates are on the left hand side.

■ Contact
Adrian Wiley
Tel: 01290 551476
E-mail:
info@sorncastle.com

■ Opening Times
1 May – 31 May inclusive and 31 August.
12-4 pm.
Last Admissions at 3.30pm.

■ Admission
Adult   £4.50
HHA Members   Free

SORN CASTLE
www.sorncastle.com

Sorn Castle is a country estate ideally situated in Ayrshire, 28 miles South of Glasgow and 60 miles West of Edinburgh.

Sorn Castle was purchased by Jamie McIntyre's Great Grandfather, Thomas McIntyre, in 1903, and the Estate has been the Family Home ever since.

The Estate extends to just over 8,500 acres of pasture land, heather clad hills, ancient woodland and the breathtaking River Ayr, that gently runs endlessly past the Castle's parapets that proudly stand above it. The original part of the Castle was built during the reign of Edward III and as each of the centuries have witnessed generations of previous owners adding their own individual extension to the Castle, the property culminated in its last significant enlargement around 1910.

In 1538 King James VI visited the Castle to attend a Marriage and since then politicians, statesmen, celebrities and distinguished guests have followed in his footsteps.

The Castle boasts all the rooms you would expect to find in a Scottish Country House, so apart from the Inner Halls, Drawing Room, Library and Dining Room there is also a Music Room with a significant Church organ along with a Games Room with a full sized snooker table.

Sorn Castle is always popular for hosting weddings, shooting parties, country weekends and corporate activities. The Castle has 12 well appointed letting rooms. Under exposed as a film location but easily achieved with the resident professional team in place.

KEY FACTS

- 12-180+ guests
- 12–4pm.
- Unlimited free parking.
- By appointment.
- Indoor and outdoor cermonies.

AUCHINLECK
Ochiltree, Ayrshire KA18 2LR
www.landmarktrust.org.uk

Once diarist James Boswell's family seat, this grand 18th Century country house has its own grounds, river, ice-house and grotto. The large dining room and its elaborate plasterwork makes any meal special while the library lends itself to conversation and contemplation, just as it did for James Boswell and Dr Johnson.
Location: Map 13:C11. OS Ref NS510 226.
Owner: The Landmark Trust
Tel: 01628 825925
E-mail: bookings@landmarktrust.org.uk
Open: Self-catering accommodation. Parts of house open Easter-Oct, Wed afternoons. The Grounds are open dawn-dusk Spring and Summer.
Admission: Free on Open Days and visits by appointment
Key facts: ℹ This building has grand, elegant rooms, a sweeping staircase, large dining and sitting rooms and plenty of open fires.
🅿 👭 🖼 ❄ ♿

CASTLE KENNEDY GARDENS
Castle Kennedy, Stranraer
Dumfries and Galloway DG9 8SJ
www.castlekennedygardens.com

Famous 75-acre gardens situated between two large natural lochs. Ruined Castle Kennedy at one end overlooking beautiful herbaceous walled garden; Lochinch Castle at the other. Proximity to the gulf-stream provides an impressive collection of rare trees, including 21 Champion Trees, magnolias, and spectacular rhododendron displays. Guided walks, children's activities, regular ranger activities, open air theatre, bird hide, gift shop, plant centre and charming tearoom - a 'must-visit'. **Location:** Map 9:D3. OS Ref NX109 610. 3m E of Stranraer on A75.
Owner: The Earl and Countess of Stair
Contact: Stair Estates **Tel:** 01776 702024/01581 400225 **Fax:** 01776 706248
E-mail: info@castlekennedygardens.com
Open: Gardens and Tearoom: 1 Apr-31 Oct: daily 10am-5pm. Feb & Mar: Weekends only. **Admission:** Adult £5.50, Child £2.00, Conc. £4.50, Family (2+2) £12.00. Groups of 20 or more 10% discount.
Key facts: ℹ 🖻 🎁 🍽 ♿ WCs 🐕 🎫 🅿 👭 On leads only. 🖼 ♠ ❄ ♿

Sorn Castle

CULZEAN CASTLE
& COUNTRY PARK ♛
Maybole, Ayrshire KA19 8LE
www.nts.org.uk

Robert Adam's 18th Century masterpiece - a real 'castle in the air' - is perched on a cliff high above the crashing waves of the Firth of Clyde. The Castle itself boasts a spectacular Oval Staircase, the impressive Armoury and the Circular Saloon, with its panoramic views over the Clyde. The extensive grounds encompass Scotland's first country park where you can explore the deer park, swan pond and miles of woodland walks.
Location: Map 13:B11. OS Ref NS232 103.
On A719, 4m west of Maybole and 12m south of Ayr. KA19 8LE
Owner: The National Trust for Scotland
Tel: 0844 493 2149 **E-mail:** culzean@nts.org.uk
Open: Please see our website or call us for up to date opening times.
Admission: Please see our website or call us for up to date prices.
Key facts: 🖻
🍴 ♿

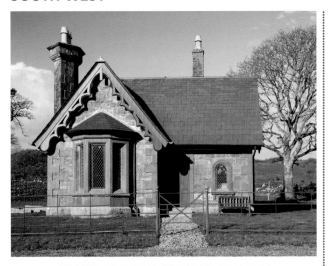

GLENMALLOCH LODGE
Newton Stewart, Dumfries And Galloway DG8 6AG
www.landmarktrust.org.uk

A fairytale cottage in a wild and beautiful glen, this diminutive former schoolroom makes a perfect hideaway or writing retreat for two, or even one.
Location: Map 9:F3.
Owner: The Landmark Trust
Tel: 01628 825925
E-mail: bookings@landmarktrust.org.uk
Open: Self-catering accommodation. Visits by appointment.
Admission: Free for visits by appointment.
Key facts: ⓘ Although not far from Newton Stewart, the Lodge feels remote and looks out over the unspoilt and geologically interesting Galloway landscape.
🅿 🚻 🖼 ✳ ♿

KELBURN CASTLE
& COUNTRY CENTRE 🏠Ⓕ
Fairlie, By Largs, Ayrshire KA29 0BE
www.kelburnestate.com

Kelburn is the home of the Earls of Glasgow and has been in the Boyle family for over 800 years. It is notable for its waterfalls, historic gardens, romantic glen and unique trees. The castle continues to be the venue of a major graffiti art installation, now considered to be in the top 10 graffiti installations in the world.
Location: Map 13:B9. OS Ref NS210 580. A78 to Largs, 2m S of Largs.
Owner: The Earl of Glasgow **Tel:** 01475 568685/568595
Fax: 01475 568121 **E-mail:** admin@kelburncountrycentre.com
Open: Country Centre: Easter-Oct: daily. Castle: Jul and Aug. Open by arrangement for groups at other times of the year.
Now available for Weddings and Special Events.
Admission: Country Centre: Adult £8.50, Child/Conc. £6.00, Under 3s Free, Family £28.00. Groups (10+): Adult, £4.50, Conc. £3.50. Castle: £2.00 extra pp.
Key facts: 🖥 🅣 ♿ Partial. 🖰 🍴 Licensed. 🎞 Jul and Aug. By arrangement at other times of the year. 🅿 🖼 🚻 In grounds, on leads. ✳

Kelburn Castle

CRAIGDARROCH HOUSE 🏠Ⓕ
Moniaive, Dumfriesshire DG3 4JB
Built by William Adam in 1729, over the old house dating from 14th Century (earliest records). The marriage home of Annie Laurie, the heroine of 'the world's greatest lovesong', who married Alexander Fergusson, 14th Laird of Craigdarroch, in 1720 and lived in the house for 33 years.
Location: Map 9:G1. OS Ref NX741 909.
S side of B729, 2m W of Moniaive, 19m WNW of Dumfries.
Owner/Contact: Mrs Carin Sykes
Tel: 01848 200202
Open: Jul: daily except Mons, 2-4pm. Please note: no WCs.
Admission: £3.00.

CAERLAVEROCK CASTLE ♨
Glencaple, Dumfries DG1 4RU
With its moat, twin towered gatehouse and imposing battlements, Caerlaverock Castle is the epitome of the medieval stronghold. Visitors can enjoy a siege warfare exhibition. **Location:** Map 10:I3. OS Ref NY025 626.
Tel: 01387 770244 **Website:** www.historic-scotland.gov.uk
Open: Please see website for up to date opening and admission details.

RAMMERSCALES 🏠Ⓕ
Lockerbie, Dumfriesshire DG11 1LD
May & June. Ring for opening times. Buses by appt.
Location: Map 10:I2. OS Ref NY080 780. Directions available on Rammerscales.co.uk **Tel:** 01387 810229 **E-mail:** malcolm@rammerscales.co.uk
Website: www.rammerscales.co.uk **Open:** May & Jun. Telephone owner for opening times. Bus tours by appointment. **Admission:** Adult £5.00.

DALMENY HOUSE
www.dalmeny.co.uk

Welcome to a family home which contains Scotland's finest French treasurers. Dine in splendor, and enjoy sea-views over superb parkland.

Dalmeny House rejoices in one of the most beautiful and unspoilt settings in Great Britain, yet it is only seven miles from Scotland's capital, Edinburgh, fifteen minutes from Edinburgh airport and less than an hour's drive from Glasgow. It is an eminently suitable venue for group visits, business functions, and special events, including product launches. Outdoor activities, such as off-road driving, can be arranged.

Dalmeny House, the family home of the Earls of Rosebery for over 300 years, boasts superb collections of porcelain and tapestries,

fine paintings by Gainsborough, Raeburn, Reynolds and Lawrence, together with the exquisite Mentmore Rothschild collection of 18th Century French furniture. There is also the Napoleonic collection, assembled by the 5th Earl of Rosebery, Prime Minister, historian and owner of three Derby winners.

The Hall, Library and Dining Room will lend a memorable sense of occasion to corporate receptions, luncheons and dinners. A wide range of entertainment can also be provided, from a clarsach player to a floodlit pipe band Beating the Retreat.

VISITOR INFORMATION

■ **Owner**
The Earl of Rosebery

■ **Address**
Dalmeny House
South Queensferry
Edinburgh
EH30 9TQ

■ **Location**
Map 13:G8
OS Ref. NT167 779
From Edinburgh A90, B924, 7m N, A90 ½m. On south shore of Firth of Forth.
Bus: From St Andrew Square to Chapel Gate 1m from House.
Taxi: Hawes Cars 0131 331 1077.
Rail: Dalmeny station 3m.

■ **Contact**
The Administrator
Tel: 0131 331 1888
Fax: 0131 331 1788
E-mail: events@dalmeny.co.uk

■ **Opening Times**
Summer
From 7 June until 29 July on Sunday-Wednesday at 2pm-5pm. Entry by Guided Tour only. Tours are 2.15pm and 3.30pm.

Winter
Open at other times by appointment only.

■ **Admission**
Summer
Adult	£10.00
Child (14-16yrs)	£7.00
OAP	£9.00
Student	£9.00
Groups (20+)	£9.00

KEY FACTS

 Fashion shows, product launches, archery, clay pigeon shooting, shows, filming, background photography, and special events. Lectures on House, contents and family history. Helicopter landing area.

 Conferences and functions, buffets, lunches, dinners.

WCs.

 Obligatory. Special interest tours can be arranged outside normal opening hours.

P 60 cars, 3 coaches. Parking for functions in front of house.

Dogs in grounds only.

HOPETOUN HOUSE 🏛️ⓕ
HOPETOUN HOUSE, SOUTH QUEENSFERRY, EDINBURGH, WEST LOTHIAN EH30 9SL
www.hopetoun.co.uk

As you approach Hopetoun House the impressive panoramic view of the main facade is breathtakingly revealed. Designed by William Bruce and then altered and extended by William Adam, Hopetoun House is one of the finest examples of 18th Century architecture in Britain. Hopetoun House is filled with stunning collections and has been home to the Hope Family since the late 1600s, with the present Lord Hopetoun and his family still living in the House. As a five star Visitor Attraction Hopetoun offers something for everyone with daily tours, 100 acres of majestic grounds with nature trails and scenic walks. The Stables Tearoom is also a must see, with traditional afternoon teas served in stunning surroundings.
Location: Map 13:F7. OS Ref NT089 790. Exit A90 at A904, Follow Brown Signs.
Owner: Hopetoun House Preservation Trust **Contact:** Reception
Tel: 0131 331 2451 **E-mail:** enquiries@hopetoun.co.uk

Open: Open Daily From Easter - last weekend Sep; 10.30am-5pm. Last admission 4pm. Groups (20+) welcome out of season by appointment.
Admission: House and Grounds: Adult £9.20; Child (5-16yrs)* £4.90; Conc/Student £8.00; Family (2+2) £25.00. Grounds only: Adult £4.25; Child (5-16yrs)* £2.50; Conc/Student £3.70; Family (2+2) £11.50. *Under 5yrs Free. Winter group rates on request. Tearoom only admission is free.
Key facts: ℹ️ Visit www.hopetoun.co.uk/whats-on-calendar.html to see our calendar of events. 📷 🍴 Private functions, wedding celebrations, banquets & gala evenings, meetings, conferences, exhibitions, incentive groups, outdoor activities, media & filming location. ♿ Lift to 1st floor, Virtual access to upper floors. WCs. 🍷 Licensed. 🎫 Daily tour @ 2pm. Groups by arrangement. 🅿️ Cars & coaches welcome 🚌 🐕 Dogs permitted (on leads) in grounds. 🏨 ♿ ♿ €

EDINBURGH CASTLE 🏰
Castle Hill, Edinburgh EH1 2NG
www.edinburghcastle.gov.uk

Edinburgh Castle, built on an extinct volcano, dominates the skyline of Scotland's capital city. Attractions include: The Honours of Scotland, The Stone of Destiny, The Great Hall, Laich Hall and St Margaret's Chapel, Prisons of War Experience, National War Memorial, the famous One O'clock Gun - fired daily Mon-Sat.
Location: Map 13:G8. OS Ref NT252 736. At the top of the Royal Mile in Edinburgh **Owner:** Historic Scotland **Tel:** 0131 225 9846
E-mail: hs.explorer@scotland.gsi.gov.uk **Open:** 1 Apr-30 Sep 9.30am to 6pm. 1 Oct-31 Mar 9.30am to 5pm. Last tickets sold 1 hour before closing. Closed Christmas Day and Boxing Day. Visit the website for New Year opening times.
Admission: Adult £16.50, Conc £13.20, Child £9.90.
Key facts: ℹ️ Disabled parking only, blue disabled badge required. 📷 🍴 Private evening hire. ♿ WCs. 🍷 🍴 🎫 Regular tours included in admission price. Check website for details. 🗣️ In 8 languages. 🏨 🐕 Assistance dogs only. 🚌 ♿ ❄️ €

GOSFORD HOUSE 🏛️ⓕ
Longniddry, East Lothian EH32 0PX
www.gosfordhouse.co.uk

1791 the 7th Earl of Wemyss, aided by Robert Adam, built one of the grandest houses in Scotland, with a 'paradise' of lakes and pleasure grounds. New wings, including the celebrated Marble Hall were added in 1891 by William Young. The house has a fine collection of paintings and furniture.
Location: Map 14:17. OS Ref NT453 786. Off A198 2m NE of Longniddry.
Owner/Contact: The Earl of Wemyss
Tel: 01875 870201
Open: Please check www.gosfordhouse.co.uk for most up to date opening times/days.
Admission: Adult £6.00, Child under 16 Free.
Key facts: 🎫
🎫 By arrangement.
🅿️ Limited for coaches. ♿

PALACE OF HOLYROODHOUSE
Edinburgh EH8 8DX
www.royalcollection.org.uk

The Palace of Holyroodhouse, the official residence of Her Majesty The Queen, stands at the end of the Royal Mile against the spectacular backdrop of Arthur's Seat. Visitors can explore Mary, Queen of Scots' historic chambers, the ten magnificent State Apartments used by The Queen, and the romantic ruins of Holyrood Abbey.

Location: Map 13:G8. OS Ref NT110 735. Central Edinburgh, end of Royal Mile.
Owner: Official Residence of Her Majesty The Queen
Contact: Ticket Sales & Information Office
Tel: +44 (0)131 556 5100
E-mail: bookinginfo@royalcollection.org.uk
Open: Please see website for opening times.
Admission: Visit www.royalcollection.org.uk for details.
Key facts: Assistance dogs welcome.

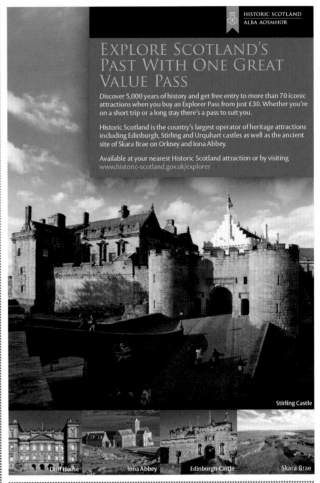

AMISFIELD MAINS
Nr Haddington, East Lothian EH41 3SA
Georgian farmhouse with gothic barn and cottage. **Location:** Map 14:I8. OS Ref NT526 755. Between Haddington and East Linton on A199.
Tel: 01875 870201 **Fax:** 01875 870620
Open: Exterior only: By appointment, Wemyss and March Estates Office, Longniddry, East Lothian EH32 0PY. **Admission:** Please contact for details.

ARNISTON HOUSE
Gorebridge, Midlothian EH23 4RY
Magnificent William Adam mansion started in 1726. Beautiful country setting beloved by Sir Walter Scott. **Location:** Map 13:H9. OS Ref NT326 595.
Tel: 01875 830515 **Website:** www.arniston-house.co.uk **Open:** May & Jun: Tue & Wed; 1 Jul-14 Sep: Tue, Wed & Sun, guided tours at 2pm & 3.30pm. Pre-arranged groups accepted. **Admission:** Adult £6.00, Child £3.00, Conc. £5.00.

BEANSTON
Nr Haddington, East Lothian EH41 3SB
Georgian farmhouse with Georgian orangery.
Location: Map 14:I8. OS Ref NT450 766. Between Haddington and East Linton on A199. **Tel:** 01875 870201 **Open:** Exterior only: By appointment, Wemyss and March Estates Office, Longniddry, East Lothian EH32 0PY.
Admission: Please contact for details.

HARELAW FARMHOUSE
Nr Longniddry, East Lothian EH32 0PH
Early 19th Century 2-storey farmhouse built as an integral part of the steading. Dovecote over entrance arch. **Location:** Map 14:I8. OS Ref NT450 766. Between Longniddry and Drem on B1377. **Tel:** 01875 870201
Open: Exteriors only: By appointment, Wemyss and March Estates Office, Longniddry, East Lothian EH32 0PY. **Admission:** Please contact for details.

LINLITHGOW PALACE
Linlithgow, West Lothian EH49 7AL
The royal pleasure palace was the birthplace of Mary Queen of Scots. Visit the great hall where Monarchs hosted banquets. **Location:** Map 13:F8. OS Ref NS 996774. **Tel:** 01506 842896 **E-mail:** hs.explorer@scotland.gsi.gov.uk
Website: www.historic-scotland.gov.uk
Open: Please see website for up to date opening and admission details.

NEWLISTON
Kirkliston, West Lothian EH29 9EB
Late Robert Adam house. 18th Century designed landscape, rhododendrons, azaleas and water features.
Location: Map 13:G8. OS Ref NT110 735. 9miles W of Edinburgh, 4miles S of Forth Road Bridge, off B800. **Tel:** 0131 333 3231
Open: 1 May-4 Jun: Wed-Sun, 2-6pm. Also by appointment.
Admission: Adult: £3.00, Children under 12: Free of charge.

RED ROW
Aberlady, East Lothian EH32 0DE
Terraced Cottages **Location:** Map 14:I7. OS Ref NT464 798. Main Street, Aberlady, East Lothian.
Tel: 01875 870201 **Fax:** 01875 870620
Open: Exterior only. By appointment, Wemyss and March Estates Office, Longniddry, East Lothian EH32 0PY. **Admission:** Please contact for details.

NEW LANARK WORLD HERITAGE SITE
New Lanark Mills, S Lanarkshire ML11 9DB
www.newlanark.org

Close to the famous Falls of Clyde, this cotton mill village c1785 became famous as the site of Robert Owen's radical reforms. Beautifully restored as a living community and attraction, the fascinating history of the village has been interpreted in New Lanark Visitor Centre.

Location: Map 13:E9. OS Ref NS880 426. 1m S of Lanark. Sat Nav code ML11 9BY. Bus service between Buchanan Bus Station in Glasgow and Lanark. Nearest train station is Lanark (1m). **Owner:** New Lanark Trust **Contact:** Trust Office **Tel:** 01555 661345 **E-mail:** visit@newlanark.org
Open: Open daily, 10–5pm Apr-Oct, 10–4pm Nov-Mar. Shops/catering open until 5pm daily. Closed 25 Dec and 1 Jan. **Admission:** Visitor Centre: Adult £8.50, Conc. (senior/student) £7.00, Child £6.00. Family (2+2) £25.00, Family (2+4) £35.00. Groups: 1 free/10 booked. **Key facts:** 🏠 📶 ♿ Suitable. WC. 📷 🍴 Licensed. 🎥 Obligatory. By arrangement. 🅿 Cars & coaches. 5 min walk. 🐕 Guide dogs. 🛏 Double, single & en suite. Self-Catering also available. ▲ ❋

COREHOUSE 🏠ⓕ
Lanark ML11 9TQ

Designed by Sir Edward Blore and built in the 1820s, Corehouse is a pioneering example of the Tudor Architectural Revival in Scotland.

Location: Map 13:E9. OS Ref NS882 416. On S bank of the Clyde above village of Kirkfieldbank. **Tel:** 01555 663126 **Open:** 2-27 May & 1-5 Aug: Sat–Wed. Tours: weekdays: 1 & 2pm, weekends: 2 & 3pm. Closed Thu & Fri.
Admission: Adult £7.00, Child (under 16yrs)/OAP £4.00.

New Lanark Mills

DRUMMOND GARDENS 🏠ⓕ
Muthill, Crieff, Perthshire PH7 4HN
www.drummondcastlegardens.co.uk

Scotland's most important formal gardens. The Italianate parterre is revealed from a viewpoint at the top of the terrace. First laid out in the 17th Century and renewed in the 1950s. The perfect setting to stroll amongst the manicured plantings and absorb the atmosphere of this special place.

Location: Map 13:E5. OS Ref NN844 181. 2m S of Crieff off the A822.
Owner: Grimsthorpe & Drummond Castle Trust, a registered charity
Contact: The Caretaker
Tel: 01764 681433
Fax: 01764 681642
E-mail: thegardens@drummondcastle.sol.co.uk
Open: Easter weekend, 1 May-31 Oct: Daily, 1-6pm. Last admission 5pm.
Admission: Adult £5.00, Child £2.00 Conc. £4.00, Groups (20+) 10% discount.
Key facts: 🏠 📶 ♿ Partial. WCs. Viewing platform. Special vehicle access, ask on arrival. 🎥 By arrangement. 🅿 🐕 Dogs on leads only. 🚻

GLAMIS CASTLE & GARDENS 🏠ⓕ
Glamis By Forfar, Angus DD8 1RJ
www.glamis-castle.co.uk

Glamis Castle is the family home of the Earls of Strathmore and Kinghorne, and has been a royal residence since 1372. It was the childhood home of Her Majesty Queen Elizabeth The Queen Mother, the birthplace of HRH Princess Margaret and the legendary setting of Shakespeare's play Macbeth.

Location: Map 13:H4. OS Ref NO386 480. Off A94.
Owner: The Earl of Strathmore & Kinghorne
Contact: Doreen Stout
Tel: 01307 840393 **Fax:** 01307 840733
E-mail: enquiries@glamis-castle.co.uk
Open: Apr-Oct, daily; 10-6pm, last admission 4.30pm. Nov-Mar groups and private tours welcome by prior arrangement.
Admission: Please see website for details.
Key facts: ℹ Visit website for details. 🏠 📶 ♿ WCs. 📷 Licensed. 🍴 Licensed. 🎥 🅿 Cars and coaches. 🐕 Grounds only. Guide dogs only. ▲

BALCARRES

Colinsburgh, Fife KY9 1HN

16th Century tower house with 19th Century additions by Burn and Bryce. Woodland and terraced gardens.

Location: Map 14:I6. OS Ref NO475 044. ½m N of Colinsburgh.

Owner: Balcarres Heritage Trust

Contact: Lord Balniel

Tel: 01333 340520

Open: Woodland & Gardens: 1 Mar-30 Sep, 2-5pm. House not open except by written appointment and 1-30 Apr, excluding Sun.

Admission: House £6.00, Garden £6.00. House & Garden £10.00.

Key facts: ⬛ Partial. ⬛ By arrangement. ⬛ Dogs on leads only.

Glamis Castle

CORTACHY ESTATE

Cortachy, Kirriemuir, Angus DD8 4LX

Countryside walks including access through woodlands to Airlie Monument on Tulloch Hill with spectacular views of the Angus Glens and Vale of Strathmore. Footpaths are waymarked and colour coded. **Location:** Map 13:H3. OS Ref N0394 596. Off the B955 Glens Road from Kirriemuir. **Owner:** Trustees of Airlie Estates

Contact: Estate Office **Tel:** 01575 570108 **Fax:** 01575 540400

E-mail: office@airlieestates.com **Website:** www.airlieestates.com

Open: Walks all year. Gardens 3-6 Apr; 4 and 18 May -7 Jun inclusive; 3 and 31 Aug. Last admission 3.30pm.

Admission: Please contact estate office for details.

Key facts: ⓘ The estate network of walks are open all year round. The gardens and grounds can be hired for the location and setting of wedding ceremonies and photographs. ⬛ ⬛ Unsuitable. ⬛ By arrangement. ⬛ Limited. ⬛ Dogs on leads only. ⬛ Licensed to hold Civil Weddings and can offer wedding receptions, either a marquee in the grounds or a reception within the Castle. ⬛

BLAIR CASTLE & GARDENS ⬛ⓔ

Blair Atholl, Pitlochry, Perthshire PH18 5TL

Blair Castle has a centuries old history as a strategic stonghold at the gateway to the Grampians and the route North to Inverness.

Location: Map 13:E3. OS Ref NN880 660.

Tel: 01796 481207 **E-mail:** bookings@blair-castle.co.uk

Website: www.blair-castle.co.uk

Open: Please see website for up to date opening and admission details.

CHARLETON HOUSE

Colinsburgh, Leven, Fife KY9 1HG

Location: Map 14:I6. OS Ref NO464 036. Off A917. 1m NW of Colinsburgh. 3m NW of Elie. **Tel:** 01333 340249

Open: 29 Aug-28 Sep: daily, 12 noon-3pm.

Guided tours obligatory, admission every ½hr. **Admission:** £12.00.

GLENEAGLES ⬛

Auchterarder, Perthshire PH3 1PJ

Gleneagles has been the home of the Haldane family since the 12th Century. The 18th Century pavilion is open to the public by written appointment.

Location: Map 13:F6. OS Ref NS931 088. 0.75 miles S of A9 on A823. 2.5m S of Auchterarder. **Tel:** 01764 682388 **Fax:** 01764 682535

E-mail: jmhaldane@gleneagles.org **Open:** By written appointment only.

HILL OF TARVIT MANSION HOUSE ⬛

Cupar, Fife KY15 5PB

Hill of Tarvit is one of Scotland's finest Edwardian mansionhouses, replete with a splendid collection of antiques, furniture, Chinese porcelain and superb paintings.

Location: Map 13:H5. OS Ref NO379 118. **Tel:** 0844 493 2185

E-mail: hilloftarvit@nts.org.uk **Website:** www.nts.org.uk

Open: Please see website for up to date opening and admission details.

HOUSE OF DUN ⬛

Montrose, Angus DD10 9LQ

The house features fine furniture, a wonderful art collection and superb plasterwork, a particular and memorable feature.

Location: Map 14:J3. OS Ref NO670 599. **Tel:** 0844 493 2144

E-mail: houseofdun@nts.org.uk **Website:** www.nts.org.uk

Open: Please see website for up to date opening and admission details.

HUNTINGTOWER CASTLE ⬛

Perth PH1 3JL

Once known as the House of Ruthven, Huntingtower Castle was a lordly residence for 300 years. The splendid painted ceilings in this castle are especially noteworthy.

Location: Map 13:F5. OS Ref NO084 252.

Tel: 01738 627 231 **Website:** www.historic-scotland.gov.uk

Open: Please see website for up to date opening and admission details.

MONZIE CASTLE ⬛ⓔ

Crieff, Perthshire PH7 4HD

Built in 1791. Destroyed by fire in 1908 and rebuilt and furnished by Sir Robert Lorimer. **Location:** Map 13:E5. OS Ref NN873 244. 2miles NE of Crieff.

Tel: 01764 653110 **Open:** 16 May-14 Jun: daily, 2-4.30pm. By appointment at other times. **Admission:** Adult £5.00, Child £1.00. Group rates available, contact property for details.

SCONE PALACE & GROUNDS ⬛ⓔ

Scone Palace, Perth PH2 6BD

1500 years ago it was the capital of the Picts. In the intervening centuries, it has been the seat of parliaments and the crowning place of the Kings of Scots.

Location: Map 13:G5. OS Ref NO114 266. **Tel:** 01738 552300

E-mail: visits@scone-palace.co.uk **Website:** www.scone-palace.co.uk

Open: Please see website for up to date opening and admission details.

STRATHTYRUM HOUSE & GARDENS ⬛

St Andrews, Fife KY16 9SF

Location: Map 14:I5. OS Ref NO490 172. Entrance from the St Andrews/ Guardbridge Road which is signposted when open. **Tel:** 01334 473600

E-mail: info@strathtyrumhouse.com **Open:** Mon - Thu weeks beginning 6,13, 20 & 27 April, 4,11 & 18 May: Guided tours at 2pm and 3pm.

Admission: Adult £5.00, Child + Concessions £2.50.

TULLIBOLE CASTLE

Crook Of Devon, Kinross KY13 0QN

Scottish tower house c1608 with ornamental fishponds, a roofless lectarn doocot, 9th Century graveyard. **Location:** Map 13:F6. OS Ref NO540 888. B9097 1m E of Crook of Devon. **Tel:** 01577 840236 **E-mail:** visit@tulbol.demon.co.uk **Website:** www.tulbol.demon.co.uk **Open:** Last week in Aug-30 Sep: Tue-Sun, 1-4pm.

Admission: Adult £5.50, Child/Conc. £3.50. Free for Doors Open weekend.

VISITOR INFORMATION

■ Owner
Duke of Argyll

■ Address
Inveraray Castle
Inveraray
Argyll
Scotland
PA32 8XE

■ Location
Map 13:A6
OS Ref. NN100 090
From Edinburgh 2½-3hrs via Glasgow. Just NE of Inveraray on A83. W shore of Loch Fyne.
Bus: Bus route stopping point within ½ mile.

■ Contact
Argyll Estates
Tel: 01499 302203
Fax: 01499 302421
For all corporate events and wedding enquiries please contact Jane Young
Email: manager@inveraray-castle.com
E-mail: enquiries@inveraray-castle.com

■ Opening Times
1st Apr - 31st Oct
Open 7 days from 10.00am to 5.45pm (Last admission 5pm).

■ Admission
Castle & Gardens\Group Rate*
Adults	£10.00	
	£8.00*	
Senior Citizens	£9.00	
	£7.20*	
Students (only valid with student card)	£9.00	
	£7.20*	
Schools	£4.00*	
Children (under 16)	£7.00	
	£5.60*	
Family Ticket (2 adults & 2 or more children)	£29.00	
Children Under 5	FREE	
Garden Only	£4.00.	

A 20% discount is allowed on groups of 20 or more persons (as shown with *)

Coach/Car Park Charge per vehicle (for non-Castle visitors)   £2.00

■ Special Events
Check website www.inveraray-castle.com for details of forthcoming events.

INVERARAY CASTLE & GARDENS 🏛Ⓕ
www.inveraray-castle.com

Inveraray Castle & Gardens - Home to the Duke & Duchess of Argyll and ancestral home of the Clan Campbell.

The ancient Royal Burgh of Inveraray lies about 60 miles north west of Glasgow by Loch Fyne in an area of spectacular natural beauty. The ruggedness of the highland scenery combines with the sheltered tidal loch, beside which nestles the present Castle built between 1745 and 1790. The Castle is home to the Duke and Duchess of Argyll. The Duke is head of the Clan Campbell and his family have lived in Inveraray since the early 15th Century. Designed by Roger Morris and decorated by Robert Mylne, the fairytale exterior belies the grandeur of its gracious interior. The Clerk of Works, William Adam, father of Robert and John, did much of the laying out of the present Royal Burgh, which is an unrivalled example of an early planned town. Visitors enter the famous Armoury Hall containing some 1,300 pieces including

Brown Bess muskets, Lochaber axes, 18th Century Scottish broadswords, and can see preserved swords from the Battle of Culloden. The fine State Dining Room and Tapestry Drawing Room contain magnificent French tapestries made especially for the Castle, fabulous examples of Scottish, English and French furniture and a wealth of other works of art. The unique collection of china, silver and family artifacts spans the generations which are identified by a genealogical display in the Clan Room.

The castle's private garden which was opened to the public in 2010 for the first time is also not to be missed, especially in springtime with its stunning displays of rhododendrons and azaleas.

KEY FACTS

ℹ️ No flash photography. Guide books in French and German translations.

🏪 A wide range of Scottish gifts, books and Clan Campbell memorabilia.

🌿 A varied selection of plants & shrubs available for purchase.

🍽 Inveraray Castle provides the perfect location for corporate events of all sizes.

♿ Partial. Disabled Toilets inside the Castle.

☕ Licenced Tearoom serving lunches, tea/coffee, soft drinks and homebaking.

🚶 Available for up to 46 people per group. Tour time: approx 1 hr.

🅿️ 100 cars. Car/coach park close to Castle.

🏛 £4.00 per child. Areas of interest include a woodland walk.

🦮 Guide dogs only.

🔔

🎫

MOUNT STUART 🏠Ⓕ ◨ ◆
ISLE OF BUTE PA20 9LR
www.mountstuart.com

One of the World's finest houses - Mount Stuart, ancestral home of the Marquess of Bute, is a stupendous example of Victorian Gothic architecture set amidst 300 acres of gloriously landscaped gardens. Spectacular interiors include the stunning White Marble Chapel and magnificent Marble Hall complete with kaleidoscopic stained glass. A Fine Art Collection and astounding architectural detail presents both stately opulence and unrivalled imagination. With something for all the family, this Award winning Visitor Attraction offers excellent restaurant facilities, Gift Shop, Tearooms, way-marked walks, picnic areas, Adventure Play Area and Contemporary Visual Arts Exhibition.

Location: Map 13:A9. OS Ref NS100 600. SW coast of Scotland,

5 miles S of Rothesay.
Owner: Mount Stuart Trust
Contact: Mount Stuart Office
Tel: 01700 503877 **Fax:** 01700 505313
E-mail: contactus@mountstuart.com
Open: Sat 28 Mar-Sun 4 Oct. May be closed occassionaly for private functions, please check website before travelling.
Admission: Please see our website for up-to-date information.
Key facts: ⓘ No photography. 🔲🚻🅃♿ Suitable. 🎦🍴🎥🅿 Ample. 🔳🖼 🖼 Exclusive - House/Self Catering - Grounds. 🔺🔽

DUART CASTLE 🏠Ⓕ
Isle Of Mull, Argyll PA64 6AP
www.duartcastle.com

The 13th Century Castle of the Clan Maclean proudly guards the sea cliffs of the Isle of Mull. Explore the ancient island fortress with dungeons, keep, state rooms, Great Hall, museum & battlements. Discover the tearoom & gift shop, cottage garden, Millennium Wood & coastal walks around Duart Point. The set for 1999 film "Entrapment" with Sean Connery.

Location: Map 12:O4. OS Ref NM750 350. Off A849, 3.5 miles from Craignure Ferry Terminal. The Duart Coach operates between the Ferry and the Castle.
Owner/Contact: Sir Lachlan Maclean Bt
Tel: 01680 812309
E-mail: guide@duartcastle.com
Open: 1-30 Apr: open Sun-Thu 11am to 4pm. Open Easter weekend.
1 May-18 Oct: open daily 10:30am to 5pm.
Admission: Adult: £6.00, Child (4-15) £3.00, Conc £5.40, Family (2+2) £15.00.
Key facts: ⓘ Summer events calendar. 🔲 Duart gift shop. 🔳 Duart tearoom. 🎥 Guided tours. 🅿 50m away. 🔳 Schools welcome. 🖼 Dogs welcome. 🔳 Duart cottage (self catering). 🔺 Weddings. 🔽

West Highlands & Islands, Loch Lomond, Stirling and Trossachs

STIRLING CASTLE

Stirling FK8 1EJ

www.stirlingcastle.gov.uk

Experience the refurbished 16th Century Royal Palace where you can explore the richly decorated King's and Queen's apartments. Other highlights include the Great Hall, Chapel Royal, Regimental Museum, Tapestry Studio and the Great Kitchens. Don't miss our guided tour where you can hear tales of the castle's history.
Location: Map 13:E7. OS Ref NS790 941. Leave the M9 at junction 10. and follow road signs for the castle.
Owner: Historic Scotland
Tel: 01786 450 000
E-mail: hs.explorer@scotland.gsi.gov.uk
Open: 1 Apr-30 Sep. 9.30am- 6pm. 1 Oct-31 Mar 9.30am to 5pm. Last ticket is sold 45 minutes before closing. Visit website for New Year opening times.
Admission: Adult £14.50, Concessions £11.00, Child £7.50.
Key facts: ⬚ ⬚ Private hire. ⬚ Partial. WCs. ⬚ Licensed. ⬚ Licensed. ⬚ Obligatory. ⬚ ⬚ Limited for coaches. Car parking is available £4.00. ⬚ ⬚ Assistance dogs only. ⬚ ⬚ €

ARDENCRAIG GARDENS

Ardencraig, Rothesay, Isle Of Bute, West Highlands PA20 9ZE
Walled garden, greenhouses, aviaries. Woodland walk from Rothesay 1 mile (Skippers Wood).
Location: Map 13:A8. OS Ref NS105 645. 2m from Rothesay
Owner: Argyll and Bute Council
Contact: Joe McCabe
Tel: 01700 504644
Open: Mon-Thu 9pm-4pm. Fri 9pm-3:30pm. Sat and Sun 1pm-4:30pm.
Admission: Free.
Key facts: ⬚ ⬚ WCs. ⬚ By arrangement. ⬚ ⬚ ⬚ Guide dogs only.

ARDTORNISH ESTATE & GARDENS

Ardtornish Estate, Morvern, Nr Oban, Argyll & Bute PA80 5UZ
30 acres of garden including over 200 species of rhododendron, extensive planting for year round interest. **Location:** Map 12:O4. OS Ref NM702 472. In Ardtornish (Highland region, nr Loch Aline) - just off the A884 to Mull. **Tel:** 01967 421 288
E-mail: stay@ardtornish.co.uk **Website:** www.ardtornishgardens.co.uk
Open: Mar-Nov, Mon-Sun, 9am-6pm. **Admission:** £4.00 per person.

CASTLE STALKER

Portnacroish, Appin, Argyll PA38 4BL
Early 15th Century tower house and seat of the Stewarts of Appin. Set on an islet 400 yds off the shore of Loch Linnhe. **Location:** Map 12:P3. OS Ref NM930 480.
Tel: 01631 730354 **E-mail:** rossallward@madasafish.com
Website: www.castlestalker.com **Open:** 29 Jun-3 Jul; 20-24 Jul; 3-7 Aug; 7-11 Sep and 21-25 Sep. Phone for app. **Admission:** Adult £15.00, Child £7.50.

The Blue Room at Mount Stuart

CRAIGSTON CASTLE 🏠
Turriff, Aberdeenshire AB53 5PX
www.craigston-castle.co.uk

Built between 1604 and 1607 by John Urquhart Tutor of Cromarty. Two wings were added in the early 1700s. The beautiful sculpted balcony, unique in Scottish architecture, depicts a piper, two grinning knights and David and Goliath. Remarkable carved oak, panels of Scottish kings' biblical heroes, originally from the family seat at Cromarty castle were mounted in doors and shutters in the early 17th Century. The house is a private home and is still owned and lived in by the Urquhart family.

Location: Map 17:D8. OS Ref NJ762 550. On B9105, 4.5m NE of Turriff.
Owner: William Pratesi Urquhart **Contact:** Claus Perch
Tel: 01888551707 **E-mail:** info@craigston.co.uk
Open: 18 Apr-26 Apr and then 10 Oct-25 Oct plus throughout the year by appointment. **Admission:** Adult £6.00, Child £2.00, Conc. £4.00. Groups: Adult £5.00, Child/School £1.00.
Key facts: ⓘ 🅣 Bespoke events can be organised with partner organisations. ♿ Very limited wheelchair access. 🎦 Obligatory. 🅿 🖼 🍴 🏨 🏠 In process of being applied for Craigston, an ideal venue for your special day.

Craigston Castle

CRATHES CASTLE, GARDEN & ESTATE ♛
Banchory, Aberdeenshire AB31 3QJ
www.nts.org.uk

Fairytale-like turrets, gargoyles of fantastic design and the ancient Horn of Leys given in 1323 by Robert the Bruce are just a few of the features of this historic castle. The Crathes gardens and estates are ideal for a family day out.
A delight at any time of year, the famous gardens feature great yew hedges and a colourful double herbaceous border. Further afield the 595-acre estate offers six separate trails to enjoy.

Location: Map 17:D12. OS Ref NO735 967. On A93, 3 miles east of Banchory. AB31 5QJ
Owner: The National Trust for Scotland
Tel: 0844 493 2166
E-mail: crathes@nts.org.uk
Open: Please see website for opening times.
Admission: Please see our website or call us for up to date prices.
Key facts: 🖼 ⓘ ♛

DELGATIE CASTLE
Turriff, Aberdeenshire AB53 5TD
www.delgatiecastle.com

'Best Visitor Experience' Award Winner. Dating from 1030 the Castle is steeped in Scottish history yet still has the atmosphere of a lived in home. It has some of the finest painted ceilings in Scotland, Mary Queen of Scots' bed-chamber. Clan Hay Centre. Scottish Home Baking Award Winner. Victorian Christmas Fayre last weekend November and first weekend December. The castle is decorated throughout with decorations, Christmas trees and much more. Santa is here for the children with a pre-christmas present, crafters in many of the rooms throughout the Castle, staff in period costume.

Location: Map 17:D9. OS Ref NJ754 506. Off A947 Aberdeen to Banff Road.
Owner: Delgatie Castle Trust **Contact:** Mrs Joan Johnson
Tel: 01888 563479 **E-mail:** joan@delgatiecastle.com
Open: Daily, 10am-5pm. 1 Oct-1 Apr 10am-4pm.
Admission: Adult £8.00, Child/Conc. £5.00, Family £21.00 (2 Adults & 2 Children), Groups (10+): £5.00.
B&B in Symbister apartment £50 per person per night.
Key facts: ⓘ No photography. 🖼 🅣 ♿ WCs. 🍴 🍴 🎦 By arrangement. 🅿 🖼 🐕 Guide dogs only. 🏨 2 self catering apartments in Castle. ❄ ♛

DUFF HOUSE
Banff AB45 3SX
www.duffhouse.org.uk

One of the finest houses built in Scotland, Duff House is a magnificent Georgian mansion designed by William Adam. Standing in extensive parkland, today it houses a beautiful collection of paintings and furniture on loan from the National Galleries of Scotland. The setting is impressively situated amid lawns fringed by woodland and enchanting follies.

Location: Map 17:D8. OS Ref NJ 690 633. Off the A97
Owner: Historic Scotland
Tel: 01261 818181
E-mail: hs.explorer@scotland.gsi.gov.uk
Open: 1 Apr-31 Oct. Open daily 11am-5pm. 1 Nov-31 Mar. Open Thu-Sun 11am-4pm.
Admission: Adult £7.10, Concession £5.70, Child £4.30.
Key facts: ⬚ ♿ Lift available.
⬚ P ⬚ ⬚ ⬚

CRIMONMOGATE
Lonmay, Fraserburgh, Aberdeenshire AB43 8SE

Situated in Aberdeenshire, Crimonmogate is a Grade A listed mansion house and one of the most easterly stately homes in Scotland, it is now owned by William and Candida, Viscount and Viscountess Petersham. Pronounced 'Crimmon-moggat', this exclusive country house stands within beautiful and seasonally-changing parkland and offers one of Aberdeenshire's most outstanding and unusual venues for corporate events, parties, dinners and weddings.

Location: Map 17:F8. OS Ref NK043 588.
Owner/Contact: Lord Petersham **Tel:** 01346 532401
E-mail: naomi@cmg-events.co.uk
Open: 1-8 May, 18-30 June, Aug 27-1 Sep. Tours at 10.30am, 11.30am, and 12.30pm, or by appointment.
Admission: Adult £7.00, Conc. £6.00, Child £5.00. Max of 12 at any one time, guided tours only.
Key facts: ⬚ Weddings & special events: max 60 in hall & up to 200 in Marquee. ⬚ Only the principal rooms are part of the tour. P ⬚ No dogs. ⬚ ⬚

BALFLUIG CASTLE
Alford, Aberdeenshire AB33 8EJ

Small 16th Century tower house, restored in 1967. Its garden and wooded park are surrounded by farmland.
Location: Map 17:D11. OS Ref NJ586 151. Alford, Aberdeenshire.
Tel: 020 7624 3200
Open: Please write to M I Tennant Esq, 30 Abbey Gardens, London NW8 9AT.

CRAIG CASTLE
Rhynie, Huntly, Aberdeenshire AB54 4LP

The Castle, a Gordon stronghold for 300 years; built round a courtyard and consists of a 16th Century L-shaped Keep, a Georgian house and an 19th Century addition. **Location:** Map 17:C10. OS Ref NJ472 259. 3m W of Rhynie and Lumsden on B9002. **Tel:** 01464 861705 **Open:** May-Sep: Wed & every 2nd weekend in each month, 2-5pm. **Admission:** Adult £5.00, Child £1.00.

DRUMMUIR CASTLE
Drummuir, By Keith, Banffshire AB55 5JE

Castellated Victorian Gothic-style castle built in 1847 by Admiral Duff. 60ft high lantern tower with fine plasterwork, family portraits and interesting artefacts.
Location: Map 17:B9. OS Ref NJ372 442. Between Keith and Dufftown, off the B9014. **Tel:** 01542 810332 **Open:** Sat 29 Aug-Sun 27 Sep: daily, 2-5pm (last tour 4.15pm). **Admission:** Adult £4.00, Child £2.50. Groups by arrangement.

KILDRUMMY CASTLE ⬚
Alford, Aberdeenshire AB33 8RA

Though ruined, the best example in Scotland of a 13th Century castle with a curtain wall, four round towers, hall and chapel of that date.
Location: Map 17:C11. OS Ref NJ455 164. **Tel:** 01975 571 331
Website: www.historic-scotland.gov.uk
Open: Please see website for up to date opening and admission details.

LICKLEYHEAD CASTLE
Auchleven, Insch, Aberdeenshire AB52 6PN

Beautifully restored Laird's Castle, built by the Leslies c1450, renovated in 1629 by John Forbes of Leslie. Boasts many interesting architectural features.
Location: Map 17:C10. OS Ref NJ628 237. 2m S of Insch on B992.
Tel: 01651 821276 **Open:** 10am-12noon. Weekdays 4-8 May, 11-15 May & 18-22 May inc. Sats only 27 Jun-29 Aug **Admission:** Free.

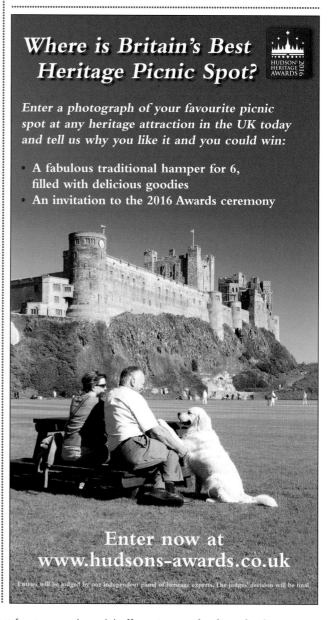

Dunvegan Castle

DUNVEGAN CASTLE & GARDENS 🏛️Ⓕ ◆

www.dunvegancastle.com

Experience living history at Dunvegan Castle, the ancestral home of the Chiefs of Clan MacLeod for 800 years.

Any visit to the Isle of Skye is incomplete without savouring the wealth of history on offer at Dunvegan Castle & Gardens, the ancestral home of the Chiefs of Clan MacLeod for 800 years. Originally designed to keep people out, it was first opened to visitors in 1933 and is one of Skye's most famous landmarks. On display are many fine oil paintings and Clan treasures, the most famous of which is the Fairy Flag. Legend has it that this sacred Banner has miraculous powers and when unfurled in battle, the Clan MacLeod will defeat their enemies. Another of the castle's great treasures is the Dunvegan Cup, a unique 'mazer' dating back to the Middle Ages.

It was gifted by the O'Neils of Ulster as a token of thanks to one of the Clan's most celebrated Chiefs, Sir Rory Mor, for his support of their cause against the marauding forces of Queen Elizabeth I of England in 1596.

Today visitors can enjoy tours of an extraordinary castle and Highland estate steeped in history and clan legend, delight in the beauty of its formal gardens, take a boat trip onto Loch Dunvegan to see the seal colony, enjoy an appetising meal at the MacLeods Table Café or browse in one of its four shops offering a wide choice to suit everyone. Over time, we have given a warm Highland welcome to visitors including Sir Walter Scott, Dr Johnson and Queen Elizabeth II and we look forward to welcoming you.

KEY FACTS

ℹ️ Boat trips to seal colony. Fishing trips & loch cruises. No photography in castle.

🛍️ Our gift shops sell a wide range of quality items, Harris Tweed products, knitwear, jewellery & small gifts.

🚻 Partial. WCs. Laptop tour of Castle available.

🍴 MacLeod Table Café (seats 76).

🚶 By appointment. Self Guided.

🅿️ 120 cars & 10 coaches. Coaches please book if possible. Seal boat trips dependent upon weather.

🎓 Welcome by arrangement. Guide available on request.

🐕 Dogs on leads only.

🏨 Self-catering holiday cottages .

Dunvegan Castle Gardens

Boat Trips to Seal Colony

VISITOR INFORMATION

■ Owner
Hugh Macleod of Macleod

■ Address
Dunvegan Castle
Dunvegan
Isle of Skye
Scotland
IV55 8WF

■ Location
Map 15:F9
OS Ref. NG250 480
1m N of village. NW corner of Skye. Kyle of Lochalsh to Dunvegan via Skye Bridge.
Rail: Inverness to Kyle of Lochalsh
Ferry: Maillaig to Armadale

■ Contact
Janet Wallwork Clarke, Executive Director
Tel: 01470 521206
Fax: 01470 521205
E-mail: info@dunvegancastle.com

■ Opening Times
1 April - 15 October
Daily 10am-5.30pm
Last admission 5pm
16 October - 31 March
Open by appointment for groups only on weekdays. Castle and Gardens closed Christmas and New Year.

■ Admission
Castle & Gardens
Adult	£11.00
Child (5-15yrs)	£8.00
Senior/Student/Group (Group min. 10 adults)	£9.00
Family Ticket (2 Adults, 3 Children)	£29.00

Gardens only
Adult	£9.00
Child (5-15yrs)	£6.00
Senior/Student/Group	£8.00

Seal Boat Trips (Prices valid with a Castle or Garden Ticket)
Adult	£6.00
Child (5-15yrs)	£4.00
Senior/Student/Group	£5.00
Infant (under 2yrs)	Free

Wildlife Loch Cruises (1 hour)
Adult from	£15.00
Child (5-15yrs) from	£10.00

Fishing Trips (2 hours)
Adult	£40.00
Child	£30.00

■ Special Events
A unique location for film, TV or advertising. Check website for details.

CAWDOR CASTLE AND GARDENS 🏰Ⓕ
CAWDOR CASTLE, NAIRN, SCOTLAND IV12 5RD
www.cawdorcastle.com

This splendid romantic castle, dating from the late 14th Century, was built as a private fortress by the Thanes of Cawdor, and remains the home of the Cawdor family to this day. The ancient medieval tower was built around the legendary holly tree. Although the house has evolved over 600 years, later additions, mainly of the 17th Century, were all built in the Scottish vernacular style. It has three gardens to enjoy: the earliest dating from the 16th Century with the symbolic gardens and maze: an 18th Century flower garden, and a 19th Century wild garden with rhododendrons and spring bulbs as well as splendid trees. Two further gardens, the Tibetan Garden and the Traditional Scottish Vegetable Garden, are at the Dower House at Auchindoune

Location: Map 16:O9. OS Ref NH850 500. From Edinburgh A9, 3.5 hrs, Inverness 20 mins, Nairn 10 mins. Main road - A9, 14m.

Owner: The Dowager Countess Cawdor
Contact: General Manager - Ian Whitaker
Tel: 01667 404401 **Fax:** 01667 404674 **E-mail:** info@cawdorcastle.com
Open: 1 May-4 Oct 2015 Daily 10am-5.30pm. Last adm 4.45pm. Groups by appointment. **Admission:** Adult £10.50, Child (5-15 yrs) £6.50, Conc. £9.50, Family (2 + up to 5) £30.00. Gardens, Grounds and Nature Trails £5.75. Adult Groups (12+) £9.00, Child Groups (12+ children, 1 adult free per 12) £6.00. Auchindoune Gardens (May-Jul only) £3.50.
Key facts: ℹ️ 9 hole golf course, whisky tasting. No photography in castle 🛍️ Gift, Highland & Wool shops. 🚻 WC. Parts of ground floor & gardens accessible. ☕ Courtyard Cafe, May-Oct. 📷 By arrangement. 🅿️ 250 cars & 25 coaches. 🎫 £6.00 per child. 🐕 Guide dogs only in castle & grounds. €

CASTLE OF MEY 🏰
Thurso, Caithness, Scotland KW14 8XH
www.castleofmey.org.uk

The home of The Queen Mother in Caithness. She bought the Castle in 1952, developed the gardens and it became her holiday home because of the beautiful surroundings and the privacy she was always afforded. There is a Visitor Centre with shop and tearoom and an Animal Centre for children. There is also a wonderful walled garden.

Location: Map 17:B2. OS Ref ND290 739. On A836 between Thurso and John O'Groats, just outside the village of Mey.
Owner: The Queen Elizabeth Castle of Mey Trust **Contact:** Shirley Farquhar
Tel: 01847 851473 **Fax:** 01847 851475 **E-mail:** enquiries@castleofmey.org.uk
Open: 13 May-30 Sep: daily, 10.20am-last entries 4pm. Closed end of Jul/early Aug. Check website or please telephone for details.
Admission: Adult £11.00, Child (5-16yrs) £6.50, Concession £9.75. Family £29.00. Booked groups (15+): £9.75. Gardens and Grounds only: Adult £6.50. Garden and Grounds family ticket £19.00.
Key facts: ℹ️ No photography in the Castle. 🛍️🎫🚻 Limited disabled access, please phone ahead for advice. ☕ Licensed. 📷🅿️ Guide dogs only. 🏠

CLAN DONALD SKYE
Armadale, Sleat, Isle of Skye IV45 8RS
www.clandonald.com

Be inspired by the magic of the restored historical gardens and walking trails threading through 40 acres of ancient woodland around the striking ruins of Armadale Castle. Discover 1500 years of the history and culture of the Highlands and the Isles in the award-winning Museum of the Isles. Explore your Scottish ancestry in the Museum's Study Centre.

Location: Map 15:H11. OS Ref NG633036. From Skye Bridge, 16 miles south of Broadford on the A851; or, take ferry from Mallaig to Amadale and follow signs.
Owner: Clan Donald Lands Trust **Contact:** Mags Macdonald
Tel: 01471 844305 **Fax:** 01471 844275 **E-mail:** office@clandonald.com
Open: Apr-Oct, 9:30am-5:30pm. Nov-Mar, gardens open dawn to dusk; Museum & Study Centre by appointment. Please check our website for any changes.
Admission: Adults £8.00, Children & Conc. £6.50, Family (2 adults & 3 children) £25.00. Groups (10 or more) £6.50 per person. Children under 5 free.
Key facts: 🛍️ 2 shops featuring Scottish designers. 🚻 Mobility aides available. ☕🍴 Local cuisine. 📷 Various languages & visually impaired. 🅿️ 🏠 Self-catering. 🏠

DUNROBIN CASTLE & GARDENS 🏛ⓕ
Golspie, Sutherland KW10 6SF
www.dunrobincastle.co.uk

Dates from the 13th Century with additions in the 17th, 18th and 19th Centuries. Wonderful furniture, paintings, library, ceremonial robes and memorabilia. Victorian museum in grounds with a fascinating collection including Pictish stones. Set in fine woodlands overlooking the sea. Magnificent formal gardens, one of few remaining French/Scottish formal parterres. Falconry displays take place in the formal gardens. **Location:** Map 16:O6. OS Ref NC850 010. 50m N of Inverness on A9. **Owner:** The Sutherland Dunrobin Trust **Contact:** Scott Morrison
Tel: 01408 633177 **Fax:** 01408 634081 **E-mail:** info@dunrobincastle.co.uk
Open: 1 Apr–15 Oct: Apr, May, Sep and Oct, Mon-Sat, 10.30am-4.30pm, Sun, 12noon-4.30pm. No Falconry on Suns. Jun, Jul and Aug, daily, 10.00am-5.00pm. Falconry displays every day. Last entry half an hour before closing. Falconry displays at 11.30am and 2pm.
Admission: Adult £10.50, Child £6.00, OAP/Student. £8.50, Family (2+3) £29.00. Groups (minimum 10): Rates on request. Rates include falconry display, museum and gardens.
Key facts: 🖼 🔲 Unsuitable for wheelchairs. 🍴 ⑪ 🔲 By arrangement. 🅿 🚻

URQUHART CASTLE 🏰
Drumnadrochit, Loch Ness, Inverness-shire IV63 6XJ
www.historic-scotland.gov.uk

Discover 1,000 years of drama, experience a glimpse of medieval life and enjoy stunning views over Loch Ness. Climb the Grant Tower that watches over the iconic loch. Peer into a miserable prison cell and imagine the splendid banquets staged in the great hall. A more comfortable view of the iconic ruin against a backdrop of lock ness and the hills of the great glen can be enjoyed from the cafe.
Location: Map 16:M10. OS Ref NH2908 5150. On Loch Ness near Drumnadrochit
Owner: Historic Scotland
Tel: 01456 450551
E-mail: hs.explorer@scotland.gsi.gov.uk
Open: 1 Apr-30 Sep 9.30am-6pm. 1-31 Oct 9.30am-5pm. 1 Nov-31 Mar 9.30am to 4.30pm. Last entry 45 minutes before closing.
Admission: Adult £8.50, Concession £6.80, Child £5.10.
Key facts: ⓘ Disability buggies are available. Photographic guide for those who have mobility difficulties. 🔲 🔲 🅿 🚻 ♿

BALLINDALLOCH CASTLE 🏛ⓕ
Ballindalloch, Banffshire AB37 9AX
Ballindalloch Castle has been occupied by its original family, the Macpherson-Grants, since 1546. You'll enjoy this beautiful home, its decor, paintings, china, furniture and family photographs. Beautiful rock and rose gardens, children's play area, a grass labyrinth and river walks. The estate is home to the famous Aberdeen-Angus cattle breed. A superb family day out. **Location:** Map 17:A9. OS Ref NJ178 366. 14m NE of Grantown-on-Spey on A9. 22m S of Elgin on A95.
Owner: Mr & Mrs Guy Macpherson-Grant **Contact:** Fenella Corr
Tel: 01807 500205 **E-mail:** enquiries@ballindallochcastle.co.uk
Website: www.ballindallochcastle.co.uk
Open: Good Friday - 30 Sep: 10.00am-3.45pm (last entry). Closed on Sats (with the exception of Easter Sat).
Admission: Castle & Grounds: Adults £10.50, Senior Citizens £9.00, Children (6-16) £5.00, Family (2+3) £27.00, Season Ticket £35.00. Grounds Only: Adults & Senior Citizens £6.00, Children £2.50, Family £13.50. **Key facts:** 🔲 ⓣ Please enquire. 🖼 Partial. 🔲 🔲 Short film. 🅿 Cars & coaches. 🚻 Designated area

THE DOUNE OF ROTHIEMURCHUS
By Aviemore PH22 1QP
The family home of the Grants of Rothiemurchus since 1560, described by Elizabeth Grant, (born 1797), in 'Memoirs of a Highland Lady is stunningly situated beside the River Spey. Visit partial restoration, exterior & grounds or the Ranger led 'Highland Lady Experience' includes completed rooms.
Location: Map 16:P11. OS Ref NH900 100. 2m S of Aviemore.
Owner: John Grant of Rothiemurchus, Earl of Dysart
Contact: Rothiemurchus Centre open daily 9.30–5.30 **Tel:** 01479 812345
E-mail: info@rothie.net **Website:** www.rothiemurchus.net
Open: Exhibition: two partly restored rooms, exterior and grounds: Apr-Aug: Mon 10-12.30pm and 2-4.30pm (or dusk) and first Mon in the month, Sep–Dec, Feb & Mar. House: Wed as part of Highland Lady Experience (booking essential) or by special arrangement excl. Xmas and New Year. Groups by arrangement.
Admission: Restoration and grounds, voluntary charitable donation; Ranger led Tours:£30.00pp (min 2 people) 2 hours; Specialist groups: on application.
Key facts: ⓘ 🔲 🔲 Obligatory. 🅿 Limited.

EILEAN DONAN CASTLE 🏛
Dornie, Kyle Of Lochalsh, Wester Ross IV40 8DX
A fortified site for eight hundred years, Eilean Donan now represents one of Scotland's most iconic images. Located at the point where three great sea lochs meet amidst stunning highland scenery on the main road to Skye. Spiritual home of Clan Macrae with century old links to Clan Mackenzie.
Location: Map 16:J10. OS Ref NG880 260. On A87 8m E of Skye Bridge.
Contact: David Win - Castle Keeper
Tel: 01599 555202
E-mail: eileandonan@btconnect.com
Website: www.eileandonancastle.com
Open: Please see our website for 2015 opening dates and times.
Admission: Please see our website for up to date admission prices.
Key facts: ⓘ 🔲 🔲 🔲 Eilean Donan holiday cottage. 🏠

Cawdor Castle

BOWHILL HOUSE & COUNTRY ESTATE
Bowhill, Selkirk TD7 5ET
Tel: 01750 22204

DUNS CASTLE
Duns, Berwickshire TD11 3NW
Tel: 01361 883211

FERNIEHIRST CASTLE
Jedburgh, Roxburghshire, Scottish Borders TD8 6NX
Tel: 01450 870051 **E-mail:** curator@clankerr.co.uk

HERMITAGE CASTLE
Scottish Borders TD9 0LU
Tel: 01387 376 222

HIRSEL ESTATE
Coldstream TD12 4LP
Tel: 01555 851536 **E-mail:** joy.hitchcock@daestates.co.uk

NEIDPATH CASTLE
Peebles, Scotland EH45 8NW
Tel: 01721 720 333

PAXTON HOUSE, GALLERY & COUNTRY PARK
Berwick-Upon-Tweed TD15 1SZ
Tel: 01289 386291 **E-mail:** info@paxtonhouse.com

SMAILHOLM TOWER
Smailholm, Kelso TD5 7PG
Tel: 01573 460365

ARDWELL GARDENS
Ardwell House, Ardwell, Stranraer, Wigtownshire DG9 9LY
Tel: 01776 860227 **E-mail:** info@ardwellestate.co.uk

BLAIRQUHAN CASTLE
Maybole, Ayrshire, Scotland KA19 7LZ
Tel: 01655 770239

DRUMLANRIG CASTLE
Thornhill, Dumfriesshire, Scotland DG3 4AQ
Tel: 01848 331555

THREAVE CASTLE
Dumfries and Galloway DG7 1TJ
Tel: 07711 223 101

DIRLETON CASTLE
North Berwick EH39 5ER
Tel: 01620 850 330

LENNOXLOVE HOUSE
Haddington, East Lothian EH41 4NZ
Tel: 01620 828614 **E-mail:** ken-buchanan@lennoxlove.com

THE HILL HOUSE
Upper Colquhoun Street, Helensburgh G84 9AJ
Tel: 0844 493 2208 **E-mail:** thehillhouse@nts.org.uk

POLLOK HOUSE
2060 Pollokshaws Road, Glasgow G43 1AT
Tel: 0844 4932202 **E-mail:** information@nts.org.uk

ARBROATH ABBEY
Arbroath, Tayside DD11 1EG
Tel: 01241 878756

ARBUTHNOTT HOUSE & GARDEN
Arbuthnott, Laurencekirk AB30 1PA
Tel: 01561 361226

DUNNINALD, CASTLE AND GARDENS
Montrose, Angus DD10 9TD
Tel: 01674 672031 **E-mail:** visitorinformation@dunninald.com

EDZELL CASTLE
Perthshire DD9 7UE
Tel: 01356 648 631

HOUSE OF PITMUIES GARDENS
Guthrie, By Forfar, Angus DD8 2SN
Tel: 01241 828245

KELLIE CASTLE & GARDEN
Pittenweem, Fife KY10 2RF
Tel: 0844 493 2184 **E-mail:** information@nts.org.uk

ST ANDREW'S CASTLE
St Andrews, Fife KY16 9AR
Tel: 01334 477196

ARDCHATTAN PRIORY GARDENS
Connel, Argyll, Scotland PA37 1RQ
Tel: 01796 481355

CASTLE FRASER & GARDEN
Sauchen, Inverurie AB51 7LD
Tel: 0131 243 9300

DRUM CASTLE & GARDEN
Drumoak, By Banchory, Aberdeenshire AB31 3EY
Tel: 0844 493 2161 **E-mail:** information@nts.org.uk

DUNOTTAR CASTLE
Stonehaven, Aberdeenshire AB39 2TL
Tel: 01569 762173 **E-mail:** dunnottarcastle@btconnect.com

FORT GEORGE
Grampian Highlands IV2 7TD
Tel: 01667 460232

FYVIE CASTLE & GARDEN
Turriff, Aberdeenshire AB53 8JS
Tel: 0844 493 2182 **E-mail:** information@nts.org.uk

HADDO HOUSE
Tarves, Ellon, Aberdeenshire AB41 0ER
Tel: 0844 493 2179 **E-mail:** information@nts.org.uk

PITMEDDEN GARDEN
Ellon, Aberdeenshire AB41 7PD
Tel: 0844 493 2177 **E-mail:** information@nts.org.uk

SKAILL HOUSE
Breckness Estate, Sandwick, Orkney, Scotland KW16 3LR
Tel: 01856 841 501

Dumfries House, Ayrshire

Gregynog Hall & Gardens,
Powys

Aberglasney House and Gardens,
Carmarthenshire

South Wales
Mid Wales
North Wales

Wales

North Wales

Mid Wales

South Wales

If you love castles and a sense of adventure, Wales is the place for you, but it is easy to miss this region's exceptional gardens and varied smaller heritage places.

New Entries for 2015:
- Cochwillan Old Hall
- Gregynog Hall & Gardens
- Plas Newydd

FONMON CASTLE 🏛ⓕ
FONMON, BARRY, VALE OF GLAMORGAN CF62 3ZN
www.fonmoncastle.com

Just 25 minutes from Cardiff and the M4, Fonmon is one of few mediaeval castles still lived in as a home, since being built c1200, it has only changed hands once. Visitors are welcomed by an experienced guide and the 45 minute tour walks through the fascinating history of the Castle, its families, architecture and interiors. The Fonmon gardens are an attraction in their own right for enthusiasts and amateurs alike and visitors are free to wander and explore. Available as an exclusive wedding and party venue, corporate and team building location, visitor attraction and host for product launches and filming.
Location: Map 2:L2. OS Ref ST047 681. 15miles W of Cardiff, 1miles W of Cardiff airport. **Owner:** Sir Brooke Boothby Bt **Contact:** Casey Govier

Tel: 01446 710206 **E-mail:** Fonmon_Castle@msn.com
Open: Public opening: 1 Apr- 30 Sep on Tue & Wed afternoons for individuals, families & small groups. Midday-5pm, no need to book. Tours at 2pm, 3pm & 4pm & last 45 mins, last entrance to gardens at 4pm. Groups 20+ welcome by appointment throughout the year. Varied hospitality options with very popular Afternoon Teas. **Admission:** Entry and tour of the Castle priced at £6.00, Children free. Access to garden and grounds is free.
Key facts: ⓘ Conferences. 🍽 By arrangement. ♿ Suitable. WCs. 🎫 Guided Tour obligatory. 🅿 Ample free parking for cars and coaches. ▣ 🐕 Guide dogs only. ⚭ Licensed for Civil Ceremonies for up to 110 people.

ABERGLASNEY GARDENS
Llangathen, Carmarthenshire SA32 8QH
www.aberglasney.org

Aberglasney is one of Wales' finest gardens - a renowned plantsman's paradise of more than 10 acres with a unique Elizabethan cloister garden at its heart. The gardens and the fully restored ground floor of Aberglasney's grade II* listed mansion are open 364 days a year. Exhibitions and events held throughout the year. **Location:** Map 5:F10. OS Ref SN579 221. Aberglasney is 12 miles east of Carmarthen and 4 miles west of Llandeilo on the A40 at Broad Oak
Owner: Aberglasney Restoration Trust (Private Charitable Trust)
Contact: Booking Department **Tel/Fax:** 01558 668998
E-mail: info@aberglasney.org
Open: All year: daily (except Christmas Day). Apr-Oct: 10am-6pm, last entry 5pm. Nov-Mar: 10.30am-4pm.
Admission: Adult £8.00, Child £4.00, Conc. £8.00, Booked groups (10+) Adult £6.80. **Key facts:** 📷 Free entry. 🍽 Free entry. 🍴 Contact for info. ♿ Mostly suitable. 🍴 Licensed. 🎫 Pre-booked for groups. 🅿 Free parking, also large coach park. ▣ 🐕 Guide dogs only. 🏠 Self Catering Holiday Cottage on site, please contact to book or go to www.aberglasney.org. ❉ Closed on Christmas Day. 🏳

ABERCAMLAIS HOUSE
Abercamlais, Brecon, Powys LD3 8EY
Splendid Grade I mansion dating from middle ages, altered extensively in early 18th Century with 19th Century additions, in extensive grounds beside the river Usk. Still in same family ownership and occupation since medieval times. Exceptional octagonal pigeon house, formerly a privy.
Location: Map 6:I10. OS Ref SN965 290. 5m W of Brecon on A40.
Owner/Contact: Mrs S Ballance
Tel: 01874 636206 **Fax:** 01874 636964
E-mail: info@abercamlais.co.uk
Website: www.abercamlais.co.uk
Open: Apr-Oct: by appointment.
Admission: Adult £5.00, Child Free.
Key facts: ⓘ No photography in house. ♿ 🎫 Obligatory. 🅿 🐕 Dogs on leads only. 🏳

CRESSELLY 🏛
Kilgetty, Pembrokeshire SA68 0SP

Home of the Allen family for 250 years. The house is of 1770 with matching wings of 1869 and contains good plasterwork and fittings of both periods. The Allens are of particular interest for their close association with the Wedgwood family of Etruria and a long tradition of foxhunting.
Location: Map 5:C11. OS Ref SN065 065. W of the A4075.
Owner/Contact: H D R Harrison-Allen Esq MFH
E-mail: hha@cresselly.com
Website: www.cresselly.com
Open: May 5-18 inclusive and Sep 1-14. Guided tours only, on the hour. Coaches at other times by arrangement.
Admission: Adult £4.00, no children under 12.
Key facts: ♿ Ground floor only. 🎫 Obligatory. 🅿 Coaches by arrangement. 🚫 🏳 ▣

LLANCAIACH FAWR MANOR
Gelligaer Road, Nelson, Treharris, Caerphilly County Borough CF46 6ER

Llancaiach Fawr is a Tudor Manor restored as it was during the Civil War year of 1645. Visitors are guided by the costumed 'servants' who love to chat about the lives of ordinary people in extraordinary times. Visitor Centre provides modern amenities and also caters for weddings, functions and B2B.
Location: Map 2:M1. OS Ref ST114 967. S side of B4254, 1m N of A472 at Nelson. **Owner:** Caerphilly County Borough Council
Contact: Lesley Edwards **Tel:** 01443 412248 **Fax:** 01443 412688
E-mail: llancaiachfawr@caerphilly.gov.uk **Website:** www.llancaiachfawr.co.uk
Open: 10am-5pm Tue to Sun and BH Mons all year round. Last entry to the Manor 4.00pm Closed 24 Dec-1 Jan inclusive. **Admission:** £7.50 Adults, £6.00 Concessions, £6.00 Child, £22.00 Family Ticket (2ad+2ch), Group discounts available (20+). **Key facts:** ⓘ No photography in Manor House. ▣ ⓑ ⓣ ⓛ Partial, WCs. ⓔ Licensed. ⓣⓣ Licensed ⓕ Obligatory. ⓟ ▣ ⓗ Dogs in grounds only. Not allowed in walled gardens of the manor. ▲ ⓦ

LLANDAFF CATHEDRAL
Llandaff Cathedral Green, Cardiff CF5 2LA

Discover Llandaff Cathedral. A holy place of peace and tranquility art, architecture and music with a very warm welcome. Over 1500 yrs of history. Works include Epstein, Piper, Pace, Rossetti, William Morris and Goscombe John. Services daily some sung by the Cathedral Choir with the Nicholson organ. Details on the Cathedral website www.llandaffcathedral.org.uk.
Discover one of the most important buildings in Wales!
Location: Map 2:L2. OS Ref ST155 397. At Cardiff Castle, drive West and cross River Taff; turn right into Cathedral Road (A4119) and follow signs to Llandaff.
Owner: Representative body of the Church In Wales **Contact:** Cathedral Office
Tel: 02920 564554 **E-mail:** admin@llandaffcathedral.org.uk
Website: www.llandaffcathedral.org.uk
Open: Every week day 9:30am-6pm, Sun 7:30am-6pm.
Admission: Free. Donations gratefully received.
Key facts: ▣ ⓛ ⓕ By arrangement. ⓟ Nearby. ▣ ⓗ Guide dogs only. ▲ ✣ ⓦ

LLANVIHANGEL COURT ⓷
Nr Abergavenny, Monmouthshire NP7 8DH

Grade I Tudor Manor. The home in the 17th Century of the Arnolds who built the imposing terraces and stone steps leading to the house. The interior has a fine hall, unusual yew staircase and many 17th Century moulded plaster ceilings. Delightful grounds. 17th Century features, notably Grade I stables.
Location: Map 6:K11. OS Ref SO433 139. 4m N of Abergavenny on A465.
Owner/Contact: Julia Johnson
Tel: 01873 890217
E-mail: jclarejohnson@googlemail.com
Website: www.llanvihangelcourt.com
Open: 1 May - 15 May & 10 Aug - 19 Aug. inclusive, daily 2.30-5.30pm. Last tour 5pm.
Admission: Entry and guide, Adult £6.00, Child/Conc. £3.00.
Key facts: ⓘ No inside photography. ⓛ Partial. ⓕ Obligatory. ⓟ Limited, no coaches. ⓗ Dogs on leads only. ▲

CASTELL COCH ✤
Tongwynlais, Cardiff CF15 7JS

A fairytale castle in the woods, Castell Coch embodies a glorious Victorian dream of the Middle Ages. The castle is a by-product of a vivid Victorian imagination, assisted by untold wealth. **Location:** Map 2:L1. OS Ref ST131 826.
Tel: 029 2081 0101 **Website:** www.cadw.wales.gov.uk
Open: Please see website for up to date opening and admission details.

DYFFRYN GARDENS ⚘
St Nicholas, Vale of Glamorgan CF5 6SU

Grade I listed gardens featuring a collection of formal lawns, intimate garden rooms an extensive arboretum and reinstated glasshouse.
Location: Map 2:L2. OS Ref ST094 717. **Tel:** 02920 593328
E-mail: dyffryn@nationaltrust.org.uk
Website: www.nationaltrust.org.uk/dyffryngardens
Open: Please see website for up to date opening and admission details.

RAGLAN CASTLE ✤
Raglan, Monmouthshire NP15 2BT

Undoubtedly the finest late medieval fortress-palace in Britain, begun in the 1430s by Sir William ap Thomas who built the mighty 'Yellow Tower'.
Location: Map 6:K12. OS Ref SO415 084. **Tel:** 01291 690228
Website: www.cadw.wales.gov.uk **Open:** Please visit www.cadw.wales.gov.uk for 2015 opening times and admission prices.

TINTERN ABBEY ✤
Tintern, Monmouthshire NP16 6SE

Tintern is the best-preserved abbey in Wales and ranks among Britain's most beautiful historic sites. The great Gothic abbey church stands almost complete to roof level. **Location:** Map 6:L12. OS Ref SO533 000.
Tel: 01291 689251 **Website:** www.cadw.wales.gov.uk **Open:** Please visit www.cadw.wales.gov.uk for 2015 opening times and admission prices.

TREBINSHWN
Llangasty, Nr Brecon, Powys LD3 7PX

16th Century mid-sized manor house. Extensively rebuilt 1780. Fine courtyard and walled garden. **Location:** Map 6:I10. OS Ref SO136 242. 1½m NW of Bwlch.
Tel: 01874 730653 **Fax:** 01874 730843
E-mail: liza.watson@trebinshunhouse.co.uk
Open: Easter-31 Aug: Mon-Tue, 10am-4.30pm. **Admission:** Free.

TREDEGAR HOUSE & PARK ⚘
Newport, South Wales NP10 8YW

Tredegar House is one of the most significant late 17th Century houses in Wales, if not the whole of the British Isles. **Location:** Map 2:M1. OS Ref ST290 852.
Tel: 01633 815880 **E-mail:** tredegar@nationaltrust.org.uk
Website: www.nationaltrust.org.uk/tredegarhouse
Open: Please see website for up to date opening and admission details.

USK CASTLE ⓷
Usk Castle, Monmouth Rd, Usk, Monmouthshire NP5 1SD

Best kept secret, romantic ruins overlooking Usk. **Location:** Map 6:K12. OS Ref SO3701SE. Off Monmouth Road in Usk. **Tel:** 01291 672563
E-mail: info@uskcastle.com **Website:** www.uskcastle.com
Open: Castle open: All year, see website. House Open: May (not Mons), 2-5pm and BHs. Guided tours only. **Admission:** £7.00; Gardens £4.00.

Aberglasney Gardens

THE HALL AT ABBEY-CWM-HIR
Nr Llandrindod Wells, Powys LD1 6PH
www.abbeycwmhir.com

In a breathtaking Mid Wales setting, the 52 room, Grade II* Hall offers tours to the public combining outstanding architecture, stunning interiors and fascinating collections - all in a family atmosphere. It is one of Wales' finest examples of Victorian Gothic Revival architecture, and is surrounded by beautiful and notable 12 acre gardens.
Location: Map 6:I8. OS Ref SO054 711. 7m NW of Llandrindod Wells, 6m E of Rhayader, 1m north of Crossgates on A483.
Owner: Paul and Victoria Humpherston **Contact:** Paul Humpherston
Tel: 01597 851727 **E-mail:** info@abbeycwmhir.com
Open: Daily and all year for prebooked tours only at 10.30am and 2pm for couples, small parties or groups. The Hall is decorated in all 52 rooms for Christmas (1 Nov-6 Jan) and Easter (Apr). **Admission:** House Tour and Gardens: Adult £16.00, Child (under 12) £5.00. Groups (10+) or repeat visitors £14.00. Gardens only: Adults £5.00. **Key facts:** i Visitors are asked to remove outside shoes for house tours, slippers can be provided. Partial. Licensed. Licensed. Obligatory. Cars and coaches. In grounds on leads.

GREGYNOG
Tregynon, Nr Newtown, Powys SY16 3PW
www.gregynog.org

Once a landed estate, now a vibrant conference centre, wedding venue and tourist destination. Set amidst 750 acres, Wales' newest National Nature Reserve and SSSI site offers 56 bedrooms and peace and tranquility. We pride ourselves on the quality of our home-produced locally sourced food from an extensive menu choice put together by our Chef. Grade 1 listed gardens, historic oak panelled rooms, an extensive library and a fine collection of furniture add to the unique ambience.
Location: Map 6:I6. OS Ref SO 084974. From the A483 follow the brown sign (Gregynog) or Bettws Cedewain. From Bettws follow Tregynon & look for large sign at end of drive. **Owner:** Gregynog **Contact:** enquiries@gregynog.org
Tel: 01686 650224 **E-mail:** enquiries@gregynog.org **Open:** Estate: every day. Cafe: please see website. **Admission:** Gardens Adult £3.00, Child £1.00.
Key facts: i Open daily from 9am. Plants for sale are on display in the Courtyard. Bespoke packages tailored to your requirements. Shop/Cafe/ some trails around the Hall. Open (except in winter) from 11am. Menu on website. Regular & various tours available - see website. Safe accessible parking. £2.50 charge. School visits welcomed - and to our Forest School. 4 of the historic rooms are licensed. Estate/grounds open all year.

HAFOD
Hafod Estate, Pontrhydygroes, Ystrad-Meurig, Ceredigion SY25 6DX
Picturesque landscape, one of the most significant in Britain located in a remote valley and improved by Col Thomas Johnes 1780-1816. Ten miles of restored walks featuring cascades, bridges and wonderful views in 500 acres of wood and parkland. The epitome of the Picturesque and Sublime. Georgian Group Award winner.
Location: Map 5:G8. OS Ref SN768 736. 15 miles E of Aberystwyth near Devils Bridge, car park, off B4574.
Owner: Natural Resources Wales **Contact:** The Hafod Trust
Tel: 01974 282568 **Fax:** 01974282579
E-mail: trust@hafod.org **Website:** www.hafod.org
Open: All year, daylight hours.
Admission: Free - guide book available at local shops or website.
Key facts: WC. Obligatory by arrangement. Dogs allowed in grounds on leads.

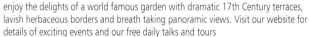

THE JUDGE'S LODGING
Broad Street, Presteigne, Powys LD8 2AD
Explore the fascinating world of the Victorian judges, their servants and felonious guests at this award-winning, totally hands-on historic house. Through sumptuous judge's apartments and the gas-lit servants' quarters below, follow an 'eavesdropping' audio tour featuring actor Robert Hardy. Damp cells, vast courtroom and new interactive local history rooms included.
Location: Map 6:K8. OS Ref SO314 644. In town centre, off A44 and A4113. Within easy reach from Herefordshire, Shropshire and mid-Wales.
Owner: Powys County Council **Contact:** Gabrielle Rivers **Tel:** 01544 260650
E-mail: info@judgeslodging.org.uk **Website:** www.judgeslodging.org.uk
Open: 1 Mar-31 Oct: Tues-Sun, 10am-5pm. 1 Nov-31 Nov: Wed-Sun, 10am-4pm, 1 Dec-22 Dec: Sat-Sun 10am-4pm. Open BH Mons.
Admission: Adult £7.50, Child £3.95, Conc. £6.50, Family £20.00. Groups (10-80): Adult £6.95, Conc. £5.95, Schools £4.95.
Key facts: i Partial. By arrangement. In town. Guide dogs only.

POWIS CASTLE & GARDEN
Welshpool, Powys SY21 8RF
Once a stark medieval fortress, Powis Castle has been transformed over 400 years into an extravagant family home with an exceptional collection of art, sculpture and furniture collected from Europe, India and the Orient. Outside you can enjoy the delights of a world famous garden with dramatic 17th Century terraces, lavish herbaceous borders and breath taking panoramic views. Visit our website for details of exciting events and our free daily talks and tours
Location: Map 6:J6. 1 mile south of Welshpool. Signed from A483.
Info line: 01938 551944 **E-mail:** powiscastle@nationaltrust.org.uk
Website: www.nationaltrust.org.uk/powis-castle
Open: 364 days. Peak times: Castle: 28 Mar-30 Sep 11am-5pm. Garden: 28 Mar-30 Sep 10am-6pm. **Admission:** Castle & Garden (Gift Aided): Adult £13.40, Child £6.70, Family (2 adults, 3 children) £33.50. See website for further details.
Key facts: i No indoor photography. Photo Copyright NTPL/Andrew Butler. Partial. Licensed. Courtyard only. Closed 25 Dec.

TREWERN HALL
Trewern, Welshpool, Powys SY21 8DT
A grade II* listed building standing in the Severn Valley. It has been described as 'one of the most handsome timber-framed houses surviving in the area'.
Location: Map 6:J6. OS Ref SJ269 113. Off A458 Welshpool-Shrewsbury Road, 4m from Welshpool. **Tel:** 01938 570243 **Open:** Please contact us for up to date opening times and admission prices.

ISCOYD PARK 🏠
NR WHITCHURCH, SHROPSHIRE SY13 3AT
www.iscoydpark.com

A red brick Georgian house in an idyllic 18th Century parkland setting situated on the Welsh side of the Shropshire/Welsh border. After extensive refurbishment of the house and gardens we are now open for Weddings, parties, photography and film shoots, conferencing and corporate events of all kinds.

The house is only let on an exclusive basis meaning there is never more than one event occurring at any time. We offer a wide range of B&B and self catering accommodation, The Secret Spa and beautiful gardens all within the context of a family home.

Location: Map 6:L4. OS Ref SJ504 421. 2m W of Whitchurch off A525.
Owner: Mr P C Godsal
Contact: Mr P L Godsal
Tel: 01948 780785
E-mail: info@iscoydpark.com
Open: House visits by written appointment.
Key facts: ⓣ Private dinners a speciality. ⓦ WCs. ⓦ Licensed. ⓦ Licensed. ⓕ Obligatory. ⓟ Limited for coaches. ⓦ ⓐ ⓦ ⓦ

DOLBELYDR
Trefnant, Denbighshire LL16 5AG
www.landmarktrust.org.uk

Set in a timeless, quiet valley this 16th Century gentry house has many of its original features, including a first floor solar open to the roof beams. It also has good claim to be the birthplace of the modern Welsh language.
Location: Map 6:I2. OS Ref SJ027 698.
Owner: The Landmark Trust
Tel: 01628 825925
E-mail: bookings@landmarktrust.org.uk
Open: Self-catering accommodation. Open days on 8 days per year. Other visits by appointment.
Admission: Free on open days and visits by appointment.
Key facts: ⓘ There is an open plan kitchen and dining area in front of a huge inglenook fireplace.
ⓟ ⓦ ⓦ ⓦ ⓦ

GWYDIR CASTLE
Llanrwst, Conwy LL26 0PN
www.gwydircastle.co.uk

Gwydir Castle is situated in the beautiful Conwy Valley and is set within a Grade I listed, 10 acre garden. Built by the illustrious Wynn family c1500, Gwydir is a fine example of a Tudor courtyard house, incorporating re-used medieval material from the dissolved Abbey of Maenan. Further additions date from c1600 and c1828. The important 1640s panelled Dining Room has now been reinstated, following its repatriation from the New York Metropolitan Museum.
Location: Map 5:H3. OS Ref SH795 610. ½m W of Llanrwst on B5106.
Owner/Contact: Mr & Mrs Welford
Tel: 01492 641687 **E-mail:** info@gwydircastle.co.uk
Open: 1 Apr-31 Oct: daily, 10am-4pm. Closed Mons & Sats (except BH weekends). Limited openings at other times. Please telephone for details.
Admission: Adult £6.00, Child £3.00, Concessions £5.50. Group discount 10%.
Key facts: ⓣ ⓦ Partial. ⓦ By arrangement. ⓕ By arrangement.
ⓟ ⓦ ⓦ ⓦ 2 doubles. ⓐ

COCHWILLAN OLD HALL
Halfway Bridge, Bangor, Gwynedd LL57 3AZ
A fine example of medieval architecture with the present house dating from 1450. It is thought to have been built by William Gryffydd who fought for Henry VII at Bosworth. Once owned in the 17th century by John Williams who became Archbishop of York. The house was restored from a barn in 1971.
Location: Map 5:G2. OS Ref OS Ref. SH606 695. 3 ½ m SE of Bangor. 1m SE of Talybont off A55
Owner: R C H Douglas Pennant
Contact: Carter Jonas
Tel: 01248 360 414
Open: By appointment.
Admission: Please telephone for details.

FFERM
Pontblyddyn, Mold, Flintshire CH7 4HN
17th Century farmhouse. Viewing is limited to 7 persons at any one time. Open by appointment. No toilets or refreshments.
Location: Map 6:J3. OS Ref SJ279 603. Access from A541 in Pontblyddyn, 3½m SE of Mold.
Owner: Dr M.C. Jones-Mortimer Will Trust
Contact: Dr Miranda Dechazal
Tel: 01352 770204
Open: 2nd Wed in every month, 2-5pm. Open by appointment.
Admission: £4.00.
Key facts: ⊠ ❋

HARTSHEATH ▯ⓔ
Pontblyddyn, Mold, Flintshire CH7 4HP
18th and 19th Century house set in parkland. Viewing is limited to 7 persons at any one time. Open by appointment. No toilets or refreshments.
Location: Map 6:J3. OS Ref SJ287 602. Access from A5104, 3.5m SE of Mold between Pontblyddyn and Penyffordd.
Owner: Dr M.C. Jones-Mortimer Will Trust
Contact: Dr Miranda Dechazal
Tel/Fax: 01352 770204
Open: 1st, 3rd & 5th Wed in every month, 2-5pm. Open by appointment.
Admission: £4.00.
Key facts: ⊠ ❋

PENRHYN CASTLE ❧
Bangor, Gwynedd LL57 4HN
Impressive Penrhyn Castle commands spectacular views of Snowdonia and the sea. Enjoy wandering around a Victorian marvel, a house where gentry were wined and dined. Discover opulence on a grand scale and a wonderful art collection. Extensive parkland and gardens offer great walks. The addition of a locomotive collection is a real treat. **Location:** Map 5:G2. OS Ref SH602 720. Satnav - LL57 4HT **Owner:** National Trust **Tel:** 01248 353084
Infoline: 01248 363219. **Facebook:** Penrhyn Castle – National Trust. **Twitter:** PenrhynCastleNT **E-mail:** penrhyncastle@nationaltrust.org.uk
Website: www.nationaltrust.org.uk/penrhyncastle **Open:** House: Feb 28–1 Nov, daily, 12pm-4.30pm. Gardens, railway museum & coffee shop: All year except Christmas day. **Admission:** NT Members Free. **Key facts:** ▢ Two shops. ⊤ ⓛ Ground floor. ⬛ Tearoom & coffee shop. ⓕ ⓕ Free taster tours 11am–12pm. Pre bookable tours. ▣ Coach & car park – 500 yds from Castle, coach drop off & disabled parking by Castle. ⬛ ⬛ On leads except in walled garden. ⛢

PLAS BRONDANW GARDENS, CAFÉ & SHOP
Plas Brondanw, Llanfrothen, Gwynedd LL48 6SW
Italianate gardens with topiary.
Location: Map 5:G4. OS Ref SH618 423. 3m N of Penrhyndeudraeth off A4085, on Croesor Road.
Owner: Trustees of the Clough Williams-Ellis Foundation.
Tel: 01766 772772 01743 239236.
E-mail: enquiries@plasbrondanw.com
Website: www.plasbrondanw.com
Open: Mar-Sep daily,10.00am-5.00pm.
Coaches accepted, please book.
Admission: Adult £4.00, Children under 12 £1.00.
Key facts: ▢ ▯ ⊤ ⬛ ⓕ ▣ ⬛ ⊠ ⬛ ⛢

PLAS NEWYDD HOUSE & GARDENS ❧
Llanfairpwll, Anglesey LL61 6DQ
On the edge of the Menai Strait in stunning surroundings, Plas Newydd is the ancestral home of the Marquess of Anglesey. The elegant 1930s restyled house is famed for its fascinating fantasy mural by the artist Rex Whistler. Join us to proudly celebrate the bicentenary of the battle of Waterloo where our first Marquess commanded the cavalry. **Location:** Map 5:F2. OS Ref SH521 696.
Owner: National Trust **Tel:** 01248 714795
Facebook: NT Plas Newydd, mon&menai. **Twitter:** NTPlasNewydd.
E-mail: plasnewydd@nationaltrust.org.uk **Website:** www.nationaltrust.org.uk/plasnewydd **Open:** House: Mar 14-Nov 4, Sat-Thu, 11am-4:30pm. Gardens: Feb 28-Dec 20, Sat-Thu, 11am-5:30pm. **Admission:** NT Members Free.
Key facts: ▢ Two shops. Secondhand bookshop. ⬛ ⊤ ⓛ Ground floor only. ⬛ Tearoom & coffee shop. ⓕ Free taster tours 11am-12pm min. of 20. Garden buggy tours. ▣ Coach and car park. 500 yds from house, transport from 50yds. ⬛ On leads in designated areas. ⬛ ❋ ⛢

TOWER ▯ⓔ
Nercwys Road, Mold, Flintshire CH7 4EW
Tower, which had been in the same family for over 500 years, is a Grade 1 listed building steeped in Welsh history and has been witness to the continuous warfare of the time. A fascinating place to visit, host a wedding or corporate event at or for an overnight stay. Bed and Breakfast – graded 5-star in 2012-13 by Visit Wales. **Location:** Map 6:J3. OS Ref SJ240 620. 1m S of Mold. SAT NAV - use CH7 4EF. **Tel:** 01352 700220
E-mail: enquiries@towerwales.co.uk
Website: www.towerwales.co.uk
Open: 4-29 May: Mon-Fri inclusive. Wed 26 Aug-Mon 31 Aug. Groups by appointment. **Admission:** Adult £5.00, Child £3.00.
Key facts: ⓘ Opening dates etc. correct at time of going to press. If travelling significant distance please phone to check details. ⊤ ⓕ Obligatory. ▣ Limited for coaches. ⬛

WERN ISAF
Penmaen Park, Llanfairfechan, Conwy LL33 0RN
This Arts and Crafts house was built in 1900 by the architect H L North as his family home and contains much of the original furniture and William Morris fabrics. Situated in a woodland garden with extensive views over the Menai Straits and Conwy Bay.
Location: Map 5:G2. OS Ref SH685 753. Off A55 midway between Bangor and Conwy.
Owner/Contact: Mrs P J Phillips
Tel: 01248 680437
Open: 16-31 Mar and 4-17 May: daily 12-2pm, except Wednesdays.
Admission: Free.

CAERNARFON CASTLE ✤
Castle Ditch, Caernarfon LL55 2AY
The most famous and perhaps the most impressive castle in Wales, built by Edward I. Distinguished by polygonal towers and colour-banded stone.
Location: Map 5:F3. OS Ref SH477 626. **Tel:** 01286 677617
Website: www.cadw.wales.gov.uk **Open:** Please visit www.cadw.wales.gov.uk for up to date opening times and admission prices.

ERDDIG ❧
Wrexham LL13 0YT
Widely acclaimed as one of Britain's finest historic houses, Erddig is a fascinating yet unpretentious early 18th Century country house.
Location: Map 6:K3. OS Ref SJ326 482. **Tel:** 01978 355314
E-mail: erddig@nationaltrust.org.uk **Website:** www.nationaltrust.org.uk/erddig
Open: Please see website for up to date opening and admission details.

PLAS MAWR ✤
High Street, Conwy LL32 8DE
The best-preserved Elizabethan town house in Britain, Plas Mawr reflects the status of its builder Robert Wynn. **Location:** Map 5:H2. OS Ref SH781 776.
Tel: 01492 580167 **Website:** www.cadw.wales.gov.uk
Open: Please visit www.cadw.wales.gov.uk for up to date 2015 opening times and admission prices.

PLAS NEWYDD
Hill Street, Llangollen, Denbighshire LL20 8AW
Lady Eleanor Butler and Miss Sarah Ponsonby captured the imagination of Regency society. They transformed a little cottage into a Gothic fantasy.
Location: Map 5:H2. OS Ref SJ218 414. **Tel:** 01978 862834
E-mail: heritage@denbighshire.gov.uk **Website:** www.denbighshire.gov.uk
Open: Please see website for up to date opening and admission details.

ABERDEUNANT ❧
Taliaris, Llandeilo, Carmarthenshire SA19 6DL
Tel: 01588 650177 **E-mail:** aberdeunant@nationaltrust.org.uk

CAERPHILLY CASTLE ✤
Caerphilly CF83 1JD
Tel: 029 2088 3143

CHEPSTOW CASTLE ✤
Chepstow, Monmouthshire NP16 5EY
Tel: 01291 624065

DINEFWR CASTLE & PARK ❧
Llandeilo, Carmarthenshire SA19 6RT
Tel: 01558 824512 **E-mail:** 01558 824512

KIDWELLY CASTLE ✤
Kidwelly, Carmarthenshire SA17 5BQ
Tel: 01554 890104

LAUGHARNE CASTLE ✤
King Street, Laugharne, Carmarthenshire SA33 4SA
Tel: 01994 427906

MARGAM COUNTRY PARK & CASTLE
Margam, Port Talbot, West Glamorgan SA13 2TJ
Tel: 01639 881635 **E-mail:** margampark@npt.gov.uk

NATIONAL BOTANIC GARDEN OF WALES
Llanarthne, Carmarthenshire SA32 8HG
Tel: 01558 667149 **E-mail:** info@gardenofwales.org.uk

PEMBROKE CASTLE
Pembroke SA71 4LA
Tel: 01646 681510 **E-mail:** info@pembrokecastle.co.uk

PICTON CASTLE & WOODLAND GARDENS ▣®
The Rhos, Nr Haverfordwest, Pembrokeshire SA62 4AS
Tel: 01437 751326 **E-mail:** info@pictoncastle.co.uk

ST FAGANS: NATIONAL HISTORY MUSEUM
Cardiff CF5 6XB
Tel: 029 2057 3500

TRETOWER COURT & CASTLE ✤
Tretower, Crickhowell NP8 1RD
Tel: 01874 730279

TUDOR MERCHANT'S HOUSE ❧
Quay Hill, Tenby, Pembrokeshire SA70 7BX
Tel: 01834 842279 **E-mail:** tudormerchantshouse@nationaltrust.org.uk

ABERYSTWYTH CASTLE
Aberystwyth, Ceredigion SY23 2AG
Tel: 01970 612125

GLANSEVERN HALL GARDENS
Glansevern, Berriew, Welshpool, Powys SY21 8AH
Tel: 01686 640644 **E-mail:** glansevern@yahoo.co.uk

LLANERCHAERON ❧
Ciliau Aeron, Nr Aberaeron, Ceredigion SA48 8DG
Tel: 01545 570200 **E-mail:** llanerchaeron@nationaltrust.org.uk

ABERCONWY HOUSE ❧
Castle Street, Conwy LL32 8AY
Tel: 01492 592246 **E-mail:** aberconwyhouse@nationaltrust.org.uk

BEAUMARIS CASTLE ✤
Beaumaris, Anglesey LL58 8AP
Tel: 01248 810361

BODRHYDDAN HALL
Bodrhyddan, Rhuddlan, Rhyl, Denbighshire LL18 5SB
Tel: 01745 590414

CHIRK CASTLE ❧
Chirk LL14 5AF
Tel: 01691 777701 **E-mail:** chirkcastle@nationaltrust.org.uk

CONWY CASTLE ✤
Conwy LL32 8AY
Tel: 01492 592358

HARLECH CASTLE ✤
Castle Square, Harlech LL46 2YH
Tel: 01766 780552

PORTMEIRION
Minffordd, Penrhyndeudraeth, Gwynedd LL48 6ER
Tel: 01766 772311 **E-mail:** enquiries@portmeirion-village.com

RHUDDLAN CASTLE ✤
Castle Street, Rhuddlan, Rhyl LL18 5AD
Tel: 01745 590777

Mount Stewart, County Down
©VisitBritain / Britain on View

Antrim
Armagh
Down
Fermanagh
Derry
Tyrone

Northern Ireland

Easy access from the mainland and new enticements for tourists from the opening of Hillsborough Castle to the trail through the locations for TV's Game of Thrones make Northern Ireland the destination of the moment.

New Entries for 2015:
• Hillsborough Castle

ANTRIM CASTLE GARDENS
RANDALSTOWN ROAD, ANTRIM BT41 4LH
www.antrim.gov.uk/antrimcastlegardens

Antrim Castle Gardens and Clotworthy House is a hidden gem waiting to be explored. After a recent £6 million restoration, the Gardens have been transformed into a unique living museum. With some features restored to their original 17th Century condition, the Gardens and Clotworthy House are now a must see attraction. Antrim Castle Gardens offers a breathtaking walk into history, but also much more, with a programme of events running all year round. While you are here why not stay for a coffee or lunch and browse the visitor shop.
Location: Map 18:N4. OS Ref J186 850. Outside Antrim town centre off A26 on A6. **Owner:** Antrim Borough Council

Contact: Samuel Hyndman - Garden Heritage Development Officer
Tel: 028 9448 1338
E-mail: culture@antrim.gov.uk
Open: All year: Mon, Wed and Fri 9.30am-5pm. Tue and Thu 9.30am–9.30pm. Sat and Sun 10am-5pm.
Admission: Free. Guided group tours by arrangement only.
Key facts: ⓘ Photographic shoots and filming by written permission only. ▣ Ⓣ Ⓚ WCs. ▣ Ⓛ Licensed. Ⓟ ▣ ⓦ Dogs on leads only. ▣ ❋ ⓦ

BALLYWALTER PARK ▣
Ballywalter, Newtownards, Co Down BT22 2PP
www.ballywalterpark.com

Ballywalter Park was built, in the Italianate Palazzo style, by Sir Charles Lanyon for Andrew Mulholland. A Gentleman's wing, was added in 1870 for Andrew's son, John Mulholland, later 1st Baron Dunleath. The house has a fine collection of original furniture and paintings, complemented by contemporary pieces.
Location: Map 18:P4. OS Ref J610 723. Off A2 on unclassified road, 1 km S of Ballywalter village. **Owner:** The Lord and Lady Dunleath **Contact:** Mrs Sharon Graham, The Estate Office **Tel:** 028 4275 8264 **Fax:** 028 4275 8818
E-mail: enq@dunleath-estates.co.uk **Open:** By prior appointment only; please contact The Estate Office. **Admission:** House or Gardens: £8.50. House & Gardens: £16.00. Groups (max 50): £8.50. Refreshments by arrangement.
Key facts: ⓘ No photography indoors. Ⓣ The house is available for corporate & incentive events, lunches & dinners. Ⓛ Lunches & dinners can be arranged by prior booking for lunch or dinner. Ⓕ Obligatory. Ⓟ ▣ Guide dogs only. ▣ Twelve en suite bedrooms available for group tours & corporate events. ❋ By appointment only. ⓦ €

CASTLE COOLE ❦
Enniskillen, Co Fermanagh BT74 6JY
www.nationaltrust.org.uk/castle-coole

Surrounded by its stunning landscape park on the edge of Enniskillen, this majestic 18th Century home of the Earls of Belmore, designed by James Wyatt, was created to impress. The surrounding wooded landscape park sloping down to Lough Coole is ideal for long walks.
Location: Map 18:I5. OS Ref H245 436.
On A4, 1½m from Enniskillen on A4, Belfast-Enniskillen road.
Owner: National Trust
Contact: House Steward
Tel: 028 6632 2690
E-mail: castlecoole@nationaltrust.org.uk
Open: Please see website for up to date opening times.
Admission: Please see website for up to date admission prices.
Key facts: ▣ Ⓣ Ⓚ Partial. WC. ▣ Ⓕ Ⓟ ▣ In grounds, on leads. ▣ ❋

CASTLE WARD HOUSE & DEMESNE ⚜

Strangford, Downpatrick, Co Down BT30 7LS

www.nationaltrust.org.uk/castle-ward

Situated in a stunning location within an 820 acre walled demesne overlooking Strangford Lough, the lawns rise up to the unique 18th Century house and its Gothic façade. This fascinating house features both Gothic and Classical styles of architectural treatment, internally and externally.

Location: Map 18:P6. OS Ref J573 498.
On A25, 7m from Downpatrick and 1½m from Strangford.
Owner: National Trust
Contact: Visitor Services Manager
Tel: 028 4488 1204
E-mail: castleward@nationaltrust.org.uk
Open: Please see website for opening times and admission prices.
Key facts: ⬚ ⬚ ⬚ ⬚ WCs. ⬚
⬚ By arrangement. ⬚ ⬚
⬚ On leads only. ⬚ Caravan park. Holiday cottages. Basecamp.
⬚ ⬚ ⬚ €

HILLSBOROUGH CASTLE
Hillsborough BT26 6AG

www.hrp.org.uk

The late Georgian mansion was built in the 1770s and is a working royal palace functioning as the official residence of the Royal Family when they are in Northern Ireland, and it has been the home of the Secretary of State since the 1970s. A tour of the house will guide you through the elegant State Rooms, still in use today, including the majestic Throne Room. Plus, don't miss the stunning 98 acres of gardens. **Location:** Map 18:N5.
Owner: Historic Royal Palaces
Tel: 028 9268 1300
E-mail: hillsboroughcastle@hrp.org.uk
Open: Apr-Sep. Please check the hrp.org.uk website before visiting.
Admission: Please check the hrp.org.uk website. By guided tour only, must book in advance.
Key facts: ⬚ Call 028 9268 1300

BARONS COURT 🏛

Newtownstewart, Omagh, Co Tyrone BT78 4EZ

The home of the Duke and Duchess of Abercorn, Barons Court was built between 1779 and 1782, and subsequently extensively remodelled by John Soane (1791), William and Richard Morrison (1819-1841), Sir Albert Richardson (1947-49) and David Hicks (1975-76).
Location: Map 18:M3. OS Ref H236 382. 5km SW of Newtownstewart.
Contact: The Agent
Tel: 028 8166 1683 **Fax:** 028 8166 2059
E-mail: info@barons-court.com **Website:** www.barons-court.com
Open: By appointment only.
Admission: Tour of House and/or Gardens £11.00pp. Tour inc. tea/coffee/scones £15.00pp. Groups max. 50.
Key facts: ⓘ No photography. ⬚ The Carriage Room in the Stable Yard.
⬚ Partial. ⬚ By arrangement. ⬚ ⬚ ⬚
⬚ Holiday cottages, 4 star rated by Northern Ireland Tourist Board. ⬚ €

DOWN CATHEDRAL

Cathedral Office, English Street, Downpatrick
County Down BT30 6AB

Built in 1183 as a Benedictine monastery, Down Cathedral is now a Cathedral of the Church of Ireland. Prominent and majestic, the cathedral is believed to have the grave of St Patrick in its grounds. There is also wonderful stained glass and a pulpit and organ of highest quality.
Location: Map 18:O6. OS Ref SB583 989. Located in Downpatrick, in the heart of English Street. Follow brown signs.
Owner: Church of Ireland **Contact:** Joy Wilkinson
Tel: 028 4461 4922 **Fax:** 028 4461 4456 **E-mail:** info@downcathedral.org
Website: www.downcathedral.org
Open: Open all year round. Mon-Sat: 9.30am - 4.00pm.
Sun: 2-4pm.
Admission: Donations. Guided tours by arrangement.
Key facts: ⬚ ⬚ ⬚ By arrangement. ⬚ Limited for cars and coaches. ⬚
⬚ Guide dogs only. ⬚

KILLYLEAGH CASTLE 🏛

Killyleagh, Downpatrick, Co Down BT30 9QA

Oldest occupied castle in Ireland. Self-catering towers available, sleeps 4-9. Swimming pool and tennis court available by arrangement. Access to garden.
Location: Map 18:O5/6. OS Ref J523 529. **Tel:** 028 4482 8261 **E-mail:** gawnrh@gmail.com **Website:** www.killyleaghcastle.com **Open:** By arrangement.
Admission: Groups (30-50) by arrangement. Around £2.50 pp.

MOUNT STEWART ⚜

Newtonards, Co Down BT22 2AD

Home of the Londonderry family since the early 18th Century, Mount Stewart was Lord Castlereagh's house and played host to many prominent political figures.
Location: Map 18:P5. OS Ref J556 703. **Tel:** 028 4278 8387
E-mail: mountstewart@nationaltrust.org.uk **Website:** www.nationaltrust.org.uk/mount-stewart **Open:** Please see website for most up to date details.

Antrim Castle Gardens

ANTRIM ROUND TOWER
16 High Street, Antrim, County Antrim BT41 4AN
Tel: 028 94428331

ARTHUR ANCESTRAL HOME
Cullybackey, County Antrim BT42 1AB
Tel: 028 2563 8494 E-mail: devel.leisure@ballymena.gov.uk

BELFAST CASTLE
Cave Hill, Antrim Road, Belfast BT15 5GR
Tel: 028 9077 6925

BENVARDEN GARDEN
Benvarden, Dervock, County Antrim BT53 6NN
Tel: 028 20741331

BOTANIC GARDENS
Stransmillis Road, Belfast BT7 1LP
Tel: 028 9031 4762

CARRICKFERGUS CASTLE
Marine Highway, Carrickfergus, County Antrim BT38 7BG
Tel: 028 9335 1273

CATHEDRAL OF CHRIST CHURCH, LISBURN
24 Castle Street, Lisburn BT28 1RG
Tel: 028 9260 2400 E-mail: sam@lisburncathedral.org

DUNLUCE CASTLE
87 Dunluce Road, Portrush, County Antrim BT57 8UY
Tel: 028 20731938

GLENARM CASTLE WALLED GARDEN
2 Castle Lane, Glenarm, Larne, County Antrim BT44 0BQ
Tel: 028 28841305

MONTALTO HOUSE
5 Craigaboney Road, Bushmills, County Antrim BT57 8XD
Tel: 028 2073 1257 E-mail: montaltohouse@btconnect.com

ST. ANNE'S CATHEDRAL
Donegall Street, Belfast BT12 2HB
Tel: 028 9032 8332

ST. PETER'S CATHEDRAL
St Peters Square, Falls Road, Belfast BT12 4BU
Tel: 028 9032 7573

SENTRY HILL
Ballycraigy Road, Newtownabbey BT36 5SY
Tel: 028 90340000

ARDRESS HOUSE ❧
64 Ardress Road, Portadown, Co Armagh BT62 1SQ
Tel: 028 8778 4753 E-mail: ardress@nationaltrust.org.uk

BENBURB CASTLE
Servite Priory, Main Street, Benburb, Co, Tyrone BT71 7JZ
Tel: 028 37548241 E-mail: servitepriory@btinternet.com

DERRYMORE ❧
Bessbrook, Newry, Co Armagh BT35 7EF
Tel: 028 8778 4753 E-mail: derrymore@nationaltrust.org.uk

GILFORD CASTLE ESTATE
Banbridge Road, Gilford BT63 6DT
Tel: 028 40623322 E-mail: gilford@irishfieldsports.com

AUDLEYS CASTLE
Strangford, County Down UK
Tel: 028 9054 3034

BANGOR ABBEY
Bangor, County Down BT20 4JF
Tel: 028 91271200

BANGOR CASTLE
Bangor, County Down BT20 4BN
Tel: 028 91270371

CLOUGH CASTLE
Clough Village, Downpatrick, County Down UK
Tel: 028 9054 3034

DUNDRUM CASTLE
Dundrum Village, Newcastle, County Down BT33 0QX
Tel: 028 9054 3034

GREENCASTLE ROYAL CASTLE
Cranfield Point, Kilkeel, County Down UK
Tel: 028 90543037

GREY ABBEY
9-11 Church Street, Greyabbey, County Down BT22 2NQ
Tel: 028 9054 6552

GREY POINT FORT
Crawfordsburn Country Park, Helens Bay, Co. Down BT19 1LE
Tel: 028 91853621

HELENS TOWER
Clandeboye Estate, Bangor BT19 1RN
Tel: 028 91852817

INCH ABBEY
Downpatrick, County Down UK
Tel: 028 9181 1491

KILCLIEF CASTLE
Strangford, County Down UK
Tel: 028 9054 3034

MAHEE CASTLE
Mahee Island, Comber, Newtownards BT23 6EP
Tel: 028 91826846

MOVILLA ABBEY
63 Movilla Road, Newtownards BT23 8EZ
Tel: 028 9181 0787

NEWRY CATHEDRAL
38 Hill Street, Newry, County Down BT34 1AT
Tel: 028 3026 2586

PORTAFERRY CASTLE
Castle Street, Portaferry, County Down BT22 1NZ
Tel: 028 90543033

THE PRIORY
Newtownards, County Down UK
Tel: 028 90543037

QUOILE CASTLE
Downpatrick, County Down BT30 7JB
Tel: 028 9054 3034

RINGHADDY CASTLE
Killyleagh, County Down UK
Tel: 028 90543037

ROWALLANE GARDEN ✻
Ballynahinch, Co Down BT24 7LH
Tel: 028 9751 0721 **E-mail:** rowallane@nationaltrust.org.uk

SKETRICK CASTLE
Whiterock, County Down BT23 6QA
Tel: 028 4278 8387

STRANGFORD CASTLE
Strangford, County Down UK
Tel: 028 9054 3034

CROM ESTATE ✻
Newtownbutler, County Fermanagh BT92 8AP
Tel: 028 6773 8118

ENNISKILLEN CASTLE ✻
Castle Barracks, Enniskillen, County Fermanagh BT74 7HL
Tel: 028 6632 5000 **E-mail:** castle@fermanagh.gov.uk

FLORENCE COURT ✻
Enniskillen, Co Fermanagh BT92 1DB
Tel: 028 6634 8249 **E-mail:** florencecourt@nationaltrust.org.uk

BELLAGHY BAWN
Castle Street, Bellaghy, County Londonderry BT45 8LA
Tel: 028 7938 6812

DUNGIVEN CASTLE
Main Street, Dungiven, Co Londonderry BT47 4LF
Tel: 028 7774 2428 **E-mail:** enquiries@dungivencastle.com

DUNGIVEN PRIORY AND O CAHANS TOMB
Dungiven, County Londonderry UK
Tel: 028 777 22074

THE GUILDHALL
Guildhall Square, Londonderry BT48 6DQ
Tel: 028 7137 7335

KINGS FORT
7 Connell Street, Limavady, Co Londonderry BT49 0HA
Tel: 028 77760304 **E-mail:** tourism@limavady.gov.uk

MOUNTSANDAL FORT
Mountsandal Road, Coleraine, Co Londonderry BT52 1PE
Tel: 027 7034 4723 **E-mail:** coleraine@nitic.net

PREHEN HOUSE
Prehen Road, Londonderry BT47 2PB
Tel: 028 7131 2829 **E-mail:** colinpeck@yahoo.com

ROUGH FORT
Limavady TIC, 7 Connell Street, Limavady BT49 0HA
Tel: 028 7084 8728

SAINT COLUMBS CATHEDRAL
London Street, Derry, County Londonderry BT48 6RQ
Tel: 028 71267313 **E-mail:** stcolumbs@ic24.net

SAMPSONS TOWER
Limavady TIC, 7 Connell Street, Limavady BT49 0HA
Tel: 028 7776 0307

SPRINGHILL HOUSE ✻
20 Springhill Road, Moneymore, Co Londonderry BT45 7NQ
Tel: 028 8674 8210 **E-mail:** springhill@nationaltrust.org.uk

THE ARGORY ✻
Moy, Dungannon, Co Tyrone BT71 6NA
Tel: 028 8778 4753 **E-mail:** argory@nationaltrust.org.uk

CASTLEDERG CASTLE
Castle Park, Castlederg, County Tyrone BT81 7AS
Tel: 028 7138 2204

HARRY AVERYS CASTLE
Old Castle Road, Newtownstewart BT82 8DY
Tel: 028 7138 2204

THE KEEP OR GOVERNORS RESIDENCE
Off Old Derry Road, Omagh, County Tyrone UK
Tel: 028 82247831 **E-mail:** omagh.tic@btconnect.com

KILLYMOON CASTLE
Killymoon Road, Cookstown, County Tyrone UK
Tel: 028 86763514

NEWTOWNSTEWART CASTLE
Townhall Street, Newtownstewart BT78 4AX
Tel: 028 6862 1588 **E-mail:** nieainfo@doeni.gov.uk

OMAGH GAOL
Old Derry Road, Omagh, County Tyrone UK
Tel: 028 82247 831 **E-mail:** omagh.tic@btconnect.com

SAINT MACARTAN'S CATHEDRAL
Clogher, County Tyrone BT76 0AD
Tel: 028 0478 1220

SIR JOHN DAVIES CASTLE
Castlederg, County Tyrone BT81 7AS
Tel: 028 7138 2204

TULLYHOGUE FORT
B162, Cookstown, County Tyrone, Northern Ireland UK
Tel: 028 86766727

SIGNPOST

RECOMMENDING THE UK'S FINEST HOTELS SINCE 1935

Motoring conditions may have changed since the founder of Signpost first took to the road in 1935, but inspectors' standards are still the same. Inspected annually, Signpost features the UK's Premier hotels who possess that something special – style, comfort, warmth of welcome, cuisine, location – which really make them worth the visit. Here are Signpost's recommendations, by region, of fantastic places to stay while you are visiting Britain's historic sites. A wonderful combination.

www.signpost.co.uk

LONDON

The Mayflower Hotel & Apartment
26-28 Trebovir Road
Earls Court
London SW5 9NJ
Tel: 0207 370 0991

New Linden Hotel
59 Leinster Square
London W2 4PS
Tel: 0207 221 4321

San Domenico House
29-31 Draycott Place
Chelsea
London SW3 2SH
Tel: 0207 581 5757

Searcys Roof Garden Rooms
30 Pavilion Road
London SW1X 0HJ
Tel: 0207 584 4921

Twenty Nevern Square Hotel
20 Nevern Square
London SW5 9PD
Tel: 0207 565 9555

SOUTH EAST

Deans Place Hotel
Seaford Road
Alfriston
East Sussex BN26 5TW
Tel: 01323 870248

Drakes Hotel
44 Marine Parade
Brighton
East Sussex BN2 1PE
Tel: 01273 696934

Flackley Ash Hotel
Peasmarsh
Nr. Rye
East Sussex TN31 6YH
Tel: 01797 230651

Hotel Una
55-56 Regency Square
Brighton
East Sussex BN1 2FF
Tel: 01273 820464

Mill House Hotel & Restaurant
Station Road
Kingham
Oxfordshire OX7 6UH
Tel: 01608 658188

The Millsteam Hotel
Bosham Lane
Bosham
Chichester
West Sussex PO18 8HL
Tel: 01243 573234

Montagu Arms Hotel
Palace Lane
Beaulieu
Hampshire SO42 7ZL
Tel: 01590 612324

Powder Mills Hotel
Powder Mill Lane
Battle
East Sussex TN33 0SP
Tel: 01424 775511

The Priory Bay Hotel
Priory Drive
Seaview
Isle of Wight PO34 5BU
Tel: 01983 613146

The White Horse Hotel
Market Place
Romsey
Hampshire SO51 8ZJ
Tel: 01794 512431

SOUTH WEST

Alexandra Hotel
Pound Street
Lyme Regis
Dorset DT7 3HZ
Tel: 01297 442010

The Berry Head Hotel
Berry Head
Brixham
Devon TQ5 9AJ
Tel: 01803 853225

Bridge House Hotel
Prout Bridge
Beaminster
Dorset DT8 3AY
Tel: 01308 862200

Budock Vean Hotel
Helford Passage
Mawnan Smith
Falmouth
Cornwall TR11 5LG
Tel: 01326 250288

The Cottage Hotel
Hope Cove
Salcombe
Devon TQ7 3HJ
Tel: 01548 561555

The Dart Marina Hotel
Sandquay Road
Dartmouth
Devon TQ6 9PH
Tel: 01803 832580

Grasmere House Hotel
70 Harnham Road
Salisbury
Wiltshire SP2 8JN
Tel: 01722 338388

Hannafore Point Hotel
Marine Drive
West Looe
Cornwall PL13 2DG
Tel: 01503 263273

Ilsington Country House Hotel
Ilsington Village
Nr Newton Abbot
Devon TQ13 9RR
Tel: 01364 661452

The Inn at Fossebridge
Fossebridge
Cheltenham
Gloucestershire GL54 3JS
Tel: 01285 720721

Langdon Court Country House Hotel
Down Thomas
Plymouth
Devon PL9 0DY
Tel: 01752 862358

The Moorings Hotel
Gorey Pier
St Martin
Jersey JE3 6EW
Tel: 01534 853633

Mortons House Hotel
45 East Street
Corfe Castle
Wareham
Dorset BH20 5EE
Tel: 01929 480988

The Pear Tree at Purton
Church End
Purton
Swindon
Wiltshire SN5 4ED
Tel: 01793 772100

Plantation House Hotel & Restaurant
Totnes Road
Ermington
Ivybridge
Devon PL21 9NS
Tel: 01548 831100

Plumber Manor
Sturminster Newton
Dorset DT10 2AF
Tel: 01258 472507

The Queens Arms
Corton Denham Road
Corton Denham
Sherbourne DT9 4LR
Tel: 01963 220317

Trevalsa Court Country House Hotel
School Hill
Mevagissey
St Austell
Cornwall PL26 6TH
Tel: 01726 842468

The White Hart Royal
High Street
Moreton-in-Marsh
Gloucestershire
GL56 0BA
Tel: 01608 650731

EAST OF ENGLAND

Broom Hall Country Hotel
Richmond Road
Saham Toney
Thetford
Norfolk IP25 7EX
Tel: 01953 882125

Hintlesham Hall Hotel
Hintlesham
Ipswich
Suffolk IP8 3NS
Tel: 01473 652334

Hotel Felix
Whitehouse Lane
Huntingdon Road
Cambridge
Cambridgeshire
CB3 0LX
Tel: 01223 277977

Maison Talbooth
Stratford Road
Dedham
Colchester
Essex CO7 6HW
Tel: 01206 321109

milsoms Kesgrave Hall
Hall Road
Kesgrave
Ipswich
Suffolk IP5 2PU
Tel: 01255 241212

The Norfolk Mead Hotel
Church Loke
Coltishall
Norwich
Norfolk NR12 7DN
Tel: 01603 737521

The Pier at Harwich
Hall Road
Kesgrave
Ipswich
Suffolk IP5 2PU
Tel: 01255 241212

Wentworth Hotel
Wentworth Road
Aldeburgh
Suffolk IP15 5BD
Tel: 01728 452312

EAST MIDLANDS

Barnsdale Lodge Hotel
The Avenue, Rutland
Water
Exton LE15 8AH
Tel: 01572 724678

Biggin Hall Hotel
Biggin by Hartington
Buxton
Derbyshire SK17 0DH
Tel: 01298 84451

The Cavendish Hotel
Church Lane
Baslow
Derbyshire DE45 1SP
Tel: 01246 582311

Langar Hall
Langar
Nottingham NG13 9HG
Tel: 01949 860559

**Losehill House
Hotel & Spa**
Edale Road
Hope
Hope Valley
Derbyshire S33 6RF
Tel: 01433 621219

The Manners Arms
Croxton Road
Knipton
Vale of Belvoir
Leicestershire
NG32 1PE
Tel: 01476 879 222

The Talbot Hotel
New Street
Oundle
Northamptonshire
PE8 4EA
Tel: 01832 273621

**Washingborough Hall
Hotel**
Church Hill
Washingborough
Lincoln LN4 1BE
Tel: 01522 790340

**Whittlebury Hall
Hotel & Spa**
Whittlebury Hall
Whittlebury
NN12 8QH
0845 400 0001

HEART OF ENGLAND

Castle House
Castle Street
Hereford
Herefordshire
HR1 2NW
Tel: 01432 356321

The Chase Hotel
Gloucester Road
Ross-on-Wye
Herefordshie HR9 5LH
Tel: 01989 763161

Cottage in the Wood
Holywell Road
Malvern Wells
Malvern WR14 4LG
Tel: 01684 577459

Eckington Manor
Manor Farm
Manor Road
Eckington
Nr. Pershore
Worcestershire
WR10 3BJ
Tel: 01386 751600

**The Mytton &
Mermaid Hotel**
Atcham
Shrewsbury
SY5 6QG
Tel: 01743 761220

Soulton Hall
Soulton
Wem
Shropshire SY4 5RS
Tel: 01939 232786

YORKSHIRE & THE HUMBER

The Blue Bell Inn
Main Street
Weaverthorpe
YO17 8EX
Tel: 01944 738204

**The Coniston Hotel
& Country Estate**
Coniston Cold
Skipton
North Yorkshire
BD23 4EA
Tel: 01756 748080

Lastingham Grange
Country House Hotel
High Street
Lastingham
North Yorkshire
YO62 6TH
Tel: 01751 417345

Raithwaite Estate
Sandsend Road
Raithwaite
Whitby
North Yorkshire
YO21 3ST
Tel: 01947 894019

**Sportsmans Arms
Hotel**
Wath-in-Nidderdale
Near Pateley Bridge
North Yorkshire
HG3 5PP
Tel: 01423 711306

The Traddock
Austwick
Nr Settle
North Yorkshire
LA2 8BY
Tel: 01524 251224

NORTH WEST

Aynsome Manor Hotel
Cartmel
Grange-over-Sands
Cumbria LA11 6HH
Tel: 015395 36653

**Borrowdale Gates
Country House Hotel**
Grange-in-Borrowdale
Keswick
Cumbria CA12 5UQ
Tel: 017687 77204

**Gilpin Hotel &
Lake House**
Crook Road
Windermere
Cumbria LA23 3NE
Tel: 015394 88818

**Holbeck Ghyll Country
House Hotel**
Holbeck Lane
Windermere
Cumbria LA23 1LU
Tel: 015394 32375

**Lovelady Shield
Country House Hotel**
Nenthead Road
Alston
Cumbria CA9 3LF
Tel: 01434 381203

Oak Bank Hotel
Broadgate
Grasmere Village
Lake District
Cumbria LA22 9TA
Tel: 015394 35217

NORTH EAST

Waren House Hotel
Waren Mill
Northumberland
NE70 7EE
Tel: 01668 214581

SCOTLAND

Atholl Palace Hotel
Pitlochry
Perthshire
Scotland PH16 5LY
Tel: 01796 472400

**Blackaddie Country
House Hotel**
Blackaddie Road
Sanquhar
Dumfries and Galloway
Scotland DG4 6JJ
Tel: 01659 50270

Coul House Hotel
Contin
By Strathpeffer
Ross-shire
Scotland IV14 9ES
Tel: 01997 421487

Craigadam House
Crocketford
Kirkpatrick Durham,
Castle Douglas
Dumfries and Galloway
Scotland DG7 3HU
Tel: 01556 650233

Duisdale House Hotel
Isle Ornsay
Sleat
Isle of Skye IV43 8QW
Tel: 01471 833202

Eddrachilles Hotel
Badcall Bay
Scourie
The Highlands
Scotland IV27 4TH
Tel: 01971 502080

**The Four Seasons
Hotel**
St Fillans
Perthshire
Scotland PH6 2NF
Tel: 01764 685333

**Roman Camp Country
House & Restaurant**
Main Street
Callander
Perthshire
Scotland FK17 8BG
Tel: 01877 330003

Toravaig House Hotel
Isle Ornsay
Sleat
Isle of Skye IV43 8QW
Tel: 01471 833202

Viewfield House
Portree
Isle of Skye
Scotland IV51 9EU
Tel: 01478 612217

WALES

**Bron Eifion
Country Hotel**
Criccieth
Gwynedd LL52 0SA
Tel: 01766 522385

**The Falcondale
Hotel & Restaurant**
Falcondale Drive
Lampeter
Ceredigion SA48 7RX
Tel: 01570 422 910

**Ffin y Parc
Country House**
Betws Road
Llanrwst
Conwy LL26 0PT
Tel: 01492 642070

**Glen Yr Afon
House Hotel**
Pontypool Road
Llanbadoc
Monmouthshire
NP15 1SY
Tel: 01291 672302

**Lake Vyrnwy
Hotel & Spa**
Lake Vyrnwy
Llanwddyn
Powys SY10 0LY
Tel: 01691 870692

Nanteos Mansion
Rhydyfelin
Aberystwyth
Ceredigion SY23 4LU
Tel: 01970 600522

Palé Hall Hotel
Pale Estate
Llandderfel
Bala
Gwynedd LL23 7PS
Tel: 01678 530285

**Penally Abbey
Country House**
Penally
Pembrokeshire SA70 7PY
Tel: 01834 843033

St Tudno Hotel
Promenade
Llandudno
Conwy LL30 2LP
Tel: 01492 874411

Trefeddian Hotel
Aberdyfi
Gwynedd LL35 0SB
Tel: 01654 767 213

Warpool Court Hotel
St Davids
Pembrokeshire
SA62 6BN
Tel: 01437 720300

West Arms
Llanarmon Dyffryn
Ceiriog
Nr Llangollen
Denbighshire LL20 7LD
Tel: 01691 600665

**Wolfscastle
Country Hotel**
Wolfscastle
Haverfordwest
Pembrokeshire
SA62 5LZ
Tel: 01437 741225

The Collector Earl's Garden, Arundel Castle

Burghley House, ©Mark Hibbert

Indexes

Plant Sales

Properties where plants are offered for sale

Great Dixter Garden

Hartland Abbey

Bruisyard Hall

Iscoyd Park

Accommodation

Properties where accommodation can be arranged

Open All Year

Properties and / or their grounds that are open for all or most of the year

Dumfries House

ENGLAND

Haddon Hall

Doddington Hall Gardens

Civil Weddings

Properties at which wedding or civil partnership ceremonies can take place

Burghley House
© Mark Hibbert

ENGLAND

Photos by MTM Studio

ELMORE COURT
Wedding and Events Venue

ENJOY MORE. LAUGH MORE. LOVE MORE.

Powderham Castle

Mount Stuart

Private Hire

Properties able to accommodate corporate functions, wedding receptions and events

Goodwood

ENGLAND

Guided Tours

Properties that offer informative guided tours

Shakespeare's Family Homes
©Amy Murrell

NORTH WEST

NORTH EAST

Members Lobby, Houses of Parliament

SCOTLAND

WALES

SOUTH WALES

MID WALES

NORTH WALES

NORTHERN IRELAND

Special Events

Arundel Castle, Sussex

Historical re-enactments, festivals, country and craft fairs, concerts, fireworks, car and steam rallies, and much more ...
(Please check dates before visiting)

Check out our on-line events calendar at www.hudsonsheritage.com or download our free Hudson's UK app for more great days out.

JANUARY

12

Great Dixter House & Gardens, Sussex
Behind the Scenes at Great Dixter

21-24

Shakespeare's Family Homes, Warwickshire
Winter School 2015

24

Alnwick Castle, Northumberland
Burns Night Party

31-7 February

Great Dixter House & Gardens, Sussex
Symposium: The Art of Gardening

FEBRUARY

7

Dover Castle, Kent
Great Tower Sleepover

14-22

Castle Howard, Yorkshire
Hearts and Flowers Children's Trail

14-22

Dover Castle, Kent
Secrets and Spies

14-22

Osborne House, Isle of Wight
Victorian Fun and Games

16-20

Audley End, Essex
Victorian Games Galore!

23

Great Dixter House & Gardens, Sussex
Behind the Scenes at Great Dixter

28

Bocconoc, Cornwall
VOTWO Glow in the Park Run

MARCH

14

Burghley House, Lincolnshire
South Gardens Opening

16

Great Dixter House & Gardens, Sussex
Behind the Scenes at Great Dixter

23

Great Dixter House & Gardens, Sussex
Succession Planting in the Mixed Border

28-29

Arundel Castle, Sussex
Life in a Medieval Castle

28-29

Bocconoc, Cornwall
CGS Spring Flower Show

28-29

Great Dixter House & Gardens, Sussex
Great Dixter Spring Plant Fair

APRIL

3-6

Blenheim Palace, Oxfordshire
Easter Weekend

4-6

Arundel Castle, Sussex
Normans and Crusaders

4-6

Castle Howard, Yorkshire
Easter Fair and Farm

6-Easter Monday

Chenies Manor House, Buckinghamshire
Children's egg races, magician,
plants for sale

11-12

Burghley House, Lincolnshire
National Gardens Scheme Open weekend

13

Great Dixter House & Gardens, Sussex
Nursery Propagation Day

14

Castle Howard, Yorkshire
Stable Courtyard Market

16-18

Blenheim Palace, Oxfordshire
CADA Antiques Fair

19

Arundel Castle, Sussex
MG Owner's Club Gathering

20

Great Dixter House & Gardens, Sussex
Behind the Scenes at Great Dixter

23-26

Shakespeare's Family Homes, Warwickshire
Shakespeare's Birthday

26

Beaulieu, Hampshire
Boatjumble

MAY

May

Clovelly, Devon
Celebration of Ales & Ciders.

2-4

Blenheim Palace, Oxfordshire
Blenheim Palace Spring Jousting Tournament

4-Early May bank holiday

Penshurst Place, Kent
Weald of Kent Craft Show

4-Early May bank holiday

Chenies Manor House, Buckinghamshire
Tulip Festival

11

Great Dixter House & Gardens, Sussex
Good Planting

11

Great Dixter House & Gardens, Sussex
Behind the Scenes at Great Dixter

12

Castle Howard, Yorkshire
Stable Courtyard Market

16-17

Beaulieu, Hampshire
Spring Autojumble

16-23

Great Dixter House & Gardens, Sussex
Symposium: The Art of Gardening

17

Bocconoc, Cornwall
Dog show

23-25

Arundel Castle, Sussex
Castle Siege

23-25

Blenheim Palace, Oxfordshire
The Blenheim Palace Food Festival

24-25

Beaulieu, Hampshire
Truckmania

25-Spring bank holiday

Chenies Manor House, Buckinghamshire
Dog Show

28

Arundel Castle, Sussex
Living History Day

29

Blenheim Palace, Oxfordshire
Churchill Memorial Concert

31

Stonor, Oxfordshire
VW Owners's Rally

JUNE

June

Clovelly, Devon
Seaweed Festival

June - First Week

Penshurst Place, Kent
Glorious Gardens week

4-8

Blenheim Palace, Oxfordshire
Gifford's Circus

8

Great Dixter House & Gardens, Sussex
Meadow Gardening

9

Castle Howard, Yorkshire
Stable Courtyard Market

13

Arundel Castle, Sussex
Town Crier's Competition

13

Great Dixter House & Gardens, Sussex
The Christopher Lloyd Lecture

13-14

Blenheim Palace, Oxfordshire
Leukaemia & Lymphoma Research Blenheim Palace Triathlon

14

Castle Howard, Yorkshire
Trail Race

15

Great Dixter House & Gardens, Sussex
Behind the Scenes at Great Dixter

19-21

Blenheim Palace, Oxfordshire
The Bleheim Palace Flower Show

20-21

Arundel Castle, Sussex
Mustering for Agincourt

20-21

Bocconoc, Cornwall
Endurance GB Ride

21

Beaulieu, Hampshire
Custom & Hot Rod Festival

21

Caerhays Castle and Garden, Cornwall
Summer Fete

22

Great Dixter House & Gardens, Sussex
Succession Planting in the Mixed Border

22

Great Dixter House & Gardens, Sussex
Miniature Hurdle Making Workshop

25-28

Castle Howard, Yorkshire
Flower Festival

27-28

Leeds Castle, Kent
Leeds Castle Triathlon

27-28

Woburn Abbey, Bedfordshire
The Woburn Abbey Garden Show

JULY

July

Bocconoc, Cornwall
Boconnoc Music Award

July

Clovelly, Devon
Clovelly Maritime Festival, Woolsery Agricultural Show, Lundy Row

July TBC

Boughton Monchelsea Place, Kent
Open Air Theatre

1

Chenies Manor House, Buckinghamshire
Plant and Garden Fair

4

Burghley House, Lincolnshire
Battle Proms Concert

11

Blenheim Palace, Oxfordshire
The Battle Proms Picnic Concert

11-12

Arundel Castle, Sussex
Privateers and Revolutionaries weekend

12

Arundel Castle, Sussex
Classic Cars Gathering

12

Beaulieu, Hampshire
Motorcycle Ride In Day

12

Stonor, Oxfordshire
Rare Plant Fair

13

Great Dixter House & Gardens, Sussex
Good Planting

14

Castle Howard, Yorkshire
Stable Courtyard Market

17

Castle Howard, Yorkshire
Robin Hood Outdoor Theatre

20

Great Dixter House & Gardens, Sussex
Behind the Scenes at Great Dixter

24-26

Bocconoc, Cornwall
Steam Fair

25-26

Castle Howard, Yorkshire
Castle Triathlon

26

Blenheim Palace, Oxfordshire
The Pre '50 American Auto Club Rally
of the Giants

30

Arundel Castle, Sussex
Living History Day

31- 2 Aug

Blenheim Palace, Oxfordshire
Blenheim Palace Summer Jousting
Tournament

AUGUST

August

Clovelly, Devon
Lifeboat Day, Clovelly Gig Regatta

1

Castle Howard, Yorkshire
Run or Dye

7-9

Capesthorne Hall, Cheshire
Rewind Festival

11

Castle Howard, Yorkshire
Stable Courtyard Market

16

Blenheim Palace, Oxfordshire
Blenheim Palace Sportive and Family
Cycling Day

23

Beaulieu, Hampshire
Supercar Showdown

24

Great Dixter House & Gardens, Sussex
Behind the Scenes at Great Dixter

27

Castle Howard, Yorkshire
Robin Hood Outdoor Theatre

28-31

Stonor, Oxfordshire
Chilterns Craft and Design Show

29-31

Arundel Castle, Sussex
History in Action (multi period)

31 Summer bank holiday

Chenies Manor House, Buckinghamshire
Dhalia Festival

SEPTEMBER

September

Clovelly, Devon
Lobster and Crab Fest

3-6

Burghley House, Lincolnshire
The Burghley Horse Trials

4-6

Penshurst Place, Kent
Weald of Kent Craft Show

4-6

Chatsworth, Derbyshire
Chatsworth Country Fair

5-6

Beaulieu, Hampshire
International Autojumble

5

Great Dixter House & Gardens, Sussex
Symposium: The Art of Gardening

7

Great Dixter House & Gardens, Sussex
Ladder Making Workshop

14

Great Dixter House & Gardens, Sussex
Nursery Propagation Day

21

Great Dixter House & Gardens, Sussex
Exotic Gardening

28

Great Dixter House & Gardens, Sussex
Behind the Scenes at Great Dixter

OCTOBER

3-4

Great Dixter House & Gardens, Sussex
Great Dixter Autumn Plant Fair

3-8 & 10-11

Burghley House, Lincolnshire
Burghley Flower Festival

19

Great Dixter House & Gardens, Sussex
Behind the Scenes at Great Dixter

26

Great Dixter House & Gardens, Sussex
Integrating and Using Bulbs

28-29

Arundel Castle, Sussex
Normans and Crusaders in the Keep

28-29

Chenies Manor House, Buckinghamshire
Spooks and Surprises

31

Great Dixter House & Gardens, Sussex
Symposium: The Art of Gardening

NOVEMBER

November

Clovelly, Devon
Clovelly Herring Festival

16

Great Dixter House & Gardens, Sussex
Behind the Scenes at Great Dixter

DECEMBER

December

Clovelly, Devon
Christmas Lights

7

Great Dixter House & Gardens, Sussex
Behind the Scenes at Great Dixter

Skipton Castle,
North Yorkshire

Maps

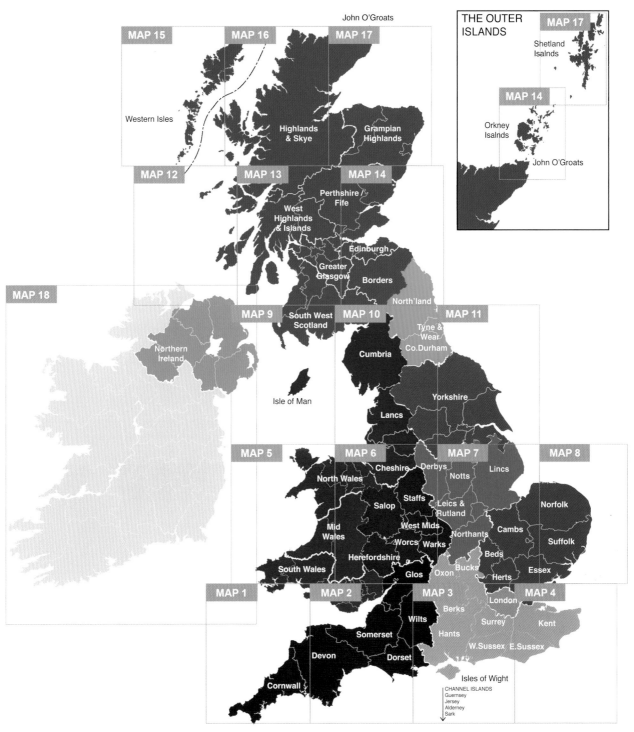

THE OUTER ISLANDS

MAP 17 — Shetland Isalnds

MAP 14 — Orkney Isalnds — John O'Groats

John O'Groats

MAP 15 — Western Isles

MAP 16 — Highlands & Skye — Grampian Highlands

MAP 17

MAP 12

MAP 13 — West Highlands & Islands — Perthshire / Fife

MAP 14 — Edinburgh — Greater Glasgow — Borders

North'land

MAP 18 — Northern Ireland

Isle of Man

MAP 9 — South West Scotland

MAP 10 — Cumbria — Lancs

MAP 11 — Tyne & Wear — Co.Durham — Yorkshire

MAP 5 — North Wales — Mid Wales — South Wales

MAP 6 — Cheshire — Staffs — Salop — West Mids — Worcs — Warks — Herefordshire — Glos

Derbys — Notts

MAP 7 — Lincs — Leics & Rutland — Northants — Beds — Bucks — Oxon — Herts

MAP 8 — Norfolk — Cambs — Suffolk — Essex

MAP 1 — Cornwall — Devon

MAP 2 — Somerset — Dorset — Wilts

MAP 3 — Berks — Hants — London — Surrey — W.Sussex — E.Sussex

MAP 4 — Kent

Isles of Wight

CHANNEL ISLANDS
Guernsey
Jersey
Alderney
Sark

MAP 1

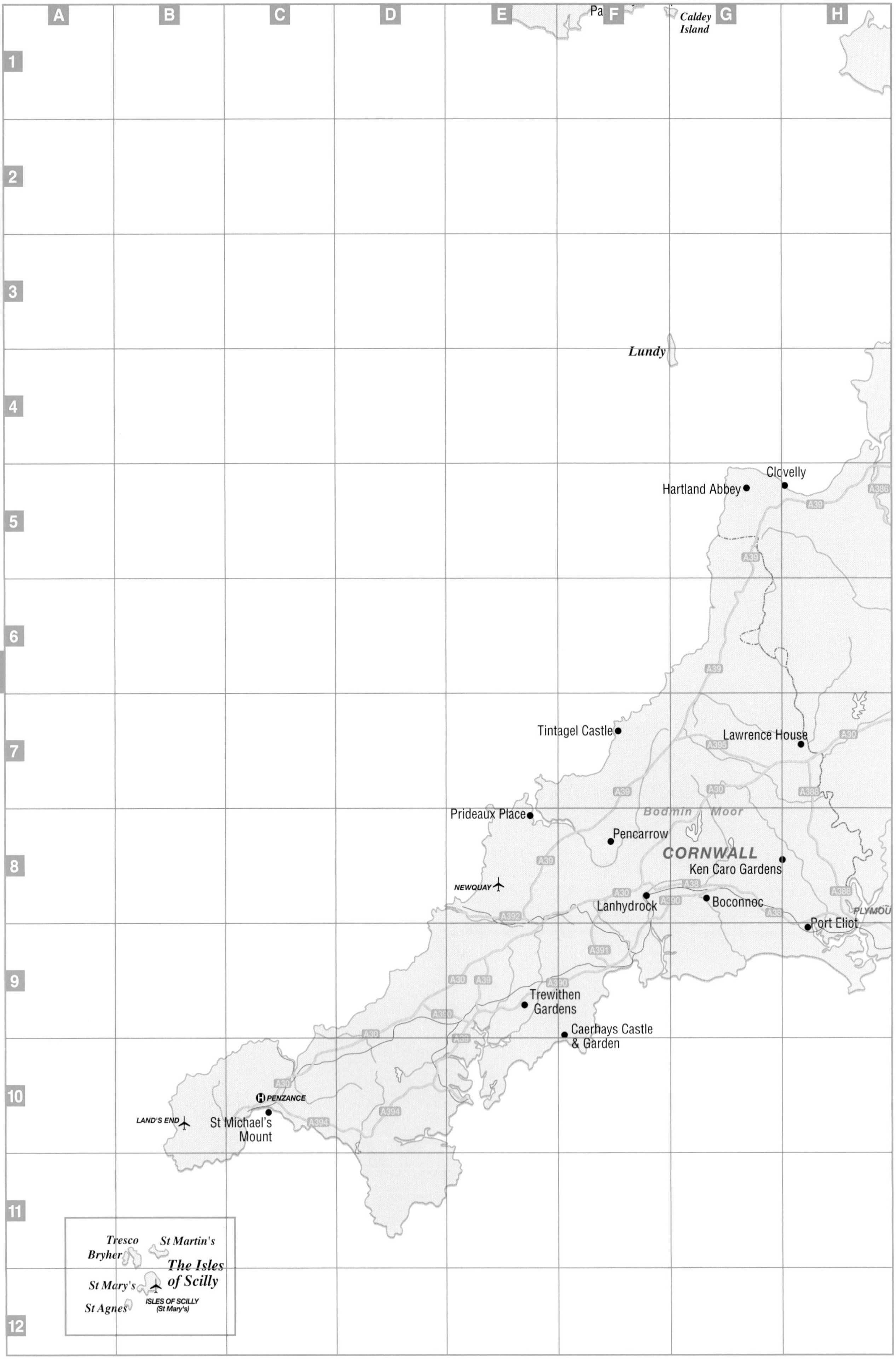

A B C D E F G H

1

2

3

Lundy

4

Clovelly
Hartland Abbey ●

5

6

7
Tintagel Castle ●   Lawrence House ●

Prideaux Place ●
Bodmin Moor

8
Pencarrow ●
CORNWALL
Ken Caro Gardens ●
NEWQUAY ✈   Boconnoc ●
Lanhydrock ●   Port Eliot ●
PLYMOUTH

9
Trewithen Gardens ●
Caerhays Castle & Garden ●

10
LAND'S END ✈   ⒣ PENZANCE
St Michael's Mount ●

11

Tresco   St Martin's
Bryher
The Isles of Scilly
St Mary's ✈
St Agnes   ISLES OF SCILLY (St Mary's)

12

Pa
Caldey Island

Weobley Castle
SWANSEA
SWANSEA

Oxwich Castle

Llancaiach Fawr Manor
RHONDDA CYNON TAFF
CAERPHILLY
Chepstow Castle
M48
SOUTH GLOUCESTERSHIRE

BRIDGEND
Castle Coch
CARDIFF
M4
NEWPORT
Tredegar House
Dyrham Park

Llandaff Cathedral
BRISTOL

VALE OF GLAMORGAN
Dyffryn Gardens
Fonmon Castle
CARDIFF

Tyntesfield
NORTH SOMERSET
BRISTOL

Building of Bath Museum
Crowe Hall
Holburne Museum of Art
Prior Park Landscape Garden
Peto Gardens at Iford Manor

Fairfield
Nunney Castle
Kentsford
Orchard
Wyndham
Dodington Hall
SOMERSET
Longleat

Exmoor
Exmoor Forest
Brendon Hills

Glastonbury Abbey

Robin Hood's Hut
Polden Hills

Castle Hill Gardens
M5
Blackdown Hills
Sandford Orcas Manor H

Sherborne Castle
Montacute House

Tiverton Castle
Stock Gayland House

DEVON
Fursdon House
Forde Abbey & Gardens
Minterne Gardens
Higher Melcombe
DORSET

Downes
Mapperton
Athelhampton House & Gardens

Castle Drogo
Great Fulford
EXETER
Cadhay
Sand
Church of Our Lady & St Ignatius
Wolfeton House

Dartmoor
Dartmoor Forest
Powderham Castle
A La Ronde
Lulworth Castle & Park

Chesil Beach

Buckfast Abbey
TORBAY
Portland Bill

Buckland Abbey
PLYMOUTH
Greenway

Hemerdon House

Shilstone

GUERNSEY

Sausmarez Manor

MAP 2

I J K L M N O P
1 2 3 4 5 6 7 8 9 10 11 12

MAP 3

A B C D E F G H

1

Chavenage
Milton Manor House
Hughenden
TWIGS Community Gardens
Stonor
Cliveden
Hall Barn
Gothic Temple
SWINDON
Ardington House
Nuffield Place
Lydiard Park
Greys Court
WINDSOR & MAIDENHEAD
Dorney Court
LYNEHAM
Mapledurham & Watermill
READING
SLOUGH
Osterley Park
HEATHROW
Kew Gdns
Kew Palace

2

Corsham Court
WEST BERKSHIRE
A329(M)
M4
BRACKNELL FOREST
Ham House
Strawberry Hill
Lacock Abbey
The Merchant's House
WOKINGHAM
Great Fosters
M3
Hampton Court
Claremont Landscape Garden
Whitehall
Bowood House
WILTSHIRE
M25
Painshill Park Landscape Garden
Hom

3

Salisbury Plain
Stratfield Saye House
SURREY
Highclere Castle, Gardens & Egyptian Exhibition
Polesden Lacey
Shalford Mill
Goddards
GATWICK

4

HAMPSHIRE
Houghton Lodge
Avington Park
Winchester City Mill
Gilbert White & The Oates Collections
Wilton House
Mompesson House
Mottisfont
Hinton Ampner Garden
Petworth House & Park
Newhouse
King John's House
Cowdray Ruins
W. SUSSEX

5

Whitsbury Down
Parham House & Gardens
Norrington Manor
Broadlands
SOUTHAMPTON
Uppark
Bramber Castle
St Mary's
St Giles House
M3
SOUTHAMPTON
M27
Wilmington Priory
A3(M)
Lancing College
Edmondsham House
New Forest
Stansted Park
Goodwood House
Denmans
SHOREHAM
Highdown Gardens

6

Kingston Lacy
BOURNEMOUTH
St Agatha's Church
Chichester Cathedral
Pallant House
Arundel Castle
Arundel Cathedral
POOLE
Beaulieu
Exbury Gardens
Highcliffe Castle
BOURNEMOUTH
Osborne House
PORTSMOUTH
Charles Dickens' Birthplace Museum

7

Clavell Tower
The Needles
ISLE OF WIGHT

Isle of Wight

8

9

10

11

12

Register for news and special offers at www.hudsonsheritage.com

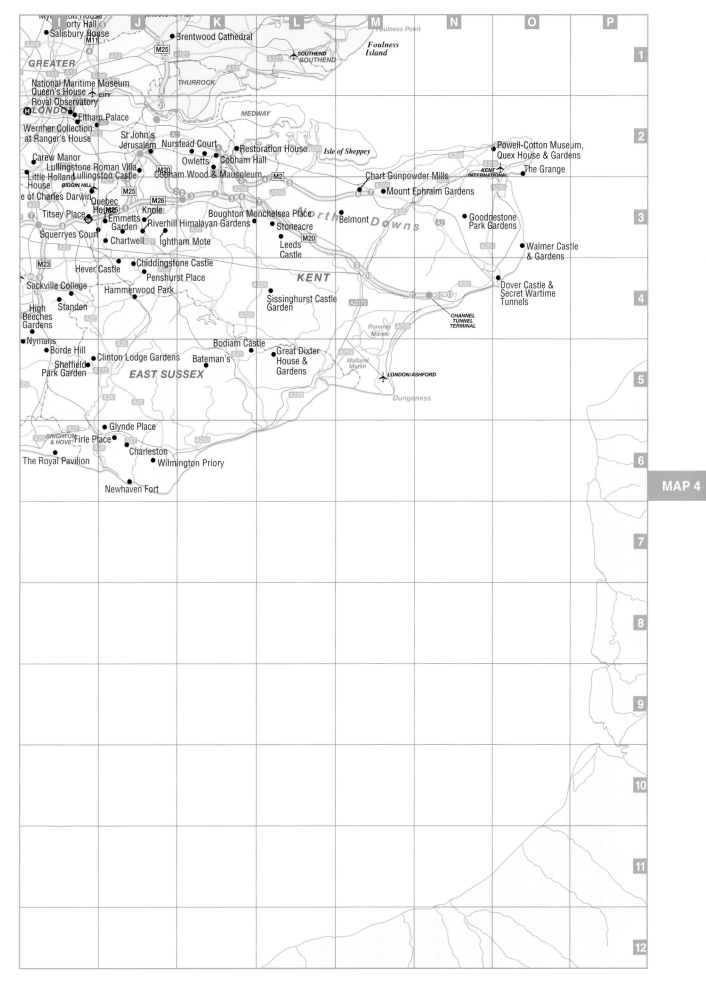

Myo... oll House
I orty Hall
Salisbury House
GREATER
A10

National Maritime Museum
Queen's House
Royal Observatory
LONDON
Eltham Palace
Wernher Collection
at Ranger's House
Carew Manor
Lullingstone Roman Villa
Little Holland Lullingstone Castle
House
BIGGIN HILL
e of Charles Darwin
Titsey Place
Squerryes Court
Chartwell

Brentwood Cathedral
M25
A12
A13
THURROCK

Foulness Point
SOUTHEND
SOUTHEND

Foulness
Island

MEDWAY

St John's
Jerusalem
Nurstead Court
Owletts
Cobham Hall
Cobham Wood & Mausoleum
A2
M2

Isle of Sheppey

Powell-Cotton Museum,
Quex House & Gardens

Chart Gunpowder Mills
KENT
INTERNATIONAL

The Grange

Mount Ephraim Gardens

Quebec
House
M25
M26
Knole
Emmetts
Garden
Riverhill Himalayan Gardens
Ightham Mote

Boughton Monchelsea Place
Stoneacre
Leeds
Castle
M20

North Downs

Belmont

Goodnestone
Park Gardens

Walmer Castle
& Gardens

Dover Castle &
Secret Wartime
Tunnels

M23
Hever Castle
Sackville College
Standen
High
Beeches
Gardens
Nymans

Chiddingstone Castle
Penshurst Place
Hammerwood Park

KENT

Sissinghurst Castle
Garden
A229
A20

CHANNEL
TUNNEL
TERMINAL

Romney
Marsh

Borde Hill
Clinton Lodge Gardens
Sheffield
Park Garden
EAST SUSSEX

Bodiam Castle
Bateman's
A21

Great Dixter
House &
Gardens

Walland
Marsh
LONDON/ASHFORD

Dungeness

Glynde Place
BRIGHTON
& HOVE
Firle Place
Charleston
The Royal Pavilion
Wilmington Priory
Newhaven Fort

MAP 4

1
2
3
4
5
6
7
8
9
10
11
12

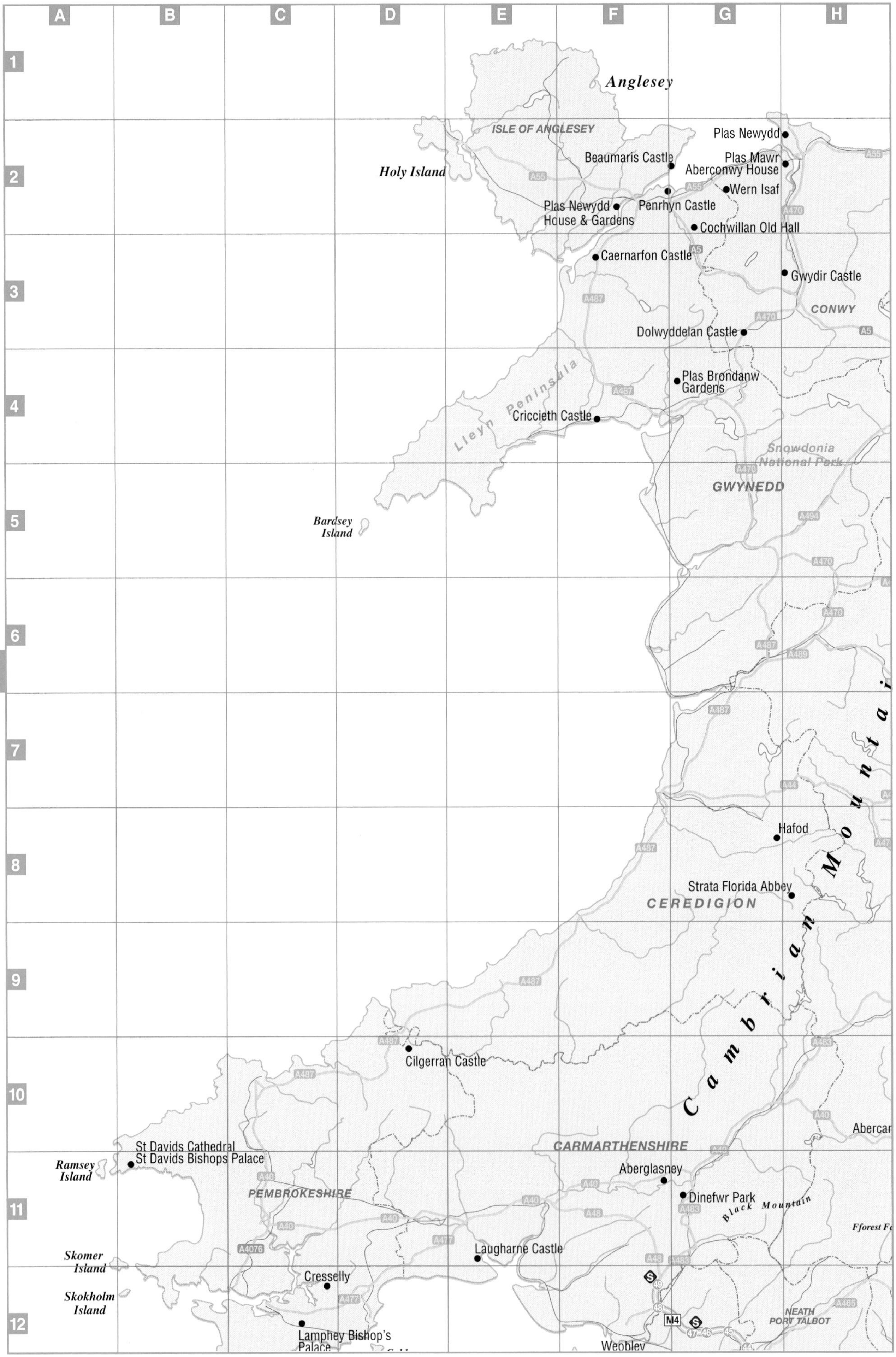

Anglesey

ISLE OF ANGLESEY

Holy Island

Plas Newydd ●

Plas Mawr ●
Beaumaris Castle ● Aberconwy House
● Wern Isaf
Plas Newydd ● Penrhyn Castle
House & Gardens ● Cochwillan Old Hall

● Caernarfon Castle

● Gwydir Castle

CONWY

● Dolwyddelan Castle

● Plas Brondanw
Gardens

Lleyn Peninsula

Criccieth Castle ●

Snowdonia
National Park

GWYNEDD

Bardsey
Island

MAP 5

● Hafod

● Strata Florida Abbey

CEREDIGION

Cambrian Mountains

● Cilgerran Castle

CARMARTHENSHIRE

Abercar

St Davids Cathedral
Ramsey ● St Davids Bishops Palace
Island

● Aberglasney

● Dinefwr Park

PEMBROKESHIRE

Black Mountain

Skomer
Island

Fforest Fa

● Laugharne Castle

Skokholm
Island

● Cresselly

Ⓢ

Ⓢ
M4 Ⓢ

NEATH
PORT TALBOT

● Lamphey Bishop's
Palace

Weobley

Register for news and special offers at www.hudsonsheritage.com

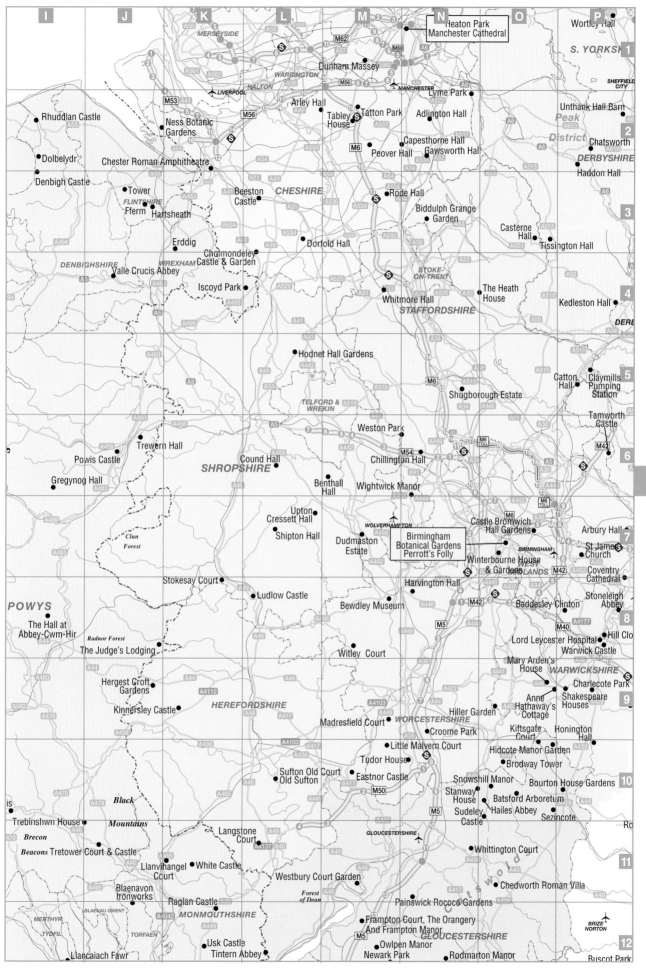

MAP 6

MAP 7

Scawby Hall
Gainsborough Old Hall

LINCOLNSHIRE WOLDS

Renishaw Hall Gardens

Welbeck Abbey
Bolsover Castle
Lincoln Castle
Doddington Hall & Gardens

Hardwick Hall
NOTTINGHAMSHIRE
LINCOLNSHIRE

Aubourn Hall

Papplewick Hall
Leadenham House
Mr Straw's House
Fulbeck Manor

NOTTINGHAM

Marston Hall
Belton House

NOTTINGHAM EAST MIDLANDS

Sandringham
Castle Rising

Melbourne Hall
Calke Abbey
Clifton House

Grimsthorpe Castle Park & Gardens
Ayscoughfee Hall Museum & Gardens

Peckover House & Garden

The Fens

LEICESTERSHIRE
RUTLAND
Burghley House

LEICESTER
PETERBOROUGH

Rockingham Castle
Elton Hall
Ely Cathedral
Old Palace
Oliver Cromwell's House

Astley Castle
Deene Park
Southwick Hall

CAMBRIDGESHIRE

Rushton Triangular Lodge
Stanford Hall
Boughton House

Cottesbrooke
Lamport Hall

The Manor, Hemingford Grey

NORTHAMPTONSHIRE
Island Hall

ose Gardens
Haddonstone Show Gardens
Kimbolton Castle

Anglesey Abbey

Holdenby House
Althorp
78 Derngate

CAMBRIDGE

ompton Verney
BEDFORDSHIRE
Turvey House
Wimpole Estate

Stoke Park Pavilions
MILTON KEYNES
Moggerhanger Park

Wakefield Lodge
Swiss Gardens

Weston Hall
Queen Anne's Summerhouse

Broughton Castle
Sulgrave Manor
Wrest Park
Audley End House & Gardens

National Trust Stowe

Woburn Abbey

ousham House
LUTON
Benington Lordship
STANSTED

BUCKINGHAMSHIRE
Ascott
HERTFORDSHIRE

enheim Palace
Waddesdon Manor
LUTON
Knebworth

Wotton House

Gorhambury House
Hatfield House

OXFORDSHIRE
Nether Winchendon House

Bodleian Library
Copped Hall

Waterperry Gardens
Chenies Manor House
Capel Manor
Hyla

Kingston Bagpuize
26A East St Helen Street

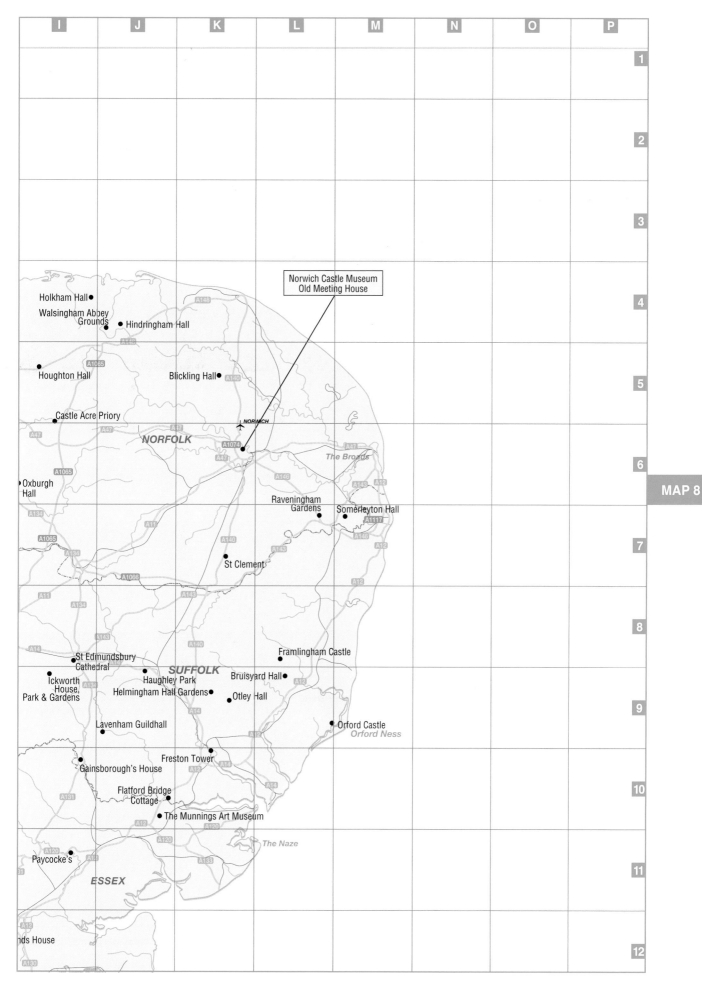

Norwich Castle Museum
Old Meeting House

Holkham Hall •

Walsingham Abbey
Grounds • • Hindringham Hall

• Houghton Hall

• Blickling Hall

• Castle Acre Priory

NORFOLK

NORWICH

The Broads

• Oxburgh
Hall

Raveningham
Gardens
Somerleyton Hall

• St Clement

Framlingham Castle •

St Edmundsbury
Cathedral

SUFFOLK
Bruisyard Hall •

Ickworth
House,
Park & Gardens

Haughley Park •
Helmingham Hall Gardens •

Otley Hall •

Lavenham Guildhall

Orford Castle
Orford Ness

Freston Tower •

Gainsborough's House

Flatford Bridge
Cottage

• The Munnings Art Museum

The Naze

Paycocke's •

ESSEX

nds House

MAP 8

MAP 9

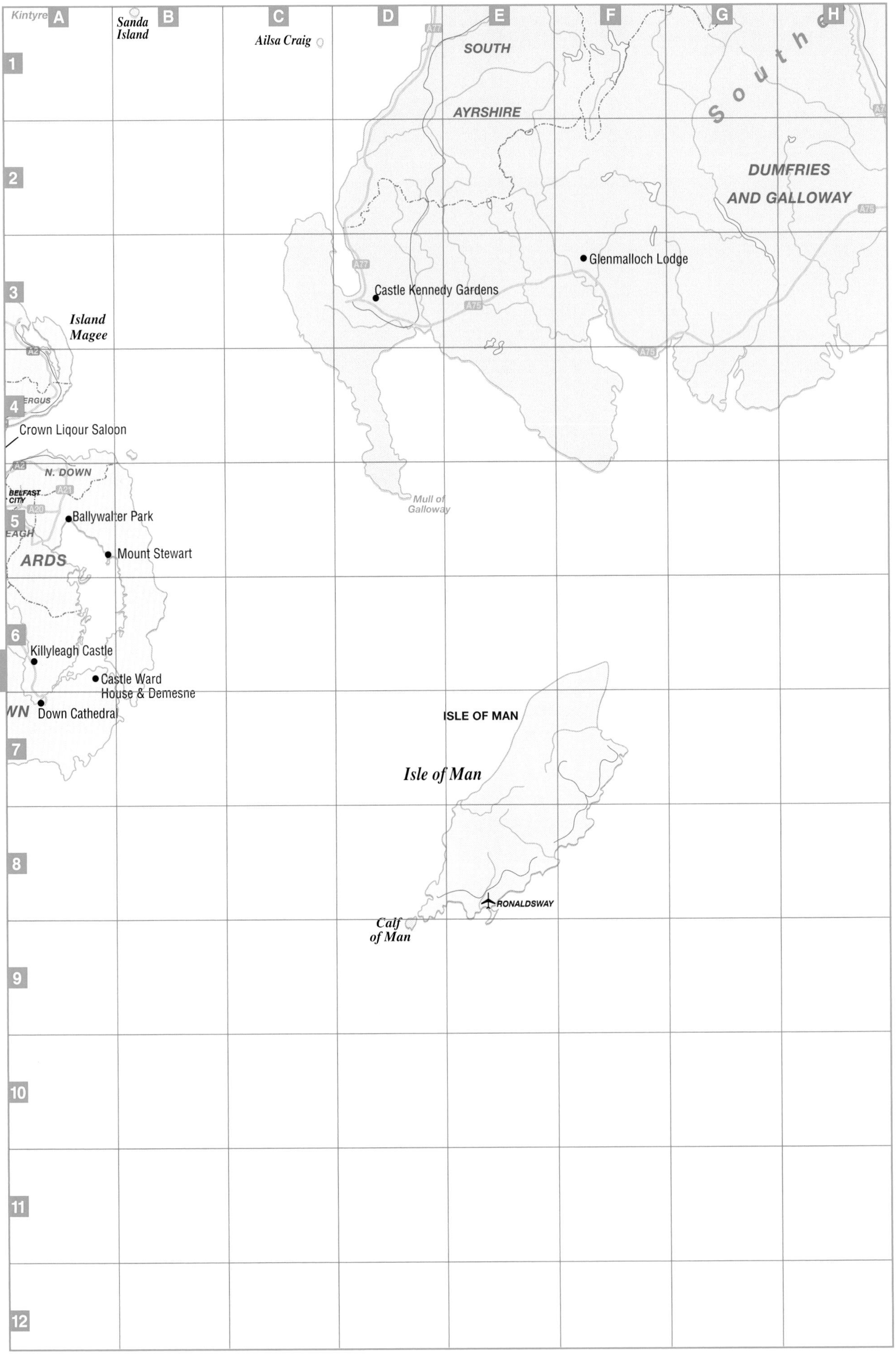

A | B | C | D | E | F | G | H

1

2

SOUTH

AYRSHIRE

South

DUMFRIES

AND GALLOWAY

Kintyre

Sanda Island

Ailsa Craig

● Glenmalloch Lodge

Castle Kennedy Gardens ●

3

Island Magee

ERGUS

Crown Liqour Saloon

N. DOWN

BELFAST CITY

EAGH

● Ballywalter Park

4

Mull of Galloway

5

ARDS

● Mount Stewart

6

Killyleagh Castle ●

● Castle Ward House & Demesne

WN ● Down Cathedral

ISLE OF MAN

Isle of Man

7

8

✈ *RONALDSWAY*

Calf of Man

9

10

11

12

394 | Register for news and special offers at www.hudsonsheritage.com

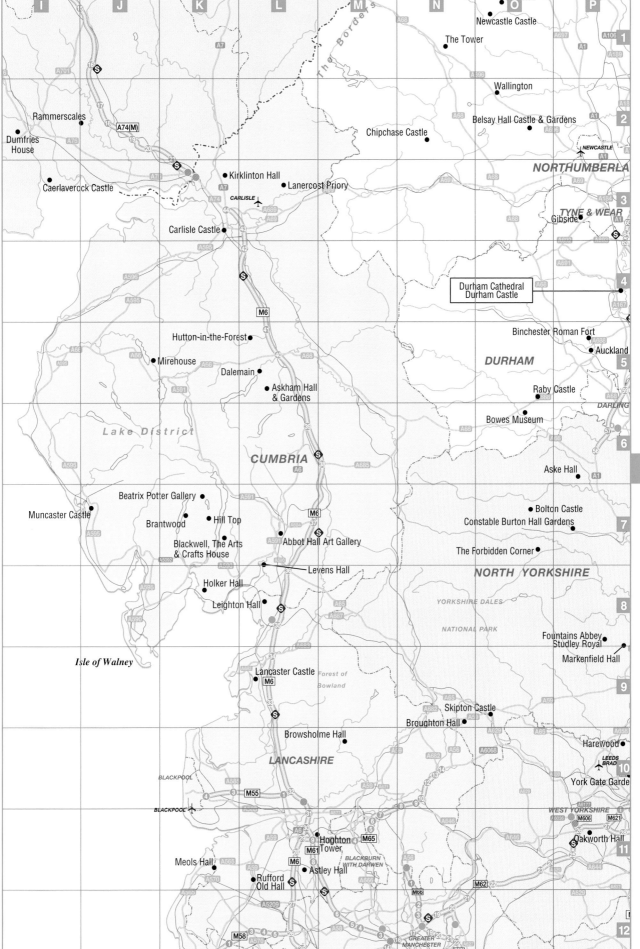

Rammerscales

Dumfries House

Caerlaverock Castle

Kirklinton Hall

Lanercost Priory

CARLISLE

Carlisle Castle

Chipchase Castle

The Tower

Newcastle Castle

Wallington

Belsay Hall Castle & Gardens

NEWCASTLE

NORTHUMBERLA

TYNE & WEAR

Gibside

Durham Cathedral
Durham Castle

Binchester Roman Fort

Auckland

DURHAM

Hutton-in-the-Forest

Mirehouse

Dalemain

Askham Hall & Gardens

Raby Castle

DARLING

Bowes Museum

Lake District

CUMBRIA

Aske Hall

Beatrix Potter Gallery

Brantwood

Hill Top

Muncaster Castle

Blackwell, The Arts & Crafts House

Abbot Hall Art Gallery

Levens Hall

Bolton Castle

Constable Burton Hall Gardens

The Forbidden Corner

NORTH YORKSHIRE

YORKSHIRE DALES

Holker Hall

Leighton Hall

NATIONAL PARK

Isle of Walney

Lancaster Castle

Forest of Bowland

Fountains Abbey
Studley Royal

Markenfield Hall

Skipton Castle

Broughton Hall

Harewood

LEEDS
BRAD

Browsholme Hall

LANCASHIRE

BLACKPOOL

BLACKPOOL

York Gate Garde

WEST YORKSHIRE

Meols Hall

Hoghton Tower

BLACKBURN WITH DARWEN

Oakworth Hall

Astley Hall

Rufford Old Hall

GREATER MANCHESTER

MAP 10

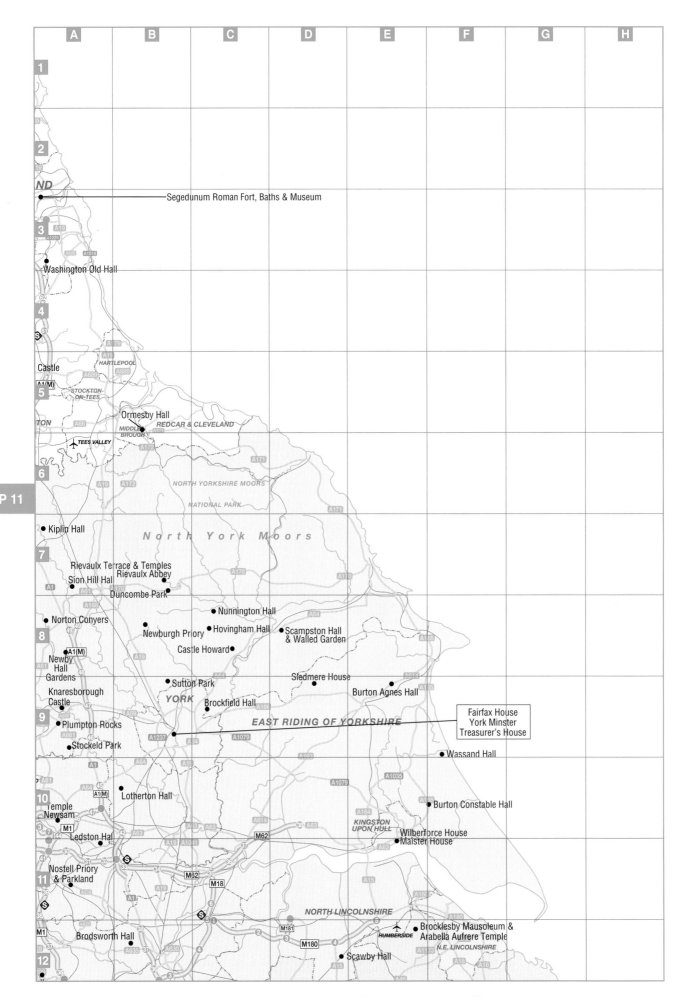

MAP 11

A **B** **C** **D** **E** **F** **G** **H**

Segedunum Roman Fort, Baths & Museum

Washington Old Hall

Castle

Ormesby Hall

REDCAR & CLEVELAND

TEES VALLEY

NORTH YORKSHIRE MOORS

NATIONAL PARK

North York Moors

Kiplin Hall

Rievaulx Terrace & Temples
Sion Hill Hall   Rievaulx Abbey
        Duncombe Park

Norton Conyers   Nunnington Hall
        Newburgh Priory ●Hovingham Hall   Scampston Hall
Newby   & Walled Garden
Hall   Castle Howard●
Gardens
        Sutton Park   Sledmere House   Burton Agnes Hall
Knaresborough   Fairfax House
Castle   Brockfield Hall   York Minster
                                        Treasurer's House
Plumpton Rocks   EAST RIDING OF YORKSHIRE
Stockeld Park   Wassand Hall

Lotherton Hall

Temple   Burton Constable Hall
Newsam
            KINGSTON
            UPON HULL
Ledston Hall   Wilberforce House
                                    Maister House
Nostell Priory
& Parkland

NORTH LINCOLNSHIRE
                            Brocklesby Mausoleum &
                            Arabella Aufrere Temple
M1   Brodsworth Hall   N.E. LINCOLNSHIRE
                HUMBERSIDE

                Scawby Hall

I J K L M N O P

Rum

Sanndraigh
(Sandray)

Eigg

alaigh
(lay)

Muck

Inner Hebrides

Coll

Oransay

Ardtornish Gardens • Castle Stalker •

Tiree

Ulva

Lismore

Isle of
Mull

Duart Castle • Kerrera

Iona

Luing

Garvellachs

Lunga

Scarba

ARGYLL
AND BUTE

MAP 12

Colonsay

Oronsay

Jura

Islay

ISLAY

Gigha

Kintyre

Arran

hull

Rathlin
Island

Giant's
Causeway

Mull of
Kintyre

Sanda
Island

W E N

(Bun an Phobail)

Ailsa Cra

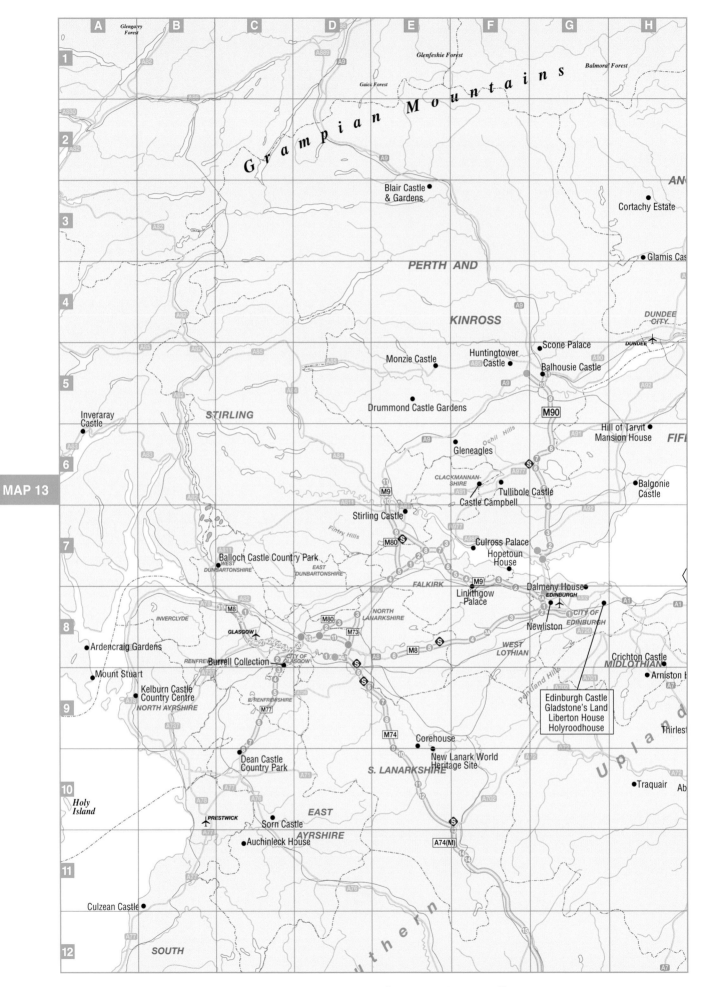

MAP 13

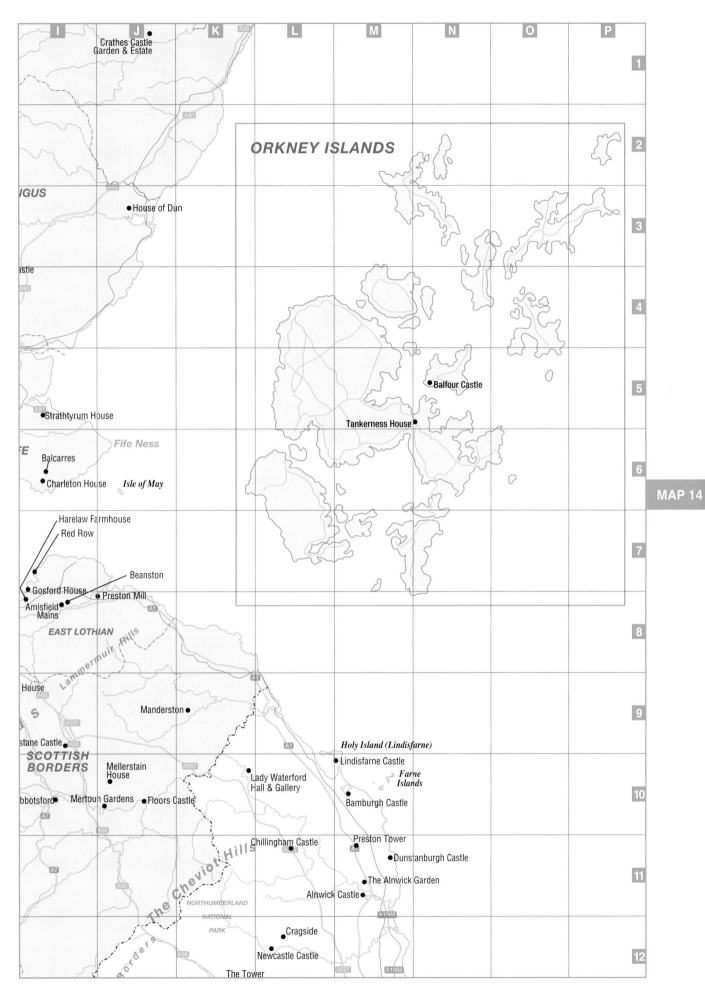

ORKNEY ISLANDS

I J K L M N O P

1
2
3
4
5
6
7
8
9
10
11
12

Crathes Castle Garden & Estate

IGUS

House of Dun

astle

Balfour Castle

Strathtyrum House

Tankerness House

Fife Ness

FE

Balcarres

Charleton House

Isle of May

Harelaw Farmhouse

Red Row

Beanston

Gosford House

Preston Mill

Amisfield
Mains

EAST LOTHIAN

Lammermuir Hills

MAP 14

House

S

**SCOTTISH
BORDERS**

Manderston

stane Castle

Holy Island (Lindisfarne)

Mellerstain
House

Lindisfarne Castle

Lady Waterford
Hall & Gallery

*Farne
Islands*

bbotsford

Mertoun Gardens

Floors Castle

Bamburgh Castle

Chillingham Castle

Preston Tower

Dunstanburgh Castle

The Cheviot Hills

NORTHUMBERLAND

NATIONAL

PARK

The Alnwick Garden

Alnwick Castle

Cragside

Newcastle Castle

The Tower

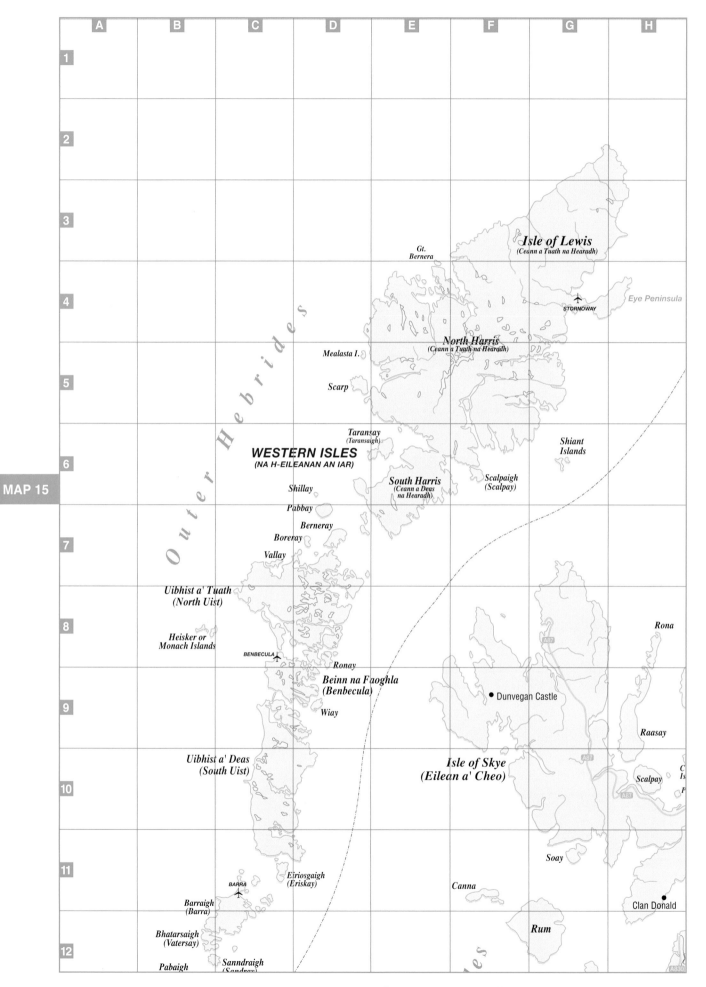

MAP 15

Register for news and special offers at www.hudsonsheritage.com

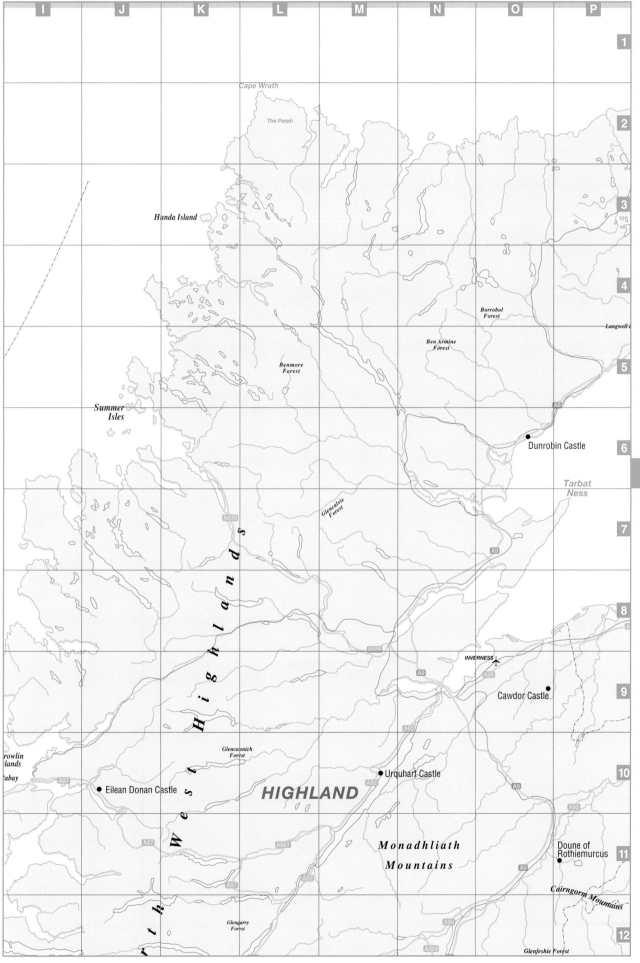

I   J   K   L   M   N   O   P

1
2
3
4
5
6
7
8
9
10
11
12

Cape Wrath

The Parph

Handa Island

Borrobol Forest

Langwell

Ben Armine Forest

Benmore Forest

Summer Isles

Dunrobin Castle

MAP 16

Tarbat Ness

Glencalvie Forest

North West Highlands

INVERNESS

Cawdor Castle

rowlin lands

abay

Glencannich Forest

HIGHLAND

Urquhart Castle

Eilean Donan Castle

Monadhliath Mountains

Doune of Rothiemurcus

Cairngorm Mountains

Glengarry Forest

Glenfeshie Forest

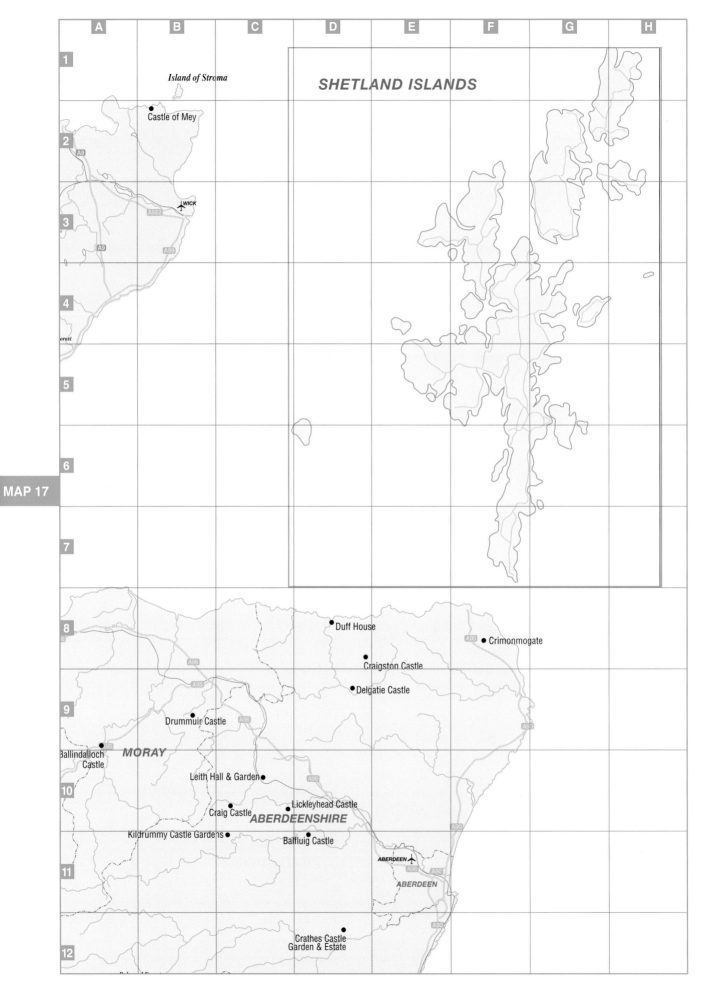

SHETLAND ISLANDS

Island of Stroma

• Castle of Mey

WICK

• Duff House

• Crimonmogate

• Craigston Castle

• Delgatie Castle

• Drummuir Castle

Ballindalloch
Castle

MORAY

Leith Hall & Garden •

• Lickleyhead Castle

Craig Castle •

ABERDEENSHIRE

Kildrummy Castle Gardens •

• Balfluig Castle

ABERDEEN

ABERDEEN

Crathes Castle
Garden & Estate

MAP 17

Register for news and special offers at www.hudsonsheritage.com

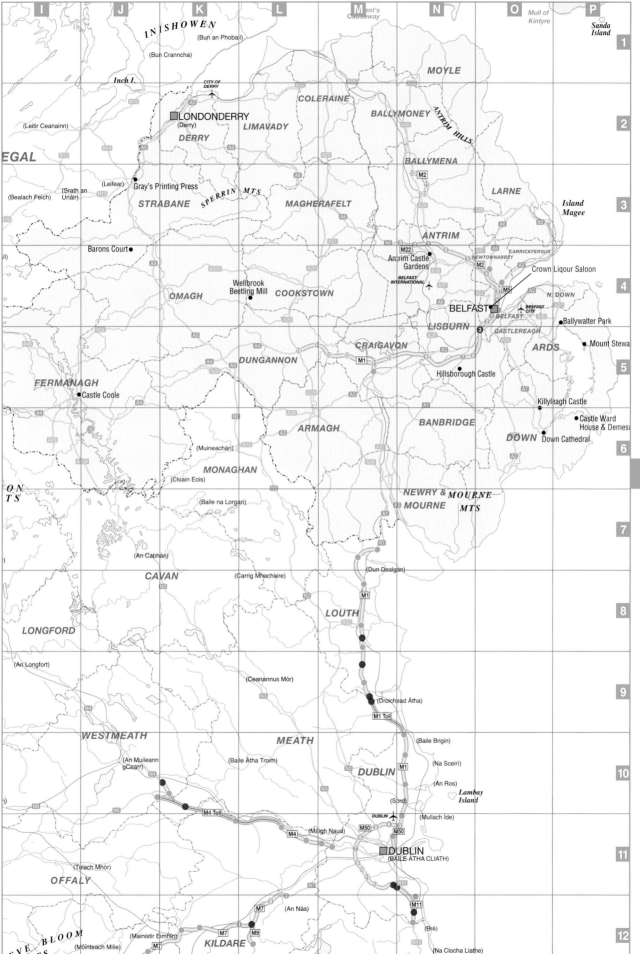

MAP 18

GREATER LONDON

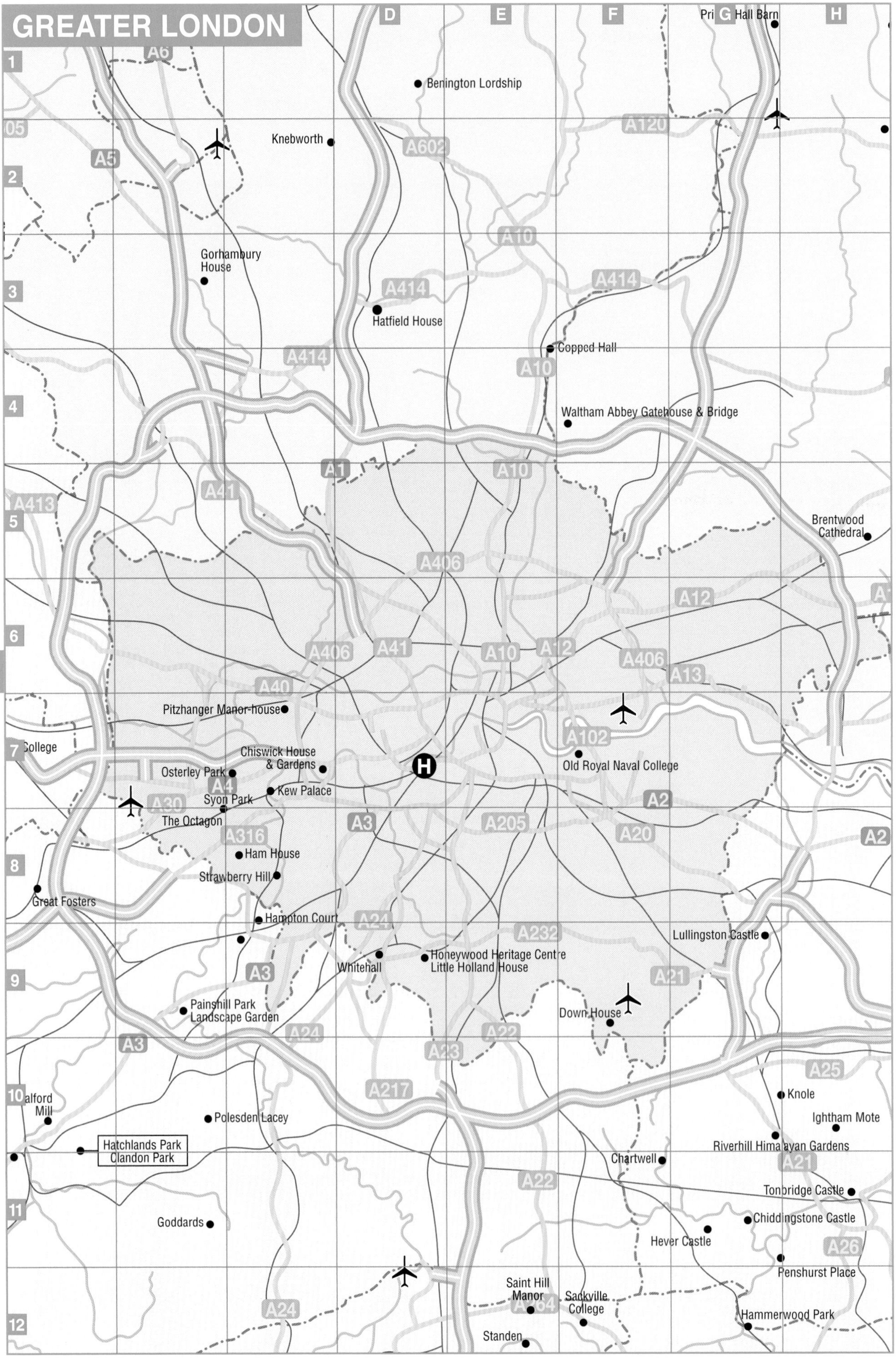

MAP 19

Benington Lordship

Knebworth

Gorhambury House

Hatfield House

Copped Hall

Waltham Abbey Gatehouse & Bridge

Pri G Hall Barn

Brentwood Cathedral

Pitzhanger Manor-house

Chiswick House & Gardens

Osterley Park

Kew Palace

Syon Park

The Octagon

Ham House

Strawberry Hill

Great Fosters

Hampton Court

Whitehall

Honeywood Heritage Centre
Little Holland House

Old Royal Naval College

Lullingstone Castle

Down House

Painshill Park
Landscape Garden

alford Mill

Polesden Lacey

Hatchlands Park
Clandon Park

Knole

Ightham Mote

Riverhill Himalayan Gardens

Chartwell

Goddards

Hever Castle

Tonbridge Castle

Chiddingstone Castle

Penshurst Place

Saint Hill Manor

Sackville College

Standen

Hammerwood Park

College

A6
05
A5
A120
A602
A10
A414
A414
A414
A1
A41
A413
A406
A12
A406
A41
A10
A12
A406
A13
A40
A102
A4
A30
A316
A3
A205
A20
A2
A2
A24
A232
A21
A3
A24
A22
A23
A217
A25
A21
A22
A26
A24
A64

404

Register for news and special offers at www.hudsonsheritage.com

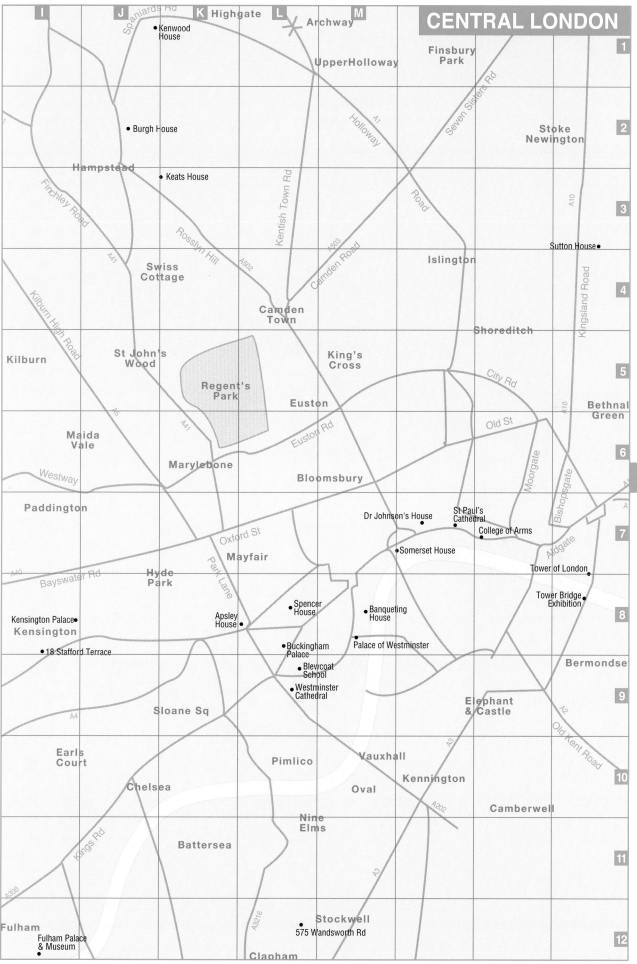

CENTRAL LONDON

MAP 20

I · J · K · Highgate · L · M
Kenwood House · Archway · UpperHolloway · Finsbury Park · Stoke Newington

Burgh House · Hampstead · Keats House · Swiss Cottage · Islington · Sutton House

Kilburn · St John's Wood · Camden Town · King's Cross · Shoreditch · Bethnal Green

Maida Vale · Regent's Park · Euston · Old St · Moorgate · Bishopsgate

Paddington · Marylebone · Bloomsbury · Dr Johnson's House · St Paul's Cathedral · College of Arms

Mayfair · Somerset House · Tower of London · Aldgate

Hyde Park · Spencer House · Banqueting House · Tower Bridge Exhibition

Kensington Palace · Kensington · Apsley House · Buckingham Palace · Palace of Westminster · Bermondsey

18 Stafford Terrace · Blewcoat School · Westminster Cathedral · Elephant & Castle

Sloane Sq · Pimlico · Vauxhall · Kennington · Camberwell

Earls Court · Chelsea · Oval

Nine Elms · Battersea

Fulham · Stockwell · 575 Wandsworth Rd

Fulham Palace & Museum · Clapham

WALES

Wo

Clapton-in-

Uphill

Parracombe

Elworthy

Upton Tower

Lar

Satterleigh

Stocklinch Otter

Devon

Luffincott

Exeter • Exeter St Martin

Bradstone

Cornwall

Princetown

West Ogwell

Torbryan

North Huish

Revelstoke

Roseland St Anthony

icestershire • Blatherwycke
• Deene

West Midlands

Aldwincle • • Steep
• Brownsover • Cranford
Northamptonshire • Co
• Holdenby • Knotting
• Richards Castle
Worcestershire • Lower Sapey
• Wolfhamcote Farndish • Offord D
Warwickshire Upton St Michael • • Northampton Car
• Billesley • Preston Deanery
• Stretford Worcester • • Churchill • Chadshunt Little Barf
Spetchley • Avon Dassett Bedfordshire
Wormsley • Moreton Croome D'Abitot Furtho • • Broughton
Jeffries • Evesham • Thornton • Lower
Yazor Strensham • • Saintbury Graver
Herefordshire • Pottesgrove
Holme Lacy • Pendock • Little Washbourne H
• Yatton Buckinghamshire • Edlesborough
• Michaelchurch Lassington Fleet Marston • • Pitstone Hertfor
• Llanrothal Shipton Sollars Hartwell
Gloucester • • Eastleach Martin ○ Oxford
• Brookthorpe Oxfordshire
Gloucestershire • Eastleach Martin ○ Oxford
Shorncote Inglesham • Chiselhampton
Ozleworth Nuneham • Shirburn Oxhey • • Li
Charfield • Tetbury • Leigh Courtenay Wallingford Kingsbury •
• Oldbury-on-the-Hill Catmore Newnham Murren
Leigh Delamere Mongewell
Bristol St Paul • Draycot Cerne • East Shefford • Lower Basildon Gre
Bristol St John Lambourn Woodlands
n-in-Gordano • Bristol St Thomas Berwick Bassett Berkshire
• Brockley Esher •
• Puxton • Pensford Wiltshire • Alton Priors
phill • Cameley • Hardington • Hartley Wintney Surre
Bampfylde Imber Chute Forest
Emborough • Everleigh • Churchill • Albury
Holcombe Old Dilton Orcheston • Sth Tidworth • Freefolk
• Otterhampton Sutton Veny • Maddington Preston Candover
Rollestone
thy • Sutton Mallet • Fisherton Idmiston Little Somborne
Berwick St Leonard • Delamere • Ashley • Itchen • Colemore
Somerset Wilton • ○ Salisbury Stoke • Privett
Langport • Stratford Tony • Eldon West Sussex
• Thurlbear • Northover West Dean Hampshire
Ottersey • • Oborne ○ Southampton • Warm
• Seavington Chichester • • North Stoke
• Stockwood • Tortington
Nether Cerne • Tarrant Crawford Church Norton
Bothenhampton Dorset • Winterborne Tomson
Winterborne Came • Whitcombe

• Portland

THE CHURCHES CONSERVATION TRUST

Fledborough
Lincoln
Great Steeping
Haltham-on-Bain
Lincolnshire
Normanton
Haceby
rthorpe
Edmondthorpe
Walpole
West Walton
King's Lynn
Islington
Wiggenhall
East
Bradenham
North Barningham · Thurgarton
Gunton
East Ruston
Booton
Brandiston
Little Witchingham
Norwich
Norwich St Augustine
Norwich St John
Moulton
Buckenham
Hellington
Heckingham
Hales
Coston
Norwich
St Laurence
Bungay
Shimpling
Frenze
South
Elmham
Ellough
Covehithe
Norfolk
Burley
Withcote
Rutland
Stamford St John
Guyhirn
Parson Drove
Barton Bendish
Feltwell
Hockwold
West
Harling
Wakerley
Deene
nerwycke
Conington
Steeple Gidding
Cambridgeshire
Aldwincle
Cranford
onshire
enby
arndish
orthampton
Preston Deanery
Knotting
Offord D'Arcy
Cambridge
Abbotsley
Little Barford
Long Stanton
Swaffham Prior
Cambridge St Peter
Cambridge All Saints
Icklingham
Sapiston
Wordwell
Stanton
Redgrave
Rickinghall
Suffolk
Stonham Parva
Badley
Claydon
Akenham
Newton
Green
Chilton
Ipswich
Washbrook
Little Wenham
Duxford
Sudbury
St Peter
Bedfordshire
Broughton
Edworth
hornton
Lower
Gravenhurst
Pottesgrove
Little
Hormead
Buckland
Halstead
West Bergholt
Chickney
Stansted
Mountfitchet
Berechurch
Little Bromley
Colchester St Leonard
Colchester St Martin
mshire
Edlesborough
Pitstone
Hertfordshire
Stanstead Abbots
Willingale
Essex
well
oton
ourn
d
Oxhey
Little Stanmore
East Horndon
Kingsbury
Oseney Crescent
Vange
Murren
sildon
London
Greater London
Higham
Cooling
Esher
Lumley Chapel
Hartley Wintney
Surrey
Albury
Luddenham
Paddlesworth
Burham
Kingsdown
East Peckham
Capel St Thomas
Goodnestone
West Stourmouth
Sandwich St Mary
Sandwich St Peter
Fordwich
Knowlton
Waldershare
Swingfield
Capel-le-Ferne
Kent
andover
emore
t
West Sussex
East Sussex
Warminghurst
North Stoke
Tortington
Preston Park
Brighton
Hove
Church Norton
er

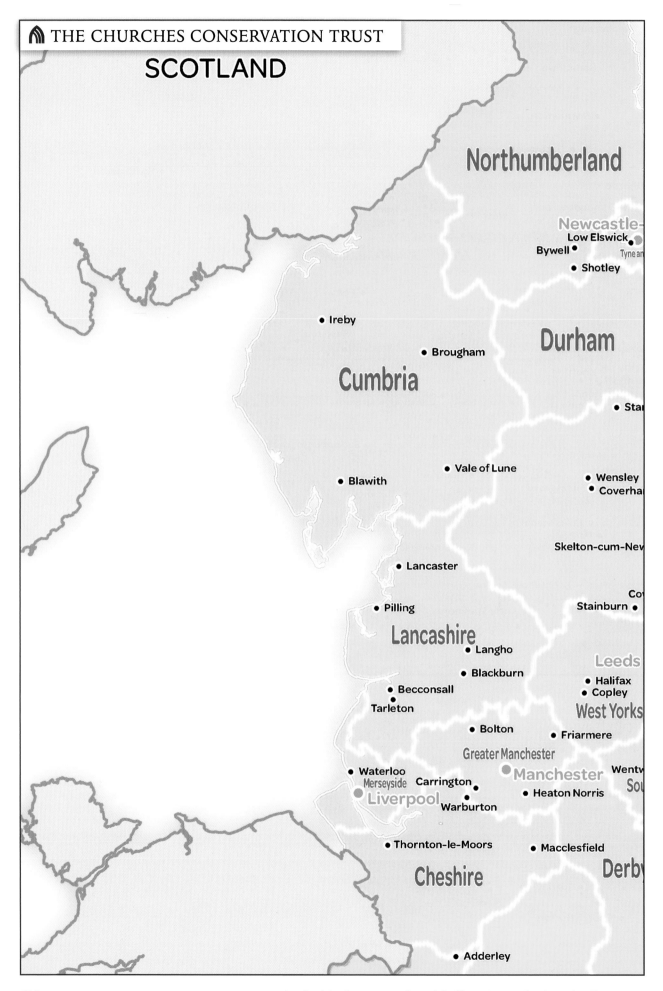

SCOTLAND

Northumberland

Newcastle-
Low Elswick
Bywell
Tyne an
Shotley

Ireby

Brougham

Durham

Cumbria

Sta

Vale of Lune

Wensley
Coverha

Blawith

Skelton-cum-Nev

Lancaster

Co
Stainburn

Pilling

Lancashire

Langho

Leeds

Blackburn

Halifax
Copley

Becconsall

West Yorks

Tarleton

Bolton

Friarmere

Greater Manchester

Wentw

Waterloo
Merseyside
Carrington
Manchester
Sou

Liverpool
Warburton
Heaton Norris

Thornton-le-Moors

Macclesfield

Cheshire

Derby

Adderley

rthumberland

Newcastle-upon-Tyne
Low Elswick
Bywell •
Tyne and Wear
• Shotley
• Sunderland

Durham

• Skelton-in-Cleveland

• Stanwick

• Fylingdales

• South Cowton

une

• Wensley
• Coverham

North Yorkshire

• Birdforth
• East Heslerton
• Wintringham

• Whenby
Skelton-cum-Newby •
• Roecliffe

• Allerton Mauleverer

Cowthorpe •
York • York Holy Trinity
Stainburn •
York St Lawrence
• Harewood
East Riding of Yorkshire
gho
• Lead
burn
Leeds • Leeds

• Halifax
• Copley

West Yorkshire

Burringham
ton
• Friarmere
Kirk Sandall •
• Barnetby
• Clixby
Manchester
• Cadeby
Redbourne •
• Waithe
South Somercotes
Manchester
Wentworth •
Edlington
Yarburgh
• Skidbrooke
South Yorkshire
Kingerby •
N Cockerington •
• Saltfleetby
• Heaton Norris
Throapham •
• Saundby
• Normanby-by-Spital
• Theddlethorpe
Buslingthorpe •
• Little Cawthorpe
Littleborough
Snarford •
Haugham •
• Milton Mausoleum •
Fledborough
• Goltho
Burwell
• Macclesfield
Low Marnham •
• Lincoln
Derbyshire
• Great Steeping
Haltham-on-Bain
Nottinghamshire
Lincolnshire
Elston •
• Normanton
Cotham
• Kedleston
ey

Sudeley Castle, Gloucestershire

© VISITBRITAIN/ROD EDWARDS

What do you think?

Help us at *Hudson's* by giving us some feedback on *Hudson's Historic Houses & Gardens*. Include your name, address and email address and your name will go into a draw for a complimentary overnight stay at a selected Signpost hotel. www.*signpost*.com.

Where do you live?
❑ London
❑ South East
❑ South West
❑ East of England
❑ East Midlands
❑ Heart of England
❑ Yorkshire & the Humber
❑ North West
❑ North East
❑ Scotland
❑ Wales
❑ Northern Ireland

What age group are you?
❑ Under 20
❑ 21- 40
❑ 41-60
❑ 61-80
❑ 80+

What is your employment status?
❑ Student
❑ Employed full time
❑ Employed part time
❑ Housewife/husband
❑ Retired

How many breaks or holidays do you take per year?
❑ 1-2
❑ 3-4
❑ 5-6
❑ 7+

Where do you take your breaks?
❑ England
❑ Scotland
❑ Wales
❑ Northern Ireland
❑ Overseas

Where do you usually stay on a break?
❑ Hotel or bed & breakfast
❑ Self catering
❑ Caravanning/Camping
❑ Friends & family
❑ Other

Do you belong to?
❑ National Trust
❑ National Trust for Scotland
❑ English Heritage
❑ Historic Scotland
❑ Cadw
❑ Friends of the HHA
❑ Royal Horticultural Society
❑ Other heritage organisation

Where did you purchase this copy of Hudson's?
❑ W H Smith
❑ Waterstones
❑ Independent bookshop
❑ Heritage attraction shop
❑ Other

Which sections did you enjoy most (grade from 1 -5)?
❑ Directory
❑ Editorial
❑ Special indexes
❑ Maps
❑ Photographs

Do you share Hudson's with friends or family?
❑ 1-2
❑ 3-4
❑ 4+

How often do you buy Hudson's?
❑ This is the first
❑ Every year
❑ Every other year
❑ Every 3-4 years
❑ Every 5-6 years
❑ Every 7-10 years

Last year did you visit an historic house or garden?
❑ Within 40 miles of home
❑ Further than 40 miles from home

How many times did you visit an historic house or garden last year?
❑ 1-2 ❑ 3-4
❑ 5-6 ❑ 7+

When you visit how much do you spend in addition to entry?
❑ £0-10 ❑ £11-20 ❑ £21-30
❑ £31-50 ❑ £50+

Do you usually use the café or restaurant?
YES/NO

Do you usually visit the shop?
YES/NO

Do you usually buy a guidebook?
YES/NO

Do you use www. hudsonsheritage.com?
YES/NO

Do you use the internet?
❑ Planning trips
❑ Buying tickets
❑ Booking accommodation
❑ Checking routes and directions on a map

Send your completed survey to:
Reader Survey
Hudson's Media Ltd
35 Thorpe Road
Peterborough
PE3 6AG

Booking Form

TOUR NAME(S)	DATES	TOUR CODES

TRAVELLERS' NAMES
Give your name as you would like it to appear on documents issued to other tour partipants – in block capitals please.

1 _____

2 _____

ROOM TYPE

Twin 2 beds	Double 1 bed	Single

YOUR DETAILS

Address (for correspondence)

_____

_____

_____

_____

Postcode

Telephone (home)

Telephone (work) _____

Mobile _____

Email _____

❏ Please tick if you do NOT want to receive updates on Martin Randall Travel's cultural tours, music festivals and London Days by email.

❏ Please tick if you do NOT want to receive Martin Randall Travel's brochures.

❏ Please tick if you do NOT want to receive updates from Hudson's.

NEXT OF KIN or Contact in case of emergency

Name

Address

Postcode

Telephone

Relationship to you

NATIONAL TRUST MEMBERSHIP NUMBERS
only applicable to the Derbyshire tour (where NT membership entails a discount).

National Trust England, Scotland or affiliate

1 _____ Expiry

2 _____ Expiry

FURTHUR INFORMATION or special requests (dietary requirements)

FELLOW TRAVELLERS

If you have made a booking for someone who does not have the same address as yourself, please give their details here. We shall then send correspondence and documents directly to them.

If you would also like the invoice to be sent to the fellow traveller's address, please tick: ❏

Name

Address

Postcode

Telephone

Email

Next of kin

Address

Postcode

PAYMENT

EITHER Deposit(s)
desposits are per person   £ _____

OR Full Payment

Full payment is required if you are booking within ten weeks of departure.

Payment can be made by cheque, credit/ debit card or bank transfer.

❏ CHEQUE. Please make cheques payable to Martin Randall Travel Ltd, and write the tour code on the back (e.g. EB 123).

❏ DEBIT OR CREDIT CARD. I wish to pay by Visa, Mastercard or Amex. Please charge my card.

Card no.

Start date   Expiry date

❏ BANK TRANSFER. Please give your surname and tour code (eg EB 123) as a reference and ask your bank to allow for all charges.
Account name: Martin Randall Travel Ltd
Royal Bank of Scotland, Drummonds, 49 Charing Cross, London SW1A 2DX
Account number 0019 6050 Sort code 16-00-38
IBAN: GB71 RBOS 1600 3800 1960 50; Swift/BIC: RBOS GB2L

Martin Randall Travel Ltd
Voysey House, Barley Mow Passage,
London, United Kingdom W4 4GF
Telephone 020 8742 3355 Fax 020 8742 7766
info@martinrandall.co.uk

I have read and agree to the Booking Conditions on behalf of all listed on this form.

Signature   Date

Index

Listed by property name in alphabetical order

The Hall at Abbey-Cwm-Hir

Manderston

St Mary's House & Gardens

Gainsborough Old Hall

G

H

Mount Ephraim Gardens

Kirklinton Hall

N

O

P

Q

R

Shakespeare's Family Homes
© Amy Murrell